PERSONAL INJURY AND CLINICAL NEGLIGENCE LITIGATION

PERSONAL INJURY AND CLINICAL NEGLIGENCE LITIGATION

Louise Marriott

Published by

College of Law Publishing,
Braboeuf Manor, Portsmouth Road, St Catherines, Guildford GU3 1HA

British Library Cataloguing-in-Publication Data
A catalogue record for this book is available from the British Library.

ISBN 978 1 915469 65 6

Typeset by Style Photosetting Ltd, Mayfield, East Sussex
Tables and index by Moira Greenhalgh, Arnside, Cumbria

Preface

The purpose of this book is to provide an introduction to the large and complex area of personal injury and clinical negligence litigation. It does not set out to cover the subject fully, neither does it purport to include all recent developments in this area of law.

Although we hope that this text will be of interest to practitioners, its aim is to provide a framework upon which the Personal Injury and Clinical Negligence course is built. Students are expected to carry out their own research into some aspects of the course and will receive further tuition in others.

The Civil Procedure Rules are amended from time to time and it is important that readers make reference to the most up-to-date provisions which can be found on the Ministry of Justice website. This is a fast-changing area of law, and practitioners must update themselves continually.

The law is generally stated as at 1 September 2023.

LOUISE MARRIOTT

Contents

Table of Cases

C

D

E

Table of Statutes

Table of Secondary Legislation

List of Abbreviations

See Chapter 2 for commonly used medical abbreviations.

ACOPs	Approved Codes of Practice
ADR	alternative dispute resolution
AEI	after the event insurance
APIL	Association of Personal Injury Lawyers
AvMA	Action against Medical Accidents
BEI	before the event insurance
CFA	conditional fee agreement
CICA	Criminal Injuries Compensation Authority
CJA 2009	Coroners and Justice Act 2009
CJCA 2015	Criminal Justice and Courts Act 2015
CLA 2018	Civil Liability Act 2018
CMCHA 2007	Corporate Manslaughter and Corporate Homicide Act 2007
CNF	Claim Notification Form
CNST	Clinical Negligence Scheme for Trusts
CPP	court proceedings pack
CPR 1998	Civil Procedure Rules 1998
CPS	Crown Prosecution Service
CRU	Compensation Recovery Unit
CTG	cardiotachograph
DBA	damages-based agreement
DCNF	Defendant Only Claim Notification Form
DHSC	Department of Health and Social Care
DPA 2018	Data Protection Act 2018
DWP	Department for Work and Pensions
DSE	display screen equipment
ECHR	European Convention on Human Rights
EL	employers' liability
ERRA 2013	Enterprise and Regulatory Reform Act 2013
FAA 1976	Fatal Accidents Act 1976
GLO	group litigation order
GMC	General Medical Council
HSE	Health and Safety Executive
HSWA 1974	Health and Safety at Work etc Act 1974
ICB	Integrated Care Board
ICSs	Integrated Care Systems
LA 1980	Limitation Act 1980
LASPO 2012	Legal Aid, Sentencing and Punishment of Offenders Act 2012
LEI	legal expenses insurance
MIB	Motor Insurers' Bureau
MID	Motor Insurance Database
NHS	National Health Service
NHSR	NHS Resolution
NMC	Nursing and Midwifery Council
OLA 1957	Occupiers' Liability Act 1957
PALS	Patient Advice and Liaison Service

PAP	pre-action protocol
PAR	police accident report
PD	Practice Direction
PHA 1997	Protection from Harassment Act 1997
PL	public liability
PPE	personal protective equipment
PTSD	post-traumatic stress disorder
QOCS	qualified one-way costs shifting
RIDDOR 2013	Reporting of Injuries, Diseases and Dangerous Occurrences Regulations 2013
RTA	road traffic accident
RTA 1988	Road Traffic Act 1988
SSP	statutory sick pay
VWF	vibration white finger
WRULD	work-related upper limb disorder

CHAPTER 1

INTRODUCTION TO THE WORK OF A PERSONAL INJURY AND CLINICAL NEGLIGENCE SOLICITOR

LEARNING OUTCOMES

After reading this chapter you will be able to:

- understand the scope and limitations of this book
- explain the similarities and differences between personal injury claims and clinical negligence claims
- set out an outline of the main steps in each type of claim
- explain how these claims are viewed from the perspectives of the claimant, the defendant and their solicitors
- appreciate that solicitors acting for claimants and defendants need to be vigilant in order to spot fraudulent claims, and understand how the courts might deal with dishonest litigants.

1.1 INTRODUCTION

The aim of this text is to provide an introduction to personal injury and clinical negligence litigation. It is assumed, however, that the basic civil litigation procedure has been studied before. Reference to the Legal Practice Guide, *Civil Litigation* and the Civil Procedure Rules 1998 (CPR 1998) may be necessary for those unfamiliar with the essential elements of High Court and county court procedure.

The terms 'personal injury litigation' and 'clinical negligence litigation' are widely used to describe claims for compensation for injuries which a client has suffered. This text will not deal with every type of claim that is encountered in practice, but it should serve as a basic introduction to a fascinating and rapidly developing area of law.

In practice, many personal injury claims will be based on either public liability, where the injury is sustained on property which is accessed by the public, or product liability, where the injury is caused by products made available to the public. However, in this text, the focus will be on the following:

(a) Road traffic accident (RTA) and other highway claims. These are usually the most straightforward type of personal injury claim. See **Chapter 3**.

(b)   Employers' liability claims. This term is used for personal injury claims where the claimant was injured in the course of employment and the employer is the defendant. Common examples of this type of personal injury claim arise where workers slip on the factory floor, fall from ladders or are caught in moving machinery. More complex cases arise where workers suffer a disease or injury which manifests itself many years after their exposure to dust, fibres, gases, fumes or noxious substances within the workplace. See **Chapter 4**.

(c)   Clinical negligence claims, which arise as a result of the negligence of doctors or other medical professionals, such as nurses, physiotherapists and dentists, or of institutional health providers, such as NHS Trusts or private hospitals. See **Chapter 5**.

(d)   Claims for psychiatric injury. These may arise in the context of any of the above types of claim, but the law in relation to claims for nervous shock and occupational stress is complex enough to warrant separate treatment in this text. See **Chapter 6**.

While the basic litigation procedures for personal injury and clinical negligence claims and the skills required of the solicitor are similar, there are differences, some of which are significant. Where the procedure for a clinical negligence claim differs notably from that of a personal injury claim, specific reference is made in the text.

Where a fatality arises from an accident in one of the above areas, special considerations arise. These are discussed in **Chapters 17** and **18**.

1.1.1   Causes of action

In most personal injury and clinical negligence cases, the claim is based on negligence. However, in relation to claims against highway authorities, and in relation to employers' liability claims resulting from incidents occurring prior to 1 October 2013, there may also be a claim arising from breaches of statutory duties. Some of the relevant statutory duties are explored in the text.

In clinical negligence claims against private hospitals and healthcare professionals who have provided advice and treatment on a private basis, there may be a claim in breach of contract. These claims lie beyond the scope of this book.

1.1.2   The CPR and the pre-action protocols

In accordance with the overriding objective set out in r 1 of the CPR 1998, personal injury and clinical negligence solicitors and their clients are required to have regard to the costs involved in pursuing the case, and to deal with the matter expeditiously and proportionately. This philosophy is to be adopted from the early days of the dispute, and reference needs to be made to the relevant pre-action protocol (PAP), which sets out the steps to be taken by the parties prior to the issue of proceedings. The full text of the PAP for Personal Injury Claims and the PAP for the Resolution of Clinical Disputes, both of which were substantially rewritten in April 2015, is set out in **Appendices 2** and **3**.

In April 2010, the Government introduced a new claims process for low value road traffic accident personal injury claims valued between £1,000 and £10,000. In July 2013, the upper financial limit was raised to £25,000 and, in addition, a similar protocol was introduced for low value employers' liability and public liability claims. The aim of these new protocols is to ensure that the process, which includes fixed time periods and fixed recoverable costs, delivers fair compensation to the claimant as soon as possible whilst keeping costs reasonable and proportionate. A further pre-action protocol came into force on 31 May 2021 – the RTA Small Claims Protocol – to supplement measures relating to whiplash claims. See **10.2** and **Chapter 21** for further detail. The Protocols, which apply only when certain criteria are fulfilled, are more prescriptive than other pre-action protocols. Consequently, this process is dealt with in some detail in **Chapter 21**, but is mentioned sparingly in the rest of the book. The full text of the Pre-action Protocol for Low Value Personal Injury (Employers' Liability and Public Liability) Claims is set out at **Appendix 4**.

In April 2018, a new protocol, the Pre-action protocol for resolution of package travel claims, was introduced. This deals with personal injury claims arising from gastric illness contracted during a package holiday, where the letter of claim is sent to the defendant after 6 May 2018 and the claim is valued at not more than £25,000. This protocol and the types of claim it covers are not dealt with in this textbook.

1.2 PERSONAL INJURY CLAIMS

1.2.1 The claimant's perspective

The aim of the claimant's personal injury solicitor is to prove that the defendant was responsible for the client's injuries and to obtain the appropriate amount of compensation. Therefore, there are two essential elements to a personal injury claim: liability and quantum. This may sound obvious, but it is important that these two elements are paramount in the solicitor's mind throughout the case.

Personal injury claims can take time to progress. At the initial interview, it should be explained to the client how it is anticipated the case will proceed and a realistic timescale should be given (although this can be difficult) as to when the matter might be settled or reach trial. The client should be informed of the basic requirements of the relevant pre-action protocol and the time limits imposed on each side. It is important that the client is kept informed as the matter proceeds. Regular letters should be sent, updating the client on the current position. If a proactive approach is taken, this will help to avoid difficulties in the future.

1.2.1.1 Liability

It is for the claimant to prove their case; the onus will therefore be on the client to persuade the court that the defendant was in breach of a statutory or common law duty owed to the client. The claimant has to prove, on a balance of probabilities, that:

(a) the defendant owed the claimant a duty of care and/or there was a relevant statutory duty;

(b) the defendant was in breach of that duty;

(c) the breach caused injury and consequential losses to the claimant which were reasonably foreseeable.

This is further explored in the context of the various types of personal injury claim dealt with in this book in **Chapters 3, 4 and 6**.

1.2.1.2 Quantum

The claimant's solicitor should have as their aim the maximisation of damages for their client, and they must take all legitimate steps to achieve that aim. The assessment of damages is dealt with in **Chapter 15** and, where there has been a fatality, in **Chapter 18**. Most solicitors working in this area acknowledge that a weariness on the part of the claimant themselves can set in if months pass and the claimant perceives that little has been done, or due to anxiety at having to attend trial. This can result in the client accepting inappropriately low offers rather than instructing the solicitor to progress the matter to trial. This should be acknowledged as a factor to be dealt with by the solicitor, and the client's concerns should be anticipated.

Medical evidence is required by the court to prove the injuries suffered by the client. Instructing a doctor may appear to be a simple task, but the choice of the appropriate doctor is significant as the value of the client's injuries will be based on the medical evidence, including the reports of the medical experts. The instruction of experts is dealt with in **Chapter 11** and a list of important medical specialities is contained in **Chapter 2**.

1.2.2   The defendant's perspective

In many cases the defendant's personal injury solicitor will be instructed only when proceedings have been issued against the defendant. At all times prior to this, where the defendant is insured, the claimant's solicitor will correspond with the defendant's insurance company. Where the insurance company believes that liability will be established, and in some low value cases where it is not economically viable to defend the claim, it will attempt to reach a settlement. The vast majority of claims are settled before trial and a substantial number of these are settled before proceedings are issued.

Many insurance companies require the insured to sign a letter of authority allowing them to act on the insured's behalf and to dispose of the case in any way that the defendant's solicitor sees fit. This is often a formality, as the terms of the insurance policy will allow the insurance company and its solicitor to have control of the case. The role of insurers is explored further at **3.3**.

Increasingly, claims are being defended on the basis that they are entirely fraudulent or that injuries and consequential loss have been fraudulently exaggerated. This is explored further at **1.4** below.

1.3   CLINICAL NEGLIGENCE CLAIMS

1.3.1   The claimant's perspective

The essential aims in a clinical negligence claim are the same as in a personal injury claim, namely, to establish liability and obtain the appropriate amount of damages. However, these are frequently not the only aims and considerations. The client's trust in a respected profession has often been lost, and the client will often lack knowledge and understanding as to what has happened to them. It must be explained to the client that they will have to prove their claim, if they are to establish liability. One of the first distinctions which has to be made between personal injury and clinical negligence cases is that the issue of liability is normally far more complicated in the latter, and there is a greater chance that the claimant's claim will fail at trial (see **Chapter 5**). However, the law relating to the quantum of damages is the same in both personal injury and clinical negligence cases.

The costs involved in a clinical negligence case are usually higher than those incurred in a personal injury case. The pre-action protocol for the resolution of clinical disputes will have to be complied with, and the initial investigations prior to commencing the claim will involve the solicitor taking instructions, obtaining the client's medical notes, and then instructing an expert to assess the notes and evidence available. However, it is only then that any preliminary view on liability can be obtained. Unlike a personal injury case, the victim's clinical negligence solicitor will never be able to give a view on liability at the first interview. It will only be when the medical notes and an expert's view are obtained that any advice on liability can be given to the client.

A common concern expressed by clients is how they will continue to be treated by the doctor/ healthcare professional if there is an ongoing 'doctor/patient' relationship, and advice and support in relation to this may be required. In addition, the solicitor will need to establish whether the client's sole concern is to pursue a damages claim or if the client has other objectives, for example to complain to the relevant NHS Trust, to report the alleged misconduct of a healthcare professional to the appropriate regulatory body and to prevent a similar event occurring in the future. In some cases, for example the death of a child, the client may not wish to pursue a claim at all but may regard the other options available as hugely important. The options available to the client in such circumstances are set out in **Chapter 5**.

1.3.2 The defendant's perspective

The defendant's clinical negligence solicitor will usually be from a firm instructed by the defendant's indemnity insurers. Where the defendant to a clinical negligence claim is the NHS, NHS Resolution (formerly the NHS Litigation Authority) will deal with the matter and will instruct a firm of solicitors from its panel for clinical negligence cases. The defendant's clinical negligence solicitor will have the same basic aims as those of the defendant's personal injury solicitor. If liability can be refuted then the case will be vigorously defended; if liability is established, the case will be settled. However, there are also special factors that the defendant's clinical negligence solicitor must consider. One important factor is that the defendant is a professional person and, while damages will not be paid by them personally, their reputation, and possibly that of their employer in the case of the NHS, will be brought into question by any admission or finding of negligence on their part. This is one of the reasons why more clinical negligence claims than personal injury claims proceed to trial. Establishing liability in a clinical negligence case is not easy. While the patient may complain that the treatment was unsuccessful, it does not follow that the doctor was negligent, and the arguments available to the defendant's solicitor to refute negligence are wider and more complicated than in a personal injury case.

1.4 FRAUDULENT AND EXAGGERATED CLAIMS

Only the most naive of those acting on behalf of claimants would believe that everything every client tells them is the truth, the whole truth and nothing but the truth. The accounts of even the most honest of people may be tainted by one or more of the following: anger, grief, confusion, a misunderstanding, a sense of indignation, a distorted perspective, an unconscious tendency to exaggerate and, of course, memory loss. Solicitors should always test the evidence of their clients and witnesses, not least of all because a story which does not stack up in the opinion of the solicitor, is likely to be found wanting should the matter be tried in court.

Solicitors acting for claimants may also encounter individuals whose aim it is to make an entirely fraudulent claim, or whose conscious exaggeration of their injuries is such as to amount to fraud. Although, as a matter of professional conduct, it is irrelevant whether a solicitor believes their client's version of events to be true or not, where a solicitor *knows their client is lying*, they should take care not to deceive or mislead the court, or to be complicit in another person's deceiving or misleading the court (SRA Code of Conduct 2019, Principles 1, 2 and 5, and paras 1.4, 2.2 and 2.4). Moreover, in circumstances where a reasonably competent lawyer would have realised that the claim was fraudulent and had no reasonable prospect of success, a wasted costs order may be made against the firm (see *Rasoul v (1) Linkevicius (2) Groupama Insurance Company Limited* [2012] 10 WLUK 194). A recent example of a case raising these sorts of issues was *Elvidge v Covea Insurance Plc* [2021] 1 WLUK 576, where a claim (£319) for was made for six physiotherapy sessions in a personal injury claim arising out of a road traffic accident. The court considered whether the solicitor with conduct of the claim had been complicit in an attempt to mislead the defendant into believing that the claimant had received genuine physiotherapy treatment when the claimant had not. The court ruled that the claimant's solicitor should have checked with the claimant on the discrepancy over the physiotherapy invoice coming to light (which was pre-trial); and on the claimant's confirmation (also pre-trial) that no treatment sessions were attended, the solicitor should have queried the invoice with the physiotherapist. The court found that, pending resolution of the discrepancy over the invoice, the solicitor should have withdrawn the physiotherapy claim and informed the defendant of the situation. This did not happen, and the physiotherapy claim proceeded. The judge ruled that it seemed to her that the solicitor had possibly failed in the duty not to mislead the court. The judge was unable to determine, on the evidence available to the court, whether or not the solicitor had knowingly misled the court. This case illustrates the importance of checking the information given by a claimant very carefully, and the potential professional conduct consequences that can follow for failing to do so.

Defendants, and particularly their insurers, are becoming increasingly wise to such matters, and they are showing a greater inclination to investigate potentially fraudulent claims thoroughly, including using covert surveillance, and to challenge them in court.

For a fascinating insight into the magnitude of the problem of fraud in relation to RTAs, the full judgment in the case of *Locke v (1) Stuart (2) Axa Corporate Solutions Services Ltd* [2011] EWHC 399 (QB) is particularly interesting. In that case, the defendant's insurers were able to use Facebook to demonstrate a connection between the claimant in that particular matter, and claimants and defendants in a number of other claims.

Claimants should be aware of the following potential outcomes of dishonesty.

1.4.1 Costs sanctions, deprivation of damages, dismissal of claims and setting aside of settlements

The practical effect of qualified one-way costs shifting (QOCS – see **9.3**), as set out in CPR, rr 44.14–44.16, is that a successful defendant in personal injury and clinical negligence claims will not be able to recover their own costs from the unsuccessful claimant. However, where a claim is found to be *fundamentally dishonest*, or where it is struck out on the grounds of disclosing no reasonable grounds for bringing the proceedings, or as an abuse of process, or for conduct likely to obstruct the just disposal of the proceedings, the shield provided by QOCS is lost and the claimant will have to pay the defendant's costs.

In *Gosling v Screwfix and another* (Cambridge County Court, 29 March 2014), which is frequently relied upon by defendants, Mr Gosling was found to be fundamentally dishonest in exaggerating his injuries following an accident at work, thus losing the protection of QOCS and being ordered to pay costs to the defendant on an indemnity basis. Despite the lack of a statutory definition of 'fundamental dishonesty', courts have not shied away from disapplying QOCS by making such findings.

Clearly, courts will not award damages in relation to a claim which is entirely fraudulent. However, they have, at times, been reluctant to deprive a claimant of damages to which the claimant is entitled either where the claimant fraudulently attempted to obtain more than their entitlement, or where the claimant lied to support the claim of another claimant. In *Shah v Ul-Haq and Others* [2009] EWCA Civ 542, the Court of Appeal held that there was no rule of law which entitled it to do so. In *Fairclough Homes Ltd v Summers* [2012] UKSC 26, the Supreme Court disagreed, stating that the court does indeed have jurisdiction to strike out a claim in such circumstances, under CPR, r 3.4(2) for abuse of process, or under its inherent jurisdiction. However, it declined to make such an order on the facts of the case. The Supreme Court made clear that the sanction was so extreme that the power to strike out should only be exercised where it was just and proportionate to do so, which is likely to be only in very exceptional cases. The Supreme Court stated that the striking out of a claim was a 'draconian step', and 'It is very difficult indeed to think of circumstances in which such a conclusion would be proportionate'.

After *Fairclough*, a number of decisions reflected a more robust approach and a greater willingness to deprive dishonest claimants of damages to which they would have been entitled if the claim had not been fraudulently exaggerated. For example, in *Barbara Fari v Homes for Haringey* [2012] 10 WLUK 270, the Central London County Court struck out the claim of a woman who had grossly exaggerated the nature and extent of her injuries. She was subsequently jailed for contempt ([2013] EWHC 3477 (QB)). Her husband was also found to be in contempt of court for dishonestly assisting her.

Since April 2015, defendants have been able to rely on s 57 of the Criminal Justice and Courts Act (CJCA) 2015 which widened the scope of 'fundamental dishonesty'. Section 57 states that where the court finds that the claimant is entitled to damages in respect of a personal injury claim and, upon the defendant's application for the dismissal of the claim the court is satisfied on the balance of probabilities that the claimant has been fundamentally dishonest in relation to the primary claim or a related claim, the court *must* dismiss the primary claim *unless* the claimant would suffer substantial injustice. See also **9.3**.

An example of this approach can be seen in *Stanton v Hunter* [2017] 3 WLUK 797, where the claimant, a taxi driver, had fallen through the roof of the defendant's outhouse and had suffered genuine injuries. The defendant had admitted liability, but had alleged contributory negligence on the part of the claimant. A recorder sitting at Liverpool County Court found that the claimant had been fundamentally dishonest, in that he had deliberately and dishonestly exaggerated the extent of his symptoms and he had been working as a taxi driver in spite of stating that he had been unable to work. The claim was dismissed in its entirety on the basis of the finding of fundamental dishonesty. No arguments were advanced on the claimant's behalf regarding 'substantial injustice' or its meaning, but it was accepted that it could not be equated with the miserable consequences likely to accrue for the claimant as a result of the judgment. Had he not been dishonest, the claimant would have been entitled to damages of £51,625, with no reduction for contributory negligence.

In *Howlett v Davies* [2017] EWCA Civ 1696, the Court of Appeal confirmed that fundamental dishonesty under r 44.15 and under s 57 of the CJCA 2015 amount to the same thing. Newey LJ approved the approach of the judge in *Gosling* who held that:

> a claimant should not be exposed to costs liability merely because he is shown to have been dishonest as to some collateral matter or perhaps as to some minor, self-contained head of damage. If, on the other hand, the dishonesty went to the root of either the whole of his claim or a substantial part of his claim ... it would be a fundamentally dishonest claim.

More recently, in *London Organising Committee of the Olympic and Paralympic Games (LOCOG) v Sinfield* [2018] EWHC 51 (QB), the High Court followed *Howlett* in finding that the fundamental dishonesty must 'substantially affect the presentation' of the case in a way which potentially adversely affected the defendant in a 'significant way'. In *LOCOG*, the claimant included a claim for the cost of employing a gardener following his injury which was found to have been exaggerated. In support of the claim in the preliminary schedule of special damages, the claimant had submitted false invoices and a false witness statement. The amount claimed for gardening was just over £14,000 (out of a total special damages claim of £33,340), representing 41.9% of the total special damages claim. In fact, the amount claimed for gardening should have been much less. As such, the court found that the claimant had presented his case on quantum in a way which could have resulted in *LOCOG* paying far more than it should have done if the claim had been presented honestly, and was therefore fundamentally dishonest.

The High Court in *LOCOG* went on to give some guidance on what is meant by 'substantial injustice' for the purposes of s 57, holding that 'something more is required than the mere loss of damages to which the claimant is entitled to establish substantial injustice'. This is a similar point to the one made by the judge in *Stanton v Hunter* (above). Mr Sinfield's claim for damages was accordingly dismissed in its entirety. *LOCOG* has been applied in numerous cases since 2018.

Where a claimant has a genuine claim but the court dismisses it in its entirely due to fundamental dishonesty, s 57(4) of the CJCA 2015 requires the court to record the amount of damages it would have awarded to the claimant for injuries genuinely suffered, but for the dismissal of the claim. When assessing costs in such proceedings, the court must deduct this amount from the amount it would otherwise have ordered the claimant to pay in respect of the costs incurred by the defendant (s 57(5)).

In certain circumstances, courts may be prepared to make punitive orders to act as a deterrent (see *Tasneem & Ors v Morley* [2013] 9 WLUK 369, when exemplary damages were awarded by the Central London County Court in recognition of the investigation costs incurred by the defendant's insurer, following a counterclaim brought by the defendant's insurer against the claimants in fraudulent crash-for-cash claims; and *Hassan v (1) Cooper (2) Accident Claims Consultants Ltd* [2015] EWHC 540 (QB), where exemplary damages were calculated by reference to the amount the original claimant had sought to obtain by fraud, including costs). See also *AXA Insurance UK Plc v Financial Claims Solutions Ltd and others* [2018] EWCA Civ 1330, which the Court of Appeal held to be a 'paradigm case of when exemplary damages should be awarded'.

In *Hayward v Zurich Insurance Co PLC* [2016] UKSC 48, the Supreme Court held that where a defendant settles a case despite suspecting fraud on the part of the claimant, and then later uncovers proof of fraud, it is entitled to set aside that settlement under the tort of deceit. In order to establish the tort of deceit, the defendant must prove that the claimant dishonestly made a material representation which was intended to, and did in fact, induce the defendant to act to its detriment. However, the Court held that the defendant's belief as to the truthfulness of the misrepresentation was not a necessary ingredient of the test, as the defendant may settle on the basis that the court would believe the misrepresentations if the matter went to trial. It was enough to show that the misrepresentation was 'a material cause' of the defendant entering into the settlement. The defendant's mere suspicion of fraud prior to the settlement is unlikely to prevent it from successfully setting it aside when proof of fraud is subsequently provided.

1.4.2 Contempt proceedings and criminal charges for fraud

Increasingly, defendants are applying for permission to pursue contempt proceedings against claimants who have manufactured or exaggerated claims, and there has been an upturn in the number of individuals being imprisoned for contempt for this type of behaviour. The rules governing contempt are found in CPR 81 and PD 81, and guidance as to its application may be found in *Royal & Sun Alliance Insurance Plc v Kosky* [2013] EWHC 835 (QB).

In *Walton v Kirk* [2009] EWHC 703 (QB), Ms Kirk had claimed damages in excess of £750,000 following a road traffic accident. Liability was admitted by the defendant's insurers, but video surveillance showed that Ms Kirk had grossly exaggerated her injuries. In the ensuing contempt proceedings, it was held that exaggeration of a claim is not automatic proof of contempt. What may matter is the degree of exaggeration and/or the circumstances in which any exaggeration is made. While the discrepancies between her witness statement and the video surveillance did not amount to a contempt of court, Ms Kirk was found guilty in relation to statements she had made to assist her personal injury claim, which the court found to be untrue. She was fined £2,500.

However, in *Motor Insurers' Bureau v Shikell & Others* [2011] EWHC 527 (QB), James Shikell claimed in excess of £1.2 million in respect of a head injury suffered in an RTA. The defendant was granted permission to bring contempt proceedings against Mr Shikell, his father, and a third man, who had signed a witness statement in support of the claim without reading it, for contempt, after surveillance revealed that he was an active, sporty man, with no significant disability. The Shikells were each sentenced to 12 months' imprisonment, and the third man was fined £750.

In *Calderdale and Huddersfield NHS Foundation Trust v Atwal* [2018] EWHC 961 (QB), the defendant trust brought committal proceedings for contempt against the claimant on the basis that he had grossly exaggerated his injuries. Mr Atwal had pursued a claim against the trust in which he alleged that injuries sustained as a result of failures in his medical care following the fracture of two fingers had left him extremely disabled, unable to work and needing help with everyday tasks such as cutting up his food. The trust admitted liability and made an early offer of settlement (£30,000) which the claimant rejected. He later presented a claim in excess of £800,000. The defendants doubted the claim that the claimant was making and carried out a number of investigations (including video surveillance and social media trawling) which revealed that Mr Atwal was working as a DJ and living in a way entirely inconsistent with the case he was presenting.

The trust alleged that Mr Atwal had attempted to interfere with the administration of justice in his clinical negligence claim by making false statements to the medical and other experts involved, intending to deceive them as to the extent of his continuing symptoms and thereby affect the correct administration of justice. Furthermore, in signing his witness evidence and schedule of loss, Mr Atwal had signed statements of truth knowing that the contents were false and that this would affect the assessment of the claim. Mr Justice Spencer accepted the case that the trust brought, finding against Mr Atwal on 14 separate allegations of contempt and sentencing him to three months in prison and ordering him to pay £75,000 toward costs.

In *McDaid v Walsall MBC* [2018] 5 WLUK 171, the claimant was found to have exaggerated an ankle injury sustained after tripping in a pothole while out running with his two dogs. He claimed that he was unable to work as a result. However, investigations revealed that he had taken part in 'Iron Man' triathlons, full and half marathons, cycling challenges and rugby following the accident and that some of these activities were uploaded to a personal fitness app. His claim was dismissed pursuant to s 57 of the CJCA 2015 as being 'fundamentally dishonest'. The claimant was subsequently sentenced to two years in prison, suspended for 12 months following a private prosecution for contempt of court brought by the defendant council.

It should be noted that criminal charges may be brought against anyone who dishonestly makes false representations contrary to s 2 of the Fraud Act 2006. Such charges may arise when the accident was genuine but the claim has been fraudulently exaggerated (see *R v W* [2013] EWCA Crim 820).

Under s 57(7) of the CJCA 2015, when sentencing a claimant for contempt for fundamental dishonesty in a personal injury claim or in relation to any criminal proceedings resulting from such a claim, or otherwise disposing of such proceedings, the court must have regard to the dismissal of the primary claim. In other words, the claimant has already been punished by the denial of damages to which he would have been entitled had he not been dishonest, and the court is required to take note of this when determining the appropriate sentence.

1.4.3 Other initiatives for combating fraudulent claims

Due to increasing concerns regarding the perceived growth in fraudulent personal injury claims, the Government has introduced a number of other measures in an attempt to tackle the problem:

(a) *Referral fees.* Sections 56–60 of the Legal Aid, Sentencing and Punishment of Offenders Act 2012 (LASPO 2012) create a regulatory offence (but not a criminal offence) for regulated persons, including solicitors, barristers, legal executives, claims management companies and insurers, to pay or receive referral fees in personal injury and fatal accident cases. See also the SRA Guidance, 'The prohibition of referral fees in LASPO 56 60', which refers to possible breaches of Principles 2, 3 and 7 if a solicitor or firm were to breach the ban on referral fees. The Guidance also makes the point that the solicitor or firm would need to demonstrate that they have fully complied with the standards set out in paras 5.1 to 5.3 of the Code of Conduct for Solicitors, and para 7.1(b) of the Code of Conduct for Firms.

(b) *Inducements to claimants.* Sections 58–61 of the CJCA 2015 prohibit providers of legal services from offering inducements, such as cash, shopping vouchers and iPads, in order to persuade others to make a personal injury claim. Again, this provision does not create a criminal offence, but relevant regulators are required to ensure that appropriate arrangements for monitoring and enforcing the restriction are in place. SRA Guidance, 'Offering inducements to potential clients or clients', states that a solicitor or firm found to be acting in breach of the ban on inducements in personal injury claims set out in the CJCA 2015 would be in breach of SRA Principles, in particular Principle 1. The SRA Guidance goes on to state that they would also very likely be in breach of SRA Principle 2. In addition, the Guidance states that para 8.8 of the Code of Conduct for Solicitors and para 7.1(c) of the Code of Conduct for Firms require that any publicity is not misleading. It states that this means any publicity must not mislead the public by offering, suggesting or implying that any inducement is being offered, in breach of the ban.

(c)   *Cold calling and nuisance texts.* Those which relate to the making of personal injury claims are prohibited under the Privacy and Electronic Communications Regulations (EC Directive) Regulations 2003 (PECR), as amended. Nevertheless, a large number of complaints reported to the Information Commissioner's Office (ICO) arising out of live or automated calls and spam texts relate to accident claims. The ICO is the main enforcer of the cold calling ban, to address concerns relating to rogue claims management companies that use information based on such methods. The Information Commissioner has several ways of taking action, including imposing a fine under the PECR of up to £500,000 against the organisation in breach or its directors. The Information Commissioner also has prosecutorial powers, and sanctions are not necessarily mutually exclusive. Paragraph 8.9 of the SRA Code of Conduct (solicitors) and para 7.1(c) of the SRA Code of Conduct (firms) state: 'You do not make unsolicited approaches to members of the public, with the exception of current or former clients, in order to advertise legal services provided by you, or your business or employer.' Further detail is given in SRA guidance as to what is and is not permitted.

(d)   *askCUE PI.* In view of the fact that most fraudulent claims are low value RTA claims, as from 1 June 2015, claimants' solicitors are required to check their clients' records held on the askCUE PI database to identify any previous incidents reported to insurers before using the Claims Portal to submit a claim under the Pre-Action Protocol for Low Value Personal Injury Claims. See para 6.3A of that Protocol and **Chapter 21** for further information.

(e)   *The Civil Liability Act (CLA) 2018.* Part 1 of this Act makes provision about whiplash claims resulting from RTAs, where the duration of the whiplash injury is unlikely to exceed two years. Part 1 of the Act was introduced to address concerns about the volume of whiplash claims being brought and to address concerns about fraudulent and exaggerated claims in this context. The Act received Royal Assent on 20 December 2018. It has introduced a definition of 'whiplash injury' and also refers to a tariff of compensation for pain, suffering and loss of amenity in respect of such claims, to be specified in regulations made by the Lord Chancellor. These regulations have now been made and the tariff set in the Whiplash Injury Regulations 2021 (SI 2021/642) which came into force on 31 May 2021. These Regulations apply to causes of action accruing on or after 31 May 2021, subject to exceptions for children, protected parties and vulnerable road users (the latter being, broadly, those not within a vehicle). They specify the total amount of damages for pain, suffering and loss of amenity that a court is permitted to award in respect of road traffic accident-related whiplash injuries that last for no longer than two years. The tariff includes amounts for any minor psychological injury suffered in the same accident. The Regulations permit the court to award a maximum 20% uplift on the tariff in exceptional circumstances. Reductions for contributory negligence still apply.

(f)   *Fixed cost medical reports.* Section 6 of the CLA 2018 also prohibits the settlement of whiplash claims resulting from road traffic accidents without appropriate medical evidence, such evidence to be specified in regulations. Regulation 4 of the Whiplash Injury Regulations 2021 specifies the medical evidence that must be provided before a regulated person (defined in s 9 of the CLA 2018 and including solicitors) may settle an RTA-related whiplash injury claim. Where the claimant lives or chooses to be examined in England or Wales, the evidence must be provided in a fixed cost medical report from an accredited medical expert identified via a search of the Medco Registration Solutions ('Medco') database, or where a more serious injury has been sustained at the same time, the General Medical Council ('GMC') Specialist Register. See also **Chapter 21**.

1.5 CONCLUSION

Personal injury and clinical negligence litigation is a diverse and expanding area. At its least complex, it may involve a claim for compensation for minor injuries suffered as a result of a road traffic accident, or, at the other extreme, it may involve representing a child who is severely disabled, allegedly as a result of being starved of oxygen at birth.

Overviews of the main steps in a typical personal injury claim and a typical clinical negligence claim are set out in **1.6** below.

This text aims to provide an introduction to personal injury and clinical negligence litigation, but reference should also be made to practitioners' works and original/primary sources. Where appropriate, reference must be made to the CPR 1998 and relevant pre-action protocols.

1.6 OVERVIEWS OF PERSONAL INJURY AND CLINICAL NEGLIGENCE CLAIMS

1.6.1 Main steps in a typical personal injury claim

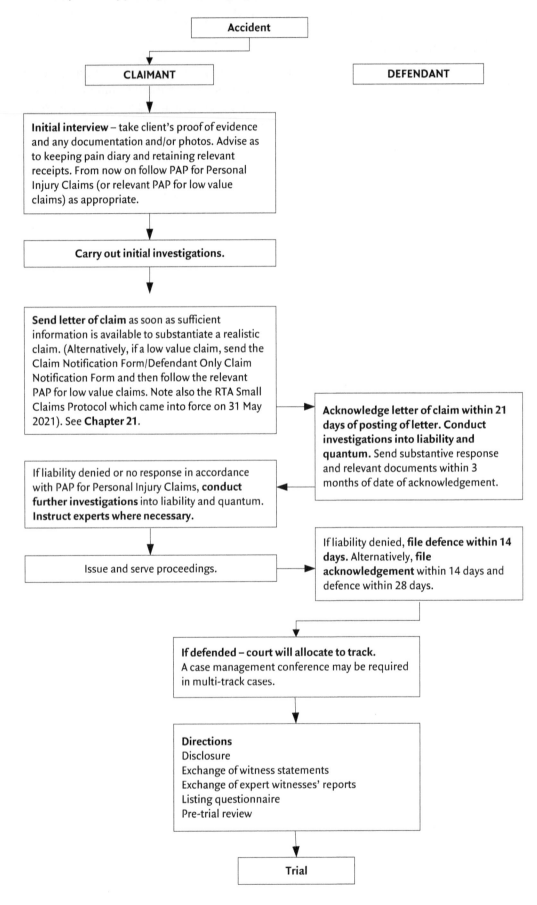

Accident

CLAIMANT

DEFENDANT

Initial interview – take client's proof of evidence and any documentation and/or photos. Advise as to keeping pain diary and retaining relevant receipts. From now on follow PAP for Personal Injury Claims (or relevant PAP for low value claims) as appropriate.

Carry out initial investigations.

Send letter of claim as soon as sufficient information is available to substantiate a realistic claim. (Alternatively, if a low value claim, send the Claim Notification Form/Defendant Only Claim Notification Form and then follow the relevant PAP for low value claims. Note also the RTA Small Claims Protocol which came into force on 31 May 2021). See **Chapter 21**.

Acknowledge letter of claim within 21 days of posting of letter. Conduct investigations into liability and quantum. Send substantive response and relevant documents within 3 months of date of acknowledgement.

If liability denied or no response in accordance with PAP for Personal Injury Claims, **conduct further investigations** into liability and quantum. **Instruct experts where necessary.**

Issue and serve proceedings.

If liability denied, **file defence within 14 days.** Alternatively, **file acknowledgement** within 14 days and defence within 28 days.

If defended – court will allocate to track.
A case management conference may be required in multi-track cases.

Directions
Disclosure
Exchange of witness statements
Exchange of expert witnesses' reports
Listing questionnaire
Pre-trial review

Trial

1.6.2 Main steps in a typical clinical negligence claim against an NHS Trust

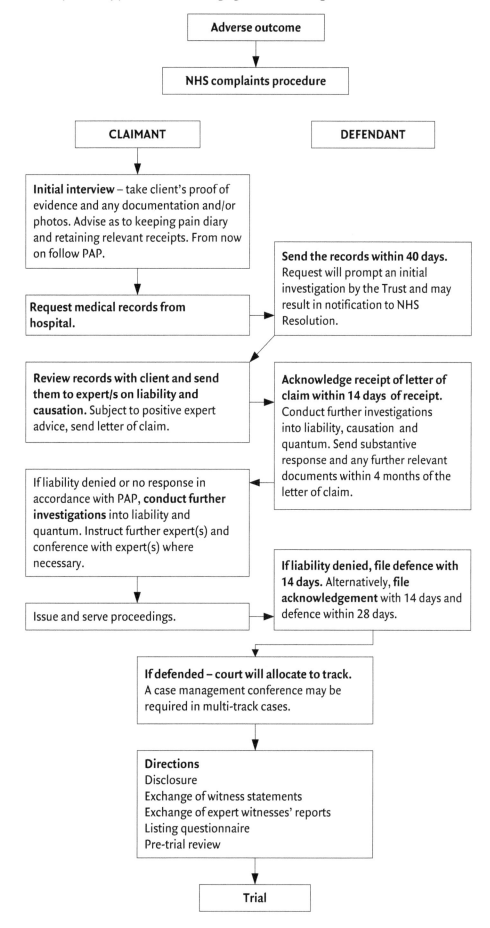

CHAPTER 2

PERSONAL INJURY AND CLINICAL NEGLIGENCE TERMINOLOGY

LEARNING OUTCOMES

After reading this chapter you will be able to:

- appreciate the importance to the personal injury/clinical negligence solicitor of acquiring a working knowledge of medical terms and abbreviations, and of understanding the nature of the most common injuries that arise and the scope of different types of medical expertise

- know where to find assistance to acquire such information and knowledge.

2.1 INTRODUCTION

A trainee or apprentice solicitor who enters the personal injury/clinical negligence department of a legal firm has to cope not only with the pressures of being able to understand fully and advise accurately on the law, but also getting to grips with unfamiliar medical terms. If a trainee is faced on their first day with their colleagues referring to claims dealing with work-related upper limb disorders (WRULD), vibration white finger (VWF), post-traumatic stress disorder (PTSD), etc, and they are unfamiliar with the terminology, they will obviously be at a disadvantage.

There can be no doubt that proficient solicitors who practise in this area have extensive medical knowledge and a detailed understanding of the terms used. This knowledge enables them to comprehend fully clients' complaints, experts' reports and medical notes, and also enables them to explain matters thoroughly to clients. For example, upon receipt of a medical report obtained following a simple road traffic accident, the solicitor must read the report carefully and then send it to the client. If the client subsequently contacts the solicitor stating that the client does not understand the terms used in the medical report, it is not acceptable for the solicitor to say, 'Neither do I'!

In addition, it is important for the trainee solicitor to have some knowledge of the areas of medical specialisation, so that appropriate experts can be instructed.

The purpose of this chapter is to assist in the understanding of the terms and abbreviations commonly found in personal injury/clinical negligence work, and of the main areas of specialisation. It should be noted, however, that a medical dictionary is an essential requirement for the personal injury solicitor, and more detailed medical texts may also be of use.

2.2 COMMON INJURIES, CONDITIONS AND MEDICAL TERMS

2.2.1 Orthopaedic injuries

Orthopaedic (bone) injuries are the most common injuries encountered in a personal injury claim. They are normally incurred as a result of falling, or from being involved in a road traffic accident.

The most common terms found in orthopaedic medical reports are as follows:

(a) *Arthrodesis* – means a joint that has been fused, either because of pre-existing joint disease or because of injury as a result of trauma to the joint.

(b) *Arthroplasty* – means that the joint has been reconstructed, often by the use of a joint implant to replace one or more parts of the components of a joint.

(c) *Contusion* – means an injury to the skin and the deeper tissues in the surrounding area which is accompanied by bleeding from damaged blood vessels. The skin, however, is not broken. The simplest form of contusion is a bruise, developing through to a contusion accompanied by a large haematoma, which is a collection of blood under the surface of the skin.

(d) *Dislocation* – means an injury which results in the bones of a joint being out of alignment or connection with one another. There is usually associated ligament and soft tissue damage.

(e) *Fracture* – means a break in the continuity of a bone.

(f) *Sprain* – means an injury in the region of a joint with associated ligament and soft tissue damage.

(g) *Subluxation* – a joint which has subluxed has undergone a partial dislocation, and subluxation is a term which is sometimes used to describe a sprain.

A client who has an orthopaedic injury may also undergo *traction*, ie a system of weights and pulleys is used to pull muscle groups, so as to reduce/immobilise fractures and put the bones back into alignment.

In general, the most common fractures occur to:

(a) *The clavicle (collar bone)* – these fractures are especially common in children and young adults, and are almost always due to falls or direct trauma to the point of the shoulder. Treatment involves wearing a sling until the pain has subsided. Surgical intervention is very rarely required and is usually indicated only if there is a risk to nearby nerves or blood vessels.

(b) *The surgical neck of the humerus (the long bone stretching from the shoulder to the elbow)* – these fractures are usually treated with a sling; but if badly displaced, are surgically treated and fixed with metal pins.

(c) *The shaft of the humerus* – these fractures can occur at any point along the humerus and are usually treated by immobilising the fracture in a plaster of Paris cast for six to eight weeks.

(d) *The radius (the bone running from the elbow to the base of the thumb)* – there are many different types of radial fracture but the most common is the Colles fracture.

(e) *The femur (the thigh bone)* – these fractures can occur at any point along the length of the femur. The most common sites are the neck or the shaft of the femur. Treatment tends to be surgical. Clients with fractures of the shaft of the femur will be placed in a Thomas splint, which immobilises the fracture.

(f) *The tibia and fibula* – these two bones make up the part of the leg from beneath the knee to the ankle. Fracture of these two bones can result from direct or indirect trauma.

(g) *The pelvis* – a number of bones which together form a ring-like structure at the base of the spine. The pelvis contains the vertebrae of the sacral spine and the hip joints, and fractures can occur at any point. Fractures to the pelvis are of two main types: first, isolated fractures of one of the bones which make up the pelvis; and, secondly, double fractures of the bones which make up the pelvic rim.

2.2.2 Hand injuries

In interpreting medical reports regarding hand injuries, a basic understanding of the anatomical position of the hand is required.

The functional parts of the hand are the wrist and the fingers. If the wrist is flexed, the hand is brought forward; if the hand is positioned as if to push someone away, it is said to be extended. The wrist is described as being 'pronated' if the palm of the hand is pointing towards the floor, and is described as being 'supinated' if the hand is positioned to receive something.

If the hand is made into a fist, the fingers are described as flexed; if the hand is opened out as if to receive something, the fingers are described as extended.

The fingers are described as the distal half of the hand, and are made up of three joints. Working from the palm of the hand out towards the end of the fingers, the three joints are the metacarpo-phalangeal joint (the knuckles), the proximal interphalangeal joint, and the distal interphalangeal joint, which is the joint nearest to the finger nails. The thumb has the same number of joints, but appears shorter because it attaches to the hand lower down; 70% of the function of the hand is provided by the thumb.

2.2.3 Head injuries

The following terms are used in relation to head injuries:

(a) *aphasia* – the loss of power of speech;

(b) *anosmia* – the loss of the sense of smell;

(c) *cerebral oedema* – a swelling of the brain;

(d) *closed head injury* – a head injury in which there is no open skull fracture;

(e) *concussion* – instantaneous loss of consciousness due to a blow on the head;

(f) *diffuse axonal injury* – a brain injury which involves shearing of the brain tissue itself;

(g) *dysphasia* – a difficulty in understanding language and in self-expression;

(h) *extradural haematoma* – a blood clot which lies immediately above the brain and its protective membranes and below the surface of the skull;

(i) *Glasgow Coma Scale* – a system of assessing neurological function;

(j) *hydrocephalus* – a condition which arises due to an increase in the amount of cerebro-spinal fluid within the cranial cavity;

(k) *hemiplegia* – paralysis of one side of the body;

(l) *intracerebral* – within the substance of the brain itself;

(m) *monoplegia* – a paralysis of one limb;

(n) *open head injury* – a head injury with an associated depressed skull fracture;

(o) *subdural haematoma* – a blood clot lying in-between the brain and its protective membranes.

2.2.4 Injuries to the skin

The following terms are used to describe injuries to the skin:

(a) *abrasion* – occurs when the surface of the skin is rubbed off due to a mechanical injury;

(b) *hypertrophy* – the overgranulation of scar tissue which can lead to disfigurement;

(c) *laceration* – a wound to the skin which has jagged, irregular edges.

2.2.5 Whiplash/soft tissue injuries

The term 'whiplash injury' is not a medical term at all, but is one which is used by lawyers and the general public to describe a whole range of symptoms suffered, in the main, by someone whose head is thrown forward in a sudden forceful jerk – literally whipped forward – and back. Both 'whiplash injury' and 'soft tissue injury' are used in legislation. The RTA Protocol provides a definition of 'soft tissue injury' (see **21.4.1**) and s 1 of the Civil Liability Act 2018 defines what is meant by 'whiplash injury' for the purposes of the Act. See **1.4.3**.

Medical practitioners may prefer to use the terms 'cervical sprain' or 'hyperextension injuries of the neck'. This type of injury is commonly associated with road traffic accidents, but it can also result from other accidents (such as tripping and slipping), sporting activities (such as biking and diving) and assaults.

The cause of the injuries associated with whiplash is the stretching and straining of the soft tissues – the tendons, ligaments and muscles – supporting the cervical spine (ie in the neck region). Symptoms can be of widely varying severity, and may include pain and stiffness in the neck, backache, tingling and numbness in the arms and possibly in the hands, headaches, dizziness, ringing in the ears, tiredness, inability to concentrate, memory loss, blurred vision, nausea and reduced libido. Typically, symptoms will not be present immediately after the accident but will develop over one or two days, and may gradually get worse before they start to improve. Most people make a full recovery within days or weeks, but where symptoms are severe, it may take much longer for them to subside.

As these injuries are to the soft tissues, they cannot always be detected by means of an MRI scan, CT scan or an x-ray, and they are otherwise difficult to diagnose accurately. This means that it is sometimes difficult to assess whether a claim is genuine or not.

2.2.6 Work-related upper limb disorders

The term 'repetitive strain injury' is commonly used by the general public to describe musculoskeletal problems of the arm and hand associated with repetitive activity, such as typing or assembly work. However, this term does not accurately reflect the fact that the condition may not be due to repetitive work and may not be the result of a strain. Consequently, the term 'work-related upper limb disorder' (WRULD) is to be preferred.

WRULDs, which are common across a wide range of occupations, may be caused by repetitive or forceful activities, including lifting or carrying heavy objects, poor posture and/or carrying out activities for long periods without adequate breaks. In some cases, a WRULD may be caused by a single strain or trauma resulting, for example, from carrying a heavy load. In other cases, problems are caused by vibration, due to the use of tools such as chainsaws, grinders or drills.

Symptoms include aches, pain, weakness, numbness, tingling, stiffness, swelling and cramp in the arm and hand, including the fingers, wrist, forearm, elbow, shoulder and neck. In many instances, rest or adjustments to the working environment (the desk layout or assembly line) or the way that work is managed will alleviate the symptoms, but in some cases the condition is permanent.

It may be possible for a precise medical diagnosis to be made, for example, carpal tunnel syndrome, tenosynovitis or vibration white finger.

Controversy surrounds claims for WRULDs due to the fact that some specific conditions, such as carpal tunnel syndrome, may be caused by factors not related to the workplace and because some WRULDs are non-specific (ie a medical diagnosis is not possible).

2.2.7 Industrial deafness

Industrial deafness claims are brought by those who have suffered hearing loss due to exposure at work to a high level of noise for a long period of time. For example, employees working in the steel industry, shipbuilding or other manufacturing industry may suffer from industrial deafness. Expert medical evidence is required to prove the loss of hearing, and evidence relating to the employee's working conditions is also required. Employers should, for example, have a system of assessing the risk from noise, provide ear protectors, and have clearly marked zones where ear protection must be worn.

2.2.8 Asbestos related conditions

Where people are exposed to asbestos, dust or fibres may be inhaled which can move to the lungs or to the pleura, which is the membrane surrounding the lungs. Where this occurs, a number of conditions of varying severity may arise.

Asbestosis is a form of *pneumoconiosis*, which is a general term applied to any chronic form of inflammation of the lungs affecting people who are liable to inhale irritating substances or particles at work. Asbestosis occurs due to the inhalation of mainly blue or brown asbestos dust, which leads to the development of widespread scarring of the lung tissue and causes severe breathing difficulties. The main hazard, however, is the potential for the development of a type of cancer called mesothelioma, which affects the lungs, the pleura or, more rarely, the ovaries.

Pleural plaques are areas of fibrosis, sometimes partly calcified, on the pleura. Typically, there are no symptoms, but there is evidence to conclude that individuals who have pleural plaques have an increased risk of developing mesothelioma.

Where these areas of fibrosis are more widespread, they can prevent the lungs from working properly and thereby cause difficulties with breathing. This is known as pleural thickening

2.2.9 Occupational asthma

Occupational asthma may develop following exposure to a precipitating factor in the workplace, for example flour.

Asthma is a breathing disorder characterised by a narrowing of the airways within the lungs. The main symptom is breathlessness and an associated cough. It is an extremely distressing condition and, if left untreated, can be fatal.

2.2.10 Occupational dermatitis

Dermatitis is an inflammation of the skin, which is usually caused by direct contact with some irritating substance.

Occupational dermatitis is the most common of all the occupational diseases.

2.2.11 Occupational stress

Following the case of *Walker v Northumberland County Council* [1995] 1 All ER 737, in which a social services officer received compensation for stress induced by his employment (he suffered a nervous breakdown), a number of occupational stress claims have been brought before the courts. Careful consideration needs to be given as to whether the particular client will satisfy the necessary criteria to persuade the court to award damages in these circumstances. Occupational stress is considered in more detail in **Chapter 6**.

2.2.12 Post-traumatic stress disorder

Post-traumatic stress disorder (PTSD) has become more prominent in recent years. This expression refers to a psychological illness in which the claimant suffers from a variety of symptoms, which may include flashbacks, panic attacks, palpitations, chest pain, nausea, constipation, diarrhoea, insomnia, eating disorders, extreme fatigue and loss of libido.

It is important that medical evidence is obtained to support the injury, so that the defendant cannot make the allegation that the claimant has simply been 'shaken up'. This type of injury must be considered by the claimant's solicitor, even if the client concentrates only on their physical injuries when asked at the first interview what injuries the client has suffered as a result of the accident. Post-traumatic stress is considered in more detail in **Chapter 6**.

2.2.13   Obstetrics

A normal labour and delivery take place in three stages. The first stage refers to the period of time it takes the cervix to dilate fully to 10 cms, and this is the longest stage of labour. The full dilation of the cervix is also associated with the rupture of the amnion, which is the tough fibrous membrane lining the cavity of the womb during pregnancy, containing amniotic fluid which supports the foetus. The rupture of the amnion is often referred to as 'the breaking of the waters'. The second stage of labour is the actual birth of the baby. The third stage is the delivery of the placenta.

If a baby is deprived of oxygen, it is said to have become 'hypoxic'. Hypoxia refers to a state where there is an inadequate supply of oxygen to maintain normal tissue function. If a baby is deemed to be in danger, it will be intubated and ventilated. This involves the insertion of an endotracheal tube into the baby's trachea to facilitate the maintenance of the baby's airway.

Once a baby is born, it is assessed using the Apgar score. This is a method of assessing a baby's condition by giving a score of 0, 1 or 2 to each of five signs: colour, heart rate, muscle tone, respiratory effort, and response to stimulation. A total score of 10 is the best Apgar score. If a baby is described as 'apnoeic', it means that it is not breathing; 'bradycardia' refers to the fact that the baby's heart is beating too slowly.

Perinatal mortality refers to the death of a foetus after the 28th week of pregnancy and to the death of the newborn child during the first week of life.

2.2.14   Cerebral palsy

Cerebral palsy is a general term used by medical practitioners to refer to a set of neurological conditions occurring in infancy or early childhood which affect movement and coordination. There are several different types of varying severity, the main ones being:

(a)   *Spastic cerebral palsy* – some of the muscles in the body are tight, stiff and weak, making control of movement of the affected arm or leg difficult. The degree of spasticity can vary significantly from case to case, but in the most severe cases the muscles in the affected limb may become permanently contracted.

(b)   *Athetoid (dyskinetic) cerebral palsy* – characterised by involuntary slow, writhing movements of the limbs and sometimes sudden muscle spasms. Sufferers have difficulty holding items or staying in one position.

(c)   *Ataxic cerebral palsy* – problems include difficulty with balance, causing unsteadiness when walking, shaky movements of the hands, making writing difficult, and speech difficulties.

(d)   *Mixed cerebral palsy* – a combination of two or more of the above.

In addition to the above symptoms, there may a lack of coordination of the muscles of the mouth, causing speech and feeding problems, visual and hearing problems, and epilepsy. The symptoms often lead others to conclude that the sufferer has learning difficulties, but the condition does not, of itself, affect intelligence.

In a minority of cases (thought to be about 1:10) cerebral palsy is caused by problems during labour and birth, such as lack of oxygen or trauma. In the majority of the remaining cases, the damage arises while the baby is developing in the womb, as a result of genetic problems, malformations of the brain or maternal infection, such as rubella or toxoplasmosis. Infantile infections (especially encephalitis or meningitis) can also be causative.

Cerebral palsy is not a progressive condition, but the strains it places upon the body can lead to further problems in later life. There is no cure, but sufferers can benefit greatly from physiotherapy, occupational therapy, speech therapy and conductive education.

2.3 AREAS OF MEDICAL SPECIALITY

In dealing with a caseload, the personal injury and clinical negligence lawyer may require expert evidence to be given by a wide range of medical specialists. The following are amongst the most common areas of expertise. In order to avoid offending medical experts, it is useful to remember that consultant surgeons are known as 'Mr' 'Mrs' or 'Ms', rather than 'Dr'.

(a) *Anaesthesia* – either renders the patient unconscious (general anaesthesia) or removes sensation in a specific area (local anaesthesia), thereby enabling surgery or other procedures to be performed without the patient incurring pain and distress. An anaesthetist assesses the patient's fitness to undergo anaesthesia, chooses and administers the appropriate drugs, monitors the patient during the operation or procedure, and supervises the recovery period. The anaesthetist also plays a major role in pain management. A consultant anaesthetist will usually have 'FRCA' (Fellow of the Royal College of Anaesthetists) after their name.

(b) *Cardiology* – the study of the diseases of the heart. A cardiologist is a physician who specialises in this branch of medicine. A cardiac surgeon carries out surgical procedures in relation to the heart. If a cardiac surgeon has also been trained in the field of vascular surgery (relating to diseases affecting the arteries and veins) and/or thoracic surgery (relating to diseases inside the thorax – the chest – including the oesophagus and the diaphragm), they will be a cardiovascular, cardiothoracic or cardiovascular thoracic surgeon. A consultant cardiologist will usually have 'MRCP' or 'FRCP' (Membership or Fellowship of one of the Royal Colleges of Physicians) after their name. A cardiac surgeon will have 'FRCS' (Fellow of the Royal College of Surgeons) after their name.

(c) *Dermatology* – deals with the diagnosis and treatment of disorders of the skin, such as eczema, psoriasis, dermatitis and skin infections, and those affecting the hair and nails. A consultant dermatologist will usually have 'MRCP' or 'FRCP' after their name.

(d) *Geriatric medicine* – relates to disorders and diseases associated with old age (usually over 65) and their social consequences. A consultant geriatrician will usually have 'MRCP' or 'FRCP' after their name.

(e) *Gynaecology* – deals with the female pelvic and urogenital organs in both the normal and diseased state. It encompasses aspects of contraception, abortion and in vitro fertilisation (IVF). Practitioners may also specialise in obstetrics (see below). A consultant gynaecologist will have 'MRCOG' or 'FRCOG' (Membership or Fellowship of the Royal College of Obstetricians and Gynaecologists) after their name.

(f) *Haematology* – the study and treatment of blood and blood disorders, such as blood clotting deficiencies, leukaemia, myeloma, lymphoma, and Hodgkin's Disease. A haematologist also deals with blood transfusions and treatments involving warfarin and heparin. A consultant haematologist will have FRCPath' (Fellowship of one of the Royal Colleges of Pathologists) after their name.

(g) *Medical oncology* – the treatment of cancer. Clinical oncologists are largely concerned with radiotherapy, whilst medical oncologists deal with the medical management of those suffering from the disease. They liaise with primary care providers, clinical oncologists and other health professionals, and providers of palliative care. The consultant oncologist may have 'MRCP' or 'FRCP', or 'FRCR' (Fellow of the Royal College of Radiologists) or 'FRCS' after their name.

(h) *Neurology* – the study of the nervous system and its disorders, ie the patient's nerves, sensory and motor functions and reflexes, and will cover injuries to the brain, neck and back, neurodegenerative disorders, epilepsy and multiple sclerosis. A consultant neurologist will have 'MRCP' or 'FRCP' after their name. A neurosurgeon operates on the brain and spine, and deals with trauma and injuries to both, with brain tumours and haemorrhages, and with spinal nerve problems. A consultant neurosurgeon will have 'FRCS' after their name.

(i) *Obstetrics* – covers pregnancy and birth, and is concerned with the health of the mother and of the foetus from conception to delivery. The obstetrician will also deal with sterilisations and infertility, cervical cancer, tumours of the ovaries and endometriosis. Both doctors and nurses can specialise in obstetrics. A consultant obstetrician will have 'MRCOG' or 'FRCOG' after their name.

(j) *Occupational health* – this deals with the effect of work on the individual's health, both mental and physical, and the effect of ill-health on the individual's work. Specialists identify and treat specific occupational illnesses and diseases, and deal with the prevention of ill-health caused by chemical, biological, physical and psychological factors arising in the workplace. The term 'occupational health' covers a number of areas, and therefore there are various specialists, including occupational physicians, occupational psychologists, occupational health nurses, occupational hygienists, disability managers, workplace counsellors, health and safety practitioners, and workplace physiotherapists. The consultant occupational physician will usually have 'FFOM' (Fellow of the Faculty of Occupational Medicine) after their name. Others specialising in this area may have a Diploma in Occupational Medicine (DOccMED).

(k) *Ophthalmology* – the diagnosis and treatment of disorders of the eye. The consultant ophthalmologist will usually have 'FRCOphth' (Fellow of the Royal College of Ophthalmologists) after their name.

(l) *Orthopaedics* – this is concerned with injuries to and disorders of the bones and muscles. Surgeons who work in this area may specialise in certain parts of the body – the knee, the hip, the spine etc. The orthopaedic surgeon will have FRCS after their name, possibly followed by (Orth) and/or (Tr & Orth) signifying their specialism in orthopaedics and trauma.

(m) *Paediatrics* – diseases and illness affecting children. A paediatrician may have a sub-speciality, eg a paediatric neurologist, a paediatric surgeon, etc. The consultant paediatrician will normally have 'MRCP' or 'FRCP' after their name, and may have 'FRCPCH' (Fellow of the Royal College of Paediatrics and Child Health).

(n) *Palliative care* – the care of patients suffering from a terminal illness, including pain control and psychological and spiritual care, and the provision of services either at home or in a hospital, hospice or day centre. It also encompasses support for the family of the patient, which continues into the bereavement period.

(o) *Pathology* – the science of the changes which the body goes through as a result of disease. A pathologist examines body samples in order to diagnose disease and undertakes post-mortem examinations in order to determine the cause of death. The consultant pathologist will have 'FRCPath' after their name.

(p) *Physiotherapy* – the use of exercise, manipulation, and heat in the treatment of disease or injury, which is often essential in the rehabilitation process. All physiotherapists will have either 'MCSP' (Member of the Chartered Society of Physiotherapy) or 'FCSP' (Fellow of the Chartered Society of Physiotherapy) after their names, and must be registered with the Health and Care Professions Council, the regulatory body for physiotherapists.

(q) *Psychiatry* – the branch of medical science which treats mental disorder and disease, and which helps with the management of individuals with learning disabilities. A psychiatrist deals with depression, PTSD, drug and substance abuse, schizophrenia, etc. A consultant psychiatrist will have 'MRCPsych' or 'FRCPsych' (Member or Fellow of the Royal Colleges of Psychiatrists) after their name.

(r) *Psychology* – the scientific study of how people think, how and why they act, react and interact as they do. It covers memory, rational/irrational thought, intelligence, learning, personality, perception and emotions. Psychology is used in promoting rehabilitation and assessing rehabilitation needs following an accident. There are a number of different branches, including educational psychology (concerned with children's learning and development), clinical psychology (concerned with reducing psychological stress in those suffering from depression, mental illness, brain injuries and the after effects of trauma), health psychology (concerned with behaviour relating to health, illness and care) and occupational psychology (relating to how people perform at work). Psychologists are not medically qualified but rather have a graduate degree in psychology plus an accredited postgraduate qualification leading to chartered status.

(s) *Rheumatology* – medical speciality concerned with the study and management of diseases of the joints and connective tissue, including rheumatoid arthritis, osteoarthritis, osteoporosis, whiplash and repetitive strain injury. A consultant rheumatologist will have 'MRCP' or 'FRCP' after their name.

2.4 COMMON ABBREVIATIONS USED IN MEDICAL RECORDS

AAL	Anterior axillary line
ACTH	Adrenocorticotrophic hormone
ADH	Antidiuretic hormone
AE	Air entry
AF	Atrial fibrillation
AFB	Acid fast bacillus (TB)
AFP	Alpha-fetoprotein
AJ	Ankle jerk (reflex)
Alk	Alkaline (phos = phosphatase)
An	Anaemia
ANF	Antinuclear factor
Anti-D	This gamma globulin must be given by injection to Rhesus negative mother who delivers/aborts Rhesus positive child/foetus to prevent mother developing antibodies which could damage a subsequent Rhesus positive baby
Apgar	Apgar score: means of recording baby's condition at and shortly after birth by observing and 'scoring' (0, 1 or 2) 5 parameters
AP	Anteroposterior
APH	Antepartum haemorrhage
ARM	Artificial rupture of membranes (labour)
ASO	Antistreptolysin O
ATN	Acute tubular necrosis
A/V	(a) Anteverted
	(b) Arterio venous
AXR	Abdominal x-ray (plain)
Ba	Barium
BD	To be given/taken twice a day
BJ	Biceps jerk (reflex, see AJ)
BMJ	British Medical Journal
BMR	Basal metabolic rate
BO	Bowels open
BP	British Pharmacopoeia
BP	Blood pressure
BS	(a) Breath sounds
	(b) Bowel sounds
	(c) Blood sugar
C_2H_5OH	Alcohol
ca	Carcinoma/cancer

Ca	Calcium
Caps	Capsules
CAT scan	Computed axial tomograph scan
CBD	Common bile duct
cc	(a) Carcinoma (cancer)
	(b) Cubic centimetre
CCF	Congestive cardiac failure
Ch VS	Chorionic villus sampling
CI	Contraindications
Cl	Clubbing (of finger or toe nails)
CLL	Chronic lymphocytic leukaemia
CML	Chronic myeloid leukaemia
CMV	Cytomegalovirus
CN I-XII	Cranial nerves 1 – 12
CNS	Central nervous system
C/O	Complaining of
CO_2	Carbon dioxide
COETT	Cuffed oral endotracheal tube
COT	Cuffed oral tube (an endotracheal tube used for ventilating a patient who cannot breathe unaided)
CPD	Cephalo-pelvic disproportion (baby too large to fit through pelvis)
CSF	Cerebro-spinal fluid
CT	Computerised tomography
CTG	Cardiotocograph (trace during labour of baby's heart and mother's contractions)
CVA	Cardiovascular accident (stroke)
CVP	Central venous pressure
CVS	Cardiovascular system
Cx	Cervix
CXR	Chest x-ray
Cy	Cyanosis
DB	Decibel
D&C	Dilation (cervical) and curettage
DM	Diabetes mellitus
DNA	Deoxyribonucleic acid (also 'did not attend')
DOA	Dead on arrival
D&V	Diarrhoea and vomiting
DVT	Deep venous thrombosis
D/W	Discussed with
Dx	Diagnosis
ECG	Electrocardiography
ECT	Electroconvulsive therapy
EDC	Expected date of confinement
EDD	Expected date of delivery
EEG	Electroencephalogram/graph (brain scan)
ENT	Ear, nose and throat
ERCP	Endoscopic retrograde choledochopancreatico/graphy/scope
ERPC	Evacuation of retained products of conception
ESR	Erythrocyte sedimentation rate (blood)
ETR	Examined through clothes
EtoH	Alcohol
ET(T)	Endotracheal (tube)
EUA	Examined under anaesthesia
FB	(a) Finger's breadth
	(b) Foreign body
FBC	Full blood count

FBS	Foetal blood sampling (a procedure which is carried out during labour to check on the baby's condition)
FH	Family history
FHH	Foetal heart heard
FHHR	Foetal heart heard regular
FHR	Foetal heart rate
FMF	Foetal movements felt
FSE	Foetal scalp electrode
FSH	Follicle-stimulating hormone
G	gram
GA	General anaesthesia
GB	Gall bladder
GFR	Glomerular filtration rate
GI	Gastro-intestinal
GIT	Gastro-intestinal tract
G6PD	Glucose 6 phosphate dehydrogenase
GP	General practitioner
GTT	Glucose tolerance test (for diabetes)
GU	Genito-urinary
GUT	Genito-urinary tract
h	Hour
Hb	Haemoglobin
Hct	Haemocrit
HOCM	Hypertrophic obstructive cardiomyopathy
HPC	History of presenting complaint
HRT	Hormone replacement therapy
HS	Heart sounds
HVS	High vaginal swab
Hx	History
ICP	Intracranial pressure
ICS	Intercostal space
IDA	Iron deficiency anaemia
IDDM	Insulin dependent diabetes mellitus
Ig	Immunoglobulin
IJ	Internal jugular vein
IM	Intramuscular
ISQ	In status quo
IT	Intrathecal
ITP	Idiopathic thrombocytopenic purpura
ITU	Intensive therapy unit
iu	International unit
IUCD	Intrauterine contraceptive device
IV	Intravenous
IVC	Inferior vena cava
IVI	Intravenous infusion (drip)
IVU	Intravenous urography
Ix	Investigations
J	Jaundice
°JACCO	No jaundice, anaemia, cyanosis, clubbing or oedema
JVP	Jugular venous pressure
K^+	Potassium
kg	Kilogram
KJ	Knee jerk (reflex, see AJ)
kPa	Kilopascal, approximately 7.5 mmHg
L	(a) Litre

	(b) Left
LA	Local anaesthesia
LBBB	Left bundle branch block
LFTs	Liver function tests
LH	Luteinising hormone
LIF	Left iliac fossa
LIH	Left inguinal hernia
LMN	Lower motor neurone
LMP	First day of the last menstrual period
LN	Lymph node
LOA	Left occiput anterior (position of baby's head at delivery, see also LOP, ROA, ROP, LOL, ROL, OA, OP)
LOC	Loss of consciousness
LOL	Left occipitolateral (see LOA)
LOP	Left occiput posterior (see LOA above)
LP	Lumbar puncture
LS	Letter sent
LSCS	Lower segment caesarean section (the 'normal' type of caesarean section)
LSKK	Liver, spleen and kidneys
LUQ	Left upper quadrant
LVF	Left ventricular failure
LVH	Left ventricular hypertrophy
mane	In the morning
mcg	Microgram
MCL	Mid clavicular line
MCV	Mean cell volume
µg	Microgram
mg	Milligram
mist	mixture
mitte 1/12	Supply/give/send/provide
ml	Millilitres
mmHg	Millimetres of mercury (pressure)
mMol	Millimol
MRI	Magnetic resonance imaging (=NMRI)
MS	Multiple sclerosis
MSU	Mid stream urine
N&V	Nausea and vomiting
Na	Sodium
$NaHCO_3$	Sodium bicarbonate
NAD	Nothing abnormal diagnosed/detected
NBM	Nil by mouth
ND	Notifiable disease
ng	Nanogram
NG	(a) Naso-gastric
	(b) Carcinoma/cancer (neoplastic growth)
NMCS	No malignant cells seen
NMR	Nuclear magnetic resonance (scan)
noct/nocte	At night
NOF	Neck of femur
N/S	Normal size
NSAID	Non-steroidal anti-inflammatory drugs
O_2	Oxygen
OA	(a) Occipito-anterior (see LOA)
	(b) Osteoarthritis
OCP	Oral contraceptive pill

OE	On examination
OP	Occipito-posterior (see LOA)
Orthop.	Orthopnoea (breathlessness on lying flat)
P	Pulse
P or p	Period
PA	Posteroanterior
PAN	Polyarteritis nodosa
PC	Post cibum (after food)
pCO_2	Partial pressure of carbon dioxide (normally in blood)
PCV	Packed cell volume
PERLA	Pupils are equal and react to light and accommodation
PE	(a) Pulmonary embolism
	(b) Pre eclampsia
PEFR	Peak expiratory flow rate
PET	Pre-eclamptic toxaemia
pg	Picogram
pH	Acidity and alkalinity scale. Low is acidic. High is alkaline. pH7 is about neutral
PH	Past/previous history
PID	(a) Pelvic inflammatory disease
	(b) Prolapsed intervertebral disc
PIP	Proximal interphalangeal
PL	Prolactin
PMH	Past/previous medical history
PND	Paroxysmal nocturnal dyspnoea
PN (R)	Percussion note (resonant)
po	Per os (by mouth)
pO_2	Partial pressure of oxygen (normally in blood)
POH	Past/previous obstetric history
POP	Plaster of Paris
PoP	Progesterone only pill
PPH	Post-partum haemorrhage
pr	Per rectum (by the rectum)
prn	As required – of eg, pain killers
PRV	Polycythaemia rubra vera
PTH	Parathyroid hormone
PTT	Prothrombin time
PU	Peptic ulcer
PV	Per vaginam (by the vagina)
QDS	To be given/taken 4 times a day
R	Right *or* respiration
RA	Rheumatoid arthritis
RBBB	Right bundle branch block
RBC	Red blood cell (erythrocyte)
RE	Rectal examination
Rh	Rhesus factor
RIC	Raised intracranial pressure
RIF	Right iliac fossa
RIH	Right inguinal hernia
ROA	Right occiput anterior (see LOA)
ROL	Right occipito-lateral (see LOA)
ROM	Range of movement
ROP	Right occiput posterior (see LOA)
RS	Respiratory system
RT	Radiotherapy
RTA	Road traffic accident

RTI	Respiratory tract infection
RUQ	Right upper quadrant
SB	Serum bilirubin
S/B	Seen by
SBE	Subacute bacterial endocarditis
SC	Subcutaneous
S/D	Systolic/diastolic (heart and circulation)
SE	Side effects
SH	Social history
SJ	Supinator jerk (reflex: see AJ)
SL	Sub linguinal (under the tongue)
SLE	Systemic lupus erythematosus
SOA	Swelling of ankles
SOB (OE)	Shortness of breath
SOS	(a) if necessary
	(b) see other sheet
SROM	Spontaneous rupture of membranes
stat	Immediately
Supp	Suppositories
SVC	Superior vena cava
SVD	Spontaneous vaginal delivery
SVT	Supraventricular tachycardia
SXR	Skull x-ray
Ts and As	Tonsils and Adenoids
TCI 2/52	To come in (to be admitted to hospital), in 2 weeks' time
tds	To be given/taken 3 times a day
TGH	To go home
THR	Total hip replacement
TIA	Transient ischaemic attack
TJ	Triceps jerk (reflex: see AJ)
TPR	Temperature, pulse and respiration
TSH	Thyroid stimulating hormone
TTA	To take away
TVF	Tactile vocal fremitus
TX	Transfusion
UC	Ulcerative colitis
U&E	Urea and electrolytes (biochemical tests)
UG	Urogenital
UMN	Upper motor neurone
URTI	Upper respiratory tract infection
USS	Ultra sound scan
UTI	Urinary tract infection
VA	Visual acuity
VE	Vaginal examination
VF	Ventricular fibrillation
VT	Ventricular tachycardia
V/V	Vulva and vagina
VVs	Varicose veins
WBC	White blood corpuscle/white blood cell count
WCC	White blood cell count
WR	Wasserman reaction
wt	Weight
XR	X-ray

2.5   DIAGRAMMATIC REPRESENTATION OF THE HUMAN SKELETON

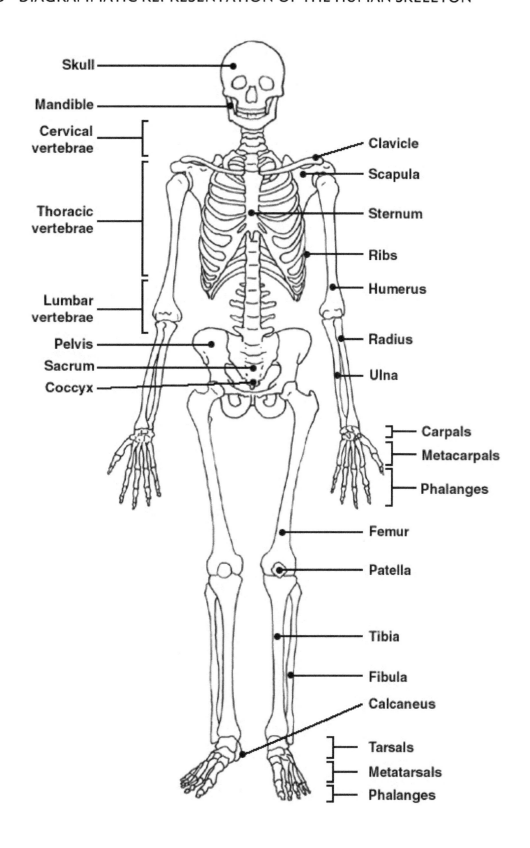

2.6 CONCLUSION

A basic understanding of the medical terms involved in personal injury and clinical negligence cases can assist the trainee when reading medical reports, and also provides an insight into the client's problems which can often be useful in the negotiation of any settlement.

2.7 FURTHER READING

Kemp and Kemp, *The Quantum of Damages* (Sweet & Maxwell Ltd)

Black's Medical Dictionary (Bloomsbury Business)

Dorland's Medical Abbreviations (Elsevier)

Other appropriate medical textbooks or online resources

ROAD TRAFFIC AND OTHER HIGHWAY CLAIMS: THE LAW

> **LEARNING OUTCOMES**
>
> After reading this chapter you will be able to:
>
> - describe how liability for road traffic accidents may be established
> - set out the circumstances in which a claimant might be held to be contributorily negligent and how damages might be reduced in such circumstances
> - explain the role of insurance and insurers in this type of claim
> - explain the role of the Motor Insurers Bureau, and the impact of the Uninsured Drivers Agreement 1999 and the Untraced Drivers Agreement 2017
> - set out the statutory duties of highway authorities and the defence under s 58 of the Highways Act 1980.

3.1 INTRODUCTION

According to the Department of Transport's statistical release on 21 January 2022, *Reported Road Casualties in Great Britain: provisional estimates year ending June 2022*, which is based on accidents reported to the police from 1 July 2021 to 30 June 2022, 1,760 people were killed in road traffic accidents. The number of people seriously injured (discounting for those who were killed) was 28,044, and the overall number of casualties of all severities was 137,013. Not surprisingly, therefore, road traffic accidents form a large part of the personal injury lawyer's casework. E-scooter statistics are now being collated by the Department for Transport. There were 1,437 casualties in collisions involving e-scooters, compared to 1,033 in the year ending June 2021. There were 12 fatalities (11 of whom were e-scooter riders; 1 a pedestrian) compared to 4 in the year ending June 2021.

A road user may be liable to an injured person, or to the estate or dependants of a deceased person, on the basis of common law negligence. A highways authority may be liable to such people on the basis of negligence and/or breach of statutory duty.

3.2 ESTABLISHING LIABILITY FOR ROAD TRAFFIC ACCIDENTS

3.2.1 The duty of one road user to another

All road users have a duty of care to avoid causing injury to others whom it may reasonably be anticipated may be injured by their actions or failure to act. The term 'road user' includes not only those driving motor vehicles or riding motorbikes or bicycles, but also their passengers, pedestrians and owners of roadside property, such as signs and bollards, and the highway itself, which in most cases will be the local highway authority.

Clearly, a driver has a duty to drive carefully so as not to cause injury to their passengers or other road users, but other examples include the duty of a driver not to park their vehicle where it might constitute a danger, the duty of a pedestrian not to step into the path of a vehicle, and the duty of the highway authority to keep the highway in good repair.

This duty of care is well-established and, in the majority of cases, will not be in dispute between the parties.

3.2.2   The standard of care

The standard of care is that of the ordinary skilful driver, and it is not lowered to take account of the fact that the driver is a learner driver (see *Nettleship v Weston* [1971] 2 QB 691).

A driver is not entitled to assume that other road users will always exercise reasonable care and skill, but a driver is not 'bound to anticipate folly in all its forms' (*London Passenger Transport Board v Upson* [1949] AC 155). Neither is the duty so high that it equates to a guarantee of the claimant's safety. In *Ahanonu v South East Kent Bus Company Limited* [2008] EWCA Civ 274, where the claimant had been trapped between the defendant's double-decker bus and a metal bollard, the Court of Appeal reversed the finding that the driver of the bus had been negligent. Lord Justice Laws said that the judge had imposed a counsel of perfection on the bus driver, thereby distorting the nature of the driver's duty, which was no more or less than a duty to take care.

This view was reiterated in *Stewart v Glaze* [2009] EWHC 704 (QB), where a driver was found not liable for injuries incurred by the claimant, who had stepped into the path of his car without warning. The judge commented that it was important to ensure the court was not guided by '20:20 hindsight'. In *Smith v Co-operative Group Ltd & Another* [2010] EWCA Civ 725, the Court of Appeal considered the case of a 13-year-old newspaper boy, who had, without looking, cycled out of a driveway across a pavement and into the path of a lorry. The defendant lorry driver had braked and swerved but could not avoid hitting the claimant. The defendant admitted that he had not sounded his horn, but relied on expert evidence that this would not have prevented the accident from occurring. The judge found against the defendant (although the claimant was held to be 60% contributory negligent), ignoring the expert evidence, and instead relying on his own opinion that, if the defendant had sounded his horn when the claimant was halfway across the pavement, the claimant would have reacted by stopping or cycling out of the way. In allowing the appeal, the Court of Appeal demonstrated its unwillingness to impose a standard of driving on motorists which amounts to a counsel of perfection. It held that the defendant had not been negligent in failing to sound his horn at the same time as being involved in emergency braking and swerving to avoid a collision.

3.2.3   Breach of duty

Each case must turn on its own facts. It is for the court to decide whether there has been any breach of the duty to take reasonable care in relation to other road users. When trying to answer this vital question, personal injury lawyers should consider legislation designed to regulate the conduct of road users and the Highway Code.

3.2.3.1   Are there any relevant criminal convictions?

Evidence of the defendant being convicted of a relevant criminal offence is of particular importance to the claimant's solicitor in order to establish breach of duty. Likewise, a relevant conviction of the claimant may assist the defendant's solicitor in negating liability or establishing contributory negligence. A conviction will be relevant where it relates to how the accident was caused or to the quantification of damages. So, for example, a defendant who was driving without insurance at the time of the accident may have been in breach of the criminal law, but a conviction for this offence will not be relevant for the purposes of civil proceedings. Convictions arising from the accident should be set out in the police accident report (see **10.10.3.1**). The following issues are some, but by no means all, of the matters for which you should look out:

(a)   *Vehicle maintenance:*

    (i)   Under s 40A of the Road Traffic Act 1988 (RTA 1988), it is an offence to use, cause or permit another to use a motor vehicle on a road when its condition is such that its use involves a danger of injury to any person.

    (ii)   Under s 41A of the RTA 1988, a person who uses a motor vehicle, or causes or permits such a vehicle to be used on a road when the vehicle does not comply with regulations governing the construction and use of brakes, steering-gear or tyres, is guilty of an offence. Current regulations relating to tyres specify a minimum tread depth, prohibit the mix of radial and cross-ply tyres, and require tyres to be inflated to the correct pressure for the vehicle.

(b)   *Poor driving.* The most important issues of relevance are as follows:

    (i)   Speeding. Driving at a speed in excess of the limit is not necessarily in itself sufficient evidence of negligence (*Quinn v Scott* [1965] 2 All ER 588). Neither will driving below the speed limit automatically negate liability (*Richardson v Butcher* [2010] EWHC 214 (QB)). Under the Highway Code, drivers should adjust their driving to the prevailing conditions and circumstances. So they must take account of the weather, available light, road layout, weight of traffic, parked vehicles or other obstructions, the presence of cyclists and motorcyclists, and the likelihood of pedestrians, particularly children, crossing the road. A driver who fails to adjust their speed in appropriate circumstances risks prosecution for dangerous or careless driving.

    (ii)   Dangerous driving. Under s 2 of the RTA 1988, it is an offence to drive dangerously on a road or other public place. For the purposes of this section, a person drives dangerously if the way they drive falls far below what would be expected of a competent and careful driver, and it would be obvious to a competent and careful driver that driving in that way, or driving the vehicle in its current state, would be dangerous. (For causing death by dangerous driving, careless driving or whilst under the influence of alcohol, see **17.3.1**.)

    (iii)   Careless and inconsiderate driving. Under s 3 of the RTA 1988, it is an offence to drive without due care and attention, or without reasonable consideration for other persons using the road. A person will drive in this way if the way they drive falls below what would be expected of a competent and careful driver.

(c)   *The influence of alcohol or drugs.* Under the RTA 1988, a person commits an offence if they:

    (i)   drive, attempt to drive, or are in charge of a motor vehicle on a road or other public place, when they are unfit to do so through drink or drugs (s 4);

    (ii)   drive or are in charge of a vehicle after consuming so much alcohol that the proportion of it in their breath, blood or urine exceeds the prescribed limit (s 5). The current prescribed limits for alcohol are 35 microgrammes of alcohol in 100 millilitres of breath; 80 milligrammes of alcohol in 100 millilitres of blood; and 107 milligrammes of alcohol in 100 millilitres of urine; or

    (iii)   drive or are in charge of a vehicle whilst there is a concentration of specified controlled drugs in excess of specified limits (s 5A). The relevant drugs and associated limits are set out in the Drug Driving (Specified Limits) (England and Wales) Regulations 2014 (SI 2014/2868). It is a defence to show that the drugs had been prescribed and the driver had followed the advice of the person who had prescribed them.

(d)   *The use of mobile phones.* Under s 41D of the RTA 1988, it is an offence to drive or supervise the driving of a motor vehicle whilst holding a hand-held mobile telephone or other interactive communication device contrary to the relevant regulations. Although it is currently not an offence to use a hands-free telephone, should an accident occur whilst the driver is using such equipment, a prosecution for careless or dangerous driving might arise.

(e)   *The wearing of seat belts and child restraints.* Under s 14 of the RTA 1988, it is an offence to drive or ride in a motor vehicle on a road without wearing a seat belt as prescribed by regulations made by the Secretary of State. In accordance with the Motor Vehicles (Wearing of Seat Belts) Regulations 1993 (SI 1993/176) (as amended), the driver must ensure that seat belts are worn, where they are available, by all passengers under the age of 14. Under s 15 of the RTA 1988, the driver must ensure that children are strapped into an appropriate child restraint. The current regulations apply only to children who are both under 1.35 metres in height and under 12 years old.

(f)   *The wearing of safety helmets.* Under s 16 of the RTA 1988, it is an offence to ride on a motor cycle without a safety helmet in accordance with the relevant regulations. Followers of the Sikh religion who are wearing a turban are exempt from this requirement.

3.2.3.2   Are there any breaches of the Highway Code?

A failure on the part of any road user to observe a provision of the Highway Code does not of itself render that person liable to criminal proceedings. Some of the rules set out in the Code, identified by the use of the words 'must' or 'must not', reflect statutory requirements, the breach of which amounts to a criminal offence, whilst others, which are in the nature of guidance, do not. In accordance with s 38(7) of the RTA 1988, all breaches of the Code may be relied upon in the civil courts to establish breach of duty. However, a breach of the Highway Code does not create a presumption of negligence but is merely one of the circumstances which the court will consider when establishing whether a breach of duty has occurred (*Powell v Phillips* [1972] 3 All ER 864, CA; *Goad v Butcher & Another* [2011] EWCA Civ 158).

The personal injury solicitor requires a good knowledge of the Code. Although the printed version must be used for all legal proceedings, you can access an adapted online version at www.gov.uk/guidance/the-highway-code.

3.2.3.3   Res ipsa loquitur

The maxim *res ipsa loquitur* is sometimes thought of as a rule of law whereby the burden of proof shifts from the claimant to the defendant. This is a misunderstanding: it is, in fact, a rule of evidence, and the burden of proof remains on the claimant throughout. Roughly translated as 'the thing speaks for itself', the maxim means that the facts of the case are sufficient proof in themselves. It may be applied in circumstances where the claimant is unable to adduce any evidence as to how or why the accident happened, but is able to show that:

(a)   the accident is such that, in the ordinary course of events, it would not have occurred without negligence; and

(b)   whatever inflicted or caused the damage was under the sole management and control of the defendant.

In such circumstances, where it appears to be more likely than not that the defendant's breach of duty led to the accident, the maxim enables the court to conclude that the claimant has established a prima facie case against the defendant. It is therefore sometimes said that the evidential burden shifts to the defendant. In order to avoid liability, the defendant must either give an explanation of what happened which is inconsistent with negligence or, where the defendant is unable to give such an explanation, demonstrate that the defendant exercised all reasonable care.

In *Ng Chun Pui & Others v Le Chuen Tat & Another* [1988] RTR 298, a coach driven by the first defendant and owned by the second defendant left the carriageway, crossed a grass verge and collided with a public bus travelling in the opposite direction. One passenger in the bus was killed and its driver and other passengers were injured. In the absence of any evidence of any mechanical defect within the defendant's coach, the claimants did not offer any evidence as to how the accident arose but relied on the maxim *res ipsa loquitur*. However, the court accepted evidence put on behalf of the defendants that the driver had been obliged to react to another, untraced vehicle, which had cut in front of him, causing him to brake and swerve, and that this reaction did not constitute a breach of duty. (Reading the full text of the judgment in this case may prove useful for furthering comprehension of *res ipsa loquitur*.)

It is not common for liability in road traffic accidents to be established on the basis of the maxim *res ipsa loquitur*, as there will usually be evidence from the claimant, in the form of eye-witness testimony and/or expert opinion, as to how and why the accident occurred. One case in which it was successfully used is *Widdowson v Newgate Meat Corporation & Others* (1997) *The Times*, 4 December. The claimant, who was suffering from mental disorder, had been walking at the side of a dual carriageway just before midnight, when he was hit by a van driven by an employee of the respondent company. Neither the claimant, who could not be considered a reliable witness, nor the driver of the van gave evidence. Having heard evidence from a psychiatrist on behalf of the claimant, the Court of Appeal held that despite the claimant's mental illness, he was aware of road safety issues, was not a risk-taker and did not have any suicidal tendencies. Moreover, it was 'pure surmise' that he fell into the van's path as a result of losing his balance. Consequently, the defendants had failed to put forward a plausible explanation.

3.2.4 Vicarious liability

Under the doctrine of vicarious liability, an employer is liable for damage caused by the negligence of an employee whilst the employee is acting in the course of their employment. So, if an employee is driving whilst carrying out work for their employer and causes a road traffic accident due to the employee's negligence, the employer will be liable for any resulting personal injury or damage to property.

You will find a more detailed analysis of vicarious liability at **4.4**.

3.2.5 Causation

The claimant will have to prove that the breach of duty caused the loss and damage complained of. The claimant will have to show that 'but for' the defendant's breach, the injuries would not have arisen. Causation will be disputed where the defendant argues:

(a)   that the cause of the injury was not the defendant's breach of duty but the claimant's own negligence. In *Whittle v Bennett* [2006] EWCA Civ 1538, a car driven by the defendant in excess of the speed limit and too close to the car in front, was involved in a collision with the claimant's car. Although the defendant's actions were negligent, the court held that the accident was caused by the gross negligence of the claimant, who had been attempting a U-turn manoeuvre on a busy single-carriage 'A' road. Courts frequently find that the negligence of the defendant and the claimant have played a part in causation, and apportion damages accordingly (see **3.2.6**).

(b)   that the accident could not have caused the injuries complained of. In recent years, it has become increasingly common for insurers to defend on this basis in low-velocity impact claims. This type of accident, where damage to the vehicles may be no more than a scratch, often results in a whiplash claim, where there are no visible signs of injury. In some instances, defendants are going further than disputing the severity of the injuries;

they are making positive allegations that the claimant has fabricated the claim. The Court of Appeal considered these types of cases in *Kearsley v Klarfeld* [2005] EWCA Civ 1510 and *Casey v Cartwright* [2006] EWCA Civ 1280, and gave guidelines as to how they should be dealt with. These guidelines are beyond the scope of this book.

3.2.6 Contributory negligence

The claimant has a duty to take care of their own safety and to take reasonable precautions against risks of injury of which the claimant was aware or ought to have been aware. The claimant's actions or failure to act might amount to a breach of this duty, and the court may conclude that the claimant was fully or partly responsible for the injury suffered. Section 1(1) of the Law Reform (Contributory Negligence) Act 1945 states:

> Where any person who suffers damage as a result partly of his own fault and partly of the fault of any other person or persons, ... the damages recoverable in respect thereof shall be reduced to such an extent as the court thinks just and equitable having regard to the claimant's share in the responsibility for the damage.

Therefore, the court will reduce the amount of damages payable by the defendant to the claimant only where the defendant is able to prove, on the balance of probabilities:

(a)   that the claimant was at fault;

(b)   that the fault was causative of the injury suffered; and

(c)   that it would be just and equitable for the claimant's damages to be reduced.

When determining the extent to which damages will be reduced, the court will apportion responsibility between the parties by looking at the relative causative potency of what each of the parties has done and their respective blameworthiness. (You may find it useful to read the full judgment in *Eagle v Chambers* [2003] EWCA Civ 1107.)

It would be rare for a court to find a pedestrian more responsible than a driver of a vehicle (and therefore reduce damages by more than 50%), unless the pedestrian suddenly moved into the path of the vehicle in circumstances where the driver could not have anticipated such a thing to happen (see *Scott v Gavigan* [2016] EWCA Civ 544, for example, where a man was held to be wholly responsible for an accident caused by his gross carelessness in running in front of an oncoming moped). The court will consider all the relevant circumstances, including whether the driver was driving in a manner appropriate for the prevailing conditions, whether the driver was aware that pedestrians were about and might step into the road, and the age of the pedestrian. Children are not expected to exercise the degree of care reasonably expected of an adult. Very young children will never be held to have been negligent, and those under the age of 12 are seldom held to be so. However, in *AB (by his mother and litigation friend CD) v Main* [2015] EWHC 3183 (QB), an eight-year-old boy who suffered serious brain injuries when he ran into the road without looking and collided with the defendant's car received a 20% reduction in damages for contributory negligence. Older children may be held to be more responsible for their actions. In the case of *Ehrari v Curry & Another* [2007] EWCA Civ 120, the claimant, who was 13 years old at the time of the accident, was held to be 70% to blame for the accident which had left her brain-damaged. The defendant driver had been travelling at no more than 20 miles per hour when the claimant stepped into the road without looking.

In the following types of cases, the courts will follow the precedents set in the cases cited:

(a)   Where a driver or passenger fails to wear a seat belt, damages will be reduced by 25% in cases where the injury would not have happened at all, or by 15% where the injuries would have been less severe (*Froom v Butcher* [1976] QB 286). From time to time, defendants attempt to argue that the court should depart from these guidelines, but the case of *Stanton v Collinson* [2010] EWCA Civ 81 highlights the court's reluctance to do so. In this case, the teenage claimant was a front seat passenger in a car driven by his friend. Neither the claimant nor the girl sitting on his lap wore a seatbelt, and when the driver lost control and crashed into an oncoming car the claimant sustained serious brain damage. In spite of the claimant's reckless behaviour, the Court of Appeal held that there was no contributory negligence as the defendant had failed to supply medical evidence proving the causal link between the claimant's failure to wear a safety belt and his injuries.

(b)   Where a motor cyclist fails to wear a crash helmet, damages will be reduced by 15% (*O'Connell v Jackson* [1972] 1 QB 270) or, where the helmet's chin strap is not fastened, by 10% (*Capps v Miller* [1989] 1 WLR 839).

(c)   Where a passenger allows themselves to be carried in a vehicle when they know the driver is drunk and should not be driving, damages will be reduced by 20% (*Owens v Brimmel* [1977] QB 859).

(d)   Although there is no legal compulsion for a cyclist to wear a helmet, and there has not been a case where damages have been reduced as a result of a cyclist's failure to wear a helmet, in *Smith v Finch* [2009] EWHC 53 (QB) the judge appeared to suggest that such a failure would amount to contributory negligence. On the facts of this case, however, the wearing of a helmet would have made no difference to the injuries sustained by the claimant.

If the claimant has contributed to their own injuries in more than one way, the court will not necessarily calculate the overall reduction simply by adding the normal percentage reductions together. So, in *Gleeson v Court* [2007] EWHC 2397 (QB), where the claimant had allowed herself to be driven in a car when she was aware that the driver was drunk (20% reduction) and had sat in the boot of the hatchback car (25% reduction), the overall reduction was 30%.

The reduction of damages as a result of contributory negligence will be a theoretical, rather than an actual, disadvantage to the motorist who has the benefit of fully comprehensive insurance which includes personal injury cover, as in that type of scenario the motorist's own insurer, being bound to indemnify them for their own injuries irrespective of blame, will cover any shortfall in damages recovered from the defendant. However, few pedestrians, particularly children, will have relevant insurance cover, and therefore they will suffer a loss in real terms from any finding of contributory negligence.

3.3 INSURANCE

3.3.1 Statutory provisions and types of policy

Under s 143(1) of the RTA 1988, any person who drives, or causes or permits another person to drive a motor vehicle on a road or other public place, must have a policy of insurance which, at the very least, covers third party risks. The minimum protection afforded by what is commonly known as a Road Traffic Act policy or third party insurance covers:

(a)   the death or bodily injury of a third party;

(b)   damage to property belonging to a third party up to £1,000,000; and

(c)   any emergency treatment, ie medical or surgical examination or treatment which is required by those suffering an injury (including a fatal injury) immediately following the accident.

A common type of policy, known as Third Party Fire & Theft, provides this minimum cover, plus cover for the policyholder's own vehicle should it be damaged or destroyed by fire or stolen. Neither of these types of policies indemnifies the policyholder where his own vehicle is damaged due to his own negligence, or where nobody was at fault.

Policies which are commonly known as 'fully comprehensive' cover the minimum risks plus damage to the policyholder's own vehicle and property. They might also cover legal expenses arising from taking or defending proceedings following an accident, but terms do vary and should be checked carefully.

3.3.2   Road Traffic Act 1988, ss 151–152

Sometimes, a situation will arise where the defendant was driving a vehicle which was covered by a policy of insurance at the time of the accident, but the insurer may have grounds to avoid paying damages to the claimant. This may arise where:

(a)   the driver of the vehicle who was responsible for the accident was insured to drive that vehicle under the terms of the policy, but the insurance company was entitled to cancel the policy due to a breach of its terms, eg driving whilst under the influence of alcohol, a failure to disclose a material fact, eg the existence of previous driving convictions or a medical condition, such as diabetes or epilepsy, or a failure to report the accident; or

(b)   the driver of the vehicle was not insured to drive the vehicle, eg where a family member or friend of the policyholder drove the vehicle, with or without the policyholder's permission, or a thief drove the vehicle.

In *Cameron v (1) Husain (2) Liverpool Victoria Insurance Co Ltd* [2017] EWCA Civ 366, the Court of Appeal held that a claimant, who was injured in a hit and run incident where the car was identified but the driver was not, was entitled to bring an action against 'The person unknown driving vehicle registration number Y598 SPS who collided with vehicle registration number KG03 ZIZ on 26 May 2013'. The Court held that where a vehicle was insured, and the insured and the registered keeper were known but the driver was not, the driver did not have to be named and s 151 applied, obliging the insurer of the car to satisfy any judgment. This decision was reversed by the Supreme Court in February 2019, on the basis that service of proceedings on the 'hit and run' driver would be impossible, thereby breaching 'the fundamental principle of justice that a person cannot be made subject to the jurisdiction of the court without having such notice of the proceedings as will enable him to be heard'. See *Cameron v Liverpool Insurance Co Ltd* [2019] UKSC 6.

In any of the situations set out at (a) and (b) above, the claimant should not be dissuaded from issuing a claim against the driver on the grounds that damages will not be recovered even if judgment is obtained. Under s 151 of the RTA 1988, the insurance company will be obliged to pay out on the judgment to the claimant, provided notice of the proceedings is given to the insurer, under s 152 of the RTA 1988, before or within seven days after commencement of the proceedings. Because it is not always clear at the start of proceedings whether or not any of the above (a) or (b) situations applies, those acting for claimants in road traffic accident cases should always send out the required notice to the insurer of the vehicle (see **12.3.2**).

Under s 151(4), there is an exception in relation to third parties who were willing passengers in a vehicle they knew or had reason to believe had been stolen or unlawfully taken.

3.3.3   The insurer's role in civil proceedings

Although a claimant is able to issue proceedings directly against the negligent driver's insurers instead of or in addition to the driver (see **10.3.1.2**), many solicitors acting for claimants will proceed only against the driver. If the claimant succeeds in obtaining judgment against the defendant driver, the insurer is obliged to pay out. Consequently, in order to protect their own position, insurers insert a clause into their policies which enables them to initiate or defend proceedings in the name of the insured. This means that the insurer will choose which firm of solicitors to use and will give instructions as to how the matter should be dealt with, including the making and accepting of any offers to settle.

3.3.4   Obtaining insurance details

Where an accident has resulted in personal injury, under s 154 of the RTA 1988, all drivers involved must supply details of their insurance to others involved in the accident. It is a criminal offence either to refuse to supply this information, or to supply false information.

In addition, the Motor Insurers' Bureau (see **3.4**) maintains the Motor Insurance Database (MID), a centralised database of motor insurance policy information of all insured UK vehicles. Insurers who underwrite motor insurance for vehicles on UK roads are obliged to be members of the MIB and to submit the policy details of all vehicles to the MID. For a small fee, those who have suffered injury and/or loss due to a motor accident, or their representatives, may make an online enquiry to obtain information regarding the insurance details of other vehicles involved (www.askmid.com).

Since November 2014, those involved in RTAs are able to use a smart mobile phone or device to check the insurance details of the other driver at the roadside. The 'askMID Roadside' service is free and can be accessed through the website mentioned above.

3.4 THE MOTOR INSURERS' BUREAU

It is not uncommon for individuals to suffer personal injury as the result of the negligence of an uninsured driver or a driver who cannot be traced. The Motor Insurers' Bureau (MIB) was founded in 1946 with the specific purpose of entering into agreements with the Government to compensate victims of negligent, uninsured drivers. All motor insurers are obliged under the RTA 1988 to be a member of the MIB and to contribute to the fund from which compensation is paid. These contributions are funded by the premiums paid by their policyholders.

In this book, we set out the main elements of the Uninsured Drivers and Untraced Drivers Agreements. However, the devil is in the detail and you are advised to carefully consider the relevant agreements, explanatory notes and application forms, which may be found on the MIB's website at www.mib.org.uk.

3.4.1 The Uninsured Drivers Agreement 2015

The Uninsured Drivers Agreement 2015 ('the 2015 Agreement') relates to claims arising from the negligence or intentional assaults of uninsured drivers who can be identified, where the incident occurred on or after 1 August 2015. Accidents occurring prior to this date are governed by older Agreements, the details of which can be found on the MIB's website.

Under the 2015 Agreement, the MIB is obliged to satisfy any judgment obtained against the defendant driver which remains unsatisfied for more than seven days, subject to the exceptions, limitations and preconditions set out in the Agreement. However, where it deems appropriate, the MIB will settle the claim prior to proceedings being commenced.

The form of the application to the MIB will depend upon the value of the claim. Where the value is not more than £25,000 and is within the scope of the Pre-Action Protocol for Low Value Personal Injury Claims in Road Traffic Accidents, the claimant should complete and send the Claim Notification Form (RTA1) through the Claims Portal, as set out in **Chapter 21**. Section H of RTA1 should be completed when there is an uninsured driver and the MIB is to be involved. If the claim falls within the Small Claims RTA Protocol (see **10.2** and **Chapter 21**) then the Small Claim Notification Form (SCNF) should be completed as specified in that Protocol and submitted to the online Official Injury Claim portal. On submission of the SCNF, the Motor Insurers' Database (MID) will be searched to identify the appropriate compensator. Where the MID does not identify a compensator, the claim will be sent to the MIB to deal with as compensator. Otherwise, for example in a small claims road traffic accident which falls outside the RTA Protocol, the application should be made by completing and returning the MIB's standard form, either online or by post and, in either case, supplying any documents in support.

Where the MIB declines to settle the matter and proceedings are necessary, the claimant's solicitors must name the MIB as second defendant (see clause 13(1) of the 2015 Agreement). If this is not done, the MIB will not usually incur a liability to the claimant. However, a claimant may not name the MIB as a party to the proceedings if the claimant initially and reasonably believes liability to be covered by an identifiable insurer. In such a case, if the claimant gives notice of the commencement of the proceedings to the MIB, notifies them promptly as soon as the claimant realises that the insurer has no responsibility, consents to the MIB being joined to the proceedings and promptly supplies relevant documentation to the MIB, the MIB cannot avoid liability on the basis of clause 13(1) (see clause 13(2)).

The onerous reporting requirements which are found in previous MIB Agreements have been omitted from the 2015 Agreement.

3.4.1.1 Exclusions from the 2015 Agreement

The MIB is not obliged to satisfy compensation claims where:

(a)   the claimant has received, or is entitled to receive or demand, payment or indemnity in respect of their losses from any other person, including an insurer, with the exception of the Criminal Injuries Compensation Authority; or

(b)   the person suffering death, injury or loss was voluntarily allowing themselves to be carried in the vehicle and, before the start of their journey in the vehicle (or after such start if they could reasonably be expected to have alighted from the vehicle), they knew or had reason to believe that the vehicle:

    (i)   had been stolen or unlawfully taken, or

    (ii)   was being used without insurance (for more details, see clause 8).

In March 2015, the Court of Appeal held in *Delaney v Secretary of State for Transport* [2015] EWCA Civ 172 that the exclusion of compensation (found in previous MIB Agreements), where a passenger knew or ought to have known that the vehicle was being used in the course or furtherance of a crime, was contrary to European law. Consequently, this provision and the provision which excluded claims where the passenger knew or ought to have known that the vehicle was being used as a means of escape from or avoidance of lawful apprehension were omitted from the 2015 Agreement.

The Supplementary Uninsured Drivers Agreement 2017 amends the 2015 Agreement by deleting the exclusion of claims for damage to the claimant's own vehicle where the claimant knew or ought to have known it was uninsured at the time of the damage, and claims resulting from terrorism, but only where the accident occurred on or after 1 March 2017 (see **3.4.1.1**).

3.4.1.2 Assignment of judgment and undertakings

In accordance with clause 15 of the 2015 Agreement, the MIB is not obliged to settle the judgment unless the claimant:

(a)   assigns the unsatisfied judgment and any order for costs made against the uninsured driver to the MIB. This enables the MIB to pursue the uninsured driver for the amount paid to the claimant;

(b)   undertakes to repay to the MIB any part of the judgment which is set aside, or any compensation received by the claimant from other sources (except the Criminal Injuries Compensation Authority) in respect of the same incident.

3.4.2 The Untraced Drivers Agreement 2017

The Untraced Drivers Agreement 2017 ('the 2017 Agreement') relates to accidents occurring on or after 1 March 2017 and requires the MIB to consider applications for compensation for victims of 'hit and run' cases where the owner or driver cannot be traced. Accidents occurring prior to March 2017 are governed by older agreements, the details of which may be found on the MIB's website.

The 2017 Agreement applies where:

(a)   the claim is in respect of the death of or bodily injury to a person or damage to property which has been caused by, or arisen out of, the use of a motor vehicle on a road or other public place in Great Britain; and

(b)   the death, bodily injury or damage to property occurred in circumstances giving rise to liability of a kind which is required to be covered by a policy of insurance; and

(c)   the person who is alleged to be liable is an unidentified person; and

(d)   the claim is made within the time limits provided for the victims of identified drivers bringing actions in tort by the Limitation Act 1980 (see **Chapter 7**).

Where a claim is made to the MIB, it must be made on the prescribed claim form, which is available on the MIB website.

3.4.2.1   Exclusions and limitations

The 2017 Agreement does not apply where:

(a)   the person suffering death, injury or damage was voluntarily allowing themselves to be carried in the vehicle and before the commencement of their journey in the vehicle (or after such commencement if they could reasonably be expected to have alighted from the vehicle) they knew or ought to have known that the vehicle:

  (i)   had been stolen or unlawfully taken, or

  (ii)   was being used without insurance; or

(b)   the claimant has received, or is entitled to receive or demand, payment or indemnity in respect of their losses from any other person, including an insurer, with the exception of the Criminal Injuries Compensation Authority.

As with the Uninsured Drivers Agreement 2015, previous exclusions prohibiting claims from those who had used a vehicle in the furtherance of a crime, from those who claimed for damage to their own vehicle which had been uninsured at the time of the incident, and from those killed, injured or suffering loss as a result of terrorism, no longer apply (see **3.4.1.1**).

Under clause 7 of the 2017 Agreement, the MIB is not liable for a claim for damage to property unless:

(a)   an award for significant personal injury has been paid to any claimant in respect of the same event. 'Significant personal injury' means bodily injury resulting in death, two nights or more of hospital in-patient treatment or three sessions or more of hospital out-patient treatment; and

(b)   the loss incurred in respect of damage to property exceeds the specified excess, which is currently £400.

3.4.2.2   Obligations upon the claimant

Clause 10 of the 2017 Agreement sets out a number of obligations which the claimant must comply with if the claim is to be allowed to progress. Non-compliance entitles the MIB to reject the claim.

The claim must be commenced by the completion and submission of the MIB's claim form, and the claimant must provide such further information, documentation or written authority to access such documentation as the MIB may reasonably require. In respect of damage to property, evidence of the fact of the damage and of the cost of repair must be produced.

In previous Untraced Drivers Agreements, there were strict time limits within which events leading to claims had to be reported to the police. By clause 10(4)(b) of the 2017 Agreement, the requirement is that the claimant, if they have not already done so, and where reasonably requested by the MIB, must report the matter to the police as soon as reasonably practicable and co-operate with any subsequent police investigation or enquiries.

The claimant, if so required by the MIB and having been granted an indemnity as to the reasonable costs incurred, must take all reasonable steps to obtain judgment against every person who may be liable in respect of the death, bodily injury or damage to property, allowing the MIB to control the steps to be taken and only acting in accordance with the MIB's reasonable instructions. The claimant must also assign to the MIB the benefit of any unsatisfied judgment, including costs obtained in proceedings. Where the claimant has commenced proceedings against a person described above without having been required to do so by the MIB, the claimant must notify the MIB as soon as reasonably practicable, and the obligations set out above in this paragraph will apply.

The Small Claims RTA Protocol, which came into force on 31 May 2021, does not apply to claims falling within the Untraced Drivers' Agreement 2017. See para 4.3(c) of the Small Claims RTA Protocol (see **10.2** and **Chapter 21**).

3.4.2.3 Investigation of claims

The MIB is under an obligation to make an award only if it is satisfied, on the balance of probabilities, that the death, bodily injury or damage was caused in such circumstances that the unidentified person would (had they been identified) have been held liable to pay damages to the applicant in respect of it.

The MIB shall investigate the claim and reach a decision as to whether it must make an award to the applicant, and where it decides to make an award, it will determine the amount. Where the MIB gives notice to the applicant that it has decided to make an award, it shall pay the award within 14 days of a written confirmation from the applicant that the applicant accepts the award.

3.4.2.4 Compensation

The MIB shall award a sum equivalent to the amount which it would have awarded to the applicant for general and special damages if the applicant had brought successful proceedings to enforce a claim for damages against the unidentified person. In calculating the sum payable, the MIB shall adopt the same method of calculation as the court would adopt in calculating damages (clause 11). Interim payments, provisional damages and periodic payments are all catered for in the 2017 Agreement.

It will include in the award a sum representing interest on the compensation payable at a rate equal to that which a court would award a successful litigant.

As mentioned above, compensation for damage to property may only be recovered where the loss exceeds £400. Clause 11(5) places further limitations on compensation for damage to property (the precise details of which are beyond the scope of this book).

3.4.2.5 Contribution towards legal costs

In accordance with clause 21, the MIB will make a contribution to any legal costs incurred by the claimant in seeking advice from a solicitor in relation to the claim. The contribution is calculated strictly in accordance with clause 21, and is the total of the fee (calculated on a sliding scale in accordance with the amount of the award), VAT charged on that fee and any reasonable disbursements.

3.5 DUTIES OF THE HIGHWAY AUTHORITY

Claims against highway authorities include those made by pedestrians who have tripped or slipped on pavements or pathways, and those made by motorists who have been injured in accidents caused by the poor state of roads. Solicitors acting for claimants injured in road traffic accidents should always consider the possibility that a highways authority may be liable to their client in addition to or instead of another road user.

3.5.1 Who is the relevant highway authority?

The local highway authority will be the local county council, metropolitan district council, unitary authority or, in London, either Transport for London or the relevant London borough council. The Secretary of State for Transport or, for roads in Wales, the Secretary of State for Wales, is the highway authority for most motorways and trunk roads.

Section 36(6) of the Highways Act 1980 (HA 1980) requires every council to keep an up-to-date list of all roads and traffic routes within its area for which it is responsible. Section 36(7) states that any person may consult the list at the council offices free of charge. Consequently, if there is any doubt as to whether it is the council who has responsibility or whether the road is in private ownership and privately maintainable, recourse can be made to the records.

It is common for neighbouring councils to enter into agency agreements, whereby one council undertakes maintenance of certain highways on behalf of the other. Ultimate responsibility remains with the statutory highway authority, and legal proceedings should be issued accordingly.

3.5.2 Duty to maintain the highway

3.5.2.1 Duty under statute and common law

Under s 41(1) of the HA 1980, a highway authority has a duty to maintain (which includes a duty to repair) any highway which is maintainable at the public expense. Section 36(2) defines a highway 'maintainable at public expense' as:

(a)   a highway constructed by a highway authority;

(b)   a highway constructed by a council within its own area, or a highway constructed outside of its area for which it has agreed to be responsible;

(c)   a trunk road;

(d)   a footpath or bridleway created or diverted by the local authority.

Highway authorities have a similar duty to maintain highways under common law (see *Dabinett v Somerset County Council* [2006] 12 WLUK 428), and breaches of both statutory and common law duties are commonly pleaded in particulars of claim. Highway authorities also have duties in common law nuisance and under s 150(1) of the HA 1980 to remove obstructions from the highway, but these are outside the ambit of this text.

In *Mills v Barnsley MBC* [1992] PIQR P291, the Court of Appeal held that 'the test of dangerousness is one of reasonable foresight of harm to users of the highway, and that each case will turn on its own facts'. The claimant in that case failed to establish that there was a breach of s 41.

3.5.2.2 Vegetation on land adjoining the highway

In *Yetkin v Mahmood and another* [2010] EWCA Civ 776, a pedestrian was struck by a car when she attempted to cross a main road from a central reservation without waiting for the lights to change in her favour. She claimed that her visibility had been seriously impaired by shrubs which the authority had planted in the central reservation. The Court of Appeal held that, although the planting of shrubs was a reasonable exercise of the authority's powers, planting shrubs which would grow to such an extent as to create a hazard on the highway was a breach of duty.

However, in *Sumner v Colborne and (1) Denbighshire County Council (2) The Welsh Ministers* [2018] EWCA Civ 1006, the Court of Appeal determined that a highway authority did not owe a duty of care to highway users to cut back vegetation on land adjoining the highway which affected visibility, where it could not be attributed to any positive act by the authority. In this case, a cyclist was injured when he was hit by a car emerging from a minor road onto a trunk road. The defendant driver of the car claimed that his visibility had been restricted by the vegetation and launched pre-emptive contribution proceedings against the respondents. There had been no previous cases where the court had to determine whether a duty of care existed as a result of a failure to act, as opposed to a positive act (as in *Yetkin*), and the Court of Appeal refused to establish such a duty in this case.

3.5.2.3   Flooding and snow and ice

Is the duty to maintain the highway limited to the surface of the road itself? In *Department of Transport, Environment and the Regions v Mott Macdonald Ltd & Others* [2006] EWCA Civ 1089, the Court of Appeal considered whether the highway authority was liable to the claimants, who had all been injured in road accidents caused by a dangerous accumulation of water on the surface of the highway, due to the longstanding blockage of the drains serving the road. In overturning the judge's decision, the Court concluded that the duties of a highway authority are not confined to the repair and the keeping in repair of the surface of the highway, and that it is obliged to maintain the drains in good repair. This duty is not limited to the repair of physical damage to the drains, but extends to the clearance of blockages. However, you should note that where a statutory authority, such as Thames Water or Severn Trent, has adopted responsibility for the drains in accordance with an agreement under the Water Industry Act 1991, it will be that authority, rather than the highway authority, which will be responsible for any accident resulting from a failure to maintain the drains.

Does the highway authority have a duty to prevent or remove the accumulation of snow or ice on the highway? It appears that there is no such duty under common law (*Sandhar v The Department of Transport, Environment and the Regions* [2004] EWHC 28 (QB)). However, s 150 of the HA 1980 requires authorities to remove any obstruction of the highway resulting from 'accumulation of snow or from the falling down of banks on the side of the highway, or from any other cause'. In addition, s 41(1A) requires highway authorities to ensure 'so far as is reasonably practicable, that safe passage along a highway is not endangered by snow or ice', and this would appear to include the need to undertake preventative gritting as well as clearing away accumulations of snow and ice. What is reasonably practicable is ultimately a matter for the courts, but one would expect highway authorities to be able to demonstrate that they have planned and implemented a winter service plan in accordance with *Well-managed Highway Infrastructure: A Code of Practice* (see **3.5.3**).

3.5.2.4   The role of contractors

Although the general rule is that employers are not liable for the torts of their independent contractors, statutory duties are non-delegable. Consequently, a highway authority which delegates responsibility for the repair and maintenance of a highway, does not escape liability to a claimant who is injured due to the negligent failure of the contractor to discharge its responsibilities.

3.5.2.5   The role of statutory undertakers

There are organisations, such as those dealing with gas, electricity, water, cable TV and telephones, which have apparatus on or under the highway. Such statutory undertakers are entitled to break up the highway under licences granted by the highway authority. They are, of course, required to take measures to ensure the highway is safe whilst the works are being carried out and to make good the highway following the completion of the works. Nevertheless, the responsibility to ensure that the highway does not pose a danger to road users remains with the highway authority and, subject to a successful defence under s 58 of the HA 1980, a claim against it for injuries caused by the dangerous condition of the highway will be successful. Where there is a possibility that a s 58 defence may be successful, claimants should commence proceedings against both the highway authority and the statutory undertaker. Where proceedings are commenced against the highway authority only, those acting for the authority should consider whether it is appropriate to issue an additional claim under CPR, Part 20, in order to pass all or part of the blame to the statutory undertaker (see **12.12**).

3.5.3   Breach of duty

In order to succeed in a claim against the highway authority, a claimant will have to prove:

(a)   that the condition of the highway made it a foreseeable danger to road users; and

(b)   the condition of the highway was due to the failure of the highway authority to maintain it; and

(c)   that the damage was caused by the dangerous condition of the highway.

In applying the foreseeability test, the danger must be foreseeable to a road user having reasonable care for his own safety. In *Rider v Rider* [1973] 1 All ER 294, Sachs LJ concluded that:

> The highway authority must provide not merely for model drivers, but for the normal run of drivers to be found on their highways, and that includes those who make the mistakes which experience and common sense teach us are likely to occur.

When considering whether the highway authority has failed to maintain the highway, reference should be made to the *Well-maintained Highway Infrastructure* Code of Practice produced by the UK Roads Liaison Group (UKRLG) and published in October 2016 ('2016 Code'). The 2016 Code replaced the 2005 Code of Practice ('Old Code') that had existed before it. The UKRLG was established in 2001, to bring together national and local government highways engineers from across the United Kingdom, to advise on roads infrastructure engineering and operational matters. UKRLG is supported by four boards, the UK Bridges; Lighting; Roads; and Traffic Management Boards, who provide specialist advice. Membership of the UKRLG is drawn from the national governments of the UK, the chairs of the Boards, and representatives of the professional bodies representing highway engineers.

The status of the 2016 Code is set out at A.1.2. This makes clear that the 'Code of Practice is not statutory but provides Highway Authorities with guidance on highways management. Adoption of the recommendations within this document is a matter for each Highway Authority, based on their own legal interpretation, risks, needs and priorities'. The 2016 Code states that each highway authority should 'adopt a risk-based approach and a risk-management regime for all aspects of highway maintenance policy ... including safety and condition inspections, and determining repair priorities ...'. The 2005 Code was more prescriptive in its guidance, for example, setting out specific categories of road with suggested frequencies of inspection. This approach has been replaced with the risk-based approach set out in the 2016 Code.

The 2016 Code proceeds on the basis that 'Adoption of a risk-based approach, taking account of the advice in the Code, will enable authorities to establish and implement levels of service appropriate to their circumstances'. The 2016 Code makes clear that this risk-based approach should be adopted for all aspects of highway infrastructure maintenance, including 'setting levels of service, inspections, responses, resilience, priorities and programmes' (see Recommendation 7 of the 2016 Code). Although the guidance and recommendations set out in the 2016 Code are not mandatory and allow discretion on the part of individual highway authorities, and although '[t]here are no prescriptive or minimum standards', courts are likely to treat the 2016 Code as a highly relevant consideration when determining whether a breach has occurred. The courts will no doubt expect highway authorities to justify their decisions and action or inaction by reference to the recommendations in the 2016 Code and the risk-based approach set out there.

In *AC v Devon CC* [2013] EWCA Civ 418, a case decided when the Old Code was still relevant, the Court of Appeal found that the first instance judge had erred in treating the Old Code as mandatory instead of guidance. The Court of Appeal made clear in its judgment that the Code did not set out mandatory rules, but that following it was evidence of good practice. The Court made clear that highways authorities must exercise their own judgement. This approach applies to the 2016 Code given that it too is a guidance document and non-mandatory. As stated above, the 2016 Code is not prescriptive in the way that the Old Code was, and it encourages a risk-based discretionary approach by highways authorities.

3.5.3.1   The statutory defence

Under s 58 of the HA 1980, a highway authority may, in its defence, prove that it had taken such care as in all the circumstances was reasonably required to ensure that the highway was not dangerous for traffic. For the purposes of such a defence, the court will attempt to balance the public and private interests, and will have regard to the following matters:

(a)   the character of the highway, and the traffic which was reasonably to be expected to use it;

(b)   the standard of maintenance appropriate for a highway of that character and used by such traffic;

(c)   the state of repair in which a reasonable person would have expected to find the highway;

(d)   whether the highway authority knew, or could reasonably have been expected to know, that the condition of the part of the highway to which the action relates was likely to cause danger to users of the highway;

(e)   where the highway authority could not reasonably have been expected to repair that part of the highway before the cause of action arose, what warning notices of its condition had been displayed.

The test under s 58 as to whether the highway authority had taken such care as in the all the circumstances was reasonably required is an objective test based on the risk, taking into account the factors set out above.

In *Crawley v Barnsley Metropolitan Borough Council* [2017] EWCA Civ 36, the claimant injured his ankle whilst out jogging on a Saturday afternoon, when he tripped on a pothole in the road. The pothole had been reported to the defendant highway authority the previous afternoon, but was not inspected until the following Monday. The defendant's policy was to carry out inspections of highways subject to complaints made on Mondays to Thursdays the following day, and those made on Fridays the following Monday. The Court of Appeal held that the pothole was a Category 1 defect (under the Old Code) which required immediate attention, and the defendant's lack of weekend cover to deal with such issues meant that it could not rely on the s 58 defence in this instance. Lack of resources does not justify a failure to provide a reasonable system of inspection and maintenance.

3.5.4   Tripping and slipping cases

Tripping and slipping claims against highway authorities under s 41 of the HA 1980 (and other land owners) are very common. They may arise, for example, as a result of uneven or unstable paving stones, broken or missing kerbstones, potholes, protruding tree roots, missing manhole covers and highway surfaces which have become slippery, such as where there is an abundance of moss or wet leaves, or an accumulation of snow or ice.

As with other claims regarding the highway, the courts have been at pains to point out that each case should turn on its own facts and that the trial judge should determine whether the highway is in a dangerous condition. The court in *Littler v Liverpool Corporation* [1968] 2 All ER 343 gave the following guidance:

> The test ... is reasonable foreseeability of danger. A length of pavement is only dangerous if, in the ordinary course of human affairs, danger may reasonably be anticipated from its continued use by the public who usually pass over it. It is a mistake to isolate and emphasise a particular difference in levels between flagstones unless that difference is such that a reasonable person who noticed and considered it would regard it as presenting a real source of danger. Uneven surfaces and differences in level

between flagstones of about an inch may cause a pedestrian ... to trip and stumble, but such characteristics have to be accepted.

When considering the point at which differing levels in a highway become dangerous to pedestrians, practitioners sometimes do refer to one inch as being the appropriate measurement. However, claimants have been successful where the difference has been as little as one-eighth of an inch (*Pitman v Southern Electricity Board* [1978] 3 All ER 901).

3.6 CONCLUSION

Road traffic accident claims are the most common type of personal injury claims, and they are, in the main, fairly straightforward. This means that the trainee solicitor or junior solicitor is likely to be dealing with this type of case when they are first introduced to personal injury work. It is useful to be aware that many lower value claims will be handled, on behalf of claimants and defendants, by individuals who have no legal qualifications, sometimes with minimal training and supervision. If the solicitor has a thorough understanding of the legal principles which govern RTA claims, they will bring clarity to the procedure and will be better able to bring about the optimum conclusion for their client in the particular circumstances of the case.

3.7 FURTHER READING AND RELEVANT WEBSITES

Uninsured Drivers Agreement 2015

Untraced Drivers Agreement 2017

www.mib.org.uk

www.askmid.com

www.ciht.org.uk/ukrlg

www.justice.gov.uk/courts/procedure-rules/civil/protocol/pre-action-protocol-for-personal-injury-claims-below-the-small-claims-limit-in-road-traffic-accidents-the-rta-small-claims-protocol

www.officialinjuryclaim.org.uk/media/1157/guide-to-making-a-claim-version-20-april-2021.pdf

www.officialinjuryclaim.org.uk/media/1176/_scnf_21-05-2021-14-02.pdf

EMPLOYERS' LIABILITY CLAIMS: THE LAW

LEARNING OUTCOMES

After reading this chapter you will be able to:

- explain the duty of care owed by an employer to an employee at common law
- explain how an employer may be liable to an employee for breach of statutory duty
- identify breaches of key health and safety regulations
- explain how an employer may be vicariously liable for the negligence of an employee
- understand the defences that are likely to be relied upon in a workplace claim
- explain the role of the Health and Safety Executive in enforcing health and safety in the workplace.

4.1 INTRODUCTION

For accidents which occurred before 1 October 2013, an employer may be personally liable to an injured employee on the basis of:

(a) common law negligence; and/or

(b) breach of statutory duty, for example under the Health and Safety at Work, etc Act 1974 (HSWA 1974), the Occupiers' Liability Act 1957 (OLA 1957) or by way of health and safety regulations made under the HSWA 1974, including pursuant to European Directives prior to Brexit.

The heads of liability are not mutually exclusive. For example, in certain circumstances the employer may be liable to the injured employee under both heads, while in other circumstances the employer may be liable only in common law negligence but not otherwise. The employer may also be vicariously liable to the injured employee where the injury was caused by a tort (eg, negligence) of another employee who was acting in the course of their employment. We consider these heads of liability below, together with the defences which are most likely to be relied upon.

For accidents which occurred on or after 1 October 2013, the Enterprise and Regulatory Reform Act (ERRA) 2013 removes the right to bring a civil claim for breach of nearly all health and safety regulations, and so for such claims employers will only be personally liable on the basis of common law negligence. We discuss the likely impact of this major change in the law below (see **4.3.3**).

In addition to civil liability, an employer who breaches health and safety regulations may face a criminal prosecution. This is also considered below, together with the role of the Health and Safety Executive (HSE) in investigating accidents.

4.2 THE EMPLOYER'S COMMON LAW DUTY OF CARE

An employer is under a duty to take reasonable care of their employees' health and safety in the course of their employment. This includes providing health checks (for example if employees are engaged in hazardous work), equipment to protect employees from injury, and medical equipment in order to mitigate the effects of any injury.

This duty to take 'reasonable care' was explained by Lord Wright in *Wilsons & Clyde Coal Co Ltd v English* [1938] AC 57 as requiring an employer to exercise due care and skill in four particular areas, ie to provide:

(a) competent staff;
(b) adequate plant and equipment;
(c) a safe system of work; and
(d) safe premises.

Many of the common law duties are confirmed or strengthened by statute and regulations, but common law rules are an important indication of how courts are likely to interpret new regulations. Each of the four areas identified by Lord Wright is discussed in further detail below.

4.2.1 Competent staff

In many cases the employer will be vicariously liable for the negligence of an employee which results in injury to a fellow worker. An employer may also be personally liable under its common law duty. The duty is on the employer to take reasonable care to provide competent fellow workers. Whether the employer has failed to take reasonable care may depend upon the knowledge that the employer has (or ought to have) of the work colleague's incompetence or inexperience, etc. In *Hudson v Ridge Manufacturing Co* [1957] 2 QB 348, the employer was held liable for continuing to employ a man who over a space of four years had habitually engaged in horseplay such as tripping people up. On the day in question he tripped the claimant, as a result of which the claimant injured his wrist. The court held that as this potentially dangerous misbehaviour had been known to the employer for a long time, and as they had failed to prevent it or remove the source of it, they were liable to the claimant for failing to take proper care of his safety.

However, in other cases involving practical jokes by fellow workers, employers have been held not liable on the basis that they could not reasonably have foreseen the behaviour that caused the injury (*Smith v Crossley Bros* (1951) 95 Sol Jo 655; *Coddington v International Harvester Co of Great Britain* (1969) 113 SJ 265).

4.2.2 Adequate plant and equipment

Accidents may also occur either because no plant or equipment is provided, or because inadequate equipment is provided. For example, if an employee suffers injuries falling from a makeshift means of gaining access to high shelves, the employer will be liable if no ladder has been provided for this purpose.

'Plant' simply means anything used in the course of work. It will include everything from large and complicated machinery (eg, a paper mill) to the most basic equipment (eg, an office chair). The duty rests on the employer to take reasonable steps to provide adequate equipment and materials to do the job, and then to maintain that equipment. For example, if an office swivel chair gives way under an employee, the employer may be liable for failing to maintain the chair, or for having inadequate provision for maintenance or renewal. The employer will also be vicariously liable if employees fail to maintain or repair such plant or equipment.

The duty to maintain plant and equipment in good order is now supplemented by the Provision and Use of Work Equipment Regulations 1998 (SI 1998/2306) (see **4.3.2.3**). When considering whether plant has been adequately maintained, the court will look to current practice, which will be different according to the type of equipment involved. Depending on the type of equipment, all or any of the following matters may be relevant, and evidence should be looked for, both when using the PAP and at the disclosure stage of litigation:

(a)   inspection and servicing records;

(b)   reports of defects, breakdown or poor running;

(c)   replacing worn-out parts or equipment;

(d)   steps taken to repair or replace equipment shown to be defective.

The frequency and method of inspection or testing that employers should adopt will depend on the nature of the equipment in question. Items which are subject to stress, such as ropes, should be inspected and, if necessary, replaced more regularly than items which are subject simply to ordinary wear and tear, such as floor coverings.

The requirement to provide adequate plant also extends to a duty to make reasonable provision of safety and protective equipment, eg goggles, safety gloves and shoes. This duty at common law is now supplemented by the Personal Protective Equipment at Work Regulations 1992 (SI 1992/2966) (see **4.3.2.4**).

If an employee is injured as a result of a latent defect in the equipment they are using, the employee may also be able to rely on the Employer's Liability (Defective Equipment) Act 1969, which imposes a form of strict liability on the employer. Section 1(1) provides:

> Where ... an employee suffers personal injury in the course of his employment in consequence of a defect in equipment provided by his employer for the purposes of the employer's business and the defect is attributable wholly or partly to the fault of a third party (whether identified or not) the injury shall be deemed to be also attributable to negligence on the part of the employer.

4.2.3 Safe system of work

The duty to provide a safe system of work is very wide and will be a question of fact to be considered in each case. It covers such things as:

(a)   the physical layout of the plant;

(b)   the method by which work is carried out;

(c)   the sequence in which work is to be carried out;

(d)   the provision of instructions;

(e)   the taking of any safety precautions;

(f)   the provision of proper warnings and notices (*Speed v Thomas Swift & Co* [1943] KB 557).

The employer must take care to see that the system is complied with, bearing in mind the fact that an employee may become careless after a time, especially if the work is of a repetitive nature (*General Cleaning Contractors Ltd v Christmas* [1953] AC 180).

EXAMPLES

In *General Cleaning Contractors Ltd v Christmas* [1953] AC 180, the claimant window cleaner was instructed by his employers in the sill method of cleaning windows. He was to hold on to the window sash whilst cleaning. A window closed on his fingers and he fell to the ground. It was held that the employers were in breach of their duty to provide a safe system of work, as they should have told the claimant to test the sashes to see if they were loose, and should have provided him with wedges.

In *Morgan v Lucas Aerospace Ltd* [1997] JPIL 4/97, 280–1, the claimant was employed in the defendants' factory to clean waste swarf (oil contaminated with metal waste) from trays underneath machinery. He had been given no formal training. Swarf caught in the machine cut through his heavy-duty glove, causing a gash to the claimant's hand. The claimant alleged this injury was caused by the defendants' failure to provide and maintain a safe system of work. In the first instance, it was held that the defendants were not absolved from the duty to provide a safe glove merely because it was difficult or expensive to obtain. If no better glove could be obtained at a reasonable price, the whole system was unsafe. The defendants appealed. On appeal, it was held that it was not necessary for the claimant to prove what alternative system of work could be adopted and which would have been safer. The claimant proved that the defendants allowed an unsafe practice to be adopted which they ought to have known to be unsafe and which they could have altered. If the gloves provided were the best available, the obligation of the defendants was to devise a system which would remove or reduce the risk of injury.

In *Johnson v Warburtons Ltd* [2014] EWCA Civ 258. The claimant was injured when his foot slipped on steps as he was exiting a side door of his lorry. There were two steps, which were steep, vertically uneven but horizontally deep. In order to use the steps a hinged flap had to be lifted vertically and secured with a catch. This was not a purpose built 'grab-point' but could be used as a handhold. There was no handrail. As he exited the lorry the claimant came down the stairs facing forwards. He was not holding onto the flap, his foot slipped off the bottom step and he fell into a gully breaking his ankle.

The steps themselves had been introduced to avoid the need for drivers to jump on and off partially deployed tail lifts, and had been specifically approved by the HSE prior to the accident. The defendant's newer fleet of lorries had been modified so that access was via three rather than two steps, however the evidence was that this was because three steps would be more comfortable to use and not due to any safety considerations. There was no specific risk assessment regarding use of the steps. Subsequent to the accident a guide was produced which suggested that the flap could be used as a handhold and that, if it was, it should be secured in an upright position.

The Claimant put his case two ways: (i) that the steps were unsuitable and posed an inherent risk of injury – they were not a safe system of work; or (ii) if that was wrong, the steps were so unsafe that drivers should have been trained in their use and advised to use the flap as a handhold.

The Court of Appeal upheld the decision of the judge at first instance who found that no training was needed and no risk assessment necessary because the need to take care was obvious.

4.2.4   Safe premises

It is accepted that the duty of care extends to the provision of safe premises. The duty applies not only to premises occupied by the employer, but also to premises occupied by a third party where the employee is working temporarily (*General Cleaning Contractors Ltd v Christmas* [1953] AC 180; *Wilson v Tyneside Window Cleaning Co* [1958] 2 QB 110). The duty is supplemented by the Workplace (Health, Safety and Welfare) Regulations 1992 (SI 1992/3004) (see **4.3.2.6**).

Slipping and tripping cases are frequent causes of negligence claims at work, as is shown by the amount of advice and preventative information available to employers from the HSE. The employer must act reasonably to ensure that floors and means of access are reasonably safe.

4.2.5   The requirement of 'reasonableness'

It should be remembered that the duty on the employer is not absolute but merely a duty to take reasonable care. Generally a high standard will be required, but it will vary according to the circumstances.

The standard of care demanded of an employer was summarised by Swanwick J in *Stokes v Guest Keen and Nettlefold Bolts & Nuts Ltd* [1968] 1 WLR 1776:

> The overall test is still the conduct of the reasonable and prudent employer, taking positive thought for the safety of his workers in the light of what he knows or ought to know; where there is a recognised and general practice which has been followed for a substantial period in similar circumstances without mishap, he is entitled to follow it, unless in the light of common sense or newer knowledge it is clearly bad; but where there is developing knowledge, he must keep abreast of it and not be too slow to apply it
>
> ...

Section 16 of the HSWA 1974 authorises Approved Codes of Practice (ACOPs), which set out guidance as to what is good practice in a particular trade and, as such, are a reflection of current informed thinking in the health and safety industry. Similarly, Guidance Notes issued by the HSE, although not binding, will be indicative of whether good working practices were being followed. It will be difficult for an employer to argue that a risk could not be foreseen where information was available in documents published by the HSE.

In *Stokes*, Swanwick J went on to say that an employer

> must weigh up the risk in terms of the likelihood of injury occurring and the potential consequences if it does; and he must balance against this the probable effectiveness of the precautions that can be taken to meet it and the expense and inconvenience they involve.

The employer must take into account the likelihood and potential gravity of an injury. It must then consider the measures necessary, and the cost involved in taking those measures, to avert the risk of injury. In *Latimer v AEC Ltd* [1953] AC 643, the claimant was one of 4,000 employees at the defendant's factory. During a night shift, the claimant slipped on the factory floor, the surface of which had become oily following recent flooding after a thunderstorm. The House of Lords held that it was reasonable for the defendant to be put on the night shift rather than close the factory until the oily surface had been rendered safe.

The duty of care is owed to each employee individually, and so all the circumstances relevant to each employee must be taken into account. A good illustration of this is the case of *Paris v Stepney Borough Council* [1951] AC 367, in which the employer was held to be negligent for failing to supply goggles to a one-eyed workman, even though it was not necessary to provide goggles to fully-sighted workers.

4.2.6   Personal nature of duty

The employer will escape liability only if the employer shows that both the employer and the person to whom the employer delegated the duty exercised reasonable care in the discharge of that duty (*Davie v New Merton Board Mills Ltd* [1959] AC 604). Therefore, the duty is not discharged, for example, merely by delegating it to an apparently competent manager, if that manager in fact fails to act competently (*Sumner v William Henderson & Sons Ltd* [1964] 1 QB 450; *McDermid v Nash Dredging & Reclamation Co Ltd* [1987] 2 All ER 878).

An employer can remain liable for the safety of an employee, even while the employee is under the control of someone else. For example, where an employee on a building site is injured whilst working on a different building site under the control and instruction of different contractors, because the employee had been sent to work for the contractors by the employee's own employer, the employer can be found liable for failing to ensure that the employee was properly trained and for failing to maintain a safe system of work, even though the employer had no control over management of that site (*Morris v Breaveglen Ltd* [1993] ICR 766, CA).

In certain circumstances both an independent contractor and an occupier of a building may also owe a duty of care to the employee of one of its subcontractors. See *EH Humphries (Norton) Ltd, Thistle Hotels v Fire Alarm Fabrication Services Ltd* [2006] EWCA Civ 1496. The judge was entitled to find in the circumstances that the defendant's right to supervise the work so as to ensure that it was carried out safely, imposed on it a duty of care which extended to the employees of the subcontractor who actually carried out the work. The defendant had been negligent in failing to obtain from the subcontractor a proper method statement of the work to be carried out, or a proper risk assessment.

4.3 BREACH OF STATUTORY DUTY

The relationship between an employer and employee is usually closely regulated by statute. The basic principles are set out below.

Legislation generally falls into one of the following categories:

(a)   The HSWA 1974, ss 2 and 3 impose obligations on employers and the self-employed to ensure, so far as reasonably practicable, the health and safety of their employees and members of the public who might be affected by their activities. A breach of s 2 or s 3 will usually give rise to criminal liability (see **4.9.3**).

(b)   Regulations (made under the HSWA 1974, s 15, including to comply with EU Directives prior to Brexit). A failure to comply with regulations may lead to a criminal prosecution by the HSE; and for accidents occurring before 1 October 2013, a breach of such regulations could also give rise to a civil claim for breach of statutory duty. However, for accidents which occur after that date, s 69 of the ERRA 2013 has removed the right to bring a civil claim for a breach of nearly all such regulations, although a breach may be relied on as evidence of negligence (see **4.3.3**).

In addition, s 16 of the HSWA 1974 authorises Approved Codes of Practice (ACOPs), which set out what is good practice in a particular trade. Unlike a breach of the 1974 Act or regulations, a failure to observe an ACOP will not give rise to criminal liability, but it will be admissible in evidence in criminal proceedings. These ACOPs will also be admissible in civil proceedings as evidence of good practice in the trade and, as such, are a reflection of current informed thinking in the health and safety industry. Similarly, Guidance Notes issued by the HSE, although not binding, will be indicative of whether good working practices were being followed.

4.3.1 Civil liability for breach of statutory duty

To be successful in a civil claim based on a breach of statutory duty, the injured employee must show that:

(a)   the breach is actionable in a civil court;
(b)   the duty is owed to the claimant by the defendant;
(c)   the claimant's loss is within the mischief of the Act;
(d)   the defendant is in breach of the duty;
(e)   the breach caused the loss.

4.3.1.1 Is the breach of duty actionable in a civil court?

Although a breach of statutory duty is primarily a crime, under s 47(2) of the HSWA 1974 it may also give rise to civil liability, except where the statute expressly provides otherwise. However, for accidents which occur on or after 1 October 2013, s 69 of the ERRA 2013 amends s 47(2) to provide that there is no right of action for breach of statutory duty in relation to a health and safety regulation, except to the extent that regulations made under s 47 make provision for this (see further **4.3.3** below). To date the only exceptions that have been provided are for pregnant workers and new mothers under the Health and Safety at Work etc Act 1974 (Civil Liability) (Exceptions) Regulations 2013 (SI 2013/1667).

4.3.1.2 Has the defendant breached their statutory duty?

The standard required of the employer to fulfil their statutory duty is a question of construction of the statute. The common words used are as follows:

(a) 'Shall' or 'shall not': these words impose an absolute duty (or 'strict') obligation to do (or not to do) the act or thing in question. It is not permissible to argue that it is impracticable, difficult or even impossible to do it (or not to do it).

(b) 'So far as reasonably practicable': when judging whether there has been a breach, the court will balance the risk against any sacrifice (eg, in terms of time, trouble or money) required to avoid the risk. In *Davies v Health & Safety Executive* [2002] EWCA Crim 2949, [2003] IRLR 170, the court considered s 40 of the HSWA 1974, which deals with the interpretation of 'reasonably practicable'. Section 40 imposes on the defendant the burden of proving to the court that it was not reasonably practicable to do more than was in fact done to satisfy the duty (the reverse burden of proof). This was attacked by the defendant as being incompatible with the presumption of innocence in Article 6(2) of the European Convention for the Protection of Human Rights and Fundamental Freedoms (ECHR) 1950. On appeal, the Court found that Article 6(2) was not breached, and confirmed that a defendant who wishes to raise a defence of reasonable practicability does have the legal burden of calling positive evidence to prove that it was not possible to have done more to prevent the death or injury. The Court justified this stance by observing that the defence should not be difficult for a defendant to prove, as the defendant will have this information to hand, whereas it would be unreasonable to place this burden on the prosecution.

(c) 'As far as practicable': this duty is stricter than 'reasonably practicable' but not an absolute duty. Lord Goddard, in *Lee v Nursery Furnishings Ltd* [1945] 1 All ER 387, described it as something that is 'capable of being carried out in action' or 'feasible'. Once something is found to be practicable then it must be done, no matter how inconvenient or expensive it may be to do it.

4.3.2 Health and safety legislation

It is not possible to set out here all the legislation currently in force; what follows is a summary of some of the regulations that are most frequently relied on in claims for personal injury.

4.3.2.1 Management of Health and Safety at Work Regulations 1999

The revised Management of Health and Safety at Work Regulations 1999 (SI 1999/3242) came into force on 29 December 1999 and replaced the Management of Health and Safety at Work Regulations 1992. These Regulations implemented European Health and Safety Directives relating to the employer's obligations in respect of health and safety for workers, and in relation to minimum health and safety requirements for the workplace as to fire safety.

The main provisions regarding employer's duties are as follows:

Risk assessment (reg 3)

All employers are required to make a suitable and sufficient assessment of the risks to health and safety of their employees, and of persons who are not in their employment but who are affected by the conduct of their undertaking. Having made an assessment of the health and safety risks, it is incumbent upon the employer to try to diminish the risks that have been identified. If the employer has five or more employees, there is a duty to record the risk assessment (reg 3(6)), and to note any significant findings of the assessment and whether any group of employees is identified as being especially at risk. The assessment should be made by asking employees how they carry out their functions, together with taking advice from a relevant health and safety expert and ergonomists. The assessment should be updated and reviewed regularly.

The duty on employers to carry out a risk assessment is likely to be one of the areas highlighted by personal injury lawyers to substantiate whether or not the employer has acted reasonably to provide a safe system of work and to establish the question of foreseeability of harm in negligence claims. In *Allison v London Underground Ltd* [2008] EWCA Civ 71, the Court of Appeal held that the employer was liable when the claimant, a tube train driver, suffered an injury as a result of prolonged use of a traction brake controller. In his judgment Smith LJ asked:

> How is the court to approach the question of what the employer ought to have known about the risks inherent in his own operations? In my view, what he ought to have known is (or should be) closely linked with the risk assessment which he is obliged to carry out under regulation 3 of the 1999 Regulations. That requires the employer to carry out a suitable and sufficient risk assessment for the purposes of identifying the measures he needs to take … [W]hat the employer *ought* to have known will be what he *would* have known if he had carried out a suitable and sufficient risk assessment.

Smith LJ went on to say:

> Plainly, a suitable and sufficient risk assessment will identify those risks in respect of which the employee needs training. Such a risk assessment will provide the basis not only for the training which the employer must give but also for other aspects of his duty, such as, for example, whether the place of work is safe or whether work equipment is safe.

The question of whether an employer has carried out a suitable and sufficient risk assessment will be a central issue in establishing liability in many cases. However, in the case of *West Sussex County Council v Fuller* [2015] EWCA Civ 189, the Court of Appeal held that, despite a failure by the appellant local authority to carry out a risk assessment before asking the claimant to deliver post around the office, the claimant's case failed because there was no causal connection between the task concerned and the injuries she sustained when she tripped on a stair whilst delivering the post.

Principles of prevention (reg 4)

According to reg 4, the principles of prevention of risk to be applied are to:

(a)   avoid risks;

(b)   evaluate the risks which cannot be avoided;

(c)   combat the risks at source;

(d)   adapt the work to the individual, especially as regards the design of workplaces, choice of work equipment, and choice of working and production methods, with a view to alleviating monotonous work and work at a pre-determined rate to reduce their effects on health;

(e)   adapt to technical progress;

(f)   replace the dangerous by the non-dangerous or less dangerous;

(g)   develop a coherent overall prevention policy which covers technology, organisation of work, working conditions, social relationships and the influence of factors relating to the working environment;

(h)   give collective protective measures priority over individual protective measures; and

(i)   give appropriate instruction to employees.

Health and safety arrangements, including review (reg 5)

Employers must make appropriate arrangements for the planning, organisation, control, monitoring and review of preventative and protective measures.

Health surveillance (reg 6)

Employers are required to have an appropriate policy on risk surveillance, having regard to the findings of risks identified by the risk assessment. For example, if the risk assessment of employees showed that there were risks to health from airborne dust, that identified risk should be kept under review by regular health checks for rises in respiratory problems in employees.

Health and safety assistance (reg 7)

Employers must appoint competent persons to assist the employer in carrying out compliance with statutory safety provisions. The Regulations require a safety audit to be carried out by accredited auditors who are suitably qualified. The audit will identify potential hazards in the workplace.

Information for employees (reg 10)

Employers must give information which is comprehensible to employees on health and safety risks and protective measures that should be adopted.

Employers' duties to 'outside workers' (reg 12)

Employers must provide information to 'outside workers' relating to hazards and the protective and preventative measures being taken.

Employee capabilities and health and safety training (reg 13)

Employers must provide adequate health and safety training to employees when first recruited and subsequently on being exposed to new risks. Such training should be repeated periodically.

Risk assessment for new or expectant mothers (reg 16)

For the purpose of reg 16, 'new or expectant mother' means an employee who is pregnant, who has given birth within the previous six months or who is breastfeeding. Where the workforce includes women of child-bearing age and the work is of a kind which could involve risk to the health and safety of a new or an expectant mother, or of the baby, the risk assessment required by reg 3 must include an assessment of that risk. If at all possible, the employee's working conditions or hours of work should be altered so as to avoid the risk. If it is not reasonable or possible to avoid the risk by these means, the employer may suspend the employee from work for so long as is necessary to avoid the risk.

Where a new or an expectant mother works at night and obtains a certificate from a registered medical practitioner or registered midwife showing it is necessary for her health and safety that she should not work for any period identified in the certificate, the employer shall suspend her from work for so long as is necessary for her health and safety.

Protection of young employees (reg 19)

A 'young person' means any person who has not attained the age of 18. In relation to young persons, reg 19 states that employers are under a duty to ensure that young persons are protected from risks which arise as a consequence of the young persons' lack of experience, or absence of awareness of existing or potential risks, or the fact that young persons have not yet fully matured. Subject to this, employers are not allowed to employ young persons for work which is beyond their physical or psychological capacity, or involves harmful exposure to agents which are toxic, carcinogenic, cause heritable genetic damage or harm to an unborn child, or which in any other way may chronically affect human health. Employers must not allow young persons to work where they may be involved in harmful exposure to radiation; nor must employers expose young employees to the risk of accidents which it may reasonably be assumed cannot be recognised or avoided by young persons owing to their insufficient attention to safety, or lack of experience or training.

Duties of employees (reg 14)

Although the main thrust of the Regulations is to confirm the obligations on employers in relation to health and safety, there are also obligations on employees, who have a duty to:

(a)   use machinery, equipment, dangerous substances or other equipment in accordance with the training and instructions which have been given to them by their employer; and

(b)   inform the employer of anything which the employee considers to represent a danger to health and safety, or any shortcomings in the employer's arrangements for health and safety.

4.3.2.2   Health and Safety (Display Screen Equipment) Regulations 1992 (as amended)

The Health and Safety (Display Screen Equipment) Regulations 1992 (SI 1992/2792) are applicable to new display screen equipment (DSE) as from 1 January 1993, and to existing DSE from 1 January 1996. However, the requirement of ongoing risk assessment applies to both old and new DSE as from 1 January 1993.

The main provisions are as follows:

(a)   Employers must make a risk assessment of workstations used by display screen workers and reduce risks identified (reg 2).

(b)   Employers must ensure that display screen workers take adequate breaks (reg 4), and must ensure that an appropriate eyesight test is carried out by a competent person (reg 5).

(c)   Employers must provide users with adequate health and safety training in the use of any workstation upon which they may be required to work (reg 6).

(d)   Employers must also provide adequate health and safety information to DSE operators, which should cover such things as information and reminders of how to reduce risks, such as early reporting of problems and provision of adjustable furniture (reg 7).

The main health problems associated with DSE operation are:

(a)   general fatigue caused by poor workstation design;

(b)   upper limb disorders, such as peritendonitis or carpal tunnel syndrome. Repetitive strain injury (RSI) is the most common problem experienced by keyboard users;

(c)   eyesight problems, such as temporary fatigue, sore eyes and headaches.

Employers should have, and be able to show that they have, an adequate policy designed to reduce risks associated with DSE work. The policy should identify hazards, such as visual fatigue, and action to be taken to reduce risk, such as provision of eyesight tests, screen filters and training in workstation adjustment.

4.3.2.3   Provision and Use of Work Equipment Regulations 1998 (as amended)

The Provision and Use of Work Equipment Regulations 1998 (SI 1998/2306) replace the Provision of Work Equipment Regulations 1992. The Regulations apply to any machine, appliance, apparatus, tool or installation for use at work (reg 2) in all types of workplaces. The Regulations are intended to ensure the provision of safe work equipment and its safe use. The main provisions are as follows:

(a)   The employer shall ensure the suitability of work equipment for the purpose for which it is provided. The equipment must be suitable, by design and construction, for the place in which it will be used and for the intended purpose (reg 4).

(b)   The employer must ensure that the equipment is maintained in an efficient state (reg 5(1)) and, if machinery has a maintenance log, that the log is kept up to date (reg 5(2)).

The wording of reg 5(1) was considered by the Court of Appeal in *Stark v Post Office* [2000] ICR 1013. The claim concerned an accident at work, where a postman was thrown from a bicycle provided by his employer when part of the front brake snapped in two. It was accepted that the defect to the bicycle would not have been detected by a rigorous inspection. Nevertheless, the Court found that the form of words used in the regulation gave rise to a finding of strict liability in relation to the provision of work equipment.

In *Ball v Street* [2005] EWCA Civ 76, the Court of Appeal reinforced the view that reg 5(1) gives rise to liability where injury is caused by machinery that is not in an efficient state of repair. The claimant was a farmer who was injured when part of a hay bailing machine fractured and ricocheted into his left eye. The Court found that notwithstanding that this was a 'freak accident', it was only necessary for the claimant to prove that the equipment failed to work efficiently and that that failure caused the accident. The Court found that the machine was no longer in good repair, neither was it in an efficient state, and such failure caused the accident. The imposition of an absolute duty by the Regulations was designed to render the task of an injured employee easier by simply requiring the employee to prove that the mechanism of the machine, that is the significant part of the machine, failed to work efficiently or was not in good repair and that such failure caused the accident. In this context 'efficient' refers to its state of repair from a health and safety standpoint and not from that of productivity.

Despite this apparent strict line taken by the courts, there have been examples where defendants have escaped liability. In *Smith v Northamptonshire County Council* [2008] EWCA Civ 181, the appellant local authority appealed against a decision that it was strictly liable under the Provision and Use of Work Equipment Regulations 1998, reg 5(1), for failure to maintain an access ramp used by the respondent employee (S) at a person's home. S was employed by the local authority as a carer/driver. As part of her duties, she was required to collect a person (C) from her home and take her by minibus to a day centre. As S was pushing C in a wheelchair down a ramp which led out from C's house, S stepped on the edge of the ramp which gave way, causing her to stumble and injure herself. The ramp had been installed by the NHS some years previously. The Court of Appeal allowed the appeal on the basis that the duty to maintain could not normally apply to something which was part of someone else's property. It could furthermore not normally apply to something in relation to which access was limited, and in relation to which, if some maintenance was necessary, consent to carry out the work was required. S's appeal to the House of Lords was dismissed. Their Lordships confirmed that control over the use of equipment is not enough. Control over the equipment must be demonstrated. This could not be achieved simply from the fact that an employer has assessed and inspected the piece of equipment in question.

(c) If the work equipment must be assembled and installed correctly in order for it to be safe to use, the employer must ensure that:

  (i) it is inspected after installation and prior to being put into service; or

  (ii) it is inspected after assembly at its new location (reg 6(1)).

(d) The employer must ensure that employees have adequate health and safety information, and, if appropriate, written instruction in the use of equipment (reg 8).

(e) The employer must ensure that anyone using the equipment has had adequate training, including as to any risks which use may entail and precautions to be adopted (reg 9). In particular, the ACOP attached to these Regulations states that induction training is particularly important when young people first enter the workplace.

(f) Employers must ensure the protection of persons from dangerous parts of machinery in the following order of precedence (reg 11):

  (i) by fixed guards if practicable; but if not

  (ii) by other guards or other protection devices if practicable; but if not

  (iii) by use of jigs, holders, push-sticks or similar protective devices where practicable; but if not

(iv)   by providing information, instruction, training and supervision as is necessary.

(g)   Employers must ensure that where equipment or the substances produced are at a very high or low temperature, there must be protection to prevent injury to any person (reg 13).

(h)   Employers must ensure that, where appropriate, equipment is provided with one or more easily accessible stop controls, and, where appropriate, emergency stop controls, and that they are clearly visible and identifiable (regs 15, 16 and 17 respectively).

(i)   Employers must ensure that, where appropriate, the equipment is provided with suitable means to isolate it from all sources of energy. This must be clearly identifiable and readily accessible. Appropriate measures must be taken to ensure that reconnection of the energy source to the equipment does not expose any person using the equipment to any risk (reg 19).

(j)   The equipment must be suitably stabilised and suitably lit (regs 20 and 21 respectively).

(k)   When maintenance is being carried out, equipment must be shut down if reasonably practicable (reg 22).

(l)   The equipment must be suitably marked with appropriate health and safety information and warning devices as appropriate (regs 23 and 24).

(m)   Due to the rising number of accidents arising out of the use and misuse of forklift trucks, there are comprehensive regulations relating to the use of mobile work equipment. The Regulations require employers to ensure that employees are not carried on mobile equipment unless it is both suitable and incorporates reasonably practicable safety features (reg 25). They also seek to reduce the risk of equipment rolling over or overturning by placing on the employer an obligation to increase the stability of the equipment by making structural alterations if necessary (regs 26–28).

4.3.2.4   Personal Protective Equipment at Work Regulations 1992 (as amended)

The Personal Protective Equipment at Work Regulations 1992 (SI 1992/2966) make provision for the supply of protective and safety equipment, eg: eye-protectors, respirators, gloves, clothing for adverse weather conditions, safety footwear, safety hats, high-visibility jackets, etc.

The main provisions are as follows:

(a)   Employers must ensure that suitable personal protective equipment (PPE) is provided to employees at risk to their health and safety while at work. Such PPE is not suitable unless (reg 4(3)):

(i)   it is appropriate to the risk involved, the conditions at the place where the exposure to the risk may occur, and the period for which it is worn;

(ii)   it takes account of ergonomic requirements and the health of persons who may wear it, and of the characteristics of the workstation of each such person;

(iii)   it is capable of fitting the wearer correctly, if necessary, after adjustments.

(b)   Before choosing PPE the employer should make an assessment to ensure that it is suitable and compatible with other work equipment used at the same time (reg 6).

(c)   Employers must ensure that PPE is maintained in an efficient state, in efficient working order and good repair, including replacing or cleaning as appropriate (reg 7). The obligation to supply protective equipment relates to identified risks. The Regulations will not be concerned with risks other than those necessitating protective equipment, and no absolute duty was intended to be imposed by reg 7(1) in relation to other risks (see *Fytche v Wincanton Logistics* [2003] EWCA Civ 874). In *Fytche*, the claimant suffered frostbite in the little toe of his right foot because there was a small hole in his boot where the steel cap met the sole. The steel-capped boots were PPE within the 1992 Regulations. The Court found that the boots were provided for the purpose of protecting the employee's foot from falling objects, and therefore his claim must fail.

(d)   Employers must ensure that where PPE is provided, employees obtain such information, instruction and training as is adequate to ensure that they know what risks the PPE will avoid or limit, the purpose of the PPE, and any action they must take to ensure efficient working of the PPE, and must ensure that this information is available to employees (reg 9).

4.3.2.5   Manual Handling Operations Regulations 1992 (as amended)

The Manual Handling Operations Regulations 1992 (SI 1992/2793), reg 2(1), provides a definition of 'manual handling operations' as any transporting of a load (including the lifting, putting down, pushing, pulling, carrying and moving thereof) by hand or bodily force. Many accidents reported to the HSE involve manual handling. Despite moves toward mechanisation in industry, there are still many jobs, such as packaging and warehouse work, requiring the day-to-day lifting of heavy objects. Many claims are brought by health service staff, who may have to lift and carry heavy patients as part of their everyday duties.

The Regulations make provision as follows:

(a)   So far as reasonably practicable, employers must avoid the need for employees to undertake any manual handling involving risk of injury (reg 4(1)(a)).

(b)   If avoidance is not reasonably practicable, employers must make an assessment of manual handling risks, and try to reduce risk of injury. The assessment should address the task, the load, the working environment and the individual's capability (reg 4(1)(b)).

In *Brazier v Dolphin Fairway Ltd* [2005] EWCA Civ 1469, at the time of the alleged injury the claimant was trying to lift down a wooden 6-feet by 6-feet pallet from a stack of pallets which was about 6-feet high. That was the system of work at C's place of employment and was known to his employer. There was a witness statement on behalf of the employer so indicating, and also using words to the effect that the pallets were 'fairly lightweight'.

The judge dismissed the claim on the basis that there was no evidence as to the weight of the pallet that was being lifted down. The judge said: 'I have no means of knowing how heavy it was or whether it was heavy enough to give rise to a foreseeable risk of injury.' He then went on to say that there was evidence that the pallet was roughly 6-feet by 6-feet, '… but I am completely at sea as to the forces and the strains which the claimant had to undergo. I have no expert engineering evidence which tells me anything about the forces of the strains.' The judge took the view that there was no evidence that the system of work that was being employed was unsafe.

On appeal (granting permission to appeal) the Court of Appeal found that it was arguable that the judge made an error of principle. Smith LJ put it like this:

> There comes a point when one does not need detailed evidence or expert evidence. The judge had evidence of a man being required to lift down a 6-feet by 6-feet wooden pallet; a pallet which when in use had to be strong enough to take considerable weight and be used with a fork lift truck. It seems to me to be arguable that no further evidence was needed to decide that a system which required someone to bring down such an object from a height of 6-feet would place that person at risk of injury.

(c)   If it is not reasonably practicable to avoid manual handling operations which involve risk of injury, employers must take steps to reduce manual handling to the lowest level reasonably practicable (reg 4(1)(b)(ii)). In the context of assessing manual handling risks for the purpose of complying with reg 4, the correct approach is for the employer to consider the particular task in the context of the particular place of work and the particular employee who has to perform that task: see *O'Neill v DSG Retail Ltd* [2002] EWCA Civ 1139. In this case the employer conceded that it had failed to give adequate training once it had recognised it was necessary to increase awareness of the risks in manual handling, and therefore it had failed to reduce the risk of injury 'to the lowest level reasonably practicable' (as required by reg 4(1)(b)(ii)).

(d)   Employees must be provided with information on the weight of each load, and the heaviest side of any load whose centre of gravity is not positioned centrally (reg 4(1)(b)(iii)).

Regulation 4 was amended by the Health and Safety (Miscellaneous Amendments) Regulations 2002 (SI 2002/2174) by the addition of the following paragraph:

(3)   In determining for the purposes of this regulation whether manual handling operations at work involve a risk of injury and in determining the appropriate steps to reduce that risk regard shall be had in particular to—

(a)   the physical suitability of the employee to carry out the operations;

(b)   the clothing, footwear or other personal effects he is wearing;

(c)   his knowledge and training;

(d)   the results of any risk assessment carried out pursuant to regulation 3 of the Management of Health and Safety at Work Regulations 1999;

(e)   whether the employee is within a group of employees identified by that assessment as being especially at risk; and

(f)   the results of any health surveillance provided pursuant to regulation 6 of the Management of Health and Safety at Work Regulations 1999.

Employees have a duty to make full use of any system of work provided by the employer to reduce manual handling risks (reg 5). As to the meaning of 'so far as reasonably practicable' in reg 4(1), see *Darrell Grant Hawkes v Southwark LBC* (unreported, 20 February 1998), Court of Appeal (Civil Division). In this case, it was found that the defendant had not carried out any risk assessment as required under the Regulations. The judge made it clear that the burden of proving what was 'reasonably practicable' lay on the defendant and that failure to carry out an assessment did not by itself prove liability, rather it was the failure to take appropriate steps to reduce risk of injury to the lowest level reasonably practicable that was at issue. See also the Lifting Operations and Lifting Equipment Regulations 1998 (SI 1998/2307), which deal with health and safety requirements with respect to lifting equipment.

4.3.2.6   Workplace (Health, Safety and Welfare) Regulations 1992

The Workplace (Health, Safety and Welfare) Regulations 1992 (SI 1992/3004) apply to all workplaces except ships, aircraft and trains, construction sites and mining operations (reg 3). The Regulations are concerned with the way in which the building and the facilities within it may affect employees.

The main provisions are as follows:

(a)   Workplace equipment, devices and systems must be maintained in efficient working order and good repair (reg 5).

(b)   There must be adequate ventilation (reg 6).

(c)   The indoor temperature during working hours must be reasonable, and thermometers must be provided to enable employees to determine the temperature (reg 7).

(d)   Workplaces must have suitable lighting, which, if reasonably practicable, should be natural light (reg 8).

(e)   Workplaces, including furniture, fittings, floors, walls and ceilings, must be kept sufficiently clean. So far as is reasonably practicable, waste materials must not be allowed to accumulate (reg 9).

(f)   Every workstation must be arranged so that it is suitable for any person likely to work there (reg 11).

(g)   Every floor or traffic route surface must be suitable for the purpose for which it is used. In particular, it must have no hole or slope, or be uneven or slippery so as to expose any person to a risk to their health or safety. So far as reasonably practicable, every floor or traffic route must be kept free of obstructions or articles which may cause a person to slip, trip or fall (reg 12). The claim in *Coates v Jaguar Cars Ltd* [2004] EWCA Civ 337 concerned an accident that occurred as the claimant was going up a number of steps at the defendant's factory. The claimant tripped on the third stair, causing him to fall and break his arm. The claimant contended that this amounted to a breach of reg 12 as, if there had been a handrail, he would not have fallen. The Court of Appeal held that there had been no reason to find that the steps posed any real risk provided that those who had used them used a sufficient degree of care, as had been the case for any other steps of this nature. The judge at first instance was correct to have dismissed the claim.

(h) Suitable and sufficient sanitary conveniences must be provided at readily accessible places. They must be adequately lit and ventilated, and kept in a clean and tidy condition (reg 20).

(i) Suitable and sufficient washing facilities must be provided, including showers if required by the nature of the work for health reasons (reg 21).

(j) An adequate supply of wholesome drinking water must be provided at the workplace, which should be readily accessible and conspicuously marked where necessary (reg 22).

4.3.2.7 Work at Height Regulations 2005

The Work at Height Regulations 2005 (SI 2005/735) impose health and safety requirements with respect to work at height where there is a risk of a fall liable to cause personal injury. They contain minimum safety and health requirements for the workplace, including minimum health and safety requirements at temporary or mobile construction sites.

Meaning of work at height

Working at height is defined in reg 2(1) as:

(a) work in any place, including a place at or below ground level;

(b) obtaining access to or egress from such place while at work, except by a staircase in a permanent workplace,

where, if measures required by these Regulations were not taken, a person could fall a distance liable to cause personal injury.

To whom do the Regulations apply?

The Regulations apply to employers, to the self-employed and to any person under an employer's control. This means that the Regulations apply not only to employees working under their employer's control, but also to contractors to the extent that they are under the control of building owners.

Duties relating to the organising and planning of work at height

Every employer is under a duty to ensure that work at height is properly planned, supervised and carried out in a safe manner, subject to its being reasonably practicable to do so. This duty includes the selection of work equipment in accordance with reg 7 (reg 4).

Persons undertaking work at height must be competent, or, if being trained, supervised by a competent person (reg 5).

Requirement for Management Regulations risk assessment

There are prescribed steps to be taken to avoid risk from work at height, including provision of a risk assessment under reg 3 of the Management Regulations (see **4.3.2.1**), which should:

(a) identify whether it is reasonably practicable to carry out the work safely otherwise than at height; and if not

(b) provide sufficient work equipment for preventing, so far as is reasonably practicable, a fall occurring and to minimise the distance or consequences should a fall occur (reg 6 and Sch 1).

Duties relating to the selection of work equipment

When selecting work equipment for use in work at height, the person concerned must give collective protection measures priority over personal protection measures; and must also take account of:

(a)   the working conditions and the risks to the safety of persons at the place where the work equipment is to be used;

(b)   in the case of work equipment for access and egress, the distance to be negotiated;

(c)   the distance and consequences of a potential fall;

(d)   the duration and frequency of use;

(e)   the need for easy and timely evacuation and rescue in an emergency;

(f)   any additional risk posed by the use, installation or removal of that work equipment, or by evacuation and rescue from it (reg 7).

The Regulations also impose duties for the avoidance of risks from fragile surfaces, falling objects and danger areas, requiring that such areas are clearly indicated (regs 9–11); and require the inspection of certain work equipment and of places of work at height (regs 12 and 13 and Sch 7).

4.3.2.8   Control of Substances Hazardous to Health Regulations 2002

The Control of Substances Hazardous to Health Regulations 2002 (SI 2002/2677) came into force on 21 November 2002, and revoked and replaced the 1994 Regulations. They provide a comprehensive and systematic approach to the control of hazardous substances at work, which include chemicals, airborne dusts, micro-organisms, biological agents and respiratory sensitisers.

The main duties on employers are as follows:

Duty to carry out a formal risk assessment

Regulation 6 provides that:

> an employer shall not carry on any work which is liable to expose any employees to any substance hazardous to health unless he has made a suitable and sufficient assessment of the risks created by that work to the health of those employees and of the steps that need to be taken to meet the requirements of these Regulations.

The assessment should be reviewed if circumstances change. In *Naylor v Volex Group Plc* [2003] EWCA Civ 222, the claimant was exposed to a hazardous substance during her employment with the defendant, and as a result suffered from industrial asthma. The defendant had carried out a risk assessment based on standards provided by the HSE which were subsequently withdrawn. The Court of Appeal held that in those circumstances a new risk assessment should have been carried out, and that the defendant was therefore in breach of reg 6.

Duty to prevent or control exposure to risks

Regulation 7 provides that the employer must ensure that the exposure of employees to hazardous substances is either prevented or, where this is not reasonably practicable, adequately controlled.

In *Dugmore v Swansea NHS Trust* [2003] 1 All ER 333, the claimant developed a severe allergy to latex as a result of wearing surgical gloves. The Court of Appeal held that the defendant should have provided vinyl gloves and was in breach of its duty to control the claimant's exposure to latex under reg 7.

The prevention or adequate control of the exposure to hazardous substances must be secured by measures other than the provision of personal protective equipment so far as is reasonably practicable. This means that the employer's first act should be to control the process or substance hazardous to health by, for example, closing off the process or machine, or by providing suitable exhaust ventilation.

Duty to ensure proper use of and to maintain personal protective equipment

Regulation 8 provides that employers must take reasonable steps to ensure that any control measure or personal protective equipment is used or applied properly.

There is also a duty on every employee to make full and proper use of such equipment, and to report any defect in it to the employer.

Regulation 9 provides that employers must ensure that any control measure is maintained in an efficient state, in efficient working order and in good repair. For example, where respiratory equipment is provided, the employer must ensure that thorough examinations and tests of that equipment are carried out at suitable intervals.

Duty to monitor exposure of employees

Regulation 10 requires monitoring to ensure the maintenance of adequate control to substances hazardous to health, or to protect the health of employees. Certain substances and processes require monitoring at specified intervals, and the results of all monitoring must be recorded and kept for at least five years. Where the monitoring relates to the personal exposure of individual employees, the records must be kept for at least 40 years.

Duty to provide health surveillance of employees where necessary

Regulation 11 requires suitable health surveillance where it is appropriate (ie, where a particular task is known to make employees susceptible to a particular injury or disease). Medical surveillance is required for certain substances or processes, and a health record must be kept in respect of each employee under surveillance for at least 40 years.

Duty to provide information and training to employees regarding hazardous substances

Regulation 12 requires an employer to provide its employee with such information, instruction and training as is suitable and sufficient for the employee to know the risks to health created by such exposure, and the precautions which should be taken.

4.3.3 The impact of the Enterprise and Regulatory Reform Act 2013

The ERRA 2013 was part of the Government's response to concerns that the UK had in recent years acquired a so-called 'compensation culture', and that health and safety legislation needed reform.

Section 69 of the ERRA 2013 amended s 47(2) of the HSWA 1974 to remove civil liability for all breaches of statutory duty occurring on or after 1 October 2013. Evidence of a breach of statutory duty might still be relied on to support a claim in negligence, but it will not constitute a cause of action in its own right. This means that an employee injured during the course of their employment will only be able to pursue a claim in common law negligence (see **4.2** above). For accidents occurring after 1 October 2013, we should still expect reference to the health and safety regulations within letters of claim, claim notification forms and particulars of claim, but with the argument that those breaches of the regulations should be seen as evidence of a breach of the common law duty to take reasonable care.

The concept of 'strict liability' will therefore disappear from employers' liability claims, and claimants such as Mr Stark, the postman in *Stark v Post Office* (see **4.3.2.3** above), will no longer be successful. Furthermore, as the claim can only be brought in negligence, the burden of proof will remain with the claimant employee throughout, rather than, as sometimes occurs under the regulations, part of that burden being on the defendant employer to show that it took all reasonably practicable steps to comply with a regulation (see **4.3.1.2**).

Where the accident occurred before 1 October 2013, a claimant employee may still make a claim both in common law negligence and for breach of statutory duty. It is usually difficult, but not impossible, to show that if the employer has complied with regulations, they have nevertheless been negligent. In *Bux v Slough Metals Ltd* [1974] 1 All ER 262, the employer was found to have complied with regulations that required the provision of goggles to its employees, and so had complied with its statutory duty, but it had failed to instruct the employee to wear the goggles and so was in breach of its common law duty. (See also *Franklin v Gramophone Co Ltd* [1948] 1 KB 542; *Close v Steel Co of Wales* [1962] AC 367.)

Equally, the employer may be liable for breach of statutory duty even though the employer has not been negligent. In *Hide v The Steeplechase Company (Cheltenham) Limited & Ors* [2013] EWCA Civ 545, the claimant jockey brought a claim in common law negligence and under reg 4 of the Provision and Use of Work Equipment Regulations 1998 (see **4.3.2.3**) for damages for injuries sustained following a fall during a race. The claim under reg 4 was based on the allegation that the guard rail with which the claimant collided was not suitable work equipment for the purpose for which it was provided. The claim failed at first instance, as the judge held that the common law concept of 'reasonable forseeability' was imported into reg 4. He decided that the way in which Mr Hide fell was unusual, and that the defendant had complied with the requirements laid down by the British Horseracing Authority. Therefore the rail was suitable under reg 4. The claimant appealed and was successful. The Court of Appeal held that the words 'reasonable forseeability' had to be construed in a way which was consistent with the limited concept of forseeability envisaged by the EU Directives which were applicable at the time. It should not be construed in the same way as the classic concept of 'reasonably foreseeable' in common law negligence. The Court of Appeal held that the burden was on the defendant to show that the incident was not 'reasonably foreseeable', ie that it was due to unforeseeable circumstances beyond its control, or to exceptional events the consequences of which could not be avoided. The defendant could not do this, and so the Court of Appeal held that although there was no negligence, there was a breach of reg 4.

It is now a decade since the ERRA 2013 came into force. In *Chadwick v RH Ovenden Ltd* [2022] EWHC 1701 (QB), the High Court considered the impact of s 69 of the ERRA 2013 on common law claims in negligence and gave the following guidance:

> ... the underlying statutory duties remain in place unchanged, certainly in relation to the criminal consequences of breach of those duties and so far as the HSE as the responsible regulator remains concerned. It also does not seem to me to be correct to say that a breach of statutory duty under HSE regulations will after ERRA 2013 automatically constitute negligence; s 69 ERRA 2013 removed the automatic link between a breach of the regulations and the right to claim damages. The most obvious situation where this occurs is where a regulation provided for strict liability for non-negligent breaches; following ERRA 2013 there is no claim in such a situation and that is a change that ERRA 2013 put into effect. Parliament has not, on the other hand, legislated in ERRA 2013 to remove or amend the common law liability of a person for negligence. [para 61]

The court went on to say:

> The reasonable steps that an employer should take are situation specific, and in particular will be influenced by the work that is to take place, and the harm that is foreseeable. It is an objective test as to whether an employer took reasonable steps and it is not for an employer to substitute their own test. An employer will be in breach of this duty if it fails to take a reasonable step even if the employer has not thought about whether or not it should take that step. [para 63]

In relation to foreseeability, the court said:

> The next question was whether the harm caused was reasonably foreseeable, because an employer's duty does not extend to harm that is not reasonably foreseeable. [para 71]

Overall, the *Chadwick* case has brought clarity in this area in respect of the duty owed by the employer where Health and Safety regulations fall to be considered post-ERRA 2013. In practice, it will be important to distinguish regulations which impose strict liability and those that require steps to be taken where 'reasonably practicable'; and as can be seen from *Chadwick*, the question of foreseeability is also important when considering liability.

4.4 VICARIOUS LIABILITY

4.4.1 Definition

An employer will be vicariously liable for their employee's torts if committed in the course of the employee's employment. Therefore, it falls to be established:

(a) whether the tort was committed by an employee; and

(b) whether that employee was acting in the course of (ie, within the scope of) the employee's employment.

4.4.2 'Course of employment'

The employee must have committed the tort 'in the course of his employment', which is less clear than might at first appear. There are many cases on the point, but the nearest to a formulation of a rule is that the employer will be liable for acts of employees if they perform an authorised act in an unauthorised way, but will not be liable for acts not sufficiently connected with authorised acts. This is examined in further detail at **4.4.3** below.

4.4.3 Disobedience of orders by employees

Having established that an employer will be liable for acts of their employees if they are acting within the course of their employment, it is necessary to examine the situation where the employee disobeys the orders of the employer in relation to the way the employee carries out their work. In *Rose v Plenty* [1976] 1 All ER 97, a milkman had been told by his employers not to allow children to help him on his rounds. Subsequently he allowed a child to assist him, and the child was injured while riding on the milk float due to the milkman's negligent driving. On appeal to the Court of Appeal, the employer was found to be vicariously liable. The Court held that the employee was doing his job but was using a method that his employers had prohibited. Nonetheless, he was still found to be working within the scope of his employment as it performed for the benefit of the defendant's business.

Contrast the above with *Lister and Others v Hesley Hall Ltd* [2001] 2 All ER 769. The facts of the case were that the warden of the school abused boys while they were resident at the school. The House of Lords held the defendant vicariously liable for the acts of its employee. The Lords said that the court should not concentrate on the nature of the actual act complained of (abuse) but on the closeness of the connection between the nature of the employment and the tort complained of. They found that the defendant employed the warden to care for the claimants. The abuse took place while he was carrying out the duties required by his employment. On that basis, the proximity between the employment and the tort complained of was very close, and therefore the defendant ought to be liable.

The Court of Appeal applied the reasoning in *Lister and Others v Hesley Hall Ltd* in the subsequent case of *Mattis v Pollock* [2003] EWCA Civ 887. There, the claimant was stabbed by a doorman of a nightclub who was employed by the defendant nightclub owner. The Court found that the defendant expected the doorman to carry out his duties in an aggressive manner; and where an employee was expected to use violence while carrying out their duties, the likelihood of establishing that an act of violence fell within the scope of their employment was greater.

However, in *Graham v Commercial Bodyworks Ltd* [2015] EWCA Civ 47, the claimant's case failed as the act of negligence by the co-worker was found not to have occurred in the 'course of employment'. The facts of the case were that the co-worker sprayed a highly flammable agent onto the claimant's overalls and then lit a cigarette, causing the claimant's overalls to set alight.

The matter was examined again by the Supreme Court in *Mohamud v WM Morrison Supermarkets Plc* [2016] UKSC 11. The claimant was kicked and punched by the defendant's employee (Mr Khan) at a petrol station, in what the judge described as a 'brutal and unprovoked' attack. The claimant brought a claim against the defendant for damages for the injuries he had sustained, on the basis that the employer was vicariously liable for the actions of its employee who worked at the petrol station.

The trial judge held that Morrison Supermarkets were not vicariously liable, and the Court of Appeal agreed, holding that the application of the test for vicarious liability in *Lister* was fact sensitive, and that, in seeking to determine whether the test was satisfied, a court had to focus closely on the facts of the case and pay careful attention to the closeness of the connection between the employee's wrongdoing and the duties the employee was employed to do.

The Supreme Court held that the required connection was not present on the facts of this case. The assault had taken place at a time when Mr Khan's supervisor had told him not to follow the claimant out of the petrol station. Mr Khan had made a positive decision to leave the petrol station and follow the claimant, and he had for 'no good or apparent reason' carried out the attack 'purely for reasons of his own'.

Further, the duties imposed on Mr Khan in terms of his interaction with customers were relatively limited, and involved no element of authority over them or responsibility for keeping order. The case could be distinguished from cases involving vicarious liability where the employee was given duties involving the clear possibility of confrontation and the use of force, or was placed in the situation where an outbreak of violence was likely, such as a night club doorman. Mr Khan's duties included no element of keeping order over customers.

The Supreme Court affirmed the established test set down in *Lister* (see above) but elaborated upon the application of the test, explaining that the court has to consider two matters:

(1) What functions or 'field of activities' were entrusted by the employer to the employee, ie what was the nature of the employee's job? This has to be addressed broadly.

(2) Whether there was a sufficient connection between the position in which the employee was employed and the employee's wrongful conduct to make it right for the employer to be held liable.

When applied to the facts of the case, the Supreme Court took a different view from the courts below and allowed the appeal, holding that there was an unbroken sequence of events between the verbal abuse in the kiosk which was 'inexcusable but within the field of activities assigned to him' and the physical violence. Although it was a gross abuse of his position, it was in connection with the business in which he was employed to serve customers.

Following on from the Supreme Court's decision in *Mohamud*, the case of *Bellman v Northampton Recruitment Ltd* [2018] EWCA Civ 2214 concerned an argument following a Christmas party which had been organised and paid for by the defendant employer. After the party ended, a group of employees, including the claimant and Mr Major, the managing director of the company, went on to a hotel where they continued to drink. At approximately 3 am there was an altercation between the claimant and Mr Major, apparently provoked by comments expressed by the claimant about a new member of staff. Mr Major let loose an expletive-filled rant about his management of the company and punched the claimant to the ground, causing the claimant to hit his head and sustain a serious head injury.

The claimant argued that the assault was in the course of and closely connected to employment and therefore that the defendant was vicariously liable for the actions of Mr Major. The judge at first instance found against the claimant, on the following basis:

> Standing back and considering matters broadly, what was taking place at 3.00 a.m. at the hotel was a drunken discussion that [a]rose after a personal choice to have yet further alcohol long after a works event had ended. Given the time and place, when the conversation was, as it was for a significant time,

on social or sporting topics, no objective observer would have seen any connection at all with the jobs of those employees of the Defendant present. That it then veered into a discussion about work cannot provide a sufficient connection to support a finding of vicarious liability against the company that employed them. It was, or without any doubt became, an entirely independent, voluntary, and discreet early hours drinking session of a very different nature to the Christmas party and unconnected with the Defendant's business. To use a hackneyed expression akin to 'a frolic' of their own.

The Court of Appeal reversed this decision and found in favour of the claimant. The Court of Appeal referred to *Mohamud* as the 'most recent and authoritative distillation of the relevant legal principles to be applied in this area of law'. In considering the two-step test mentioned above, the Court found that the participants were in attendance 'qua staff and managing director', even at the follow-on hotel drinking session, and that Mr Major's remit as managing director was wide. The Court of Appeal decided:

> given the whole context, and despite the time and place at which the assault occurred, Mr Major's position of seniority persisted and was a significant factor. He was in a dominant position and had a supervisory role which enabled him to assert his authority over the staff who were present and to re-assert that authority when he thought it was necessary ... In all the circumstances, therefore, as a matter of law, having conducted an evaluative judgment based upon the primary facts as found, there is sufficient connection between Mr Major's field of activities and the assault to render it just that NR should be vicariously liable for his actions.

Two recent decisions have highlighted that it is not necessary for there to be a formal contract of employment in existence to impose vicarious liability. In *Armes v Nottinghamshire County Council* [2017] UKSC 60, the Supreme Court found a local authority vicariously liable for the abuse committed by foster parents it had appointed. In *Various Claimants v Barclays Bank plc* [2017] EWHC 1929 (QB), a claim was brought against the defendant bank on the basis that it was vicariously liable for the sexual abuse the claimants had suffered at the hands of an independent doctor. The doctor had been instructed by the bank to carry out medical examinations as part of the selection process for potential employees of the bank. The defence was that the doctor was not an employee but an independent contractor for whom the bank was therefore not liable. The High Court rejected that defence, holding that, as the bank had directed the questions the doctor should ask and the examinations he should carry out, the relationship was akin to one of employment. Furthermore, the abuse perpetrated during the examinations was 'inextricably linked' to that quasi-employment.

4.5 OCCUPIERS' LIABILITY

4.5.1 Occupiers' liability to lawful visitors

The OLA 1957 replaces common law rules concerning the duty owed by an occupier to a lawful visitor.

Under s 1(1), 'occupier' is given the same meaning as at common law (s 1(2)), the test for which was said by Lord Denning, in *Wheat v E Lacon & Co Ltd* [1966] AC 552, to be 'who is in sufficient control?'.

A 'visitor' is a person who would be treated as an invitee or a licensee at common law (s 1(2)), and who therefore is a lawful visitor (as opposed to a trespasser). The duty of care extends not only to the visitor's person, but also to his property (s 1(3)).

4.5.2 The nature of the duty of care

The common duty of care is a duty to take such care as in all the circumstances of the case is reasonable to see that the visitor will be reasonably safe in using the premises for the purposes for which he is invited or permitted by the occupier to be there (s 2(2)).

The common duty of care does not impose on an occupier any obligation to a visitor in respect of risks willingly accepted as his by the visitor (s 2(5)).

4.5.3   Discharging the duty of care

The duty is to take 'such care as ... in all the circumstances ... is reasonable', taking into account the degree of care, and of want of care, which would ordinarily be looked for in such a visitor (s 2(3)). So, for example, an occupier must expect children to be less careful than adults. A warning may discharge the duty of care if it is enough to enable the visitor to be reasonably safe (s 2(4)).

In *Tomlinson v Congleton Borough Council and Another* [2002] EWCA Civ 309, [2003] 2 WLR 1120, the claimant was injured when diving into a lake despite signs prohibiting swimming and warning that to do so was dangerous. The defendants argued that the risk of danger was an obvious one which the claimant had willingly accepted; that they owed the claimant no duty of care; or if they did, that it had been discharged by the display of warning notices.

The Court of Appeal agreed with the court of first instance and found in favour of the claimant. The House of Lords overturned the Court of Appeal decision on the basis that it would be unreasonable to impose a duty to protect people from self-inflicted injuries that they sustained when voluntarily taking risks in the face of obvious warnings. Even if the local authority had owed the claimant a duty of care, that duty would not extend to preventing the claimant from diving or warning him against dangers that were obvious. Their Lordships took the view that it was not appropriate to find in favour of the claimant and thereby impose a duty on local authorities to protect those foolish enough to ignore clear warnings. This would be at the expense of the vast majority of people, who might find that they were barred from all manner of recreational activities on public land for fear that they might injure themselves and decide to sue the local authority. See *Tomlinson v Congleton BC* [2003] UKHL 47.

4.5.4   Employing an independent contractor

Where injury is caused to a visitor by a danger due to the faulty execution of any work of construction, maintenance or repair by an independent contractor employed by the occupier, the occupier will not be treated by this reason alone as answerable for the danger if in all the circumstances (s 2(4)(b)):

(a)   he had acted reasonably in entrusting the work to an independent contractor; and

(b)   he had taken such steps (if any) as he reasonably ought in order to satisfy himself that:

      (i)   the contractor was competent, and

      (ii)   that the work had been properly done.

The duty of care under the Act is therefore delegable to an independent contractor. This should be contrasted with the personal nature of the common duty of care owed to an employee, which is non-delegable (see *Wilsons & Clyde Coal Co Ltd v English* [1938] AC 57; and **4.2.6** above).

4.5.5   Exclusion or modification of duty of care

By s 2(1) of the OLA 1957, an occupier may extend, restrict, modify or exclude their duty to any visitor. However, this must be read subject to s 2 of the Unfair Contract Terms Act 1977, under which, in the case of business liability:

(a)   a person cannot by reference to any contract term, or to a notice given to persons generally or to particular persons, exclude or restrict his liability for death or personal injury resulting from negligence;

(b)   in the case of other loss or damage, a person cannot so exclude or restrict his liability for negligence except in so far as the term or notice satisfies the requirement of reasonableness.

4.6   REMOTENESS OF DAMAGE

The defendant will be liable to the claimant only if it can be proved that it was foreseeable that the claimant would suffer damage of the kind that the claimant did in fact suffer. The claimant will generally recover for:

(a)   damage which was reasonably foreseeable; or

(b)   damage which can be shown to flow as a direct consequence of the breach.

Once damage is established as foreseeable (no matter how small), the claimant can recover for the full extent of the injury even if this was unforeseeable (*Smith v Leech Brain & Co Ltd* [1962] 2 QB 405).

4.7   CAUSATION

Whether the claimant can establish causation is a question of fact to be decided by the judge in each case. The basic test both for common law negligence and breach of statutory duty is the 'but for' test. In *Clough v First Choice Holidays and Flights Ltd* [2006] EWCA Civ 15 at [44], Sir Igor Judge said that the term 'but for'

> encapsulates a principle understood by lawyers, but applied literally, or as if the two words embody the entire principle, the words can mislead. ... The claimant is required to establish a causal link between the negligence of the defendant and his injuries, or, in short, that his injuries were indeed consequent on the negligence.

The claimant is not required to show that the breach is the sole cause of the loss; it is sufficient if the breach materially contributed to the loss (*Bonnington Castings Ltd v Wardlaw* [1956] AC 613). To determine who caused the accident, the courts apply common sense to the facts of the case. If a number of people can be shown to have been at fault, that does not necessarily mean that they all caused the accident; it is a question of looking at the facts and deciding which factors are too remote and which are not (*Stapley v Gypsum Mines Ltd* [1953] AC 663).

4.7.1   Disease claims

In most straightforward personal injury claims the issue of causation will be clear. However, this may not be so in occupational disease cases, where two or more defendants have negligently exposed an employee to work practices that may prove injurious to health. This was the situation in the House of Lords' ruling in *Fairchild v Glenhaven Funeral Services Ltd and Others; Fox v Spousal (Midlands) Ltd; Matthews v Associated Portland Cement Manufacturers (1978) Ltd and Others* [2002] UKHL 22, [2002] 3 All ER 305. Here, during the course of his career with more than one employer, the claimant had been exposed to asbestos dust which in later years manifested itself as mesothelioma, a particular type of asbestos-related cancer for which there is no cure. The House of Lords found that where there had been employment with more than one employer and:

(a)   both employers had a duty to take reasonable care to prevent the claimant from inhaling asbestos dust; and

(b)   both were in breach of that duty; and

(c)   the claimant did subsequently suffer from mesothelioma,

then the claimant could recover damages from both former employers. In these circumstances it was not necessary to satisfy the 'but for' causation test. It was enough that the claimant was able to prove that a defendant had materially increased his risk of injury. In his speech to the House, Lord Bingham of Cornhill said that 'such injustice as may be involved in imposing liability on a duty breaking employer is heavily outweighed by the injustice of denying redress to a victim'.

The case of *Barker v Corus (UK) plc & Others* [2006] UKHL 20 was another House of Lords decision following hot on the heels of *Fairchild v Glenhaven Funeral Services*. In *Barker v Corus*, the

House of Lords concluded that where it was established that a number of employers were liable, on the basis that they had negligently exposed an employee to asbestos and thereby created a risk of mesothelioma which did in fact occur, those employers should be liable to the claimant only to the extent of the share of the risk created by their breach of duty. To understand this case, it is necessary to take a step back to the previous state of the law. Prior to this judgment, if there were a number of employers all of whom were negligent to some degree, the claimant would simply sue all of them and claim joint and several liability (ie sue all potential defendants for 100% of the loss and let them apportion the blame between them). This allowed the claimant to gain damages in full from one defendant in circumstances where the others might be insolvent or uninsured. Not surprisingly, defendants and their insurers were keen to resist this.

The facts of the case are as follows. The employer (Corus) appealed against a decision of the Court of Appeal in respect of its liability for damages for negligently exposing Mr Barker to asbestos dust, from which he ultimately died, having contracted mesothelioma. During his career he had worked at three stages where he was exposed to asbestos dust. The first two episodes were due to breaches of duty by his then employers. However, the third instance occurred when he was self-employed, and arose from his failure to take reasonable care for his own safety.

The Court of Appeal held that the defendant was jointly and severally liable with the first employer, but subject to a 20% reduction for B's contributory negligence while he was self-employed.

The defendant submitted that it should not be liable at all as a matter of causation, since there had been a period when B, and no one else, had been responsible for his exposure to asbestos dust; and submitted, amongst other things, that it should be severally liable only according to the share of the risk created by its breach of duty.

By a majority decision the House of Lords held that a defendant who is found liable under the *Fairchild* exception to the usual rule of causation, will be liable only to the extent that it contributed to the risk.

Fairchild constitutes an exception to the normal principles of causation. In the House of Lords judgment it was accepted that there might well be instances when the same principle should be applied to other circumstances. However, those circumstances are likely to be strictly controlled by the courts.

In *Sanderson v Hull* [2008] EWCA Civ 1211, the claimant alleged that she had been infected by the campylobacter bacterium as a result of her employer's breach of duty during the course of her employment as a turkey plucker. At first instance the judge held that her case fell within the *Fairchild* exception. However, the Court of Appeal disagreed. The Court did not accept that this was a case where it was impossible for the claimant to show that 'but for' negligence on the part of her employer there would have been no injury. The appeal judges stated that the conditions set out in *Fairchild* in respect of mesothelioma cases, which might justify a relaxation of the test, were not intended to exclude the application of the exception to other diseases, but an essential element is the impossibility of the claimant satisfying the 'but for' test: mere difficulty of proof is not enough. However, more recently, in *Heneghan v Manchester Dry Docks Limited* [2016] EWCA Civ 86, the *Fairchild* exception was held to apply where the claimant developed lung cancer from exposure to asbestos during the course of employment with different employers, and, following *Barker*, damages were apportioned according to the extent to which each defendant had contributed to the overall exposure and therefore the risk of harm to the claimant.

4.7.2 The Compensation Act 2006

Because of the implications of the House of Lords' ruling in *Barker v Corus*, Parliament acted quickly to negate its effect in the form of s 3 of the Compensation Act 2006, which came into force on 26 July 2006. The effect of s 3 is that where mesothelioma is contracted as a result of negligent exposure to asbestos in the course of employment with more than one employer, the employers will be jointly and severally liable for the damage caused. This means that the employee can claim compensation in full from any one of the negligent employers, who may in turn claim against the remaining employers for a contribution according to their share of the blame. Section 3 strictly only applies to mesothelioma cases, but it may be that, following *Heneghan* (see above **4.7.1**), efforts will be made to extend it to asbestos-induced lung cancer claims.

4.8 THE MESOTHELIOMA ACT 2014 AND THE DIFFUSE MESOTHELIOMA PAYMENT SCHEMES

Mesothelioma is a cancer of the lining of internal organs, such as the lungs or stomach, and almost always arises from exposure to asbestos. Life expectancy from diagnosis is between eight and nine months, on average. The long time that mesothelioma takes to develop – sometimes 40 to 50 years after exposure before symptoms appear – means that some workers were negligently exposed to asbestos at work but their employers are no longer in existence to make a claim against. Insurance records from the time are also often incomplete. The Diffuse Mesothelioma Payment Schemes (DMPS) have been introduced in response to the difficulties faced by sufferers in obtaining compensation through a civil claim for damages and the fact that death usually occurs within months of diagnosis. There are two such schemes in operation at present, both of which are administered by the DWP.

The Mesothelioma Act 2014 established the latest DMPS, which provides for lump sum payments to be made to sufferers who were exposed to asbestos either negligently or in breach of statutory duty by their employer(s) and who are unable to bring a claim for damages because they cannot trace the employer or that employer's EL insurer. It is funded by a levy on insurance companies and applies where mesothelioma was diagnosed after 25 July 2012.

The DMPS 2008, which is a 'no fault' scheme, continues to operate where the diagnosis is before 25 July 2012. It applies where the mesothelioma is unrelated to the employment of the sufferer (for instance, where the claimant was self-employed), or to a family member who was exposed via the worker's overalls.

The details of these schemes are beyond the scope of this textbook but can be found by consulting the schemes themselves on the gov.uk website.

4.9 DEFENCES

4.9.1 *Volenti non fit injuria*

Where the defence of *volenti non fit injuria* applies, if a person engages in an event, being aware of and accepting the risks inherent in that event, they cannot later complain of, or seek compensation for, an injury suffered during the event. In order to establish the defence, the claimant must be shown not only to have perceived the existence of danger, but also to have appreciated it fully and voluntarily accepted the risk.

In *ICI v Shatwell* [1965] AC 656, two brothers, both experienced shotfirers, agreed to test detonators without obeying safety regulations imposed by their employer. Both were injured when one of the detonators exploded. One of the brothers sued his employer on the basis that ICI were vicariously liable for injuries caused to him by the negligence of his fellow worker. The Court held that ICI were not liable. Shatwell had voluntarily consented to a risk of which he was well aware. The Court went on to say that the defence of *volenti non fit injuria* should be available where the employer is not itself in breach of statutory duty and is not vicariously in breach of any statutory duty through neglect of some person of superior rank to the claimant and whose commands the claimant is bound to obey, or who has some special and different duty of care.

It is important to note that in *ICI v Shatwell* there was no breach of statutory duty by the employer. The defence is not available to an employer on whom a statutory obligation is imposed as against liability for the employer's own breach of that obligation.

While *volenti non fit injuria* may be a defence in theory, in practice it is rarely successful; an employee will not often consent freely to run the risk of injury with full knowledge of that risk. The only real defence to a work-based claim will therefore be contributory negligence.

4.9.2 Claimant's contributory negligence

The contributory negligence of the claimant may sometimes reduce the damages to be awarded against the defendant. It is for the judge to decide the proportion of responsibility of the claimant and to reduce the amount of damages accordingly.

The Law Reform (Contributory Negligence) Act 1945, s 1 provides:

> [If] any person suffers damage as a result partly of his own fault and partly of the fault of any other person … damages recoverable in respect thereof shall be reduced by such extent as the court thinks just and equitable having regard to the claimant's share in responsibility for the damage.

'Fault' is defined by s 4 as 'negligence, breach of statutory duty, or other act or omission which gives rise to a liability in tort or, apart from this Act, gives rise to the defence of contributory negligence'.

The question for the court, when considering contributory negligence, is whether the claimant acted reasonably in taking the risk (*AC Billings & Son Ltd v Riden* [1958] AC 240). Whether the claim is in negligence or for breach of statutory duty, there cannot be a finding of 100% contributory negligence (see *Anderson v Newham College of Further Education* [2002] EWCA Civ 505).

In assessing the claimant's conduct, allowance will be made for the claimant's working conditions. Mere inadvertence by the employee will generally not be sufficient for contributory negligence, for example where the employee is engrossed in their work or is in a hurry to get on with their job. The relative age and experience of the claimant will also be a relevant consideration for the court when deciding questions of contributory negligence. Disobedience or reckless disregard for the employer's orders are far more likely to give rise to a finding of contributory negligence.

In *Eyres v Atkinsons Kitchens & Bathrooms* [2007] EWCA Civ 365, the defendant was the claimant's employer. The claimant asserted that the defendant was liable in negligence and/or for breach of statutory duty because it caused or permitted him to drive when he was too tired after having worked excessively long hours without a proper break.

At the time of the accident, the claimant was a 20-year-old kitchen fitter employed by the defendant. Long hours, resulting in good money, were accepted by all the defendant's employees to be normal. If the work took them far from their factory base, the fitters, including the claimant, tended to prefer a long drive back to Bradford and getting home late rather than staying away overnight. The claimant was held to be 25% to blame for his injuries because he had not been wearing a seat belt. The Court was asked to consider the degree of culpability of the claimant, as he had, whilst driving, become tired and liable to fall asleep.

The Court concluded that the claimant had to bear some further responsibility for the accident, but went on to say that the claimant was in that predicament because his employer had put him there. His employer was next to him, fast asleep. His employer was doing nothing to guard against the very risk of injury from which he ought to have been saving his employee. Bearing in mind the relative blameworthiness of the parties' respective faults and their degrees of responsibility, the judge assessed the claimant's overall contributory negligence at 33%.

In *Sherlock v Chester City Council* [2004] EWCA Civ 201, the claimant was a joiner who lost his thumb and index finger in an accident when using a circular saw provided by his employer. He claimed that his employer was both negligent, for failing to carry out an appropriate risk assessment, and in breach of statutory duty in relation to breaches of reg 3 of the Management of Health and Safety at Work Regulations 1999, reg 20 of the Provision and Use of Work Equipment Regulations 1998, and reg 4 of the Manual Handling Operations Regulations 1992. On appeal to the Court of Appeal, Arden LJ considered whether it was appropriate for there to be findings of contributory negligence in a breach of statutory duty case:

> There may be some justification for the view [that the findings of contributory negligence are not appropriate] in cases of momentary inattention by an employee. But where a risk has been consciously accepted by an employee, it seems to me that different considerations may arise. That is particularly so where the employee is skilled and the precaution in question is neither esoteric nor one which he could not take himself ... In those circumstances it seems to me that the appellant can properly be required to bear the greater responsibility. I would assess his responsibility for the accident at 60 per cent.

When considering contributory negligence, it should be remembered that many statutory duties apply to employees and not employers. For example, the Management of Health and Safety at Work Regulations 1999, reg 14 places a duty on employees to use equipment in accordance with training and instructions.

The case of *Blackmore (Executrix of the Estate of Cyril Hollow, Deceased) v Department for Communities & Local Government* [2017] EWCA Civ 1136 illustrates that there is no reason in principle for distinguishing between a claimant who contributed to their injury by conduct related to their work and one who contributed by conduct unrelated to their work. It also gives some insight into the proper approach to be taken in such cases. The deceased had died of lung cancer, which medical experts agreed had been caused by the combined effect of exposure to asbestos during the course of his employment and many years of smoking. The sole issue in dispute concerned the appropriate apportionment. The Court of Appeal held that the judge at first instance had been correct to reject the argument that apportionment should be based on a precise mathematical calculation of the relative proportions by which exposure to asbestos and smoking increased the risk of contracting lung cancer. The Law Reform (Contributory Negligence) Act 1945 required the court to compare the respective fault of the parties, recognising their respective duties, powers and resources. On these facts, the employer's blameworthiness in exposing the deceased to asbestos in circumstances where the risks to health were well known was greater than the deceased's smoking, particularly as he had smoked for many years before the associated risks had become known. The judge's apportionment of contributory negligence at 30% was held to be within the range of options available to him.

4.10 ENFORCEMENT OF HEALTH AND SAFETY AT WORK

The function of enforcement is carried out by:

(a) the HSE, which deals broadly with industrial working environments;

(b) various specialist agencies appointed on behalf of the HSE (eg, the Hazardous Installations Directorate);

(c) local authorities, which deal broadly with non-industrial working environments such as the retail, office, leisure and catering sectors.

4.10.1 Health and safety inspectors

Health and safety inspectors have wide powers to enter premises and carry out investigations. As a result of an investigation revealing a contravention, an inspector may:

(a) issue an improvement notice requiring any contravention to be remedied;

(b) serve a prohibition notice requiring the contravention to be remedied and fixing a time after which the activity is prohibited unless remedied;

(c) commence a criminal prosecution (which may give rise to a relevant conviction that can be used against the employer by the employee in subsequent civil proceedings).

4.10.2 The employer's duty to report, maintain and implement safety provisions

The following are the principal requirements imposed on an employer:

(a)   An employer who employs five or more persons must have written details of the employer's policy in regard to the organisation, control, monitoring and review of health and safety measures.

(b)   An employer is under a duty to report certain accidents, diseases and dangerous occurrences to the HSE via its website at www.hse.gov.uk/riddor. This enables the HSE to consider an investigation of the incident. Not all accidents need to be reported. A RIDDOR report is required only when it is work related and the injury is of a type which is 'reportable' under the Reporting of Injuries, Diseases and Dangerous Occurrences Regulations 2013 (RIDDOR) (SI 2013/1471). The list of 'reportable injuries' includes the death of any person (workers and non-workers) and certain 'specified injuries' to workers. The specified injuries listed in reg 4 are:

- fractures, other than to fingers, thumbs and toes
- amputations
- any injury likely to lead to permanent loss of sight or reduction in sight
- any crush injury to the head or torso causing damage to the brain or internal organs
- serious burns (including scalding) which cover more than 10% of the body or causes significant damage to the eyes, respiratory system or other vital organs
- any scalping requiring hospital treatment
- any loss of consciousness caused by head injury or asphyxia
- any other injury arising from working in an enclosed space which leads to hypothermia or heat-induced illness, requires resuscitation or admittance to hospital for more than 24 hours.

In addition to deaths and specified injuries, accidents must be reported when they result in an employee or self-employed person being away from work or unable to perform their normal work duties for more than seven consecutive days as the result of their injury. This seven-day period does not include the day of the accident, but does include weekends and rest days. There is also a requirement to report certain occupational diseases, dangerous occurrences and gas incidents.

(c)   All occurrences which result in a RIDDOR report or a worker being unable to work for three days or more must be recorded, and details of the injuries must be kept in an accident book. The records must be kept for at least three years.

(d)   The employer may (and in certain circumstances must) have a safety representative to represent the health and safety interests of the employees. Such a representative has wide powers to investigate potential hazards and dangerous occurrences, and to follow up complaints made by employees.

(e)   In addition to the safety representative, the employer may (and in certain circumstances must) have a safety committee, the function of which includes:

(i)   the studying of accidents and notifiable diseases in order to recommend corrective measures to management;

(ii)   making recommendations on safety training;

(iii) examining reports of the HSE and safety representatives;

(iv)   making recommendations on developing/changing safety rules.

(f)   Subject to certain exceptions, an employer is required by the Employers' Liability (Compulsory Insurance) Act 1969 to take out insurance against liability to the employer's own employees.

4.10.3 Employers' liability – enforcement through criminal proceedings

4.10.3.1 Prosecution of health and safety offences

Criminal prosecutions may be brought against both the company and individual directors for breaches of the HSWA 1974.

Section 2(1) is the key provision of the HSWA 1974. It states that: 'It shall be the duty of every employer to ensure, so far as is reasonably practicable, the health, safety and welfare at work of all his employees'.

The Court of Appeal established in R v Gateway Foodmarkets Ltd [1997] 3 All ER 78 that the HSWA 1974, s 2(1) imposed a duty of strict liability. This is qualified only by the defence that the employer has done everything reasonably practicable to ensure that no person's health and safety are put at risk. The defendants appealed against their conviction for failing to do everything reasonable to ensure the safety of their employees. The facts of the case were that a supermarket manager died after falling down an open lift shaft which he had been trying to repair. He had entered the room to free the lift, which had become jammed, by hand – a regular though unauthorised practice of which head office was unaware – but failed to notice that the trap door had been left open by contractors. The Court dismissed the company's appeal and held that s 2(1) of the HSWA 1974 was to be interpreted so as to impose liability in the event of a failure to ensure safety unless all reasonable precautions had been taken not only by the company itself, but also by its servants and agents on its behalf.

In R v HTM Ltd [2006] EWCA Crim 1156, the Court reaffirmed that a defendant to a charge under ss 2, 3 or 4 of the HSWA 1974, could adduce evidence in support of its case that it had taken all reasonable steps to eliminate the likelihood of the relevant risk occurring. In a preparatory hearing, the judge ruled that evidence of foreseeability was admissible as it was relevant to the case alleged against the defendant, particularly with regard to the reasonable practicability of the employer ensuring the health, safety and welfare of its employees, and that the Management of Health and Safety at Work Regulations 1999, reg 21 did not preclude the defendant from relying upon any act or default of its employees in its defence. The defendant was entitled to put before the jury evidence to show that what had happened was purely the fault of one or both of its employees. If the jury were persuaded that everything had been done by or on behalf of the defendant to prevent the accident from happening, the defendant would be entitled to be acquitted: R v Gateway Foodmarkets Ltd applied.

In the cases of R v Tangerine Confectionery; R v Veolia ES (UK) Ltd [2011] EWCA Crim 2015, the Court of Appeal gave further guidance on the relevance of foreseeability in such cases. The appeals, which were dealt with together, involved two companies which had been convicted of offences under the HSWA 1974. Tangerine Confectionery had been prosecuted after an employee was killed attempting to unblock a sweet-making machine. It was convicted of a breach of s 2 of the HSWA 1974 and fined £300,000. However, it appealed on the basis that the risk of the employee's making an inexplicable decision not to isolate the machine before entering it was not foreseeable, and therefore the employer could not have been expected to guard against it. Veolia, a waste company, was convicted of breaches of ss 2 and 3 of the HSWA 1974 and fined £225,000, following an accident in which a worker collecting litter from the roadside was killed when hit by a car driven by a member of the public. Veolia appealed on the basis that the risk arose from the negligent driving of a member of the public and was not something over which the employer had any control. Both appeals were rejected by the Court of Appeal, which held that foreseeability of risk is relevant but it is only the risk that needs to be foreseeable (such as an employee being crushed by the arms of a sweet-making machine) and not the mechanics of the actual events which occurred.

4.10.3.2 Punishment of health and safety offences

The maximum sentence whether tried summarily or on indictment is an unlimited fine. Following concern at the inconsistency and low level of fines being imposed for offences under the HSWA 1974, the Sentencing Council issued the Definitive Guideline for Health and Safety Offences, Corporate Manslaughter and Food and Hygiene Offences ('the Definitive Guideline'), which applies to all cases which are sentenced after 1 February 2016 regardless of the date of the offence.

Full details of the Definitive Guideline are beyond the scope of this book but, in brief, it sets out starting points and offence ranges for each type of offence. For an offence under s 2 of the HSWA 1974, the range is between £50 and £10 million. In considering the level of fine to impose, the Definitive Guideline states that the fine must reflect the seriousness of the offence and the court must take into account the financial circumstances of the offender. The fine must be 'sufficiently substantial to have a real economic impact which will bring home to both management and shareholders the need to comply with health and safety legislation'.

By way of example, in April 2017, Bakkavor Foods Ltd was fined after a worker died when plastic bales fell on top of him. An investigation by the HSE found that there was unsafe stacking of bales of plastic. Bakkavor had failed to implement properly planned safe systems of work for its employees who were exposed during the stacking of the bales. There was also no formal training in stacking bales and a lack of monitoring in the bale area. Bakkavor pleaded guilty to breaches of s 2(1) of the HSWA 1974 and was fined £2 million.

Where an accident results in death and the evidence indicates that a serious criminal offence other than a health and safety offence may have been committed, the HSE is required to liaise with the Crown Prosecution Service in deciding whether to prosecute. This is dealt with in more detail in **Chapter 17**.

4.11 CONCLUSION

Negligence is the relevant cause of action for this area of personal injury litigation, with *Wilsons & Clyde Coal v English* setting out the standard of the duty of care owed. However, even for accidents that occur after 1 October 2013, breaches of statutory duty will continue to be an important part of a claimant's case in establishing negligence against an employer, and so it remains important for claimants' solicitors to consider possible breaches of regulations in order to maximise the clients' chances of success and fully consider the claim.

Defendants' solicitors need to be alert to possible arguments of contributory negligence on the part of the claimant, although there is generally less scope for substantial reductions for contributory negligence in work-based claims than in RTA claims. It is important that the solicitors for both sides regularly review the evidence available, including all relevant health and safety documentation which can often hold the key to establishing liability or refuting it, and which it is essential for a claimant's solicitor to obtain at an early stage.

An example of an EL case may be found in **Appendix 1**.

4.12 FURTHER READING AND RELEVANT WEBSITES

The above is merely an overview of the law as it relates to liability in EL claims. For a more detailed consideration of the subject, reference should be made to the following sources of information:

Redgrave, Hendy and Ford, *Redgrave's Health and Safety* (Butterworths)

Munkman, *Employer's Liability* (Butterworths)

Tolley's Health and Safety at Work Handbook (Tolley)

www.hse.gov.uk

www.hse.gov.uk/riddor/

www.gov.uk

www.sentencingcouncil.org.uk

CHAPTER 5

CLINICAL NEGLIGENCE: THE LAW

> **LEARNING OUTCOMES**
>
> After reading this chapter you will be able to:
>
> - set out the nature and scope of the duty of care owed by institutional health providers and individual medical practitioners
> - explain how the *Bolam* test is used to determine whether there has been a breach of duty
> - appreciate that causation is a more complicated issue in clinical negligence cases than in personal injury cases
> - set out the role of NHS Resolution, the structure of the NHS and the operation of the NHS complaints procedure.

5.1 INTRODUCTION

Clinical negligence claims arise when a medical practitioner, such as a doctor, nurse, midwife or dentist, or an institutional health provider, such as an NHS or Foundation Trust or a private hospital, breaches their or its duty of care to the claimant, who is injured as a result of the breach. The claimant may seek legal advice following an adverse outcome from medical treatment, for example an unexpected injury or condition, a worsening of the original condition, an increased length of stay in hospital, a subsequent unplanned re-admission, a transfer to the intensive care unit, or perhaps even the death of the patient. However, whereas in the case of an accident on the highway or in the workplace it is generally a straightforward matter to establish breach and causation, this is not so in clinical negligence claims. The fact that the claimant has had an unexpected or disappointing outcome from the medical treatment received by the client does not necessarily mean that the healthcare provider failed to act with reasonable care and skill. Even where a breach can be established, it may not be possible to show that the breach caused the injury, as the underlying medical condition may have led to the same outcome for the patient in any event.

From the outset, the claimant's solicitor will need to manage the client's expectations with sympathetic tact and diplomacy. The client may struggle to understand why the case is not as clear-cut as the client had imagined and, in the absence of a very careful explanation, may feel that the solicitor is simply incompetent. The client may have objectives other than compensation, such as an explanation as to what went wrong, an apology, the punishment of those responsible and the assurance that similar mistakes will not happen in the future. These options should be explored with the client and the shortcomings of each option highlighted. For instance, the NHS complaints procedure will not lead to the payment of compensation. The NHS complaints procedure and the disciplinary procedures followed by the General Medical Council and the Nursing and Midwifery Council are dealt with in **5.9** and **5.11** below.

Clinical negligence claims are, in the main, more complex than personal injury claims, and should therefore be handled only by those solicitors who have the required specialist skills. For a number of reasons, including the implicit allegations of professional incompetence, the high levels of compensation awards and the need for NHS bodies in particular to maintain the confidence and support of the public, claims are frequently defended.

Where a patient has been treated privately and a certain outcome had been anticipated, such as in the case of cosmetic surgery or dentistry, a claim may be brought for breach of contract. However, most claims against NHS bodies and private doctors and hospitals are brought under the tort of negligence. If the claim is to be successful, the claimant must show, on a balance of probabilities, that the essential elements are proved, ie:

(a)   that the medical practitioner or institutional health provider owed the claimant a duty of care;

(b)   that the medical practitioner or institutional health provider breached that duty;

(c)   that the claimant suffered injury and losses as a result of that breach of duty, which were reasonably foreseeable.

Each of these three elements is examined in detail below.

5.2   THE DUTY OF CARE

5.2.1   The medical practitioner

It is clear that a doctor, nurse, midwife or other medical practitioner owes a duty of care to their patients. This is unlikely to be a matter in dispute between the parties. The duty of care owed by a doctor is wide-ranging but would encompass, for example:

(a)   properly assessing the patient's condition by taking account of the symptoms, the patient's views and an examination, where necessary;

(b)   working within the limits of personal competence;

(c)   keeping professional knowledge and skills up to date;

(d)   prescribing drugs or administering treatment only where in possession of adequate knowledge of the patient's health and where satisfied that the drugs or treatment are appropriate for the patient's needs;

(e)   keeping clear, accurate and legible records;

(f)   being readily accessible when on duty;

(g)   consulting and taking advice from colleagues, where necessary; and

(h)   referring a patient to another practitioner, where this in the patient's best interests.

5.2.2   The institutional health provider

Where a medical practitioner is an employee of an NHS or Foundation Trust, the institutional health provider will be vicariously liable for its employees' breaches of duty. However, the NHS or Foundation Trust itself owes a duty of care to the patient, and can be sued for negligence without the claimant having to prove negligence on the part of an individual medical practitioner. The leading case in this area is *Wilsher v Essex Area Health Authority* [1988] AC 1074, in which it was held that an institutional health provider has a duty to provide services of doctors of sufficient skill and that there was no reason why a health authority could not be liable for a failure to provide such services.

The duty of care owed by an institutional health provider encompasses, for example:

(a)　the provision of staff with the appropriate levels of knowledge, experience and ability;

(b)　the provision of adequate instruction, training and supervision of staff;

(c)　the provision of equipment which is reasonably suitable for the patient's needs and is maintained in good working order;

(d)　ensuring that the working conditions within the hospital are not such that they lead to levels of fatigue or stress which pose a risk to the patient; and

(e)　ensuring that appropriate systems are in place for the storage and retrieval of patients' records.

In respect of private treatment, the doctors and some other healthcare providers will usually be independent contractors. Where it is their breach of duty which has led to the claim, vicarious liability is not applicable. A private hospital is vicariously liable for the breaches of duty of its own employees, such as nurses, and it will also owe a duty to provide appropriate services and equipment.

5.3　BREACH OF THE DUTY OF CARE

5.3.1　The *Bolam* test

Some errors made by doctors are clearly in breach of their duty of care, for example where a swab is left in the patient during an operation, where the wrong limb is amputated or where an incorrect drug is administered. Such errors are known as 'never events' in the NHS and, when they arise, liability is unlikely to be disputed. However, difficulty arises in cases where a medical practitioner exercises their professional judgement and decides to take one course of action rather than another, or perhaps decides not to act at all. In the realms of diagnosis and treatment, there is scope for genuine differences of opinion, and a doctor will not necessarily be negligent because the decisions they took did not result in the outcome the patient was hoping for.

Consequently, in clinical negligence claims, the normal 'reasonable person' test is modified. In order to show a breach of duty, the claimant must show that the doctor has followed a course of action which is not supported by any reasonable body of medical opinion. This has become known as the *Bolam* test after the case of *Bolam v Friern Hospital Management Committee* [1957] 1 WLR 582, in which it was held that:

> The test as to whether there has been negligence or not is not the test of the man on top of the Clapham omnibus because he has a special skill. The test is the standard of the ordinary skilled man exercising and professing to have that special skill. A man need not possess the highest expert skill; it is well established law that it is sufficient if he exercises the ordinary skill of an ordinary competent man exercising that particular art ... A doctor is not guilty of negligence if he has acted in accordance with a practice accepted as proper by a reasonable body of medical men skilled in that particular art ... a doctor is not negligent, if he is acting in accordance with such a practice, merely because there is a body of opinion which takes the contrary view.

Thus, if the defendant NHS body can show that the doctor (or other medical practitioner) it employed acted in accordance with a reasonable body of opinion, it will have a defence to the claim. The word 'reasonable' is important, because it is possible that a sizeable group of doctors might hold firm and honest beliefs which are rejected by their peers, for example because they are outdated or have been disproved.

This point was addressed when the House of Lords considered the *Bolam* test in *Bolitho v City and Hackney Health Authority* [1997] 3 WLR 1151 (see **5.5.4** for the facts of this case). It held:

> The court is not bound to hold that a defendant doctor escapes liability for negligent treatment or diagnosis just because he leads evidence from a number of medical experts who are genuinely of the opinion that the defendant's treatment or diagnosis accorded with sound medical practice. ... The court has to be satisfied that the exponents of the body of opinion relied upon can demonstrate that such opinion has a logical basis.

Practitioners sometimes refer to the *Bolam* test as the 10% rule. It is said that if 10% of the doctors in the country would have taken the same course of action, and that action has a logical basis, then it will not be a negligent act.

The following further clarifications should be noted:

(a)   A medical practitioner will be judged in accordance with the reasonable body of opinion which existed at the time of the alleged negligent act. It would be inequitable to consider medical practice which exists at the time of trial, as advances in knowledge and practice are almost inevitable.

(b)   A medical practitioner will normally be judged in accordance with the standard of reasonably competent practitioners of the same rank in the same discipline, eg the competence of a junior registrar obstetrician is assessed by reference to that of other junior registrar obstetricians rather than that of consultant obstetricians. The required standard of care and skill for the post held is not reduced to take account of the relative youth and/or inexperience of the post-holder. Medical practitioners have a responsibility to ensure that they do not practise beyond the confines of their knowledge and experience, and they should seek to obtain advice and assistance from more knowledgeable and experienced personnel where appropriate. Where a doctor works in a more senior role than their knowledge and experience would indicate, it is likely that a higher standard of care, as appropriate to the post, will be applied (see *Wilsher v Essex Area Health Authority* [1988] AC 1074 and *FB (Suing by her Mother and Litigation Friend, WAC) v Princess Alexandra Hospital NHS Trust* [2017] EWCA Civ 334). Moreover, an NHS body will be in breach of duty if it fails to provide medical practitioners of the required level of skill and experience for the task in hand.

(c)   In cases of misdiagnosis, the *Bolam* test may not be the appropriate test. In *Muller v King's College Hospital NHS Foundation Trust* [2017] EWHC 128 (QB), a histopathologist had examined a biopsy of tissue taken from the sole of the claimant's foot and had diagnosed a non-malignant ulcer when it was, in fact, a malignant melanoma. The evidence of the defendant's expert was that the misdiagnosis could easily have been made by a histopathologist acting with reasonable care and skill and therefore, applying *Bolam*, the histopathologist had not been negligent. Kerr J distinguished 'pure treatment' cases, such as the *Bolam* case, from cases where the issue was one of pure diagnosis, where 'there is no weighing of risks against benefits and no decision to treat or not to treat; just a diagnostic ... decision which is either right or wrong, and either negligent or not negligent'. He noted the approach of the Court of Appeal in *Penney and others v East Kent HA* [2000] Lloyd's Rep Med 41 (relating to false negative reports of cervical smear tests) and expressed disappointment that the Court of Appeal had not endorsed the trial judge's proposition that *Bolam* did not apply. In the circumstances, Kerr J felt unable to reject the notion that *Bolam* applies in such cases, but rather applied the exception set out in *Bolitho*, and found that the defendant's expert's evidence had failed to stand up to logical analysis.

5.4   RES IPSA LOQUITUR

The maxim *res ipsa loquitur* may be applied in clinical negligence cases in circumstances where the claimant is unable to adduce any evidence as to how or why the injury has occurred but asserts that it would not have occurred in the absence of the defendant's negligence (see **3.2.3.3**).

In *Cassidy v Ministry of Health* [1951] 2 KB 343, the claimant attended a hospital due to a problem affecting two fingers on one hand, but following an operation and post-operative treatment, the whole hand was affected. The court held that he was entitled to rely on the maxim *res ipsa loquitur* and that the defendant had failed to explain how the injury could have occurred without negligence.

The approach to *res ipsa loquitur* in clinical negligence litigation was reviewed by the Court of Appeal in *Ratcliffe v Plymouth and Torbay Health Authority* [1998] EWCA Civ 206. Dismissing the claimant's appeal, the Court of Appeal expressed surprise at the suggestion that courts were having difficulty in assessing the applicability of the doctrine to cases involving allegations of clinical negligence, and reviewed the relevant principles in detail.

Lord Justice Brooke made the following points:

(a) The maxim applies where the claimant relies on the happening of the thing itself to raise the inference of negligence, which is supported by ordinary human experience, and with no need for expert evidence.

(b) The maxim can be applied in that form to simple situations in the clinical negligence field (a surgeon cutting off a right foot instead of the left; a swab left in the operation site; a patient who wakes up in the course of a surgical operation despite a general anaesthetic).

(c) In practice, in contested clinical negligence cases the evidence of a claimant which establishes the *res* is likely to be buttressed by expert evidence to the effect that the matter complained of does not ordinarily occur in the absence of negligence.

(d) The position may then be reached at the close of the claimant's case that the judge would be entitled to infer negligence on the defendant's part unless the defendant can then adduce some evidence which discharges the inference.

(e) This evidence may be to the effect that there is a plausible explanation of what may have happened which does not rely on negligence on the defendant's part.

(f) Alternatively, the defendant's evidence may satisfy the judge on the balance of probabilities that the medical practitioner did exercise proper care. If the untoward outcome is extremely rare, or is impossible to explain in the light of the current state of medical knowledge, the judge will be bound to exercise great care in evaluating the evidence before making such a finding.

The judgment goes some way in explaining why *res ipsa loquitur* is not commonly pleaded in such cases. Whilst it is commonplace for a claimant not to have full knowledge of what had occurred, particularly if the procedure was an operation carried out under anaesthetic, in practical terms, few cases are brought to trial without full disclosure of relevant information being supplied by the defendant, and both sides will rely on expert evidence. Consequently, by the time the matter comes to trial, and as was said in *Ratcliffe*, most claimants will be able to particularise allegations of negligence and the trial opens 'not in the vacuum of available evidence and explanation' as sometimes occurs in road traffic accident cases. The court will be able to decide the case on the evidence which is presented.

5.5 CAUSATION

In a clinical negligence claim, the claimant will argue that, as a result of the negligent treatment by the doctor or hospital, they suffered an unexpected injury or condition, their pre-existing injury or condition became worse, they failed to recover from that condition, or the chances of them recovering diminished. Where a patient has died, their estate or dependants may argue that the death was caused by negligent treatment.

However, the issue of causation which is likely to be admitted (subject to liability) in personal injury cases, is likely to be hotly disputed by the defendant in clinical negligence cases. In personal injury cases, the claimant is normally fit and well prior to the accident, and it is clearly the accident which caused the injury. In contrast, in clinical negligence cases, the adverse outcome complained of can arise as a result of many different variables, and it may be difficult to show that 'but for' the breach, this outcome would not have arisen.

Also, in contrast with personal injury cases, in clinical negligence cases, the term 'liability' is usually confined to matters relating to breach of duty. 'Causation' is dealt with separately and the evidence of a further medical expert may be required. Consequently, where the defendant admits liability prior to trial, the claimant's solicitor should seek confirmation that the defendant also admits causation.

5.5.1 The 'but for' test

The claimant has to satisfy the court, on a balance of probabilities, that, but for the defendant's breach of duty, the claimant would not have suffered the injury complained of. If, for example, a failure to treat a patient has made no difference because the claimant would have died in any event, the claimant's death will not have been caused by negligence.

In *Barnett v Chelsea and Kensington Hospital Management Committee* [1969] 1 QB 428, three night-watchmen attended a casualty department complaining of vomiting after drinking tea three hours previously. The men were sent home with instructions to go to bed, and if necessary to call their own doctors. They went away but one of them died later that night, and the cause of death was subsequently found to be arsenic poisoning. In an action brought by the widow, the defendant was found to be in breach of duty. However, the court found that the deceased would have died of the poisoning even if he had been treated with all the necessary care. Therefore, the claimant had failed to establish on the balance of probabilities that the defendant's negligence caused the deceased's death.

The claimant does not have to prove that the defendant's breach of duty was the sole cause of the injury. It is enough for the claimant to show that the breach made a material (ie something more than minimal) contribution towards the injury. In *Bailey v Ministry of Defence* [2008] EWCA Civ 883, the claimant, who underwent a medical procedure at the defendant's hospital, was not properly resuscitated and, due to the subsequent deterioration in her condition, had to undergo three further procedures shortly after. It was argued on her behalf that she would have needed only one additional procedure had she been properly resuscitated after the first operation. As a result of weakness due to the procedures, and the development of pancreatitis, which was a natural complication not attributable to negligence, the claimant inhaled vomit, went into cardiac arrest and suffered brain damage. The Court of Appeal upheld the trial judge's finding that it was not possible to say whether the weakness had been caused mainly by the negligence or by the pancreatitis, that each had contributed materially to the overall weakness, and it was that overall weakness that caused her inability to respond to the vomit and her subsequent injuries. Consequently, the finding against the defendant was upheld.

In *Williams v Bermuda Hospitals Board* [2016] UKPC 4, the Privy Council upheld the test on material contribution as set out in *Bailey*. Mr Williams attended A&E complaining of abdominal pain, and a scan was arranged. In fact, he was suffering from appendicitis. There was a delay in scanning and operating on Mr Williams, and the appendix ruptured, leading to a large accumulation of pus and subsequent damage to the heart and lungs. At first instance, the claim failed. Although the Court found that the defendant was negligent in that the operation had been carried out at least 2 hours and 20 minutes later than it should have been, Mr Williams had not been able to prove that a better outcome would have resulted from an earlier operation. The Court of Appeal of Bermuda overturned this decision on the grounds that the delay in treatment had 'materially contributed' to his injuries.

It is important to appreciate the difference between injuries which are 'divisible', ie where it is possible to distinguish the extent of the injury which the claimant would have suffered in any event from those injuries which resulted directly from the defendant's negligence, and those which are 'indivisible'. Where injuries are divisible, the defendant will be liable only for the proportion resulting from its negligence. Where injuries are indivisible and the defendant materially contributed to the cause of the injury, the defendant will be liable for the claimant's injuries in full (for damages where there are pre-existing injuries or conditions, see **15.3.1.4**).

5.5.2 Causation and loss of a chance

As the claimant must prove causation on a balance of probabilities, the courts have held that a claimant cannot claim for the loss of a prospect of recovery where the chance of recovery is less than probable. In *Hotson v East Berkshire Health Authority* [1987] AC 750, a 13-year-old boy, was climbing a tree to which a rope was attached when he lost his grip and fell 12 feet to the ground. He was subsequently taken to hospital, where the staff failed to diagnose a fracture and sent him home to rest. When he returned to the hospital, the correct diagnosis was made. As a result of the initial failure to give a correct diagnosis, he was left with a disability of the hip and a risk of future osteoarthritis. At first instance, the trial judge found that if the health authority had correctly diagnosed and treated the claimant when he first attended hospital, there was a high probability (which he assessed at a 75% risk) that his injury would have followed the same course it had followed. In other words, the doctor's delay in making the correct diagnosis had denied the claimant a 25% chance that, if given immediate treatment, he would have made a complete recovery. Accordingly, the claimant was awarded 25% of the appropriate damages. The defendant's appeal to the Court of Appeal was dismissed, but the House of Lords overturned the decision. The claimant had failed to prove causation as the lost chances of recovery, being less than 50%, were less than probable.

This approach was confirmed in the case of *Gregg v Scott* [2005] UKHL 2. The claimant, Mr Gregg, visited his GP, Dr Scott, because he had discovered a lump under his left arm. Dr Scott negligently misdiagnosed the lump as a lipoma or benign fatty tumour and therefore as non-cancerous. Nine months later, the claimant went to a new GP who was more cautious and referred him on to a specialist. It was then that he discovered that he had cancer of a lymph gland. By that time the tumour had spread and he had to undergo painful chemotherapy. The claimant sued Dr Scott, alleging that he should have referred the claimant to hospital and that, if he had done so, the condition would have been diagnosed earlier and there would have been a significant likelihood of a cure. Although the claimant could claim for the extra pain and suffering caused by the defendant, the claimant tried to sue on the basis that he had suffered a loss due to diminished chances of surviving the cancer. On appeal to the House of Lords, their Lordships found in favour of the defendant on the basis that the claimant was unable to prove that the negligence had caused or materially contributed to the injury. It had not been shown that, on the balance of probabilities, the delay in commencing the claimant's treatment had affected the course of the claimant's illness or prospects of survival, which had never been as good as even. Further, liability for the loss of a chance of a more favourable outcome should not be introduced into personal injury claims.

5.5.3 Causation and failure to attend

In *Bolitho v City and Hackney Health Authority* [1997] 3 WLR 1151, the House of Lords considered causation in the context of a doctor's breach of duty in failing to attend a child. The child claimant (aged 2 years) who had been treated for croup at St Bartholomew's Hospital, was discharged but then readmitted. He suffered episodes of extreme breathing difficulties and, during one such episode, the nurse called for a doctor to attend. The senior registrar was dealing with a clinic and was unable to attend, and the senior house officer did not attend either because the batteries of her pager were flat. The child subsequently suffered cardiac arrest which led to brain damage. The defendant accepted that the failure to attend the child was in breach of duty, but it disputed that the failure was causative of any damage. It was agreed that if the child had been intubated (to create an airway), the child would not have suffered the cardiac arrest and consequently would not have incurred brain damage. The senior registrar gave evidence to the effect that she would not have intubated had she attended. There was a dispute between experts called by the parties as to whether intubation would have been the appropriate course of action to take in those circumstances, bearing in mind the risks associated with that procedure. The House of Lords dealt with the case by taking a two-stage approach:

(a)   The court first considered what the doctor would have done if she had attended the child. This was a fact-finding exercise and the *Bolam* test was not relevant at this stage. From the senior registrar's evidence, it was accepted by the court that she would not have intubated the child and that the senior house officer would not have done so without her permission.

(b)   The court went on to consider whether the failure to intubate would have been negligent. At this point the *Bolam* test was relevant, and the court found that a reasonable body of medical opinion would support the registrar's decision not to intubate.

Consequently, their Lordships found in favour of the defendant.

5.6   CONSENT

The patient's consent is required by the medical practitioner before any sort of operation is performed or treatment (such as an injection of drugs or manipulation of a limb) administered. The consent must be freely given and informed. It need not be in writing, although, in relation to surgical procedures, it invariably will be, and the patient will be asked to sign a consent form. However, it should be noted that a signed consent form is evidence that consent was given but not necessarily that consent was valid, ie freely given by someone with capacity, following full disclosure of all the relevant facts.

The standard NHS consent forms are drafted widely so as to allow a surgeon to deal with any procedure that the surgeon deems to be necessary, in the patient's best interests, during the course of the operation. However, the surgeon would be justified in carrying out such additional measures only where they were closely related to the initial procedure, or where they became necessary due to an emergency.

In *Williamson v East London and City Health Authority* [1998] Lloyd's Rep Med 6, the claimant agreed to an operation to replace a leaking silicone breast implant. Immediately prior to the operation, the surgeon noted that the situation was worse than had originally been thought, but did not tell the claimant that she intended to carry out a more extensive procedure than she had initially planned, and no further consent form was signed. A mastectomy was performed without the patient's consent and the patient sued the health authority. The court found that the clinician did not properly or sufficiently inform the claimant of her intention to increase the scope of the operation, the claimant had not consented to the operation, and accordingly damages were awarded in respect of the claimant's pain and suffering.

Where treatment is less risky, oral consent is common. It may also be implied by the very fact that the patient has consulted the doctor.

If the medical practitioner acts without consent, this may lead to a criminal prosecution for battery and to civil proceedings under the tort of trespass to the person (or battery in particular). The basis of these actions is that the interference with the physical integrity of the patient was intentional. (A consideration of the tort of battery lies beyond the scope of this book.)

However, where the medical practitioner seeks the consent of the patient and advises the patient, in broad terms, of the nature of the operation or treatment, but fails to advise of all the associated risks, the consent may not be fully 'informed' but it will not be invalidated (see

Chatterton v Gerson [1981] QB 432). This failure to advise fully may lead to civil proceedings in negligence (see **5.6.4**).

Where the patient suffers from a mental incapacity and thereby falls under Pt IV of the Mental Health Act 1983, the patient's consent is not required for any medical treatment necessary for the management of their mental disorder. (A consideration of the treatment of those who are mentally incapacitated also falls outside the scope of this book.)

5.6.1 Emergency treatment

In some instances, for example in emergencies, it may not be possible to obtain consent. Where treatment is necessary to save the life or preserve the health of the patient in such circumstances, a failure to obtain consent will not render the doctor liable in civil or criminal proceedings (see *Connolly v Croydon Health Services NHS Trust* [2015] EWHC 1339 (QB)).

5.6.2 Consent by children

Section 8(1) of the Family Law Reform Act 1969 provides a presumption that a child may give valid consent for medical treatment at the age of 16. This area of the law was examined closely in *Gillick v West Norfolk and Wisbech Area Health Authority and Department of Health and Social Security* [1986] AC 112, in which it was held that the important point is the degree of understanding by the child of what is going to happen. In that case, it was stated that 'the parental right to control a minor child deriving from parental duty was a dwindling right which existed only in so far as it was required for the child's protection; that the extent and duration of the right could not be ascertained by a fixed age, but depended on the degree of intelligence and understanding of that particular child'.

5.6.3 Refusal of consent

The basic proposition is that an adult of sound mind has the right to autonomy and self-determination, and therefore can refuse to consent to medical treatment, even where this may lead to their death. Many of the reported cases deal with women who are in the later stages of pregnancy, and where the medical practitioners, concerned to protect the foetus as well as the mother, apply for a declaration from the court that it would be lawful to carry out the required medical procedure without the mother's consent. These cases show that the court is not able to take the interests of a foetus into account. In *St George's Hospital NHS Trust v S; R v Collins and others, ex p S* [1998] 3 All ER 673, the Court of Appeal said:

> In our judgment while pregnancy increases the personal responsibilities of a woman it does not diminish her entitlement to decide whether or not to undergo medical treatment. Although human, and protected by the law in a number of different ways ... an unborn child is not a separate person from its mother. Its need for medical assistance does not prevail over her rights. She is entitled not to be forced to submit to an invasion of her body against her will, whether her own life or that of her unborn child depends on it. Her right is not reduced or diminished merely because her decision to exercise it may appear morally repugnant. The declaration in this case involved the removal of the baby from within the body of her mother under physical compulsion. Unless lawfully justified, this constituted an infringement of the mother's autonomy. Of themselves, the perceived needs of the foetus did not provide the necessary justification.

In the case of *Re MB (An Adult: Medical Treatment)* (1997) 38 BMLR 175, a woman who was 40 weeks pregnant and in labour refused to consent to a caesarean section because she had a phobia about needles and therefore could not consent to anaesthesia. Her life and that of her unborn child were therefore at risk. The Court of Appeal held that a competent woman could choose to reject medical intervention, even on irrational grounds, ie where the decision was so outrageous in its defiance of logic or of morally accepted standards that no sensible person could have arrived at it. However, in this case, the appellant's fear of needles had made her incapable of making a decision in relation to anaesthesia and had therefore rendered her temporarily incompetent.

5.6.4 Failure to advise of risk

5.6.4.1 Breach of duty

In order that consent to the proposed treatment may be fully informed, the medical practitioner must, so far as is possible, advise the patient of the risks involved in treatment and the likelihood and nature of any side-effects. Where a patient asks a question, the medical practitioner must answer the question honestly. Clearly, a failure to advise a patient about a substantial risk of grave adverse consequences will be negligent, whether or not the patient asks a specific question; but what about where the risks are very small and there is no specific question?

Until fairly recently, the decision in the case of *Sidaway v Board of Governors of the Bethlem Royal Hospital and the Maudsley Hospital* [1985] AC 871 governed the nature of the obligation placed upon the doctor to tell the patient about the risks of proposed treatments and procedures. In that case, it was held by the majority that the *Bolam* test should be applied. In other words, if a reasonable body of clinicians would not have advised the patient of the risk in those circumstances, there was no breach of duty. The decision sat uneasily with the general recognition that the relationship between doctor and patient was, in practice, becoming less paternalistic and more co-operative.

In *Montgomery v Lanarkshire Health Board* [2015] UKSC 11, the Supreme Court held that the analysis of the law by the majority in *Sidaway* was unsatisfactory. Following *Montgomery*, the situation is as follows:

(a)   An adult of sound mind is entitled to determine which, if any, of the available forms of treatment to undergo, and consent to such treatment must be obtained before treatment interfering with bodily integrity is undertaken.

(b)   Medical practitioners are under a duty to take reasonable care to ensure that patients are aware of any material risks involved in any recommended treatment, and of any reasonable alternative or variant treatments. There are exceptions: for example, where an unconscious patient requires urgent treatment, where a patient makes it clear they do not wish to be informed of the risks, and where a doctor reasonably believes that disclosure would be seriously detrimental to the patient's health.

(c)   The test of materiality is whether, in the circumstances, a reasonable person in the patient's position would be likely to attach significance to the risk, or the doctor was (or should reasonably be) aware that the particular patient would be likely to attach significance to it. The *Bolam* test is not relevant.

This approach was confirmed by the Court of Appeal in *Webster v Burton Hospitals NHS Foundation Trust* [2017] EWCA Civ 62, which concerned a child who had been born 11 days after the expected date of delivery, and who suffered brain injury some 2 or 3 days before his birth. A scan carried out a few weeks earlier had shown anomalies, and the defendant accepted that the failure to arrange further scans had been negligent. It was also accepted that, had labour been induced on the expected date of delivery or on any day up to 3 days before the date of his birth, the child would have avoided injury. The Court of Appeal held that the child's mother should have been warned of the increased risk associated with delayed delivery, and, had she been so warned, she would have chosen to have been induced sufficiently early to have avoided the brain injury suffered by her son.

5.6.4.2 Causation

In a case where informed consent has not been obtained, the claimant must demonstrate, using the 'but for' test, that the breach of duty has caused the injury (see **5.5.1**). In many instances, it will be a straightforward matter for the court to determine whether or not the patient would have consented to the operation anyway. If a patient, made fully aware of the risks involved in the recommended procedure or treatment, would have consented, causation is not established; if the patient would not have so consented, causation is established.

However, sometimes the matter is not so straightforward. In *Chester v Afshar* [2004] UKHL 41, the House of Lords modified conventional causation principles on policy grounds. The claimant, who consulted the defendant consultant neurosurgeon for back pain, was not warned of a small (1–2%) risk that the proposed operation, no matter how expertly performed, could result in a serious complication, causing partial paralysis. The operation was not performed negligently but, unfortunately, the risk materialised. The difficulty in this case was that the claimant was unable to say that she would never have had the operation had she known of the risk; merely that she would not have had it as soon as she did, as she would have explored other options first. Moreover, the failure to warn had not increased the risk, which was inherent in the operation and liable to occur randomly, irrespective of the degree of care and skill of the surgeon. Consequently, the 'but for' test strictly applied could not be satisfied. The House of Lords found in the claimant's favour and, in so doing, veered away from conventional causation principles. The ratio of the decision is that where there is a negligent failure to warn of a particular risk from an operation, and the injury is intimately connected to the duty to warn, then the injury is to be regarded as being caused by the breach of the duty to warn.

The facts of *Chester v Afshar* are unusual and must be regarded as a modest departure from the established principles of causation. (See *Duce v Worcester Acute Hospitals NHS Trust* [2018] EWCA Civ 1307, where the appellant's argument that it created a free-standing alternative test to causation in consent cases was rejected.) Moreover, where a claimant seeks to rely on the exceptional principle of causation set out in *Chester v Afshar*, the claimant must plead the point and support it with evidence (*Correia v University Hospital of North Staffordshire NHS Trust* [2017] EWCA Civ 356).

5.7   THE ROLE OF NHS RESOLUTION

NHS Resolution (NHSR) is an arm's length body of the Department of Health and Social Care. It handles clinical negligence claims against NHS bodies and administers a risk-pooling scheme, the Clinical Negligence Scheme for Trusts (CNST), which provides unlimited cover for members of the scheme and their employees against such claims. Membership of the CNST is voluntary, but all NHS and Foundation Trusts are currently members of the scheme. Independent sector providers of NHS care can also join. Members contribute to the scheme in accordance with the level of risk they pose. For example, hospitals that perform high-risk procedures, such as obstetrics, have higher levels of contributions than those which do not.

From 1 April 2019, NHSR has been operating a new state indemnity scheme for general practice in England called the Clinical Negligence Scheme for General Practice (CNSGP). The scheme covers clinical negligence liabilities arising in general practice in relation to incidents that occurred on or after 1 April 2019. CNSGP provides a fully comprehensive indemnity for all claims within its scope. Previously, GPs, as self-employed health professionals, were not part of the scheme and were required to carry their own indemnity insurance.

(Health professionals who provide advice and treatment on a private basis are not covered by the scheme and must carry their own indemnity insurance.)

NHSR relies on a panel of solicitors' firms which are specialised in clinical negligence litigation to handle defence work on their behalf. Fewer than 1% of cases referred to NHSR are concluded at trial.

The NHSR 'Reporting claims to NHS Resolution September 2022' sets out the requirements for when and how a member should report a new claim to NHSR. Various situations – such as a serious incident where investigations suggest there have been failings in the care provided which might lead to a large value claim (more than £500,000), a disclosure request suggesting the possibility of a claim of whatever value, or the receipt of a letter of claim, Part 36 offer or proceedings – require notification to be given within specified time limits. The purpose of timely notification is to enable NHSR to carry out appropriate investigations and to consider whether any pro-active steps, such as an early admission, offer or apology, could be taken to avoid proceedings being issued.

The establishing of NHSR in April 2017 was accompanied by the release of a five-year plan for future change. The intention was for a radical refocus from simply defending NHS litigation claims to the early settlement of cases, learning from any previous mistakes and the prevention of errors. Central to this approach was the need for Trusts all over the country to learn from litigation cases they have been involved in and share experiences. NHS Resolution published its strategy, 'Advise, Resolve, Learn', on 22 May 2022, setting out its strategy up to 2025. Further reading on NHSR is available on its website.

5.8 THE STRUCTURE OF THE NHS

Solicitors acting for clients who have suffered as a result of alleged poor NHS treatment must acquire an understanding of the structure of the NHS, and the responsibilities of each body within that structure, to enable them to determine where complaints should be addressed and the identity of the appropriate defendant, should proceedings be necessary.

On 1 April 2013, as a result of the implementation of the provisions of the Health and Social Care Act 2012, fundamental changes were made, the full extent of which is beyond the scope of this book. However, an outline of the responsibilities of those bodies is as follows:

(a) The Department of Health and Social Care, under the leadership of the Secretary of State for Health and Social Care, is responsible for standards of health and social care and is accountable to Parliament. It provides strategic leadership to the health and care system, the basis of which is set out in the NHS Mandate published by the Secretary of State in November 2012.

(b) NHS England (formerly the NHS Commissioning Board) is an independent body which has a statutory obligation to pursue the objectives found in the NHS Mandate. It is responsible for improving health outcomes for people in England by driving up the quality of care, by commissioning specialist services and primary care (GP services, dental services, pharmacy, and certain aspects of optical services), through the local area teams, and by allocating resources to, and overseeing the work of, the clinical commissioning groups (see below).

(c) Clinical commissioning groups (CCGs) were responsible for about 60% of the NHS budget and commissioned most secondary care services. This included planned hospital care, rehabilitative care, urgent and emergency care (including out-of-hours and NHS 111), most community health services and mental health and learning disability and/or autism services. Services could be commissioned from any provider that met NHS standards and costs, including charities and private sector providers. As a result of the Health and Care Act 2022, CCGs were abolished on 1 July 2022 and replaced by 42 statutory Integrated Care Systems (ICSs). Each ICS consists of an Integrated Care Board (ICB) established by the Integrated Care Boards Establishment Order 2022 (which came into force on 1 July 2022). ICSs are geographically based partnerships that bring together providers and those commissioning NHS services with local authorities and other local partner organisations to plan, coordinate and commission health (and care) services. In summary, ICBs will take on the NHS planning/coordination role previously carried out by the CCGs and will also be able to contract with suppliers to deliver NHS services.

(d) Providers of primary and secondary care. These will be the defendants in civil proceedings, and complaints about the services provided will usually be made directly to them, at least in the first instance.

(i)   Primary care. This is the first point of contact for most people experiencing health problems and is delivered by a wide range of independent contractors, such as GPs, dentists, opticians and pharmacists. It also includes NHS walk-in centres and NHS 111.

Those who are not primary care providers (see (ii)–(iv) below) are sometimes referred to as secondary care providers.

(ii)   Hospital care. Hospitals in England are managed by acute trusts, many of which are NHS Hospital Trusts. However, Foundation Trusts were introduced in 2004 with the aim of decentralising health services and tailoring them to meet the needs of the local population. They have more financial and operational freedom than NHS Hospital Trusts. The aim was that all NHS Trusts, including those providing community care or mental health services (see below), would have become Foundation Trusts by 2016, but some trusts have remained as NHS Hospital Trusts.

(iii)   Community care services. Care trusts manage integrated services between health and social care which arise from joint working agreements between the NHS and local authorities. Services include those provided by district nurses and health visitors.

(iv)   Mental health services. Mental health trusts (the majority of which have foundation status) oversee the specialist care required by those with mental health problems, such as severe anxiety or psychotic illness. Services include counselling, psychological therapies, community and family support and more specialist care. Services may be provided in partnership with other primary and secondary care providers and local authorities.

The Care Quality Commission is the independent regulator of all health and social care services in England. Its role is to ensure that the care provided by hospitals, dentists, ambulances, care homes and services in people's own homes and elsewhere meets national standards of quality and safety by regulating, monitoring and inspecting those services and sharing its findings with the public.

In March 2012, the Department of Health published the 'NHS Constitution for England' (the 'Constitution'), which establishes the principles and values of the NHS in England. It sets out the rights and responsibilities of patients, public and staff, and the pledges which the NHS is committed to achieve. Further information is set out in the Handbook to the NHS Constitution for England (the 'Handbook'). The Secretary of State for Health and Social Care, NHS bodies, private and voluntary sector providers of NHS services, and local authorities exercising public health functions are statutorily obliged to take account of the Constitution. NHS England and ICBs are obliged to promote the Constitution. The Constitution has been updated since its inception, the most recent update being (at the time of writing) on 17 August 2023. The most recent update to the Handbook (at the time of writing) was on 17 August 2023.

5.9 THE NHS COMPLAINTS PROCEDURE

In April 2009, the Government introduced a simplified two-stage process for handling complaints about NHS services in accordance with the Local Authority Social Services and National Health Service Complaints (England) Regulations 2009 (SI 2009/309) ('the Complaints Regulations'). The procedure, which is set out at **5.9.1** applies to complaints concerning all NHS staff, whether they are GPs, hospital doctors, nursing staff, ambulance crew, administrators or cleaners. The procedure is not relevant where treatment has not been funded by the NHS, even where that treatment was provided in an NHS hospital. A complaint by a patient may encompass any expression of dissatisfaction, from a complaint about the food or politeness of staff, to one about diagnosis or treatment (ie a clinical complaint), and may be made orally, in writing or electronically.

The purpose of the complaints procedure is to enable complaints to be dealt with simply and swiftly, at a local level if at all possible. Speedy resolution of the complaint to the complainant's satisfaction may avoid the instigation of civil proceedings, especially where the adverse outcome has not resulted in particularly serious consequences for a patient.

When advising a client about the right to complain in relation to NHS care, and how to go about it, there are a number of matters for the solicitor to explain:

(a)   The complaints procedure does not provide for the payment of compensation to the complainant, although some NHS Trusts operate a policy of offering limited compensation, and the proposed NHS Redress Scheme would, in the event it were to become operational, provide a formal basis for such payments (see **5.10**). Therefore, particularly in relation to those who have suffered severe injury and consequential financial loss, the complaints procedure is unlikely to provide a complete solution in itself.

(b)   Notwithstanding (a) above, generally it is advisable to exhaust the complaints procedure before commencing proceedings. In addition to ensuring that the complainant's voice does not go unheard, the complaints procedure will mean that the matter is investigated quickly by the relevant NHS body, while events are still fresh in the minds of those involved. This may provide the claimant's solicitor with valuable information for civil proceedings, should they be necessary. In the past, it was common for the complaints procedure to be suspended as soon as legal proceedings were commenced, or where there was a stated intention to commence proceedings. This should no longer happen.

(c)   In accordance with the guidance 'Openness and honesty when things go wrong: the professional duty of candour', issued by the General Medical Council and the Nursing and Midwifery Council in June 2015 (updated most recently in February 2022), healthcare professionals must tell the patient (or their advocate, carer or family) when things go wrong. They should also apologise, offer an appropriate remedy or support to put matters right, and give a full explanation of the short- and long-term effects of what has happened. It should be noted that an apology, an offer of treatment or other redress does not, of itself, amount to an admission of negligence (Compensation Act 2006, s 2).

(d)   The purpose of the procedure is to satisfy complaints, rather than apportion blame amongst staff, and it is separate from disciplinary procedures. A complaint may bring the shortcomings of individual members of staff to the notice of the management of an NHS body, which may then consider taking action in accordance with its internal disciplinary procedures. Negligence amounting to gross misconduct may lead to dismissal and/or a referral of the matter by the NHS body to an individual's professional body. However, a complainant should not assume that this will happen, and the complainant may wish to seize the initiative and bring the matter to the attention of the appropriate professional body themselves (see **5.11**).

(e)   There are various sources of information and bodies that will provide assistance regarding the complaints procedure:

(i)   Basic information as to how to complain and how the complaint will be dealt with may be found on the NHS website (www.nhs.uk).

(ii)   Each NHS Trust has its own complaints policy, and this is normally found on the Trust's own website.

(iii) There is a Patient Advice and Liaison Service (PALS) within each Trust, which is staffed by NHS employees and volunteers. Its role is to provide confidential advice and assistance to patients, their relatives, visitors to the hospital and staff members, with the aim of resolving problems and concerns quickly, wherever possible. It does not investigate formal complaints but it can provide advice as to the complaints procedure, and it will refer complainants on to the Independent Complaints Advocacy Service. Information about PALS may be found on the NHS website, including details of how to find local PALS contacts. Individual PALS have their own websites.

(iv) The Independent Complaints Advocacy Service (ICAS) is an organisation which is independent of the NHS. Its staff, known as advocates, can assist with all stages of the complaints procedure, for example writing letters of complaint, contacting third parties on the complainant's behalf and attending meetings with the complainant. Other organisations may be found at www.theadvocacypeople .org.uk and www.voiceability.org.

(v) The Citizens Advice Bureau and law centres can also provide help and assistance.

The complaints procedure involves two stages, local resolution and, if the complainant remains dissatisfied, referral to the Health Service Commissioner. However, complaints may be made to the Care Quality Commission or to the ICS where appropriate.

5.9.1 Local resolution

Local resolution is a key part and the first stage of the complaints procedure. Complaints are most likely to be voiced to staff on the spot, and it is these front-line staff or their departmental managers who are the people best placed to make the initial response. The aim is to resolve problems and answer concerns of patients and their families immediately and informally if possible, thereby reducing the need for legal proceedings and the associated cost to the public purse.

Regulation 3 of the Complaints Regulations requires each NHS body to make arrangements for the handling and consideration of complaints. These arrangements must be such as to ensure that

(a) complaints are dealt with efficiently;

(b) complaints are properly investigated;

(c) complainants are treated with respect and courtesy;

(d) complainants receive, so far as is reasonably practical—

(i) assistance to enable them to understand the procedure in relation to complaints; or

(ii) advice on where they may obtain such assistance;

(e) complainants receive a timely and appropriate response;

(f) complainants are told the outcome of the investigation of their complaint; and

(g) action is taken if necessary in the light of the outcome of a complaint.

Each NHS body must designate a person, known as a 'responsible person' to be responsible for ensuring compliance with the arrangements and, in particular, ensuring that action is taken if necessary in the light of the outcome of the complaint. This will be the Chief Executive Officer (CEO), although the CEO may authorise others to act on the CEO's behalf. Each NHS body must also designate a person as a 'complaints manager', to be responsible for managing the procedures for handling and considering complaints. The responsible person and the complaints manager may be the same person.

A complaint should be made within 12 months of the date the matter complained of occurred or, if later, the date when it came to the notice of the complainant. However, the time limit shall not apply where the NHS body is satisfied that the complainant had good reasons for not making the complaint within the time limit and, notwithstanding the delay, it is still possible to investigate the complaint effectively and fairly.

Unless a complaint is made orally and is resolved to the complainant's satisfaction not later than the next working day after the day on which the complaint was made, a complaint must be dealt with in accordance with the procedures set out in the Complaints Regulations. This means that the NHS body should:

(a)   acknowledge the complaint not later than three working days after the day on which it receives the complaint;

(b)   investigate the complaint in a manner appropriate to resolve it speedily and efficiently, and, during the investigation, keep the complainant informed, as far as reasonably practicable, as to the progress of the investigation;

(c)   as soon as reasonably practicable after completing the investigation, send a response to the complainant setting out how the complaint has been considered, its conclusions, a confirmation that it is satisfied that any necessary action has been taken or is proposed to be taken, and details of the complainant's right to take the complaint to the Health Service Commissioner;

(d)   provide the response within six months commencing on the day on which the complaint was received, or such longer period as may be agreed by the NHS body and the complainant, or set out in writing to the complainant the reasons why this has not been possible and provide a response as soon as possible thereafter.

Each NHS body must maintain systems for monitoring complaints, and must prepare an annual report which is made available to any person on request.

5.9.2   The Parliamentary and Health Service Ombudsman and the Public Service Ombudsman for Wales

The Parliamentary and Health Service Ombudsman ('the Ombudsman') deals with complaints arising in England about the NHS and other government departments and public organisations (www.ombudsman.org.uk); the Public Service Ombudsman for Wales (www.ombudsman.wales) deals with complaints about public services in Wales. There are separate ombudsmen for Scotland and Northern Ireland.

The Ombudsman, who is independent of the NHS and the Government, will investigate complaints where the NHS body has refused to investigate a complaint on the basis that it is outside the time limit, or where a complaint has been dealt with by the NHS complaints procedure and the complainant is still dissatisfied. Complaints which have not been through the local resolution process are unlikely to be considered by the Ombudsman. The complaint should generally be made within one year of the event complained of, although there is discretion to extend this limit in cases where there is good reason for the delay.

Where the Ombudsman finds in favour of the complainant, in accordance with the Principles for Remedy, the Ombudsman will recommend that the health authority offers a remedy which will return the complainant to the position the complainant would have been in had the service provided to the complainant been of the proper standard, or compensate the complainant appropriately where this is not possible.

The remedies which may be recommended by the Ombudsman include:

(a)   an apology, an explanation, and acknowledgment of responsibility;

(b)   remedial action, such as reviewing or changing a decision on the service given to the complainant, revising published material, revising procedures to prevent recurrence of that particular problem, training or supervising staff, or any combination of these;

(c)   financial compensation for out-of-pocket expenses.

Although the Ombudsman has no power to enforce recommendations made, they are generally followed.

The Ombudsman publishes annual reports regarding the Ombudsman's investigations, which are available on the website.

5.10 PLANS FOR REFORM

According to the cross-party Health and Social Care Committee (a House of Commons Select Committee), figures show that in 2021, over £2 billion was spent from the NHS budget to settle claims and pay legal costs arising from clinical negligence claims, with this figure expected to more than double by 2031. Many argue that the current approach to compensation in clinical negligence claims is too generous to claimants, is crippling the NHS and is adversely affecting front-line services.

A number of initiatives are looking at the problem in order to effect change. Key amongst those initiatives are the following:

(a) In February 2018, the Department of Health and Social Care published its response to its consultation on the introduction of fixed recoverable costs in lower value clinical negligence cases. A Civil Justice Council (CJC) working group, made up of representatives from all sides of the debate, was set up to:

(i)   consider and recommend an improved process for clinical negligence claims, where the claim has a value of £25,000 or less;

(ii) draw up a structure for fixed recoverable costs, together with figures, including figures for expert reports;

(iii) consider the possible effects on patient safety;

(iv) consider how expert reports should be commissioned and funded, including the feasibility of single joint experts for at least some claims;

(v)   report with recommendations.

The CJC published its report with recommendations in October 2019. Following on from this, in September 2021, the parliamentary Health and Social Care Committee launched an inquiry/call for evidence 'to examine the case for the reform of NHS litigation against a background of a significant increase in costs, and concerns that the clinical negligence process fails to do enough to encourage lessons being learnt which promote future patient safety'.

On 31 January 2022 the Department of Health and Social Care (DHSC) published a consultation on Fixed Recoverable Costs for Lower Value Clinical Negligence Claims, which ran until 22 April 2022. The Government published its response to the consultation in September 2023, stating that a fixed recoverable costs regime will come into force in April 2024 for clinical negligence claims that settle pre-issue for between £1,001 and £25,000.

(b) Part 2 of the Civil Liability Act 2018 (CLA 2018), which received Royal Assent on 20 December 2018, amends the Damages Act 1996 in respect of the personal injury discount rate. The amendments provide for periodic reviews of the discount rate to take place, the first of these to be started within 90 days of commencement of the CLA 2018. This first review has already happened, as a result of which the discount rate has been set at −0.25% from 5 August 2019 (rather than the previous −0.75%). Each subsequent review must be started within five years following the previous review. The CLA 2018 provides a mechanism for the Lord Chancellor to set the discount rate, having taken the advice of an expert panel (for subsequent reviews) and using for all reviews a low risk investment profile, rather than the no risk profile previously used, with the aim of providing no more and no less than 100% compensation for the injury sustained. The next discount rate review will take place in 2024. See **Chapter 15** for further reading on this subject.

5.11 DISCIPLINARY PROCEEDINGS

Those who have been injured or who have lost a loved one as a result of a clinical error may be keen to see those responsible punished, and the solicitor will need to give advice regarding the appropriate disciplinary procedures. A detailed consideration of the conduct of the proceedings lies beyond the scope of this book.

5.11.1 Disciplinary proceedings against doctors

Doctors must be registered with the General Medical Council (GMC) in order to practise medicine in the UK. The GMC has responsibility for investigating complaints about doctors, and it can take action if the doctor's fitness to practise is impaired due to any of the following grounds:

(a)   misconduct;

(b)   poor performance;

(c)   receipt of a criminal conviction or caution;

(d)   physical or mental ill-health;

(e)   determination by a regulatory body either in the British Isles or overseas.

The GMC's procedures are divided into two separate stages: 'investigation' and 'adjudication'. At the investigation stage, cases are investigated to assess whether the matter is sufficiently serious to warrant referral for adjudication. The adjudication stage consists of a hearing of those cases which have been referred to a Fitness to Practise Panel.

A Fitness to Practise Panel may come to any of the following conclusions:

(a)   the doctor's fitness to practise is not impaired and no further action should be taken;

(b)   the doctor's fitness to practise is not impaired but they are required to give an undertaking, eg to have further training or to work only under supervision;

(c)   the doctor's fitness to practise is not impaired but a warning should be issued;

(d)   the doctor's fitness to practise is impaired and –

    (i)   conditions should be placed on the doctor's registration (for example, restricting the doctor to certain areas of practise or stating that the doctor must be supervised), or

    (ii)   the doctor's name should be suspended from the medical register, or

    (iii)   the doctor's name should be erased from the medical register.

An appeal may be made by either side within 28 days.

5.11.2 Disciplinary proceedings against nurses and midwives

The Nursing and Midwifery Council (NMC) is the regulatory body for nurses and midwives. The NMC has a duty to investigate once an allegation has been made against a member to the effect that the practitioner's fitness to practise is impaired due to:

(a)   misconduct;

(b)   lack of competence;

(c)   a conviction or caution;

(d)   physical or mental ill-health; or

(e)   where a different healthcare profession has already determined that the practitioner is unfit to practise.

The sanctions which may be imposed at the end of the procedure are as follows:

(a)   the issue of a caution;

(b)   the removal of the practitioner from the register for a specified period, after which the practitioner may apply for their name to be restored; or

(c)   the removal of the practitioner from the register indefinitely.

5.12 CRIMINAL PROCEEDINGS

The CPS may bring a prosecution for manslaughter against a medical practitioner following an incidence of gross clinical negligence which results in the death of a patient (see **17.3.3**).

5.13 CONCLUSION

Clinical negligence claims are, in the main, more complex than personal injury claims and should be handled only by those practitioners who have the required specialist skills. The claimant's chances of success are generally less than in personal injury claims, largely due to the increased difficulties in establishing breach of duty (see the *Bolam* test) and causation.

The claimant's solicitor's job may be made more difficult by their client's ambivalent attitude towards taking action against medical practitioners, particularly where a relationship with those practitioners is ongoing. A sound knowledge of the NHS complaints procedure and the procedures of the relevant disciplinary bodies is required.

5.14 FURTHER READING AND RELEVANT WEBSITES

For reading on the structure of the NHS: https://commonslibrary.parliament.uk/research-briefings/cbp-7206/

The General Medical Council's website: www.gmc-uk.org

The Care Quality Commission's website: www.cqc.org.uk

The NHS Mandate: www.gov.uk/government/publications/the-nhs-mandate

The NHS Constitution: www.gov.uk/publications/the-nhs-constitution-for-england

The Handbook to the NHS Constitution: www.gov.uk/government/publications/supplements-to-the-nhs-constitution-for-england

https://committees.parliament.uk/committee/81/health-and-social-care-committee/

NHS England: www.england.nhs.uk/

CLAIMS FOR PSYCHIATRIC INJURY

LEARNING OUTCOMES

After reading this chapter you will be able to:

- explain what is meant by the term 'nervous shock'
- identify whether a person is a primary or a secondary victim
- understand the control mechanisms that apply to claims brought by secondary victims
- explain what must be established in order to make a claim for occupational stress.

6.1 INTRODUCTION

Not all accidents result in physical injury. Claims for psychiatric injury or illness have risen markedly in recent years, and are usually awarded in a claim arising from an accident (so-called 'nervous shock 'claims) or as a consequence of occupational stress. The purpose of this chapter is to examine some particular issues that arise when dealing with these types of claim.

6.2 CLAIMS FOR NERVOUS SHOCK

There have been a number of high-profile nervous shock cases arising out of disasters such as Hillsborough, which involved a crush at the Sheffield Wednesday FC stadium in 1989. In the Hillsborough case, a number of claims were brought against the police by spectators and relatives of the victims who were present at the stadium or who had seen the disaster unfolding on the television (*Alcock v Chief Constable of South Yorkshire Police* [1992] 1 AC 310). Other claims were brought by police officers who had been on duty in the stadium and who were traumatised by what they saw (*White v Chief Constable of South Yorkshire* [1999] 2 AC 455). These cases establish certain 'control mechanisms' that limit liability for psychiatric injury.

6.2.1 What is nervous shock?

In order to claim for psychiatric injury there must be expert medical evidence that the claimant has suffered a recognised psychiatric illness which is more than temporary grief, fright or emotional distress. In recent years the courts have recognised a wide range of psychiatric injuries, including chronic fatigue syndrome (*Page v Smith* [1996] AC 155), pathological grief disorder (*Vernon v Bosley* [1997] 1 All ER 577) and post-traumatic stress disorder (PTSD) (*Alcock v Chief Constable of South Yorkshire* Police [1992] 1 AC 310). In establishing whether a claimant has suffered a recognisable psychiatric illness, a medical expert is likely to refer to two main systems of classification of psychiatric illnesses currently used in the UK:

(a)   The *Diagnostic and Statistical Manual of Mental Disorders of the American Psychiatric Association*. This is currently in its 5th edition (DSM-5-TR). The 5th edition (DSM-5) was published in 2013 to replace the previous DSM-IV. DSM-5-TR was published in June 2022, to include a new disorder – Prolonged Grief Disorder (PGD). DSM-5-TR also included text revisions, hence the letters 'TR' in the title of the latest version.

(b)   The *World Health Organisation International Classification of Mental and Behavioural Disorders*. A new version, ICD-11, and the first update to be developed and published in two decades, officially came into effect from 1 January 2022 to replace the 10th edition (ICD-10).

One of the most common psychiatric illnesses that arises is PTSD, for example, following a life-threatening experience or exposure to the sudden death of a close relative, the symptoms of which are listed at **2.2.12**.

6.2.2   Primary and secondary victims

In order to bring a claim for negligently inflicted psychiatric illness, a person must fall into one of two categories established by the House of Lords in *Alcock v Chief Constable of South Yorkshire Police* [1992] 1 AC 310. Primary victims will normally be involved in the events as participants, but it will be relatively rare for a primary victim directly involved in the events not to suffer any physical injury as well. Secondary victims are normally witnesses of injury caused to primary victims, and have not suffered physical injury themselves but have suffered psychologically from what they saw or heard. The key importance of this classification between primary and secondary victims is that if the claimant can show that they are a primary victim then they are likely to be treated more favourably by the courts.

6.2.2.1   Primary victims

A primary victim must show that some personal injury (ie, physical injury or psychiatric injury) was reasonably foreseeable as a result of the defendant's negligence so as to bring the victim within the scope of the defendant's duty of care. No distinction should be made between a physical or a psychiatric injury.

The case of *Page v Smith* [1996] AC 155 was the first time that the House of Lords had considered a claim brought by a primary victim. The claimant's car was involved in a collision with a car driven by the defendant. The collision was not severe, and the claimant suffered no physical injuries, but he claimed damages on the basis that shortly after the accident he suffered a recurrence of chronic fatigue syndrome from which he had suffered 20 years before. The House of Lords held that as a participant in the accident he was a primary victim, and therefore it was not necessary for him to show that the psychiatric harm he suffered was foreseeable in a person of normal fortitude. It made no difference that the claimant was predisposed to psychiatric illness – the normal 'egg-shell skull' rule applied so that the defendant had to take his victim as he found him.

In *Corr v IBC Vehicles* [2006] EWCA Civ 331, the claimant brought proceedings under the Fatal Accidents Act following the suicide of her husband, who had been badly injured in a factory accident whilst employed by the defendant. He suffered PTSD as a result of the factory accident which resulted in deep depression, and some six years after the accident he committed suicide by jumping off the roof of a multi-storey car park. The Court of Appeal held that the claimant did not need to establish that at the time of the accident the deceased's suicide had been reasonably foreseeable, as the suicide flowed from the psychiatric illness for which the defendant was admittedly responsible. The Court of Appeal's decision was affirmed by the Houses of Lords – see [2008] UKHL 13.

In *Johnstone v NEI International Combustion Limited* [2007] UKHL 39, the House of Lords rejected claims by workers who had been negligently exposed to asbestos by the defendants and who had developed clinical depression as a consequence of being told that they had pleural plaques which indicated a risk of future illness. It was argued on behalf of the claimants that they should be regarded as primary victims and should therefore be entitled to recover damages regardless of whether or not psychiatric injury was a foreseeable consequence of the defendants' negligence. The House of Lords rejected this argument on the basis that the illness had been caused by the fear of the possibility of an unfavourable event which had not actually happened and was therefore not actionable.

6.2.2.2 Secondary victims

A secondary victim must show that it was reasonably foreseeable that a person of reasonable fortitude would have suffered some psychiatric injury. Foreseeability of psychiatric injury is of critical importance to secondary victims, as they will normally be outside the scope of persons who might suffer foreseeable physical injury.

In addition to the test of reasonable fortitude, *Alcock v Chief Constable of South Yorkshire Police* [1992] 1 AC 310 established that a secondary victim must satisfy three further control mechanisms if the victim is to succeed in a claim for damages for psychiatric injury:

(a) *A close tie of love and affection to the immediate victim.* In *Alcock*, the claimants were various relations of the immediate victims, some of whom had been present at the Hillsborough football stadium and some of whom had watched the disaster unfold on television. The House of Lords held that there is a rebuttable presumption of sufficiently close ties between spouses, parents and children, but that in all other cases the closeness of the tie had to be proved. One claimant had been present at the ground and witnessed the incident in which his two brothers were killed, but his claim failed because he did not produce evidence of a close tie of love and affection to his brothers. However, in a subsequent case, damages were awarded to the half-brother of one of the Hillsborough victims because the judge found evidence that he was particularly close to his half-brother.

(b) *Closeness in time and space to the incident or its aftermath.* In *Alcock*, several claimants were not present at the ground but went there subsequently to identify the bodies of their relatives. The earliest had arrived between eight and nine hours after the accident, which was held by the House of Lords not to be part of the immediate aftermath.

Subsequent decisions have seen a relaxation in the courts' approach to what constitutes the immediate aftermath. In *Walters v North Glamorgan NHS Trust* [2002] EWHC 321 (QB), [2002] All ER (D) 65, the mother of a baby claimed psychiatric injury as a result of witnessing her child's decline and death due to misdiagnosis at the treating hospital. The period from first onset of injury to death was 36 hours. The claimant issued proceedings against the hospital for damages. The court found that although clearly not a primary victim, she could succeed as a secondary victim if her psychiatric injury was induced by shock as a result of the sudden appreciation by sight or sound of a horrifying event or its immediate aftermath. The court found that the whole period of 36 hours could be seen in law as a horrifying event, and the claimant was therefore entitled to recover damages.

In *Galli-Atkinson v Seghal* [2003] EWCA Civ 697, the claimant appealed to the Court of Appeal following a decision dismissing her claim for nervous shock. The facts of the case were such that the claimant was present at the immediate aftermath of a road traffic accident at which her daughter had died. At that time, she was told of the death of her daughter, but did not see the body until some hours later in the mortuary. It was only when she viewed the body that the claimant broke down and suffered the psychiatric condition that formed the basis of her claim. On appeal, the Court found that, provided events retained sufficient proximity, the subsequent viewing of the body could be seen as part of the aftermath of the incident, and on that basis the claim could succeed.

In *Taylor v A Novo (UK) Ltd* [2013] EWCA Civ 194, the claimant's mother suffered a head injury at work which the claimant did not witness. Some three weeks later, the claimant witnessed her mother die as a result of a pulmonary embolism which was caused by the original injury. The claimant brought a claim for damages for psychiatric injury which succeeded at first instance. However, the Court of Appeal reversed the decision, holding that the lack of physical and temporal connection between the sudden and unexpected death and the original accident meant that the claim had to fail.

In *Wild & Another v Southend University Hospital NHS Foundation Trust* [2014] EWHC 4053 (QB), a father's claim following the discovery that his unborn son had died in the womb failed. Negligence was admitted by the defendant, on the basis of a failure to note foetal growth rate at antenatal appointments, and it was accepted that, but for the negligence of the hospital staff, labour would have been induced earlier and the baby would have survived. The mother's claim for psychiatric injuries as a primary victim was settled, but the father's claim as a secondary victim failed. The judge concluded that the father's experience was analogous to those who witnessed the Hillsborough disaster unfolding on television in *Alcock* and experienced distress and anxiety about their loved ones, but held that being present when the baby's death was confirmed did not qualify as 'witnessing horrific events leading to death or serious injury'.

(c)   *The claimant must suffer 'nervous shock' through witnessing a sudden shocking event with his own unaided senses.* In *Alcock*, the House of Lords confirmed that the secondary victim must establish that the psychiatric illness was induced by a shock or, in the words of Lord Ackner, 'the sudden appreciation by sight or sound of a horrifying event, which violently agitates the mind'. Some of the claimants in *Alcock* had watched the events at Hillsborough unfold via live television broadcasts. This was held to be insufficient to satisfy the test of proximity, because watching the events on television was not felt to be equivalent to witnessing the events at first hand.

In *Ronayne v Liverpool Women's Hospital NHS Foundation Trust* [2015] EWCA Civ 588, the claimant brought a claim for damages, alleging that he was a secondary victim and had sustained PTSD caused by the shock of seeing his wife's deterioration in hospital due to injuries caused by the Trust's negligence. The claimant's wife had recently undergone a hysterectomy but, due to a negligently misplaced suture, developed septicaemia and peritonitis and was admitted to the A&E department for emergency surgery. During the next 36 hours, the claimant witnessed her deterioration, which resulted in her being connected to a ventilator, drips and monitors and becoming swollen, with her 'arms, legs and face blown up because of the amount of fluid'. He subsequently described his wife's appearance as resembling 'the Michelin man'. The claimant succeeded at first instance but the defendant appealed, arguing that there was no qualifying 'event', in the sense that it was neither sudden nor sufficiently shocking. The Court of Appeal overturned the trial judge's decision, holding that the judge was wrong to regard the events of the 36 hours as one event and distinguished this case from that of *Walters* (above), which Tomlinson LJ described as 'a seamless tale with an obvious beginning and an equally obvious end'. In contrast, Mr Ronayne had suffered a 'series of events over a period of time' which did not have the necessary element of suddenness. The Court of Appeal also found that the appearance of the claimant's wife in hospital was as would ordinarily be expected of a person in hospital in the same circumstances and that, by objective standards, it was not horrifying.

In *Tanner v Sarkar* [2016] 12 WLUK 259 (HHJ Buckingham, Great Grimsby CC), the claimant was a child (aged 16 at trial and aged 5 at the time of the relevant events) whose case was that she sustained a psychiatric injury from witnessing the death of her 2-year-old brother in an ambulance, following the defendant GP's negligent failure urgently to refer the brother for hospital treatment for sepsis, the previous day. The judge decided that the claim should be dismissed, finding that the claimant failed to satisfy the key control mechanisms on such claims. The relevant 'event' was the appointment with the GP, which was not shocking, not the consequential events in the ambulance.

However, in RE *(a child) v Calderdale and Huddersfield NHS Foundation Trust* [2017] EWHC 824 (QB), there was a successful claim by a mother and grandmother for psychiatric injuries sustained following sight of the baby during a mismanaged birth. The baby had become stuck in the birth canal following crowning of the baby's head due to shoulder dystocia. Goss J held that the mother was entitled to damages as a primary victim on the basis that, at the point the negligence occurred, the baby was not a legally separate entity, still being in the birth canal. In the alternative, she was a secondary victim (as was the grandmother who was present at the birth) and satisfied the criteria in *Alcock* and *Ronayne* that there must be a sudden appreciation of an objectively horrifying event.

6.2.2.3 Employee victims

In *White v Chief Constable of South Yorkshire* [1999] 2 AC 455, the claimants were police officers who were severely traumatised by their duties at the aftermath of the Hillsborough Stadium disaster. They claimed compensation for their psychiatric injuries against the police service. It was conceded that none of the claimants had been exposed to any personal physical danger, but their case was that the Chief Constable was vicariously liable for the negligence of the police officer who caused the catastrophe by admitting the crowd into the pens. The claimants argued that by the negligent creation of the horrific situation, the Chief Constable was in breach of his duty not to expose the claimants to unnecessary risk of injury and was consequently liable for their injuries. The House of Lords rejected their claims and confirmed that unless employees can show a risk of physical injury (and therefore fall into the category of primary victims), they will be treated as secondary victims and therefore subject to the control tests established in *Alcock* (see **6.2.2.2**). Part of the reason for this was undoubtedly public policy – since all the claims for compensation by relatives of the victims had already been rejected, it could – and did – cause a public furore if police officers were compensated in seemingly less deserving cases. The effect of this decision is that the *Alcock* test applies to all psychiatric injury claims where physical injury is not reasonably foreseeable; employees do not get special consideration.

In *Young v Charles Church (Southern) Ltd* (1998) 39 BMLR 146, a case which pre-dated the ERRA 2013 (see **4.3.1**), it was established that an employee who suffered psychiatric illness after seeing a workmate electrocuted close to him could recover damages against his employer as a primary victim because of the risk to himself of physical injury. The court decided that the ambit of the relevant health and safety regulations was not limited to physical electrocution. The statutory provisions gave protection to employees from kinds of injury which could be foreseen as likely to occur when the electrical cable or equipment was allowed to become a source of danger to them. This included psychiatric illness caused to the claimant by the shock of seeing his workmate electrocuted in circumstances where he was fortunate to escape electrocution himself. The Court found that the employer was both negligent and in breach of statutory duty. Following the ERRA 2013, breach of statutory duty would be used as evidence of negligence (see **4.3** above).

Contrast the above case with *Hunter v British Coal Corp* [1999] QB 140, CA. The claimant was a driver in a coalmine. His vehicle struck a hydrant, causing it to leak. With the help of a workmate, he tried to stop the flow but failed. He left the scene in search of help. When the claimant was 30 metres away, the hydrant burst, and he was told that someone was injured. On his way back to the scene, he was told that the workmate who had been helping him had died. The claimant thought he was responsible and suffered nervous shock and depression. He brought proceedings for damages against his employers. It was held that a claimant who believes they have been the cause of another's death in an accident caused by the defendant's negligence could recover damages as a primary victim if they were directly involved as a participant in the incident. However, a claimant who was not at the scene could not recover damages as a primary victim merely because the claimant felt responsible for the incident. In this case, the claimant was not involved in the incident in which the workmate died as he was 30 metres away and suffered psychiatric injury only on being told of the death some 15 minutes later. Therefore, there was not sufficient proximity in time and space with the incident. Also, the illness triggered by the death was not a foreseeable consequence of the defendant's breach of duty of care, as it was an abnormal reaction to being told of the workmate's death, triggered by an irrational feeling that the claimant was responsible.

6.2.2.4 Professional rescuers

Before *White v Chief Constable of South Yorkshire and Others* [1999] 2 AC 455 it had been thought that rescuers were automatically to be treated as primary victims. However, in *White* the House of Lords rejected the police officers' claims for psychiatric injury, stating that there was no authority for placing rescuers in a special position. The decision was based on two factors:

(a)　the problem of applying a definition to delineate the class of rescuers that could claim; and

(b)　the fact that, if the law did allow the claims to succeed, the result would be unacceptable to the ordinary person, who would think it wrong that police officers should have the right to compensation for psychiatric injury out of public funds when bereaved relatives did not. Fairness demanded that the appeal be allowed, and the claims were therefore dismissed.

A rescuer who is not exposed to danger of physical injury, or who does not believe themselves to have been so exposed, is therefore classified as a secondary victim who must satisfy the control mechanisms set out in *Alcock* before they can recover damages for pure psychiatric injury.

In *Stephen John Monk v (1) PC Harrington Ltd (2) HTC Plant Ltd (3) Multiplex Constructions Ltd* [2008] EWHC 1879 (QB), the claimant had been working as a self-employed foreman on site during the construction of Wembley Stadium. While he was working, a temporary platform fell 60 feet onto two fellow workers. One of the men died from his injuries shortly after the accident, the other suffered a broken leg. Having arrived at the scene of the accident, the claimant tried to help both men and, specifically, to comfort the man with the broken leg. Thereafter, as a result of the accident, he began to suffer from symptoms of PTSD, which ultimately caused him to stop work. The defendant admitted liability for the accident, and the claimant claimed damages for psychiatric injury on the grounds that his involvement in the accident was such that he fulfilled the necessary conditions to recover compensation as a rescuer; and even if he was unable to bring himself within the rescuer category of primary victim, he could nevertheless establish the necessary proximity to the accident, which he believed he had caused, in order that he could be regarded as an unwilling participant.

While it was accepted by the court that the claimant had provided significant help and comfort to the injured men, and that this assistance entitled him to be regarded as a rescuer, the claimant could not show on the evidence that he had reasonably believed that he was putting his own safety at risk. He could not therefore establish himself as a primary victim on the basis of his acts as a rescuer. As for the second ground advanced by the claimant – that he was a primary victim as an unwilling participant – it was held that he had to show that his injuries were induced by a genuine belief that he had caused another person's injury or death, and there was no reasonable basis for such a belief in this case. Therefore, it was not reasonably foreseeable that someone in his position would suffer psychiatric injury as a result of such a belief.

6.2.2.5 Bystanders as victims

A 'mere bystander' will be unable to claim damages for pure psychiatric injury as they will be unable to satisfy control mechanisms for a secondary victim outlined at **6.2.2.2** above. This is well illustrated by the case of *McFarlane v EE Caledonia Ltd* [1994] 2 All ER 1, which arose out of the Piper Alpha oil rig disaster. The claimant had been off duty on a support vessel some 550 metres away when he witnessed the explosions and consequent destruction of the oil rig, which resulted in the death of 164 men. His claim failed as he was not himself in any danger, and it had not been shown that it was reasonably foreseeable that a man of ordinary fortitude would have suffered a psychiatric injury as a result of what he saw.

6.3 OCCUPATIONAL STRESS

6.3.1 The meaning of occupational stress

Stress is a feature of nearly every workplace, and indeed is often seen as desirable to motivate and encourage people. However, too much pressure can lead to psychological problems and physical ill-health.

In trying to come to some workable definition of 'occupational stress', Hale LJ, in *Hatton v Sutherland; Barber v Somerset County Council; Jones v Sandwell Metropolitan Borough Council; Bishop v Baker Refractories Ltd* [2002] EWCA Civ 76, [2002] 2 All ER 1, referred to three documents which she said the Court had found particularly helpful:

(a)   *Stress in the Public Sector – Nurses, Police, Social Workers and Teachers* (1988) defines stress as 'an excess of demands upon an individual in excess of their ability to cope'.

(b)   *Managing Occupational Stress: a Guide for Managers and Teachers in the School Sector* (Education Service Advisory Committee of the Health and Safety Commission, 1990) defines stress as 'a process that can occur when there is an unresolved mismatch between the perceived pressures of the work situation and an individual's ability to "cope"'.

(c)   The HSE website (www.hse.gov.uk/stress/) defines stress as follows:

> The adverse reaction people have to excessive pressures or other types of demand placed upon them. Workers feel stress when they can't cope with pressures and other issues ...
>
> Stress is not an illness but it can make you ill.

In *Hatton v Sutherland*, the judge concluded that harmful levels of stress are more likely to occur in situations where people feel powerless or trapped, and are therefore much more likely to affect people at junior levels; and, secondly, stress is a psychological phenomenon which can lead to either physical or mental ill-health, or both.

More recently, the HSE published the Management Standards, which provide guidance to assist employers to identify, manage and control the risks from work related stress.

6.3.2 Duty of care

In *Petch v Commissioners of Customs and Excise* [1993] ICR 789, it was accepted that the ordinary principles of employers' liability applied to claims for psychiatric illness arising from employment. Although the claim in *Petch* failed, Colman J, in *Walker v Northumberland County Council* [1995] 1 All ER 737, applied the same principles in upholding the claim. In this case, Mr Walker was a conscientious but overworked manager of a social work area office, with a heavy and emotionally demanding workload of child abuse cases. Although he complained and asked for help and for extra leave, the judge held that his first mental breakdown was not foreseeable. There was liability, however, when he returned to work with a promise of extra help, which did not materialise, and he experienced a second breakdown only a few months later.

Petch and *Walker* have both been cited with approval by the Court of Appeal in *Garrett v Camden LBC* [2001] EWCA Civ 395.

6.3.3 Reasonable foreseeability, breach of duty and causation – the *Hatton* guidelines

In *Hatton v Sutherland & Others* [2002] EWCA Civ 76, the Court of Appeal set out guidance for courts to follow in occupational stress cases which was approved by the House of Lords in *Barber v Somerset CC* [2004] UKHL 13. Hale LJ set out the guidance as follows:

(1)   There are no special control mechanisms applying to claims for psychiatric (or physical) illness or injury arising from the stress of doing the work the employee is required to do. The ordinary principles of employer's liability apply.

(2)   The threshold question is whether this kind of harm to this particular employee was reasonably foreseeable: this has two components (a) an injury to health (as distinct from occupational stress) which (b) is attributable to stress at work (as distinct from other factors).

(3)   Foreseeability depends upon what the employer knows (or ought reasonably to know) about the individual employee. Because of the nature of mental disorder, it is harder to foresee than physical injury, but may be easier to foresee in a known individual than in the population at large. An employer is usually entitled to assume that the employee can withstand the normal pressures of the job unless he knows of some particular problem or vulnerability.

(4)   The test is the same whatever the employment: there are no occupations which should be regarded as intrinsically dangerous to mental health.

(5)   Factors likely to be relevant in answering the threshold question include:

(a)   The nature and extent of the work done by the employee. Is the workload much more than is normal for the particular job? Is the work particularly intellectually or emotionally demanding for this employee? Are demands being made of this employee unreasonable when compared with the demands made of others in the same or comparable jobs? Or are there signs that others doing this job are suffering harmful levels of stress? Is there an abnormal level of sickness or absenteeism in the same job or the same department?

(b)   Signs from the employee of impending harm to health. Has he a particular problem or vulnerability? Has he already suffered from illness attributable to stress at work? Have there recently been frequent or prolonged absences which are uncharacteristic of him? Is there reason to think that these are attributable to stress at work, for example because of complaints or warnings from him or others?

(6)   The employer is generally entitled to take what he is told by his employee at face value, unless he has good reason to think to the contrary. He does not generally have to make searching enquiries of the employee or seek permission to make further enquiries of his medical advisers.

(7)   To trigger a duty to take steps, the indications of impending harm to health arising from stress at work must be plain enough for any reasonable employer to realise that he should do something about it.

(8)   The employer is only in breach of duty if he has failed to take the steps which are reasonable in the circumstances, bearing in mind the magnitude of the risk of harm occurring, the gravity of the harm which may occur, the costs and practicability of preventing it, and the justifications for running the risk.

(9)   The size and scope of the employer's operation, its resources and the demands it faces are relevant in deciding what is reasonable; these include the interests of other employees and the need to treat them fairly, for example, in any redistribution of duties.

(10)   An employer can only reasonably be expected to take steps which are likely to do some good: the court is likely to need expert evidence on this.

(11)   An employer who offers a confidential advice service, with referral to appropriate counselling or treatment services, is unlikely to be found in breach of duty.

(12)   If the only reasonable and effective step would have been to dismiss or demote the employee, the employer will not be in breach of duty in allowing a willing employee to continue in the job.

(13)   In all cases, therefore, it is necessary to identify the steps which the employer both could and should have taken before finding him in breach of his duty of care.

(14)   The claimant must show that that breach of duty has caused or materially contributed to the harm suffered. It is not enough to show that occupational stress has caused the harm.

(15)   Where the harm suffered has more than one cause, the employer should only pay for that proportion of the harm suffered which is attributable to his wrongdoing, unless the harm is truly indivisible. It is for the defendant to raise the question of apportionment.

(16)   The assessment of damages will take account of any pre-existing disorder or vulnerability and of the chance that the claimant would have succumbed to a stress related disorder in any event.

Young v Post Office [2002] EWCA Civ 661 was decided after *Hatton v Sutherland* and considered whether it is the responsibility of the claimant to inform the employer if the claimant is unable to cope, and whether the claimant will be contributorily negligent if they fail to do so. The claimant had worked for the Post Office for a number of years and had been promoted to workshop manager. He had no direct line manager, and when a new computer system was introduced he was expected to familiarise himself with it without formal training. The claimant began to show signs of stress and eventually suffered a nervous breakdown, and subsequently took four months off work to recover. Arrangements were made to allow the claimant to return to work gradually and on a flexible basis. When the claimant returned to work he quickly shouldered the burden of the management position that had led to his breakdown. Seven weeks later the claimant was again unable to continue due to stress and left. The defendants contended that they had done all that they could in offering a less stressful work pattern for the claimant. On appeal, the Court found for the claimant, as it was plainly foreseeable that there might be a recurrence if appropriate steps were not taken when the claimant returned to work, and the employer owed a duty to take such steps. Although the employer had told the claimant that he could adopt a flexible approach to his work, the reality was that he was a hardworking and conscientious employee, and it was foreseeable that he would quickly revert to overworking, and the employer had a duty to ensure that help was on hand. Regarding the allegation of contributory negligence, the Court found that this was not relevant in this case and would be unusual but was 'theoretically possible'.

The High Court decision in *Barlow v Broxbourne Borough Council* [2003] EWHC 50 (QB), [2003] All ER (D) 208 (Jan), provides an example of the application of the principles set out by the Court of Appeal in *Hatton v Sutherland*. B had initially been employed as a gardener and had obtained several promotions to become senior operations manager in 1993. B's claim was based on two broad grounds: systematic victimisation and 'general' bullying. He alleged that from approximately 1997 he had been deliberately victimised and bullied by senior members of the council's staff, which had caused him to suffer emotional distress and psychological injury. The alleged 'victimisation' and 'bullying' had included receipt of lengthy letters detailing B's non-performance, threats of disciplinary action and, at times, abusive language. Medical experts for each party were agreed that B had suffered a moderately severe depressive episode. Consequently, B had been unable to continue working for the council. B argued that he had been exposed to such stress at work that he had developed a stress-related illness which had prevented him from remaining in the council's employ. However, B's claim failed on the following grounds:

(a) The actions of the council and its employees did not give rise to a foreseeable risk of injury. Hale LJ's guidelines in *Hatton v Sutherland* applied. In the circumstances, it was not necessary for the court to consider causation issues.

(b) The council could not have reasonably known or foreseen that the conduct complained of by B would have caused him harm.

(c) Nothing in B's behaviour, at the time, had given any cause for concern about the risk of psychiatric illness.

This judgment assists the defendant by confirming that the alleged incidents of bullying and/or harassment must be considered in context. In the context of the claimant's working environment, the use of bad language (which was not disputed at trial) and the actions of his line managers in highlighting areas of non-performance, did not amount to victimisation or bullying.

In *Intel Corporation (UK) Limited v Daw* [2007] EWCA Civ 70, Pill LJ approved of the guidance in *Hatton* but warned courts against following it too rigidly:

> A very considerable amount of helpful guidance is given in *Hatton*. That does not preclude or excuse the trial judge either from conducting a vigorous fact-finding exercise, as the trial judge in this case did, or deciding which parts of the guidance are relevant to the particular circumstances. The reference to counselling services in *Hatton* does not make such services a panacea by which employers can discharge their duty of care in all cases. The respondent, a loyal and capable employee, pointed out the serious management failings which were causing her stress and the failure to take action was that of management. The consequences of that failure are not avoided by the provision of counsellors who

might have brought home to management that action was required. On the judge's findings, the managers knew it was required.

This approach was endorsed by the Court of Appeal in *Dickins v O2 plc* [2008] EWCA Civ 1144, when the Court upheld the trial judge's decision to award the claimant damages for injury caused by occupational stress.

Ms Dickins' job involved the preparation of management and regulatory accounts. She found one particular audit in February 2002 'extremely stressful'. She had a short holiday but returned to work exhausted, and on 11 March 2002 she asked her line manager for a different and less stressful job. As there were no vacancies available at the time, Ms Dickins was told that the matter would be reviewed in three months. On 23 April 2002 she requested a six-month sabbatical. She said she was stressed out, was having a real struggle to get out of bed in the mornings and to get to work on time because she felt so drained of physical and mental energy, and she did not know how long she could carry on before being off sick. She was advised to access O2's confidential counselling helpline, and was told that her request for a sabbatical would be considered. On 30 May 2002 Ms Dickins repeated her concerns during her appraisal and was referred to occupational health, albeit with some delay. Before any appointment was fixed, she suffered a breakdown and never returned to work.

The Court of Appeal upheld the judge's finding that psychiatric injury was reasonably foreseeable from 23 April 2002 onwards. There was sufficient indication of impending harm to health, given the claimant's description of the seriousness of her symptoms and the important background context that these problems had not come 'out of the blue'. The fact that the claimant had been mentioning difficulties over a period of time was significant, given that she was usually a conscientious employee.

The Court of Appeal also agreed with the trial judge that the defendant employer was in breach of duty in not sending her home and in not making an immediate referral to occupational health.

In *Connor v Surrey County Council* [2010] EWCA Civ 286, the claimant, a head teacher in a primary school, was awarded damages against the defendant local education authority for its failure to have regard to the effect of its conduct on her health or to give her the support she needed, which resulted in her suffering severe depression. The defendant raised in its defence the issue of foreseeability of injury, and argued that there were no signs of impending harm to the claimant's health, particularly as she had not been absent from work prior to her breakdown. However, the judge held that the fact that the claimant had not been absent from work was irrelevant; the risk was apparent from comments made by the claimant and others, and action should have been taken to respond to it. The decision at first instance was upheld by the Court of Appeal.

It seems clear from these decisions that, in an appropriate case, it may not be necessary to show that the claimant has previously suffered a breakdown if the claimant's words and actions in the recent past would alert a reasonable employer to the risk of illness. Furthermore, whereas *Hatton* had indicated that an employer who offered a confidential counselling service was unlikely to be found in breach of duty, the recent cases cast doubt over whether the provision of such a service will exonerate an employer. More recently, in *Yapp v Foreign and Commonwealth Office* [2014] EWCA Civ 1512, the Court of Appeal held that the claimant's claim for psychiatric injuries should fail. In a judgment that provides an extremely useful summary of the authorities on this subject, Underhill LJ stated that it would 'be exceptional that an apparently robust employee, with no history of any psychiatric ill-health, will develop a depressive illness as a result even of a very serious setback at work', but that 'each case depends on its own facts, and in principle the employer's conduct in a particular case might be so devastating that it was foreseeable that even a person of ordinary robustness might develop a depressive illness as a result'. Each case is highly fact-specific but, for a helpful reminder of some common issues, the full judgment in *Easton v B&Q Plc* [2015] EWHC 880 (QB) is also recommended reading.

6.3.4 Causation

Having established a breach of duty, it is still necessary to prove that the particular breach of duty caused the harm. Where there are several different possible causes (as will often be the case with stress-related illness), the claimant may have difficulty proving that the employer's breach of duty was one of them. This will be a particular problem if, as in *Garrett v Camden LBC* [2001] EWCA Civ 395, the main cause was a vulnerable personality which the employer knew nothing about. However, the employee does not have to prove that the breach of duty was the sole cause of the claimant's ill-health: it is enough to show that it made a material contribution (see *Bonnington Castings Ltd v Wardlaw* [1956] AC 613). Expert medical evidence will be crucial in determining causation.

6.3.5 Damages

The *Hatton* guidelines (see **6.3.3**) suggested that an employer found liable for psychiatric injury caused by occupational stress should pay only for that proportion of the injury caused by the employer's wrongdoing and not for any part of the injury caused by other factors. However, in *Dickins v O2*, the Court of Appeal was critical of the trial judge's decision to reduce the total damages by 50% for the other non-tortious factors which had contributed to the claimant's illness. In the Court's view, albeit *obiter*, the injury was indivisible, and so an employer should be liable for the whole injury if it is proved that the tort has made more than a minimal contribution to the injury.

Further guidance by the Court of Appeal on the issue of apportionment was given in *BAE Systems (Operations) Ltd v Konczak* [2017] EWCA Civ 1188. Following *Dickins v O2*, it seemed for a time that no reduction should be made for the other stresses which contributed to a claimant's illness and that a more appropriate route may have been for defendants to argue that particular heads of damage (eg loss of future earnings) should be discounted to reflect the fact that a claimant might in any event have suffered a breakdown at some time in the future. However, *BAE Systems v Konczak* made clear that there is a distinction between guidelines 15 and 16 of the *Hatton* guidelines. Guideline 15 is applicable to cases where the injury in question is regarded as having multiple causes, one or more of which is, or are, attributable to the wrongful acts of the employer but one or more of which is/are not. A sensible attempt at apportionment should be made and the employer should pay only for the proportion of harm which is attributable to the employer's wrongdoing, unless the harm is truly indivisible. Guideline 16 relates to a pre-existing disorder or vulnerability, which is not treated as a cause in itself but which might have led to a similar injury (for which the employer would not have been responsible) even if the wrong had not been committed. The Court of Appeal noted:

> The distinction between pre-existing vulnerability and concurrent cause may be debatable, and even if it is legitimate it may be difficult to apply in particular cases. There may also be cases where both propositions are in play. It may in many or most cases not be necessary for a court or tribunal to worry too much about where exactly to draw the line. Both propositions are tools which enable a tribunal to avoid over-compensation in these difficult cases. Nevertheless they are clearly treated as conceptually distinct.

6.4 CLAIMS UNDER THE PROTECTION FROM HARASSMENT ACT 1997

The Protection from Harassment Act 1997 (PHA 1997) provides an alternative cause of action for employees who experience harassment in the workplace by a colleague.

Section 1 of the PHA 1997 provides that 'a person must not pursue a course of conduct: (a) which amounts to harassment of another, and (b) which he knows or ought to know amounts to harassment of another'.

Although there is no specific definition of harassment, the PHA 1997 does stipulate that references to harassing a person include alarming or causing the person distress; a course of conduct must involve at least two occasions; and that conduct includes speech (s 7).

In contrast to a claim at common law, under the PHA 1997 a claimant needs only to prove that they have experienced 'anxiety' as a result of the harassment. This is a significantly lower hurdle than establishing 'a recognisable psychiatric condition' required for a successful non-physical injury claim under established common law principles. In addition, a claimant has six years to bring a claim, rather than three years (s 6).

In *Majrowski v Guy's and St Thomas's NHS Trust* [2006] UKHL 34 the House of Lords held that to succeed under the PHA 1997, a claimant must show that the conduct complained of is 'oppressive and unacceptable' as opposed to merely unattractive, unreasonable or regrettable. The primary focus is on whether the conduct is oppressive and unacceptable, albeit the court must keep in mind that it must be of an order which 'would sustain criminal liability'.

In *Veakins v Kier Islington Ltd* [2009] EWCA Civ 1288 the Court of Appeal allowed the claimant's appeal in a harassment at work claim as the trial judge had applied the wrong legal test.

The claimant was an electrician employed by the defendant for two years before she went on long-term sick leave with depression after which she never returned to work. She alleged that she was victimised by her supervisor for some two to three months during which her supervisor had made it clear that she did not like her, had singled her out from other employees for no reason and had 'made her life hell'.

The trial judge decided that the claimant's allegations, even though unchallenged by the defendant, did not amount to harassment under the PHA 1997. Relying on the Court of Appeal decision in *Conn v The Council of the City of Sunderland* [2007] EWCA Civ 1492 the trial judge held that this conduct would not justify any criminal prosecution and dismissed the claim.

The claimant's appeal to the Court of Appeal was allowed. The Court of Appeal agreed that the conduct must be grave to constitute harassment under the PHA 1997 but the judge had failed to apply the primary legal test set out by the House of Lords in *Majrowski*. Under that primary test the judge was required to consider whether the conduct had crossed the boundary from the 'unattractive and unreasonable' to conduct which is 'oppressive and unacceptable'.

On the undisputed evidence of the claimant, the Court of Appeal held that this was such a case where the conduct was extraordinary and that boundary had been crossed. The trial judge had undervalued the evidence. The claimant's account was of victimisation, demoralisation and reduction of a substantially reasonable and usually robust woman to a state of clinical depression. This was, the Court of Appeal felt, to have self-evidently crossed the line into conduct which was 'oppressive and unreasonable'.

6.5 CONCLUSION

The main points to bear in mind when bringing a claim for psychiatric injury are as follows:

- To claim damages for nervous shock there must be evidence of a recognised psychiatric illness.
- It is necessary to identify whether the client is a primary victim (directly involved in the accident) or a secondary victim (a witness/bystander).
- If the client is a secondary victim, the client must satisfy the control mechanisms laid down in *Alcock* to establish closeness to the victim and the incident itself.
- There are no special control mechanisms in claims for occupational stress – the ordinary principles of employers' liability apply.
- The injury to the individual employee must have been reasonably foreseeable.

- In order to establish a breach of duty, it will be necessary to identify the steps the employer could and should have taken to prevent harm.
- The provision of a counselling service will not automatically exonerate an employer.

6.6 FURTHER READING AND RELEVANT WEBSITES

Butterworths Personal Injury Litigation Service

Marshall, *Compensation for Stress at Work* (LexisNexis Butterworths)

Law Commission Consultation Paper, *Liability for Psychiatric Illness* 1995 (Law Com No 137)

www.hse.gov.uk/stress

LIMITATION OF ACTIONS

LEARNING OUTCOMES

After reading this chapter you will be able to:

- set out the law as it relates to limitation in cases involving a claim for personal injuries and a claim following a fatal accident
- appreciate that the court may use its discretion to disapply the limitation period, and set out the factors which it takes into consideration
- apply the law to real-life situations.

7.1 INTRODUCTION

The law relating to limitation is fairly complex and can cause difficulties for the unwary. Each year, there is a steady flow of case law relevant to this area, partly because clients seek legal advice far too late, but also because solicitors sometimes breach the duty of care owed to their clients by failing to ensure that proceedings are issued within the limitation period. Consequently, one of the first priorities for the claimant's solicitor will be to identify when the limitation period ends and, having established this, to mark the file with that date and enter it into the diary system.

The principal statute dealing with limitation issues is the Limitation Act 1980 (LA 1980).

For the purpose of limitation in a personal injury claim, 'personal injury' includes any disease and any impairment of a person's physical or mental condition (s 38).

7.2 THE LIMITATION PERIOD

Under ss 11 and 12 of the LA 1980, where a claimant claims damages for negligence, nuisance or breach of duty, and that claim consists of or includes a claim for personal injuries, the claimant must normally commence their claim (ie the claim form must be issued, or received by the court in order to be issued) within three years from:

(a) the date on which the cause of action accrued; or

(b) the date of knowledge (if later) of the person injured (s 11(4); see **7.3** below).

When calculating the three-year period (generally referred to as the 'primary' limitation period), the day on which the cause of action accrued is excluded (s 2). Therefore, in a simple road traffic accident case, generally the claimant has three years from the incident (excluding the date of the incident) in which to commence the claim. If the last date of this period is a Saturday, Sunday or Bank Holiday, the time is extended until the next day when the courts are open and the claim can be issued.

It is important to note the distinction between when a claim is 'brought' for limitation purposes and when it is issued by the court. CPR, PD 7A, para 6.1 sets out the position as follows:

> 6.1   Proceedings are started when the court issues a claim form at the request of the claimant (see rule 7.2) but where the claim form as issued was received in the court office on a date earlier than the date on which it was issued by the court, the claim is 'brought' for the purposes of the Limitation Act 1980 and any other relevant statute on that earlier date.

The general effect of this was confirmed in *Barnes v St Helens MBC* [2006] EWCA Civ 1372, in which the Court of Appeal held that the expiry of the limitation period was fixed by reference to something that the claimant had to do, rather than something which someone else such as the court has to do. Once the claimant had taken all reasonable steps to set the process in motion, the risk of any delay was transferred to the court. Therefore, if a claimant established that the claim form was delivered in due time to the court office, accompanied by a request to issue and the appropriate fee, that was sufficient to stop the limitation clock running.

The position is less clear when the appropriate fee has not been sent to the court. In *Atha & Co Solicitors v Liddle* [2018] EWHC 1751 (QB) the court received the claim form a few days before the limitation period expired. The statement of value on the claim form valued the claim at between £10,000 and £25,000 and the fee of £1,250 based on that valuation was included. The court duly issued the claim a few days later. Soon afterwards, the claimant's solicitors wrote to the defendant saying that the value of the claim could not be calculated without further investigation by medical experts and therefore refused to accept a Part 36 offer of £25,000. The defendant applied to strike out the claim as an abuse of process. At first instance, the judge held that there was no abuse of process as the value of the claim was genuinely unknown at the time of drafting of the claim form. On appeal, the High Court disagreed, finding that the claimant's solicitors had deliberately misstated the value of the claim and therefore there had been an abuse of process. However, the abuse was not 'sufficiently egregious' to justify striking out the claim. The defendant argued in the alternative for summary judgment on the basis that as the appropriate fee had not been sent, the claim had not been brought in time. This was rejected by the High Court judge who held that the abuse of process had had no effect on the timing of the issue of proceedings and that therefore proceedings had been brought in time for limitation purposes. Mr Justice Turner concluded that 'the time is now ripe for authoritative guidance from the Court of Appeal' on this contentious subject. In *Butters v Hayes* [2021] EWCA Civ 252, the Court of Appeal considered whether non-payment of a court fee means that time continues to run for limitation purposes in respect of a new claim within existing proceedings (ie where the claimant seeks to amend an existing claim). The Court of Appeal considered the relevant case law, including *Barnes* and *Atha*, and stated, 'Tempting though it is to seek to resolve the question, it is unnecessary for us to do so for the purposes of the present appeal. That said, my provisional view is that there is force in the concerns expressed in a number of cases about the disallowing of a claim on limitation grounds merely because of an inadvertent miscalculation of a court fee.' The Court of Appeal noted the range of other responses available to the court to control any abuse of its processes.

Where the three-year period has expired, the claimant is not prohibited from commencing proceedings, although if the claimant does so, the defendant may seek to have the claim struck out on the grounds that it is statute-barred. However, the claimant may apply to the court for the limitation to be disapplied under s 33 of the LA 1980 (see **7.8**).

7.3   DATE OF KNOWLEDGE

A claimant may work in an environment which, for example, exposes the claimant to injurious dust particles such as asbestos dust or coal dust. It may be many years before an illness or disease manifests itself, and it may be some time later before the claimant realises what the cause of their illness is. Similarly, in a clinical negligence context, a patient may be fully aware of their pain and suffering but assume that it is entirely due to an underlying illness, rather than due to negligent advice from or treatment by a doctor or other medical practitioner. In such circumstances, it is not unusual for a claimant to issue proceedings many years after the expiry of the three-year limitation period and to seek to rely on a later date of knowledge under s 14 of the LA 1980. Where the claimant seeks to do so, the burden of proof rests with the claimant.

7.3.1   Section 14 of the Limitation Act 1980

Section 14 of the LA 1980 defines 'date of knowledge' for the purpose of ss 11 and 12 as follows:

(1) In sections 11 and 12 of this Act references to a person's date of knowledge are references to the date on which he first had knowledge of the following facts—

    (a)   that the injury in question was significant; and

    (b)   that the injury was attributable in whole or in part to the act or omission which is alleged to constitute negligence, nuisance or breach of duty; and

    (c)   the identity of the defendant; and

    (d)   if it is alleged that the act or omission was that of a person other than the defendant, the identity of that person and the additional facts supporting the bringing of an action against the defendant;

and knowledge that any acts or omissions did or did not, as a matter of law, involve negligence, nuisance or breach of duty is irrelevant.

(2) For the purposes of this section an injury is significant if the person whose date of knowledge is in question would reasonably have considered it sufficiently serious to justify his instituting proceedings for damages against a defendant who did not dispute liability and was able to satisfy a judgment.

(3) For the purposes of this section a person's knowledge includes knowledge which he might reasonably have been expected to acquire—

    (a)   from facts observable or ascertainable by him; or

    (b)   from facts ascertainable by him with the help of medical or other appropriate expert advice which it is reasonable for him to seek;

but a person shall not be fixed under this subsection with knowledge of a fact ascertainable only with the help of expert advice so long as he has taken all reasonable steps to obtain (and, where appropriate, to act on) that advice.

7.3.2   The meaning of knowledge and the starting of the clock

In *Halford v Brookes* [1991] 3 All ER 559, it was stated that knowledge does not mean 'know for certain and beyond the possibility of contradiction', but rather 'know with sufficient confidence to justify embarking on the preliminaries to issue of proceedings, such as submitting a claim to the proposed defendant, taking legal advice and other advice and collecting evidence'.

Consequently, the date of a claimant's knowledge is the date on which the claimant first knew enough of the various matters set out in s 14(1) to begin to investigate whether the claimant has a claim against the defendant. For example, where a specialist told the claimant that he had an inhaled disease or industrial injury and the only source for this could be his work for the defendants (*Corbin v Penfold Metallising Co Ltd* [2000] Lloyd's Rep Med 247), or where the claimant was told by a community worker that his deafness could have been caused by his work in a mill (*Ali v Courtaulds Textiles Limited* [1999] Lloyd's Rep Med 301).

It should be noted that knowledge will be present even though the claimant's psychological condition leads to a state of denial. In *TCD v (1) Harrow Council (2) Worcester County Council (3) Birmingham City Council* [2008] EWHC 3048 (QB), the clamant sought damages in relation to child abuse suffered from 1975 and 1981. The fact that her psychological or mental state 'may have meant that she was in denial and/or could not face reliving her abuse for the purposes of the claim', was not relevant for the purposes of determining her knowledge (although it was relevant in relation to the exercise of discretion under s 33 – see **7.8**).

Although it may be possible to identify a specific date when it is clear that the claimant had the requisite knowledge, the court may determine that the claimant should have acquired this knowledge at an earlier date.

7.3.3   Actual and constructive knowledge

Where a claimant wishes to rely on a later date of knowledge, the claimant will seek to fix that date as being the date when they actually acquired the requisite knowledge. This is known as 'actual knowledge'. The defendant, though, may argue that the claimant had actual knowledge of these matters at an earlier date and/or *should* have obtained knowledge at an earlier date, and that the claimant is thereby fixed with 'constructive knowledge'.

7.3.3.1   Actual knowledge

When considering the question of actual knowledge, claimants will often seek to rely on a date when they were told that their injury or illness was caused by the defendant's actions, usually by a doctor or a solicitor. However, the court may determine that a claimant had actual knowledge at an earlier date.

In *Spargo v North Essex District Health Authority* [1997] 8 Med LR 125, the court held that a subjective test was to be applied, namely 'What did the claimant know?' and not 'What would a reasonable layman realise?' The facts of the case were that the claimant had been diagnosed as suffering from selective brain damage and was compulsorily detained in hospital from 1975 until 1981. The proceedings were not issued until 1993, although the claimant had first consulted solicitors in 1986. At this time, she did not know whether she had a case but felt clear in her own mind that her suffering was attributable to a mistaken diagnosis. It was held on appeal that because the claimant was clear in her own mind that a connection existed between her suffering and the misdiagnosis when she first sought legal advice in 1986, it was not necessary for the court to enquire further whether a rational lay person would have been willing to say that he knew of a connection between the suffering and the misdiagnosis without first obtaining a medical confirmation.

In *Ministry of Defence v AB and others* [2012] UKSC 9, the Supreme Court looked at limitation as a preliminary issue in the context of nine conjoined cases. The claimants, all veteran servicemen, claimed that they had suffered numerous illnesses as a result of exposure to ionising radiation during nuclear tests carried out by the British Government in the 1950s. At first instance, it was held that actual and constructive knowledge arose only when each veteran had been made aware of the Rowland Study in 2007, which was the first credible scientific evidence that the exposure could cause the illnesses complained of. Although, applying that test, none of the cases was statute-barred, five of the veterans had already formed a strong belief that exposure to radiation had caused their illnesses, and this was sufficient to amount to actual knowledge. These cases would have been statute-barred had the court not exercised its discretion under s 33 to disapply the limitation period (see **7.8** below).

The Court of Appeal and the Supreme Court determined that the wrong approach had been taken in relation to the date of knowledge, and that the discretion to disapply the limitation period should not be exercised. The claimants had argued that they had not known that their illnesses were attributable to the acts or omissions of the defendant more than three years prior to issue of proceedings; they might have believed this to be the case, but the Act required knowledge. However, the Court of Appeal unanimously and the Supreme Court by a majority held that a reasonable belief (ie more than a fanciful suggestion) that the defendant was responsible amounted to knowledge. All that was required was sufficient knowledge to justify further investigation and commencement of the preliminaries to making a claim.

For the purposes of establishing knowledge, it was irrelevant that the claimants were still not in a position, after many years of investigation and campaigning, to establish causation. However this, and the lapse of time, led to the Court determining that time should not be extended under s 33.

It is possible that a claimant may be fixed with actual knowledge of certain facts even if a medical expert has advised the claimant that this was not the case. In *Sniezek v Bundy (Letchworth) Ltd* [2000] PIQR P213, the Court of Appeal ruled that the claimant had the knowledge from the date when he went to complain to his doctor of severe symptoms but was assured that there was no link between the illness and his work. The Court decided that the claimant knew that his severe throat symptoms, which had persisted for five years, were a significant injury, and that he had always attributed them to his work. The fact that a doctor subsequently advised him that this was not the case, did not change the fact that he had actual knowledge.

7.3.3.2 Constructive knowledge

Where a claimant is not fixed with actual knowledge, they may be fixed with constructive knowledge in accordance with s 14(3) of the LA 1980.

In accordance with s 14(3) (see **7.3.1**), a claimant cannot argue that they did not have the requisite knowledge due to their ignorance of the law, or because they failed to make further enquiries or seek appropriate advice. The test is an objective one: knowledge which would have been obtained by a reasonable person in the same circumstances as the claimant will be imputed to the claimant. So, there is an assumption that a reasonable person who had suffered a significant injury would be sufficiently curious about the cause of the injury that they would seek expert advice (see *Adams v Bracknell Forest BC* [2004] UKHL 29), unless there were reasons why a reasonable person in their position would not have done so (see *Johnson v Ministry of Defence* [2012] EWCA Civ 1505).

In *Collins v Secretary of State for Business, Innovation and Skills and Stenna Line Irish Sea Ferries Ltd* [2014] EWCA Civ 717, the claimant, who had been exposed to asbestos when he worked as a docker between 1947 and 1967, and who had developed lung cancer in 2002 (although he had made a full recovery), commenced proceedings in 2012. At first instance, the court determined that actual knowledge took place in 2009, when the claimant saw an advertisement by personal injury solicitors, but that constructive knowledge had occurred in 2003, after he had been diagnosed with cancer and allowing time for him recover from the shock of diagnosis. This was on the basis that a reasonable person would have asked their doctor about the possible causes of the cancer, and that it was inevitable that the doctor would have mentioned the claimant's exposure to asbestos. The Court of Appeal upheld this decision. This case is also important in relation to the exercise of the court's discretion to disapply the limitation period under s 33 of the LA 1980 (see **7.8**).

The objective nature of the test was confirmed by the House of Lords in *A v Hoare* [2008] UKHL 6, when it was said that the correct approach was to ask what the claimant knew about their injury, add any 'objective' knowledge which might be imputed to the claimant under s 14(3) and then ask whether a reasonable person with that knowledge would have considered the injury sufficiently serious to justify them instituting proceedings. Once the court has determined what the claimant knew and what they should be treated as having known, the actual claimant drops out of the picture, and judges should not consider the claimant's intelligence. Consequently, the effect of any psychological injuries resulting from the breach of duty upon what the claimant could reasonably have been expected to do is irrelevant when considering constructive knowledge. (However, this will be considered by the court when deciding whether to exercise its discretion under s 33 to disapply the limitation period – see **7.8.**)

In *Forbes v Wandsworth Health Authority* [1997] QB 402, the claimant, who suffered from poor circulation, underwent surgery for a by-pass operation. This was not a success and a further by-pass was performed the next day. Unfortunately, the second operation was too late to be successful and the claimant was told that it was necessary to amputate his leg to prevent gangrene, to which he agreed. The sole allegation was that the authority had been negligent not to perform the second operation sooner. The claimant did not seek advice until seven years after the limitation period had expired. The Court of Appeal held by a majority that the claimant was deemed to have constructive knowledge as soon as he had had time to overcome the shock of the injury, take stock of his disability and seek advice.

In *Kew v Bettamix Ltd (formerly Tarmac Roadstone Southern Ltd) & Others* [2006] EWCA Civ 1535, the claimant issued proceedings in respect of injuries suffered from his exposure to vibrating equipment during his employment with the defendants. As early as 1991 the claimant had experienced numbness in his fingers, but had thought this was due to his age. On 29 March 2000, following a routine occupational health care assessment, he was informed by means of a letter from an occupational physician that his symptoms might be attributable to his exposure to vibration at work. The Court held that it was necessary for the claimant to have sufficient knowledge to make it reasonable for him to seek to acquire further knowledge of the link between his injury and his prior working conditions. He did not have such knowledge until 29 March 2000, when he received the physician's letter. Although he was not told about the causative link at that time, he knew that there was a real possibility that his working conditions had caused his symptoms, and a reasonable person would have investigated further. He was therefore fixed with constructive knowledge at that date.

In *Pierce v Doncaster MBC* [2008] EWCA Civ 1416, the Court of Appeal considered the knowledge of a man who claimed damages from the local authority for its failure to take him into care when he was a child. The claimant's actual knowledge arose when he saw his care records, shortly before issuing proceedings. However, constructive knowledge took place several years earlier, when he had requested his files but had failed to take up the appointment to view them, even though the authority had offered to pay his train fare.

In *Whiston v London Strategic Health Authority* [2010] EWCA Civ 195, the claimant suffered from cerebral palsy caused at the time of his birth, but he was highly intelligent and lived a full life. The claimant's mother had told him that he had been delivered by forceps and that he had been starved of oxygen at birth, but she did not tell him that she thought the junior doctor attending her may have been at fault until 2005, when she was prompted to do so by a deterioration in the claimant's condition. Proceedings were commenced in 2006, when the claimant was 32 years old, more than 11 years after the expiry of the limitation period. Although the Court of Appeal accepted that a person who suffers from a disability at birth is more likely to be accepting of his disability, and therefore less likely to ask questions, than a person who suffers an injury during adult life, it held that a reasonable person in his position would have wanted to know more about the circumstances of his birth and would have asked his mother, particularly as she was a nurse and a trained midwife. Consequently, it concluded that the claimant had constructive knowledge of the facts which he discovered from his mother in 2005 no later than when he was in his early 20s, in about 1998.

It is not necessary for the court to specify an exact date when constructive knowledge took place. In *White v EON and Others* [2008] EWCA Civ 1463, the claimant claimed damages for vibration white finger (VWF) caused whilst working for the defendant between 1962 and 1996. He argued that he first had the requisite knowledge in the summer of 2003, when he saw an advert from a claims company describing the symptoms of VWF. At first instance, the judge dismissed his claim on the basis that he knew he had a significant injury and it was reasonable for him to have obtained medical advice which would have led to his linking that injury to his employment. Consequently, he had constructive knowledge at the end of 1996. On appeal, the claimant's argument that it was illogical for the judge to have plucked the end of 1996 as the date of constructive knowledge, because nothing significant happened at that point to have led to that knowledge, was dismissed by the Court of Appeal. The Court held that the end of 1996 was the *latest time* at which the claimant could be fixed with constructive knowledge, as the claimant's symptoms had reached a plateau by that time.

The issue of constructive knowledge of the identity of the defendant was considered in *Henderson v Temple Pier Co Ltd* [1998] 1 WLR 1540. In this case, it was held that, where a claimant instructed solicitors to bring a claim for damages, on the proper construction of s 14(3) of the LA 1980 the claimant was fixed with constructive knowledge of facts which the solicitor ought to have acquired.

7.3.4 The injury was 'significant'

In order to determine whether the claimant was aware that the injury was significant, further guidance is provided in s 14(2). This states that an injury is significant if the claimant would reasonably have considered it sufficiently serious to justify instituting proceedings against a defendant who did not dispute liability and was able to satisfy a judgment.

In *McCoubrey v Ministry of Defence* [2007] EWCA Civ 17, the Court of Appeal considered the case of a soldier who, during a training exercise in 1993, had been deafened by a thunderflash which had been thrown negligently into his trench. The claimant had known almost immediately that he had suffered the injury, and this had been confirmed by medical examinations. However, he had continued working in the army without complaint until 2003, when he was told that he could not accompany his unit to Iraq because of his disability. At that stage, he became aware of the consequences of the injury, consulted solicitors and issued proceedings. It was held that time had started to run in 1993, as soon as the claimant had become aware of his deafness. When determining whether an injury is 'significant', the court should consider the gravity of the injury and not its effect, or perceived effect, on the personal life or career of the claimant.

If an injury is significant, the fact that the symptoms attributable to it subsequently became worse is irrelevant for purpose of determining when knowledge took place (see *Brooks v JP Coates (UK) Ltd* [1984] 1 All ER 702). The date of knowledge is not affected by the fact that the consequences turned out to be more serious than was initially thought.

Moreover, in cases of multiple illnesses arising from the same course of events, time starts to run as soon as the claimant has knowledge of the first injury that could be said to be significant, irrespective of whether the claimant might learn of other injuries much later.

7.3.5 Attributable to the act or omission

'Attributable' means 'capable of being attributable to' and not necessarily 'caused by'. The knowledge of the 'act or omission' does not necessarily include knowledge that the act or omission is actionable in law. For example, if the claimant has asthma but does not know that this is due to their working conditions, time does not start to run. However, if the claimant is aware that their asthma is capable of being attributed to those working conditions, time starts to run even though the claimant may not know that their employer may have been to blame.

In *Dobbie v Medway Health Authority* [1994] 1 WLR 1234, CA, Mrs Dobbie had surgery to remove a lump in her breast. It was only during the operation that the surgeon took the decision to perform a mastectomy (removal of the breast), as he believed the lump was cancerous. In fact, the lump was not cancerous and the mastectomy had been unnecessary. Mrs Dobbie accepted at the time that the surgeon had acted reasonably and it was her good fortune that the lump was not cancerous. It was only several years later, when she heard about a similar case, that Mrs Dobbie took legal advice and commenced proceedings. The Court of Appeal held that she knew of the removal of her breast and the psychological and physical harm which followed within months of the operation, and she knew it to be significant. She also knew that her injury was the result of an act or omission of the health authority and, therefore, time began to run even though she did not appreciate until later that this act or omission may have been negligent.

7.3.6 The identity of the defendant

In most cases the claimant will know who is responsible for the claimant's injuries, but s 14(1)(c) will assist a claimant where there is a delay in identifying the defendant, eg in the case of a hit and run motor accident (assuming an application is not made to the Motor Insurers' Bureau – see **3.4**).

The identity of the defendant may prove problematic in cases involving corporate groups. In *Simpson v Norwest Holst Southern Ltd* [1980] 2 All ER 471, the claimant worked on a building site, and his contract of employment stated that he was employed by Norwest Holst Group. However, this did not identify his employer because at least four companies made up Norwest Holst Group, including Norwest Holst Ltd and Norwest Construction Co Ltd, and the claimant's payslips stated simply that his employer was 'Norwest Holst'. In the circumstances, the Court of Appeal found for the claimant, on the basis that neither the contract nor the payslips identified the employer, and it was not reasonable to expect the claimant to request further particulars of the identity of his employer prior to the expiry of his primary limitation period. For a case on similar facts, see *Rush v JNR (SMD) Ltd* (CA, 11 October 1999) [2000] CP Rep 12, where it was held that knowledge of a number of potential defendants was not sufficient knowledge for the purpose of s 14.

7.4 PERSONS UNDER A DISABILITY

Under s 38(2) of the LA 1980, a person is under a disability 'while he is an infant' (a person who has not attained the age of 18) or 'lacks capacity (within the meaning of the Mental Capacity Act 2005) to conduct legal proceedings'.

Under s 28(6), while a person is under a disability, they may bring a claim at any time up to three years from the date when they ceased to be under a disability. Consequently, where a child is injured, limitation does not start to run until the child reaches their 18th birthday and it expires on their 21st birthday.

Where a person lacks capacity within the meaning of the Mental Capacity Act 2005, thereby being under a disability for the purposes of the LA 1980, the start of the limitation period is delayed only if the person was under such disability when the cause of action first accrued. If the disability comes into existence after that date, time continues to run. However, under s 33(3) of the LA 1980 (see **7.8**) the court will have regard to any period or periods of disability when it considers its discretion to disapply the limitation period.

7.5 LIMITATION IN ASSAULT CASES

Until January 2008, the limitation period in relation to acts of deliberate assault, including indecent assault, followed the House of Lords' decision in the case of *Stubbings v Webb* [1993] AC 498, which involved child abuse at a children's home. The House of Lords held that deliberate assault did not fall under s 11(1) actions for 'negligence, nuisance or breach of duty' but under s 2, and therefore the correct limitation period was six years from the date of the cause of action (or the age of 18 in the case of a child) rather than three years. However, there was no discretion to disapply the period under s 33, which led to unfairness in cases where the victim had been a child or otherwise vulnerable at the time of the assault and, as a result, lacked the psychological capacity to bring a claim.

The House of Lords departed from this approach in *A v Hoare* [2008] UKHL 6, the facts of which were as follows. In 1988, the claimant had been subjected to a serious sexual assault by Hoare, who was subsequently convicted of attempted rape and sentenced to life imprisonment. The claimant had not brought civil proceedings against him within the six-year limitation period as Hoare did not have the financial means to pay any damages that the court might award. However, in 2004, whilst on day release from prison, Hoare purchased a lottery ticket and won over £7 million. When the claimant heard of the defendant's windfall, she commenced proceedings against him, seeking to rely on the court's discretion to disapply the limitation period under s 33. The House of Lords heard the claimant's appeal against the decision that her claim was statute-barred, together with four other cases, all relating to the abuse of children in children's homes.

The House of Lords held that *Stubbings* had been wrongly decided, and extended the meaning of claims under 'negligence, nuisance or breach of duty' to include deliberate assault. Consequently, the limitation period in assault cases was three years. The House of Lords remitted the matter to the judge, for them to reconsider whether the court was able to exercise its discretion under s 33 to disapply this limitation period, taking into account the House of Lords' decision (see **7.8**).

7.6 CLAIMS FOLLOWING FATAL ACCIDENTS

Claims on behalf of the deceased's estate and on behalf of the deceased's dependants are generally brought together. Nevertheless, there are slight differences in how limitation is dealt with.

7.6.1 Claims under the Law Reform (Miscellaneous Provisions) Act 1934

Where a claim is brought on behalf of the deceased's estate, s 11(5) of the LA 1980 provides that if the injured person died before expiration of the limitation period of three years as set out in s 11(4), the limitation period is three years from:

(a)   the date of death; or

(b)   the date of the personal representative's knowledge,

whichever is the later. If there is more than one personal representative and they have differing dates of knowledge, time runs from the earliest date of knowledge (s 11(7)).

If the injured person died after the expiry of the primary limitation period under s 11(4) without commencing proceedings for the personal injuries that they had suffered, or if the person died before the expiration of the primary limitation period and their personal representatives failed to commence proceedings within three years of death or date of later knowledge, the claim is statute-barred. However, in both instances, the court does have a general discretion to override the above provisions and disapply the limitation period under s 33 of the LA 1980 (see **7.8**).

7.6.2 Claims under the Fatal Accidents Act 1976

In relation to claims brought by the dependants of the deceased, s 12(2) of the LA 1980 provides that if the injured person died before the expiration of the limitation period of three years as set out in s 11(4), the limitation period is three years from:

(a)   the date of death; or

(b)   the date of knowledge of the person for whose benefit the claim is brought,

whichever is the later.

Where there is more than one dependant, the limitation period is applied separately to each one, taking into account the date of knowledge of each dependant. Moreover, if any dependant is a child, time does not start to run for that dependant until they reach 18, and the claim will not become time-barred until they have reached the age of 21.

If the dependants fail to commence their claim within the three-year limitation period, an application can be made under s 33 to disapply the limitation period.

Where the injured person failed to commence a personal injury claim within three years of the cause of action and subsequently died as a result of their injuries, a claim under the FAA 1976 cannot be brought by the dependants. This is because s 12(1) of the LA 1980 provides that a claim under the FAA 1976 cannot be brought if death occurred when the person injured could no longer maintain a claim and recover damages in respect of the injury, whether because of a limitation problem or for any other reason. In other words, the dependants of the deceased are not in a better position than the deceased would have been. When considering whether a claim brought by the deceased person would have been time-barred, no account may be made of the possibility that the court would have exercised its discretion under s 33 to disapply the limitation period. However, the court may exercise its discretion to disapply the primary limitation period in respect of the dependants' action. See s 12(1) of the LA 1980.

7.7   OTHER PERIODS OF LIMITATION

Although in the vast majority of personal injury cases the three-year rule will apply, it is possible that a special rule applies, for example in regard to claims relating to aircraft under the Carriage by Air Act 1961 or the Warsaw Convention, or relating to vessels used for navigation under the Maritime Conventions Act 1911 or the Merchant Shipping Act 1995. In these cases, the limitation period is generally two years.

The most common form of special rule is in respect of contributions between tortfeasors under the Civil Liability (Contribution) Act 1978, where no claim to recover a contribution may be brought after the expiration of two years from the date on which the right accrued. This is generally the date on which judgment was given against the person who is seeking the contribution, or the date when they pay or agree to pay compensation.

7.8   THE COURT'S DISCRETION TO OVERRIDE THE LIMITATION PERIOD

Section 33 of the LA 1980 gives the court a wide and unfettered discretion to disapply the three-year limitation period. Section 33(1) provides that:

> If it appears to the court that it would be equitable to allow an action to proceed having regard to the degree to which—
>
> (a)   the provisions of section 11 [, 11A, 11B] or 12 of this Act prejudice the plaintiff or any person whom he represents; and
>
> (b)   any decision of the court under this subsection would prejudice the defendant or any person whom he represents;
>
> the court may direct that those provisions shall not apply to the action, or shall not apply to any specified cause of action to which the action relates.

The onus rests upon the claimant to show why the limitation period should be disapplied (*Halford v Brookes* [1991] 3 All ER 559).

Under s 33(3), the court is required to have regard to all the circumstances of the case, and it will attempt to balance the needs of the parties by seeking to avoid prejudice caused to the claimant by depriving the claimant of the right to continue with the claim, or prejudice caused to the defendant by allowing the matter to continue when the defendant has been deprived of the ability to defend themselves.

The court is specifically directed to six factors, which are outlined below:

(a)   the length and reasons for the delay on the part of the claimant;

(b)   the effect of any delay on the cogency of the evidence;

(c)   the conduct of the defendant following the date of the cause of action;

(d)   the duration of any disability (within the meaning of the Mental Capacity Act 2005) suffered by the claimant after the cause of action arose;

(e)   the conduct of the claimant after the claimant became aware that they might have a claim against the defendant;

(f)   the steps taken by the claimant to obtain medical, legal or other expert advice, and the nature of any advice received.

'Delay' in s 33(3)(a) and (b) is the delay since the expiry of the limitation period. However, the court may consider the overall delay when having regard to all the circumstances of the case. See *McDonnell & Another v Walker* [2009] EWCA Civ 1257 and *Cairn-Jones v Tyler* [2010] EWCA Civ 1642.

Guidance in relation to s 33(3)(a) was provided by the Court of Appeal in *Coad v Cornwall and Isles of Scilly Health Authority* [1997] 1 WLR 189, CA. The Court held that it must apply a subjective test when determining why the claimant had delayed, the length of the delay and whether the reason was good or bad. There was no requirement for the claimant to provide a 'reasonable' explanation.

In *Collins v Secretary of State for Business, etc* (see **7.3.3.2**), in a decision which is thought to have serious implications for long-tail disease claims, the Court of Appeal confirmed that the period of time between the defendant's breach of duty and the commencement of the limitation period (ie a later date of knowledge) must be part of 'the circumstances of the case' within the meaning of s 33(3), although the weight attached to pre-knowledge delay will be less than that attached to post-knowledge delay. There had been a period of some 50 years between the alleged breaches of duty and the date of constructive knowledge, and this lengthy delay had a detrimental effect on the cogency of the evidence. Taking this and other issues into account, the judge at first instance had been correct to refuse to exercise his discretion.

When considering s 33(3)(b), the extent to which evidence is less cogent, the Court of Appeal highlighted the importance of written evidence when memories of witnesses are unreliable due to the lapse of time (see *Farthing v North East Essex Health Authority* [1998] Lloyd's Rep Med 37, CA). In 1981, the claimant had had a hysterectomy which was negligently performed, but proceedings were not issued until 1995. When considering her application under s 33, the court found that due to the lapse of time a number of the witnesses had died, or had moved abroad and could recall little of the events in question. However, the Court of Appeal further found that because there was considerable evidence available in the form of the medical records and a letter from the surgeon to the claimant's GP written shortly after the operation, there would be little need for reliance on memory alone and consequently the appeal should be allowed.

In *McArdle v Marmion* [2013] NIQB 123, the court exercised its discretion where there had been an inexcusable and unjustifiable delay of 17 years, because the large amount of evidence collected at the time of the accident meant the ability to conduct a defence had not been diminished.

In *TCD v Harrow Council and Others* (see **7.3.2**), it was argued on behalf of the claimant that she had been unable to confront some aspects of the abuse to the extent that would be necessary for the purposes of litigation, and that she had delayed proceedings until her children were older. Nevertheless, the judge repeated what was said in *Hoare* (see **7.5**), that not everyone who brings a late claim for damages for sexual abuse, however genuine his or her complaint, can expect the court to exercise the s 33 discretion favourably. He refused to exercise his discretion in relation to the claims against two of the authorities on the grounds that the long delay meant that evidence was not forthcoming and the defendants were therefore severely prejudiced. (Discretion was not exercised in relation to the third claim due to the weakness of the claim.)

In relation to s 33(3)(c), where the court is satisfied that the defendants have brought upon themselves the prejudice that they claim to suffer, that should be taken into account and the prejudice should be significantly discounted. In the case of *Hammond v West Lancashire Health*

Authority [1998] Lloyd's Rep Med 146, CA, the defendants claimed prejudice to their case as they had destroyed the deceased's x-rays after three years had elapsed. The Court held that the destruction of the x-rays was a policy implemented by the defendants, and which had no regard for the time limits of the LA 1980. Consequently, although the prejudice caused to their case should still be taken into account, it would be significantly discounted.

These factors are guidelines only, and the court is entitled to take into account any other matter which it considers to be relevant. For example, the time of notification of the claim to the defendant is of extreme importance in ascertaining prejudice, although there is no specific reference to this in s 33. In addition, the court is entitled to consider the ultimate prospects of the claim being successful. In *TCD v Harrow Council and Others* (see above), the judge refused to grant discretion in relation to the case against Worcester County Council on the grounds that the claim had no realistic prospects of success. (Also see *Forbes v Wandsworth Health Authority* at **7.3.3.2**).

In the case of *Hoare* (see **7.5**), the House of Lords remitted the matter to the judge to reconsider the application of s 33 in accordance with the opinions of their Lordships. In *A v Hoare* [2008] EWHC 1573 (QB), the parties agreed that the main reason why the claimant had not commenced proceedings within the limitation period was because the defendant had been impecunious and, because he had been serving a life sentence, this was unlikely to change. The claimant had commenced proceedings in 2004, almost 14 years after expiry of the three-year limitation period, principally because she had learned that the defendant had won £7 million on the lottery. It was also agreed that there was no reported authority on the court being asked to exercise its discretion under s 33 on the grounds that the defendant was impecunious. However, the judge determined that this was a relevant factor when considering the exercise of the discretion to disapply the limitation period. In doing so, he took into account the fact that the defendant's own actions were the cause of his impecuniosity. The judge found in favour of the claimant and exercised his discretion under s 33. (The full judgment in this case may aid understanding of the application of s 33.)

Where the proceedings are brought against the defendant outside the limitation period as a result of the negligence of the claimant's solicitor, and the claim is not allowed to proceed, the claimant may have a claim against their own solicitor. It has been argued by defendants that the fact that the claimant has a cast-iron claim against the claimant's own solicitor provides an overwhelming reason why the limitation period should not be disapplied; the claimant will not be prejudiced because the claimant can pursue an alternative claim against their solicitor (rather than the defendant). However, although the ability to claim against the solicitor is a factor for the court to bear in mind, it is not an absolute bar against disapplying the limitation period under s 33.

The court considered this issue in *Steeds v Peverel Management Services Ltd* [2001] EWCA Civ 419. In this case, solicitors issued proceedings 49 days outside of the limitation period. On appeal, the court found that the district judge at first instance was wrong to treat the claimant's good claim against his own solicitors as justification for refusing to exercise a discretion under s 33. The better view was that the existence of a claim against his own solicitors was a relevant factor in weighing the degree of prejudice suffered by the defendant in not being able to rely on the limitation period as a defence. To that end, it would always be relevant to consider when the defendant first had notification of the claim. On the facts of the case, the judgment was set aside and the court exercised its discretion under s 33, as it was unlikely that the defendants were caused any appreciable prejudice and it was equitable to allow the claim to continue allowing for all of the circumstances of the case.

However in *McDonnell v Walker* (see **7.8**), the Court of Appeal refused to disapply the limitation period as the defendant had been forensically disadvantaged by a substantial period of inexcusable delay.

It has also been argued by defendants that the loss of the limitation defence itself, and the subsequent requirement to pay damages, is a prejudice which must be taken into account by the court when considering the exercise of the s 33 discretion. In *Cain v Francis; McKay v Hamlani* [2008] EWCA Civ 1451, both road traffic accident claims, the Court of Appeal considered the so-called 'windfall defence', which arises where the defendant has no defence other than one based on limitation due to the claimant's solicitors failing to issue proceedings on time. In each case, the defendant had admitted liability but, in the course of negotiating damages, the claimant's solicitors had missed the limitation deadline. In *Cain*, where there was a delay of just one day, the judge refused to exercise his discretion; in *McKay*, the delay was one year, but the judge exercised his discretion and allowed the case to proceed. In order to establish a consistency of approach, as opposed to a 'lottery for litigants', the Court of Appeal dealt with both cases together.

The Court of Appeal held that the defendant had a right to a fair opportunity to defend himself and had a complete procedural defence under s 11, which would remove the obligation for him to pay damages. However, fairness and justice meant that the obligation to pay damages should be removed only if the passage of time had significantly damaged the defendant's opportunity to defend himself. Parliament could not have intended the financial consequences for the defendant to be a consideration relevant to the exercise of discretion under s 33. The important factor is whether the defendant is able to defend themselves, and therefore it would always be important to consider when the defendant was notified of the claim against them, and whether it was still possible for them to investigate the claim and gather evidence. This judgment has brought clarity to this area, and is likely to result in the court exercising its discretion under s 33 in more claims which were issued late but where the defendant's ability to defend themselves is not prejudiced.

7.9 DEALING WITH LIMITATION ISSUES IN PRACTICE

Failure to issue proceedings within the limitation period is a major source of negligence claims against solicitors. Although this chapter includes the law and procedure relevant to an application under s 33 to override the limitation period (see **7.8** above), prevention is better than cure. It is therefore essential that the claimant's solicitor establishes a routine of checking and rechecking the limitation period on the files for which they are responsible. There may also be many other files for which the solicitor is not responsible, but which may pass through that solicitor's hands on a regular basis. Such files are often the source of limitation problems, as one solicitor may assume (wrongly) that the responsibility for checking limitation resides with someone else, and the date of limitation may go unnoticed. To avoid this, the solicitor should adopt a routine of checking for limitation on every file in which they are involved.

Needless to say, as the expiry of the limitation period provides the defendant with a significant, although not always watertight defence, those acting for defendants should always keep a watchful eye open for limitation issues.

7.9.1 Initial instructions

At the first interview, the claimant's solicitor should note the date of the cause of action and calculate the limitation period from this date. This can be verified by checking, for example, the relevant hospital A&E notes, the employer's accident report book, or police reports. If they are satisfied that there is sufficient time for them to investigate the matter and commence proceedings within the limitation period, they should mark the file with the expiry date and enter the date into the file management system, to ensure that limitation does not become a problem at a later stage.

If the limitation period has already expired, the solicitor will need to take account of this fact when carrying out the risk assessment. Where there appear to be no grounds for relying on a later date of knowledge or persuading the court to exercise its discretion under s 33, the client should be advised accordingly. *Carlton v Fulchers (a Firm)* [1997] PNLR 337, CA, provides a valuable illustration as to how a solicitor can be found to be negligent due to a failure to be aware of limitation problems. In this case, even though the claimant did not consult the solicitor until after the three-year limitation period had expired, the solicitor was held liable due to his failure to advise of the possibility of an application under s 33.

Where the primary limitation period has expired and there are good arguments relating to later knowledge and/or s 33, the claimant's solicitor should issue proceedings without further delay. They may delay the service of the claim form and follow the procedure as set out in **7.9.2**.

In clinical negligence cases, where there is a possibility of legal aid funding, further delays resulting from applying for such funding must be avoided, and therefore the solicitor should apply for emergency assistance from the Legal Aid Agency.

7.9.2 Protective proceedings and standstill agreements

The court does not have the power to extend the limitation period before it has expired, so in circumstances where the claimant's solicitor has insufficient time to investigate the matter and carry out the steps set out in the relevant pre-action protocol before time runs out, the options available to them to secure their client's position are:

(a)   obtain the defendant's agreement not to plead a limitation defence;

(b)   enter a standstill agreement with the defendant; or

(c)   commence protective proceedings.

Obtaining the defendant's agreement not to plead a limitation defence effectively places the parties in the position they would be in if proceedings were commenced within the limitation period. However, as many defendants would not be prepared to enter into such an agreement, the remaining options are more likely.

Where the parties enter a standstill agreement, the defendant agrees not to rely on a limitation defence from a specified date, usually the date of the agreement, until the defendant serves notice on the claimant that the defendant wishes to restart the clock. This has the effect of freezing time at the specified date. Generally, such agreements specify that a month's notice must be given by the defendant. The case of *Gold Shipping Navigation Co SA v Lulu Maritime Ltd* [2009] EWHC 1365 (Admlty), regarding a shipping dispute, demonstrates how important it is to take care when drawing up such an agreement. In that case, clumsy drafting almost prevented one party from pursuing its claim.

The claimant's solicitor may initiate protective proceedings in order to safeguard their client's position. The steps which should be taken are as follows:

(a)   The claim form should be issued, which will stop the clock for limitation purposes, but should not be served upon the defendant. Under CPR, r 7.5(1), where the claim form is to be served within the jurisdiction, it must be served within four months of being issued. This provides the claimant's solicitor with some time to investigate the matter and comply with the relevant protocol. The particulars of claim must be served upon the defendant within 14 days after service of the claim form (CPR, r 7.4(1)(b)), but it too must be served within four months of the claim form being issued (CPR, r 7.4(2)).

(b)   The claimant's solicitor should contact the defendant and notify them of the situation without delay. The date when the defendant first became aware of the claim or potential claim will be a relevant factor if the court is asked to consider whether the time limit should be disapplied under s 33.

(c)   Both parties should then follow the relevant protocol. However, there may not be time to follow the protocol to the letter, eg there may not be time to allow the defendant three months to investigate the matter under the personal injury pre-action protocol.

(d)   Where time allowed for service of the claim form is about to expire, the claimant's solicitor should make an interim application to the court for an extension of the time limit relating to service (CPR, r 7.6). The application must be made in accordance with CPR, Part 23 and supported by evidence. It is vital that this application is made within the four months allowed for service of the claim form, as the powers of the court to grant an extension where the application is made after the expiry of this period are limited to when the court has been unable to serve the claim form, the claimant has taken all reasonable steps to serve it but has been unable to do so and, in either case, the application for the extension has been made promptly (CPR, r 7.6(3)).

(e)   Where an application is made within the four-month time period, it is likely that the court will grant an extension of time for the service of the claim form. If so, it will also make directions in order to manage the case.

7.9.3   Commencing proceedings

Rule 16.4(1)(a) of the CPR states that the particulars of claim should include a concise statement of the facts on which the claimant relies. It therefore follows that where a claim is issued outside the primary limitation period, the particulars of claim should, where relevant, include a statement that the claimant relies on a later date of knowledge, and the date should be specified.

It will be for the claimant to prove the later date of knowledge, and therefore this issue should be addressed in the witness statements of the claimant and any other witness who can give evidence on this point.

In practice, where there is a limitation problem and the parties have discussed this prior to commencement of proceedings, the claimant's solicitor will deal with the limitation issue in the particulars of claim. However, if the matter has not been discussed before issue of proceedings, some solicitors acting for claimants will not pre-empt a defence by raising the limitation problem in the particulars of claim, on the basis that it is not in their client's interests to do so. If the defendant is not aware of the existence of the rules relating to limitation, or does not notice that the limitation period has expired, the defendant may admit the claim.

7.9.4   The defence

The defendant's solicitor should carefully check each particulars of claim for limitation problems. Where the claim form was issued outside the primary limitation period, they will need to address the issue in the defence. Where the claimant has relied on a later date of knowledge and the defendant seeks to rely on an earlier date of knowledge, whether actual or constructive, they should give details.

The defendant will have to prove any earlier date of knowledge they seek to rely on. It is unlikely that the defendant will be able to call witnesses of their own in this regard; rather, the defendant will usually be obliged to extract the necessary information from the claimant and any other witness(es) during cross-examination.

7.9.5   Dealing with limitation as a preliminary issue

In most cases, the limitation problem will be dealt with as a preliminary issue. The defendant should consider bringing the issue to a head either by applying for the claim to be stayed under CPR, r 3.1(f) or, in a clear case, by applying for summary judgment under CPR, r 24.2(a)(i). The claimant should respond by giving notice of their intention to ask the court to exercise its discretion to disapply the limitation period under s 33. Both parties should address the matter fully in the supporting witness statements. This will enable the court to consider the matter before trial.

If the defendant does not bring the matter to the court's attention by making an application, the claimant's solicitor should consider doing so by making an application under s 33.

Whilst the courts will normally seek to deal with limitation as a preliminary issue wherever feasible, there will be circumstances where it is not appropriate to do so. In the case of *J, K & P v Archbishop of Birmingham & Trustees of the Birmingham Archdiocese of the Roman Catholic Church* (QBD, 25 July 2008), which involved the alleged victims of child sexual abuse, the court held that it was not appropriate due to the large overlap of evidence and the additional stress on the victims having to give their evidence twice.

7.10 CONCLUSION

Practitioners must be alert to limitation issues and maintain a good working knowledge of the key sections of the LA 1980. The courts' interpretation of the statutory provisions, particularly in relation to actual and constructive knowledge and the discretion to disapply the limitation period, is something of a moveable feast, and therefore practitioners must keep an eye out for relevant case law.

Sound case management processes and an exemplary diary system are essential for claimants' solicitors. There is claimant's limitation checklist at **7.11** below.

7.11 CLAIMANT'S LIMITATION CHECKLIST

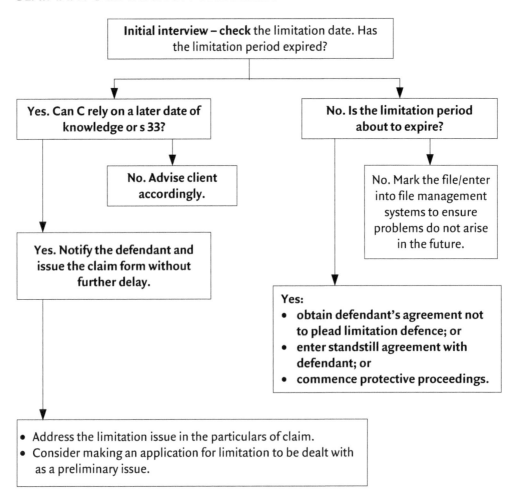

THE FIRST INTERVIEW

LEARNING OUTCOMES

After reading this chapter you will be able to:

- identify the important matters that must be dealt with during the first interview
- identify any urgent action that needs to be taken
- take a proof of evidence.

8.1 INTRODUCTION

The first interview is the cornerstone of the solicitor/client relationship, and it is therefore worthwhile making the effort to get it right. The Law Society's Guide on Engaging Clients, published on 21 April 2020, contains useful guidance on this topic and may be obtained from The Law Society website, together with associated guides/guidance. Reference should also be made to *Skills for Lawyers*, in particular Chapter 11, which deals with how to conduct an interview. The interview will normally last at least an hour. The client should tell their own story, and the solicitor will often complete a long and detailed accident questionnaire, prior to drafting a proof of evidence. Detailed preparation at this stage will save a great deal of time later. The matters that should be considered in preparation for this first interview are examined below.

You should note that conduct requirements, such as checking for conflicts of interest and obtaining evidence of identity, are not dealt with in this book, but should be strictly followed.

8.2 FUNDING

Many people are wary of solicitors' charges, and are reluctant even to approach a solicitor in order to enquire about making a personal injury or clinical negligence claim. Consequently, some firms offer a free, fixed fee or reduced cost initial interview, in which they can give preliminary advice about the viability of the claim and provide information about costs and funding options.

Should the solicitor be instructed in relation to the matter, in accordance with para 8.7 of the SRA Code of Conduct 2019 (solicitors), they must ensure that the client receives the best possible information about how their matter will be priced and, at the time of engagement, the likely overall cost of the matter. This includes information about funding options, disbursements which may arise and potential liability for inter parties' costs. Funding is discussed in more detail in **Chapter 9**.

8.3 URGENT MATTERS

If an urgent matter comes to light during the first interview, the solicitor should bear in mind the question of funding prior to making lengthy or expensive investigations on the client's behalf, and should consider making an application for emergency public (legal aid) funding if appropriate.

8.3.1 Limitation

Limitation is discussed in detail in **Chapter 7**. At the first interview in a personal injury or clinical negligence claim, it may become apparent that:

(a)   the three-year primary limitation period is about to expire (see **7.2**). If so, the solicitor should consider entering into a standstill agreement with the defendant or issuing protective proceedings immediately (see **7.9.2**);

(b)   the three-year primary limitation period has recently expired. If so, consideration should be given to issuing proceedings as soon as possible, including in the claim form or particulars of claim, a request for a direction that the limitation period should be disapplied (see **7.8**). Thereafter, the solicitor should inform the defendant without delay that proceedings have been issued, to minimise any claim by the defendant of prejudice due to the passage of time;

(c)   there is a question as to the client's 'date of knowledge' of the injury complained of. The client should be questioned closely regarding the earliest date on which the client realised they might have a cause of action, and how they came to that conclusion. The client's medical records should be obtained without delay in order to confirm the precise date of knowledge. Proceedings can then be issued as in point (b) above, and thereafter it can be argued that the limitation period has not yet expired because the client's date of knowledge of the injury is within the last three years. If this is not successful, an application should be made for the court to exercise its discretion and disapply the limitation period (see **7.8**).

Having established when the primary limitation period is due to expire, it is important that the time limit is recorded separately from the file in a diary system. The file itself may be similarly marked with the date on which limitation expires. This double recording of the primary limitation period is good practice, as failure to issue the claim within the limitation period is a common pitfall, and one which may lead to a negligence claim by the claimant against their solicitor.

8.3.2 Photographs

In most personal injury cases, persons seeking advice following an accident will do so relatively soon after the accident occurs. If this is the case, a task, which is often overlooked, will be to secure photographic evidence.

8.3.2.1 The client

The client may attend the interview with an array of bruises and abrasions (soft tissue injuries). These will heal or fade relatively quickly, and an important piece of the claimant's evidence will be lost. The claimant's solicitor should therefore ensure that good colour photographs are taken of the client's injuries for subsequent disclosure. Such photographs will form very tangible evidence of the severity of the injuries sustained, when the case comes to be considered some months or years in the future. In cases where the client may suffer embarrassment at being photographed, or indeed in any case where a degree of sensitivity is needed, specialist medical photographers are available, for example at larger teaching hospitals.

8.3.2.2 The location of the accident

In road traffic accidents, it may be necessary to visit the location of the accident in order to take photographs and draw up sketch plans of important features of the road and landscape. In many cases, it will be more cost-effective to use images from internet-based resources such as Google Maps. In any event, be aware that photographs and other images which are not taken close to the date of the accident may show seasonable and other differences which may affect their usefulness.

Where accidents at work are concerned, it is good practice to obtain photographs of any machinery or equipment involved. Any delay may mean that the equipment involved is replaced and/or disposed of. Similarly, if the accident involves allegations of a defect in a floor surface, it would be helpful to obtain photographic evidence of that floor surface before it is corrected.

8.4 ADVISING THE CLIENT

It is important for the solicitor not to lose sight of the fact that the client has come into the office seeking some meaningful advice, which the client hopes will lead them to a decision as to whether they have an actionable case against some other party. The client therefore needs to have the best information available, in a form that they can understand, so that the client can make an informed decision as to what to do next. It is best to set out the strengths and weaknesses of the case, based on what has been said by the client. The importance of the limitation period should be explained to the client if this is likely to be an issue. The solicitor should also explain to the client that it is for the client to prove their case on the balance of probabilities by evidence and that anything short of this is not enough. The client should be informed of the basis of their case, and the level of proof needed by the court to prove it. The client should be left in no doubt that it is the client's case, to be proved by the client's evidence, and that the client bears the risk that their case may fail. As such, the client should think seriously prior to instructing the solicitor to issue proceedings. The solicitor should give an indication as to whether they believe that the case is likely to succeed, but the solicitor should make it clear that the assessment is based on the limited information available at this early stage. In any event, if the solicitor is considering taking the client's case but will be paid under a CFA or a DBA, it will be necessary for the solicitor to conduct an assessment of risk at an early stage in order to decide whether or not to accept the client's instructions on that basis.

It may be that the solicitor advising the client will be required to produce to their senior colleagues a report, from which they will make a risk assessment in relation to whether or not the client should be accepted on a CFA or DBA basis. The risk assessment report may also consider such things as whether it is proposed that the client covers their own disbursements, or whether the firm is prepared to fund them on the client's behalf. The client is likely to press for an indication of the likely level of damages that may be recovered. Giving a firm indication based on inadequate information should be resisted. Instead, the solicitor should explain to the client why an assessment would be premature at this stage. The solicitor will not be in a position to assess the value of the claim until medical evidence dealing with diagnosis and prognosis has been obtained.

One reason for not giving a provisional indication of the likely level of damages is that the client may be found to have been contributorily negligent. This principle should be explained to the client, first to try to elicit whether the client has any reason to believe that it will be relevant to their claim and, secondly, to act as a warning to the client that it is likely that the opposition will try to allege that the client was contributorily negligent.

The client should also be advised that they must prove every head (or type) of loss against their opponent. Although it is the case that the client is able to claim all that the client lost as a direct result of the accident, the client must also be in a position to prove every head of that loss to the court if they wish to recover damages in respect of it. It should therefore be explained to the client that damages are made up of general damages (for pain, suffering and loss of amenity) and special damages (everything the client has had physically to pay for and other quantifiable losses as a direct result of the accident). For a detailed analysis of the subject of damages, see **Chapter 15**.

It will assist greatly, when it comes to proving the losses, if the client has kept a detailed record or account of their out-of-pocket expenses. To this end, the client should be advised at the first interview to keep all receipts for expenses incurred as a direct result of the accident, and that it is their responsibility to do so. Common examples are prescriptions, the cost of items lost or damaged beyond repair in the accident, and taxi fares to the out-patient or physiotherapy departments. Similarly, with respect to general damages for pain and suffering, although the client's distress may be keen at the first interview, by the time of trial their recollection may have dimmed, to the extent that they have forgotten many of the minor losses of function they suffered in the early stages of recovery from their injuries. The client should therefore be advised to keep a diary if they do not already do so, to record, for example, the fact that they are unable to sleep due to pain, or are unable to dress themselves unaided or to do housework, and to record how long these disabilities last. Any number of tasks, either recreational or work-related, should be recorded so that they are not forgotten later when it comes to preparing the client's witness statement.

It is particularly important in clinical negligence cases that the client is made aware of the difficulties in pursuing the claim successfully, and especially that the client (if acting for the claimant) must establish not only a breach of duty, but also that the breach was causative of the damage that resulted (as opposed to the underlying illness or injury being the root cause of the loss). If the client is paying for the litigation privately, the high costs involved must be explained to the client clearly. The solicitor should also explain the difficulty in giving a preliminary view on liability without first obtaining all the client's medical notes and at least one expert's views.

8.5 THE CLIENT'S PROOF OF EVIDENCE

Client questionnaires are used frequently in personal injury work. The questionnaires are designed to elicit certain basic information about the client and the accident. Increasingly, law firms 'capture' these basic data about the client by keying the details into a case management system. This has the advantage that once 'captured', the data are available for use subsequently throughout the life of the claim.

The client's proof of evidence should contain all the information the client has regarding the events in question and the people involved. It is, in effect, a rough copy of the witness statement, and it may well include irrelevant material and suspicions that cannot be proven by evidence. Although these matters will be edited out when the witness statement is drafted in readiness for exchange, it is important to include them in the proof as they may lead the solicitor to other evidence or lines of enquiry.

8.5.1 Contents of the proof

The proof should commence with the client's full name, address, date of birth and National Insurance number. It should state the client's occupation and marital/civil partnership status. If the client was admitted to hospital, it should state their hospital number. The proof is intended for use by the client's solicitor and barrister, and, subsequently, in the preparation of the client's witness statement; as such, it should be the fullest possible statement from the client relating to the incident, the events immediately following the incident and its long-term effects. The client should begin their narrative at the earliest point in time that they feel to be relevant.

Following the client's personal details, the proof should next detail the date, time and location of the incident. It should then follow through chronologically and meticulously:

(a)   the events leading up to the incident;

(b)   the circumstances of the accident, including a clear explanation of the mechanics of the accident itself;

(c)   what happened immediately after the incident;

(d)   why the client feels that the incident was caused by the negligence of some other person;

(e)   what medical treatment was given and injuries incurred; and

(f)   how the client feels that the incident has affected their day-to-day life.

The solicitor should bear in mind that the proof will form the basis of the witness statement, and that, usually, the witness statement will be ordered to stand as the witness's evidence-in-chief at the trial. It is important, therefore, that the proof is detailed in its description of how the incident actually happened, and the effect the incident has had on the client's day-to-day life. All aspects of the client's life should therefore be considered in the proof. The following areas should always be covered, including an estimate in weeks or months of how long the incapacity affected the client's life, or confirmation that the incapacity is still continuing:

(a)   Everyday tasks which the client is unable to do for themselves, eg dressing, bathing, housework, shopping, driving. This will be important if a claim is made for loss incurred in employing someone else to carry out these tasks.

(b)   Recreational activities such as sports, hobbies, gardening, DIY in maintaining the home and the family car. The client's inability to participate in sports will have an effect on the client's loss of amenity claim for general damages. The client should also be asked whether they are a member of any sports team or club, and about any prizes or trophies they have won as further evidence of their level of commitment. The inability to carry out jobs of maintenance around the home will similarly affect a claim for loss of amenity. If the client gives evidence that DIY is a hobby, details should be obtained of any projects the client has undertaken. This will also affect the client's special damages and/or future financial loss claim for the labour element of the cost of having to employ someone else to fulfil those tasks in the future.

(c)   Whether and to what extent the injury has affected the claimant's sex life. This area of loss of amenity should always be broached with the client, as the stress of an accident can often bring about a degree of sexual dysfunction, even if the injury itself would not immediately suggest that such was the case.

(d)   Specifically, whether the incident will affect the client's ability to continue with their employment, and the extent to which the client is affected. It may be obvious that the client will never work again, or will be unable to work in their pre-incident position but will have to retrain, or that the client intends to return to their pre-incident employment but is unsure whether they will cope. Details should also be obtained as to the client's position if they were to be made redundant, and the degree of difficulty they would have in obtaining similar employment elsewhere because of their injuries.

It is important that all of the above issues are considered and, if relevant, that they are covered in the proof in some detail, as there is little point in the client and/or the client's solicitor knowing the extent to which the incident has ruined the client's life, if this is not articulated sufficiently to the court. If a matter is not covered in the client's witness statement, the chances are the court will never hear of it; and if the court is not made aware of all relevant matters, the claimant's solicitor has not achieved one of their main aims, that of maximising the client's damages based on the available evidence.

Before finishing the proof of evidence in personal injury cases, the client should always be asked whether they have had any pre-existing incident injury which may affect the current case.

The proof of evidence should always end with the client's signature and the date on which it was prepared so that, if the client dies prior to the conclusion of the case, the proof of evidence will still be of use evidentially.

8.5.2   Proofs of evidence in relation to different types of incident

The following types of incident will require the proof of evidence to cover certain areas in particular detail.

8.5.2.1   Road traffic incidents

When taking the proof in the case of a road incident, it is important first to have in mind the stretch of road in question. A large-scale map of the area in question is invaluable at this stage, as it will cut short any unproductive argument as to how or where, for example, the road bends. If the client has difficulty explaining how the incident happened, it can be useful to get the client to draw a sketch of the relative positions of the vehicles involved, or to use toy cars to illustrate what happened. Care should be taken to ensure that the client is entirely clear about the following matters:

(a)   the direction in which the client was travelling;

(b)   the time of day;

(c)   whether there was anyone else in the car with the client;

(d)   the weather conditions;

(e)   the speed of travel;

(f)   familiarity with the car;

(g)   familiarity with the road;

(h)   whether there were any witnesses;

(i)   the make and registration numbers of all vehicles involved;

(j)   who the client believes to be responsible for the incident and why;

(k)   what happened immediately after the incident;

(l)   exactly what the client said to anyone after the incident;

(m)   exactly what anyone said to the client, and whether anyone else heard what was said;

(n)   whether the police were called and, if not, why not;

(o)   if the police were called, which police force and the name of the officer attending;

(p)   whether the client is aware of any pending prosecutions (eg, whether the client was warned that the client themselves might be prosecuted, or that the client might be needed as a witness in the prosecution of the other driver);

(q)   whether the client is comprehensively insured and the amount of excess the client has to pay on their own insurance policy (the client's uninsured loss);

(r)   whether the client is the owner of the vehicle, and details of the owner if the client is not.

If the client wrote anything down at the time of the incident, such as the name and address of the other driver(s), this should be retained. If the client explains what happened, for example by referring to the offside and nearside of his vehicle, the solicitor should check that the client understands what is meant by those terms. Clients may believe that they have to speak to their solicitor using words which they would not normally use in everyday speech, and consequently they may use words that they do not fully understand. For the avoidance of doubt, the solicitor should check with the client that when referring to a vehicle's 'offside' the client means the driver's side, and that 'nearside' refers to the side of the vehicle nearest the gutter.

In road traffic cases, it is vitally important to trace and interview witnesses as soon as possible. It is unlikely that the witnesses will be known to the client and they may prove difficult to trace if not contacted immediately, and in any event their memory of the events will fade quickly and will therefore be of less use evidentially. The question of whether there are any independent third party witnesses is of central importance, because the case will be much easier to prove if an independent witness can be found who is prepared to give evidence to a court that they saw the incident and believe that the cause of the incident was the fault of the other driver. If the client does not have any details of witnesses, the police accident report may have statements from witnesses whom the solicitor can contact. The police should be notified of all incidents involving personal injury, and will prepare a report on the incident including witness statements (see **10.10.3.1**).

8.5.2.2 Tripping/slipping incidents on public roads and pavements

Tripping and slipping incidents occurring on public roads and pavements are governed by s 41 of the Highways Act 1980, under which the highway authority (usually the local district or borough council responsible for the area in which the fall or trip took place) has a duty to maintain the highway, which includes the pavements used by the public (see **3.5**). It is for the claimant to show that the highway was not reasonably safe. Uneven paving stones or the sites of road improvements with poor temporary surfaces usually claim the most victims. Local authorities sometimes contract out such road improvement works to independent contractors, in which case it may be advisable to sue both the contractor responsible for the safety of the site and the local authority which delegated the improvement work to them. If the client can show that the highway was not reasonably safe, the authority must show that it has taken such care as in all the circumstances was reasonably required to ensure that the highway was not dangerous.

Applying the above principle to the client's proof, it will be necessary to ask the client:

(a)   the time of day;

(b)   the weather conditions;

(c)   whether the client was in a hurry or was running at the time of the incident;

(d)   whether the client was carrying anything which obscured the client's view or which may have caused the client to go off balance (eg several heavy bags);

(e)   whether there was a warning sign to take care and, if so, what the sign said;

(f)   whether there were any witnesses;

(g)   what sort of shoes the client was wearing; and

(h)   the exact location of the incident.

It will then be necessary to obtain photographs of the location without delay, as the local authority may act quickly to repair the relevant area in order to show that it has taken such care as was reasonably required in the circumstances.

8.5.2.3 Incidents at work

The nature of the work process that gave rise to the incident must be thoroughly understood from the outset if the case is to be dealt with properly. The client should be asked to explain:

(a)   their job title;

(b)   what that involves in the work process;

(c)   the level of training or instruction received;

(d)   the level of seniority held by the client;

(e)   the level of supervision over the client;

(f)   whether the client can recall any written or oral confirmation of their work duties;

(g)   a description of the client's usual duties;

(h)   what the client was doing on the day and at the time in question that gave rise to the incident;

(i)   whether anything out of the ordinary occurred that day;

(j)   details of other similar incidents known to the client;

(k)   any representations made by a trade union about the machine or system of work;

(l)   any comments made at health and safety meetings;

(m)   any witnesses to the incident or the unsafe practice.

Trips and slips make up a large proportion of incidents in the workplace and therefore, in addition to the above questions, the client should be asked such questions as are relevant from **8.5.2.2** above.

EXAMPLE

John is an instrument artificer employed to work at a chemical plant. Part of his duties is to check the temperature of certain chemicals stored in large tanks above ground on the site. On the day of the accident, John climbed to the top of a storage tank and removed the outer cover. Without warning, John was blown backwards by excess pressure in the tank, causing him to fall from the tank approximately 4 metres to the ground. Because the chemical was corrosive on contact with the skin, John suffered burns to his face and hands, as well as a damaged spine and broken left leg. John tells you that he has done the same task many times before without incident, but he believes that whoever last checked that particular tank failed adequately to secure the inner seal, so that when he next opened the outer seal the sudden change in pressure was like releasing a cork from a bottle. John tells you that he is usually accompanied by a fellow employee when doing these checks, as the company's safety policy requires this. On the day of the incident, his colleague had telephoned in sick, but the duty manager had not called in anyone else to take his place. John also tells you that the company used to have a nurse on site to deal with minor injuries, but when the last nurse ceased to be employed she was not replaced. John believes that this was because of the expense involved. John also believes that his burns would not be so severe if he had received first aid more quickly.

In the above example, if, when describing any part of his duties, John becomes unclear, he should be asked to explain it again, perhaps drawing a sketch to assist his narrative. It is important that there is no misunderstanding at this stage, as the solicitor will probably use this information as the basis for John's statement of case. In addition, if the solicitor is unsure from the client's explanation precisely how the incident happened, it is also likely that a judge will be similarly confused. It is therefore vitally important that any ambiguity is resolved at this point. If ambiguity remains, facilities should be sought for a site inspection. Where the place of work is privately-owned property, and may be a dangerous environment for the visitor, the solicitor must always seek permission from the employer for a site inspection. The inspection can be carried out with the claimant's expert engineer if the accident involves a piece of machinery.

In the above example, it is necessary to include in the proof of evidence John's suspicions as to:

(a)   the cause of the incident;

(b)   disregard of safety policy; and

(c)   his belief that the burns were worsened by delay in treatment.

All these matters will have to be checked, however, as the chemical engineer who inspects the plant may conclude that the incident had a completely different cause, possibly involving contributory negligence by John himself. It may be apparent to the engineer that the tank is fitted with a large pressure gauge that John should have checked prior to opening the tank.

Similarly, the company safety policy may specify that rubber gloves and a full-face mask must be worn when working with corrosive chemicals, and that the burn time for that particular chemical is less than 30 seconds, in which case having medical personnel on site would have made no difference to John's injuries.

8.5.2.4 Clinical negligence claims

In a clinical negligence claim, the client is likely to be in a more confused or uncertain position than in a personal injury matter. While a client is normally able to explain, for example, what occurred during a road traffic incident, in a clinical negligence claim the client may not understand the treatment and care received from a medical practitioner. The terminology will be unfamiliar and, in the case of alleged negligence during hospital treatment, the client may not be able to recall or identify the treating doctors or nurses.

When obtaining a proof of evidence in a clinical negligence case on behalf of a claimant, it is important that every detail is obtained, such as what exactly was said when the claimant attended at the hospital or when the client was asked to sign the consent form.

Unless the alleged negligent act arises out of an illness not previously suffered by the client, full details of any previous medical problems should be obtained. Other matters contained in the proof of evidence could be as follows:

(a)   the symptoms which led the client to seek medical advice;

(b)   the information given by the client to the doctor;

(c)   any questions asked by the doctor (eg, where the client went to their GP complaining of headaches, whether the doctor asked whether the client had hit their head or whether the client had been sick – questions which would lead a competent GP to suspect a severe head injury);

(d)   whether the client was given details of a diagnosis at that time;

(e)   what form of treatment was prescribed;

(f)   whether the treatment was explained to the client, and whether the client was warned of any potential risks and the likely consequences of not receiving treatment;

(g)   the name of the doctor who treated the client and the doctor's status;

(h)   whether the client was receiving treatment from different doctors;

(i)   whether the client asked for a second opinion;

(j)   whether any witnesses were present at the consultation;

(k)   any previous medical problems which could have affected the client;

(l)   whether the client has complained to the hospital/doctor;

(m)   whether the client has received any reply or relevant correspondence;

(n)   whether an apology has been received.

This should be followed by details of the injury in the normal fashion.

In certain cases, it can be useful to ask what prompted the client to contact a solicitor. In some cases, the client is advised by other medical professionals to seek legal advice as they believe that a mistake may have been made.

EXAMPLE

A client injures her leg playing hockey and attends at the local A&E department. The department is busy and, although the client is sent for an x-ray, the house officer fails to spot the fracture and discharges the client immediately. The client is in considerable pain for a number of weeks and eventually visits her GP, who refers her back to the hospital for another x-ray. In such circumstances, the client may be told that in fact the leg is fractured and that it was missed when the client first attended. Such information is clearly of assistance in assessing liability.

8.6 WELFARE BENEFITS

It will be necessary to advise the client of the welfare benefits the client may be entitled to receive because of the incident. It may be months or years before the claim is settled, and if the client is unfit for work, they may experience financial difficulties and feel pressured into accepting the first offer of compensation from the defendant. The solicitor should give the client general advice on the types of benefits that may be available in view of the client's inability or decreased capacity to work, and that may assist with the costs of mobility issues, household tasks and child care requirements.

The law relating to state welfare benefits is complex and subject to frequent amendment. In particular, the Welfare Reform Act 2012 and related regulations have brought in recent reforms. Details of the benefits which may be available are beyond the scope of this book. If the solicitor is not fully familiar with the current situation regarding available benefits, and the firm does not have a welfare rights adviser, the solicitor should give only general advice and tell the client to contact Jobcentre Plus (an agency of the Department for Work and Pensions (DWP)) for further information. The client must act quickly when seeking welfare benefits, as it is not always possible to back-date them.

The client should be advised that where the client does qualify for benefits, if their damages claim is successful there may be some recoupment under the Social Security (Recovery of Benefits) Act 1997. This area is considered in detail in **Chapter 16.**

Lastly, when considering eligibility for benefits, it is necessary to have regard to whether the receipt of compensation will take the claimant out of financial eligibility for means-tested benefits. In B (A Child) v Secretary of State for Social Security [2001] 1 WLR 1404, B was injured in a road traffic accident and rendered quadriplegic. B sued by his litigation friend and Court of Protection receiver, SB. The claimant appealed a decision of the Social Security Commissioner that he was not entitled to income support because payments 'falling to be treated as income' under a structured settlement took him beyond the limit on income for the purpose of claiming income support. B appealed, arguing that guidance from the Department of Social Security (now the DWP), while not directly on point, suggested that, as long as the compensation was held on trust and payments were made on a discretionary basis and were not used to fund items that would normally be paid for using benefits, then those payments would not affect benefit entitlement. The Court of Appeal was not persuaded by this argument, and ruled that the agreement, as part of the structured settlement, to make regular payments for a fixed number of years was in fact a 'typical example of an annuity' and was therefore 'capital treated as income' under reg 41(2) of the Income Support (General) Regulations 1987 (SI 1987/1967). The essential difference in this case is that the compensation was paid to the Court of Protection, which would hold the money for the benefit of the patient, rather than simply held on discretionary trust.

8.7 REHABILITATION, EARLY INTERVENTION AND MEDICAL TREATMENT

Where the client has not fully recovered from their injuries at the time of the first interview, the solicitor should explore the possibility of rehabilitation with the client. It has long been recognised that a claimant's long-term prognosis can be dramatically improved by the intervention of rehabilitative treatment at the earliest possible opportunity. Examples of such early treatment include surgery, physiotherapy, counselling, occupational therapy, speech therapy and also adaptations to the claimant's home to make the client's life easier.

The problem in the past was that many claimants were not able to find the funds to pay for the necessary treatment until after their claims for damages for personal injuries were settled. However, over time, insurance companies began to see the clear benefits of early intervention for themselves, even if liability had not yet been determined. Extra sessions of physiotherapy, for example, might speed up the claimant's recovery rate to enable the client to return to work earlier than otherwise expected, if expected to return to work at all, and this might result in a smaller claim for damages.

The Rehabilitation Code (the 'Code'), which was drafted as a collaborative effort between insurers and personal injury lawyers, was first introduced in 1999 and updated in 2007. A revised Rehabilitation Code became operational from 1 December 2015 (see **Appendix 5**). Its aim, as set out in the introduction to the Code, is to promote the use of rehabilitation and early intervention in the claims process so that the injured person makes the best and quickest possible medical, social and psychological recovery. The Code is designed to apply whatever the severity of the injury suffered by the client.

The Code provides a framework within which all those involved in the claim can work together to ensure that the claimant's needs are assessed at an early stage and appropriate treatment provided as a matter of priority. Both claimants' solicitors and insurers should consider whether rehabilitation is appropriate (see both the Pre-Action Protocol for Personal Injury Claims and the Pre-Action Protocol for the Resolution of Clinical Disputes) and, if so, to raise the matter with the other party. It should be noted that the provisions of the Code itself are not mandatory and that the aims of the Code might be achieved by means of an alternative framework agreed between the parties.

For the details of the provisions of the Code, you are referred to the Code itself. Further assistance can be found in APIL's Best Practice Guide on Rehabilitation, 3rd edn (updated November 2015).

8.8 CONCLUSION

If the first interview is handled correctly, it should save the claimant's solicitor a great deal of time in the future. As personal injury litigation is 'front loaded', much of the essential work is covered during or shortly after the first interview. If essential matters have been missed, old ground will need to be covered again, which will lead to delay and upset for the client, and may allow the opposition to gain the advantage. An overview of matters to be considered is set out below at **8.10**.

8.9 FURTHER READING

www.lawsociety.org.uk/topics/client-care/engaging-clients

Skills for Lawyers 2023/24 (CLP)

APIL, Best Practice Guide on Rehabilitation, 3rd edn (updated November 2015) (available online)

8.10   OVERVIEW OF MATTERS TO BE CONSIDERED AT THE FIRST INTERVIEW

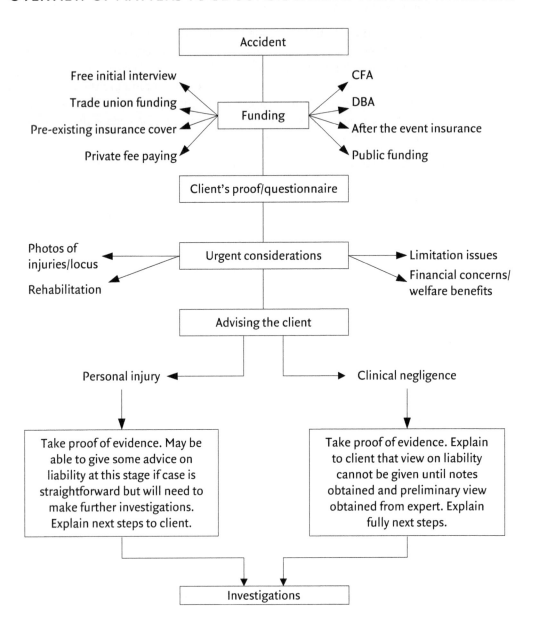

CHAPTER 9

Methods of Funding and Qualified One-Way Costs Shifting

LEARNING OUTCOMES

After reading this chapter you will be able to:

- describe the methods of funding available to a client
- explain how a conditional fee agreement operates
- explain how a damages-based agreement operates
- understand how qualified one-way costs shifting works.

9.1 INTRODUCTION

The ways in which personal injury and clinical negligence claims may be funded and costs recovered by both sides underwent many changes following the Legal Aid, Sentencing and Punishment of Offenders Act 2012 (LASPO 2012), which came into operation on 1 April 2013. The so-called 'big bang' introduced a new method of funding in the form of damages-based agreements (DBAs), placed restrictions on the recovery of costs by prohibiting in all but a few cases the recovery of success fees and insurance premiums, and introduced a new regime of qualified one-way costs shifting (QOCS).

9.2 METHODS OF FUNDING

9.2.1 Advising the client – the Code of Conduct

Paragraph 8 of the SRA Code of Conduct 2019 for Solicitors (the 'Code') sets out requirements for providing clients with information. Paragraph 8.7 relates to how a solicitor should advise a client about costs and funding their claim. It states that the solicitor and the firm should ensure that clients receive the best possible information about how their matter will be priced and, both at the time of engagement and when appropriate as their matter progresses, about the likely overall cost of the matter and any costs incurred. Paragraph 8.6 is also relevant. This requires that you give clients information in a way they can understand. This includes ensuring that clients are in a position to make informed decisions about the services they need, how their matter will be handled and the options available to them. Principle 7 – acting in the best interests of the client – is also relevant in this context.

Overall, therefore, solicitors should bear these specific provisions of the Code in mind when advising on the funding options outlined below.

9.2.2 Public funding

9.2.2.1 Is legal aid still available?

The majority of personal injury and clinical negligence cases are now outside the scope of public funding, with the exception of:

(a)   claims involving neurological injury to a child resulting in severe disability, which arises during pregnancy, childbirth, or in the eight week postnatal period; and

(b)   cases which the Director of Legal Aid Casework determines to be 'exceptional' on the basis that to deny legal aid would be a breach of the individual's human rights.

The detail of how to apply for legal aid in such cases is beyond the scope of this book and so what follows is a brief summary.

9.2.2.2 Funding in clinical negligence cases

LASPO 2012 removed all claims for damages for clinical negligence from the scope of civil legal aid, with one exception: clinical negligence during pregnancy, child birth or the postnatal period (eight weeks), which causes a child to suffer severe disability due to a neurological injury.

The conditions which must be met are set out in LASPO 2012, Sch 1, Pt 1, para 23. They are that:

(a)   clinical negligence caused a neurological injury to the individual (V) and, as a result of the neurological injury, V is severely disabled; and

(b)   the clinical negligence occurred:

(i)   while V was in his or her mother's womb; or

(ii)   during or after V's birth but before the end of the following period:

- if V was born before the beginning of the 37th week of pregnancy, the period of eight weeks beginning with the first day of what would have been that week; or

- if V was born during or after the 37th week of pregnancy, the period of eight weeks beginning with the day of V's birth.

Paragraph 23(5) provides that 'disabled' means 'physical or mentally disabled' and defines 'birth' as 'the moment when an individual first has a life separate from his or her mother'.

The most common scenario is likely to be obstetric negligence where mismanagement of a mother's labour leads to deprivation of oxygen to the baby resulting in brain injury. Alternatively it could be that a serious illness (eg meningitis) is not diagnosed in the early weeks of a baby's life either by a GP or hospital staff.

In addition to falling within the scope of claims described above, it will be necessary for the client to satisfy both financial criteria (under the Civil Legal Aid (Financial Resources and Payment for Services) Regulations 2013 (SI 2013/480) as amended) and merits criteria which are contained in the Civil Legal Aid (Merits Criteria) Regulations 2013 (SI 2013/104) ('Merits Criteria Regulations'). There are essentially two levels of funding which may be granted in the clinical negligence context – Investigative Representation and Full Representation.

Investigative Representation

Investigative Representation will be granted only where: (i) the prospects of success on a claim are not clear and substantial investigative work needs to be undertaken before the prospects of success can be determined; (ii) the LAA has reasonable grounds for believing that, once the investigative work to be carried out under Investigative Representation is completed, the case will satisfy the criteria for Full Representation and, in particular, will meet both the cost benefit and the prospects of success criterion set out in the Merits Criteria Regulations; and (iii) the individual's claim is primarily a claim for damages exceeding £5,000 or, if not, the case is of significant wider public interest. The applicant will also need to satisfy the Standard Criteria set out at reg 39 of the Merits Criteria Regulations. Certificates limited to Investigative Representation will usually be subject to a limitation that the certificate covers only the obtaining of medical notes and records, obtaining one medical report per specialism, complying with all steps under the clinical disputes pre-action protocol, considering relevant evidence with counsel or an external solicitor with higher court advocacy rights and experts if necessary, and thereafter obtaining counsel's opinion, up to and including settling proceedings if counsel so advises. A costs limitation for this work will also be specified.

Investigative Representation may be refused if the client has not pursued the NHS complaints procedure and it is still possible for the client to do so (see Merits Criteria Regulations, reg 39(d)).

Criteria for granting of Full Representation

To qualify for Full Representation, both the 'cost–benefit' criteria and the 'prospects of success' criteria must be met. In terms of prospects of success, these must not be 'poor' or 'borderline' as defined in the Merits Criteria Regulations, subject to a few narrow exceptions in borderline cases, but must be at least 'moderate' (50–60%). The cost–benefit criteria, which relate to likely costs versus likely damages, are set out at reg 5 of the Merits Criteria Regulations and are as follows:

(a)   For cases with 80% or more prospects of success, ie where the prospects of success are 'very good', likely damages must exceed the likely costs.

(b)   For 60–80% prospects of success, ie the prospects of success are 'good', likely damages must be at least twice the likely costs.

(c)   For cases with 50–60% prospects of success, ie the prospects of success are moderate, likely damages must be at least four times the likely costs.

If the prospects of success and the cost–benefit criteria set out above are satisfied, and the solicitor has decided that legal aid is an appropriate form of funding for the claim, the solicitor should make an application for Full Representation after the investigative stage. The certificate will then be issued if the relevant criteria are satisfied, and will normally be limited to all steps up to and including exchange of witness statements and expert reports and CPR Part 35 questioning of experts, and thereafter obtaining counsel's opinion or the opinion of an external solicitor with higher court advocacy rights.

In the event that the claimant wishes to proceed to full trial, the cost–benefit criteria above will be reapplied to the case; if the criteria are satisfied then application can be made once again to amend the scope of the Full Representation certificate to cover the cost of trial.

9.2.2.3   'Exceptional funding'

If a case falls outside the scope of the civil legal services specified in Part 1 of Sch 1 to LASPO 2012 (ie fall outside the scope of legal aid), funding may still be provided if the case is deemed 'exceptional'.

Section 10(3) of LASPO 2012 sets out the test for determination of exceptional funding as follows:

(3)   For the purposes of subsection (2), an exceptional case determination is a determination—

(a)   that it is necessary to make the services available to the individual under this Part because failure to do so would be a breach of—

(i)   the individual's Convention rights (within the meaning of the Human Rights Act 1998), or

> (ii)   any rights of the individual to the provision of legal services that are enforceable EU rights, or
>
> (b)   that it is appropriate to do so, in the particular circumstances of the case, having regard to any risk that failure to do so would be such a breach

The Lord Chancellor has issued guidance for both inquest and non-inquest cases which would otherwise not qualify for legal aid. Inquest cases are discussed further in **Chapter 17**. As for non-inquest cases, the guidance makes it clear that the overarching question is whether the client will be unable to present their case effectively and without obvious unfairness in proceedings. This threshold is high.

The same means criteria apply to legal aid under the exceptional funding scheme as to general cases, and it will only be available to those claimants of qualifying means who do not have any form of alternative funding, such as before the event (BTE) insurance, and are unable to secure a conditional fee agreement (CFA) or a DBA. A possible type of claim that may succeed in an application for exceptional funding is a clinical negligence claim of moderate to high value where the claimant has failed to find a solicitor to accept it as a CFA or a DBA because its merits appear to be moderate rather than good. All clinical negligence claims require medical expert evidence on breach of duty, causation and quantum and involve complex issues of law. It may therefore be possible to assert that the claimant could not represent themselves and should therefore qualify for exceptional funding.

9.2.3   Conditional fee agreements

The decline in legal aid has led to a huge increase in CFAs. Under s 58 of the Courts and Legal Services Act 1990 (CLSA 1990), a solicitor and client can agree that the client will have to pay their own solicitor's costs only in certain agreed circumstances or conditions, the condition usually being that the client wins their case (hence 'conditional fee agreement').

Conditional fee agreements have undergone important changes following LASPO 2012, and so what follows is a summary of the position that is in force since those changes came into operation on 1 April 2013. The Law Society issued a model CFA in 2014 which could be found on its website. This has been withdrawn and no Law Society model agreement for use in personal injury and clinical negligence cases is currently available. The Law Society's website states that the model CFA will be reviewed in light of the court's decision in *Belsner v CAM Legal Services Ltd* [2020] EWHC 2755 (QB). This case centred around CPR, r 46.9(2) and informed consent in relation to costs recovery. In *Belsner v CAM Legal Services Ltd* [2022] EWCA Civ 1387 the Court of Appeal ruled that r 46.9(2) did not apply on the facts of the case because the matter had settled pre-action and therefore fell within the definition of non-contentious proceedings. The Law Society website states that a revised model CFA will be issued in due course.

9.2.3.1   Formal requirements

A CFA is enforceable only if it meets the requirements of ss 58 and 58A of the CLSA 1990, which provide that a CFA:

(a)   must be in writing;

(b)   must state the percentage success fee to be applied (up to a maximum of 100%); and

(c)   may not be used in family and criminal proceedings.

The CFA must be signed by the client and by the legal representative.

There are no statutory requirements regarding information to be given to the client over and above the requirements of the SRA Principles and Codes of Conduct 2019 (see **9.2**). Any breaches of the Code will be a professional conduct issue and therefore a matter for the SRA to deal with, but it will not render the CFA unlawful/unenforceable. However, a breach of the CLSA 1990 will render a CFA unenforceable and will prevent the solicitor from recovering any costs.

9.2.3.2   The success fee

If the claim is successful, the solicitor will normally expect to receive an enhanced fee to reflect their 'success'. The enhancement on the fee is a percentage increase on the solicitor's normal fee and not a percentage of damages. The percentage increase on the solicitor's fee is agreed in writing between the client and the solicitor prior to the litigation, and will take into account a number of factors discussed below (see **9.2.5**), including the likelihood of winning the case.

The success fee can be up to 100% of the basic fee. However, for CFAs entered into from 1 April 2013, art 5 of the Conditional Fee Agreements Order 2013 (SI 2013/689) imposes a cap in proceeds at first instance on the recoverable success fee in personal injury and clinical negligence claims of 25% of general damages for pain, suffering and loss of amenity and past losses, net of any sums recoupable by the Compensation Recovery Unit (see **Chapter 16**). This means that the success fee cannot be taken from damages for future losses, such as future care costs.

9.2.3.3   Recovery of the success fee

Prior to 1 April 2013, if the client won their case and the opponent was ordered to pay the client's costs, these would include the success fee to the extent that it was 'reasonable'. However, for CFAs entered into from that date, s 44 of LASPO 2012 provides that the success fee may no longer be claimed from the other side and so will be paid by the client out of the client's damages. As success fees are no longer recoverable as part of costs, the requirement that existed prior to 1 April 2013 to notify your opponent that you have entered into a CFA (or taken out after the event insurance (AEI)) has gone.

9.2.3.4   Conditional fees and counsel

Where there is a CFA between client and solicitor, counsel's fees are usually dealt with in one of two ways:

(a)   The solicitor enters into a separate CFA with the barrister, in which case:
  (i)   if the client wins the case, the barrister's basic fee will be recovered as a disbursement from the opponent. The solicitor will pay the barrister's 'uplift' agreed in the barrister's CFA, but will have regard to this expense when agreeing the solicitor's own fee 'uplift' with the client;
  (ii)   if the client loses the case, the client will owe the barrister nothing.
(b)   There is no CFA between the barrister and the solicitor, in which case:
  (i)   if the client wins the case and has been paying the barrister's fees on account (ie, up front), there will be no extra success fee to pay, and the barrister's fees can be recovered from the opponent in the usual way;
  (ii)   if the client wins the case and has not been paying the barrister's fees on account, the solicitor will recover that disbursement from the opponent. Because of this greater outlay by the solicitor (and greater financial loss to the firm in the event that the client loses), the solicitor will charge an extra success fee in the event that the client wins;
  (iii)   if the client loses the case and has not been paying the barrister's fees on account, the solicitor is liable to pay them, and will not be able to pass this loss on to the client.

9.2.4   Damages-based agreements

Damages-based agreements were introduced as a method of funding for civil litigation by s 45 of LASPO 2012. Under a DBA, solicitors are not paid if they lose a case, but they may take a percentage of the damages recovered for their client as their fee if the case is successful. Damages-based agreements differ from CFAs because, under a DBA, the payment received by the solicitor is calculated as a percentage of the damages awarded to the client, rather than as an uplift on the solicitor's base costs.

In order to be enforceable, the DBA must comply with s 58AA of the CLSA 1990 and the Damages-Based Agreements Regulations 2013 (SI 2013/609) (DBA Regulations 2013). In summary, to be enforceable the DBA must:

(a) be in writing;

(b) specify:

    (i) the claim or proceedings or parts of them to which the agreement relates;

    (ii) the circumstances in which the representative's payment, expenses and costs, or part of them, are payable; and

    (iii) the reason for setting the amount of the payment at the level agreed; and

(c) not provide for a payment above an amount which, including VAT, is equal to 25% of the combined sums awarded for general damages for pain, suffering and loss of amenity (PSLA) and past pecuniary losses.

9.2.4.1 How do DBAs work?

Costs are recoverable on what is known as the 'Ontario model', since the regime is based on the system that operates in Ontario, Canada. Regulation 4 of the DBA Regulations 2013 states:

(1)   ... a damages-based agreement must not require an amount to be paid by the client other than—

    (a)   the payment, net of—

        (i)   any costs (including fixed costs under Part 45 of the Civil Procedure Rules 1998); and

        (ii)   where relevant, any sum in respect of disbursements incurred by the representative in respect of counsel's fees that have been paid or are payable by another party to the proceedings by agreement or order; and

    (b)   any expenses incurred by the representative, net of any amount which has been paid or is payable by another party to the proceedings by agreement or order.

In other words, the claimant's recoverable costs will be assessed in the conventional way, ie how many hours were reasonably spent on the case, what is a reasonable rate for those hours, etc. If the fee agreed with the solicitor is higher than the figure arrived at through that exercise, the claimant will have to pay the shortfall out of the damages.

EXAMPLE 1

The claimant (C) has entered into a DBA with their solicitor which provides for a contingency fee of 25% and is awarded damages of £100,000. C owes the solicitor £25,000.

If the costs recoverable from the defendant are assessed at £15,000, then C has to pay C's solicitor the excess £10,000 out of C's damages – ie, C receives £90,000 of the damages.

Accordingly, the existence of a DBA will not increase the amount of the defendant's costs liability. It may, however, decrease the defendant's costs liability. This is because the indemnity principle applies to DBAs, so that the claimant cannot recover more in costs from an opponent than the client is liable to pay their own lawyer. Therefore, if the agreed contingency fee is lower than the figure arrived at through a traditional costs assessment, the defendant will only have to pay the lower amount.

EXAMPLE 2

Continuing the scenario in Example 1 above, if the assessed costs are £30,000 then the defendant only has to pay the lower contingency fee figure of £25,000 due to the indemnity principle, and there is nothing further for C to pay their solicitor.

9.2.4.2   The 25% cap

Regulation 4(2) of the DBA Regulations 2013 provides that:

> (2)   In a claim for personal injuries—
>
>   (a)   the only sums recovered by the client from which the payment shall be met are—
>
>   (i)   general damages for pain, suffering and loss of amenity; and
>
>   (ii)   damages for pecuniary loss other than future pecuniary loss, net of any sums recoverable by the Compensation Recovery Unit of the Department for Work and Pensions; and
>
>   (b)   ... a damages-based agreement must not provide for a payment above an amount which, including VAT, is equal to 25% of the combined sums in paragraph (2)(a)(i) and (ii) which are ultimately recovered by the client.

EXAMPLE 3

Mr Brown enters into a DBA with his solicitor which provides for a contingency fee of 25%. Mr Brown is awarded £70,000 damages for PSLA, £30,000 for past loss of earnings and £400,000 for future loss of earnings. The contingency fee will be £25,000 (25% of the combined sums for PSLA and past loss of earnings). The £400,000 awarded to Mr Brown for future losses cannot be touched.

The 25% cap will apply only to claims or proceedings at first instance, not to appeals (DBA Regulations 2013, reg 4(4)).

9.2.5   Risk assessment for CFAs and DBAs

In order to decide:

(a)   whether to take a potential claim on *at all* on a CFA or DBA basis; and

(b)   once the decision has been made to accept the client's case on that basis, what is the appropriate level of fee to apply to the agreement,

it will be necessary for the claimant's solicitor to undertake assessment of the risk of the potential claim in every case.

The method of risk assessment adopted will differ from one firm to another, with some adopting paper-based systems and others utilising computer software to capture basic information and assist in speeding up the risk assessment process. Whichever method is used, the underlying principles are the same.

Principles of risk assessment

The *Oxford English Dictionary* defines 'risk' as 'the chance or possibility of loss or bad consequence'. If a solicitors' firm accepts a case on a 'no win, no fee' basis, it exposes itself to the risk of loss in not getting paid for the work it has done on behalf of the client. However, this is only half of the equation. There is equally the chance of a successful outcome. So risk assessment can be seen as the process of balancing the risk of losing against the chance of winning. That is easy enough to say, but rather more difficult to quantify objectively in a way that gives predictable and workable results. Nevertheless, this is exactly what a personal injury practitioner has to do when deciding whether or not to take a case on a CFA or DBA basis.

Practice of risk assessment

In practice, the skill of the personal injury practitioner will be in the ability to spot the factors relevant to risk and then go on to assess the severity of that risk. The majority of firms make use of a checklist for this purpose, which may be paper or electronically based.

The factors relevant to risk (or hazards) will include anything that could harm the claim. The risk will be the percentage chance that the factor will actually occur.

Common risk factors will include:

(a) *The facts*: is the client a credible witness and are there any other witnesses who will confirm the client's version?

(b) *Liability*: will the client be able to show that there was a relevant duty of care and that this duty has been breached?

(c) *Causation*: will the client be able to show that the injuries sustained are causally linked to the accident?

(d) *Limitation*: are there any issues due to limitation of claims or delay (ie 'stale' or lost evidence)?

(e) *The potential defendant*: is the opponent a 'viable' source of damages – does the defendant carry insurance or have funds to meet a damages claim, and have insurance details been confirmed?

(f) *Loss and damage*: can the losses sustained be proved by way of medical and other forms of evidence?

The second stage in the risk assessment is to assess the chance of each of the above risk factors actually occurring and harming the viability of the case. To do this, each factor needs to be categorised or 'scored' in some way. This can be done by giving each factor a percentage, or a score between 1 and 10 or, more simply still, by assessing it as a high, medium or low risk.

Based on the result (or score) from the above assessment, a risk assessment co-ordinator (usually a partner in the firm) will judge whether to accept the case on a conditional or contingency fee basis and, if so, on what level of success fee or percentage of likely damages. In the event that the risk assessor is unable to do so, because of insufficient information being available, the file will be passed back to the case worker for further investigation, for example obtaining witness statements or contacting the police for clarification of key issues.

In the event that the claim is accepted on a CFA or DBA basis, it is essential to record the reasoning behind the decision and the reason for the success fee or percentage of prospective damages claimed, as this will be needed in the event that the claim is successful and either the client (or the opponent in the case of a CFA entered into prior to 1 April 2013) wishes to challenge the level of the success fee or percentage.

9.2.6 After the event insurance

The client's potential liability to pay the other side's costs and disbursements and the client's own disbursements can be insured against by what is often referred to as 'after the event' insurance (AEI). The risk of having to pay the other side's costs has greatly diminished following the introduction of qualified one-way costs shifting (see **9.3** below) but nevertheless there may still be potential costs that an unsuccessful client may be liable to pay.

As the name suggests, AEI is taken out only once the need for the legal action has become apparent but before the proceedings have commenced. Here, the insurance is not against the risk of litigation but merely against the risk of having to pay the other side's costs and disbursements should the litigation fail, and it can cover the cost of the party's own disbursements as well. This type of insurance can be obtained alongside a CFA, a DBA or on its own. If necessary, many AEI insurers will arrange a loan to the client to fund both the disbursements and the cost of the AEI premium. If the client wins, the interest on the loan is not recoverable from the opponent but is usually deducted from the damages recovered.

9.2.6.1 Can the premium be recovered?

As with success fees, for AEI policies entered into before 1 April 2013 the AEI premium for insuring against liability to pay the other side's costs and disbursements is recoverable from the losing party provided it is reasonable. However, for policies entered into after 1 April 2013, the premium will not be recoverable from the other side.

Clinical negligence proceedings are treated as a special category. Regulation 3 of the Recovery of Costs Insurance Premiums in Clinical Negligence Proceedings (No 2) Regulations 2013 (SI 2013/739) states:

(1)   A costs order made in favour of a party to clinical negligence proceedings who has taken out a costs insurance policy may include provision requiring the payment of an amount in respect of all or part of the premium of that policy if—

(a)   the financial value of the claim for damages in respect of clinical negligence is more than £1,000; and

(b)   the costs insurance policy insures against the risk of incurring a liability to pay for an expert report or reports relating to liability or causation in respect of clinical negligence (or against that risk and other risks).

(2)   The amount of the premium that may be required to be paid under the costs order shall not exceed that part of the premium which relates to the risk of incurring liability to pay for an expert report or reports relating to liability or causation in respect of clinical negligence in connection with the proceedings.

Therefore, in clinical negligence cases, a party may recover the cost of an AEI premium taken out to cover the risk of having to pay for their own or the other side's costs in relation to obtaining expert evidence on liability and causation (but not quantum). The reasoning behind this exception to the normal rules is that clinical negligence claimants should not be deterred from pursuing their case by the unusually heavy burden of expert evidence required in such cases.

9.2.6.2   Staged AEI premiums

There are many different types of AEI policy, and it is important to shop around to find one that is appropriate for a client's particular case, but note that FSMA rules apply here. One popular form of AEI is where the premiums are 'staged'.

The way this works is as follows: with traditional AEI insurance, the underwriter considers the level of risk of the claimant losing and sets a premium accordingly. In so doing, the underwriter bears in mind that the majority of claims are settled either pre- or post-issue of proceedings, but long before trial. Another big tranche of claims will fight on at least until directions are complied with (so that each side has had the benefit of full disclosure from the opposition) and will then settle before being set down for trial. Only a small number of claims will go on to trial. By staging premiums at these trigger points (pre-issue, on setting down for trial, commencement of trial), the insurer can set a lower premium earlier on (accurately reflecting the risk) and an appropriately larger premium only for those cases that do not settle at an early stage. Clearly, a claim which does not settle until trial has a much greater prospect of going to trial, and is therefore much more likely actually to fail on liability and land the insurer with a big bill for the other side's costs. Hence the nearer the claim is to trial, the higher the AEI premium should be.

9.2.7   Legal expenses insurance

The client may have legal expenses insurance (known as 'before the event' or 'BTE' insurance) as a part of either the client's home or motor insurance policy, or as an extra service from the client's credit card provider, or as an extra for which the client has paid an additional premium. This is something that the client may either be unaware of or have forgotten, and it is therefore important that this is considered at the first interview.

Where the client has the benefit of a BTE insurance policy, the presumption is that the client will use it rather than take out additional insurance in the form of an AEI policy. There is no need to enter into a CFA or DBA because BTE insurance generally covers both sides' costs. However, the level and type of cover available under the BTE policy should be checked to make sure it is suitable. Many BTE policies have a limit of indemnity of £25,000, which may not be sufficient to cover the larger multi-track cases. If the cover is insufficient then it may well be reasonable to enter into a CFA or DBA and to take out AEI instead.

In *Sarwar v Alam* [2001] EWCA Civ 1401, the claimant had taken out an AEI policy when there was the opportunity to benefit from an existing legal expenses insurance policy or BTE insurance. In the costs-only proceedings, the issue was whether the AEI premium was recoverable. The Court of Appeal gave guidance that although a solicitor is not obliged to embark on a 'treasure hunt' in relation to pre-existing insurance, a solicitor should develop a practice of sending a standard letter requesting sight of:

(a)   any relevant motor insurance policy;

(b)   any household insurance policy;

(c)   any stand-alone BTE insurance policy belonging to the client and/or any spouse or partner living in the same household, and, if possible, their driver (if they are an injured passenger), in advance of the first interview.

A decision then needs to be made about whether any legal expenses insurance policy is satisfactory. The Court emphasised that the decision related to small road traffic accident claims with a quantum of £5,000 or less and that enquiries should be proportionate. (See also *Kilby v Gawith* [2008] EWCA Civ 812.)

As with trade union-funded work (see **9.2.8** below), the insurer may have nominated firms of solicitors who must be instructed to undertake the insured's claim. If the insured is free to instruct the solicitor of their choice, it is usual for the insurer to require the solicitor to report to it regularly on the progress of the case. In terms of confidentiality, it is essential for the solicitor to explain to the client at the outset that a term of the insurance is that the insurer has the right to receive reports on the viability of the case and whether or not it is worthwhile to continue with it. The progress of the case can be slowed down considerably by the obligation on the solicitor to report back to the insurer to seek approval (and therefore funding) to continue with the claim to the next stage.

9.2.7.1   Choice of solicitor under legal expenses insurance policies

The Insurance Companies (Legal Expenses Insurance) Regulations 1990 (SI 1990/1159) gave effect to Directive 87/344/EEC and are still in force. The Regulations cover, amongst other things, BTE insurance cover in respect of road traffic accidents. Regulation 6 of the 1990 Regulations specifies:

> 6.   Freedom to choose a lawyer
>
> (1)   Where under a legal expenses insurance contract recourse is had to a lawyer ... to defend, represent or serve the interests of the insured in any *enquiry or proceedings*, the insured shall be free to choose that lawyer (or other person). (emphasis added)

The interpretation given to the term 'enquiry or proceedings' will determine whether or not the insured person does have freedom to choose their own lawyer. Some insurance companies providing legal expenses insurance (LEI) cover put a narrow interpretation on it, saying that only when there are actual court proceedings is there any freedom for the policy holder to choose. The insurer will often prefer to refer the insured's claim to its panel of solicitors only, effectively concentrating the bulk of claims to so-called 'panel firms'. Not all LEI providers operate panels of preferred solicitors but many do, citing quality assurance and consistency of claims handling as the rationale for insisting on operating panels to which to channel claims. Non-panel firms may be forced to advise clients that they should avail themselves of pre-existing LEI cover rather than take up the non-panel solicitors' offer to work on the basis of a CFA or DBA. Non-panel solicitors will often take the view that the wording of reg 6(1) of the 1990 Regulations should be given a wide interpretation, and 'enquiry or proceedings' will encompass the work undertaken at pre-issue stage under the pre-action protocol. Their justification for this is due to the 'front loading' of litigation, where much of the work and advice is, of necessity, conducted before the issue of proceedings.

A case which illustrates many of the points outlined above is *Chappell v De Bora's of Exeter* (SCCO, 2004). This is a Supreme Court Costs Office case in which the costs claim of a non-panel local firm of solicitors was allowed despite the existence of pre-existing LEI. The facts briefly are as follows. The claimant's claim was in respect of the personal injuries she suffered when she fell down some steps at the defendant's shop in Exeter. The claimant, who lived near Exeter, instructed solicitors in Exeter. They entered into a CFA with a success fee of 71%. They also arranged a policy of AEI and corresponded with DAS, the legal expenses insurers with whom the claimant had an existing BTE insurance policy. DAS said that, under the terms of her policy with them, the claimant was obliged to instruct solicitors who were on their panel for any work which had to be done before the issue of proceedings, although she was entitled to instruct the solicitors of her choice for the purpose of the proceedings themselves should proceedings be necessary. The claimant's solicitors (who were not on the DAS panel) undertook the usual pre-proceedings work, including sending the letter of claim, taking witness evidence and obtaining two medical reports. The defendant's solicitors eventually offered to settle the matter for £31,156 plus costs. This offer was accepted, but the issue of costs could not be agreed and, following detailed assessment, the defendant was given permission to appeal on the issue of whether it was reasonable for the claimant to enter into a CFA with a success fee and AEI with the solicitors of her choice, when BTE insurance was available but the claimant's chosen solicitors were not on the BTE insurers' panel.

The defendant's counsel submitted that the onus was on the claimant to show why it was reasonable, on the standard basis, that the more expensive route of proceedings under a CFA with AEI should have been adopted. He submitted that solicitors on the DAS panel up and down the country conducted very many cases no less serious and complex than the present case on a regular basis. He accepted what the Master of the Rolls had said in *Sarwar v Alam* (see **9.2.7** above).

> In this case we are concerned only with a relatively small personal injury claim in a road traffic accident. We are not concerned with claims which look as if they will exceed about £5,000, and we are not concerned with any other type of BTE claim. We have no doubt that, if a claimant possesses pre-existing BTE cover which appears to be satisfactory for a claim of that size, then in the ordinary course of things that claimant should be referred to the relevant BTE insurers.

The claimant's counsel submitted that this was not a straightforward case and that the amount of the damages, in excess of £31,000, reflected those complexities. It had been reasonable for the claimant to go to solicitors in Exeter to handle her case rather than to solicitors in Bristol or Salisbury. He submitted that the costs which the district judge had allowed were proportionate in relation to a multi-track case of this nature. The judge concluded that it was reasonable in a case of this kind for the claimant to instruct the solicitors of her choice in Exeter rather than DAS panel solicitors, the nearest of whom would have been many miles away from where she lived. Accordingly, he dismissed the appeal in so far as it related to the claimant's choice of solicitor.

9.2.8 Trade unions

If the client has had an accident at work and belongs to a trade union, the client may be entitled to receive free access to legal advice as part of the client's trade union membership. This is something of which the client may not be aware initially, and the solicitor should therefore cover this point at the first interview.

If the client is entitled to advice through their trade union, the trade union may have its own legal department or nominated solicitors which it always uses. If this is the case, the solicitor first consulted by the client is unlikely to be instructed, but should nevertheless advise the client to seek advice from the trade union on this point. The advantage to the client, if the client is able to procure the support of trade union funding, is that, provided the client has paid their membership fees to the trade union, they will have the full financial support of the trade union behind them. The client's solicitor will still have to convince the trade union as to the merits of the case, and will also be obliged to report on the case prior to proceeding with it. However, the claimant will not have to worry that part of their damages may be taken away to pay the client's legal expenses, as would be the case if the client were funded either through public (ie legal aid) funding or via a CFA or DBA.

9.2.9 Private fee-paying clients

Some clients will have no alternative but to fund their cases privately, or may choose to do so in any event. In such circumstances the solicitor is required under the SRA Code to explain to the client fully their liability for costs and disbursements. The solicitor should give the best information on costs that they can, including likely disbursements and the hourly rate that the solicitor proposes to charge (as to which see **9.2.1** above and *Legal Foundations*, Professional Conduct).

9.3   QUALIFIED ONE-WAY COSTS SHIFTING

On 1 April 2013, 'qualified one-way costs shifting' (QOCS) was introduced for personal injury and clinical negligence claims. This means that although a defendant will still generally be ordered to pay the costs of a successful claimant, subject to certain exceptions, a defendant will not recover their own costs if they successfully defend the claim. The rules are contained in CPR, rr 44.13–44.17 and PD 44 General Rules About Costs, paras 12.1–12.7.

9.3.1   When will QOCS apply?

Rule 44.13(1) provides that QOCS applies to proceedings which include a claim for damages:

(a)   for personal injuries;

(b)   under the Fatal Accidents Act 1976; or

(c)   which arises out of death or personal injury and survives for the benefit of an estate by virtue of s 1(1) of the Law Reform (Miscellaneous Provisions) Act 1934.

It also applies where a person brings a counterclaim or an additional claim for such damages.

The Court of Appeal decision in *Howe v MIB* [2017] EWCA Civ 932 confirmed that QOCS also applies to claims brought against the MIB.

CPR, r 44.13(1) makes clear that QOCS does not apply to applications for pre-action disclosure or cases where CPR, r 44.17 applies (in effect, in respect of a funding arrangement entered into before 1 April 2013). See also **9.3.3** below.

9.3.2   How does it work?

Up until 5 April 2023, CPR, r 44.14 set out the basic rule that:

(1)   ... orders for costs made against a claimant may be enforced without the permission of the court but only to the extent that the aggregate amount in money terms of such orders does not exceed the aggregate amount in money terms of any orders for damages and interest made in favour of the claimant.

(2)   Orders for costs made against a claimant may only be enforced after the proceedings have been concluded and the costs have been assessed or agreed.

Rule 44.14 therefore permitted costs orders to be made and enforced against claimants, but only to the extent that those costs did not exceed the total damages the claimant recovered. Therefore, the effect was that a claimant who lost (and so had no damages against which an order for costs could be enforced) would not have to pay the defendant's costs. However, it did not preclude a successful claimant being deprived of all or part of their costs, or ordered to pay the defendant's costs, in other circumstances. Enforcement of any such costs order cannot take place until after the conclusion of the proceedings. The intention was to enable costs orders to be made in the usual way against a claimant who failed to beat a Part 36 offer, lost an application or failed to comply with court orders and directions.

In *Cartwright v Venduct Engineering Ltd* [2018] EWCA Civ 1654, the Court of Appeal held that in a case where there are multiple defendants and the claimant has lost or discontinued against one, the winning defendant is in principle entitled to enforce the costs order against a claimant who has obtained some damages, even though the source of the claimant's damages is another defendant. The Court stated that any other result would give claimants carte blanche to commence claims against as many defendants as they like without any adverse consequences and would encourage the bringing of hopeless claims. However, the Court of Appeal went on to point out that CPR, r 44.14(1) only allowed enforcement of costs orders against damages obtained by way of a court order. In *Cartwright*, the damages were due by way of a schedule to a *Tomlin* order and were therefore not part of the order itself. It concluded that there was consequently no court order for damages against which the costs could be enforced. It was also agreed that as the acceptance of a Part 36 offer does not require an order of the court, settlement in consequence of acceptance of a Part 36 offer would also fall outside CPR, r 44.14(1) (as it was then drafted), and a costs order would not be enforceable against damages obtained as a result of such a settlement.

CPR, r 44.14(1) has been amended as from 6 April 2023 and states:

(1)   … orders for costs made against a claimant may be enforced without the permission of the court but only to the extent that the aggregate amount in money terms of such orders does not exceed the aggregate amount in money terms of any orders for, or agreements to pay or settle a claim for, damages, costs and interest made in favour of the claimant.

(2)   For the purposes of this Section, orders for costs includes orders for costs deemed to have been made (either against the claimant or in favour of the claimant) as set out in rule 44.9.

(3)   Orders for costs made against a claimant may only be enforced after the proceedings have been concluded and the costs have been assessed or agreed.

The amendment to r 44.14(1) means that, as from 6 April 2023, defendants will be able to set off costs orders against agreements to pay or settle a claim, which would include a Part 36 offer accepted before trial and any settlement by way of a *Tomlin* order. ATE insurance will therefore need to be considered in this context.

The pre-6 April 2023 QOCS regime will continue to apply to claims in which proceedings were issued prior to 6 April 2023.

9.3.3   Exceptions when QOCS will not apply

Rules 44.15 and 44.16 set out the exceptions:

(a)   *The claim is found on the balance of probabilities to be 'fundamentally dishonest'*. PD 44 (ie Practice Direction Costs), para 12.4 provides that the court will normally direct that allegations of fundamental dishonesty will be determined at trial. The intention is that sham accidents and other totally dishonest claims will lose the protection of QOCS. In *Gosling v Screwfix and another* (Cambridge County Court, 29 March 2014), it was held that the claim was fundamentally dishonest for the purposes of QOCS and, as a result, the claimant was ordered to pay the defendant's costs on the indemnity basis. The judge found that the claimant had suffered an injury and had not been dishonest about the accident circumstances. However, the claimant had significantly exaggerated the extent of his ongoing symptoms, and the effect of the discovery of this deceit reduced the value of his claim by half. See also *Murphy v Wye Valley NHS Trust* [2022] 10 WLUK 119 for an example of a clinical negligence claim involving issues of fundamental dishonesty. Here, the claimant was ordered to repay a £50,000 interim payment and to pay the defendant's costs on the indemnity basis.

The term 'fundamental dishonesty' has now been incorporated into s 57 of the Criminal Justice and Courts Act 2015 (see **1.4**) which applies to all proceedings issued on or after 13 April 2015. Section 57 provides as follows:

(1)   This section applies where, in proceedings on a claim for damages in respect of personal injury ('the primary claim')—

    (a)   the court finds that the claimant is entitled to damages in respect of the claim, but

    (b)   on an application by the defendant for the dismissal of the claim under this section, the court is satisfied on the balance of probabilities that the claimant has been fundamentally dishonest in relation to the primary claim or a related claim.

(2)   The court must dismiss the primary claim, unless it is satisfied that the claimant would suffer substantial injustice if the claim were dismissed.

(3)   The duty under subsection (2) includes the dismissal of any element of the primary claim in respect of which the claimant has not been dishonest.

(4)   The court's order dismissing the claim must record the amount of damages that the court would have awarded to the claimant in respect of the primary claim but for the dismissal of the claim.

(5)   When assessing costs in the proceedings, a court which dismisses a claim under this section must deduct the amount recorded in accordance with subsection (4) from the amount which it would otherwise order the claimant to pay in respect of costs incurred by the defendant.

In *LOCOG v Sinfield* [2018] EWHC 51 (QB) the High Court provided some guidance on the approach courts should take when applying s 57. Mr Justice Knowles said:

Where an application is made by a defendant for the dismissal of a claim under s 57 the court should:

a.   Firstly, consider whether the claimant is entitled to damages in respect of the claim. If he concludes that the claimant is not so entitled, that is the end of the matter, although the judge may have to go on to consider whether to disapply QOCS pursuant to CPR r 44.16.

b.   If the judge concludes that the claimant is entitled to damages, the judge must determine whether the defendant has proved to the civil standard that the claimant has been fundamentally dishonest in relation to the primary claim and/or a related claim in the sense that I have explained.

c.   If the judge is so satisfied then the judge must dismiss the claim including, by virtue of s 57(3), any element of the primary claim in respect of which the claimant has not been dishonest unless, in accordance with s 57(2), the judge is satisfied that the claimant would suffer substantial injustice if the claim were dismissed.

(b)   *The claim is struck out as disclosing no reasonable grounds for bringing the proceedings, or as an abuse of process, or for conduct likely to obstruct the just disposal of the proceedings.*

(c)   *The proceedings include a claim which is made for the financial benefit of a person other than the claimant.* PD 44, para 12.2 gives examples of such claims as subrogated claims for damages for the repair of a motor vehicle in an RTA or for credit hire of a replacement vehicle where the beneficiary of the claim is the claimant's insurer. The intention here is to prevent insurers persuading a lay claimant to make a claim for a minor personal injury and to include the claim for repairs or car hire, thereby enabling the insurer to obtain the benefit of QOCS. In such a case, the rules expressly give the court the power to make a costs order against a person other than the claimant, ie generally the injured claimant will retain the QOCS protection for the injury element of the claim.

9.4   CONCLUSION

Personal injury lawyers are facing challenging times following the implementation of these recent rules on costs and funding, and it will take time before we can assess their true impact.

The introduction of QOCS was aimed at counter-balancing the impact on personal injury claimants of the decision to abolish recoverability of CFA success fees and, in particular, ATE insurance premiums. The intention behind QOCS was to make ATE insurance unnecessary for personal injury actions, since the claimant would not normally be liable for the defendant's costs if the claim failed. However, even under the regime that operated up to 5 April 2023 (and still continues to operate for claims issued by that date):

(a)   The fact that the claimant can lose the QOCS protection where the defendant has made a Part 36 offer means that the claimant will potentially be back on risk for costs whenever a Part 36 offer is made, should the matter proceed to trial, though only up to the amount of the claimant's damages. If ATE cover is available in respect of this risk, and is taken out, the premium will not be recoverable.

(b)   After the event insurance is also taken out, normally, to cover own disbursements as well as adverse costs. The Government has carved out from the reforms the cost of ATE premiums to cover expert reports on liability and causation in clinical negligence cases, but the cost of ATE cover in respect of other disbursements will not be recoverable.

The amendments to the QOCS regime from 6 April 2023 increase the potential costs risks to claimants in personal injury and clinical negligence claims. Claimants' solicitors should advise carefully and comprehensively on the costs risks and the protection needed to mitigate these, for example through ATE insurance.

CHAPTER 10

INVESTIGATING THE CLAIM AND PRELIMINARY STEPS

LEARNING OUTCOMES

After reading this chapter you will be able to:

- set out the main requirements of the pre-action protocols for personal injury claims, disease and illness claims, and clinical disputes, and the Practice Direction on pre-action conduct
- identify the appropriate defendant in personal injury and clinical negligence cases
- set out the preliminary steps in such cases
- draft an appropriate letter of claim on behalf of the claimant
- respond appropriately on behalf of the defendant
- appreciate the different types of evidence which may be available and understand how to go about collecting such evidence.

10.1 INTRODUCTION

During the first interview, the claimant's solicitor will have taken a proof of evidence from their client, who may have been able to supply additional evidence, such as documents or photographs. However, in all but the most straightforward low value personal injury cases, further information will be required before the claimant's solicitor is able to send either the Claim Notification Form (CNF) in a case falling within the scope of one of the low value pre-action protocols, or a letter of claim in all other cases. In all cases where settlement is not reached prior to commencement, full investigations must be made before proceedings are issued.

The defendant may contact their solicitor immediately after the incident which has given rise to the potential claim, but in many cases the defendant's solicitor or the defendant's insurer's solicitor will become involved only after the letter of claim or the CNF has been received. In any event, the defendant's solicitor must also make full investigations and, where a claim is to be defended, gather evidence in support of their client's case.

Solicitors acting for both parties should be keen to gather evidence quickly, while events are fresh in the minds of clients and witnesses, and before real and documentary evidence is repaired, misplaced or destroyed. In this chapter, the investigations that should be made will be outlined. This chapter will also deal with the procedural steps that must be taken before proceedings are issued. In this regard, the parties and their solicitors are guided by the relevant pre-action protocols (PAPs).

10.2 PRE-ACTION PROTOCOLS

Solicitors dealing with personal injury and clinical negligence claims must be familiar with the PAPs relating to these claims and the associated Practice Direction. There are a number of protocols, and it is important to ensure that the correct one is consulted for each individual claim. Sanctions may be imposed by the court for non-compliance with the requirements of the PAPs, although the court is unlikely to be concerned with minor or technical shortcomings.

The protocols considered in this book are as follows:

(a)   PAP for Personal Injury Claims (revised April 2015 and updated subsequently). This is primarily designed for PI claims which are likely to be allocated to the fast track, and to the entirety of such claims (for example, to any property damage resulting from the incident causing the injury). It does not apply to cases which would properly fall under any of the other PAPs listed below; but, if a case commenced under either of the Low Value PAPs ((d) and (e) below) exits the Portal for any reason, it would then fall under this PAP. This PAP is equally appropriate to higher value claims, and the spirit (if not the letter) of the PAP should be followed for claims which could potentially be allocated to the multi-track. This PAP is set out in full in **Appendix 2**.

(b)   PAP for Disease and Illness Claims. This is the correct protocol to use for all personal injury claims where the injury takes the form of an illness or disease, eg mesothelioma, asthma or dermatitis, which arises through working in or occupying premises or using products (and which do not fall under the PAP for Low Value Personal Injury (Employers' Liability and Public Liability) Claims). These claims are likely to be complex and therefore unsuitable for fast track procedures, even where the value is less than £25,000. This PAP is not reproduced in this book, but may be found on the Justice.Gov.UK website. (CPR, PD 3D, which gives further assistance in relation to mesothelioma claims, is beyond the scope of this book.)

(c)   PAP for the Resolution of Clinical Disputes (revised April 2015 and updated subsequently). This is the correct protocol to use for claims against hospitals, GPs, dentists and other healthcare providers (both NHS and private) which involve an injury that is alleged to be the result of clinical negligence. The PAP recognises that it is in the interests of everyone involved – patients, healthcare professionals and providers – that patients' concerns, complaints and claims are dealt with quickly, efficiently and professionally, and that the patient/clinician relationship is preserved if at all possible, not least because the patient may need further treatment. This PAP is set out in full in **Appendix 3**.

(d)   PAP for Low Value Personal Injury Claims in Road Traffic Accidents. This is the correct protocol to use where a claim for general and special damages for personal injury resulting from an RTA (excluding damage to the vehicle and hire costs) is valued at no more than £25,000, where the small claims track would not be the normal track for the claim, and where the CNF was sent on or after 31 May 2021. (The previous version of this PAP, dealing with claims of up to £10,000, shall continue to have effect in respect of any claim where the CNF was sent on or after 31 July 2013 but before 31 May 2021.)

Recent changes have been made to the PAP for Low Value Personal Injury Claims in Road Traffic Accidents and the small claims limit for personal injury claims arising out of road traffic accidents. These changes have coincided with the coming into force of the Whiplash Injury Regulations 2021 (SI 2021/642) on 31 May 2021. Regulation 2 of the Whiplash Injury Regulations 2021 sets a tariff for the total amount of damages for pain, suffering and loss of amenity payable in relation to whiplash injuries and associated minor psychological injuries lasting up to a maximum of 2 years. The maximum amount of compensation payable under the tariff is £4,345. In addition, the small claims limit has been increased in relation to road traffic accidents, to £5,000 (see further below), and a new pre-action protocol was also brought into force on 31 May 2021 – the Pre-Action Protocol for Personal Injury Claims below the Small Claims Limit in Road Traffic Accidents ('RTA Small Claims Protocol'). Furthermore, a new free and independent online service has been developed by the MIB on behalf of the Ministry of Justice – Official Injury Claim – to deal with road traffic accident claims falling within the small claims limit. A new Practice Direction 27B has also been brought into force: Practice Direction 27B – Claims under the Pre-Action Protocol for Personal Injury Claims below the Small Claims Limit in Road Traffic Accidents – Court Procedure.

In light of these recent changes, CPR, r 26 was amended. The current position is that the small claims track would not be the normal track where the claim has an overall financial value of more than £10,000 or where the value of any claim for pain suffering and loss of amenity is more than:

(i)   £5,000 where the claim arises from a road traffic accident which occurred in England and Wales after 31 May 2021 (this reflects the changes explained above), except where (ii) below applies;

(ii)   £1,000 where the claim arises from a road traffic accident where the accident occurred before 31 May 2021, or where on the date that the proceedings are started: the claimant is a child or protected party (unless r 26.11 applies); the claimant was a vulnerable road user (namely that the claimant was using a motorcycle, or was a pillion or sidecar passenger, using a wheelchair or mobility scooter, a bicycle or other pedal cycle, riding a horse or was a pedestrian when the accident occurred); the claimant is an undischarged bankrupt; or (unless r 26.11 applies) the claimant or defendant acts as a personal representative of a deceased person. See r 26.10 and r 26.11.

Rule 26.11 relates to children and protected parties and in effect sets out exemptions from the RTA Small Claims Protocol altogether. Rule 26.11 states:

(1)   The fast track is the normal track where a claim—

    (a)   is for personal injuries arising from a road traffic accident which occurs on or after 31st May 2021;

    (b)   is made by—

        (i)   a child or a protected party; or

        (ii)   a person who, on the date the claim was first presented via the Pre-Action Protocol for Low Value Personal Injury Claims in Road Traffic Accidents, was a child; and

    (c)   consists of, or includes, a claim for a whiplash injury.

(2)   Where this rule applies, the claim must not be allocated to the small claims track.

(3)   'Whiplash injury' has the meaning ascribed to it by paragraph 1.2(38) of the Pre-Action Protocol for Personal Injury Claims Below the Small Claims Limit in Road Traffic Accidents.

Paragraph 4.1A of the PAP for Low Value Claims in Road Traffic Accidents is an amending paragraph which mirrors r 26.11. Paragraph 4.1A makes clear that the low value (as opposed to the small claims) RTA protocol applies to a claim for whiplash injury where the claimant is a child, and where the claim arises from a road traffic accident after 31 May 2021 and the claim is worth no more than the low value protocol upper limit.

There are some general exclusions, set out in para 4.5 of the PAP for Low Value Claims in Road Traffic Accidents, such as where the claimant or defendant is either a personal representative of a deceased person or is a protected party (for protected party, see **Chapter 20**). Paragraph 4.1A also explicitly makes clear that the low value protocol does not apply to protected parties.

Claims commenced under this PAP may cease to be governed by it in a number of circumstances, such as where the defendant defends the claim or admits negligence but alleges contributory negligence (other than simple failure to wear a safety belt). The PAP is not reproduced in this book, but the main elements of the PAP and the associated practice direction are set out in **Chapter 21**.

Whilst the focus of this book is on fast-track and multi-track claims, it is necessary to understand the recent changes to the small claims track and the pre-action protocols in relation to road traffic accident claims, as well as the Whiplash Injury Regulations 2021 that were brought into force on 31 May 2021 following the enactment of the Civil Liability Act 2018. Understanding these changes enables a fuller understanding of the PAP for Low Value Claims in Road Traffic Accidents. A reasonably detailed explanation of the recent changes has been set out above, but further reference should be made to the Whiplash Injury Regulations 2021, CPR Part 26, Practice Direction 27B and the protocols themselves.

(e)   PAP for Low Value Personal Injury (Employers' Liability and Public Liability) Claims. This is the correct protocol to use where damages for personal injury in an employers' liability or public liability claim are valued at no more than £25,000 on a full liability basis (excluding interest) and the accident occurred on or after 31 July 2013 or, in a disease claim, no letter of claim was sent before 31 July 2013 (although there are exclusions – see para 4.3 of the PAP). As in (d) above, there are circumstances where claims commenced under this PAP may cease to be governed by it. This PAP is set out in full in **Appendix 4** and is covered in more depth in **Chapter 21**.

In addition to these protocols, there is a Practice Direction on pre-action conduct ('PD Pre-action Conduct') which describes the conduct the court will normally expect of the prospective parties prior to the start of the proceedings.

The PAPs deal with such matters as the letter of claim and the defendant's response, but before the claimant's solicitor can think about writing the letter of claim, they will need to investigate the matter further and ensure that they have identified the correct defendant.

10.3   IDENTIFYING THE DEFENDANT

One of the first issues for the claimant's solicitor to deal with is the identification of the defendant and, in many cases, this will be straightforward. However, this question should always be addressed carefully by the claimant's solicitor, as sometimes the issue may not be as simple as it appears, and it is crucial to issue proceedings within the primary limitation period against the correct defendant.

Generally, there is little point in pursuing a claim against a defendant unless the defendant is insured, or has the means with which to pay the judgment sum. It is important to note that, for the purposes of the two PAPs for low value claims, the CNF will be sent to the insurer and it will be necessary, therefore, to make a reasonable attempt to identify the insurer. The means of doing so are set out at **10.3.1** and **10.3.2** below.

10.3.1   Road traffic incidents and other highway claims

In a road traffic accident claim, it is necessary to establish not only the name of the driver of the vehicle and his insurance position, but also the name of the owner of the vehicle and of his insurer. Under the Motor Vehicles (Compulsory Insurance) (Information Centre and Compensation Body) Regulations 2003 (SI 2003/37) which implemented the Fourth EU Motor

Insurance Directive, it is a requirement that the insurer of a vehicle must be readily identifiable from the vehicle registration number. Therefore, when trying to trace the owner and insurer of a vehicle involved in a road traffic accident, if the claimant has taken down the registration of the other driver's vehicle, the solicitor should be able to trace the insurance details. The UK insurance industry has met this requirement by introducing the Motor Insurance Database (MID), which provides details of all vehicles and their associated insurance policies. Individual firms of solicitors can apply for a licence to operate the MID system, allowing them almost instant access to insurance details of third parties, accessed by means of the vehicle registration mark. A savvy client may have used the 'askMID Roadside' service to obtain these details at the time of the accident (see **3.3.4**).

10.3.1.1 Driving in the course of employment

Frequently, the driver may be using a vehicle owned and insured by their employer. In such cases, the claim would normally be issued against the employer (or vehicle operator in the case of commercial vehicles). If it is unclear whether or not the driver was acting within the course of employment, it is usual to sue both the driver and the employer. Similarly, if protective proceedings are necessary to avoid the claim being statute-barred under the Limitation Act 1980 (see **7.9.2**), and there is insufficient time to investigate the issue of vicarious liability properly, the claim should be issued against both driver and employer.

10.3.1.2 Insured drivers – naming the insurer as defendant

Under reg 3 of the European Communities (Rights against Insurers) Regulations 2002 (SI 2002/3061), as amended by the Motor Vehicles (Compulsory Insurance and Rights Against Insurers) (Amendment) (EU Exit) Regulations 2020 (SI 2020/945), where a claimant has a claim in tort against an insured person arising out of an accident, the claimant has a direct right of action in the courts against the driver's insurer. This means that the claimant can issue proceedings against the insurer alone, or in addition to the driver. How this is dealt with in practice varies. Some solicitors acting for claimants always issue proceedings directly against insurers where they are able to do so; some never do so. On a practical level, it is unlikely to make any measurable difference to how the proceedings are conducted or to the final outcome. Where a driver is insured, it will be the insurance company and its solicitors who will determine how the proceedings are conducted, and it will be the insurance company who will pay up, should liability be established, whether or not it is named as a defendant. Under the terms of the policy, the driver will be obliged to cooperate with the insurer in defending the matter, including giving evidence at trial if necessary, whether or not the driver is named as a defendant.

10.3.1.3 Invalid insurance – Road Traffic Act 1988, ss 151 and 152

Sometimes, a situation will arise where a vehicle was covered by a policy of insurance at the time of the accident, but the policy did not cover the driver or the insurer has grounds to void the policy. The claimant should not be dissuaded from commencing proceeding against the driver on the grounds that the driver may be impecunious, as the insurance company will be obliged to pay out on the judgment to the claimant, provided the correct notice is given (see **3.3** and **12.3.2**).

10.3.1.4 Uninsured drivers

Where an accident occurring on or after 1 August 2015 is caused by an uninsured driver, an application should be made to the Motor Insurers' Bureau (MIB) under the Uninsured Drivers' Agreement 2015, and under previous versions of the Agreement for accidents occurring before that date (see **3.4.1**). If the MIB declines liability, proceedings should be commenced against the driver, as first defendant, and the MIB, as second defendant. If the driver is found to be liable, the MIB must satisfy the judgment, provided the claimant has followed the steps set out in the Agreement. For accidents occurring on or after 1 March 2017, the Supplementary

Uninsured Drivers Agreement England, Scotland and Wales 2017 applies. From that time onwards, the 2015 Agreement continues to apply in all respects except as provided for by the amendments set out in the 2017 supplementary agreement.

10.3.1.5   Untraced drivers

Where the accident is caused by a 'hit and run' driver who cannot be traced, it will not be possible to commence court proceedings. Instead, an application should be made to the MIB on behalf of the injured party under the Untraced Drivers Agreement England, Scotland and Wales 2017 (or the 2003 Agreement where the accident occurred before 1 March 2017). This scheme is considered in **3.4.2**.

10.3.1.6   Highway authorities, statutory undertakers and other owners of the highway

Where there are indications that the actions or omissions of a highway authority, statutory undertaker or some other owner of the highway have caused or contributed to the claimant's accident, enquiries may be made of the local council in order to identify who that body is. Every council is obliged to keep and allow access to records detailing the ownership of highway land within its area (see **3.5.1**); and it will also have information about any activities of statutory undertakers on highway land, as the council operates a licensing system (see **3.5.2.4**). Whilst highway authorities and statutory undertakers will always have public liability insurance, other owners of the highway may not.

10.3.2   Employers' liability claims

If an incident occurs at work, notwithstanding that the incident was caused by another employee or someone acting as agent for the employer, provided that person was acting in the course of employment, it is usual to sue the employer only (see **4.4**). (Although the defendant will generally be the employer, a claim may also be made against the occupier of the premises, or against the person with control of the premises if different from the employer. This lies beyond the scope of this book.) All employers should have appropriate insurance, although a minority of rogue employers may not, and the claimant's solicitor should carry out a database search through the Employers' Liability Tracing Office in order to establish the identity of the insurer.

10.3.3   Cases involving negligence of doctors and medical staff

10.3.3.1   Claims arising out of NHS hospital treatment

If the claim arises out of treatment in a hospital by an employee of the NHS, the relevant NHS Trust or Foundation Trust is named as the defendant. It is not appropriate to sue individual doctors or nurses in the direct employment of the Trust.

In order to identify the name and address of the relevant Trust, a search can be made on the NHS website at www.nhs.uk by typing in the name of the hospital.

NHS Resolution, an arm's length body of the Department for Health and Social Care, is responsible for handling all clinical negligence claims against NHS bodies and their employees, who are indemnified under the Clinical Negligence Scheme for Trusts. NHS Resolution has a panel of firms of solicitors to deal with such claims on its behalf (see **5.7**).

10.3.3.2   General practitioners

General practitioners (GPs) are almost always self-employed, and they contract their services to the NHS. A GP is liable for their own acts and for the acts of their employees. General practitioners often operate in partnerships, and in such cases, the claim may be issued against the individual GP concerned or against the partnership. General practitioners have until recently carried indemnity insurance from an organisation such as the Medical Defence Union or the Medical Protection Society. In April 2019, however, NHS Resolution started operating the state indemnity scheme for general practice in England, known as the Clinical Negligence Scheme for General Practice (CNSGP). The CNSGP covers clinical negligence liabilities arising in general practice in relation to incidents that occurred on or after 1 April 2019.

10.3.3.3 Private hospitals and clinics

If the claim arises out of treatment in a private hospital or clinic, the decision as to who should be named as the defendant will depend upon the basis of the claim. The doctors and some other healthcare providers will usually be independent contractors. Where it is their breach of duty which has led to the claim, the claim should be issued against them as individuals, as vicarious liability is not applicable. They will be indemnified by their own medical defence organisations.

The hospital or clinic will provide premises and equipment for the use of independent contractors and will employ the staff who run and administer the hospital or clinic, and this will usually include nursing staff. If the claim arises as a result of defective or inadequate premises or equipment or the actions of employees, the hospital or clinic should be named as defendant. It will carry its own insurance. The hospital or clinic will advise the claimant's solicitor as to the position of individuals who are employed or who otherwise use their premises.

10.3.3.4 Private treatment from dentists

A dentist treating private patients is not under any statutory or professional requirement to have insurance cover in respect of professional negligence – although the majority are insured.

10.4 CLINICAL NEGLIGENCE CLAIMS – PRELIMINARY STEPS

The PAP for the Resolution of Clinical Disputes assumes that the patient's medical records will be provided by the health care provider *before* the letter of claim is sent. It may also be necessary for the claimant's solicitor to instruct an expert to look at the records and advise as to liability and/or causation prior to the letter of claim.

10.4.1 Obtaining medical records

The claimant's solicitor should obtain a copy of their client's records from their GP and from the hospital where the claimant was treated, in order to build up a full picture of the client's health prior to the incident and of the treatment the client received. The GP's records should contain notes of symptoms, medication and treatment, referrals to hospital, reports back from hospital doctors and referrals to other professionals such as occupational therapists, physiotherapists or community nurses. The hospital records will contain details of the client's admission, the client's consents to treatment, x-rays, photographs, print-outs from monitoring equipment, nursing records and comments made by the doctors who were treating the client.

The claimant's solicitor should ensure that they obtain all the notes, not just those which are supplied and marked relevant to the matter in hand, as background history may be highly relevant. In *Wickham v Dwyer* (1995) *Current Law Weekly*, 1 January, the court held that it was for the expert to determine whether or not there was any information of any irrelevance contained within the notes, and therefore it was fair to allow the solicitors and experts access to the full notes.

Until all records have been traced and disclosed, the solicitor will not be in a position to instruct an expert to review the evidence and form a view on liability and/or causation. Early and full disclosure is the key to successful clinical negligence litigation as, without this, it may be impossible for the claimant and the claimant's solicitor to know exactly what happened.

10.4.1.1   Right of access to medical records

Records of living individuals

The Data Protection Act 2018 (DPA 2018) gives the right to living individuals to access their personal health records. For the purposes of the Act, 'records' may be handwritten or in a computerised form, and will include imaging records, such as x-rays, photographs and print-outs from monitoring equipment.

Records of deceased individuals

The Access to Health Records Act 1990 governs access to the health records of individuals who have died. Access may be requested only by a personal representative or a person who may have a claim arising out of the death (s 3(1)(f)).

10.4.1.2   Procedure for obtaining access to medical records

Paragraph 3.2 of the PAP for the Resolution of Clinical Disputes states that a request for records by the claimant should:

(a)   provide sufficient information to alert the defendant where an adverse outcome has been serious or has had serious consequences or may constitute a notifiable safety incident;

(b)   be as specific as possible about the records which are required for an initial investigation of the claim (including, for example, a continuous copy of the CTG trace in birth injury cases); and

(c)   include a request for any relevant guidelines, analyses, protocols or policies and any documents created in relation to an adverse incident, notifiable safety incident or complaint.

Paragraph 3.3 states that the requests should be made using the Law Society and Department of Health approved standard form, which can be found at Annex B of the PAP, adapted as necessary. The form requires the solicitor to obtain their client's signature to indicate the client's informed consent to the release of the records.

Paragraph 3.4 states that the copy records should be provided within 40 days of the request and for a cost not exceeding the charges permissible under the Access to Health Records Act 1990 and/or the DPA 1998. The DPA 2018 repealed the DPA 1998, implementing the General Data Protection Regulation (Regulation (EU) 2016/679). As a result, the general rule is that, as from 25 May 2018, no charges for access to records are permissible. If the defendant is unable to comply with the 40-day time limit, the problem should be explained quickly and details given of what is being done to resolve it (para 3.6). Ultimately, an application can be made to the court under r 31.16 of the CPR for an order for pre-action disclosure. The court has the power to impose costs sanctions for unreasonable delay in providing records (para 3.7).

Under para 3.8, if either party requires additional health records from a third party healthcare provider, co-operation from that third party is expected. Rule 31.17 of the CPR sets out the procedure for applying to the court for pre-action disclosure by third parties (see **10.10.3**).

10.4.1.3   The content of medical records

Medical records may be in paper or electronic form and will, of course, vary from case to case. The following is a sample of the records that a solicitor may expect to receive from a hospital:

(a)   *Admission details/record sheet.* These should give the date and the time of admission, the record number, the name of the ward and the name of the consultant in charge of the case.

(b)   *In-patient notes.* These include casualty notes (where appropriate), personal details of the patient, a detailed history of the patient and of the initial examination, daily progress and record notes, discharge notes, a copy of the letter to the GP giving details of the patient's treatment and a general report to the GP.

(c) *Nursing records*. Nursing records are detailed notes made by nursing staff including temperature charts, vital signs, test results, results of all investigations carried out, and details of drugs prescribed and taken.

(d) *Letters of referral*. These include referrals from GPs, responses to GPs following consultation or complaint of a missed appointment, and comments on the patient's demeanour and attitude.

(e) *Records of x-rays*. These include other films taken. Copies of the x-rays and films themselves are not supplied automatically (only the record of the fact that the x-ray was carried out) and copies of the films will have to be obtained separately.

(f) *Anaesthetic details*. These are details of the examination of the patient prior to an operation, a record of the drugs administered during pre-medication and during the operation itself.

(g) *Patient consent forms*. These forms show what treatments the patient consented to have performed on them.

(h) *Internal enquiry reports*. Where an internal enquiry has been held and the dominant purpose of that enquiry was not in contemplation of litigation, the enquiry notes will be discoverable.

(i) *Obstetric cases*. The following documents should also be supplied:
   (i) progress of labour cards;
   (ii) cardiotachograph (CTG) traces showing foetal contractions;
   (iii) partogram (showing labour in chart form);
   (iv) ante-natal records;
   (v) neo-natal records;
   (vi) paediatric notes.

Information that a solicitor may expect to receive from a GP will include the doctor's own notes, reports of any investigations requested by them, letters of referral to hospitals or consultants and any responses, letters from hospital regarding out-patient clinic attendances and treatment, and in-patient discharge summaries.

10.4.1.4 Examining the records

The solicitor should ensure (as far as possible) that the notes or records supplied to them are complete and are in chronological order, which will show the pattern of the disease or problem and its treatment, and may also highlight missing documents or records. Where the claimant's solicitor suspects that a document or documents may be missing, or where documents have been badly copied or are otherwise illegible, they should raise the issue with the records holder, since an incomplete set of records may distort the overall picture and thus give a false impression of the claim. It may be necessary to make an appointment with the GP or hospital to inspect the original documents. It is also helpful for the solicitor to go through the records with the client to ensure that the treatment shown on the records accords with the client's recollection of what actually occurred. The records should be supplied to the solicitor and not direct to the expert, so that the solicitor has an opportunity to check them through before instructing the expert to prepare their report.

10.4.2 Instructing an expert on liability and/or causation

In clinical negligence cases, it will be necessary to instruct one or more medical experts to consider the claimant's medical records and provide an opinion on matters relating to breach of duty and causation. Frequently, it will be appropriate to do this before the letter of claim is sent. In due course, other medical experts will deal with issues relating to quantum. Expert evidence is dealt with in **Chapter 11**.

10.5 EMPLOYERS' LIABILITY CLAIMS FOR DISEASE AND ILLNESS – PRELIMINARY STEPS

Disease and illness claims are very difficult to establish, particularly the so-called 'long-tail' claims, where the illness or disease manifests itself many years after exposure to the causative substance or working conditions (see **4.7**). It will not be possible for the claimant's solicitor to assess whether there is a claim with a reasonable chance of success until they have seen all relevant medical records and obtained the claimant's occupational records from the potential defendant, who will be either the claimant's current employer or a former employer. These notes will enable the claimant's solicitor to draw up a chronology of events and map the progress of the disease. They may need a medical expert to advise as to causation before the letter of claim is sent.

Medical records should be obtained as outlined in **10.4**.

10.5.1 Obtaining occupational records

In accordance with para 4 of the PAP for Disease and Illness Claims, the claimant's solicitor should write to the potential defendant, the client's employer or former employer, requesting the claimant's occupational records, including health and personnel records, before the letter of claim is sent. The DPA 2018 applies. Sufficient information should be given in the letter of request to alert the potential defendant or their insurer to the fact that a potential disease claim is being investigated. A specimen letter and request form to be used for this purpose are set out at Annexes A and A1 of the Protocol.

Records should be provided within a maximum of 40 days of the request, free of charge. The Protocol suggests that as a matter of good practice, the potential defendant should also disclose any product data documents which the claimant has requested which may resolve a causation issue. Where documents are not provided within 40 days and no information is forthcoming from the defendant to explain the reasons for the delay, the claimant should apply to the court for an order for pre-action disclosure (see **10.10.2**).

The claimant's solicitor should also seek to obtain relevant occupational records held by other bodies or individuals who have employed the claimant in the past.

10.6 LETTER OF NOTIFICATION

In many instances, the potential defendant will be aware of the possibility of a claim before the letter of claim is sent. Where this is not the case, the claimant's solicitor may wish to give the potential defendant early notification before they are in possession of sufficient information to enable them to send the letter of claim, as follows:

(a) Personal injury claims: In accordance with para 3.3 of the PAP for Personal Injury Claims, this will not start the clock ticking for the purposes of the time limit set for the defendant's response. However, the Letter of Notification should be acknowledged by the proposed defendant within 14 days of receipt.

(b) Clinical negligence cases: A template for the recommended contents is set out in Annex C1 to the PAP for the Resolution of Clinical Disputes. On receipt, the defendant should acknowledge receipt within 14 days, identify who will be dealing with the matter, and consider what investigations/preliminary steps need to be taken and what information could be passed to the claimant in order to narrow the issues or facilitate early resolution. In addition, a copy of the letter should be sent to NHS Resolution or any relevant medical defence organisation or indemnity provider.

10.7 LETTER OF CLAIM

10.7.1 Purpose

The purpose of the letter of claim is:

(a) to notify the likely defendant of the proposed claim and to set out sufficient information to enable him to assess liability and the likely size and heads of claim without necessarily addressing quantum in detail;

(b) to obtain details of the defendant's insurers (where not already known). In personal injury claims, the claimant must send two copies of the letter to the defendant with a request that one copy is forwarded to the defendant's insurers, which ensures that the insurers are involved at the earliest possible date. In clinical negligence cases against an NHS Trust, a copy of the letter of claim should be sent by the claimant to NHS Resolution; and

(c) to request access to relevant documents which the defendant might hold and which the claimant has not yet seen.

10.7.2 Contents

The precise wording contained in the three PAPs differs, and therefore reference to the relevant protocol should be made in order to determine precisely what the letter of claim should contain in each type of case. Each PAP has a specimen letter of claim set out in the Appendices, which should be followed, although the required detail will depend on the facts of each case. However, as a general approach, the letter should contain the following:

(a) a clear summary of the facts on which the claim is based;

(b) the main allegations of negligence/breach of statutory duty (and an outline of the causal link where this is likely to be in dispute);

(c) an indication of the nature of all of the injuries that have been sustained, including current condition and prognosis where relevant;

(d) an indication of other financial losses; and

(e) a request for early disclosure of relevant documentation held by the defendant. It is best practice for the claimant's solicitor to assist the defendant by identifying those documents which they believe are material (see **10.10.1**).

In the majority of cases, witness statements and the reports of experts would not be enclosed with the letter of claim. However, where the claimant's solicitor feels that such evidence demonstrates a very strong case on liability, they may decide that disclosure at this stage may lead to an admission of liability by the defendant.

The claimant's solicitor may make an offer to settle in the letter of claim, by setting out what their client would be willing to accept in full and final settlement of the matter. However, in many cases, a detailed investigation into quantum will not have been undertaken by the claimant's solicitor, and therefore an offer should not be made.

The letter of claim does not have the same status as a statement of case, and so the claimant will not be held to the content of the letter. Nevertheless, the claimant's solicitor should be as accurate as possible, in order to avoid credibility issues if the matter goes to trial.

10.8 CLAIMS NOTIFICATION FORM – LOW VALUE CLAIMS

Where a claim falls under one of the low value claims PAPs (see **10.2** above and **Chapter 21**), the claimant's solicitor commences the process by completing and sending the Claim Notification Form (CNF) to the defendant's insurer electronically through the Portal at www.claimsportal.org.uk and, in the case of EL or public liability (PL) claims, sending the Defendant Only CNF (DCNF) to the defendant electronically through the Portal. In EL or PL cases where it is not possible to serve the defendant electronically, and in RTA cases, the DCNF should be sent to the defendant by first class post at the same time as sending the CNF to the insurer, or as soon as practicable thereafter.

All boxes in the CNF and DCNF which are marked as mandatory must be completed, and a reasonable attempt made to complete those boxes which are not marked as mandatory. The statement of truth in the CNF must be signed by the claimant or the claimant's legal representative where the client has authorised the solicitor to do so and the representative can provide written evidence of that authorisation. Where the claimant is a child, the statement of truth may be signed by the parent or guardian. On the electronically completed CNF, the person may enter their name in the signature box to satisfy this requirement.

See Document 2 in **Appendix 1** for a completed CNF.

10.9 RESPONSE TO THE LETTER OF CLAIM OR CNF

10.9.1 Personal injury claims

In personal injury claims where the claim does not fall under one of the low value protocols or under the PAP for personal injury claims below the small claims limit in RTAs, the defendant has 21 calendar days of the date of the posting of the letter of claim to send a preliminary response to the claimant. In this letter, the defendant should identify their insurer, if any, and highlight any significant omissions from the letter of claim. If there is no reply from the defendant or the defendant's insurer within that period, the claimant is entitled to issue proceedings.

The defendant has three months from the date of acknowledging the claim to investigate the matter and provide a substantive response. Where the claim is denied, reasons for the denial and any alternative versions of events should be set out. Any documents material to the issues (which are not privileged from inspection) should be enclosed. The individual PAPs give further information as to what information should be included.

See Document 4 of the Case Study in **Appendix 1** for an example of a defendant's letter denying liability.

10.9.2 Clinical negligence claims

In clinical negligence claims, the defendant has less time to respond. The letter of claim must be acknowledged within 14 days of receipt and the person dealing with the matter should be identified. Where the claim is denied, full reasons for the denial should be provided within four months of the letter of claim. A template for the letter of response is at Annex C3 of the PAP for the resolution of clinical disputes (see **Appendix 4**).

10.9.3 Low value claims

Where one of the low value PAPs applies, the insurer must send to the claimant's solicitor an electronic acknowledgement of the CNF the day after its receipt. It must then complete the 'Insurer Response' section of the CNF and send it to the claimant within 15 business days of the acknowledgment in the case of RTAs and 30 days in the case of EL and PL cases. Where the defendant denies liability, brief reasons must be given.

If the insurer fails to respond within this time limit, denies liability, alleges contributory negligence (other than failure to wear a seatbelt in a RTA) or states that the information in the CNF is inadequate, the claim exits the low value PAP and continues in accordance with the relevant non-low value PAP. In accordance with para 5.5 of the PAP for Personal Injury Claims, where this happens, the CNF can be used as a letter of claim, unless the defendant notifies the claimant that there is inadequate information on the CNF. The insurer/defendant then has 30 days from the date of acknowledgment of the claim to investigate the matter and serve a full response on the claimant.

10.10 ACQUIRING EVIDENCE IN RESPECT OF LIABILITY

Although the claimant's solicitor will have obtained sufficient evidence to justify the dispatch of the CNF or letter of claim, where the defendant denies liability, they will need to obtain further evidence in order to ensure that liability can be proved at trial, if need be.

10.10.1 Documents held by the defendant

The claimant's solicitor will have no difficulties in obtaining documents which are in the possession of their client, or documents to which the public have access. However, many of the documents which will give real insight into the causes of the accident will be in the possession of the proposed defendant.

The PAPs are designed to encourage parties to have an open-handed approach to litigation, and this requires each party to allow the other to see relevant documents at an early stage. In clinical negligence claims and in occupational disease and illness claims, the relevant PAPs envisage that the claimant will obtain medical records or occupational health records prior to the sending of the letter of claim (see **10.4** and **10.5**). In all other cases, where the defendant denies liability, the defendant should enclose with their letter of reply copies of all documents in their possession which are material to the issues between the parties and which would be likely to be ordered to be disclosed by the court, either on an application for pre-action disclosure or on disclosure during proceedings. In clinical negligence and occupational disease and illness claims, the defendant should disclose any relevant documents they have not yet disclosed.

10.10.1.1 Documents relevant to personal injury claims

Annex C to the PAP for personal injury claims contains lists of documents which are likely to be in the defendant's possession in various types of claim, and in the letter of claim the claimant's solicitor should set out which documents they require, should liability not be admitted. However, Annex C does not provide an exhaustive list of what the defendant may have and there might be other relevant documents, including, for example, minutes of meetings, memorandums between in-house departments or individuals, and reports. With experience, the personal injury solicitor will obtain an understanding of the types of documents which might be available in certain circumstances, but the claimant's solicitor should always listen carefully to what their client and other witnesses have to say, as they may know of the existence of documentation without understanding its relevance.

It is important to remember that, for the purpose of disclosure, the term 'document' is not restricted to written documents but includes anything in which information of any description is recorded. It therefore includes audiotapes, videotapes, photographs and electronic documents such as e-mails. Footage from CCTV cameras is becoming increasingly available, and in workplace claims, it is possible that the employer had installed a CCTV camera in, for example, a factory, warehouse or supermarket, which has captured images of the accident.

10.10.1.2 Documents relevant to employer liability claims

A list of documents which the defendant employer may be expected to have following an accident at work are set out in Annex C to the PAP for personal injury claims. However, the following documents may require an explanation:

(a) *The Accident Book*. Under the Reporting of Injuries, Diseases and Dangerous Occurrences Regulations 2013 (RIDDOR 2013), employers are required to keep an accident book of an approved type where details of all accidents that occur on the premises must be recorded. The claimant's solicitor should not only ask the employer for a copy of the relevant page from the accident book, but should also consider whether the book itself should be inspected for evidence of similar incidents in the past.

See Document 5 of the Case Study in **Appendix 1** for an example of a report from an employer's accident book.

(b) *RIDDOR report to the HSE*. Employers are required to report certain classes of injury or disease sustained by people at work and specified dangerous occurrences. The RIDDOR 2013 require the responsible person (ie the safety officer/manager) to inform the HSE electronically, and to follow it up with written confirmation within 10 days. The defendant should retain a copy of the report in its files.

The reportable occurrences include:

(i)   the death of any person;

(ii)   any person suffering a specified major injury;

(iii)   any person suffering an injury which is not major but which results in the person being away from work or unable to do the full range of their normal duties for more than seven days;

(iv)   any person suffering from a work-related disease;

(v)   where there has been a dangerous occurrence. Dangerous occurrences are listed in Sch 2 to RIDDOR 2013 and include such things as dangerous occurrences involving overhead electric lines, biological agents and radiation generators, as well as occurrences in mines, at quarries, on the railways and at off-shore installations.

See Document 6 of the Case Study in **Appendix 1** for an example of a report to the HSE – RIDDOR.

10.10.2 Application for pre-action disclosure and inspection

Where the claimant's solicitor believes the proposed defendant has relevant documentation which the proposed defendant has not disclosed in compliance with the protocol, and the proposed defendant has failed to respond to written requests to do so, an application for disclosure prior to the start of proceedings can be made under s 33 of the Senior Courts Act 1981 or s 52 of the County Courts Act 1984. The application must be supported by appropriate evidence, and the procedure is the same in both the High Court and county court. Under r 31.16, the court may make an order for disclosure only where:

(a)   the respondent is likely to be a party to subsequent proceedings;

(b)   the applicant is also likely to be a party to the proceedings;

(c)   if proceedings had started, the respondent's duty by way of standard disclosure, set out in rule 31.16, would extend to the documents or classes of documents of which the applicant seeks disclosure; and

(d)   disclosure before proceedings have started is desirable in order to—

(i)   dispose fairly of the anticipated proceedings; or

(ii)   assist the dispute to be resolved without proceedings; or

(iii)   save costs.

An order under r 31.16 will specify the documents or class of documents which the respondent must disclose and require the respondent, when making such disclosure, to specify any of those documents which the respondent no longer has, or which the respondent claims the right or duty to withhold from inspection. The order may also specify the time and place for disclosure and inspection to take place.

10.10.3 Documents held by third parties

Relevant documents may also be held by third parties. In some instances, for example where documents are held by the police or the HSE, the claimant's solicitor will generally be able to obtain copies, although they may be frustrated by the delay. Where documents contain the claimant's personal data, for example occupational records held by someone other than the proposed defendant, the claimant is entitled to see them under the DPA 2018.

In other cases, where a third party holds documents and it is under no statutory obligation to disclose them, the claimant's solicitor should make a polite request, offering to pay all the reasonable costs associated with providing access to or copies of the documents. If the third party refuses to cooperate, generally the claimant's solicitor cannot apply to the court for an order of disclosure and inspection until proceedings have commenced (see CPR, r 31.17). The court does have an equitable power to make a pre-action order for disclosure against third parties, but this will be exercised only in rare circumstances, a consideration of which lies beyond the scope of this book.

10.10.3.1 Documents relevant to RTAs – the police accident report

In the case of a road traffic incident, it may be useful to obtain a copy of the police accident report (PAR), if one exists. Some police forces use different terminology, eg 'collision report'. The following should be borne in mind:

(a)   The PAR will contain statements from the parties and a sketch plan, as well as the police officer's comments on the condition of the vehicles, the road surface, the weather conditions and details of any criminal proceedings that have been commenced as a result of the accident. It may also include photographs and witness statements. Some PARs contain more useful information than others and, bearing in mind that a fee will be payable, it may be advisable to ask what the PAR does contain before seeking to obtain a copy.

(b)   In order to obtain a copy of the PAR, the solicitor should contact the accident records department at the police force headquarters for the area in which the accident occurred (not the police officer assigned to the case). The letter should include details of the date, time and place of the accident, the registration numbers of the vehicles and the full names of those involved.

(c)   The PAR will not be released until the conclusion of any criminal investigation and proceedings. If the defendant is convicted of an offence which is relevant to the issue of negligence, it is likely that the defendant (or more likely the defendant's insurers) will want to settle the proceedings, and therefore it will not be necessary to obtain a copy of the PAR.

(d)   A fee is payable for the PAR. The amount of the fee varies, depending upon the relevant police force, the length and nature of the report and the type of accident.

(e)   On payment of a further fee, the police officer who prepared the PAR may be interviewed, in the presence of a senior officer. (If the matter goes to trial, police officers will give evidence in civil proceedings, but they must be witness summonsed and a further fee will be payable.)

(f)   If there is no PAR, it is still possible to obtain copies of police notebooks and witness statements on payment of a fee. Because reports may be destroyed (in some cases after as little as one year), a request for a report should be made promptly, notwithstanding that the report will not actually be released until the conclusion of criminal investigations.

10.10.3.2 Documents relevant to work-based claims – HSE reports

Health and Safety Executive reports are the equivalent of police reports in the field of industrial incidents. Generally, the same rules apply as with police reports, although, due to lack of resources, a report may only be available in the case of very serious injury or death.

The HSE officer responsible for the factory or workplace concerned should be approached with a request for a copy of their report. As with the PAR, the HSE report will not be available until after any criminal prosecution has been dealt with. If the HSE is unwilling to provide a copy of its report voluntarily, it may be necessary to wait until after proceedings have been commenced and then make an application for non-party disclosure.

The HSE will also have other relevant documentation, such as the RIDDOR and correspondence with the defendant regarding the incident. However, the defendant should have a copy of these documents in its own files and may possibly have a copy of the HSE report. All these documents should be disclosed to the claimant with other relevant documents it holds.

10.10.4   Real evidence

Real evidence is a material object, such as a piece of machinery, an article of personal protective clothing, etc, which is relevant to the issues of the case. Where it is practicable for the item to be produced at court, the claimant's solicitor should take appropriate steps to obtain the item, instruct an expert to examine it where necessary, and then put it into safe-keeping until it is required. If it is impracticable for an item (eg a large piece of machinery) to be produced at court, photographs should be taken.

10.10.5   Photographs and sketch plans of the location of the accident

In road traffic cases, it is usually necessary to produce photographs and sketch plans of the location of the accident for two reasons. First, the layout of the road may change between the date of accident and the date of trial, and/or the road may appear different depending on whether it is photographed in summer or in winter, especially if there are lots of trees or vegetation which could obscure a driver's view. Secondly, it may be necessary to try to show the location from the perspective of the car drivers at the time. An aerial view or plan of a road junction will do nothing, for example, to prove to a court how badly the approach of a vehicle was obscured by trees and bushes or roadside property. The solicitor should not lose sight of the fact that they must be able to prove to the court what could or could not be seen from a particular vantage point. It is open to the court to visit the site of the accident, but this may not be practicable, and in any event, it would take an inordinate amount of time. The solicitor should always visit the site if possible, in order to get a feel for the case.

Police accident reports (see **10.10.3.1**) often contain good quality photographs which can be purchased on payment of an extra fee per print, and which may prove helpful in showing not only the severity and location of the damage to each vehicle, but also the final position on the road in which the vehicles were immediately following the accident. This evidence may assume significance at a later date, or may contradict the oral evidence of the witnesses. It is, however, important to read the PAR closely, as it will confirm whether or not the vehicles were moved from their original resting position prior to the taking of the photographs.

In road traffic cases, the photographer should mark on a plan the precise location from which each photograph was taken and the direction in which the camera was pointing.

Site visits in non-road traffic cases are no less important. For example, in a case where the client has tripped on a broken pavement, it is not uncommon for the local authority, upon receiving intimation of a possible claim, to send a team of operatives to mend the offending paving stone. It is therefore vitally important to secure good quality photographs of the pavement, etc as soon as possible, usually on the same day that the client is interviewed. Photographs must contain some indication of scale, and it is therefore necessary to place an item, such as a ruler, within the photograph.

In modern times, the availability of mobile telephones with inbuilt cameras means that claimants or their friends or family members may have taken relevant photographs of the site at or about the time of the accident. Whilst such photographs may have some use, particularly in low-value cases, it is not good practice to entrust the taking of photographs to the client, who may underestimate the importance of the task and forget about it until it is too late. Photographs taken by the client may be out of focus, underexposed or otherwise taken in a manner which will not help the client's case. A good example of this can be found in *Flynn v Leeds City Council*, 10 September 2004, where the claimant was injured when she tripped on the edge of an uneven paving stone. She claimed that the discrepancy between the heights of the paving stones was over an inch and that the pavement was therefore dangerous to pedestrians. Photographs of the paving stones, with the alleged discrepancy highlighted by the presence of a 50 pence piece and a ruler, had been taken by the claimant's partner, who happened to be a litigation solicitor. The defendant claimed that these photographs appeared to have been 'massaged slightly'. The judge did not feel that anything sinister was being suggested, but he accepted that the 50 pence piece appeared to be leaning at an angle and that there may have been some slight excavation of material between the paving stones. The claimant failed to prove that the discrepancy between the paving stones was a dangerous one and the judge found in favour of the defendant.

10.10.6 Evidence of criminal convictions

If the proposed defendant is charged with a criminal offence in relation to the incident which caused the injury to the claimant, ideally the claimant's solicitor should attend the proceedings to note the evidence. The date of the proceedings may be obtained from the police or the HSE, as appropriate.

Any resulting conviction of the defendant which is relevant to the issues in civil proceedings (ie relevant when seeking to prove or disprove negligence or breach of statutory duty) may be referred to in the civil proceedings (Civil Evidence Act 1968, s 11). In an RTA claim, for example, a conviction for speeding or dangerous driving arising out of the incident itself is a relevant conviction. However, a conviction for driving without insurance at the time of the accident, or a previous conviction for driving with excess alcohol in the blood, is not a relevant conviction, as it does not prove that the defendant was negligent at the time of the accident.

For the purposes of the civil proceedings, the defendant will be taken to have committed the offence 'unless the contrary is proved'. The defendant may seek to argue that they should not have been convicted, but if they do so, the burden of proving this on the balance of probabilities will pass to the defendant. In most cases where there is a relevant conviction, the defendant will seek to settle the matter.

Where a claimant is convicted for failing to wear a safety belt or a safety helmet, the conviction is relevant to the issue of damages as it indicates contributory negligence.

Should the matter go to trial, the party seeking to rely on the conviction will need to produce a certificate from the convicting court in order to prove the conviction.

10.10.7 Evidence of lay witnesses

Witnesses should be contacted and interviewed by the claimant's solicitor as soon as possible. The defendant's solicitor, in the normal course of events, will be instructed at a later date than the claimant's solicitor, but they too should contact and interview witnesses without delay. Where a witness is not interviewed at an early stage, their memory of the events may fade or they may become untraceable. If the claimant was injured at work and the witness is a fellow employee of the claimant, the witness may be concerned about their employer's reaction and become increasingly reluctant to speak to the claimant's solicitor. Witnesses to road incidents are often initially enthusiastic, but later decide that they have little to gain and would rather not get involved. For this reason, the solicitor should not delay in contacting the witness and obtaining a proof of evidence, or at the very least a letter confirming what the witness saw and/or heard and that they are prepared to make a statement to that effect.

In a straightforward case, it may not be necessary to interview the witness. If their letter of response is sufficiently clear, a proof can be prepared from it and from any questionnaire the witness may also have been sent. A copy of the proof should be forwarded for approval and signature by the witness. This should be accompanied by a stamped addressed envelope and covering letter, requesting the witness to read the proof carefully and make any amendments or additions that the witness feels to be necessary before signing and dating the document for return in the envelope provided. The witness is a volunteer to the client's cause and should be thanked accordingly for the time and trouble taken on the client's behalf.

The proof of evidence, once converted into a formal witness statement and exchanged with the other side, will form the basis of the witness's evidence to be relied on at trial and will stand as the evidence-in-chief of that witness. Furthermore, the statement may have to be used at the trial under the Civil Evidence Act 1995 if the witness subsequently becomes unavailable. Consequently, it should contain all the relevant evidence the witness can give and, needless to say, it should be the truth. In accordance with r 22.1 of the CPR, the witness statement must conclude with a statement of truth, and this must be signed by the witness themselves.

In an EL case, it may be advisable for the claimant's solicitor to obtain statements from individuals, such as shop stewards or co-workers, who, although they may not have seen the accident, may know of other similar accidents in the past, or be able to give background information on policy changes that may have taken place within the organisation. In road incident or tripping cases, people living or working adjacent to the location of the incident may be able to give useful information relating to similar incidents that have happened in the past, and even as to the identities of past claimants in similar incidents, or information on how long the defect has been in existence.

10.10.8 Expert evidence

Almost all cases will involve some expert evidence. There may be a requirement for non-medical experts, such as engineers or RTA reconstruction experts, but most experts will be from the medical field. In clinical injury cases, experts will be required in respect of liability, causation and quantum. In most personal injury cases, the evidence of a medical expert will relate to quantum rather than liability, although there will be some cases where a medical opinion in relation to causation will be required, for example where the claimant has suffered a disease or illness. Consequently, the claimant's solicitor will not normally seek to obtain a report from a medical expert until they are satisfied that the claimant has a strong case on liability, or liability has been admitted by the defendant. See **Chapter 11** for a detailed consideration of the role of experts.

10.11 ACQUIRING EVIDENCE IN RESPECT OF QUANTUM

10.11.1 Evidence of lost earnings

The client's loss of earnings is likely to form a significant part of the claim for special damages. See **Chapter 15** for a detailed consideration of this point.

10.11.1.1 Obtaining details from employers

In an EL claim against the claimant's current employer, a request for details of the claimant's earnings should be set out in the letter of claim. In other cases, the claimant's solicitor should write to the client's employer to ask for details of earnings for 13 weeks prior to the incident and for a copy of the client's contract of employment. The loss of earnings details should be set out to show weekly earnings (both gross and net) so as to reveal a pattern over 13 weeks.

10.11.1.2 Self-employed clients

Documentary evidence in the form of the client's previous year's trading accounts (or longer if appropriate) should be obtained if possible, together with other evidence of contracts or offers of work that had to be turned down as a result of the incident. The client's accountant, business associates and colleagues in the same area of work should be approached to assist in this.

10.11.1.3 Unemployed clients

Even if the client is unemployed, evidence should be obtained of the claimant's last employer and of the likelihood of the claimant obtaining suitable work which the claimant could have undertaken but for the accident, as evidence of earning capacity. Colleagues in the same area of business and employment agencies should be approached for evidence of availability of work within the client's specialism and the level of possible earnings.

10.11.2 Evidence of other special damages

During the first interview with the client, the claimant's solicitor should ask the claimant to keep details of any articles damaged in the accident, repair costs, private medical treatment, journeys to hospital, parking tickets, etc which have resulted from the accident, and to retain any relevant quotes, invoices, receipts or tickets. Where the defendant admits liability, or where the court finds in favour of the claimant, many of these items will be admitted by the defendant, provided evidence is produced.

10.11.3 Evidence of pain, suffering and loss of amenity

10.11.3.1 Medical records

It may be necessary to obtain copies of the claimant's medical records from the claimant's GP and/or from a hospital where the claimant was treated (see **10.4.1**) in order to prove the extent of the claimant's suffering and, if necessary, disprove that any pre-existing condition contributed to the injuries suffered by the claimant.

10.11.3.2 Medical experts

Medical experts provide crucial evidence for the assessment of general damages for pain, suffering and loss of amenity. In a fairly straightforward case, one medical expert of an appropriate specialisation will be able to deal with all aspects of liability and quantum in their report. In more complex cases, such as where the claimant has suffered major brain trauma, several experts might be required, including, for example, a neurologist, a neuropsychologist, an occupational therapist, and an expert on the need for care and general support.

10.11.3.3 Lay witnesses

The claimant's own testimony is important. During the first interview, the claimant's solicitor should ask their client to keep a pain diary. The claimant should set out the extent of their suffering and its effect on the claimant's life in their witness statement.

The evidence of members of the claimant's family, friends and work colleagues may also provide a valuable insight into the impact of the accident.

10.11.3.4 Photographs

Photographs of the injuries immediately after the accident, during the various stages of recovery and as at the date of trial, where they are continuing, are also very useful.

10.12 CONCLUSION

The claimant's solicitor is obliged, under the overriding objective found in r 1 of the CPR and under the PAPs, to be fully prepared before proceedings are commenced. Once proceedings have been issued, the court will actively manage the case and will require the parties to deal with each step of the proceedings in accordance with the timetable it lays down in the order for directions. Where a solicitor fails to prepare adequately prior to issue and consequently is unable to comply with the directions within the specified time limits, the court may impose cost penalties.

The essential element when gathering evidence at the preliminary stage is to act quickly. A failure to act on the client's instructions as soon as they are received can have disastrous consequences for the subsequent conduct of the litigation. In extreme cases, this may seriously prejudice the client's chances of success and can amount to negligence on the part of the solicitor.

INSTRUCTING EXPERTS

LEARNING OUTCOMES

After reading this chapter you will be able to:

- understand the role of experts in personal injury and clinical negligence cases

- appreciate the different types of expert who might be instructed

- explain the expert's overriding duty to the court and the court's case management powers in relation to experts

- write a letter of instruction to an expert.

11.1 INTRODUCTION

In almost every personal injury or clinical negligence case, the claimant's solicitor will instruct at least one medical expert. Commonly, an expert will prepare a report on the claimant's injuries for quantum purposes, which is often referred to as a report on condition and prognosis. In clinical negligence and disease and illness claims, medical evidence will not only be required in order to assist the court in assessing damages, but will also be necessary in order to prove liability and/or causation. Indeed, the claimant's solicitor may be unable to understand precisely what happened to the claimant, and therefore advise the claimant in relation to the claim, until such evidence has been obtained. In some personal injury cases, other types of experts, such as accident reconstruction experts or engineers, may be required for liability purposes.

The purpose of this chapter is to examine the role of experts and the matters that must be considered when instructing an expert in a personal injury or clinical negligence case.

With regard to the procedural law, the practitioner must have a sound grasp of CPR Part 35 and the accompanying Practice Direction, which govern the use of experts in civil trials. In addition, the Guidance for the Instruction of Experts in Civil Claims 2014 (the 'Guidance') provides guidance on the interpretation of and compliance with Part 35 and PD 35 in the interests of good practice.

11.1.1   Who is an expert?

An expert is an individual with a high level of skill, knowledge and experience in a particular area which is outside the knowledge of the court. The expert will be permitted to give their opinion when the court would otherwise be unable properly to understand the factual evidence which has been placed before it and requires the expert's assistance in order to determine a matter of dispute between the parties. This evidence should be presented in a clear and concise way so that the court can use the information to reach its own conclusions.

The court is not obliged to accept the evidence of an expert. In *Armstrong and Another v First York Ltd* [2005] EWCA Civ 277, the Court of Appeal held that the trial judge had been entitled to reject the evidence of a forensic motor vehicle engineer who had been jointly instructed by the parties. The two claimants had allegedly sustained neck and spinal injuries when their car had been hit by a bus owned by the defendant. The expert's evidence was that there had been insufficient force generated by the impact to cause the injuries claimed. Although the trial judge found that the expert's evidence had been flawless, this could not be reconciled with his belief that the claimants were credible and honest witnesses. Consequently, he was entitled to find that there must have been a flaw in the expert's evidence, even though he had not been able to identify that flaw. In the Court of Appeal case of *Huntley v Simmons* [2010] EWCA Civ 54, Waller LJ stated that:

> the evidence of experts is important evidence but it is nevertheless only evidence which the judge must assess with all other evidence. Ultimately issues of fact and assessment are for the judge. Of course if there is no evidence to contradict the evidence of experts it will need very good reason for the judge not to accept it and he must not take on the role of expert so as to, in effect, give evidence himself. So far as Joint Statements are concerned parties can agree the evidence but (as happened in this case) it can be agreed that the joint statements can be put in evidence without the need to call the two experts simply because they do not disagree; but either party is entitled to make clear that the opinion expressed in the joint statement is simply evidence that must be assessed as part of all the evidence.

In *Stewart v Glaze* [2009] EWHC 704 (QB), the judge said that although the expert could be of considerable assistance, it was the primary factual evidence which was of the greatest importance, and that expert evidence should not be elevated into a fixed framework or formula against which the defendant's actions were to be judged rigidly with mathematical precision.

11.1.2   The expert's overriding duty to the court

Rule 35.3 of the CPR states that it is the duty of experts to help the court on matters within their expertise, and that this duty overrides any obligation to the person from whom experts have received instructions or by whom they are paid.

Paragraph 2 of PD 35 gives the following guidance as to the nature of that duty:

2.1   Expert evidence should be the independent product of the expert uninfluenced by the pressures of litigation.

2.2   Experts should assist the court by providing objective, unbiased opinion on matters within their expertise, and should not assume the role of an advocate.

2.3   Experts should consider all material facts, including those which might detract from their opinions.

2.4   Experts should make it clear:

(a)   when a question or issue falls outside their expertise; and

(b)   when they are not able to reach a definite opinion, for example because they have insufficient information.

2.5   If, after producing a report, an expert changes his view on any material matter, such change of view should be communicated to all the parties without delay, and when appropriate to the court.

Paragraphs 9 to 15 of the Guidance set out further guidance on the duties and obligations of experts. In particular, para 10 provides that experts are under an obligation to assist the court in dealing with cases in accordance with the overriding objective set out in r 1 of the CPR.

Paragraph 11 of the Guidance offers a test for independence as being, 'Would the expert express the same opinion if given the same instructions by an opposing party?', and goes on to say that experts should not take it upon themselves to promote the point of view of the party instructing them or engage in the role of advocates or mediators.

In accordance with para 3.1 of PD 35, the expert's report should be addressed to the court and not to the party from whom the expert has received instructions.

The case of *EXP v Barker* [2017] EWCA Civ 63 serves as a useful reminder of the importance of the independence and impartiality of expert evidence. The claimant brought a claim against Dr Barker, a neuroradiologist, alleging that he had negligently failed to identify and report a cerebral artery aneurysm following an earlier MRI scan. The issue for the trial judge was whether the MRI scan did indicate the presence of an aneurysm which a reasonably competent neuroradiologist would have identified and reported.

Both parties called expert evidence on the issue. It became apparent during cross-examination that the connection between Dr Barker and his expert Dr Molyneux had been 'lengthy and extensive':

> Dr Molyneux had trained Dr Barker during his seven years of specialist radiology training, and in particular had trained him for two and a half years as a registrar and senior registrar in neuroradiology, including the particular area of interventional radiology in which Dr Molyneux specialised and in which Dr Barker had a special interest. It is clear that they had worked together closely over a substantial period. They had written together a paper for the 14th International Symposium on radiology, ... and Dr Molyneux told the Court that they might have co-operated on other papers which he could no longer specifically recall. Dr Molyneux helped Dr Barker to obtain foreign placements ... Dr Barker accepted that Dr Molyneux had guided and inspired his practice, and Dr Molyneux had helped Dr Barker become a consultant in Southampton. They had also been officers together on the committee of the British Society of Radiologists, Dr Barker having been Treasurer at the time when Dr Molyneux, being a committee member, was nominated President.

The claimant's application to have the evidence of Dr Molyneux excluded failed but, in giving judgment for the claimant, the judge stated:

> Where the core issue in a case turns, as it does here, on the court's ability to evaluate the competing and finely balanced medical judgements of rival experts, the court's confidence in the independence and impartiality of the respective experts must play an important role. I have to say, with considerable regret, that by reason of the matters set out earlier in this judgment my confidence in Dr Molyneux's independence and objectivity has been very substantially undermined. On the other hand I have complete confidence in the independence and objectivity of Dr Butler, and I much prefer to accept his judgement ...

The defendant's appeal was dismissed. The Court of Appeal held that the judge had been entitled to take the view that the weight to be attached to Dr Molyneux's evidence was considerably diminished, and indeed would have been justified in excluding it altogether.

11.2 CASE MANAGEMENT AND THE USE OF EXPERTS

11.2.1 General principles

Rule 35.1 states that expert evidence should be 'restricted to that which is reasonably required to resolve the proceedings', and solicitors should be mindful that the court's permission is required before a party may call an expert or put in evidence an expert's report (CPR, r 35.4(1)). In determining whether a party should be entitled to use an expert, the court will be governed by the overriding objective found in r 1 of the CPR, in particular ensuring that the parties are on an equal footing, saving expense and dealing with the case in ways which are proportionate.

Specific new rules apply to whiplash claims under the RTA Low Value Protocol and are set out in **Chapter 21**, which also discusses the recent additional new rules that apply to whiplash claims as a result of the Civil Liability Act 2018 and the Whiplash Injury Regulations 2021 (SI 2021/642). For all other types of claim, the following should be noted:

(a)   Generally, permission will be sought in the directions questionnaire. When permission is sought, parties must provide an estimate of the costs of the proposed expert evidence and identify the field in which expert evidence is required, the issues the expert will address and, where practicable, the name of the proposed expert (CPR, r 35.4(2)). Where permission is granted, it shall be in relation only to the expert named or the field identified, and the issues which may be addressed may also be specified. Where a claim has been allocated to the small claims track or the fast track, permission will normally be given for evidence from only one expert on a particular issue (CPR, r 35.4(3A)). If necessary, further directions relating to the use of experts may be given on listing or upon the application of a party.

(b)   Usually, the claimant's solicitor will be obliged to instruct an expert before permission is given by the court for the use of that expert. In clinical negligence and disease and illness claims, it will be necessary for the claimant's solicitor to instruct an expert in order to advise in relation to liability and/or causation before the letter of claim is sent and, in almost all cases, a medical report will be attached to the particulars of claim. This is well understood by the court, and there is unlikely to be a problem in obtaining permission for the use of such an expert. Solicitors instructed by both claimants and defendants should give careful consideration as to whether it is necessary to instruct any other expert prior to permission being given. The court may decide that expert evidence is not required at all, or may determine that a single joint expert should be used. The client should be informed of the risks of instructing an expert before permission has been given, ie that the client may not be permitted to use the expert's evidence and costs relating to that expert will not be recoverable even where the client is successful in the claim.

(c)   The PAP for Personal Injury Claims encourages the joint selection of experts, mostly medical experts for quantum purposes but also experts dealing with liability, where appropriate (PAP, para 7.2). In accordance with para 7.3, before a party instructs an expert, they must provide their opponent with a list of one or more experts whom the party considers to be suitable for the case. In many cases, the claimant's solicitor will do this in the letter of claim and three names are usually supplied. The defendant then has 14 days within which to communicate any objections they have to any expert appearing on the list, and the claimant's solicitor is thereby able to select a mutually acceptable expert. The expert is instructed only by the claimant's solicitor (and in this respect, joint selection differs from joint instruction as envisaged by CPR, r 35.7 – see (d) below), but there is a presumption in fast-track cases that the defendant will not be permitted to instruct their own expert in relation to that issue. Where the defendant objects to all the experts suggested by the claimant, the defendant may instruct their own expert. However, if the matter proceeds, the court will consider whether the defendant acted reasonably in this regard.

In *Edwards-Tubb v JD Wetherspoon Plc* [2011] EWCA Civ 136, the claimant, Mr Edwards-Tubb, brought a claim arising out of a fall at work in October 2005. His employer, JD Wetherspoon, accepted liability. The issue related to damages and causation.

The claimant in the pre-action letter of claim gave notice to the defendant of three medical experts he wished to instruct. The defendant raised no objection and the claimant obtained a report from one of those experts, Mr Jackson. It was accepted that this was not a joint instruction and the report would remain privileged unless and until disclosed.

Proceedings were issued close to limitation. Shortly before service, the claimant disclosed a medical report from a Mr Khan, who was not originally nominated. The defendant sought an order that disclosure of the original report by Mr Jackson should be made a condition of the permission which the claimant needed to rely on Mr Khan.

The main issue before the Court of Appeal was whether the Court's power to impose a condition on the permission granted to rely on a particular expert could be utilised to require the disclosure of another expert report. The Court concluded that, before the claimant could rely on the second expert report, the claimant should disclose the findings of the first expert report.

The Court was mindful of exercising its power under CPR, r 35.4 so as to discourage 'expert shopping'. In the circumstances of the case, expert A had been instructed for the purposes of the litigation. A factor which held significant weight for the Court of Appeal was that the parties had embarked upon the pre-action protocol procedure of co-operation in the selection of experts. This is not something which is generally undertaken under the pre-action protocol for the resolution of clinical disputes, and it remains to be seen whether the Court would impose such a condition upon a request for leave to rely upon a particular expert where there has been no pre-action discussion in relation to the instruction of experts.

(d)   Where the parties wish to submit expert evidence on a particular issue, the court has the power, under CPR, r 35.7, to direct that a single joint expert be used. See **11.2.2** below.

(e)   A party will be entitled to use the report or call the expert at trial only if the report has been disclosed to the other parties to the action in accordance with CPR, r 35.13, unless the court gives permission.

(f)   At trial, expert evidence is to be given by means of a written report unless the court gives permission for the expert to give oral evidence. In small claims and fast track cases, permission will be given for an expert to attend a hearing only if it is necessary in the interests of justice (CPR, r 35.5).

(g)   In accordance with para 11.1 of PD 35, at any stage in the proceedings the court may direct that some or all of the experts from like disciplines shall give their evidence concurrently. This is known as hot-tubbing and may include, for example, the judge inviting the experts, in turn, to give their views, or the judge questioning one witness and then asking the other witness to comment on the answers given.

11.2.2 The single joint expert

A 'single joint expert' is defined in CPR, r 35.2(2) as an expert instructed to prepare a report for the court on behalf of two or more parties (including the claimant) to the proceedings. Under CPR, r 35.7, where two or more parties wish to submit expert evidence on a particular issue, the court may direct that the evidence on that issue be given by a single joint expert. In fast track cases, the court is likely to direct that a single joint expert be used unless there is good reason not to do so (PD 28, para 3.9(4)). Similar wording is used in PD 29, para 4.10(4) in relation to multi-track cases, but the insertion of the words 'on any appropriate issue' reflects the reality that there will be more issues in a multi-track case which will not be suitable for a single joint expert to determine. Paragraph 35 of the Guidance provides that, in the early stages of a dispute, when investigations, tests, site inspections, photographs, plans or other preliminary expert tasks are necessary, consideration should be given to the instruction of a single joint expert, especially where such matters are not expected to be contentious. Generally, single joint experts are more likely to be used to determine issues in relation to quantum than issues relating to liability or causation. In clinical negligence and illness and disease cases, it is recognised that single joint experts are less likely to be acceptable to the parties, and the pre-action protocols state that the courts are less prescriptive as to the use of experts in these types of claim.

Where the parties are unable to agree who the single joint expert should be, the court may select an expert from a list provided by the parties, or direct how the expert should be selected (CPR, 35.7(2)). Paragraph 38 of the Guidance requires parties to try to agree instructions to single joint experts, but allows for each party to give instructions in default of such an agreement. Where each party gives instructions to the expert, they should supply a copy of those instructions to the other side (CPR, r 35.8). Unless the court otherwise directs, the instructing parties are jointly and severally liable for the expert's fees and expenses.

11.2.3   Directions relating to the use of experts

In fast track cases, standard directions given on allocation in relation to expert evidence will order the use of the written report of a single joint expert or, where permission is given for the parties to use their own experts, order the disclosure of experts' reports by way of simultaneous exchange (usually within 14 weeks of allocation). Where the reports are not agreed, a discussion between the experts in accordance with CPR, r 35.12(1) and the preparation of a report under r 35.12(3) (PD 28, para 3.9) are required. In addition, the court may direct that a party put written questions to an expert instructed by another party or to a single joint expert about the expert's report (CPR, r 35.6). Bearing in mind the tight timetable between allocation and trial (30 weeks), little time will be available for these steps.

Directions in multi-track cases are tailored to the requirements of each individual case and are likely to be more complex. Where the parties are permitted to use their own experts on any issue, typical directions will include:

(a)   exchange of reports, either simultaneously or sequentially;

(b)   the service of written questions to the experts and the service of answers;

(c)   the agreement of expert reports where possible;

(d)   where agreement is not possible, a without prejudice meetings between the experts in order to try to resolve the matters upon which they are unable to agree, and the subsequent filing of a report setting out the points upon which they agree and disagree;

(e)   permission for the experts to give oral evidence at trial or that the reports shall stand as evidence.

The time allowed for each step outlined above will be dependent upon the complexities of the individual case and, in some cases, the availability of the experts themselves.

11.3   AREAS OF EXPERTISE

The number and variety of experts available to prepare reports are often surprising to those unfamiliar with this area. The following are examples of experts who provide reports.

11.3.1   Medical experts

Medical experts are usually required in order to assist the court in relation to the assessment of damages. In other words, they will report on the condition and prognosis of the claimant and the cost of living with the particular injury suffered by the claimant. In a simple, low-value case, a report from a general practitioner may be sufficient, but in a complex, high-value case, experts in several areas of medical expertise may be required. The types of medical experts who may assist in this regard are numerous, but may include doctors of various specialities, occupational therapists, behavioural therapists, speech therapists and physiotherapists.

In clinical negligence cases, it will be necessary to instruct an expert to advise in relation to liability and possibly causation. A consultant should be instructed with expertise in the same speciality as the doctor who is alleged to have been negligent.

A list of the most common areas of medical expertise can be found at **2.3**.

11.3.2 Other experts

In road traffic accidents, the following types of experts may be helpful in order to establish liability:

(a)   accident investigators to reconstruct the events leading up to the road traffic accident;

(b)   mechanical engineers to examine the vehicles involved in the accident, to identify damage or to investigate if any mechanical defects were present in the vehicle.

In employers' liability cases, the following types of experts may be helpful to establish liability:

(a)   general consulting engineers to provide reports on machinery, systems of work, slipping accidents;

(b)   mining engineers;

(c)   ergonomics experts;

(d)   bio-engineers;

(e)   pharmacologists.

When dealing with quantum, in addition to doctors of the appropriate speciality, the following experts may be useful in relation to condition and prognosis and the costs of living with a particular injury:

(a)   occupational therapists;

(b)   behavioural therapists;

(c)   speech therapists;

(d)   physiotherapists;

(e)   employment consultants.

When dealing with quantum, the following experts may be useful in relation to financial loss and the investment of damages:

(a)   employment consultants;

(b)   accountants;

(c)   actuaries.

11.3.3 Specific experts

The following types of experts warrant further attention.

11.3.3.1 Accident reconstruction experts

In more serious RTA claims, an accident reconstruction expert may be required. If the claimant's solicitor is instructed immediately following the accident, the accident reconstruction expert should be contacted without delay and requested to attend the scene of the accident in order to examine any skid marks, etc. It may also be appropriate for the expert to examine the vehicles involved in the accident, and the claimant's solicitor should take appropriate steps to ensure that the vehicles are not disposed of or repaired prior to the expert carrying out their examination. The evidence of tachographs will be particularly useful. The reconstruction expert will want to see the PAR and any associated reports prepared by the police, such as a police reconstruction report, and proofs of evidence from anyone involved in the accident or anyone who witnessed the accident. They will then be in a position to provide an opinion as to the cause of the accident.

11.3.3.2 Consulting engineers

Many personal injury claims involve machinery or systems of work (especially EL claims), and in such cases it may be thought appropriate for a consulting engineer to be instructed to prepare a report on the machinery involved or the system of work undertaken.

> **EXAMPLE**
>
> A client is injured while driving a fork-lift truck and alleges that the steering wheel failed to respond while she was driving it. It is part of the client's case that the employer failed adequately to maintain the fork-lift truck. If the truck has not been modified prior to the solicitor being instructed, a consulting engineer may be instructed to examine the vehicle and its maintenance records. The solicitor will therefore obtain an expert's view as to whether the appropriate system of maintenance was adopted and attempt to identify the cause of the accident.

The expert will need to inspect the machinery, and the permission of the proposed defendants (who are normally the claimant's employers in such cases) is required. If this is not granted then it will be necessary to apply to court for an order for preservation and inspection.

Where both parties are given permission to instruct their own experts, it is common for them to attend the scene of the accident at the same time in order to conduct a joint inspection. This has the advantage of saving costs and time, as the engineers can agree on measurements and technical details.

11.3.3.3 Clinical case managers

In certain high-value/severe injury cases, a clinical case manager may be appointed to consider the claimant's appropriate care regime. In *Wright (by her litigation friend Karen Fay) v Kevin Sullivan* [2005] EWCA Civ 656, it was held that the clinical case manager would owe a duty to the claimant to work in the claimant's best interests and should not be jointly appointed. The evidence given by such a witness is evidence of fact and not expert opinion.

11.4 HOW TO FIND AN EXPERT

New rules relating to whiplash claims under the Low Value RTA Protocol and under the Whiplash Injury Regulations 2021 and the Pre-Action Protocol for Personal Injury Claims below the Small Claims Limit in RTAs all provide that an accredited medical expert must be selected via MedCo (www.MedCo.org.uk) (see **Chapter 21**). In all other cases, there is no such restriction on who may be instructed, and it is vital that the solicitor responsible instructs the correct person to provide expert evidence in the case. Many firms will have their own in-house directory of experts, which should be referred to in the first instance. Frequently, other fee-earners will have inserted comments about the expert alongside the entry in the directory. Information such as how well the expert gave evidence in court, can be extremely useful. If an in-house directory of experts is not available or is inappropriate then other sources can be used.

The following sources may also be of use:

(a) The Association of Personal Injury Lawyers. This organisation provides information to members on appropriate experts.

(b) Action against Medical Accidents (AvMA).

(c) The Academy of Experts.

(d) Expert Witness Institute.

(e) The *New Law Journal* and *Solicitor's Journal* regularly issue expert witness supplements which carry advertisements from experts who are prepared to provide reports for the purposes of litigation.

(f)   Many professional institutes also prepare a directory of expert witnesses.

(g)   The Medico-Legal Society publishes reports which may reveal the name of a suitable expert.

11.4.1   The use of medical agencies

Increasingly, solicitors rely on medical agencies to source suitable experts to write reports. The rise in popularity of medical agencies has come about due to the growth of large personal injury practices which accept claims from clients anywhere in England and Wales. It is necessary to find a medical expert (or better still a choice of experts in the same specialism) who is sufficiently local to the home of the client. Without the assistance of a national agency to co-ordinate this search, this would represent something of a headache for the claimant's solicitor.

Medical agencies are able to provide a choice of experts local to the client, and they will send copies of the CVs of those experts direct to the solicitor, together with an indication of the waiting time for preparation of the report. Subject to the arrangement they have with the instructing solicitor, they may also attempt to agree the choice of expert with the defendant insurer direct, obtain the client's medical records, arrange the medical appointment for the client and forward the subsequent report direct to the solicitor. The agency will charge a fee for this service which, if reasonable, will be allowed as part of the disbursements incurred on the claim at assessment of costs stage.

In the case of *Woollard v Fowler* [2006] EWHC 90051 (Costs), 12 April 2006, the court held that it was entirely proper that a payment made by a solicitor to such an agency should be treated as a disbursement under the fixed costs regime in section II of Part 45 of the CPR 1998, and therefore as recoverable in full from the losing party. However, this case needs to be read in the light the low value pre-action protocols for RTA and EL/PL claims and associated costs rules set out in section III of Part 45 of the CPR 1998.

The PAP for personal injury claims states that where a claimant wishes to use a medical agency, the defendant's prior consent should be sought and, if the defendant so requests, the medical agency should provide in advance the names of the doctors whom they are considering instructing (para 7.4).

11.5   KEY QUALITIES TO LOOK FOR IN AN EXPERT

A number of key qualities must be looked for when selecting an expert:

(a)   Is the individual appropriately qualified to deal with the matter and does the individual have the relevant practical experience in the area? If not, the court is unlikely to consider the individual to be an expert.

(b)   Can the expert be regarded as impartial? In *Liverpool Roman Catholic Archdiocesan Trustees Inc v Goldberg (No 2)* [2001] Lloyd's Rep PN 518, the evidence of an expert was disregarded due to his close relationship with the defendant.

(c)   Is the expert usually instructed on behalf of defendants when you are instructed by a claimant, or vice versa? Although all experts have an overriding duty to the court and should give the same evidence in a particular case no matter who is instructing them, it is unwise to instruct an expert who has an impressive record of appearing against the type of client you are representing.

(d)   Does the expert have sufficient time to deal with the case properly? A good expert will refuse instructions when they have insufficient time, but this will not always happen. Whether the case is a personal injury or clinical negligence claim, the expert will have to spend considerable time on the matter, either examining the papers or the claimant, or inspecting a vehicle, a piece of machinery or the scene of the accident.

(e)   Can the expert provide a clear and comprehensive report?

(f)   Does the expert have experience in litigation of this type? Do they prepare reports and attend at trial regularly to give evidence? Only a small percentage of cases proceed to trial, and thus an expert may claim to have been involved in, say, 200 cases but may have given evidence in only a few of them (especially as, in the fast track, expert evidence is normally given in written form). It cannot be assumed that the case will settle and, however good the written report might be, convincing oral testimony (where allowed by the court) and the ability to withstand tough cross-examination are essential. The expert's general reputation should be checked with their colleagues who practise in the same area.

11.6   PRELIMINARY ENQUIRIES OF THE EXPERT

Once a party has decided to instruct an expert in relation to any issue in a case and an appropriate expert has been identified, the solicitor should approach the expert with a number of preliminary enquiries, in order to establish whether they are willing and able to act in relation to the matter. Some health practitioners may be reluctant to provide reports for claimants in clinical negligence cases, and their views on this must be obtained. Even if the expert has been used by the solicitor before, it is good practice to send a preliminary letter to establish whether the proposed expert has any personal or professional connection with others who may be involved in the case, such as one of the parties, a health professional who is alleged to have been negligent or experts instructed by another party. Even though experts have an overriding duty to the court, it is preferable to avoid any possibility of bias or allegations of bias.

The preliminary letter to the expert might usefully cover the following matters:

(a)   request confirmation that the expert deals with the appropriate speciality, has the necessary qualifications and experience, and is familiar with the general duties of an expert;

(b)   request confirmation that they are willing to accept instructions to provide a report and, where time is an important consideration, details of when the report will be available;

(c)   request confirmation that the expert is prepared to carry out any necessary post-initial report work, such as attending conference with counsel and attending experts' meetings;

(d)   request confirmation that they would be willing to provide oral evidence to support their written report, if required;

(e)   inform the expert of the identity of the potential defendant and, in a clinical negligence claim, the name of any health professional who is alleged to have been negligent;

(f)   obtain details of the expert's charging rate and/or to explain that the client has the benefit of public funding; and

(g)   confirm on whose behalf the solicitor is acting (but without giving any view on liability).

(h)   where the expert is a medical expert and relevant medical records have been obtained, confirm that this is the case (however, they must not be forwarded to the expert at this stage).

If the expert is prepared to act in response to an initial letter of enquiry then a full letter of instruction should be sent.

11.7   LETTER OF INSTRUCTION

The nature of the letter of instruction to a medical expert will, of course, be determined by what it is the expert is required to do.

11.7.1   Instructing medical experts in relation to quantum

Generally, in an RTA claim or an EL claim not involving illness or disease, the only medical expert instructed will be required to examine the claimant in order to provide a condition and prognosis report for quantum purposes. Medical experts will also be required for quantum purposes in clinical negligence and disease and illness claims. The specimen letter of instruction to a medical expert which is set out at Annex D to the PAP for personal injury claims (see **Appendix 2**) is often suitable for this purpose.

It may be necessary to provide the expert with copies of the claimant's medical records where they relate to the injuries sustained and/or the treatment received by the claimant as a result of the defendant's alleged negligence, or where there is a pre-existing condition which may have an impact on the assessment of damages.

The heading of the letter should contain: the client's full name, address, date of birth, date of the accident, the client's telephone number and, if considered appropriate, details of the hospital where the client was treated. It is important that the letter of instruction makes it clear on whose behalf the solicitor is acting and whether the notice of appointment should be sent directly to the claimant or via the claimant's solicitor.

Where a defendant is given permission to instruct an expert to examine the claimant and provide a report on condition and prognosis, specific questions included in the letter of instruction may require the expert to comment, for example, on the reasonableness of the special damages claim, ie did the client reasonably need assistance with gardening and, if so, for how long?

11.7.2   Instructing medical experts in relation to liability and causation

In clinical negligence and disease and illness claims, it will be necessary to instruct a medical expert of an appropriate speciality to advise in relation to liability and/or causation. These experts may not need to examine the claimant and their expert opinion may be primarily based on the claimant's medical records, copies of which should be enclosed. The letter of instruction may include the following matters:

(a)   a chronology of the events/factual resumé to which the expert can refer. A concise overview of the events should be available for the expert to consider;

(b)   a brief explanation of the relevant standard of care, with reference to the *Bolam* test as modified by *Bolitho* (see **5.3**). In the case of *Sharpe v Southend Health Authority* [1997] 8 Med LR 299, the court stated that an expert in a clinical negligence case should make it clear in the expert's report whether the approach adopted by the defendant was in accordance with a responsible body of medical practitioners, even if the expert themselves would have adopted a different approach. If it is not known that the expert is aware of this point, then this must also be mentioned in the letter of instruction;

(c)   a reminder that it will be necessary to establish a causational link between the identified negligence and injury;

(d)   an offer for the expert to meet the claimant if they so wish. This may not be necessary but the facility should be made available;

(e)   the date by which the report is needed;

(f)   who is responsible for the fee;

(g)   a request that the expert consider whether all relevant notes have been disclosed and, if not, what further notes should be obtained;

(h)   a request that the expert advise as to whether any other type of expert evidence is required in addition to their own;

(i)   a request that the expert make reference to medical publications to support their case. The expert should be asked to refer to texts and authoritative works that were available at the time of the incident (see *Breeze v Ahmad* [2005] EWCA Civ 223);

(j)   specific questions that the expert is required to answer;

(k)   a reminder that the expert may be required to attend a conference with counsel at the appropriate time;

(l)   a reminder as to how the expert should structure the report.

The medical notes must not be sent to the expert without first being checked by the solicitor to ensure that they are complete and in order. Identical ring binders should be prepared, with copies of paginated medical notes included, in date order, indexed and divided into relevant sections. A ring binder of notes should be prepared for each expert, counsel and the solicitor.

11.8   THE EXPERT'S REPORT

Practice Direction 35, para 3.2 states that an expert's report must:

(1)   give details of the expert's qualifications;

(2)   give details of any literature or other material which the expert has relied on in making the report;

(3)   contain a statement setting out the substance of all facts and instructions given to the expert which are material to the opinions expressed in the report or upon which those opinions are based;

(4)   make clear which of the facts stated in the report are within the expert's own knowledge;

(5)   say who carried out any examination, measurement, test or experiment which the expert has used for the report, give the qualifications of that person, and say whether or not the test or experiment has been carried out under the expert's supervision;

(6)   where there is a range of opinion on the matters dealt with in the report –

    (a)   summarise the range of opinion, and

    (b)   give reasons for his own opinion;

(7)   contain a summary of the conclusions reached;

(8)   if the expert is not able to give his opinion without qualification, state the qualification; and

(9)   contain a statement that the expert –

    (a)   understands his duty to the court, and has complied with that duty; and

    (b)   is aware of the requirements of Part 35, this practice direction and the Guidance for the Instruction of Experts in Civil Claims 2014.

In relation to the requirement for a statement of the substance of the instructions given to the expert, it should be noted that r 35.10(4) specifically states that the instructions are not privileged. However, the court will not normally order disclosure of any specific document or allow cross-examination of the expert on the instructions, unless there are reasonable grounds to believe that the statement of instructions given to the expert is inaccurate or incomplete (see also *Lucas v Barking, Havering and Redbridge Hospitals NHS Trust* [2003] EWCA Civ 1102, [2003] All ER (D) 379 (Jul)).

Once an expert's report has been received, it should be read (and understood) by the solicitor and sent to the client for the client's approval. It should then be disclosed to the other party in accordance with the order for directions.

A specimen medical report may be found in **Appendix 1** at Document 8.

11.9   CONFERENCE WITH EXPERT AND COUNSEL WHERE EXPERT INSTRUCTED BY ONE PARTY

11.9.1   The initial conference prior to proceedings being issued

11.9.1.1   Personal injury

An initial conference prior to proceedings being issued is not normally necessary in personal injury cases, but consideration should be given to this approach if the claimant is resistant to the solicitor's advice that the claim is likely to fail, or if the matter is unusually complicated.

11.9.1.2 Clinical negligence and illness and disease claims

In clinical negligence and illness and disease cases, because the issues involved are likely to be complex, it may be appropriate to arrange a conference with the expert, counsel and the client after the initial medical report on liability and/or causation has been provided. This will provide an opportunity to examine all the issues in full, to test the expert's evidence and ensure that the expert chosen is the appropriate person to be instructed, and to determine whether proceedings should be issued. An initial conference at this stage is also appropriate when the medical report is unfavourable and it appears that the claim should not proceed.

The conference also provides a valuable opportunity to satisfy the client that every possibility has been investigated, that the client is not being sidelined by the legal process and that there is no medical conspiracy against the client.

Consideration should be given to instructing counsel to produce a written advice following the conference, to ensure that all matters have been dealt with. During the conference, a detailed note should be taken of matters covered. This note should be sent to all the experts who attended the conference to confirm that it accurately records the views they expressed.

If the case is going to proceed, the next stage is the drafting of the letter of claim which is to be sent to the potential defendant.

11.9.2 Conference with counsel after proceedings issued

11.9.2.1 Personal injury

In the vast majority of personal injury cases, proceedings will be issued without the need for a conference with counsel, and many low-value cases proceed to trial without such a conference. In more complex personal injury cases, the solicitor and counsel will want to be sure that the expert has studied all the papers sent to them, has understood the facts of the case, and that they have excellent communication skills. These and other matters can be assessed at a conference.

11.9.2.2 Clinical negligence

In addition to the conference prior to the issue of proceedings in a clinical negligence case, it is common to have a further conference after the exchange of lay witness statements to check whether all the experts can still support the case. A further conference is normally arranged prior to the trial to review matters.

11.10 CONCLUSION

The role that the expert has in a personal injury or clinical negligence case is a significant one. The importance of the selection of the correct individual cannot be overestimated. The key points are summarised below at **11.12**.

11.11 FURTHER READING

Pre-action Protocol for Personal Injury Claims

Pre-action Protocol for the Resolution of Clinical Disputes

Guidance for the Instruction of Experts in Civil Claims 2014

CPR, Part 35 and PD 35

11.12   KEY POINTS

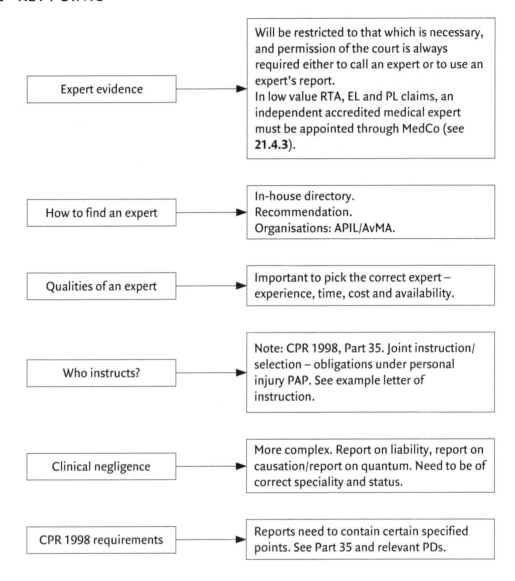

Expert evidence	Will be restricted to that which is necessary, and permission of the court is always required either to call an expert or to use an expert's report. In low value RTA, EL and PL claims, an independent accredited medical expert must be appointed through MedCo (see **21.4.3**).
How to find an expert	In-house directory. Recommendation. Organisations: APIL/AvMA.
Qualities of an expert	Important to pick the correct expert – experience, time, cost and availability.
Who instructs?	Note: CPR 1998, Part 35. Joint instruction/selection – obligations under personal injury PAP. See example letter of instruction.
Clinical negligence	More complex. Report on liability, report on causation/report on quantum. Need to be of correct speciality and status.
CPR 1998 requirements	Reports need to contain certain specified points. See Part 35 and relevant PDs.

COMMENCEMENT OF PROCEEDINGS

LEARNING OUTCOMES

After reading this chapter you will be able to:

- set out the main matters to be considered before and upon the issue of proceedings
- explain where and how proceedings are issued
- draft appropriate Particulars of Claim and Defence
- explain what additional claims are and how such claims are made.

12.1 INTRODUCTION

Where the defendant has denied liability, or where the defendant has failed to respond within the time limits set out in the relevant PAP (see **10.2**), the claimant is entitled to commence proceedings by issuing and serving the claim form.

It is usually to the claimant's advantage to begin proceedings early for the following reasons:

(a) To avoid problems with the limitation period. In personal injury litigation, proceedings must normally be commenced within three years of the accident occurring (see **Chapter 7**). Ongoing negotiations with the proposed defendant/defendant's insurers do not have the automatic effect of extending the limitation period, and in any event, negotiations may continue after proceedings have been commenced.

(b) To avoid further delay in so-called 'long-tail' occupational disease and illness claims, and in some clinical negligence claims where claimants will be relying on a later date of knowledge in order to overcome limitation problems. Claimants may have suffered from poor health for many years, and it is important that their claims are progressed with expedition.

(c)   To exert pressure on the defendant/defendant's insurers to act in relation to the claim. In personal injury cases, it will often precipitate the defendant's file moving from the insurance company claims department to the insurer's nominated solicitors, who may be more willing to negotiate.

(d)   In practice, judgment usually carries entitlement to interest and costs. A settlement achieved prior to the commencement of proceedings does not carry such an entitlement (although the claimant's solicitor will always want to include in any such settlement an element in respect of interest and costs). After proceedings have been issued, if there is any argument by the defendant as to how much of the claimant's costs the defendant should pay on settlement, the claimant's solicitor can have those costs assessed by the court.

(e)   Commencing proceedings enables the claimant to apply to the court for an interim payment in the event that a voluntary payment cannot be negotiated.

12.2   PRE-ISSUE CHECKLIST

Unless the limitation period is about to expire (in which case see **7.9.2**), proceedings should not be commenced until the claimant's solicitor is satisfied that:

(a)   the period allowed by the relevant PAP for the defendant to respond to the letter of claim (or the CNF/DCNF in a case falling under one of the low value protocols) has expired and either the defendant has not responded or the defendant has denied liability;

(b)   a full investigation of the matter has been conducted and the claimant's solicitor is in possession of all relevant evidence in relation to liability and quantum;

(c)   a re-evaluation of the risk assessment has been carried out which takes into account the defendant's response to the letter of claim, the documents supplied by the defendant and other evidence obtained following the dispatch of the letter of claim. Where the risk assessment indicates that the claim is unlikely to succeed, the claimant's solicitor should not issue proceedings but should try to settle the matter, if at all possible, or alternatively advise the client that it is not possible to proceed with the matter, whichever is appropriate;

(d)   the requirements of the relevant PAP have been complied with. In particular, an approach has been made to the proposed defendant with the aim of settling the matter without the need for litigation;

(e)   the claimant's solicitor is ready to process the claim once proceedings have started, in accordance with the directions and the associated timetable which will be set out by the court on allocation. The court will actively manage the claim and, in fast-track cases in particular, there will be limited time to prepare for each stage of the proceedings. The court will not be best pleased if the claimant's solicitor is unable to keep to the timetable due to inadequate preparation prior to issue;

(f)   where the client has before the event insurance (BEI) or after the event insurance (AEI), the insurer has given permission for proceedings to be commenced;

(g)   the claimant understands the situation and has given instructions for the matter to proceed.

12.3   MATTERS TO CONSIDER UPON ISSUE

Additional steps must be taken in certain circumstances before, at the time of, or shortly following the issue of proceedings. The claimant's solicitor needs to be suitably organised before proceedings are issued, as the consequences of failing to carry out the required steps may be severe.

12.3.1 Medical report and schedule of past and future loss and expense

A medical report and a schedule setting out past and future loss and expense should be served with the particulars of claim. Medical experts can be extremely busy and there may be a lengthy delay in obtaining an appointment for the claimant. Schedules in relation to substantial claims may be complex and cannot be put together overnight. Bearing in mind the fact that the particulars of claim must be served within 14 days of service of the claim form, the claimant's solicitor should be wary of issuing proceedings until these documents are available.

12.3.2 Notice in road traffic cases: Road Traffic Act 1988, ss 151 and 152

In RTA claims, where the claimant is entitled to require an insurance company to settle the judgment under s 151 of the Road Traffic Act 1988 (see **3.3.2** and **10.3.1.3**), the claimant must give the insurer notification of the claim under s 152, either before or within seven days after the commencement of the claim. It makes sense to give this notification as soon as possible, although some solicitors may choose to wait until commencement and then serve the notice on the insurers with a copy of the claim form and particulars of claim. There is no prescribed form for the notice.

12.4 ISSUING PROCEEDINGS

12.4.1 Where to issue

All tort proceedings may be issued in the county court. Proceedings which include a claim for damages for personal injury may be commenced in the High Court only where the total claim is worth at least £50,000 unless an enactment requires it to be commenced in the High Court (CPR, PD 7A, paras 2.2 and 2.3).

When calculating the value of the claim for case management purposes, the claimant must disregard interest and costs, any possible counterclaim or finding of contributory negligence which may be made against the claimant, and any recoupment of benefits by the Compensation Recovery Unit (CPR, r 16.3(6)).

The procedure for issuing proceedings is dealt with in **Civil Litigation**, but it is worth saying here that all designated money claims which are to be commenced in the county court must be issued in the County Court Money Claims Centre.

12.4.2 Claim form – statements of value

In accordance with CPR, r 16.2(c), where the claimant is making a claim for money, the claim form must contain a statement of value in accordance with CPR, r 16.3. This will be used to determine the amount of the court fee to be paid by the claimant upon issue of proceedings, and will assist the court to allocate the matter to the appropriate track.

In claims for damages, it is impossible to give anything more than an approximation of how much the claim is likely to be worth. Consequently, in the recent past, it was sufficient to state that the claimant expects to recover:

(a)   not more than £10,000;

(b)   more than £10,000 but not more than £25,000; or

(c)   more than £25,000.

However, as a result of changes to how issue fees are calculated, claimants' solicitors must now try to calculate the maximum value of a claim with greater precision than in the past. There are specified fees for claims at various levels up to £10,000, which means that the figures for the relevant level should be set out as the value. Fees for claims greater than £10,000 but no more than £200,000 are calculated as 5% of the amount claimed inclusive of interest. This means that valuing the claim at 'more than £10,000 but not more than £25,000' would automatically attract a fee of £1,250, being 5% of £25,000, even if damages are unlikely to exceed, say, £16,000.

Although it is clearly appropriate to be more precise when valuing the claim, this is not without its difficulties. Problems may arise if it is subsequently discovered that damages are likely to exceed the amount initially set out as the value in the claim form, as an inadequate issue fee will have been paid. Conversely, it would not be acting in the client's best interests to overvalue the claim and pay a greater issue fee than is required. Moreover, unsuccessful defendants may use any overvaluation to challenge the amount of the issue fee sought in the claimant's costs application at the end of the case.

At the moment, there is no universal approach to this dilemma. However, it is suggested that the best approach is to calculate the value of the claim, allow some margin for error, and give a more precise upper limit in the 'Value' section of the claim form than those set out in (a) to (c) above.

Particular care should be taken to pay the correct fee in cases where limitation is about to expire to avoid an allegation that the claim is statute barred on the basis that the claim has not been brought in time because the proper fee was not paid (see **7.2**).

See Document 10 of the Case Study in **Appendix 1** for an example of a claim form.

If a claim is to be issued in the High Court, it must state that the claimant reasonably expects to recover £50,000 or more; or must state that some other enactment provides that the claim may be commenced in the High Court and specify that enactment (CPR, r 16.3(5)(b) and (c)).

In a claim for non-road traffic personal injuries, subject to CPR, r 16.3(3A) and (3AA), the claimant must state on the claim form whether the amount which the claimant reasonably expects to recover in general damages for pain, suffering and loss of amenity is either not more than £1,500 or more than £1,500 (CPR, r 16.3(3)). This is to enable the court to allocate the claim to the correct track should a defence be filed (see **13.3**).

In relation to road traffic accident claims, CPR, r 16.3(3A) states that where a claim for personal injuries arises from a road traffic accident which occurred on or after 31 May 2021 (when the Whiplash Regulations came into force) and rr 26.5A, 26.6A or 26.6B do not apply to the claim, the claimant must state in the claim form whether the amount which the claimant expects to recover as general damages for pain, suffering and loss of amenity is:

(i)   not more than £5,000; or

(ii)   more than £5,000.

CPR, r 16.3(3AA) provides that where a personal injury claim arises from a road traffic accident and CPR, r 26.6A applies to that claim, the claimant must state in the claim form whether the amount which the claimant expects to recover as general damages for pain, suffering and loss of amenity is:

(i)   not more than £1,000; or

(ii)   more than £1,000.

The above statements of value are relevant to the small claim thresholds in different types of personal injury claim.

12.5 PARTICULARS OF CLAIM

The particulars of claim must be contained in or served with the claim form, or be served on the defendant by the claimant within 14 days after service of the claim form. In any event, particulars of claim must be served on the defendant no later than the latest time for serving a claim form (ie, within four months after date of issue of the claim form).

It is vital that the particulars of claim are drafted carefully. They should set out the basis of the claim clearly, accurately and comprehensively. If they do not do this, the worst case scenario is that the claim will be struck out for failing to disclose reasonable grounds for bringing the claim (CPR, r 3.4(2)(a)) or summary judgment will be given against the claimant (CPR, r 24.2). At the very least, the claimant's solicitor will give an impression of sloppiness or incompetence.

12.5.1 Structure and content of the particulars of claim

The formalities set out in PD 5A, para 2.2 and the main principles of drafting are discussed in *Civil Litigation*. A suggested structure for particulars of claim in a personal injury case can be found at **12.15** below, and an example is included in the Case Study at **Appendix 1(11)**. Particulars of claim in clinical negligence cases and in more complex personal injury cases are generally drafted by counsel.

Rule 16.4 of the CPR and PD 16 deal with the contents of the particulars of claim. The particulars must include, *inter alia*:

(a) a concise statement of the facts on which the claimant relies. When drafting, it is useful to remember that the claimant will need to prove that the defendant owed the claimant a duty of care and/or there was a statutory duty, that this duty was breached by the defendant, and that this caused injury and loss which was reasonably foreseeable. As far as is reasonably possible, the particulars should deal with these elements in separate, consecutively numbered paragraphs, with one allegation in each paragraph and in a chronological order.

Although the CPR allow references to evidence and statutory provisions, the particulars should deal with the 'bare bones' of the claim, and it is therefore preferable not to include these details unless the information is specifically required. Four examples of where evidence or statutory provisions should be set out are as follows:

(i) Where the claimant wishes to rely on the evidence of a medical expert, a medical report should be attached to the particulars (see (c) below).

(ii) Where the claimant alleges breach of statutory duty, such as in an employer's liability case, the relevant statutory provisions should be set out.

(iii) Where the claimant relies on a criminal conviction of the defendant (see (f) below).

(iv) Where the claimant is seeking an order for provisional damages (see (h) below).

(b) for the purposes of assessing damages, the claimant's date of birth and brief details of the claimant's injuries. The main points of the medical report (see (c) below) can be summarised for this purpose but, especially in a high value claim, it is important to ensure that all the relevant information is included, ie the immediate impact of the accident, the duration of any stay in hospital, the number and nature of any operations or other treatments, continuing pain and disability, the practical effects on the claimant's life, disability in the labour market, loss of congenial employment, etc;

(c) reference to a report from a medical expert detailing the injuries and their past, current and future effect on the claimant. The report must be served with or attached to the particulars of claim. In a soft tissue injury claim, the medical report must be a fixed cost medical report (PD 16, para 4.3A). The first report (if there is more than one) must be from an accredited medical expert selected via the MedCo Portal (PD 16, para 4.3A);

(d) details of past and future expenses and losses, which should be provided in a schedule attached to the particulars;

(e) where the claimant seeks interest, this must be pleaded by reference to the Senior Courts Act 1981 or the County Courts Act 1984, depending on whether the claim is to be issued in the High Court or the County Court. The amount of interest which may be claimed, and the period for which it may be claimed, differs in relation to special damages and damages for pain, suffering and loss of amenity (see **15.6**). Consequently, where the amount sought is considerable or the calculation of damages complex, the plea for interest may be set out in detail. However, it is common practice, particularly in low value claims, to claim interest at such rates and for such periods as the court thinks fit.

Where appropriate in the circumstances of the case, the particulars may also contain:

(f)   where the claimant is relying on a relevant conviction of the defendant, the nature of the conviction, the date of conviction, the name of the convicting court and the issue in the claim to which it relates;

(g)   where the claimant is relying on a later date of knowledge for the purposes of limitation (see **Chapter 7**), details of the date of knowledge (PD 16, para 8.2);

(h)   where the claimant is seeking provisional damages, a statement to that effect and his grounds for claiming them. Further guidance as to what must be set out is found in PD 16, para 4.4, namely:

(i)   that the claimant is seeking the award under either s 32A of the Senior Courts Act 1981 or s 51 of the County Courts Act 1984,

(ii)   that there is a chance that at some future time he will develop some serious disease or suffer some serious deterioration in his physical or mental condition, and

(iii)   the disease or type of deterioration in respect of which an application may be made at a future date;

(i)   where the claim relates to a fatal accident, a statement by the claimant covering:

(i)   the fact that it is brought under the Fatal Accidents Act 1976,

(ii)   the dependants on whose behalf the claim is made,

(iii)   the date of birth of each dependant, and

(iv)   details of the nature of the dependency claim.

The particulars of claim and the schedule of special damages must also contain a statement of truth, ie that the claimant (and if the claimant is acting as a litigation friend, the litigation friend) believes that the facts stated in the document are true. This may be signed by the claimant (or litigation friend), or by the solicitor on their behalf (CPR, r 22).

See Document 11 of the Case Study in **Appendix 1** for an example of Particulars of Claim, Document 8 for an example of a medical report and Document 12 for a Schedule of Past and Future Expenses and Losses.

12.6 SERVICE OF PROCEEDINGS

After the claim form has been issued, it must be served within four months after the date of issue. This may be extended, however, with permission of the court. If the claim form is to be served out of the jurisdiction, the period for service is six months.

See *Civil Litigation* for the rules governing the service of court documents.

12.7 ACKNOWLEDGEMENT OF SERVICE

The defendant may respond to the claim by:

(a)   defending the claim; or

(b)   admitting the claim; or

(c)   acknowledging service of the claim form.

If the defendant makes no response to the claim, the claimant may enter default judgment.

Where the defendant is unable to file a defence in time, they may gain extra time by acknowledging service. The time for acknowledgement of service is 14 days from the service of the claim form, unless the claim form indicates that the particulars of claim are to follow separately, in which case the defendant does not have to acknowledge service until 14 days after service of those particulars of claim. The acknowledgement of service form must be signed by the defendant or the defendant's legal representative, and must include an address for service for the defendant which must be within the jurisdiction.

On receipt of such an acknowledgement of service, the court must notify the claimant in writing of this.

12.8 THE DEFENCE

The defendant must file a defence within 14 days of service of the particulars of claim, or, if the defendant has filed an acknowledgement of service, within 28 days after service of the particulars of claim.

The parties may agree an extension of time for filing of the defence of up to 28 days. The defendant must give the court written notice of any such agreement.

12.8.1 Contents of the defence

The defence must deal with every allegation set out in the particulars of claim by admitting, denying or not admitting (neither admitting nor denying) each allegation. This will be an easier task if the particulars have dealt with one allegation per paragraph.

The following should also be noted.

(a) Where allegations are denied, the defendant must give reasons for that denial and, where relevant, give the defendant's own version of the facts. If the defendant disputes the claimant's statement of value, the defendant must give reasons for doing so and, if possible, give their own estimate of value.

(b) Where the defendant wishes to make an allegation of fraud, and there is reasonable evidence to establish a prima facie case of fraud, it is best practice to specifically plead this in the defence. However, in *Howlett v Davies* [2017] EWCA Civ 1696, the Court of Appeal held that a failure to plead fraud did not preclude a finding of fundamental dishonesty (see **1.4**).

(c) Where the defendant wishes to rely on the fact that they took all reasonable care or on a statutory defence, such as s 58 of the Highways Act 1980, the defendant should say so.

(d) Where the defendant claims that the claimant was themselves negligent, and therefore contributed to the accident or increased the severity of their injuries, the particulars of the claimant's negligence should be set out in the defence.

(e) The defendant should give details of the expiry period of any limitation period on which the defendant wishes to rely (PD 16, para 11.3).

(f) If the claimant has attached a medical report to their particulars of claim, the defendant should state whether the defendant admits, denies or does not admit the matters contained in it, and give reasons for any matters denied. For example, the defendant may claim that the claimant has failed to mitigate loss, that the injuries were not caused by the alleged negligence but rather by some pre-existing condition, or that the claimant has fraudulently made or exaggerated the claim. If the defendant has obtained their own medical report on the claimant, the defendant should attach it to the defence.

(g) If the claimant has attached a schedule of past and future expenses and losses to the particulars of claim, the defendant must include with the defence a counter-schedule stating which items the defendant agrees, disputes, or neither agrees nor disputes but has no knowledge of. If items are disputed, an alternative figure must be supplied.

(h)   The defence must contain a statement that the defendant, or, if the defendant is conducting proceedings with a litigation friend, the litigation friend, believes the facts stated in it are true. The statement of truth may be signed either by the defendant (or litigation friend), or by their legal representative.

(i)   Unless the defendant has already acknowledged service, the defendant must give an address for service which is within the jurisdiction.

12.9   THE COUNTERCLAIM

If a defendant wishes to make a counterclaim against a claimant, the defendant should file the counterclaim with the defence (CPR, r 20.4). Provided the counterclaim is filed at the same time as the defence, the defendant will not need permission of the court to make the counterclaim. Generally, the counterclaim will form part of the same document as the defence and will follow on from the defence.

12.10   THE REPLY TO DEFENCE AND DEFENCE TO COUNTERCLAIM

The claimant may file a reply to the defence, but if the claimant does not do so, they will not be deemed to admit the matters raised in the defence. The reply must respond to any matters in the defence which have not been dealt with in the particulars of the claim, and must contain a statement of truth.

The claimant may file a reply and a certificate of reply when they file their directions questionnaire (see **13.2**). If the claimant does serve a reply, the claimant must also serve it on all other parties.

Where there is a counterclaim and the claimant disputes the counterclaim, the claimant must file a defence to it within the usual 14-day period. This will be way of a reply to the defence and a defence to the counterclaim. If the claimant does not file a defence to the counterclaim, the defendant will be entitled to enter judgment in respect of the counterclaim.

The particulars of claim, defence and reply are said to be the statements of case. No subsequent statements of case may be filed without the court's permission.

12.11   AMENDMENT TO STATEMENTS OF CASE

Sometimes, the claimant's solicitor may need to amend the particulars of claim. Where this arises before the particulars have been served on the defendant, the amendments may be made without the court's permission. On occasion, the defence may highlight a need for an amendment, for example the need to add a further defendant, or even to pursue a different defendant. Amendments may be made at any time after service, provided the defendant gives their written consent. Where consent is not forthcoming, the permission of the court must be sought (see CPR, rr 17 and 23).

In *Goode v Martin* [2001] EWCA Civ 1899, [2002] 1 WLR 1828, the claimant sought permission to amend her statement of claim after the expiry of the limitation period. The amendment consisted of a response to the defendant's version of events and no new facts were being introduced. The claimant also argued that if the amendment could not be allowed under a conventional approach to r 17.4, a less conventional approach should be adopted to comply with Article 6 of the European Convention on Human Rights.

The court found that because the claimant's new cause of action arose out of the same facts that were in issue in the original claim, she should be allowed to add to her claim the alternative plea proposed. The Court of Appeal agreed with the claimant that to prevent the claimant from putting her alternative case before the court would impose an impediment on her access to the court that would have to be justified. It was possible to interpret r 17.4 in such a way as to allow the claimant's amendment, and that should be done to comply with Article 6 of the Convention.

12.12 ADDITIONAL CLAIMS (CPR, PART 20)

Part 20 of the CPR applies to:

(a)   a counterclaim by a defendant against the claimant or against the claimant and some other person;

(b)   an additional claim by a defendant against any person (whether or not already a party) for contribution or indemnity or some other remedy; and

(c)   where an additional claim has been made against a person who is not already a party, any additional claim made by that person against any other person (whether or not already a party) (CPR, r 20.2).

Such claims (other than counterclaims) are sometimes referred to as third party proceedings.

In accordance with s 1(1) of the Civil Liability (Contribution) Act 1978, 'any person liable in respect of any damage suffered by another person may recover contribution from any other person liable in respect of the same damage (whether jointly with him or otherwise)'.

The 'contribution' which a defendant may seek from a third party may be either:

(a)   *an indemnity* – this arises though a contractual relationship between the defendant and the third party (such as where a product supplied by the defendant to the claimant causes injury to the claimant, but was manufactured and supplied to the defendant by the third party), or a statutory obligation placed on the third party (such as where a gas company fails to reinstate a road properly and the claimant, who was injured in a road traffic accident caused by defects in the road surface, brings proceedings against the local highway authority). The claimant has a cause of action against the defendant, but the court may order the third party to recompense the defendant in respect of the full amount of the damages the defendant is ordered to pay the claimant. The important point to note is that an indemnity does not exonerate the defendant; the defendant remains liable to the claimant. Consequently, if the third party were to become insolvent, the claimant would be able to recover the judgment sum from the defendant; or

(b)   *a contribution* – this arises where either or both of two parties, the defendant and the third party, have been negligent or in breach of contract or of statutory duty (such as in a road traffic accident where the claimant, who was a passenger in Car A, issues proceeding against the defendant, the driver of Car B, but the defendant alleges that the driver of Car A, the third party, was fully or partially responsible for the accident). In such a case, the defendant seeks a contribution which may be equal to or less than the claimant's loss.

It is common for defendants to claim both an indemnity and a contribution in the alternative.

12.12.1 Making an 'additional claim'

Where a defendant wishes to make a counterclaim against someone other than the claimant, or where the defendant wishes to claim an indemnity or a contribution from someone else in respect of the damages which the defendant may be ordered to pay to the claimant, the defendant's solicitor should take the appropriate steps set out in CPR, Part 20 and PD 20 to ensure that the court is able to apportion blame and liability to pay compensation. The appropriate steps for each type of claim are as follows:

(a)   a defendant who wishes to seek damages (ie counterclaim) against someone who is not already a party to the proceedings. The defendant must apply to the court for an order that that person be added as an additional party. The application may be made without notice unless the court orders otherwise (CPR, r 20.5);

(b)   a defendant who wishes to seek a contribution or an indemnity from a co-defendant. Once the defendant has filed their acknowledgement of service or defence, the defendant may proceed with their additional claim against the co-defendant by filing a notice stating the nature and grounds of the defendant's claim and serving it upon the co-defendant. Provided the defendant serves the notice with their defence, the defendant will not require the court's permission. Otherwise, the defendant must seek the court's permission (CPR, r 20.6);

(c)   a defendant who wishes to seek a contribution or an indemnity in respect of the claimant's losses from someone who is not already a party to the proceedings (commonly known as 'third party proceedings'). The defendant must issue an additional claim and serve it on the third party, together with particulars of claim, the forms for defending and admitting the claim and acknowledging service, a copy of the statements of case which have been served in the main claim, and any other document the court directs. Provided the claim is issued before or at the same time as the defence is filed, the court's permission is not required. Otherwise, the court's permission will be necessary (CPR, r 20.7);

(d)   where an additional claim has been made against a third party, when that third party wishes to seek a contribution or an indemnity from someone else, whether or not already a party. Where a new party is introduced, the procedure is the same as in (c) above.

12.12.2   Obtaining permission to issue an additional claim

Where permission is required for an additional claim, an application notice must be filed and served, together with a copy of the proposed additional claim and a witness statement setting out the matters contained in PD 20, paras 2.1 to 2.3, namely:

(a)   the stage the proceedings have reached;

(b)   the nature of the additional claim to be made, or details of the question or issue which needs to be decided;

(c)   a summary of the facts on which the additional claim in based;

(d)   the name and address of the proposed additional party;

(e)   where there has been a delay, an explanation for the delay. The court will be concerned to ensure that the late introduction of an additional party will not cause prejudice to any existing party; and

(f)   a timetable of the proceedings to date.

12.12.3   Case management in relation to an additional claim

The court will be keen to ensure that counterclaims and other additional claims are managed in the most convenient and effective manner. Where the defendant to an additional claim files a defence, a case management hearing will take place to enable the court to consider the future conduct of the proceedings (PD 20, para 3.1). In accordance with PD 20, para 3.3, the court may treat the hearing as a summary judgment hearing, order that the Part 20 proceedings be dismissed and/or make appropriate directions.

12.12.4   Example of an additional claim

Carol was injured in a road traffic accident when her car was hit by a vehicle driven by Darren. Darren had failed to stop at a junction. Carol (the claimant) issued proceedings in negligence against Darren (the defendant). The day before the accident, Darren had taken his car to be serviced by Tyrone, who had fitted new brake pads. Darren alleges that when he tried to apply his brakes they failed to work, and this was the cause of the accident. Darren makes an additional claim against Tyrone (the third party). Tyrone alleges that the brakes failed because the brake pads he fitted to Darren's car, which were purchased from Fab-Brakes Limited, were defective. Tyrone makes an additional claim against Fab-Brakes Limited (the fourth party).

12.13 GROUP LITIGATION

Engaging in group litigation is time-consuming, difficult and therefore costly. Group litigation results when there are a number of prospective claimants who have a common interest or common defendant arising out of a common incident. An example of group litigation is that brought by a number of families following the drowning of 51 passengers of the pleasure boat *Marchioness*, which sank after being hit by the dredger *Bowbelle* on the Thames in 1989.

The relevant rule of the CPR 1998 governing group litigation can be found at Part 19, with its accompanying PD 19B. Part 19 provides for the making of a group litigation order (GLO) at the request of the parties where there are, or are likely to be, a number of similar claims. The aim of the GLO is to 'steer' the group litigation by ensuring that the case is managed to suit the needs of multi-party litigation.

The GLO seeks to ensure that all cases that are eligible to join the group do so and are then all treated in like manner to ensure consistency of result. The GLO must include specific directions for the maintenance of a group register, specify the GLO issues, and appoint a particular court and particular judge to oversee the case management process. By giving one court/judge 'ownership' of the management process, the case can be more effectively managed than if all potential claimants were allowed to issue and deal with their case at any court of their choosing. The managing judge appointed to the group litigation will quickly amass specialist knowledge in relation to that particular group litigation, and will therefore be able to deal with matters as they arise more quickly and effectively.

The details of group litigation are beyond the scope of this book but recourse should be had, as a starting point, to PD 19B and to The Law Society's Multi-Party Action Information Service.

12.14 CONCLUSION

Generally, it is in the claimant's interests for proceedings to be commenced as early as possible. Nevertheless, the claimant's solicitor should ensure that the matter has been investigated as thoroughly as possible, and that all preliminary steps to protect the client's position and to comply with the overriding objective set out in r 1 and the relevant pre-action protocol are complied with prior to issue of proceedings.

Practitioners require a good working knowledge of the rules which govern whether the proceedings should be commenced in the county court or High Court, and where and how they should be issued. A sound understanding of what should be contained in the Particulars of Claim and the Defence, and competent drafting skills are essential.

12.15 SUGGESTED STRUCTURE OF PARTICULARS OF CLAIM IN PERSONAL INJURY CASE

Court inserts case number

IN THE HIGH COURT OF JUSTICE ETC

Parties

PARTICULARS OF CLAIM

- Describe parties to establish duty of care if necessary

- Succinctly describe what happened

- Allege breach of statutory duty/duty of care

PARTICULARS OF BREACH OF STATUTORY DUTY

Where relevant, set out the breaches with specific reference to the relevant statutory provisions. Be as comprehensive as possible.

PARTICULARS OF NEGLIGENCE

Set out what the defendant did or did not do which constitutes negligence. Be as specific as possible. Where you have set out breaches of statutory duty, state here 'The Claimant repeats the allegations of breach of statutory duty as allegations of negligence', then particularise negligence.

- Criminal conviction (if relevant) – nature of conviction, date of conviction, name of convicting court and the issue in the claim to which it relates

- Allege injury and loss caused

PARTICULARS OF INJURY

- Date of birth
- Summary of injuries, treatment and continuing effect on claimant
- Weakening in labour market (*Smith v Manchester*)
- Refer to attached medical report(s)

PARTICULARS OF LOSS

- Refer to attached schedule

- Claim for interest

- Remedies sought (the prayer)
  AND THE CLAIMANT CLAIMS

- Statement of truth

- Ending

Note: in EL cases where the accident occurred on or after 1 October 2013, save in limited circumstances, breach of statutory duty does not give rise to civil liability. Consequently, there will not be Particulars of Breach of Statutory Duty, although such breaches may be cited to support allegations of negligence. Particulars of Breach of Statutory Duty continue to be relevant in other types of personal injury cases, eg a claim against a highway authority for failure to maintain a highway under s 41(1) of the Highways Act 1980.

Case Management and Interim Applications

LEARNING OUTCOMES

After reading this chapter you will be able to:

- explain why and how and upon what criteria claims are allocated to the appropriate track, and the court's role in managing cases
- set out the standard directions together with the timeframe for fast track cases, and explain how directions are dealt with in multi-track cases
- explain what an interim payment is, the grounds and procedure for obtaining an interim payment, and how the amount of an interim payment is determined.

13.1 INTRODUCTION

Case management is one of the key elements of the CPR 1998. The overriding objective of the CPR, as set out in CPR, r 1.1, is to enable the court to deal with cases justly and at proportionate cost. In accordance with CPR, r 1.4, the court must further the overriding objective by actively managing cases, and r 1.3 requires solicitors and their clients to assist the court in furthering the overriding objective. Dealing with cases justly and at proportionate cost includes allotting to each case an appropriate share of the court's resources (r 1.1(2)(e)), which, in the first instance, requires the court to ensure that cases are dealt with in the appropriate court and are allocated to the appropriate track. It also means that the court will enforce compliance with rules, practice directions and orders (r 1.1(2)(f)), and it has various sanctions at its disposal in order to enable it to do so.

The bulk of the activities which require active management by the court arise in the period between the filing of the defence and trial, or earlier settlement. During this period, the case is allocated to the appropriate track and the parties receive from the court a set of directions, setting out a number of steps which must be taken within specified time limits. The aim of these directions is to encourage settlement and, where this is not possible, ensure the matter is properly prepared for trial.

This chapter contains a brief account of some of the main issues relating to case management and interim applications which are relevant to personal injury and clinical negligence cases. See **Civil Litigation** for a more in-depth consideration of this area.

13.2 DIRECTIONS QUESTIONNAIRE

Where a claim is defended, upon receipt of the defence, the court will make a provisional decision regarding the appropriate track for the case and will serve on the parties a notice of the proposed allocation (CPR, r 26.4). The factors relevant to allocation are set out at **13.3** below.

The notice of the proposed allocation requires each party to complete the relevant directions questionnaire (N180 for small track cases; N181 for fast track and multi-track cases), return it to the court office stated in the notice and serve copies on all other parties by the date specified on the notice. Parties are advised as to where the directions questionnaire may be obtained, unless a party is not legally represented, in which case a copy of the questionnaire will be enclosed with the notice. RTA claims falling within the small claims RTA protocol have their own prescribed procedure. This is not considered further in this chapter in any great detail, the focus of this book being generally on fast-track and multi-track claims. See **10.2** for further detail.

Where a case is suitable for allocation to the fast track or multi-track, parties are also required to file proposed or agreed directions (see **13.5** and **13.6** below). Low value RTA and EL/PL claims have their own prescribed procedures and are not considered further in this chapter. See **Chapter 21** for further detail.

See Document 16 of the Case Study at **Appendix 1** for an example of a directions questionnaire.

13.2.1 Stay to allow settlement of case

A party returning their directions questionnaire may request a stay of up to one month while the parties try to settle the case. Where all parties request a stay, or where the court, of its own initiative, considers such a stay would be appropriate, the court will direct a stay for one month. The court may also extend the period of the stay until such a date or such a period as it considers appropriate. If proceedings are settled during the stay, the claimant must inform the court.

13.2.2 Transfer of proceedings between courts

The court has the power to transfer cases between the High Court and the county courts and within district registries of the High Court (CPR, r 30.1, and see Part 30 generally). It may do so of its own volition, or upon application by a party to the proceedings. Where the matter has been commenced in the county court and a party believes that it is suitable for trial in the High Court or vice versa, it should set out its reasons in the directions questionnaire.

The court may transfer designated money claims issued in the County Court Money Claims Centre (see **12.4.1**) to the claimant's preferred court or the defendant's home court as appropriate (CPR, r 26.2A). Parties should set out in the directions questionnaire the court in which they would like the matter to be dealt with, and should reach an agreement on this point, if possible.

13.3 ALLOCATION TO TRACK

In accordance with CPR, r 26.7, personal injury and clinical negligence claims are allocated to the appropriate track within a three-tier system largely in accordance with the value of the claim as a whole and the value of the claim for damages for 'personal injuries' suffered, ie that part of the damages which relates to pain, suffering and loss of amenity.

The *small claims track* is the normal track in claims for personal injuries where:

(a) the value of the claim as a whole is not more than £10,000; and

(b) the value of any claim for damages for personal injuries is not more than:

  (i) £5,000 in a claim for personal injuries arising from a road traffic accident in England and Wales, except where r 26.10 applies (see (ii) below);

  (ii) £1,000 where the claim arises from a road traffic accident where the accident occurred before 31 May 2021, or where on the date that the proceedings are started: the claimant is a child or protected party (unless r 26.11 applies); the claimant was a vulnerable road user (namely that the claimant was using a motor cycle, or was a pillion or sidecar passenger, using a wheelchair or mobility scooter, a bicycle or other pedal cycle, riding a horse or was a pedestrian when the accident occurred); the claimant is an undischarged bankrupt; or (unless r 26.11 applies) the claimant or defendant acts as a personal representative of a deceased person. See r 26.7, r 26.10 and r 26.11. Rule 26.11 relates to children and protected parties and in effect sets out exemptions from the RTA Small Claims Protocol altogether. See **10.2** for further detail;

  (iii) £1,500 in any other claim for personal injuries.

The *fast track* is the normal track for any claim for which the small claims track is not the normal track and which has a value of not more than £25,000. However, such a case will be allocated to the fast track only if the court considers that:

(a) the trial is likely to last for no longer than one day; and

(b) oral expert evidence at trial will be limited to one expert per party in relation to a maximum of two expert fields.

The *multi-track* is the normal track for any claim for which the small claims track or the fast track is not the normal track.

Once the court has allocated a claim to a track, it will notify all parties, and it will also serve them with copies of the allocation questionnaire provided by all other parties and a copy of any further information provided by a party about their case.

Factors taken into account

When allocating a case, the court may take into account the following factors (CPR, r 26.13):

(a) the financial value of the claim (or amount in dispute if different);

(b) the nature of remedy sought;

(c) the likely complexity of the facts, law or evidence;

(d) the number of parties or likely parties;

(e) the value of any counterclaim or other claim and the complexity of any matters relating to it;

(f) the amount of oral evidence that may be required;

(g) the importance of the claim to persons who are not parties to the proceedings;

(h) the views expressed by the parties;

(i) the circumstances of the parties.

When assessing the value of the claim for the purposes of track allocation, the court will disregard any amounts not in dispute, interest, costs and any possible finding of contributory negligence which may be made against the claimant (CPR, r 26.13(2)).

If the statements of case are later amended and it becomes clear that the case has been allocated to an inappropriate track, the court may subsequently re-allocate a claim to a different track (CPR, r 26.18).

13.4   THE SMALL CLAIMS TRACK

The small claims track has been specifically designed to enable individuals to pursue or defend a claim without the need to instruct solicitors. A consideration of the procedure for these claims is generally beyond the scope of this book. However, the Pre-Action Protocol for Personal Injury Claims below the Small Claims Limit in Road Traffic Accidents ('RTA Small Claims Protocol'), which came into force on 31 May 2021, is discussed to some degree at **10.2**. See also the RTA Small Claims Protocol itself and CPR Practice Direction 27B.

13.5   THE FAST TRACK

Case management of cases allocated to the fast track (see CPR Part 28) will generally be by directions given at allocation and, later, on the filing of the pre-trial checklists (listing questionnaires). The court will seek to give directions without the need for a hearing wherever possible, and sanctions will be imposed upon parties or their legal representatives whose default makes a hearing necessary.

Generally, the court will give standard directions for the management of the case, based on what is set out below, which will not be more than 30 weeks from allocation to trial. Although the parties may seek to agree directions, they are unlikely to be approved if they are not based on the following:

Disclosure	4 weeks
Exchange of witness statements	10 weeks
Exchange of experts' reports	14 weeks
Pre-trial checklists, listing questionnaires sent out by court	20 weeks
Pre-trial checklists, listing questionnaires filed by parties	22 weeks
Trial	30 weeks

When giving directions relating to the trial, the court may fix a trial date but would more usually set a 'trial period', a three-week period within which the trial will take place.

From 1 October 2023, a new intermediate track will be introduced. Part 28 will deal with the fast and the intermediate track. The fast track is the normal track for claims up to a value of £25,000 where the trial is likely to last for no longer that one day and oral expert evidence is limited to one expert per party in two expert fields. The new intermediate track will be for simpler cases (which would otherwise have been allocated to the multi-track) where the damages are valued at up to £100,000. As from 1 October 2023, fixed recoverable costs will be extended across the fast track (but will not apply to clinical negligence claims). The new intermediate track will have four bands of complexity, with associated fixed recoverable costs for each. There will be new standard directions for the intermediate track.

The new rules on fixed recoverable costs on the fast track will apply to claims where proceedings are issued on or after 1 October 2023, except for personal injury claims. The new fixed recoverable costs regime will apply to personal injury claims where the cause of action accrues on or after 1 October 2023; and will only apply to disease claims where the letter of claim has not been sent to the defendant before 1 October 2023.

As a result, from 1 October 2023 there will be substantial changes to Part 45 (Fixed Costs) with a new Practice Direction to Part 45 setting out the relevant tables of costs, as well as changes to Part 26 and Part 28 and their Practice Directions.

13.6 THE MULTI-TRACK

Where the value of the claim is more than £25,000, or where other factors make it unsuitable for the fast track (and, as from 1 October 2023 the claim is not allocated to the intermediate track), the claim will be allocated to the multi-track (see CPR, Part 29). Claims which are just above the financial limit and which are fairly straightforward will be allocated to the intermediate track where the cause of action accrues after 1 October 2023. As a result, the claims allocated to the multi-track will be those of high value where the issues, evidence and law are extremely complex. The court will adopt a flexible approach in order to manage the claim in accordance with its needs. When allocating a case to the multi-track, the court will either:

(a) use the information contained in the directions questionnaires and any draft directions submitted by the parties in order to give directions for case management and set a timetable; or

(b) fix a case management conference or a pre-trial review, or both, when it will hear from the parties and then give such directions relating to management of the case as it thinks fit.

In accordance with CPR, r 29.1(2), when drafting case management directions, both the parties and the court should take as their starting point any relevant model directions and standard directions, which can be found online at www.justice.gov.uk/courts/procedure-rules/civil, and adapt them as appropriate to the circumstances of the particular case.

13.7 THE CASE MANAGEMENT CONFERENCE AND PRE-TRIAL REVIEW

Where the court decides that directions cannot be given without hearing directly from the parties, it may, at any time after the filing of the defence, fix a date for a case management conference and/or, after the return of the directions questionnaires, set a date for a pre-trial review. Where a party is legally represented, any case management conference or pre-trial review called by the court must be attended by a legal representative who is familiar with the case and has the authority to take decisions regarding the management of the case. It is therefore important that the solicitors have obtained their client's instructions regarding all matters which are likely to be dealt with at the hearing. The court will expect the parties to be in a position to deal with all outstanding matters regarding the conduct of the case, and to reach an agreement regarding these matters wherever possible. It is increasingly common for case management conferences to be conducted over the telephone.

Personal injury and clinical negligence claims are generally subject to the costs management provisions in CPR Part 3. However, CPR, r 3.12(1) makes it clear that those provisions will not apply to a claim brought by or on behalf of a child or to any claim subject to fixed costs unless the court orders otherwise.

13.7.1 Case management in relation to an additional claim

Where the defendant to an additional claim (see **12.12**) files a defence, a case management hearing will take place to enable the court to consider the future conduct of the proceedings and give appropriate directions. It is obliged to ensure, in so far as it is practicable, that the original claim and all additional claims are managed together (CPR, r 20.13). In accordance with PD 20, para 5.3, at the hearing the court may:

(a) treat the hearing as a summary judgment hearing;

(b) order that the additional claim be dismissed;

(c)   give directions about the way any claim, question or issue set out in or arising from the additional claim should be dealt with;

(d)   give directions as to the part, if any, the additional defendant will take at the trial of the claim;

(e)   give directions about the extent to which the additional defendant is to be bound by any judgment or decision to be made in the claim.

Paragraph 7 of PD 20 sets out how parties should be described in the proceedings when there are additional claims. In summary, the claimant and defendants in the original claim should be referred to as such, and additional parties should be referred to as 'Third Party' or 'Fourth Party', depending on the order in which they were joined to the proceedings.

13.8   DISCLOSURE AND INSPECTION OF DOCUMENTS

Recent changes to the rules relating to disclosure and inspection of documents in multi-track cases require parties to file and serve a disclosure report, which includes an estimate of the costs associated with the disclosure process. However, it should be noted that where a multi-track claim includes a claim for personal injuries, it is exempt from this requirement. Consequently, parties are not required to give more than standard disclosure in fast track and multi-track cases unless the court directs otherwise (see CPR, r 31.5(2)).

Standard disclosure (CPR, r 31.6) means that a party is required to disclose only:

(a)   the documents on which he relies;

(b)   the documents which could adversely affect his own case, adversely affect another's case or support another party's case; and

(c)   all documents which he is required to disclose by any Practice Direction.

The court may dispense with or limit standard disclosure, and the parties can agree in writing to dispense with or limit any part of standard disclosure. The duty of standard disclosure continues throughout the proceedings, and if a document comes to a party's notice at any time, that party must immediately notify every other party. Privileged documents, however, should be listed as such in the party's list of documents, but should not be offered for inspection.

13.8.1   Procedure

Each party must make and serve a list of documents, which must identify the documents 'in a convenient order and manner as concisely as possible' (CPR, r 31.10(3)). The list must indicate documents which are no longer in the party's control, if any, and state what has happened to those documents and when they were last in the party's control.

The list must include a disclosure statement by the party (CPR, r 31.10):

(a)   setting out the extent of the search made to locate the documents;

(b)   certifying that the party understands the duty of disclosure and that, to the best of his knowledge, he has carried out that duty.

13.8.2   Specific disclosure

Where a party believes that the other party has failed to carry out their duty of disclosure and inspection under CPR Part 31, they may apply for an order for specific disclosure under CPR, r 31.12. An order for specific disclosure can require a party to disclose specified documents or classes of documents, or carry out a search for specified documents and disclose any documents located as a result of that search.

An application for specific disclosure must be supported by evidence. The court will order specific disclosure only if necessary to dispose fairly of the claim or save costs.

For applications for an order for pre-action disclosure, see **10.10.2**.

13.9 THE EVIDENCE OF LAY WITNESSES

As part of its management powers, the court will decide the issues on which it requires evidence, the nature of that evidence and the way in which the evidence should be placed before the court (see CPR Part 32).

Facts should normally be proved at the trial by oral evidence of witnesses, and at any other hearing by the written evidence of witnesses. The court may allow a witness to give evidence by any means, which includes by means of a video link.

13.9.1 Procedure

According to CPR, r 32.4(1): 'A witness statement is a written statement signed by a person which contains the evidence which that person would be allowed to give orally.' A witness statement must comply with the requirements set out in PD 32 (CPR, r 32.8).

The court will normally give directions that each party serve the witness statements of the oral evidence on which they intend to rely at the trial. The directions usually envisage that simultaneous exchange will take place, but that the court may give directions as to the order in which such witness statements are to be served and whether or not the statements are to be filed.

If a witness statement has been served and a party wishes to rely on that evidence at trial, the party must call the witness to give oral evidence unless the court otherwise orders.

13.9.2 Statements to stand as evidence-in-chief

Where a witness is called to give oral evidence, their statement shall stand as evidence-in-chief, unless the court orders otherwise (CPR, r 32.5(2)).

The witness giving the oral evidence may amplify the witness statement, and give evidence in relation to new matters that have arisen since the statement was served. However, the witness may do this only if the court considers there is a good reason not to confine the evidence to the contents of the statement that has been served, and the court's permission is required.

Evidence in proceedings other than at the trial (ie on an interim application) should be by witness statement, unless the court or a particular Practice Direction otherwise directs.

13.9.3 Witness summary

Where a party is required to serve a witness statement and they are unable to obtain such a statement, for example because the witness refuses to communicate with the party's solicitor, the party may apply to the court for permission to serve only a witness summary instead (CPR, r 32.9). This application should be made without notice. The witness summary is a summary of the evidence which would otherwise go into a witness statement, or, if the evidence is not known, matters about which the party serving the witness summary will question the witness.

Where a witness statement or a witness summary is not served, the party will not be able to call that witness to give oral evidence unless the court allows it.

13.10 EXPERT EVIDENCE

The duties of experts in relation to court proceedings and the directions which the courts are likely to make are dealt with in Part 35 of the CPR (see **Chapter 11** generally and **11.2** for case management and the use of experts).

13.11   USE OF PLANS, PHOTOGRAPHS AND MODELS AT TRIAL

Where a party wishes to use evidence such as plans, photographs or models, or other evidence:

(a)   which is not contained in a witness statement, affidavit or expert's report;

(b)   which is not given orally at trial;

(c)   which has already been disclosed in relation to hearsay evidence;

the party wishing to use the evidence must disclose their intention to do so not later than the latest date for serving witness statements (CPR, r 33.6).

If the evidence forms part of expert evidence, it must be disclosed when the expert's report is itself served on the other party. Having disclosed such evidence, the party must give every other party an opportunity to inspect it and agree its admission without further proof.

13.12   PRE-TRIAL CHECKLIST (LISTING QUESTIONNAIRE)

In accordance with the order for directions and unless the court considers that the claim can proceed to trial without one, the court will send each party a pre-trial checklist (listing questionnaire) to complete and return to the court by the date specified in the notice of allocation (CPR, r 28.4 (fast track); CPR, r 29.6 (multi-track)). The date specified for filing a pre-trial checklist (listing questionnaire) is not more than eight weeks before the trial date.

If a party fails to file a completed pre-trial checklist within the time limit, or fails to give all the information requested, or the court thinks it is necessary, the court may fix a listing hearing or give such other directions as it thinks appropriate. If no party files the completed pre-trial checklist by the date specified, the court will order that unless a completed pre-trial checklist is filed within seven days from service of the court's order, the claim, defence and any counterclaim will be struck out without further order of the court. See CPR, r 28.4(3) and CPR, r 29.6(3). Relief from sanction would then need to be sought.

On receipt of the pre-trial checklist, the court may decide to hold a pre-trial review, or cancel a pre-trial review if it has already decided to hold one, having regard to the circumstances of the case.

Using the information given in the pre-trial checklists or at the pre-trial review or listing hearing, the court will set a timetable for the trial, including confirming or fixing the trial date and setting out any further steps that need to be taken by the parties prior to the trial.

The court will give each party at least three weeks' notice of the trial date. Only in exceptional circumstances will the notice period be shorter than this.

13.13   VARIATION OF CASE MANAGEMENT TIMETABLE

The parties may agree in writing to extend the dates for the carrying out of any steps set out in the directions subject to CPR, r 29.5. This states that if a party wishes to vary any of the dates which the court has fixed for:

(a)   a case management conference;

(b)   a pre-trial review;

(c)   the return of a pre-trial checklist;

(d)   the trial;

they may do so only with permission of the court. The parties should not agree to make any other variations to the timetable which would make it impossible for them to comply with the time limits set for the above steps.

13.14 INTERIM APPLICATIONS

Interim applications are applications which are made by either party between the issue of proceedings and trial. The general rules governing such applications are set out in CPR Part 23, but practitioners should be aware that some types of application are governed by specific rules. For a detailed consideration of interim applications, see **Civil Litigation**. This text will deal with the following types of application:

(a)   interim payments;

(b)   specific disclosure – see **13.8.2** above; and

(c)   specific disclosure against a non-party.

13.15 INTERIM PAYMENTS

An interim payment is a payment made to the claimant, prior to the conclusion of the matter, in partial settlement of the claim. It is defined as 'a payment on account of any damages, debt or other sum (excluding any costs) which that party may be held liable to pay to or for the benefit of another party to the proceedings if a final judgment or order of the court in the proceedings is given or made in favour of that other party' (Senior Courts Act 1981, s 32(5) and County Courts Act 1984, s 50(5)).

In a multi-track case where liability has been admitted or proven, or where the claimant can demonstrate a strong case on liability, an interim payment will assist in mitigating the effects of financial hardship caused by the often lengthy period between the accident and the determination of the claim. Interim payments are particularly important where the claimant has suffered catastrophic injuries or disablement and requires access to a substantial sum of money in order to pay for accommodation and/or a care regime.

An interim payment cannot be made in a small claims track case and, whilst not forbidden in a fast track case, will be rarely made due both to the value of the claim and to the relatively short period of time from issue of proceedings to trial. For interim payments in cases falling under one of the low value pre-action protocols, see **21.4**.

Where the grounds for making an order are satisfied, the court has a discretionary power to order that the defendant make an interim payment under r 25.6 of the CPR. The order may specify that such payment be made by instalments, and more than one order may be made during the lifetime of a claim. Where the claimant is a child or a protected party (see **Chapter 20**), the payment will usually be made to the Court of Protection.

In accordance with CPR, r 25.9, where an interim payment has been made either voluntarily or pursuant to a court order, unless the defendant agrees, this shall not be disclosed to the trial judge until all questions of liability and quantum have been decided.

13.15.1 Grounds for making the order

In accordance with CPR, r 25.7(1), the court may order an interim payment only if:

(a)   the defendant admits liability; or

(b)   the claimant has a judgment for damages to be assessed; or

(c)   if the matter were to proceed to trial, the claimant would obtain judgment for a substantial amount of money.

The court will take into account the defendant's ability to pay the interim payment before making an order.

In a claim where there are two or more defendants, the court may make an order for interim payment against any of them if it is satisfied that, if the claim went to trial, the claimant would obtain judgment for substantial damages against at least one of the defendants although it cannot determine which. It will do so only where all the defendants are either insured or they are a public body, or liability will be met by the MIB.

Although a claimant will normally set out in their application why the interim payment is required, they are not obliged to show that there is a *need* for the payment. In *Stringman v McCardle* [1994] 1 WLR 1653, Stuart-Smith LJ said: 'It should be noted that the plaintiff does not have to demonstrate any particular need over and above the general need that a plaintiff has to be paid his or her damages as soon as reasonably may be done.'

13.15.2 Procedure

Before making an application to the court for an interim payment, the claimant's solicitor should contact the defendant's solicitor and request that the defendant make a voluntary interim payment. The defendant may be amenable to such a request; if the payment is to fund treatment or rehabilitation costs, this may reduce the final award of damages and interest payments will be reduced. However, where the claimant is a child or protected party, the permission of the court is required before an interim payment is made (PD 25B, para 1.2).

A claimant may not seek an interim payment until after the time for acknowledging service has expired (CPR, r 25.6(1)).

The application should be made using Form N244 and must be supported by evidence. Although the evidence may be set out on the application form itself, generally it will be set out in a supporting witness statement. Paragraph 2.1 of PD25B states that the evidence must deal with the following:

(1)   the sum of money sought by way of an interim payment,

(2)   the items or matters in respect of which the interim payment is sought,

(3)   the sum of money for which final judgment is likely to be given,

(4)   the reasons for believing that the conditions set out in rule 25.7 are satisfied,

(5)   any other relevant matters,

(6)   in claims for personal injuries, details of special damages and past and future loss, and

(7)   in a claim under the Fatal Accidents Act 1976, details of the person(s) on whose behalf the claim is made and the nature of the claim.

Paragraph 2.2 of PD 25B states that any documents in support of the application should be exhibited, including, in personal injuries claims, the medical report(s).

The application notice and witness statement in support must be served on the defendant (the respondent) at least 14 days before the hearing date for the application. If the defendant wishes to rely on a witness statement in response to the application, they must file and serve a copy of that witness statement at least seven days before the hearing of the application; and if the claimant (the applicant) wishes to file a further witness statement in reply, the claimant must do so at least three days before the hearing.

Where the claimant has been in receipt of recoverable benefits which will fall to be repaid by the defendant to the Compensation Recovery Unit (CRU) (see **Chapter 16**), the defendant should obtain a certificate of recoverable benefits in advance of the hearing of the interim application and file this with the court.

13.15.3 The amount of the interim payment

When dealing with an application for an interim payment, the court will seek to avoid making an overpayment which may lead to the claimant having to repay money to the defendant (see **13.15.4**). In accordance with CPR, r 25.7(4) and (5), the amount of the interim payment must not exceed a reasonable proportion of the likely amount of the final judgment, taking into account contributory negligence and any relevant set-off or counterclaim.

Where there is a large discrepancy between what the claimant and the defendant believe will be ultimately awarded, the court will first look at the amount of special damages which have already accrued and the amount of special damages which will arise prior to the date of trial. There can be a large degree of certainty as to the likely amount of damages to be awarded in this respect. The court will then attempt to determine what the court is likely to award in respect of pain, suffering and loss of amenity, etc, and future loss of earnings and costs of care, which is much more speculative.

Defendants have sought to limit the size of interim payments by arguing:

(a) that allowing substantial interim payments to cover the cost of purchasing new accommodation and/or an expensive care regime, in circumstances where the defendant argues that the accommodation or care regime is excessive for the claimant's needs, distorts the 'level playing field' against defendants. When quantum is ultimately considered by the court, it is considerably harder for the defendants to argue this point when the accommodation has already been purchased and the care regime is up and running, and where expert witnesses are able to give evidence as to how the claimant's needs are being met. In *Spillman v Bradfield Riding Centre* [2007] EWHC 89 (QB), the claimant, a minor, suffered serious head injuries when she was kicked by a horse at the defendant's riding school. The application for an interim payment to fund special care and to enable her parents to purchase a larger house, which they argued was necessary for her benefit, was rejected at first instance. At appeal, the defendant unsuccessfully argued that if the interim payment was ordered in the amount sought by the claimant, the head of damage would become self-fulfilling as, at the date of trial, the claimant would have benefited from the accommodation and care to which the defendants argued she was not entitled. The Court of Appeal stated that the purpose of ordering only a 'reasonable proportion' was to avoid prejudice to a defendant who may have overpaid if a final award was not as substantial as had been anticipated. The Court decided that 75% of the amount proposed by the defendant as the final award was sufficient to protect against overpayment;

(b) that allowing a substantial interim payment may prevent the court at trial from awarding periodical payments (see **15.5**) because there will be insufficient damages left to be paid. This argument is particularly relevant to cases where the claimant's life expectancy has been reduced significantly. Where it is likely that the final judgment would involve an order for periodical payments to be made, the court has to consider what is the 'likely amount' for the purposes of CPR, r 25.7(4). In *Braithwaite v Homerton University Hospitals Foundation Trust* [2008] EWHC 353 (QB), the court held that the likely amount of the final judgment was the capital sum plus a periodical sum payable during the life of the claimant. Consequently, the court must be confident that the amount of the proposed interim payment is not in excess of the capital sum ultimately awarded at trial.

There is no specific rule as to what constitutes a 'reasonable proportion', but decided cases appear to suggest that the courts will order a maximum of 75% of the likely final award of damages.

For guidance in cases where an interim payment is sought and where the final judgment is likely to include a periodical payment order, see the Court of Appeal's judgment in *Cobham Hire Services Ltd v Eeles* [2009] EWCA Civ 204.

It should be noted that where recoverable benefits have been received by the claimant, the claimant will receive the interim payment net of the amount of the benefits. The defendant will pay an amount equal to the recoverable benefits to the CRU.

13.15.4 Repayment and variation

In accordance with r 25.8 of the CPR, where a defendant has made an interim payment either voluntarily or pursuant to an order, the court may order that all or part of that sum be repaid by the claimant, or that the defendant be reimbursed by another defendant.

In addition, where a defendant makes an interim payment which it transpires exceeds the defendant's liability under the final judgment, the court may award interest on the overpaid amount from the date the interim payment was made.

13.16 SPECIFIC DISCLOSURE OF DOCUMENTS HELD BY A THIRD PARTY

Once proceedings have been commenced, the court may make an order for specific disclosure of documents against a non-party under CPR, r 31.17(3), only where:

(a)   the documents of which disclosure is sought are likely to support the case of the applicant or adversely affect the case of one or other of the parties to the proceedings; and

(b)   disclosure is necessary to dispose fairly of the claim or save costs.

The application must be supported by appropriate evidence. An order under r 31.17 will specify the documents or class of documents which must be disclosed, and require the respondent to make disclosure or specify any of those documents which are no longer in the respondent's possession or for which the respondent claims the right or duty to withhold from inspection. The order may specify a time and place for such disclosure and inspection.

13.17 CONCLUSION

When proceedings are defended, upon completion of the directions questionnaires, the case will be allocated to the appropriate track, and may be transferred from the court of issue to another court where appropriate. The court will then actively manage the matter in accordance with the overriding objective set out in CPR, r 1, and will require the parties and their solicitors to cooperate fully in achieving that objective. The parties will be expected to do their best to settle the matter as soon as possible and without the need for a court hearing.

Directions will be issued as are appropriate for the track to which the case has been allocated, and practitioners must do all they can to ensure that steps are taken within the specified time limits.

Solicitors acting for claimants and defendants may make interim applications to the court in relation to diverse issues such as time extensions, specific disclosure and interim payments, either where agreement cannot be reached between the parties or where the CPR require the court's involvement. Where possible, such applications should be made at the time of case management conferences, pre-trial reviews or at the same time as other applications, in order to save court time and costs.

Sound case management systems and procedures are essential, as judges are increasingly intolerant of avoidable delays and mistakes which lead to unnecessary applications.

CHAPTER 14

NEGOTIATIONS, ALTERNATIVE DISPUTE RESOLUTION AND TRIAL

LEARNING OUTCOMES

After reading this chapter you will be able to:

- understand how to prepare for and conduct a negotiation on behalf of the client
- draw up an appropriate consent order
- draft a Part 36 offer including provisional damages or periodical payments
- identify steps necessary to prepare a case for trial.

14.1 INTRODUCTION

Over 90% of personal injury claims and many clinical negligence claims settle without trial. It is usually the case that the solicitor's skill in arguing their client's claim with the other side's representative, rather than their ability to argue the case at trial, will determine the level of damages. For this reason, the personal injury solicitor is more likely to become a skilled negotiator than a trial advocate.

In order to avoid a potential negligence claim, it is imperative that the claimant solicitor is absolutely sure that the client's medical prognosis is clear prior to proceeding to settle the claim, or to advising the client that it is appropriate to settle the claim. In this regard the solicitor will rely heavily on the medical report and the prognosis for recovery contained within it. It should be stressed to the client that the prognosis is only an estimate, and if the client does not feel that they have recovered then the solicitor cannot advise the client to settle their claim prematurely. It should be pointed out to the client that the compensation offered by the defendant is a 'once and for all payment', and the client therefore cannot (normally) return at a future date to obtain further compensation if the prognosis for recovery should prove to be incorrect.

This chapter aims to summarise the main factors to take into account when negotiating, and considers other methods of alternative dispute resolution (ADR) which may be used in personal injury and clinical negligence cases (including cases within the low value protocols). Inevitably there will be cases which are not capable of settlement and which must proceed to trial, in which case it is vital to prepare properly as a poorly presented case will not impress a judge. The steps that should be taken to prepare the case for trial are also explained below (but note that, for cases which are proceeding within the low value protocols, different procedures apply and reference should instead be made to **Chapter 21**).

14.2 PROFESSIONAL CONDUCT

As a matter of conduct, a solicitor does not have ostensible authority to settle a client's claim until after proceedings have been issued. It is imperative for the solicitor to seek the client's specific instructions prior to settling a claim. For example, even if the client instructs their solicitor that the solicitor can settle the client's claim as long as the client receives at least £1,000, the solicitor should, when negotiating with the defence, stipulate that any agreement is 'subject to the client's instructions'. In this way, if the client should change their mind (which the client may do at any time), the solicitor will not have committed the client to the settlement irrevocably. A solicitor acting for the defendant must be careful not to exceed any authority they have been given to settle by their insurance client.

Negotiations should always be entered into on an expressly 'without prejudice' basis. When talking to an insurer in person or on the telephone, it is advisable for the solicitor to preface anything they say by stating expressly at the outset that the entire conversation is without prejudice to their client's claim.

14.3 NEGOTIATING WITH INSURANCE COMPANIES AND DEFENCE SOLICITORS

Claims can be settled by agreement being reached between the parties at any stage. The pre-action protocols encourage early disclosure of information to facilitate this. Claimant solicitors have in the past considered that defendant insurers will not make reasonable offers for settlement prior to issue of proceedings. For this reason, many claimant solicitors have tended to issue proceedings first and negotiate second. This strategy is not encouraged by the CPR 1998. The pre-action protocols require that attempts be made to settle disputes. For a detailed consideration of the protocols, see **Chapter 10** (and **Chapter 21** for the low value protocols).

When negotiating with the defendant's insurer or its solicitor, a firm approach should be taken by the claimant's solicitor. They must be alert to the fact that the insurer is in business to make money for its shareholders, and its employees are employed to ensure that as little money as possible is paid out in damages. Therefore, the claimant's solicitor should not delay in issuing proceedings, after the pre-action protocol has been complied with if the defendant has failed or refused to make an acceptable response. Failure to do so is likely to be a failure to act in the best interests of the client.

14.4 PREPARING FOR THE NEGOTIATION

Prior to any negotiation, the solicitor should first become familiar with the file, noting specifically any matters likely to increase the level of damages, such as the risk of osteoarthritis or permanent scarring. There is a risk that the solicitor will fail to remember the file adequately because they may be running many very similar claims at any one time. When reviewing the file it is good practice to build up a profile of the severity of the injuries by reading the medical reports and the client's statement. Matters relevant to each head of loss should be noted, so that the solicitor has a list of areas of loss without having to make reference to the specifics of the claim itself.

EXAMPLE

Client A is aged 56. She suffered injuries to her left shoulder and abrasions to both arms and legs when she tripped over a loose paving stone in her local high street. She is a keen gardener and likes to attend aerobics once a week, and enjoys walking her dog in the countryside near her home. Her husband took early retirement due to ill-health and is not able to assist her much, but he has been driving her to the doctor and to physiotherapy, and has been helping her bathe and dress herself. Day-to-day cleaning of the house and gardening has been undertaken by friends and relations.

The profile in such a case would be along the lines of the following:

General damages claim:

(a)   female aged 56, therefore likely to take some time for injuries to mend, danger of osteoarthritis revealed in medical report;

(b)   report revealed split fracture to the clavicle (collar bone) together with a tear to the *latissimus dorsi* (muscle beneath the shoulder) and associated soft tissue damage;

(c)   medical intervention involved substantial and uncomfortable strapping to render the injury immobile followed by light physiotherapy. Physiotherapy continued for 20 weeks;

(d)   reasonably fit, unable to undertake pastimes such as aerobics and walking in countryside for X weeks.

Special damages:

(a)   clothes and personal items lost or damaged in the accident;

(b)   mileage claim for travel to and from hospital/physiotherapy;

(c)   prescription charges;

(d)   daily care necessary;

(e)   husband unable to care on his own due to his own ill-health;

(f)   cleaning of house and garden maintenance undertaken by others.

Having built up such a profile, the next stage is for the solicitor to become familiar with the likely level of damages to be awarded in such a claim. Such familiarity comes with experience. The method of approach to calculation of damages is considered in detail in **Chapter 15**.

In addition to reviewing quantum, the solicitor must ensure that they have a good grasp of the facts of the accident and the evidence supporting the case on liability. The solicitor must undertake a thorough review of all statements of case, witness statements and other documents disclosed, and consideration should be given to possible arguments of contributory negligence.

The client should be aware that any form of litigation carries with it a certain amount of risk that the claim will fail because the evidence may not come up to proof at trial. Because of this 'litigation risk', it is likely that the defence solicitor will seek some reduction in damages because the claimant is being spared the upset and risk of failure at trial.

If acting for the defendant, the solicitor must obtain a certificate of recoverable benefit from the DWP before making any offer in settlement so that any relevant benefits can be taken into account.

14.5 CONDUCTING THE NEGOTIATION

The technique of negotiation is discussed in **Skills for Lawyers**. When conducting negotiations, it is worth bearing in mind the following:

(a) Settlement should not be entered into prematurely. If proceedings are never issued and the defendant's insurers make clear that they do not contest the case, argument will centre on quantum, and it will be fairly safe to negotiate. If, however, the matter is contested, it is unwise to negotiate prior to disclosure of each side's evidence. For this reason, many solicitors believe that settlement should not be contemplated prior to the exchange of witness evidence. Once the solicitor has considered the evidence, they can then assist the client to make an informed decision as to whether the client should accept a settlement.

(b) The solicitor must never negotiate when unprepared. The file must be considered thoroughly prior to proceeding with negotiations. If the solicitor receives a surprise telephone call from a defendant insurer seeking a settlement, it is better for the solicitor to call back later, after having considered the case afresh.

(c) The defence should be invited to put forward its settlement figure with supporting argument as to why that figure is correct. Comments should be kept to a minimum and further negotiations postponed while the offer is considered. This is easiest to do if negotiating over the telephone, as negotiation can be cut short and re-established later with minimum difficulty. The telephone has the added advantage that the person making an offer cannot see the reaction of the recipient of the call, and will be unable to gauge how well or how badly the offer is received. The claimant's solicitor should never disclose their valuation of the claim first in negotiations, and should not reveal any figures until they believe the defendant is putting forward a realistic amount.

(d) The defence opening offer is unlikely to be the best it is prepared to come up with. All offers must, however, be put to the client. A solicitor has a duty to act in the best interests of their client, and this includes obtaining the best possible settlement figure.

(e) An offer by the defence to pay the claimant's costs to date should not sway the solicitor into advising their client to accept an offer. If the defence is offering to settle, it is effectively admitting (albeit without prejudice) that there is merit in the claim, and it would normally be obliged to pay the claimant's reasonable costs if the case went to trial.

(f) Often the solicitor has specific instructions to try to settle the case on the client's behalf. In such circumstances, they may seek confirmation that a settlement will be agreed as long as the client will receive at least £x. If this is the case, the solicitor must be careful not to jump at the first offer simply because it will secure for the client the minimum that the client requires and will usually also secure payment of the solicitor's costs.

(g) Consideration of the defendant's offer should not be rushed. Any attempt to force an agreement quickly should be regarded as spurious. The defence would not have made an offer if it was happy to take the case to trial. Therefore, regardless of whether a time limit is placed on the offer, it is likely that unless fresh evidence comes to light strengthening the defence case, an offer once made will remain open. By making an offer at all the defence is saying that it would far rather pay than fight.

(h) When negotiating, defendant insurers will often offer to 'split the difference' if agreement cannot be reached on a particular head of loss. This is a favourite tactic that the claimant solicitor should consider carefully before accepting. On the face of it, it may appear to be a generous offer, bringing negotiations to a speedy conclusion. On closer scrutiny, it may be a ploy which results in the loss of a substantial portion of the client's legitimate expectation in a particular head of damages.

14.6 NEGOTIATING IN CLINICAL NEGLIGENCE CLAIMS

When considering negotiation in the context of clinical negligence claims, the following additional points should be borne in mind.

(a) In many cases, the NHS complaints procedure will already have been put to use, and there may therefore be greater clarity as regards the issues of the claim.

(b) It is unlikely that any negotiations with a view to settlement will be made prior to full recourse to the clinical disputes PAP. Only after both sides have had access to full disclosure and expert opinion will it be possible for any meaningful negotiation to take place.

(c) In straightforward claims of low value, negotiating tactics as outlined above may be appropriate. In relation to more complex claims, it is more likely that there would be a meeting of the parties' solicitors, with or without experts, to try to narrow as many issues as possible. In appropriate cases, counsel for both sides may be asked to discuss the case informally to try to narrow areas in dispute.

14.7 ALTERNATIVE DISPUTE RESOLUTION

The use of ADR is likely to become more important in the resolution of disputes, as the overriding objective (stated in Part 1 of the CPR 1998) encourages its prompt use as a way of furthering the overriding objective and to aid prompt settlement. Most disputes are capable of resolution either by discussion and negotiation, or by trial on the issues. The rules encourage the use of alternatives to litigation as a first resort and of litigation as a last resort. **Civil Litigation** explains ADR in detail.

14.7.1 Different types of ADR

All of the methods of ADR are mechanisms which aim to bring the parties together to obtain a consensual agreement rather than a ruling which is forced upon them. The main types of ADR available today are as follows:

14.7.1.1 Mediation

In mediation, a neutral third party is chosen by the parties as their intermediary (mediator). The mediator is likely to meet the opposing parties separately to try to establish some common ground before finally bringing the parties together to try to reach an agreement.

14.7.1.2 Conciliation

Conciliation is a similar process to mediation. However, the conciliator is likely to take a more interventionist approach by taking a more central role. The mediator will often consider the case as put forward by both sides, and then suggest terms of settlement which the mediator feels to be most appropriate.

14.7.1.3 The mini-trial

The format and content of a mini-trial is much more like a trial. It will be chaired by a neutral mediator who will sit with a representative from each party.

14.7.2 Case management conference

At the case management conference/pre-trial review, the parties will be told to confirm whether the question of ADR has been considered and also to confirm, if it has not, why this is the case.

When considering the conduct of the parties, the judge is entitled to consider the parties' unreasonable refusal to use ADR, as this is central to the ethos of how to deal with disputes in accordance with Part 1 of the CPR 1998. Where ADR has been refused, or where a party has later failed to co-operate with ADR, the court is entitled to take that into account when considering what costs order to make, or whether to make any costs order at all.

14.7.3 ADR and personal injury claims

Use of the pre-action protocol will ensure that the parties are better able to obtain a greater depth of knowledge about the case against them than in the past. Full use of pre-action disclosure, and preliminary disclosure of key documents, will enable each side to obtain a far better view of the issues of the case in relation to liability, and will therefore allow them to make a far better and earlier assessment of their client's case.

At the stage where the parties complete their directions questionnaire, they will be asked whether they would like their proceedings to be stayed while they try to settle the case by way of ADR.

Because the court is very likely to ask whether the parties are interested in attempting ADR, and whether the possibility of ADR has been discussed with the client prior to any case management conference, it follows that the solicitor will need to ask their client at an early stage whether the client would be interested in pursuing the matter by way of ADR, and must explain to the client what this will entail.

In *Halsey v Milton Keynes General NHS Trust* [2004] EWCA Civ 576, the Trust refused to refer the matter to mediation as it was of the steadfast view that there had been no negligence and therefore referral to ADR would increase costs and delay. The claim was dismissed by the court. When the court came to consider the question of costs, it stated that when deciding whether a successful party had acted unreasonably in refusing to agree to ADR, the court should bear in mind the advantages of ADR over the court process and have regard to all of the circumstances of the particular case. The following factors were found to be of relevance:

(a)   the nature of the dispute;

(b)   the merits of the case;

(c)   the extent to which other settlement methods had been attempted;

(d)   whether the costs of ADR would be disproportionately high;

(e)   whether any delay in setting up and attending the ADR would have been prejudicial;

(f)   whether the ADR had a reasonable prospect of success.

14.7.4 The timing of ADR

It is likely that in complicated cases ADR will not be appropriate until such time as statements of case and disclosure of documents by both sides have been dealt with. Only then will ADR be a practical alternative to a trial. It is therefore likely that parties in cases which were initially felt to be unsuitable for ADR may find that ADR is a possibility once the case is at the case management conference stage.

14.7.5 Procedure following failed ADR

Where the parties have attempted ADR and this has failed to produce a settlement, the parties are likely to wish to fall back on their original court proceedings or intended court proceedings.

At this stage, if proceedings have already been issued, the solicitor for the claimant will need to apply promptly for further directions in the case so that the matter may proceed swiftly to trial.

However, although ADR may fail to produce a settlement, it may produce a degree of information about the other side's case which prior to ADR had not been clear. If this is so, it may be that an offer to settle or payment should be considered by either party or both parties.

14.7.6 ADR in clinical negligence cases

Although the majority of clinical negligence claims do settle, due to their relative complexity they often do so at a very late stage. NHS Resolution, which handles clinical negligence claims (see **5.7**), encourages the use of ADR, and the Clinical Disputes Forum has also produced a guide on the use of mediation in clinical negligence disputes.

The guidance aims to:

(a)   ensure that the use of ADR is considered by clients and solicitors at key points in clinical negligence claims;

(b)   require solicitors to report to their regional office at various stages in the litigation, explaining why ADR has not been pursued if appropriate;

(c)   explain the approach regional offices should take in deciding whether to limit a certificate to work necessary to progress ADR;

(d)   help the parties set up mediation.

14.7.6.1   When should ADR be considered in clinical negligence claims?

The parties should keep the possibilities of ADR in mind at all times. However, at the outset of litigation ADR is not likely to be appropriate until the PAP for use in clinical negligence claims has been complied with, because the client and their solicitor are unlikely to have information available to enter into a fair settlement of the claim.

Once the clinical negligence PAP has been complied with, solicitors should consider with their clients the use of ADR at the following stages:

(a)   prior to issue of proceedings;

(b)   before and immediately after a case management conference;

(c)   before and immediately after pre-trial review;

(d)   whenever the other side offers ADR;

(e)   whenever the new parties are specifically asked to consider ADR by the court.

If at any of the above points it is decided by the client or solicitor not to pursue ADR, the reason for that decision should be recorded on the solicitor's file.

14.7.6.2   Cases where ADR may not be appropriate

The following types of claims may not be suitable for ADR:

(a)   where essential basic information (such as relevant medical records, key expert evidence on liability and causation) is not available;

(b)   where there is no clear prognosis for the condition of the client and time is needed to see how the client progresses before settlement can be considered;

(c)   ADR is unnecessary as all parties are already negotiating effectively;

(d)   proceedings need to be issued urgently in order for the claim to be within the relevant limitation period;

(e)   the claim includes a future cost of care claim and information is needed as to quantum before any settlement can be discussed;

(f)   the case is a 'test case' and requires a ruling from a court in order to lay down a precedent for future claims;

(g)   ADR would not be a cost-effective way of dealing with the claim because there is no reason to believe that the claim will be resolved more quickly or cheaply by using it.

14.7.7   NHS complaints procedure

The complaints procedure (which is dealt with in detail in **Chapter 5**) is designed specifically to provide an explanation to patients in cases where they have felt sufficiently concerned about the healthcare received to make a complaint. The procedure is not designed or able to give compensation to patients. It is useful if the only or main issue at stake is for an explanation or an apology to be obtained, or simply to find more information to help the patient to come to terms with an event, or to help the patient decide whether to take further action and, if so, what form this should take.

14.7.8 Mediation

Mediation may be appropriate in some cases where the parties agree. This may be seen as particularly useful when there are allegations of clinical negligence, as ADR will be conducted in private, and this is something which is likely to appeal to medical practitioners who may not wish the allegations to be made public and reportable, as would be the case if the matter were to proceed in open court to a trial.

14.8   FUNDING ANY SETTLEMENT

In nearly all personal injury cases, there will not be a problem with the financing of any settlement, as the defendant will have been required to be insured in respect of the potential liability and a commercial insurer will normally meet any settlement.

In clinical negligence cases too, the defendant will normally not have a problem with the financing of any settlement but the administration of the settlement can be rather more complicated in certain cases. NHS Resolution administers the Clinical Negligence Scheme for Trusts (CNST), which is a scheme for handling clinical negligence claims against NHS Trusts. The CNST came into being as a result of concern over the financing of damages claims, and key objects of the scheme are to protect NHS Trusts and improve the quality of risk management. The CNST is not an insurance scheme but a mutual fund (see **5.7** above).

The administration of any settlement is normally of little concern to claimant solicitors, but practitioners may become frustrated by the delays which can arise with insurance companies in personal injury cases and also the NHS Resolution, as they operate a system whereby certain levels of settlement have to be given specific approvals.

14.9   COURT ORDERS

It is good practice to obtain a court order formally stating the terms of the settlement. A settlement on behalf of a minor should always be contained in a court order (see **Chapter 20**). The court will charge a fee for sealing the consent order.

14.9.1   Advantages of obtaining a court order

The advantages of obtaining an order are:

(a)   payment of interest and costs can be dealt with specifically;
(b)   if the amount stated in the order is not paid, the order can be enforced in the same way as any other judgment;
(c)   if costs cannot be agreed, they can be assessed by the court if there is provision for this in the order;
(d)   if the client has legal aid funding, there will need to be an order for legal aid assessment.

The order should contain a provision that the claim be stayed rather than dismissed, and the stay should contain provision for a return to court in the event that the terms of the stay are not complied with.

14.9.2   Drawing up the consent order

The procedure for drawing up a consent order is:

(a)   it must be drawn up in the agreed terms;
(b)   it must be expressed as being 'by consent';
(c)   it must be signed by solicitors or counsel for the parties;
(d)   it must be presented to the court for entry and sealing.

An order takes effect from the date given, unless the court orders otherwise. An order for payment of money (including costs) must be complied with within 14 days, unless the order or any rule of the CPR specifies otherwise. When drafting a consent order, the guiding principle is that the order shows where the money is to come from to satisfy the order and where that money will go.

EXAMPLE

In a case where a settlement is achieved by which the defendant agrees to pay £12,000 plus costs to be assessed if not agreed, the order should state:

(a)   that the claim is stayed on payment of £12,000;

(b)   that the £12,000 is to be paid by the defendant within a given timescale (usually 14 days);

(c)   where the money is to go (in this case to the claimant). In a case involving a minor the money will usually be ordered to be invested by the court;

(d)   who is to bear the costs. If this has been agreed, the figures should be stated with a time limit for payment. Usually, the provision will be for costs to be assessed if not agreed;

(e)   whether legal aid assessment is needed; and

(f)   liberty to apply – which simply allows the parties to return to the court if there is subsequently a disagreement as to what the terms of the order mean or because the terms have not been complied with.

If there had been an interim payment in the above example, this should also be reflected in the terms of the order. The order should state that the amount agreed in full and final settlement takes into account the interim payment, specifying the amount and the date the interim payment was given, or the date of the court order so ordering it to be paid. An example of a consent order may be found in **Appendix 1** at Document 22.

14.10   PART 36 OFFERS

If negotiations do not result in a settlement, consideration should be given to making a Part 36 offer in order to place the opponent under some pressure as to costs. For a detailed discussion of the form, content and costs consequences of Part 36 offers, reference should be made to *Civil Litigation*. There are also special provisions in Part 36 for claims brought within the low value protocols, which are dealt with at **21.7**. Part 36 does not apply to small claims (CPR, r 27.2(1)(g)).

In personal injury, including clinical negligence, cases, in addition to the above basic requirements as to content for a Part 36 offer, further information must be set out in the offer if the claim involves future pecuniary loss, provisional damages or the deduction of State benefits. That information is summarised below.

14.10.1   Special provisions applicable to Part 36 offers and personal injury claims for future pecuniary loss

It is possible to make an offer to settle a claim involving future pecuniary loss either by way of a lump sum, or by way of periodical payments or a combination of both (see **Chapter 15**). To be treated as a Part 36 offer with all the costs consequences that follow, the offer must explicitly set out the amounts which relate to the lump sum and periodical payments, and the duration of the periodical payments. If the offer is accepted, in addition to serving a notice of acceptance, the claimant must apply to the court for an order for an award of damages in the form of periodical payments. This must be done within seven days of the date of acceptance.

Rule 36.18 provides as follows:

(3)   A Part 36 offer to which this rule applies may contain an offer to pay, or an offer to accept—

(a)   the whole or part of the damages for future pecuniary loss in the form of—

    (i)   a lump sum; or

    (ii)   periodical payments; or

    (iii)   both a lump sum and periodical payments;

(b)   the whole or part of any other damages in the form of a lump sum.

(4)   A Part 36 offer to which this rule applies—

(a)   must state the amount of any offer to pay the whole or part of any damages in the form of a lump sum;

(b)   may state—

    (i)   what part of the lump sum, if any, relates to damages for future pecuniary loss; and

    (ii)   what part relates to other damages to be accepted in the form of a lump sum;

(c)   must state what part of the offer relates to damages for future pecuniary loss to be paid or accepted in the form of periodical payments and must specify—

    (i)   the amount and duration of the periodical payments;

    (ii)   the amount of any payments for substantial capital purchases and when they are to be made; and

    (iii)   that each amount is to vary by reference to the retail prices index (or to some other named index, or that it is not to vary by reference to any index); and

(d)   must state either that any damages which take the form of periodical payments will be funded in a way which ensures that the continuity of payment is reasonably secure in accordance with section 2(4) of the Damages Act 1996 or how such damages are to be paid and how the continuity of their payment is to be secured.

(5)   Rule 36.6 applies to the extent that a Part 36 offer by a defendant under this rule includes an offer to pay all or part of any damages in the form of a lump sum.

(6)   Where the offeror makes a Part 36 offer to which this rule applies and which offers to pay or to accept damages in the form of both a lump sum and periodical payments, the offeree may only give notice of acceptance of the offer as a whole.

(7)   If the offeree accepts a Part 36 offer which includes payment of any part of the damages in the form of periodical payments, the claimant must, within 7 days of the date of acceptance, apply to the court for an order for an award of damages in the form of periodical payments under rule 41.8.

14.10.2   Special provisions applicable to Part 36 offers and provisional damages

If the claim is for provisional damages (see **15.4**), an offer to settle must specify whether or not the offeror is offering to agree to the making of an award for provisional damages. If so, the offer must state:

(a)   the damages offered;

(b)   the conditions to trigger a further claim;

(c)   the period within which such further claim may be made.

Once the offer is accepted, the claimant must, within seven days, apply to the court for an order.

Rule 36.19 provides:

(1)   An offeror may make a Part 36 offer in respect of a claim which includes a claim for provisional damages.

(2)   Where he does so, the Part 36 offer must specify whether or not the offeror is proposing that the settlement shall include an award of provisional damages.

(3)   Where the offeror is offering to agree to the making of an award of provisional damages the Part 36 offer must also state—

(a)   that the sum offered is in satisfaction of the claim for damages on the assumption that the injured person will not develop the disease or suffer the type of deterioration specified in the offer;

(b)   that the offer is subject to the condition that the claimant must make any claim for further damages within a limited period; and

(c)   what that period is.

(4)   Rule 36.6 applies to the extent that a Part 36 offer by a defendant includes an offer to agree to the making of an award of provisional damages.

(5)   If the offeree accepts the Part 36 offer, the claimant must, within 7 days of the date of acceptance, apply to the court for an order for an award of provisional damages under rule 41.2.

14.10.3   Compensation recovery and Part 36 offers – deduction of benefits

A Part 36 offer in a personal injury claim (including a clinical negligence claim) may state that the offer is made without regard to any liability for recoverable benefits, ie it is a net offer and the compensator will pay benefits in addition.

Alternatively, the offer should state that it is intended to include any deductible CRU benefits.

According to r 36.22, the offer must state:

(a)   the amount of gross compensation before CRU benefits are offset;

(b)   the name of any deductible benefit;

(c)   the amount of any deductible benefit by which the gross amount is reduced; and

(d)   the net amount of compensation after deduction.

Remember, when calculating what benefits can be offset, that specific benefits can be offset only against certain heads of claim and must not exceed the amount claimed under that head. Where it is agreed or alleged that the claimant was contributorily negligent, the damages from which benefits can be offset must be net of the deduction for contributory negligence.

For the purpose of establishing whether the claimant has failed to obtain a judgment more advantageous than a defendant's Part 36 offer, the sums to be considered are those after deduction of the deductible benefits. In other words, the court will look at what sum the claimant was offered net of benefits and what sum the claimant recovered net of benefits.

Where the claimant accepts a Part 36 offer out of time and the CRU repayment has increased, CPR, r 36.22 states that the court may direct that the additional benefits should be deducted from the net offer.

14.10.4   Part 36 and interim payments

In *El Gamal v Synergy Lifestyle Ltd* [2018] EWCA Civ 210, it was held that where an interim payment is made following a Part 36 offer, there is a presumption that the interim payment is made on account of the sum offered in the Part 36 offer. If the defendant does not wish the Part 36 offer to be reduced by the interim payment in this way, the defendant should state this in the offer.

14.10.5   QOCS and Part 36

Rule 44.14 of the CPR allows a costs order to be made against a claimant who fails to beat a defendant's Part 36 offer to settle. The usual order will require the claimant to pay the defendant's costs from the end of the relevant offer period. However, the claimant's liability for the defendant's costs in these circumstances will be capped at the level of damages and interest (and costs in cases issued on or after 6 April 2023) recovered by the claimant (see **9.3.2**). After the event insurance may be available to cover this risk but any insurance premium will not be recoverable as part of the costs of the case.

14.11   PREPARATION FOR TRIAL

14.11.1   Outstanding orders

Once it becomes apparent that the case will proceed to trial as no satisfactory Part 36 offer has been received, the claimant's solicitor should undertake a thorough stocktaking of the file to ensure that all directions or other orders of the court have been complied with. Any outstanding matters in the claimant's own file should be attended to without further delay, and any outstanding matters for the defendant to attend to should be chased by issuing an interim application for judgment in default of compliance with the direction/other order if necessary (a so-called 'unless' order).

14.11.2   Experts

Experts' reports will usually have been exchanged in accordance with directions. Provision of joint experts and agreed expert evidence is dealt with in **Chapter 11**.

14.11.3   Use of counsel

The solicitor may not have instructed counsel before this stage if the claim has been straightforward. If the case has been complex, as is likely in a clinical negligence case, counsel will probably have been involved at an early stage, from drafting documents to advising on evidence. It is usual for the barrister who drafted the statements of case also to be briefed for the trial. As counsel will be handling the witnesses at trial, it may be thought to be appropriate to send the witness statements to counsel for approval before exchange to ensure that an important area concerning the conduct of the case at trial is not overlooked. It may be more cost-efficient to brief counsel for the trial than for the solicitor to attend. However, with trial on the fast track limited to one day, and with fixed costs of trial in such cases, it may be that a solicitor-advocate will undertake the advocacy of this type of claim.

If the case involves complex elements, such as clinical negligence, catastrophic injuries, or difficult questions of fact or law, consideration should be given to whether it would be appropriate to instruct leading counsel; junior counsel will usually advise the solicitor if they think that this would be appropriate. The solicitor should advise the client accordingly of the extra cost involved and, if the client is funded by legal aid, seek authority from the Legal Aid Agency to instruct leading counsel. The client should also be advised that if leading counsel is instructed, and this is disallowed on assessment, the cost will ultimately be borne by the client in the form of the statutory charge on the client's damages in cases where the claimant was legally aided.

14.11.4   Narrowing the issues

When preparing for trial the solicitor should ask, 'What do I have to prove?' A review should be made of the case file to ascertain areas of agreement which are no longer in issue. One useful device may be a list comprising two columns: the left-hand column listing the facts which have to be proved (eg, that the claimant was driving the car; that an accident occurred; the date of the accident; the place of the accident; an itemised list of the losses, etc); and the right-hand column indicating whether the fact is admitted by the opponent.

Admissions will normally be found in the statements of case or in open correspondence.

14.11.5   Schedule of special damages

Note that CPR, PD 22, para 1.4(3) requires that a statement of truth is included in a schedule or counter-schedule of expenses and losses, and in any amendments to such a schedule or counter-schedule, whether or not the schedule is contained in a statement of case.

The claimant's solicitor must check that the schedule of special damages is up to date, and if necessary, serve an updated schedule of special damages. Ideally, this should be the final schedule (although it may have to be revised again if there is a significant delay before the trial), the purpose of which is to identify the areas of agreement and disagreement between the parties. With this in mind, the following format could be usefully employed (the figures are merely for illustration):

Item of claim	Claimant's figure	Defendant's figure	Discrepancy
Purchase of wheelchair	£350	£350	Nil
Loss of future earnings	£50,000 (multiplicand = £5,000, multiplier = 10)	£32,000 (multiplicand = £4,000, multiplier = 8)	£18,000

The defendant's solicitor should be sent the updated schedule of special damages, with a covering letter requesting that they agree it or specify the items they are not prepared to agree, and giving a time limit for the reply. It should be pointed out that if they fail to reply, the claimant's solicitors will have to issue a witness summons for any persons necessary to prove the amounts claimed by the claimant in the schedule of special damages, and the claimant will ask for the costs of this exercise to be paid by the defendant in any event.

In clinical negligence claims, where special damages claims may often to involve substantial amounts of money, it is more likely that the defence will seek to query items claimed as special damages. For this reason, the directions will normally require that the defendant also provide a counter-schedule of special damages itemising the areas of disagreement.

14.11.6 Trial bundles

In both the High Court and the County Court, bundles of documents upon which the parties intend to rely must be lodged within the appropriate time, for use by the trial judge.

The bundle must be paginated and indexed. The medical records must be complete and in good order to enable medical experts to study them easily. X-rays or scans included in the bundle should be clearly identified. Scans may be several feet long and should be professionally copied if possible. The index to the trial bundle is normally agreed with the defendant.

The quality of preparation of bundles varies enormously, and this can have serious implications for the client's case if preparation is not undertaken properly. Although there are rules governing the content of the bundles, there is very little guidance on how the documents should be presented. When preparing the bundle, the aim should be to enable whoever is conducting the trial to turn to any document at any time with the minimum of fuss or delay, and that all others concerned with the case can do likewise. The more documents there are in the bundle, the more difficult this task becomes. In a straightforward road traffic claim, there will be few documents and, as such, the bundle should be relatively easy to prepare. In serious cases involving multiple injuries or in clinical negligence cases, however, the documents are likely to extend to many hundreds of pages. In such cases, it is even more important that the court is not hindered by trying to find documents that should be readily to hand. Poor preparation of the case will not impress the judge, neither will it go unnoticed. Documents will need to be split into a number of smaller bundles which are easier to handle. Using colour-coded lever arch files is often a good method, with a separate file for each class of document. As a matter of courtesy, if counsel has been instructed, the solicitor may wish to send the proposed index to the core bundle of documents to counsel in advance of the trial, so that counsel has the opportunity to ask for further items to be included if necessary.

14.11.7 Use of visual aids

Plans, photographs and models can be of enormous value at the trial as an aid to clarity, thereby shortening the length of the trial (avoiding long testimony of a witness) and saving costs. A judge may more readily understand the testimony of a witness if that witness is allowed to refer to a plan or photograph. Medical experts can often supply good quality colour diagrams, anatomical illustrations or models to make their testimony more comprehensible. In clinical negligence cases, it is worth the extra time and effort to find good visual aids. A judge is unlikely to have in-depth medical knowledge, and attempts to help the judge fully comprehend the circumstances giving rise to the alleged negligence are likely to be gratefully received.

Visual aids must be disclosed to the opponent in advance. No plan, photograph or model will be receivable in evidence at trial unless the party wishing to use the evidence discloses it no later than the latest date for serving witness statements, exhibited as appropriate.

A video-recording is more useful than photographs in the case of 'movement'. Two common examples are:

(a)   a video-recording of an industrial process;

(b)   a video-recording showing the difficulties of the claimant in coping with their injuries (a 'day in the life'). Although the claimant should call, in addition to their own evidence, members of the claimant's family or friends to give evidence as to how the claimant manages with the injuries sustained (evidence of the claimant's bodily and mental condition before and after the accident), a video film (eg, showing the medical assistance required, such as physiotherapy or even surgery) may illustrate the situation more clearly.

If the photographs or other visual aids are agreed, they are admissible in the absence of the maker. If they are not agreed, the maker must be called to prove their authenticity.

The solicitor should ensure at the trial that there are enough copies of photographs for the use of the judge, advocates and witnesses.

14.12   THE TRIAL

14.12.1   The morning of the trial

The solicitor should arrive early to ensure that they have time:

(a)   to check with the clerk to the court that the court has the trial bundles, and place a bundle in the witness-box;

(b)   to ensure that counsel has arrived and consider any last-minute questions they may have;

(c)   to meet the client on their arrival and attempt to put the client at ease;

(d)   to introduce counsel to the client (if they have not already met in conference);

(e)   to ensure that an interview room is reserved for the pre-trial conference with counsel.

14.12.2   Advice to clients and witnesses

The case will often turn on how well or how badly the witnesses give their evidence, and how they are perceived by the judge. The client and other witnesses should be reminded that they will not be able to take their statements into the witness-box. The solicitor should run through the procedure to be adopted when giving oral evidence with the witnesses, as follows:

(a)   explain the procedure on taking the oath, and whether the client wishes to affirm;

(b)   remind the witness that all responses should be addressed to the judge regardless of who asked the question; and

(c)   that the judge must be addressed in the appropriate manner; and

(d)   go through the order in which the witnesses will be examined.

Each witness's statement will normally stand as evidence-in-chief, in which case the witness's evidence will move to being cross-examined almost immediately.

It is important to allay the client's fears about giving oral evidence. The solicitor should advise the client to speak slowly and directly to the judge, just as if there were no one else in the room. The judge will be writing notes, and therefore the witness should watch the judge's pen and resume speaking only when the judge has finished writing.

It is unlikely that the client and lay witnesses will have given evidence before. They should be advised that if they do not understand the question they should say so, and to take their evidence slowly, answer only the question put to them and not to engage in questioning opposing counsel or offer unsolicited opinions of their own. It is up to the solicitor to keep their witnesses in check and ensure that they do not embarrass the client or harm the client's case.

14.12.3 Conduct of the trial

Counsel (if instructed) will have the conduct of the trial, and the solicitor's function will be to sit behind counsel and take full notes of evidence and proceedings. For the purpose of time costing, a note should be made of the start time, any adjournments and the time the trial finishes. The questions asked by counsel should be noted, as well as the responses given, as counsel will not be able to make any notes while on their feet.

14.12.4 Order of evidence

Although evidence is usually given by the claimant first, followed by the defence, in clinical negligence cases all witnesses of fact may be called first, followed by witnesses giving evidence of opinion. This is because the facts themselves are often complex and it assists the judge greatly if the facts are first laid out clearly by hearing evidence from the witnesses of fact for the claimant, followed directly by those of the defence. The object is to clarify the areas of disagreement so that experts can concentrate their efforts there, and shorten the length of trial. However, the parties must apply to the trial judge on the first day of the trial to use this procedure, as the order of evidence in the judge's court will be decided by the individual judge as a matter of discretion.

14.12.5 Judgment

The solicitor should take a careful note of the judgment delivered by the judge at the end of the case, as it may be crucial if the client decides to appeal.

Counsel must be made aware of any specific orders which may be necessary. In addition, counsel must be informed about any Part 36 offers which may have a bearing on costs.

The solicitor should also check the pre-trial orders to see if costs were reserved in any interim proceedings, and if so, that this is brought to the attention of the judge so that a costs order can be made in relation to that application.

The judgment should be fully explained to the client, which can be undertaken by counsel.

14.12.6 The order

Following trial in the county court, the court will draw up the order, which should be checked carefully to ensure that it reflects the judge's decision, as mistakes are sometimes made by the court staff.

14.13 CONCLUSION

Most cases settle, and taking a case to trial will be the exception rather than the rule in personal injury litigation. The court, as we have seen, actively encourages parties to negotiate and attempt to settle at every opportunity. Nevertheless, every case must be approached from the standpoint that it will go to trial, and must be prepared accordingly. It is important to keep a case under review as the case progresses. In particular, any Part 36 offers should be kept under review and, if necessary, withdrawn if further evidence comes to light which alters your views of quantum and/or liability.

14.14   FURTHER READING

The Civil Court Practice (the Green Book) (LexisNexis Butterworths)

Civil Procedure (the White Book) (Sweet & Maxwell)

Skills for Lawyers 2023–24 (CLP)

https://resolution.nhs.uk/services/claims-management/clinical-schemes/clinical-negligence-scheme-for-trusts/

The Quantification of Damages

LEARNING OUTCOMES

After reading this chapter you will be able to:

- explain what special damages are and how the main items of loss are calculated
- explain what general damages for pain, suffering and loss of amenity are, and how such damages are quantified
- explain what general damages for future financial loss are and how they are calculated
- draft a schedule of past and future expenses and losses
- set out and apply the law in relation to provisional damages
- explain the court's power to make an order for periodical payments and set out the procedure for obtaining such an order
- set out how interest is calculated in personal injury and clinical negligence claims.

15.1 INTRODUCTION

In cases of catastrophic injury, claims for damages may amount to several million pounds. For example, in one extreme case in November 2012, a teenage girl left paralysed following a road traffic accident was awarded a lump sum plus annual payments thought to total over £23 million over her lifetime. Of course, the vast majority of claims are settled or determined for considerably smaller amounts, most within the fast track limit of £25,000.

The aim of the claimant's solicitor is to establish liability against the defendant and to achieve the highest possible level of damages for their client (without falsifying or exaggerating the claim). The primary aim of the defendant's solicitor is to defeat the claimant's claim. However, if they cannot prevent their client being found liable for the claimant's injuries and loss, their fallback position is to minimise the level of damages their client is obliged to pay. It therefore follows that the task of valuing the claimant's losses is just as important to those representing defendants as it is to those representing claimants. Although the claimant and defendant will usually only be interested in the final amount of the award, the personal injury solicitor must fully understand the various heads of damages which the court can order, to ensure that they can achieve the best possible result for their client. However, even the most experienced personal injury lawyer will be able to quantify the damages only approximately, and therefore solicitors should take care to manage their client's expectations. It is generally a wise claimant's solicitor who gives their client a slightly lower assessment of the likely damages, and generally a wise defendant's solicitor who gives their client a slightly higher assessment.

In negligence, the aim of the award of damages is to restore the claimant to the position that they were in prior to the accident. Of course, it is impossible to take away the pain and suffering associated with a personal injury, particularly as, in many cases, there will be lasting physical and/or psychological disability. The award of monetary compensation is the only remedy available to the court and, particularly in cases of catastrophic injury, claimants and their families will cope better with the physical, mental, social and financial consequences of the injuries where appropriate monetary compensation is received.

In most cases, the claimant will receive a lump sum award in full and final settlement of the claim, which means the claimant will not be able to return to court at a later date to seek additional compensation (see provisional damages and periodical payments at **15.4** and **15.5** below for exceptions to this rule). It is therefore important that the claimant's solicitor is thorough in their investigations to identify all losses. Where the case is determined at trial, damages are assessed as at the date of the trial (or, in 'split trials', at a later hearing), and therefore detailed and up-to-date evidence, such as an updated loss of earnings calculation and medical report, should be provided to the court. Most claims are settled through negotiation, but it is equally important for the claimant's solicitor to have detailed and up-to-date evidence available whenever quantum is discussed with the defendant's solicitor.

15.1.1 Heads of damage

The following heads of damage can be claimed in personal injury and clinical negligence cases:

(a) Special damages (also known as past pecuniary loss). These are the financial losses which the claimant has incurred prior to trial, and they are capable of fairly precise calculation.

(b) General damages. These are damages that cannot be calculated precisely and therefore require the application of certain formulaic approaches plus a little educated guesswork. They can be split into two categories:

(i) Non-pecuniary loss. This is the element of the compensation award that does not reflect financial losses at all but rather reflects the claimant's pain, suffering and loss of amenity.

(ii) Future pecuniary loss. Although this element of the compensation reflects financial losses, such as future loss of earnings or the cost of the care which the claimant will require, it cannot be calculated precisely as it is impossible to say with precision, for example, how long the claimant will live, what the claimant would have earned had they not been injured or how much the claimant's care requirements will cost in future years.

Terminology may create problems for the unwary, as some practitioners use the term special damages' when referring to all items of pecuniary loss, both past and future, and the term 'general damages' is used routinely in case reporting to mean pain, suffering and loss of amenity only. It goes without saying that, when negotiating a settlement, solicitors must be precise about the nature of the damages to which they are referring. In this text, the terminology is given its traditional meaning as set out in (a) and (b) above.

The distinction between special damages and the two heads of general damages is significant not only in the method of calculation, but also with regard to the level of interest awarded by the court (see **15.6**).

15.2 SPECIAL DAMAGES – 'PAST PECUNIARY LOSS'

Special damages are the items of financial loss incurred by the claimant between the date of the accident and the date of trial which can be specifically calculated.

The main heads of special damages are:

(a) loss of earnings;

(b) clothing and personal effects;

(c) cost of medical care and expenses;

(d) cost of care and quasi-nursing services;

(e) cost of DIY, gardening and housework services;

(f) cost of aids and appliances;

(g) cost of alternative and/or adapted accommodation;

(h) transport costs.

In RTA cases, there may also be:

(i) cost of repairs to or replacement of the claimant's vehicle;

(j) vehicle recovery and storage charges;

(k) loss of use of a motor vehicle or hire of a substitute vehicle;

(l) loss of a no claims bonus and wasted road fund licence.

You should note that some of the above heads will also be relevant to any general damages claim for future pecuniary loss.

15.2.1 Loss of earnings up to the date of the trial

In most cases, there will be a claim for loss of earnings up to the date of trial. The claimant is entitled to recover their net loss of earnings, ie what the claimant would have earned after tax, National Insurance and contractual pension payments.

In many cases, where the claimant was in regular employment, it will be reasonably straightforward to determine precisely how much the claimant has lost. In other cases, the calculation will not be so precise. For example, where the claimant's pre-accident wages varied markedly from week to week, or where there has been a fairly lengthy period of time between the accident and trial and the claimant argues that they would have been promoted to a more lucrative position had they still been working.

15.2.1.1 Calculating loss of earnings

The starting point in the calculation is to determine the claimant's average net wage for the period immediately prior to the accident. The common approach is to obtain, from the claimant's wage slips or bank statements or from the claimant's employer, details of the claimant's earnings for the 13-week period prior to the accident. Where that 13-week period is not representative of the claimant's average pre-accident wage, a longer period, for example six months, should be considered. Whatever period is looked at, appropriate adjustments should be made to take account of any overtime, bonus payments, benefits such as company cars or commission that the claimant would have earned had they been at work. Further adjustments should be made to take account of any pay increase, promotion, or further benefits which the claimant would have obtained during the period from the date of the cause of action to trial.

In some cases, such as where the claimant had obtained a job immediately prior to the accident and a clear pattern of pre-accident wages cannot be provided, or where there has been a lengthy period between the date of the accident and the assessment of damages, it may be useful to obtain details of a comparative earner. This involves identifying someone who was in a similar post and earning a similar salary to the claimant immediately prior to the accident, and determining what the earnings pattern of the comparative earner had been and, where appropriate, tracking their career progression and salary increases during the period up to trial. Clearly, it would be most useful if the comparative earner is employed by the claimant's employer, but where this is not possible, a comparative earner from a similar business or organisation can be used.

Some claimants have more complex employment histories, such as where they worked on short-term contracts or were self-employed. In such circumstances, more detailed enquiries must be made in order to provide evidence of income lost before the trial. Self-employed claimants should be asked to supply copies of their accounts and/or tax returns for the year prior to the accident, or a longer period if one year's figures are not representative. This information may be difficult to obtain, leaving scope for those representing defendants to argue that losses have been exaggerated. It may be necessary to obtain a report from an accountant (the term 'forensic accountant' is often used for those who specialise in this area).

In an attempt to establish details of how much the claimant would have earned between the accident and trial in cases where an erratic employment history is presented, reference can be made to the Annual Survey of Hours and Earnings produced by the Office for National Statistics, which is a statistical analysis of earnings throughout the country. This can provide details of average earnings for particular industries or occupations on a national or regional basis, and can be useful in attempting to persuade the defendant to accept that the claimant would have received a particular wage.

Very few employees receive no income whatsoever while absent from work, and so the calculation of the claimant's lost earnings is not simply a case of multiplying the net weekly loss by the number of weeks' absence. Such an approach would place the claimant in a better financial position than they would have been in had the accident not occurred. A detailed examination of what income the claimant received while absent from work is required, as certain types of income have to be credited in calculating the net loss figure.

15.2.1.2   Items which must be accounted for in the calculation

The following are the most common items which must be accounted for in the net loss of earnings figure (for both past and future loss of earnings calculations), ie these amounts must be deducted from the net salary in order to calculate the total loss of earnings:

(a)   *Tax refunds received due to absence from work as a result of the accident.* A claimant who is an employee will generally pay income tax on the Pay As You Earn (PAYE) system. To a certain extent this system is a payment of tax in advance, as it assumes that the claimant's earnings will continue throughout the whole of the forthcoming year. In the event of the claimant's absence from work, the claimant may then have paid too much tax. In this case, the claimant may receive a tax rebate via their employer. An amount equivalent to the whole of the rebate has to be given credit for in the calculation of wage loss (*Hartley v Sandholme Iron Co Ltd* [1975] QB 600). Occasionally, instead of a 'cash-in-hand' tax rebate, the claimant may receive a tax credit against future tax liability, so that on return to work the claimant pays no tax for a period (a 'tax holiday'). A sum equivalent to this tax credit also has to be given credit for in the calculation of the wage loss (*Brayson v Wilmot-Breedon* [1976] CLY 682).

(b)   *Sums paid to the claimant by the claimant's employer.* Whether sums equivalent to such payments fall to be deducted from the damages depends on the basis of the payment and the identity of the tortfeasor.

The following are the most common situations:

(i)   The sum is paid under a legal obligation (eg, under the claimant's contract of employment) and is not refundable by the claimant to their employer. An amount equivalent to the whole of the payment should be deducted from the damages.

(ii) The sum is paid under a legal obligation (eg, under the contract of employment) and must be repaid by the claimant to their employer out of any damages the claimant receives from the defendant. Such a payment is effectively a loan and, as such, is not deducted when assessing the damages.

(iii) The sum is paid *ex gratia* by the employer who is not the tortfeasor. Such a payment is effectively a 'charitable' payment and is not to be deducted when assessing the damages (*Cunningham v Harrison* [1973] 3 All ER 463).

(iv) The sum is paid *ex gratia* by the employer who is the tortfeasor. An amount equivalent to the whole of the payment may (in certain circumstances) be deducted from the damages (*Hussain v New Taplow Paper Mills Ltd* [1988] AC 514).

(v) The claimant receives statutory sick pay (SSP) from their employer. This is not a recoverable benefit to the DWP (see **Chapter 16**), and therefore an amount equivalent to the whole payment should be deducted (the contract of employment may need to be examined in case the employer is entitled to claw back the SSP in some way). See also *Palfrey v Greater London Council* [1985] ICR 437.

(c) *Any saving to an injured person attributable to their maintenance wholly or partly at public expense.* This would apply where the claimant was, for example, admitted into an NHS hospital, a nursing home or other institution. The savings must be calculated and set off against any claim for income lost as a result of the injuries (Administration of Justice Act 1982, s 5). In practice, this deduction is overlooked because in most cases the sums saved are *de minimis*. (While in hospital the claimant will generally have to meet the same household expenses such as rent, mortgage and council tax; any saving will usually be only in regard to the cost of food. This saving is then so small as to be ignored.)

(d) *Redundancy payments.* An equivalent amount is to be deducted in full from the damages calculation when redundancy occurs as a result of the injury caused by the accident (*Colledge v Bass Mitchells & Butlers* [1988] 1 All ER 536).

(e) *Benefits outside the ambit of the Social Security (Recovery of Benefits) Act 1997.* A sum equivalent to certain benefits received by the claimant as a result of the accident will be deducted from the judgment sum or negotiated settlement by the defendant and paid directly to the Compensation Recovery Unit (see **Chapter 16**). However, when calculating the award, benefits which are not subject to offsetting are potentially deductible. In *Clenshaw v Tanner* [2002] EWCA Civ 1848, the Court of Appeal held that as the claimant was not required to reimburse the local authority for receipt of housing benefit, if he was allowed to recover for loss of earnings in full, he would be overcompensated to the extent of the housing benefit. Consequently, the housing benefit payments were deducted from the loss of earnings award. It therefore follows that, potentially, other benefits, such as council tax benefit, child tax credit, working tax credit, motability payments, etc are deductible.

15.2.1.3 Items which are not accounted for

The following items are the most common payments to be left out of account in assessing an award for loss of past (and future) earnings:

(a) *State retirement pension.* The State retirement pension is ignored in assessing an award for loss of past and future earnings (*Hewson v Downs* [1970] 1 QB 73).

(b) *Pensions received.* The general rule is that if the claimant receives a pension, this cannot be set against the claim for loss of earnings. However, if there is a separate claim for loss of pension rights, for example since the claimant is unable to work and will receive less pension in the future, any pension the claimant does receive may be offset against the claim for loss of pension rights (*Parry v Cleaver* [1970] AC 1; *Smoker v London Fire and Civil Defence Authority* [1991] 2 All ER 449; *Longden v British Coal Corporation* [1997] 3 WLR 1336.

(c) *Insurance moneys.* Where a claimant has taken out an insurance policy specifically to cover themselves against the risk of sustaining personal injuries, or where such cover is an incidental' benefit to other types of insurance, such as motor insurance, the claimant may receive a payment as a result of injuries caused by the defendant's negligence. In such cases, the payment is usually a fixed sum according to the type of injury; for example, in the event of a loss of a specified limb, the insurance company will pay the insured the sum of £5,000.

The claimant need not give credit for moneys received under such a policy against the damages payable by the defendant, provided the claimant paid for or contributed to the policy premiums. The justification is that the defendant should not benefit from the fact that the claimant had the foresight to take out the cover and pay the premium (*Bradburn v Great Western Railway Co* (1874–75) LR 10 Exch 1; *McCamley v Cammell Laird Shipbuilders Ltd* [1990] 1 All ER 854). Where the claimant does not pay for or contribute to the policy, as where the employer sets up a non-contributory group personal accident insurance policy, credit must be given (see *Pirelli v Gaca* [2004] EWCA Civ 373).

In cases where credit does not have to be given to the defendant, the terms of the insurance policy should be checked carefully. There will often be a provision (particularly in motor insurance) which obliges a policyholder to reimburse the insurance company for any sum it paid to the insured under the policy in respect of a loss for which the insured receives compensation from a third party. In such a case, the claimant will not receive any financial benefit from commencing proceedings, but the insurance company may insist on commencing and conducting proceedings in the claimant's name.

(d) *Charitable payments.* If money is received by the claimant as a charitable payment (even if it is on an informal basis such as the proceeds of a collection taken among the claimant's friends) then the claimant is not required to give credit for such payment against the damages received. The justification is that as a matter of policy, people should not be discouraged from making such payments to the victims of accidents. However, the exact circumstances and sources of the *ex gratia* payment must be considered. In *Williams v BOC Gases Ltd* [2000] PIQR Q253, the Court of Appeal held that where an employer (who was the tortfeasor) made an *ex gratia* payment on termination of the claimant's employment on the basis that it was to be treated as an advance against any damages that might be awarded in respect of any claim the claimant had against the employer, credit had to be given for that amount in a subsequent personal injury claim.

15.2.2   Clothing and personal effects

Where the claimant has been injured as a result of an accident, there may be damage to items of clothing and other personal effects, such as mobile telephones, laptop computers, watches, etc. Where such items are damaged beyond repair, the claimant is entitled to claim their pre-accident value, and appropriate documentary evidence (such as receipts or valuations) should be provided. Solicitors acting for defendants will be keen to ensure that items have not been overvalued by the claimant and that discounts are given in respect of items which were not brand-new at the time of the accident. This type of loss does not arise in clinical negligence cases.

15.2.3   Cost of medical care and expenses

The claimant is entitled to recover all medical expenses reasonably incurred as a result of the defendant's breach of duty, for example prescriptions, over-the-counter drugs, and private medical care and treatment. However, where the claimant has been treated as an in-patient, only the cost of the medical care may be claimed; the claimant cannot claim for the 'hotel' element included in the cost of staying in hospital, for example the proportion of the fees that relate to the provision of meals, heating and lighting (*Lim Poh Choo v Camden and Islington Area Health Authority* [1979] 2 All ER 910).

Treatment may be in relation to essential matters (such as a colostomy), non-emergency, non-life threatening matters (such as dealing with bed sores), or incidental treatments (such as IVF, required, for example, where a claimant is unable to father a child naturally due to a spinal cord injury). The courts will allow the costs of numerous types of therapeutic care, such as psychiatric assistance, physiotherapy and occupational therapy, and may allow the cost of alternative medical treatments, such as acupuncture. The availability of free NHS treatment is ignored (Law Reform (Personal Injuries) Act 1948, s 2(4); see also *Eagle v Chambers* [2004] EWCA Civ 1033), although a claimant cannot be treated free under the NHS and then claim for private treatment.

In cases where there are long waiting lists under the NHS, if the claimant does not themselves raise the matter, the claimant's solicitor should suggest that the client undergo private medical treatment in an attempt to speed the recovery period. Indeed, where the claimant has a strong case on liability, the defendant's solicitors may well suggest this, as prompt treatment may reduce the level of damages ultimately payable by the defendant. Reference should be made to the Rehabilitation Code (para 5 of the PAP for Personal Injury Claims; see **Appendix 2**, and see also the Rehabilitation Code at **Appendix 5**), which requires the parties to co-operate in order to assess and provide for the claimant's rehabilitation needs.

> **EXAMPLE**
>
> A 10-year-old girl is injured and has to undergo major abdominal surgery at the local hospital, which leaves her with a large surgical incision. As part of her general damages award, she will claim for pain and suffering relating to the scarring. It is also likely that she will claim that she will suffer psychological problems in relation to the embarrassment of wearing swimming costumes throughout her teenage years and perhaps in later life. In such a case, the claimant should undergo specialist plastic surgery in an attempt to reduce the significance of the scarring and the potential psychological problems, which, in turn, will reduce the level of damages that the defendant will pay.

Future private medical care may also be claimed as part of the future pecuniary loss head of general damages (see **15.3.5**), provided it is reasonably likely to be incurred.

15.2.4 Cost of care and quasi-nursing services

In cases where the claimant is seriously injured, the cost of providing care and quasi-nursing services may form a substantial part of both the special damages claim for past pecuniary losses and the general damages claim for future pecuniary losses (see **15.3.5**). The cost of such services may also form part of the special damages claim where injuries have been less severe. In most cases, at least some of the care will have been provided gratuitously, by a member of the claimant's family or a close friend. As with medical care and expenses, the claimant is under no obligation to use care services provided by the NHS.

15.2.4.1 Professional care

Where care services are provided on a commercial basis, they can be recovered from the defendant provided they are reasonable in amount and are reasonably incurred as a result of the injuries. The claimant will bear the burden of proving that they needed the level of care provided/will need the level claimed for.

15.2.4.2 Gratuitous care

In relation to gratuitous care, the carer is unable to make a claim against the defendant due to the general principle that a third party cannot claim in respect of losses the third party has incurred as a result of the claimant's injuries. However, the claimant may recover the value of care services provided to the claimant on a gratuitous basis, so long as such services were rendered necessary by the negligence of the defendant. In other words, the care provided must be over and above that which the claimant would have normally received from the carer. So, for example, where a mother is severely injured and her child slightly injured in a road traffic accident as a result of the defendant's negligence, it is not possible for the child to claim damages for the care element from the defendant, as the mother would normally provide such care. The appropriate course is for the mother to include, as part of her damages claim, the costs of the care of the child which she can no longer provide herself (see *Buckley v Farrow and Buckley* [1997] PIQR Q78).

The value of gratuitous services may be claimed by the claimant irrespective of whether the third party has been put to actual expense in providing those services, for example by incurring loss of earnings, and it is unnecessary for there to be any agreement between the claimant and the third party as to reimbursement for the services.

Initially, courts were reluctant to award damages for the cost of gratuitous care except in the most serious cases. However, in *Giambrone & Others v JMC Holidays Ltd (formerly t/a Sunworld Holidays Ltd)* [2004] EWCA Civ 158, holiday makers who had developed gastro-enteritis at the defendant's hotel, which persisted for more than 14 days, were able to recover for gratuitous care provided by family members once they had returned home. The Court of Appeal rejected the defendant's argument that an award for the value of such services should be made only in serious cases or where the claimant could point to a demonstrable financial expense in providing the necessary care. Consequently, claimants' solicitors should always include a claim for gratuitous care when it has been provided.

As has already been said, the claim for the value of the services is made by the claimant, not by the third party, as it is the claimant's loss (their need for the services) which is being compensated. However, although it is the claimant who obtains the award for the value of the services, the damages are held by the claimant in trust for the carer. Therefore, where the carer is also the defendant (eg, where a wife is injured as a result of her husband's negligent driving and the husband provides quasi-nursing services to her), the claimant cannot recover the value of those services from the defendant/carer, as the claimant would have to repay the damages to the defendant/carer (*Hunt v Severs* [1994] 2 AC 350).

15.2.4.3   The valuation of gratuitous care

In the case of professional services, the claimant is entitled to the reasonable fee payable for those services; but in the case of gratuitous care where no fee is incurred, the valuation may be more problematical. Each case will be assessed on its own facts.

Where the relative or spouse has given up work in order to look after the claimant, and has thereby incurred loss of earnings, the lost earnings will be recoverable, provided they were reasonably incurred.

Where there is no loss of income by the third party, the court will normally take account of what it would cost to employ professional help. In this regard, there has been a recent tendency to favour the standard hourly rate paid at spinal point 2 (prior to April 2019, spinal point 8) of the National Joint Council for Local Government Services table. This rate, currently £10.60 from 1 April 2022 to 31 March 2023, represents the standard hourly earnings rate for home care workers. (At the time of writing, the rate for the financial year from 1 April 2023 is still be decided – pay negotiations in this area take some time to conclude.) The rate may be weighted to take account of location and also whether care is provided during the night or in extremely difficult circumstances. (See *Massey v Tameside & Glossop Acute Services NHS Trust* [2007] EWHC 317 (Admin), where the court found that the spinal point flat rate did not adequately recompense a mother who provided particularly demanding services during the night and at weekends to her claimant son.) In addition, the court will normally apply a discount of somewhere between 20 and 30%, to reflect the absence of tax and National Insurance deductions, travelling costs to and from work, the profit element associated with commercial care services and the fact that professional carers might be more efficient.

If the claimant seeks a rate in excess of the commercial rate, the claimant has the onus of proving the higher value (*Rialas v Mitchell* (1984) *The Times*, 17 July, where the claimant justified care at home which was approximately twice the cost of care in an institution) (see also *Fitzgerald v Ford* [1996] PIQR Q72).

15.2.5 Cost of DIY, gardening and housework services

The claimant is entitled to recover from the defendant the reasonable costs of obtaining DIY, gardening and housework services which the claimant used to provide for themselves but has been unable to do as a result of the accident. The services may be provided commercially or gratuitously, and there may be a claim for past loss under special damages and/or a general damages claim for future loss.

In the case of *Mehmetemin v Craig Farrell* [2017] EWHC 103 (QB), the court held that dog walking by a relative (in this case, the claimant's husband) was claimable in exactly the same way as DIY services, and it was irrelevant that the relative might enjoy walking the dogs. In this case, the amount of hours allowed per week was reduced to take account of shared dog walking with the claimant, and a 25% reduction to a commercial dog walking hourly rate was applied. It should be noted that the appropriate multiplier for future loss is the life expectancy of the dog, rather than the active life expectancy of the claimant.

15.2.6 Costs of aids and appliances

The claimant may require specific aids or equipment to enable the claimant to cope better with their disabilities. Such items will result in one-off payments, and where this expense has been incurred before the trial, it will form part of the claim for special damages. However, such items may be required at regular intervals after trial and throughout the claimant's life, and therefore the replacement cost must be included within any future loss calculation.

The types of aids and appliances which a claimant may require are too numerous to list here, but the following are a few examples:

(a)   adaptations to the family car to allow the claimant to drive;

(b)   wheelchairs (defendants may argue that these can be provided free by the State, in which case the claimant's solicitors should argue that these would not be suitable if that is the position);

(c)   special beds;

(d)   incontinence pads;

(e)   odour control in the house due to incontinence;

(f)   hoists, to assist in moving the claimant in and out of bed;

(g)   tilting chairs;

(h)   exercise equipment, such as stationary cycles;

(i)   therapy balls, to help with mobility.

15.2.7 Cost of alternative accommodation and/or adaptations

Where a disabled claimant is living at home, it is possible that the accommodation the claimant had prior to the accident is no longer suitable. It may require alterations and adaptations, such as the installation of ramps for a wheelchair or a hoist for access to the bath, alterations to the internal layout of the premises to facilitate access to bedrooms and bathrooms, or the creation of extra storage space to accommodate wheelchairs and other aids or appliances. It may be necessary to create accommodation for a resident nurse or carer. Where such alterations and adaptations do not add value to the accommodation, the cost may be recovered in full from the defendant. If the expense has been incurred prior to trial, it will form part of the special damages calculation. If not, it will form part of the future loss calculation.

Some alterations, such as an extension, may be expensive, but they will add value to the accommodation and, in such cases, the added value must be accounted for in the claim for damages.

In some circumstances, the claimant's existing home may be incapable of adaptation and it is not then unreasonable for the claimant to move to more suitable accommodation. Provided that accommodation is reasonable for the claimant's needs, they will be entitled to purchase a home which is more expensive than their previous one. Clearly, the claimant will incur expenses in the move which are recoverable from the defendant. However, if the claimant were entitled to recover from the defendant the purchase price of the more expensive new property less the proceeds from the sale of the claimant's previous home, then the claimant would be overcompensated. The claimant would benefit from a more expensive house than perhaps they would otherwise have been able to buy, and the capital value of the property would remain intact on their death and represent a windfall to the claimant's estate.

In such circumstances, the solution developed by the courts until very recently has been to say that the loss is not a straightforward capital loss, ie the cost of buying a larger house less the proceeds from the sale of the previous house, but rather the loss of the net income which that capital sum would have earned had it been invested. This lost income is not calculated by reference to a normal commercial rate of interest but in accordance with the rate chosen by the Court of Appeal in *Roberts v Johnstone* [1988] 3 WLR 1247 of 2% which it was held represented the real rate of return on a risk-free investment at that time.

Subsequently, in 2001, the Lord Chancellor set the discount rate (see **15.3.4.2**) at 2.5%, and since then that was the rate that had consistently been used in calculating this head of loss. However, following the decision by the Lord Chancellor to reduce the discount rate to –0.75% from 20 March 2017, this approach was thrown into doubt. To illustrate why, consider the following example, which sets out the *Roberts v Johnstone* calculation using both the old 2.5% and the previous –0.75% discount rates by way of comparison:

EXAMPLE

The claimant, Abdul, is 39 at the time of the trial and has, as a result of catastrophic injuries, been confined to a wheelchair. Prior to the accident, he was living in a third-floor flat which is wholly unsuitable for his needs following the accident. He therefore needs to sell his flat which is valued at £200,000 and purchase a bungalow which will suit his needs and will cost £300,000. Following the approach set down in *Roberts v Johnstone*, the calculation of damages to compensate Abdul for the extra expense of purchasing a new home will be as follows:

Using a 2.5% discount rate	Using a –0.75% discount rate
Capital outlay = £100,000	Capital outlay = £100,000
Annual loss of interest on capital outlay (£100,000 x 2.5%) = £2,500	Annual loss of interest on capital outlay (£100,000 x –0.75%) = –£750
Mulitipler for future loss of interest (Table 1 pecuniary loss for life, male, aged 39 at trial, 2.5% discount rate) = 26.70	Mulitipler for future loss of interest (Table 1 pecuniary loss for life, male, aged 39 at trial, –0.75% discount rate) = 55.60
Loss = £2,500 x 26.70 = £66,750	Loss = –£750 x 55.60 = –£41,700

Therefore, whereas under the 2.5% discount rate, Abdul would be entitled to £66,750 to compensate him for needing appropriate housing, under the –0.75% discount rate Abdul would owe the defendant £41,700.

The personal injury discount rate changed further, from 5 August 2019, to –0.25% (see **5.10** and **Chapter 15**). The calculation in the example above, using a discount rate of –0.25% and a corresponding multiplier from Table 1 of 48.81, would result in Abdul owing the defendant

£12,202.50. In the recent case of *Swift v Carpenter* [2018] EWHC 2060 (QB), the claimant proposed four alternative approaches – that there should be a *Roberts v Johnstone* calculation using a 2% rate of investment, that the defendant pay the full capital cost of an interest only mortgage for life, that an interest only mortgage for life be funded by periodical payments, or that the defendant pay the greatly increased costs of privately renting specialised accommodation for life. All were rejected by the court on the same basis as in *JR v Sheffield Teaching Hospitals* [2017] EWHC 1245 (QB). In the *JR* case, the court followed the approach in *Roberts v Johnstone*, namely that damages for accommodation costs should not represent the full capital value of the asset since that would remain intact at the claimant's death and thereby represent a windfall to the claimant's estate. The court found that there was no justification for adopting another approach.

However, in *Swift v Carpenter* [2020] EWCA Civ 1467, the Court of Appeal decided that the formula in *Roberts v Johnstone* no longer achieved fair and reasonable compensation in circumstances where a claimant needed to buy a more expensive home, had a long life expectancy and where the discount rate at the time was low or negative. The Court of Appeal decided that *Roberts v Johnstone* was not a statement of principle but rather was authoritative guidance which the Court could reconsider if current conditions justified it. The Court of Appeal decided that it *would* reconsider the guidance given current high property prices and the negative discount rate, which meant in its view that fair and reasonable compensation could not be achieved applying *Roberts v Johnstone*. The Court of Appeal acknowledged that a windfall should be avoided, and came up with an approach based on the capital value needed to fund the property purchase less the market value of the reversionary interest in that property at the assumed date of the claimant's death. This is a complex area and detailed reading of *Johnstone* and *Swift* would be required in practice.

15.2.8   Travelling costs

The claimant is entitled to claim reasonable travelling costs, whether by private car or other transport, such as buses, trains and taxis, which have arisen as a result of the accident. The costs of travelling to hospitals, doctors, physiotherapists, etc are all claimable. Although the cost of travelling to a medical expert for the purposes of the litigation is more properly claimed as legal costs rather than as damages, it is common to see them in the claim for special damages.

Where the claimant uses their own vehicle, there is usually a dispute between the parties regarding the reasonable amount payable for mileage. Claimants may seek to rely on the amount HM Revenue and Customs allows employees to claim for business mileage before tax is charged – currently 45p per mile for up to 10,000 miles per year and 25p per mile for any additional miles in respect of cars or vans. There is a flat rate for motorcycles of 24p per mile. The defendant may seek to rely on figures based on running costs, such as those provided by the AA and the RAC, which tend to be lower.

In many cases, family members and friends will incur additional travelling expenses, for example by visiting the claimant whilst they are in hospital. The claimant is able to claim such expenses as part of the claimant's loss (because they have a need for the visit), but it will be necessary to prove that they were reasonably incurred as a result of the claimant's injuries. Consequently, only those expenses which exceed what the family member or friend would have ordinarily spent on visiting the claimant can be recovered.

> **EXAMPLE**
>
> The claimant, Klaus, lived with his girlfriend, Natalya, prior to the accident. Ordinarily, Natalya would not have incurred any expense in seeing him, so all travelling expenses associated with visiting him in hospital can be claimed. On the other hand, if she had lived several miles away from Klaus, a claim could be made only in respect of the costs which were over and above the normal travelling costs. If the hospital is further away than Klaus's house, or she visits him more frequently than she would have otherwise done, a claim should be made for the additional expense.

Where there is a claim for future travelling costs, these can be calculated by means of a multiplicand and multiplier (see **15.3.4**). A claim for parking charges should also be made where appropriate.

15.2.9   Repairs to or replacement of the claimant's vehicle; recovery and storage costs

Where the claimant's vehicle is damaged beyond repair, the claimant is entitled to claim its pre-accident value, less any salvage price obtained. Where the vehicle has been repaired, the claimant is entitled to the reasonable costs of the repairs. The claimant will also be able to claim any reasonable costs incurred in recovering the vehicle from the accident site and storage costs prior to repair or disposal. As the claimant is under an obligation to mitigate their losses, the claimant should not allow their vehicle to languish in storage facilities for too long or they may find themselves unable to recover all of the associated charges.

15.2.10   Loss of use of a motor vehicle or hire of substitute vehicle

Where the claimant's vehicle is damaged and is off the road whilst being repaired, the claimant is entitled to claim for the hire of a replacement vehicle, although the claimant must act reasonably in doing so. Where the claimant has hired a vehicle at their own immediate cost, the defendant should challenge such a claim where the hire vehicle is of a more expensive type than the claimant's own vehicle, where it has additional features at extra cost, where the hire period is longer than it ought reasonably to have been, or where the basic hire rate is unreasonably high.

More commonly in recent years, a claimant will hire a replacement vehicle from a credit hire company, which means there is no immediate cost to the claimant and the claimant contracts to pay the hire charges to the hire company at the end of the hire period. The cost of credit hire is generally higher than basic hire rates, sometimes significantly so, and it is common for other benefits to be included, eg insurance to cover legal costs and hire charges insofar as they are not recoverable from the defendant. Consequently, even in cases where liability and the majority of heads of damage are agreed, credit hire remains a fiercely fought bone of contention between the parties. There is a significant amount of case law governing this complex area which goes beyond the scope of this book, but the following matters should be noted:

(a)   *The agreement must be enforceable by the credit hire company against the claimant under the Consumer Credit Act 1974.* If it is unenforceable, the claimant has suffered no loss that may be recouped from the defendant.

(b)   *The claimant must show a need to hire a replacement vehicle.* Generally, this is easy to satisfy, but nevertheless evidence of need should be provided. Examples of where there may not be a need are where the claimant is in hospital or abroad at any time during the hire period, or where the claimant has access to an equivalent spare replacement vehicle without depriving another driver, such as a spouse or partner, of that vehicle.

(c)   *The claimant is entitled to hire an equivalent vehicle.* The claimant cannot recover the cost of the hire of a better, more expensive vehicle, if vehicles of an equivalent value to the damaged vehicle were reasonably available at less cost. The burden of proof is on the defendant to show a failure to mitigate. The question of what amounts to an appropriate and available vehicle is more difficult in relation to prestige cars, and expert evidence may be required. If the claimant obtains a less expensive replacement vehicle, the claimant can recover only the cost of the vehicle supplied.

(d) *The period of repair must be reasonable.* The court will take into account the start and end dates and what happened to the vehicle at all times between those dates and state the number of days for which the hire charge is recoverable. If damage was minor and the vehicle was in a driveable condition, the claimant may only recover hire charges for the period when it was necessary for the vehicle to be off the road for inspection and repair purposes. Repairs must be undertaken in a timely manner, but again the burden is upon the defendant to show that the claimant failed to mitigate the loss. This requires evidence of conduct on the claimant's part, or on the part of someone for whom the claimant is in law responsible, or a break in the chain of causation by a third party or intervening event. For example, did the claimant unreasonably delay in getting their vehicle to a garage or fail to make enquiries if repairs were delayed?

(e) *The hire rate must be reasonable.* The hire rate must of itself be reasonable, and savings made by hiring on a weekly or longer rate, rather than on a daily rate, should be considered. Unrecoverable extras need to be removed. Of significant importance is the court's consideration of the claimant's own financial position. If the claimant is found to be *impecunious*, in other words, at the time of entering the agreement the claimant was unable to pay for car hire charges without having to make unreasonable sacrifices, then the claimant is entitled to recover the credit hire rate. On the other hand, if the claimant was not impecunious, and the defendant can prove that the basic hire rate for a vehicle of the same or similar type to the claimant's own vehicle was less than the credit hire rate paid, the claimant will be able to recover only the basic hire rate. In *Stevens v Equity Syndicate Management Ltd* [2015] EWCA Civ 93, the Court of Appeal held that the court should use the lowest of the basic hire rates available for a vehicle of an equivalent type from a mainstream supplier or, if unavailable from a reputable local supplier, in the broad geographical area.

As an alternative to claiming for hire charges, a claimant may claim damages for loss of use of their vehicle whilst it is off the road. A weekly amount should be claimed, and this will reflect the level of inconvenience and hardship incurred by the claimant's having to rely on other means of transport. Special damages claims for loss of use of a motor vehicle have decreased in recent years, as the claimant is more likely to hire a substitute vehicle, as set out above. However, such claims are still relevant where the claimant is no longer able to drive, and in such cases there might also be a general damages claim for the future loss of use of a motor vehicle.

15.2.11 No-claims bonus

Under the terms of an insurance policy, a no-claims bonus (NCB) will entitle the policyholder to a discount on their annual premiums where the policyholder has not made any claims under the policy for a specified period. Where there is a NCB of five years or more, the policyholder may be entitled to a discount of as much as 60% to 75% and, as premiums are becoming increasingly expensive, the loss of the NCB may represent a significant monetary loss to the claimant. The claimant will lose the NCB where, as a result of being involved in an accident, the insurance company has to make payments to either the claimant or a third party under the terms of the policy, and is unable to recoup such losses from anyone else. As it is a NCB and not a no-fault bonus, it is immaterial whether the claimant was at fault or not. Where the claimant has lost their NCB, or is at risk of doing so, the loss should be included in the claim for damages. If, ultimately, the claimant's insurer is able to recover all its losses from the defendant (or more usually the defendant's insurer), the NCB will not be lost and the defendant's solicitor should ensure that the claim for the NCB is withdrawn.

15.2.12   Evidence of items of special damages

It is for the claimant to prove all items of special damages, and details should be set out in the appropriate witness statement(s). Where damaged items are capable of repair or services are required, the claimant should obtain two or three estimates in order to demonstrate that the costs incurred are reasonable. A decision to use a more expensive service provider should be explained in full. The claimant should be reminded at the outset of the case that they should retain documentary evidence (such as receipts, estimates and valuations) wherever possible. Defendants' solicitors should challenge items that cannot be supported by appropriate evidence. Where there is no documentary evidence, it is open to the claimant to attempt to prove the loss by their own oral testimony at trial, but see *Hughes v Addis* [2000] 3 WLUK 650, where the Court of Appeal upheld the judge's decision not to allow petrol costs where no receipts were supplied.

15.3   GENERAL DAMAGES

General damages are those which are not capable of precise mathematical calculation. They may be divided into:

(a)   pain, suffering and loss of amenity (sometimes known as non-pecuniary loss); and

(b)   financial losses incurred from the date of trial (or date of assessment of damages) for as long as court deems the losses will continue into the future (sometimes known as future pecuniary loss).

The main heads of general damages are:

(a)   pain, suffering and loss of amenity;

(b)   handicap in the labour market;

(c)   loss of congenial employment;

(d)   future loss of earnings;

(e)   future cost of medical expenses and care/non-medical care and aids and appliances;

(f)   lost pension.

15.3.1   Pain, suffering and loss of amenity

15.3.1.1   Damages for pain and suffering

Awards of damages under this head are designed to compensate the claimant for the pain and suffering attributable to any physical injury and psychological illness caused by the defendant's actions, from the moment of the accident to the date of trial, when damages are assessed, and, where appropriate, future pain and suffering.

The award is made on the basis of a subjective test, ie a consideration of the pain and suffering of this particular claimant.

15.3.1.2   Damages for loss of amenity

Strictly speaking, there is a separate head of damages known as 'loss of amenity', but compensation for this loss is usually included with compensation for pain and suffering. This element is designed to compensate the claimant for the loss of enjoyment of life which has resulted from the accident. Examples under this head include interference with the claimant's sex life, or the loss or impairment of the claimant's enjoyment of holidays, sports, hobbies and other pursuits.

The award for loss of amenity is based on an objective test (in contrast to pain and suffering), and thus may be awarded irrespective of whether the claimant is personally aware of the loss, for example if the claimant is unconscious (*West v Shephard* [1964] AC 326).

Although the test is primarily objective, it does have subjective overtones in so far as the court will have regard to the claimant's former lifestyle. This may be particularly pertinent where the claimant was formerly a very active person (eg a keen sportsperson) and can no longer pursue the sport. Although the claimant's pain and suffering may be the same as that of another person with a similar disability, their loss of amenity may be greater and, as such, the total award for pain and suffering and loss of amenity may be greater.

Damages for loss of congenial employment (see **15.3.3**) may also be argued under this head, but increasingly, the courts are making separate reference to these types of damages.

15.3.1.3 Quantification of damages for pain, suffering and loss of amenity

There is no minimum award which must be made for pain, suffering and loss of amenity (however, only exceptionally would an injury not be worth, for example, £500 or £750); neither is there any maximum.

The award is incapable of precise mathematical calculation. The solicitor's first step is to examine the claimant's witness statement and the medical report in order to identify details of the following:

(a) The claimant's life prior to the accident. This will be relevant to the loss of amenity claim.

(b) The pain and suffering associated with the accident itself and the immediate aftermath. What were the injuries? How did the claimant react? Was the claimant taken to hospital by ambulance?

(c) Any periods of time the claimant was in hospital, and the number and nature of any operations or other medical procedures the claimant had to undergo.

(d) The short-term/long-term prognosis. Will the claimant recover in full? If not, what will his continuing pain/disabilities be, and how long will they continue?

(e) Is there a risk of any future degeneration (eg, osteoporosis)?

(f) What has been/will be the effect of the injuries on the claimant's lifestyle?

In attempting to value the claim, courts will refer to the awards made in comparable cases, so the solicitor's next step is to carry out the relevant research. As no two cases are exactly alike (for example, there may be differences in relation to the sex and age of the claimant, the injuries suffered and the effect on the claimant's life), this is not as straightforward as it might appear.

A useful starting point is the Judicial College's *Guidelines for the Assessment of General Damages in Personal Injury Cases*, currently in their 16th edition, published in April 2022 by Oxford University Press. The *Guidelines* are commonly used by personal injury lawyers and judges to obtain a ball-park figure for the claimant's injuries. (An online version of the *Guidelines* may be found on Lawtel Personal Injury on Westlaw.) The *Guidelines* are based on an analysis of previous judgments and provide an easy reference to broad categories of injuries, such as head injuries, psychiatric damages, injuries affecting the senses, injuries to internal organs, etc. These categories are further divided, so, for example, the section on orthopaedic injuries is divided into neck injuries, back injuries, shoulder injuries, etc. Lastly, each of these sub-categories is divided into severe, serious, moderate and minor classifications, with an indication of what each of these types of injuries are worth.

You should not base your assessment of the claimant's losses solely on the *Guidelines* but rather should make reference to specific comparable cases. The importance of comparable cases was stressed by the Court of Appeal in *Dureau v Evans* [1996] PIQR Q18, when it commented on the limited assistance provided by the *Guidelines* in relation to claimants who have suffered multiple injuries. Similarly, in *Reed v Sunderland Health Authority* (1998) *The Times*, 16 October, it was held that while the *Guidelines* were an important source of information, they did not have the force of law, and the Court of Appeal is unlikely to overturn a decision if the *Guidelines* are not followed precisely (see *Davies v Inman* [1999] PIQR Q26).

Traditionally, solicitors looking for comparable cases would use specialist sources in hard copy, such as:

(a)   Kemp and Kemp, *The Quantum of Damages* (Sweet & Maxwell);

(b)   *Butterworths Personal Injury Service*;

(c)   *Personal Injuries and Quantum Reports* (Sweet & Maxwell);

(d)   *Current Law* (Sweet & Maxwell);

(e)   *Personal and Medical Injuries Law Letter* (IBC).

However, solicitors will now almost invariably use online services, such as Butterworth's Personal Injury Service (LexisNexis) or Lawtel on Westlaw (which includes access to Kemp and Kemp), to identify comparable cases.

Once a comparable case has been found, the relevant figure is that relating to pain, suffering and loss of amenity. Remember the difficulties associated with terminology. Frequently, the case reports will helpfully set out a figure for pain, suffering and loss of amenity, but sometimes they will refer to 'general damages'. If it is clear from the facts of the case that there are no future losses, or alternatively a figure for future losses appears, it is safe to assume that the term 'general damages' is the award for pain, suffering and loss of amenity. If it is unsafe to make such an assumption, further investigations will need to be made.

There will be differences between the claimant's situation and the circumstances of the claimants in the comparable case so, once the relevant figure in the comparable case has been identified, adjustments will need to be made in order to take account of the following matters:

(a)   *Sex/gender* – this may not be as important as it once was. For example, traditionally, female claimants received higher awards for facial scarring than male claimants with similar injuries. This was based on the assumption that a woman's appearance is of greater importance than a man's appearance and, consequently, disfigurement causes greater suffering for women. This differentiation based on gender was removed in September 2017 in the 14th edition of the *Guidelines*. Each case turns on its facts.

(b)   *Age of the victim* – in cases of permanent disability, younger victims tend to get more compensation than older victims as the young will suffer longer. On the other hand, some injuries will have a more severe impact on an older claimant than on a younger one. Again, each case turns on its facts.

(c)   *Loss of amenity* – this is heavily influenced by whether the victim had a previously active lifestyle.

(d)   *Limb injuries* – injuries to dominant limbs attract higher awards than injuries to non-dominant limbs.

(e)   *Inflation* – previous awards must be inflated to present-day values. The inflation table in Kemp and Kemp, *The Quantum of Damages*, can be used for that purpose although online sources, such as Lawtel on Westlaw, provide both original and inflated figures in their quantum reports. Lawtel also has an online inflation calculator which is very easy to use (see Kemp Practice Tools).

(f)   *2000 uplift* – in the case of *Heil v Rankin and Another* [2000] 2 WLR 1173, the Court of Appeal considered the level of damages for pain and suffering, concluded that they were too low, and stated that there should be staged increases for all future cases where the value of awards for pain and suffering was in excess of £10,000. Consequently, when seeking to rely on a pre-March 2000 case in excess of £10,000, a conversion table (such as that found in *Quantum* 2/2000, 18 April 2000 (Sweet & Maxwell)) must be used to update the award, which will then need to be inflated to present-day values. The inflated figures provided in Lawtel's quantum reports take account of *Heil v Rankin*, and their online calculator will do this automatically, where relevant. The *Guidelines* also take the increases into account.

(g) *2013 uplift* – following the Court of Appeal's revised decision in *Simmons v Castle* [2012] EWCA Civ 1039, in order to mitigate the effects of the 2013 reforms to the civil litigation costs regime, a 10% uplift is to be applied for damages for pain, suffering and loss of amenity in all cases where judgment is given after 1 April 2013, except where the claimant had entered into a CFA before that date (LASPO 2012, s 44(6)). The idea is that this increase will be used by the claimant to pay for any success fee owed to the claimant's solicitor, as this will no longer be recoverable from a losing defendant. The *Guidelines* from then on, up to and including the 15th edition, had two columns, one providing figures for general damages with the uplift, and one without. The column without the uplift relates to those transitional cases funded by a CFA entered into before 1 April 2013 with a recoverable success fee. The column with the uplift took into account the *Simmons v Castle* 10% increase. The 16th edition of the *Guidelines* does not include the pre-*Simmons* alternative (ie the non-uplifted figures). As the introduction to the 16th edition explains: 'We have decided to remove figures for general damages which do not include the *Simmons* 10% uplift. Apart from mesothelioma cases, there are now likely to be vanishingly few ongoing cases in which the pre-uplift figures will be relevant. The view of the editorial team is that the number is now insufficient to justify the inclusion of both figures. However, for those who may need to identify the pre-uplift figure, we provide the formula in the Note on page xvii of this edition.'

When carrying out the research relating to a client who has sustained multiple injuries, it is extremely unlikely that an exactly matching comparable case will be found. The accepted approach is to identify the most serious injury, find a comparable award for that injury and then take account of awards made for the other injuries. It will not normally be appropriate simply to bolt the separate awards together, as the court will seek to compensate the claimant for the totality of the claimant's pain and suffering, and some discount will be required in recognition of this.

15.3.1.4 Damages where there are pre-existing injuries or conditions

One of the arguments that the defendant may use to bar or limit recovery of loss for pain and suffering is that the whole or part of the claimant's injuries or disabilities is due to a pre-existing condition.

The egg-shell skull rule means that the defendant must 'take the victim as he finds him'. In other words, where a claimant has a *pre-existing disposition or vulnerability to injury*, and the negligent act caused greater damage to that particular claimant than it would have caused to someone without that disposition or vulnerability, the defendant will be held liable for the entirety of the claimant's injuries, and not simply for the injuries that a less vulnerable victim would have suffered.

However, where a claimant has a *pre-existing injury and/or condition* (as opposed to a pre-existing disposition or vulnerability), the rule does not mean that the defendant will be liable for all injuries and disabilities suffered by the claimant post-accident, where such injuries and disabilities are distinguishable and severable. Rather, the defendant will be liable for the full extent of the *aggravation or exacerbation* of the claimant's pre-existing injuries and/or condition.

This approach was reaffirmed by the Court of Appeal in *Reaney v University Hospital of North Staffordshire NHS Trust & Anor* [2015] EWCA Civ 1119. Mrs Reaney was admitted into hospital with an illness that resulted in paralysis below the mid-thoracic level, although this was not caused by negligence. At this stage, had she returned home, she would have been able to live a largely independent life, with some family support and about 7 hours' local authority support per week. However, her condition was much worsened as a result of the defendants' negligence. During an extended period of hospitalisation, she developed deep pressure sores, which caused an infection of the bone marrow, hip dislocation, serious contractures of the lower limbs, increased lower limb spasticity, and a resulting steep rise in her care needs.

The Court of Appeal overturned the first instance decision that all of Mrs Reaney's care and other needs were caused by the defendants' negligence, on the basis that the needs caused by the negligence were *of the same kind* as her pre-existing needs. Consequently, the claimant was entitled to damages relating only to the increased need for care. It went on to say that in cases where the needs caused by the negligence *were of a different kind* to pre-existing needs, those needs would be caused in their entirety by the negligence. Hence, parties will need to consider whether needs are qualitatively different from that which had been previously needed, or quantitatively different, ie more of the same.

Where there has been a worsening of a pre-existing condition and the defendant is able to show that the claimant would eventually have suffered similar symptoms in any event, damages will be restricted to those arising during the acceleration period, ie the period of time by which the symptoms have been brought forward by reason of the defendant's negligence.

> **EXAMPLE**
>
> Saira suffered from a degenerative condition of the spine prior to her involvement in a RTA caused by the defendant's negligence. The defendant argues that this condition would eventually have generated the symptoms of which Saira is now complaining, and that the defendant's actions have merely accelerated Saira's disabilities. The defendant is able to prove that, but for the defendant's actions, Saira's symptoms would have developed in five years' time in any event. The court will apply the 'acceleration period' approach and the defendant will be liable only for a five-year period for injury, loss and damage.

15.3.1.5   Evidence

Although the medical evidence will be the primary matter to which the court will have regard in determining the award for pain, suffering and loss of amenity, the claimant will also give evidence of their injuries at trial. It is important that details are contained within the client's witness statement. It is surprising how many clients forget the exact details of the difficulties they had immediately post-accident or post-operation, and it is good practice for the claimant's solicitor to suggest that a diary is kept by the client, detailing the pain and practical difficulties that were suffered. It may also be helpful to obtain evidence from others, such as the claimant's spouse, civil partner or partner and family members, or the claimant's employer, as to the effect of the injuries on the claimant.

15.3.2   Handicap in the labour market

Where a claimant is able to continue to work following an accident but may lose their job at some stage in the future and will subsequently face difficulties in obtaining another job because of their disability, eg it will take the claimant longer to find a job and/or the claimant may have to accept less lucrative employment, then the claimant may be compensated for their so-called 'handicap in the labour market' or, to put it another way, for the claimant's loss of earning capacity. This will be the case even where, at the time of the trial, the claimant's earnings are the same as they were before the accident. For the court to award such damages, the claimant should have suffered a 'weakening' of their competitive position in the open labour market. In practice, this is referred to as a *Smith v Manchester* claim (see *Smith v Manchester Corporation* (1974) 17 KIR 1).

This type of award is not appropriate where the claimant will never be able to return to work, as the claimant will then be compensated by a claim for future lost earnings using the multiplier and multiplicand method and reference to the Ogden tables (see **15.3.4**). Examples of cases where a *Smith v Manchester* award may be considered appropriate include the following:

(a)   The claimant has returned to work after the accident and thus has no continuing loss of earnings claim. However, the claimant has suffered a weakening of their position in the labour market due to their injuries.

(b)   The claimant has returned to work and is earning less than they did prior to the accident. In addition, the claimant has suffered a weakening of their position in the labour market. The court will take all the circumstances into account and may order a *Smith v Manchester* award to cover all these losses or, alternatively, order damages for future loss of earnings and earning capacity calculated by using a multiplier, multiplicand and the Ogden tables (see **15.3.4** for future loss of earnings and *Billett v Ministry of Defence* [2015] EWCA Civ 773 below). Alternatively, there is nothing to prevent a court in these circumstances from ordering damages for future loss of earnings using the multiplier/multiplicand approach *plus* a *Smith v Manchester* award for the handicap on the labour market.

(c)   The claimant is still absent from work at the time of the trial as a result of the injuries suffered in the accident, but expects to return to their job at some time in the future when they have recovered further. However, when the claimant does so, their position in the labour market will be weaker than it would otherwise have been. In such circumstances, the court's approach may be any of the alternatives as set out in (b) above.

In deciding whether a *Smith v Manchester* award is appropriate, the court will:

(a)   consider whether there is a 'substantial' or 'real' risk that the claimant will lose their present job at some time before the estimated end of their working life; and if there is

(b)   assess and quantify the present value of the loss which the claimant will suffer if that risk materialises. In doing so, the court will have regard to the degree of risk, the time when it is likely to materialise and the factors, both favourable and unfavourable, which may affect the claimant's chance of getting another job at all or an equally well-paid job.

When seeking to establish whether there is a risk that the claimant will lose their job, the courts have given the words 'substantial' or 'real' a liberal interpretation, so that what is required to be shown is that the risk is 'real' rather than 'speculative'. The risk might lie in the nature of the injuries themselves, which might make it impossible for the claimant to continue in that line of work. Alternatively, the risk might lie in matters that have nothing to do with the injuries, such as a contraction in the industry in which the claimant is employed, or their employer's business restructuring.

Once the first test has been satisfied, the court will attempt to assess and quantify the risk and calculate the appropriate damages. The court has to anticipate what would be the claimant's chances of getting an equally well-paid job if the claimant were forced onto the labour market. This head of damages is notoriously hard to quantify as the court will consider each individual case on its own facts, but a common approach is to award between zero to two years' net loss of earnings as at the date of trial. However, the Court of Appeal in *Foster v Tyne and Wear County Council* [1986] 1 All ER 567 stated that there was no 'conventional' figure for damages under this head, and awarded a sum equivalent to four years' net salary.

A *Smith v Manchester* award should normally be claimed in the particulars of claim (*Chan Wai Tong v Li Ping Sum* [1985] AC 446). However, the Court of Appeal, in *Thorn v Powergen* [1997] PIQR Q71, upheld a decision allowing a *Smith v Manchester* award in a case where it had not been claimed specifically but was found by the trial judge to be implied due to the nature of the injuries revealed by the medical evidence.

Evidence of the effect of the claimant's injuries on their ability to maintain their current employment position and on the claimant's future job prospects should be set out in the medical report as well as in the claimant's own witness statement. If the risk to continued employment relates to matters concerning the employer's business, evidence of, for example, likely redundancies, may be obtained from managers, co-workers or trade unions. In addition, evidence must be obtained concerning the claimant's future job prospects, including any skills the claimant possesses (eg, a labourer of 50 years of age with no qualifications will find it difficult to retrain if they lose their job), the prospects of the industry in which the claimant works and any unusual local problems that may be relevant to the claimant. It may be necessary to instruct an employment consultant to provide information about these matters, or to obtain relevant information from other sources, for example the Annual Survey of Hours and Earnings. The expert would consider the client's injuries and personal qualifications, and analyse employment statistics and local press advertisements in order to report on the severity of the handicap on the labour market.

In recent years, there has been an increasing tendency for claimants to pursue damages for loss of future earnings capacity by means of the multiplier/multiplicand/Ogden tables approach rather than a *Smith v Manchester* award. The justification is that the former offers increased mathematical precision in calculating loss due to tables A–D of the Ogden tables, which enable account to be taken for contingencies other than mortality, although the tendency for this approach to lead to higher awards is undoubtedly a factor.

In *Billett v Ministry of Defence*, the Court of Appeal considered how the court should assess damages for loss of future earning capacity in circumstances where the claimant suffers from a minor disability, is in steady employment and is earning at their full pre-accident rate. In that case, the decision of the court at first instance to award damages calculated by use of the Ogden tables was overturned. Jackson LJ observed: 'In the present case that exercise is no more scientific than the broad-brush judgment which the court makes when carrying out a *Smith v Manchester* assessment.' Consequently, a *Smith v Manchester* award was more appropriate and the award for loss of future earnings was reduced from £99,000 to £45,000, roughly equivalent to two years' net earnings. The conclusion to be drawn from this case is that the court will look at the specific circumstances of each case and determine which approach is the most suitable.

15.3.3 Loss of congenial employment

The concept of compensating the claimant for a loss of job satisfaction has been accepted by the courts for some time. In *Morris v Johnson Mathey & Co* (1967) 112 SJ 32, a precious metal worker, aged 52, sustained a serious injury to his left hand, which left him incapable of continuing his craft. His employers found him alternative employment as a storeman, which he described as 'at times rather boring'. Edmund-Davies LJ stated:

> [T]he joy of the craftsman in his craft is beyond price. But the court has to give some monetary value to the loss of craft. The court should give consideration to the fact that a craftsman had to replace his craft with humdrum work.

Traditionally, the award was incorporated within the award for pain, suffering and loss of amenity, but it is now well established that the court will normally make a separate award under this heading. Generally, those who received such awards were deprived of jobs which have a vocational element or where a period of training is required, such as firemen, nurses, members of the armed forces, dancers, actors, and craftsmen such as carpenters. Those employed in repetitive manual work, such as factory workers, are unlikely to be able to convince a court that they found their job rewarding. However, claimants' solicitors should listen carefully to what their clients have to say on this point, as courts will judge each case on its facts. In *McCrae v (1) Chase International Express Ltd (2) Justin Smith* [2004] PIQR P21, the Court of Appeal overturned an award made to a motor-cycle courier on the basis that it was not satisfied with the evidence in support of the claim, but said that that an award might otherwise have been appropriate. In *Lane v The Personal Representatives of Deborah Lake (Deceased)* [2007] All ER (D) 258, the defendant tried to argue that this award should be reserved for policemen, firemen, etc, but this was rejected by the judge on the basis that such an award 'should be confined to those who truly have suffered a loss under this head and not be awarded merely by reference to the type of employment nor automatically as an extra'.

Awards tend to be in the range of £5,000 to £10,000. In *Willbye (by her mother and next friend) v Gibbons* [2003] EWCA Civ 372, the Court of Appeal reduced an award of £15,000 which had been made to a girl who had been 12 years old at the time of the accident and who had wanted to become a nursery nurse. It said that it was important to keep this head of damages in proportion and reduced the award to £5,000. Nevertheless, higher awards will be made in appropriate circumstances. One of the highest awards made so far was in *Appleton v Medhat Mohammed El Safty* [2007] EWHC 631 (QB), to a footballer who had been playing for West Bromwich Albion before clinical negligence cut short his career. The Court of Appeal found the facts of this case to be exceptional and awarded £25,000.

Any evidence relating to a loss of congenial employment claim must be included within the witness statements for exchange. In particular, the claimant must give full details of the nature of their previous employment, any training or qualifications required, their career progression, etc, so that the loss of job satisfaction can be proved.

15.3.4 Future loss of earnings

Damages for loss of earnings after the date of trial will be assessed as general damages. The court will need to determine what the claimant would have earned, had the claimant not been injured, up to the time the claimant would have ordinarily retired or for a specified period, if the claimant is expected to recover sufficiently to be able to work in the future. Even the most straightforward case will require the court to tackle uncertainty, and the more complex the case, the more 'crystal ball gazing' will be required.

Under the conventional method of calculating future loss of earnings, a lump sum award will be calculated using a multiplier and a multiplicand. The object is to assess the amount of money which can be invested today which will represent a fund which should last for precisely the period of the lost earnings. In other words, the capital sum is invested, the claimant periodically draws out from the fund what the claimant would have earned throughout the period of loss, and the fund gradually decreases until it is exhausted at the very end of the period of loss. That is, at least, the theory.

15.3.4.1 The multiplicand

The multiplicand is the figure which represents the claimant's annual loss, so where a claimant is not able to work at all, it will be the net annual earnings that the claimant would have received had they not been injured. Where the claimant is able to work but will earn less than their pre-accident salary, the multiplicand is the difference between the two net annual earnings. The items to be included or ignored in the calculation of the multiplicand are the same as for pre-trial earnings, as identified at **15.2.1**.

15.3.4.2 The multiplier

The multiplier is based on the period of likely future loss. This will depend on the facts of the case. For example, in the case of a male claimant who will never work again, the period of loss will normally extend until his likely retirement age (normally 60 or 65, although the recent 8th edition has inserted new tables for both men and women, to reflect retirement ages of 68 and up to 80). The period of loss is taken from the date of trial, as pre-trial losses will be claimed as special damages.

The period of loss is then converted into a multiplier. Following the House of Lords' decision in the joint appeals of *Page v Sheerness Steel Co Ltd; Wells v Wells; Thomas v Brighton Health Authority* [1998] 3 WLR 329, it can now be assumed that the starting point when attempting to identify the multiplier is to use the Government's actuarial tables (the Ogden tables; see **Appendix 6**). The current version of the Ogden tables is the 8th edition. These were published by the Government Actuary in July 2020 (updated in August 2022). These tables reflect the current discount rate in England and Wales of –0.25%. This became the applicable discount rate for personal injury claims from 5 August 2019. See **Appendix 6**.

The multipliers in Tables 1 to 34 are based on mortality rates for the United Kingdom, with different tables for males and females, and a discount to take account of accelerated receipt (ie the claimant will receive a lump sum which they can invest). The tables cover loss for life, loss of earnings and pension loss.

In order to find the appropriate multiplier for loss of earnings, the solicitor will;

(a)　identify the correct table for loss of earnings from Tables 3 to 18 by using the claimant's sex and anticipated retirement age had it not been for the accident;

(b)　find the claimant's age at the date of trial along the left-hand vertical column;

(c)　find the correct discount rate along the top horizontal line. The discount rate reflects the anticipated net return on investment of the lump sum (after tax and allowing for inflation) over the period of the loss for which it is awarded. The rate was changed from 2.5% to –0.75% on 20 March 2017, and had the effect of greatly increasing awards for future losses. To illustrate this point, using the example given at **15.3.4.3**, Simon's damages for future loss of earnings with a discount rate of 2.5% would have been £262,600, whereas, with a discount rate of –0.75%, it was £357,400. Following the first review of the discount rate under the Civil Liability Act 2018 (CLA 2018), which received Royal Assent on 20 December 2018, the discount rate was changed again on 5 August 2019. This resulted in the current rate of minus 0.25% (–0.25%). (See **5.10** for the changes made by CLA 2018 to the mechanisms by which the discount rate will be set in the future and the timescales involved.)

(d)　identify the appropriate multiplier, which can be found where the relevant vertical and horizontal columns meet;

(e)　consider whether further discounts are appropriate to take account of other 'risks and vicissitudes of life', such as the possibility that there would be periods when the claimant would not have been earning due to ill-health unrelated to the claim, or loss of employment. The factors which are to be taken into account are as follows:

(i)　whether the claimant was employed or not at the time of the accident. Employed includes being self-employed or being on a government training scheme;

(ii)　whether the claimant was disabled or not at the time of the accident. A claimant is considered to be disabled for the purposes of the Ogden tables if they have an illness or a disability which has or is expected to last for over a year or is a progressive illness; satisfies the Disability Discrimination Act 1995 definition that the disability has a substantial adverse effect on the claimant's ability to carry out normal day-to-day activities; *and* the impairment affects either the kind or the amount of paid work the claimant can do;

(iii)　the claimant's level of educational attainment at the time of the accident. There are three levels: Level 3 is a degree or equivalent and higher; Level 2 is GCSE grades A* to C/9 to 4, up to A levels and equivalent; Level 1 is below GCSE grade C or CSE grade 1 or no qualifications.

Section B of the Ogden tables gives further information regarding these discounts and how they should be applied (see **Appendix 6**).

15.3.4.3　The calculation

In order to determine the amount for future loss of earnings, the multiplicand is multiplied by the amended multiplier.

EXAMPLE

Abidemi was 43 when the accident occurred and 45 at trial. He was employed as a labourer prior to the accident, earning £20,000 per annum. He was not disabled, had no qualifications and was due to retire 65. As a result of the accident, Abidemi will be unable to do any kind of work for the rest of his life.

> (a)   As he is male and his retirement age is 65, the correct table is Table 9;
>
> (b)   Using his age at trial, 45, and the –0.25% rate of return, a multiplier of 19.84 is identified.
>
> (c)   Account for risks other than mortality, ie for Abidemi being employed, not disabled and having no qualifications. Table A is the correct table as Abidemi is male, would have retired at 65, and was not disabled. Identify the correct age bracket on the left hand side (45–49) and, across the top, identify the correct column. This is the third column (headed O), as he was employed but without qualifications. The correct discount figure is 0.85.
>
> (d)   The amended multiplier is 19.84 x 0.85 = 16.86
>
> (e)   The future loss of earnings 16.86 x £20,000 = £337,200

15.3.4.4   Career progression and loss of earnings

In cases where the period of loss will continue for many years into the future, it is particularly important to ensure that account is taken of likely periodic changes to the claimant's income. The claimant will want to point to anticipated career progressions where, for example, the claimant was a junior doctor, a trainee solicitor or a junior officer in the armed forces. In such cases, the court will either:

(a)   determine an average multiplicand, based upon the likely earnings throughout the period of loss, which will then be applied to the full period of the loss; or

(b)   use stepped multiplicands for each stage of the claimant's career. Generally, this will result in a lower multiplicand at the beginning and possibly at the very end of the period of loss, with one or more higher multiplicands to represent the likely career progression that would have been followed.

In *Collett v Smith and Middlesbrough Football & Athletics Company (1986) Ltd* [2008] EWHC 1962 (QB), the court was required to assess damages in relation to a young man whose promising football career had been cut short, at the age of 18, as a result of a negligent tackle. In assessing damages for future loss of earnings at £3,854,328, the court was obliged to make decisions on such issues as the level at which he would have played football and at what remuneration, how long he would have played for, whether his career would otherwise have been cut short by injury and whether he would have gone on to work as a coach or manager.

The amount of 'crystal ball gazing' which the court will of necessity have to undertake in this exercise is increased in cases where the claimant was a child at the time of the accident. If the child is old enough to have attended school, taken a few exams and shown some interest in one career or another, it might be possible to anticipate a likely career progression. With a younger child, this will be much more difficult. The court will take into account the following evidence, where available:

(a)   the nature of the employment of the claimant's parents and siblings;

(b)   any qualifications obtained so far;

(c)   evidence from the claimant's former teachers, club leaders, sports trainers, etc regarding the claimant's abilities and personality;

(d)   neuropsychological evidence of the claimant's pre-accident IQ;

(e)   the claimant's own evidence and personality, as demonstrated in the witness-box.

15.3.4.5   Evidence

The importance of expert evidence in such a case is vital. Medical evidence can provide an indication as to what work the claimant will be capable of undertaking, both at present and in the future. This, together with evidence of the claimant's employment prospects, will assist the court in determining what will happen to the claimant in the future, which, while often appearing unsatisfactory to many clients, is usually the approach that the court will take.

15.3.5 Future cost of medical expenses, care and quasi-nursing services, and aids and appliances

In cases of catastrophic injury, it is possible that the claim for the cost of future care and quasi-nursing services will exceed the claim for future loss of earnings. This is because the need for care will often continue beyond the claimant's normal retirement age, plus the fact that specialist care is extremely expensive. It must be remembered that the cost and type of care may change in the future. For example, a severely injured child's costs of care will increase as they become older because it is unlikely that the child's parents will be able to look after them when they are elderly and, as such, increased professional help will be required.

The calculation for the future cost of care is carried out in the same way as set out in **15.3.4**. However, when identifying the multiplier, the correct table will be either Table 1 or Table 2, depending upon whether the claimant is male or female. In addition, following the House of Lords' decision in *Page v Sheerness Steel Co Ltd; Wells v Wells; Thomas v Brighton Health Authority* (see **15.3.4.2**), it is not appropriate to discount whole life multipliers.

The cost of medical expenses and aids and appliances may also be dealt with using a multiplier from Tables 1 or 2 and a multiplicand where a continuing need can be demonstrated. For example, the claimant may include the cost of a wheelchair as part of their special damages claim. That wheelchair will not last the claimant for the rest of their life, and therefore the replacement cost will need to be annualised. So, where the cost of a wheelchair is £1,000 and it would have a life span of five years, the multiplicand would be £200. Generally, the annual cost of items relevant to the same period of loss are added together to produce one multiplicand.

Alternatively, the claimant may require an operation which will not need to be repeated, or an appliance which will not need to be replaced. In such cases, a one-off payment should be included in the claim.

15.3.6 Loss of pension

In more serious cases, where the claimant does not return to work or returns on a lower wage, consideration must be given to a claim for lost pension. The claimant's pension is normally based upon their period of service with the company and the salary that they would have earned at retirement age. Reference should be made to specialist texts on this subject.

15.4 PROVISIONAL DAMAGES

15.4.1 The problem which provisional damages are intended to solve

When the court awards damages or the parties agree a settlement, it will be on the basis of a full and final settlement of the claim. Consequently, the normal rule is that the claimant is unable to return to court to ask for a further award to be made, even where the claimant's condition has seriously deteriorated.

This being the case, the claimant's solicitor should ensure that the claimant is properly compensated, by ensuring that expert medical evidence deals with any deterioration that is likely to arise in the future. Where the court is satisfied that the claimant is more than 50% likely to suffer a specified deterioration in their condition, the court will award damages on the basis that the deterioration *will* occur and a provisional damages order is not appropriate. The problem lies in cases where the deterioration, although possible, is less than probable.

> **EXAMPLE**
>
> Ladonya is injured. At the time of the trial she has no loss of sight, but there is a 10% possibility that in the future she will lose the sight in one eye. Bearing in mind that quantum for pain and suffering and loss of amenity for the total loss of sight in one eye is approximately £30,000, how does the judge award damages to Ladonya?
>
> If the judge awards £3,000 (10% of £30,000) and Ladonya does lose the sight in her eye in the future, Ladonya will be under-compensated by £27,000 but cannot return to court for more damages. If Ladonya does not lose the sight in her eye in the future, Ladonya is unjustly enriched by £3,000 and the defendant cannot recover the excess damages.

Provisional damages are aimed at solving the above problem by providing an exception to the basic rule. In certain limited circumstances the claimant can be compensated for their injuries with the proviso that if a specific condition occurs in the future, the claimant will be allowed to return to court so that further damages may be awarded.

15.4.2 The statutory provisions

Rule 41.2 of the CPR states that the court may make an order for provisional damages, provided the claim is included in the particulars of claim and the court is satisfied that s 32A of the Senior Courts Act 1981 or s 51 of the County Courts Act 1984 applies.

In accordance with s 32A of the Senior Courts Act 1981, an order for provisional damages may be made where there is:

> a chance that at some definite or indefinite time in the future the injured person will, as a result of the act or omission which gave rise to the cause of action, develop some serious disease or suffer some serious deterioration in his physical or mental condition.

A similar provision is found in s 51 of the County Courts Act 1984.

If the court considers that there is a suitable case for provisional damages (see CPR, Part 41 and PD 41), it will:

(a)   assess damages on the assumption that the injured person will not develop the disease or suffer the deterioration in their condition;

(b)   identify the disease or deterioration that has been disregarded;

(c)   stipulate a period (which may be indefinite) during which the claimant may return to court for further damages if they develop the disease or suffers the deterioration;

(d)   make an order that relevant documents are to be kept by the court.

If the claimant subsequently suffers the specified disease or deterioration within the specified time frame, the claimant may apply to the court for further damages. The order will set out with precision the circumstances which must arise before the claimant is allowed to return to court, as it will wish to avoid a situation where there is a subsequent dispute as to whether the proper circumstances had arisen.

15.4.2.1 'Chance'

The expression 'chance' is not defined in the legislation. It clearly indicates something less than a probability, ie less than 50% likelihood, and in *Curi v Colina* [1998] EWCA Civ 1326, the Court of Appeal said there had to be a 'possibility but no more than a possibility'. However, it must be measurable rather than merely fanciful (*Willson v Ministry of Defence* [1991] 1 All ER 638, where it was held that the possibility that the claimant would incur further injury from a fall as a result of an ankle injury was not evidence of 'serious deterioration' as it might not ever happen).

In order to be measurable, the chance should be expressed in terms of a percentage figure. The courts have been prepared to make an order for provisional damages where the likelihood of deterioration has been expressed in terms of single figure percentages, but an award should not be made where the risk is *de minimis*. In *Chewings v (1) Williams & (2) Abertawe Bro Morgannwg University NHS Trust* [2009] EWHC 2490 (QB), the claimant sought provisional damages, reserving the right to claim further damages should he suffer a below the knee amputation of his right leg. One of the issues for the court to determine was whether the risk of amputation was more than fanciful. In allowing the award, the court held that the chance of amputation was more than fanciful and, although it was difficult to ascribe a precise percentage to it, if it were necessary to do so, it would be about 2%.

If there is doubt as to whether the case is appropriate for a provisional damages claim then advice from a solicitor or barrister with expertise in this area should be sought.

15.4.2.2 'Serious deterioration'

'Serious deterioration' is not defined in the legislation. In *Willson*, it was held that 'serious deterioration' meant:

(a) a clear and severable risk of deterioration (not merely the natural progression of the injury); and

(b) something beyond ordinary deterioration.

On the facts of *Willson*, the court held that the chance of arthritis was merely a natural progression of the injury and was not a suitable case for provisional damages. The most common examples of conditions in which provisional damages have been awarded in practice are where there is the chance of the claimant suffering from epilepsy, or from a disease such as cancer or asbestosis as a result of exposure to a dangerous substance.

15.4.3 Procedural approach

The claim for provisional damages must be included in the particulars of claim, and if the possibility of provisional damages emerges after these documents have been served, the documents must be amended. Part 16 of the CPR 1998 and the accompanying Practice Direction set out the necessary information which must be included. Where a case settles before proceedings are issued and the parties agree that an order for provisional damages should be made, the matter should be brought before the court using Part 8 proceedings.

The court will be slow to make an order for provisional damages, on the basis that finality is better for all parties. Evidence is therefore very important, and the medical report should address the issues with precision. In particular, it should set out the nature of the deterioration, the chance of deterioration by means of a percentage figure and an anticipated time frame.

The only basis for an award of provisional damages is a court order. Any application by consent for an order awarding provisional damages should follow the procedure set out in Part 23 of the CPR 1998.

If the specified disease or deterioration occurs within the specified period, the claimant must give at least 28 days' written notice to the defendant of their intention to apply for further damages.

Ideally, such an application should be made within the time limit set out in the original order. However, although the CPR do not expressly authorise an extension where an application is made after the expiry of the time limit, they do not exclude it. In *Blythe v Ministry of Defence* [2013] All ER (D) 326 (Nov), CA, the Court of Appeal held that the facts of a case might justify an extension in such circumstances in furtherance of the overriding objective.

15.4.4 The claimant's and defendant's perspectives

Even where the claimant's claim falls within the realm of provisional damages, the claimant may not want to pursue this option, preferring instead that the claim is satisfied once and for all by the award of a lump sum. The defendant will also usually prefer the matter to be dealt with by one lump sum award, and thus in such a case be prepared to negotiate an additional amount to take account of the risk of deterioration in an attempt to persuade the claimant to abandon their claim for provisional damages.

The claimant's solicitor must advise their client of the implications of each option, preferably in writing, and obtain their instructions, again preferably in writing. The claimant must appreciate that if they choose to accept a lump sum in full and final settlement, they will not be able to return to court to ask for additional compensation should their condition deteriorate, no matter how serious the deterioration is. Alternatively, if the court makes an order for provisional damages, the claimant will be able to return to court only if the specified deterioration occurs within the specified time limit.

Solicitors must ensure that they preserve their own files for the appropriate length of time.

15.4.5 Provisional damages and the Fatal Accidents Act 1976

Section 3 of the Damages Act 1996 allows an application to the court under the FAA 1976 where a person is awarded provisional damages and subsequently dies.

15.4.6 Provisional damages and Part 36 of the CPR

Where there is a claim for provisional damages and the defendant makes a Part 36 offer, the offer notice must specify whether or not the settlement includes the making of a provisional damages award (see **14.10.2**).

15.5 PERIODICAL PAYMENTS

15.5.1 The problems which periodical payments are intended to solve

The assessment of damages, particularly in relation to future pecuniary loss, depends upon matters which are uncertain and unpredictable. Consequently, a lump sum payment may result in the following:

(a) over-compensation, leading to unfairness to the defendant. A claimant may die early and the claimant's beneficiaries be unjustly enriched;

(b) under-compensation, leading to a lack of financial security for the claimant. Where a claimant will be dependent on care for many years, the money may run out;

(c) a lack of prudence on the part of the claimant or the claimant's family. Few have experience of managing large sums of money, and inappropriate spending or unwise investment may dissipate the fund;

(d) a lack of flexibility. The general rule is that the claimant cannot return to court if their condition deteriorates (unless there is an order for provisional damages, see **15.4** above).

These problems will be less severe where the court orders periodical payments to be made. Here, the court will assess the annual needs of the claimant in order to calculate the amount of the periodic payments; the payments rise in accordance with inflation and are paid, free of tax, to the end of claimant's life. In addition, the management and administration involved in the investment of damages is transferred from the claimant to the defendant, but as the payments must be secure, the continuity of the payments is guaranteed.

15.5.2 The statutory provisions

15.5.2.1 The court's power to make an order for periodical payments

Under s 2 of the Damages Act 1996 (as amended by s 100 of the Courts Act 2003), where an order for damages includes an amount for future pecuniary loss in respect of personal injury, the court must consider whether an order for periodical payments is appropriate. Where there is a claim for damages in respect of future pecuniary loss, such as the future loss of earnings or the future costs of care, the court can order that the damages wholly or partly take the form of periodical payments, and it can do so without obtaining the consent of the parties.

The court can make an order for periodic payments in respect of other damages, such as past pecuniary loss and pain, suffering and loss of amenity, only where both parties consent (s 2(2)).

Under s 2(3), the court can make such an order only where it is satisfied that the continuity of payment is reasonably secure. Section 2(4) states that a payment is 'reasonably secure' where:

(a)   it is protected by a guarantee given under s 6 of or Schedule 1 to the Act;

(b)   it is protected by a scheme under s 213 of the Financial Services and Markets Act 2000; or

(c)   the source of payment is a government or health service body.

Where none of the above applies, a defendant may be able to prove that payment is reasonably secure by purchasing a life annuity for the claimant's benefit, which would be protected by the Financial Services Compensation Scheme or by some other means.

15.5.2.2   The order

Under CPR, r 41.8(1), where the court awards damages in the form of periodical payments, it must specify:

(a)   the annual amount awarded, how each payment is to be made during the year and at what intervals;

(b)   the amount awarded for future—

(i)   loss of earnings and other income; and

(ii)   care and medical costs and other recurring or capital costs;

(c)   that the claimant's annual future pecuniary losses, as assessed by the court, are to be paid for the duration of the claimant's life, or such other period as the court orders; and

(d)   that the amount of the payments shall vary annually by reference to the retail prices index, unless the court orders otherwise under section 2(9) of the 1996 Act.

15.5.2.3   Indexation

Under s 2(8) of the Damages Act 1996, the payments will rise by reference to the Retail Price Index (RPI), although s 2(9) allows for s 2(8) to be disapplied or its effect modified. There has been much controversy as to whether the RPI is the appropriate index as it is based on prices, which historically have not risen as sharply as wages. In the provision of care services, it has been wages that have been driving the cost up, and it is therefore argued that the Aggregate Annual Survey of Hours and Earnings (ASHE 6115) is the appropriate index to use. In *Tameside and Glossop Acute Services NHS Trust v Thompstone* [2008] EWCA Civ 5, the Court of Appeal settled this debate by endorsing the use of ASHE 6115.

15.5.2.4   Variation

In accordance with the Damages (Variation of Periodical Payments) Order 2005 (SI 2005/841), where the court is satisfied that, at some time in the future, the claimant will:

(a)   as a result of the act or omission which gave rise to the cause of action, develop some serious disease or suffer some serious deterioration; or

(b)   enjoy some significant improvement in his physical or mental condition, where that condition had been adversely affected as a result of that act or omission;

the court can include in an order for periodical payments an order that they may be varied. The consent of the parties is not required. The wording is similar to that used for provisional damages (see **15.4**), and it is thought that the courts will apply the same strict criteria before including a provision for variation in a periodical payments order.

15.5.3 Procedural approach

In accordance with CPR, r 41.5, the party should address whether or not it considers periodical payments to be appropriate in its statement of case and set out the particulars of the circumstances it relies on. If a statement of case does not address the matter at all, or does not set out sufficient particulars, the court may order the party to rectify the situation.

The power to make an order for periodical payments must be exercised in accordance with CPR, r 41.7, which states that when considering whether to make such an order, the court must have regard to 'all the circumstances of the case and in particular the form of award which best meets the claimant's needs, having regard to the factors set out in Practice Direction 41B'. Practice Direction 41B, para 1 states that these factors include:

(1) the scale of the annual payments taking into account any deductions for contributory negligence;

(2) the form of the award preferred by the claimant including

    (a) the reasons for the claimant's preference; and

    (b) the nature of any financial advice received by the claimant when considering the form of the award; and

(3) the form of the award preferred by the defendant including the reasons for the defendant's preference.

Although the court must have regard to the wishes of the parties, ultimately it must decide what order best meets the claimant's needs, and this may not necessarily coincide with what the claimant prefers. The claimant's solicitor must instruct an independent financial adviser to report on the form of order which they consider is in the best interests of the claimant. However, in the *Tameside* case (see **15.5.2.3**), the Court of Appeal stated that it was able to have regard to the defendant's preferences without the need for the defendant to call evidence on this point. It went on to say that only in rare cases would it be appropriate for the defendant to call expert evidence in order to seek to demonstrate that the form of order preferred by the claimant would not best meet the claimant's needs.

15.5.4 The claimant's and defendant's perspectives

Generally speaking, claimants are not keen on the idea of periodical payments, preferring all damages to be paid as a lump sum. This gives them more control over their finances, and may be particularly important to the claimant who is keen to provide for their family in the event of their death. Defendants differ in their approach, and some may be deterred by the need to manage the fund on behalf of the claimant. However, where cases involve large claims for the cost of future care, defendants will usually prefer periodical payments, because they will assist with cash-flow and will prevent large over-payments where the claimant dies early.

15.6 INTEREST

A claim for interest should be included in the court proceedings. In the majority of personal injury cases, the court will award interest (simple, not compound) in addition to the basic damages. The purpose of an interest award is to compensate the claimant for having to wait to receive compensation. Interest in a personal injury claim is generally awarded in accordance with the following guidelines:

(a) Special damages carry interest at half the short-term investment/special account rate from the date of the accident to the date of trial. For the seven years prior to February 2009, the special account rate was 6%. On 1 July 2009, it was reduced to 0.5%, and in 2020 was reduced further to 0.1%. The rate, from 2 September 2022, is 1.75% per annum (therefore half the special account rate is 0.875%). In *Roberts v Johnstone* [1989] QB 878, it was held that damages for unpaid past services of care and attendance should be awarded in a similar manner to any other items of special damages.

It should also be noted that following the case of *Wadley v Surrey County Council* [1999] 2 All ER 334, the House of Lords confirmed that when calculating interest on special damages, the court should disregard deductible State benefits; interest is claimed on the gross amount.

(b) Damages for pain and suffering and loss of amenity carry interest from date of service of proceedings to the date of trial at 2% per annum, following the case of *Felmai Lawrence v Chief Constable of Staffordshire* [2000] All ER (D) 894.

(c) Damages for future losses carry no interest (as, by definition, the losses have not yet been incurred).

(d) General damages for a handicap on the labour market carry no interest.

It should be noted that these are general guidelines, but the court does have a discretion to depart from them in exceptional cases. In Kemp and Kemp, *The Quantum of Damages*, it is argued that while the general approach for special damages stated above is appropriate for regular losses between the accident and trial (eg, weekly wage loss), it is not satisfactory where the claimant had incurred a large, one-off item of expenditure shortly after the accident. In such circumstances, the claimant would be under-compensated by the application of the normal interest rule, and therefore, it is argued, interest should be awarded at the full rate on such items.

Interest is awarded to mitigate the effects of delay. However, if the delay is the fault of the claimant, this may be a 'special reason' not to award full interest (*Birkett v Hayes* [1982] 2 All ER 710). This point was raised in the case of *Beahan v Stoneham* [2001] 1 WLUK 187, where an appeal from an assessment of damages in a claim for personal injuries was allowed in part where the trial judge failed to reduce interest on damages. The matter concerned a case where there was a significant delay in proceeding with the claim (see also *Spittle v Bunney* [1988] 1 WLR 847). The court held that the judiciary should be more ready to mark their disapproval of delay in this matter.

15.6.1 Calculation of interest

The calculation of interest on general damages should not present any problem. However, the calculation of interest on special damages can be more difficult. Traditionally, solicitors used the Nelson–Jones table, printed annually in the *Law Society's Gazette*. However, online calculators are quicker and easier to use.

The inclusion of interest on the settlement of a case must not be forgotten by the claimant's solicitor.

15.7 THE SCHEDULE OF PAST AND FUTURE LOSS AND EXPENSE

In accordance with PD 16, para 4.2, the claimant must attach to their particulars of claim a schedule setting out details of any past and future expenses and losses claimed (see **12.5.1** and **Appendix 1(12)**). Where the defendant disputes the information contained in the schedule, the defendant should serve a counter-schedule (being in effect part of the defence). Both the schedule and the counter-schedule should be revised for the trial.

15.8 CONCLUSION

Subject to liability being established, the aim of the claimant's solicitor is to recover the highest possible award of damages on behalf of their client (without falsifying or exaggerating the claim), and the aim of the defendant's solicitor is to minimise the award. Both require an in-depth understanding of the rules which govern what may be recovered under the heads of special damages for pecuniary losses incurred up to the date of the trial or earlier settlement, and general damages for non-pecuniary loss and future pecuniary loss.

The claimant's solicitor should make thorough enquiries of their client to ensure that all pecuniary losses and expenses are included in the schedule of loss, as the client may not appreciate the true cost of their losses and expenditure thus far or the possible financial implications stretching out into the future. The schedule should be updated as required as the matter progresses. The defendant's solicitor should not be afraid to challenge the inclusion of items of loss or the amounts claimed where it is appropriate to do so.

General damages for pain, suffering and loss of amenity, and for handicap in the labour market and loss of congenial employment, are not capable of precise mathematical calculation. Nevertheless, the courts have adopted an approach to quantifying these heads of damage which aims to ensure, in so far as possible, that comparable cases receive comparable amounts in damages. The starting point for practitioners when calculating an appropriate award for pain, suffering and loss of amenity is the *Guidelines for the Assessment of General Damages in Personal Injury Cases*, but research of reported cases involving similar injuries will also be necessary.

Future pecuniary losses, such as the loss of earnings or the cost of care, are calculated by means of a multiplicand, a figure representing the claimant's net annual loss, and a multiplier, a figure which is based on a best guess of how long the incapacity will continue into the future and is found by reference to the Ogden tables.

In the vast majority of cases, lump sum damages are awarded in full and final settlement of the claim, which means that the award cannot be changed in the event that the claimant makes a substantial recovery or suffers an unexpected deterioration. However, an exception to this rule exists where the court makes an order for provisional damages, enabling the claimant to return to court to seek a further award of damages in the event that a specified condition or deterioration occurs within a specified (or, in some instances, unspecified) time period. A further exception arises where the court makes an order for periodical payments, where an annual sum is paid to the claimant in accordance with the claimant's needs, usually in addition to lump sum damages. Such payments may be increased, decreased or stopped on the application of either party, where the claimant's needs have changed.

Proceedings should always include a claim for interest, as this may be a considerable amount, but practitioners should be aware that different rules apply to different heads of damage and that there is no interest on future losses.

15.9 FURTHER READING

Kemp and Kemp, *The Quantum of Damages* (Sweet & Maxwell)

Ogden tables (8th edn)

Judicial College, *Guidelines for the Assessment of General Damages in Personal Injury Cases* (OUP)

Facts and Figures (Sweet & Maxwell)

CHAPTER 16

RECOVERY OF BENEFITS AND NHS CHARGES

LEARNING OUTCOMES

After reading this chapter you will be able to:

- explain how the Compensation Recovery Unit (CRU) recovers benefits paid to a claimant as a result of an accident or disease
- explain how the cost of NHS treatment provided to a claimant as a result of an accident or disease is recovered from a defendant who is found liable
- identify which benefits may be set off against each head of damage by way of 'like for like' offsetting
- describe the steps that each party must take in order to comply with the CRU system.

16.1 INTRODUCTION

Where a claimant has received State benefits as a result of an accident or disease and is subsequently awarded compensation, the Department for Work and Pensions (DWP) will seek to recover those benefits from the defendant (or the defendant's insurer) via a system operated by the Compensation Recovery Unit (CRU). The CRU is also responsible for collecting from a defendant the cost of any NHS treatment that a claimant has received following an accident. The purpose of this chapter is to explain how these systems of recovery operate and how they may affect a compensation payment.

16.2   RECOVERY OF BENEFITS – KEY FEATURES OF THE SYSTEM

The legislation on the recovery scheme is predominantly contained in the Social Security (Recovery of Benefits) Act 1997 ('the 1997 Act'). The key features of the scheme are as follows:

(a)   No person should be compensated twice in respect of the same accident or disease.

(b)   A defendant cannot make a compensation payment (other than an exempt payment) without first applying to the CRU for a Certificate. The defendant (or 'compensator') must pay to the DWP an amount equal to the total amount of the recoverable benefits on the Certificate when the defendant pays compensation to the claimant.

(c)   In some circumstances it may be possible for the compensator to deduct some or all of the amount they have had to repay to the DWP from the compensation award (a practice known as 'offsetting'; see **16.4**).

(d)   The compensator is responsible for repayment of *all* relevant benefits paid to the injured person, regardless of whether the compensator is able to offset the full amount out of that person's damages. However, recovery of a lump sum paid cannot exceed the amount of compensation paid.

The main regulations relevant to the scheme are found in the Social Security (Recovery of Benefits) Regulations 1997 (SI 1997/2205), as amended by paras 149–152 of Sch 7 to the Social Security Act 1998.

16.3   KEY DEFINITIONS

There are several key definitions in the 1997 Act:

16.3.1   The meaning of 'compensation payment'

A compensation payment is a payment made by a person (whether on his own behalf or not) to or in respect of any other person in consequence of any accident, injury or disease suffered by the other (s 1 of the 1997 Act). This is a very wide definition and is designed to cover payments made by the defendant or the defendant's insurer.

16.3.2   The meaning of 'compensator'

The compensator means the person, company or agent who is paying the compensation, usually an insurance company, on behalf of the insured.

16.3.3   The meaning of 'recoverable benefit'

A recoverable benefit is any listed benefit which has been or is likely to be paid during the relevant period in respect of an accident, injury or disease (s 1 of the 1997 Act).

'Recoverable benefits' are listed in Sch 2 to the 1997 Act and are reproduced at **16.4.2**.

16.3.4   The meaning of 'relevant period'

Recovery of benefits can occur only in respect of losses during what the 1997 Act terms 'the relevant period'.

The relevant period begins on:

(a)   the day following an accident or injury; or

(b)   in the case of a disease, the date on which a listed benefit was first claimed in consequence of the disease.

The relevant period ends on:

(a)   the day a compensation payment is made in final discharge of a claim; or

(b)   the date five years after the relevant period begins, whichever comes first.

16.4 COMPENSATION SUBJECT TO OFFSETTING

16.4.1 Heads of damage subject to offsetting

Offsetting of recoverable benefits is allowed only against specified areas of loss. The three specified areas subject to offsetting are:

(a)   compensation for loss of earnings;

(b)   compensation for cost of care; and

(c)   compensation for loss of mobility.

Scope for offsetting is further limited by the fact that it is only allowed on a 'like-for-like' basis (see below at **16.4.2**).

Therefore, the overall effect of the legislation is that, in relation to benefits:

(a)   it allows offsetting only against certain items of special damage; and

(b)   it ensures that general damages for pain suffering and loss of amenity, loss of congenial employment, handicap on the labour market and all future losses are protected from offsetting.

The position in relation to lump sums, however, is different (see below at **16.4.3**).

16.4.2 'Like-for-like' offsetting

Having established that only special damages can be the subject of offsetting, Sch 2 to the 1997 Act further safeguards special damages as it allows only 'like-for-like' offsetting. This means that only benefits which closely correspond to the relevant head of loss can be set against damages awarded in respect of that head of loss, as set out in the table below. For example, you will see that attendance allowance can be recouped only from compensation for cost of care, and not from compensation for loss of earnings.

EXAMPLE

A claimant agrees to accept compensation totalling £100,000 which is broken down as follows: £40,000 for pain, suffering and loss of amenity (PSLA), £30,000 for loss of earnings, and £30,000 for the cost of care.

The Certificate shows that the claimant has received incapacity benefit totalling £5,000, income support totalling £10,000 and attendance allowance amounting to £10,000.

The compensator (the defendant's insurer) may not offset any of the benefits against the PSLA element of the award, but may offset the incapacity benefit and income support against the loss of earnings award. The compensator therefore deducts a total of £15,000 from the loss of earnings sum, leaving £15,000 to be paid to the claimant.

Similarly the compensator may offset the £10,000 attendance allowance against the damages for cost of care, leaving £20,000 to be paid to the claimant.

The claimant has settled the claim for £100,000 but following offsetting the claimant receives £75,000 (the claimant has already received the remaining £25,000 in benefits so double compensation is avoided).

In addition to paying the claimant £75,000, the compensator must now pay £25,000 to the DWP, representing the amount of recoverable benefits.

If compensation for cost of care is less than the amount actually paid out in listed benefits during the relevant period, the claimant will receive nothing in respect of that head of loss; *however*, any excess in benefits for cost of care which has not so far been offset, cannot be offset against any other head of compensation. In this instance, the burden of paying off the excess falls on the compensator (usually the insurance company) and will be refunded to the DWP, so that the State will always achieve 100% recovery, the only question being how much will be out of compensation, and how much will be paid by the compensator.

Table to illustrate like-for-like offsetting

Head of compensation	Benefit
1. Compensation for earnings lost during relevant period	Disability Working Allowance Employment and Support Allowance Incapacity Benefit Income Support Industrial Injuries Disablement Benefit Invalidity Pension Invalidity Allowance Jobseeker's Allowance Reduced Earnings Allowance Severe Disablement Allowance Sickness Benefit Unemployability Supplement Unemployment Benefit Universal Credit
2. Compensation for cost of care incurred during the relevant period	Attendance Allowance Care Component of Disability Living Allowance Industrial Injuries Disablement Benefit increase for Constant Attendance Allowance or Exceptionally Severe Disablement Allowance Living Component of Personal Independence Payment
3. Compensation for loss of mobility during the relevant period	Mobility Allowance Mobility Component of Disability Living Allowance Mobility Component of Personal Independence Payment

Statutory Sick Pay paid on or after 6 April 1994 is not a recoverable benefit.

The DWP Guidance Note Z1, which can be found on the gov.uk website, provides general guidance, including further details of damages that do and do not fall within Sch 2. General information/guidance can be found at: www.gov.uk/government/publications/recovery-of-benefits-and-or-lump-sum-payments-and-nhs-charges-technical-guidance.

In *Griffiths and Others v British Coal Corporation and the Department of Trade and Industry* [2001] EWCA Civ 336, it was held that an award of interest on damages for past loss of earnings fell within the definition of 'compensation for earnings lost' in Sch 2 to the 1997 Act and was therefore subject to reduction on account of payments by the defendant to the DWP under the compensation recovery rules. In the same case, it was also held that any compensation for services in the nature of care, gratuitously rendered, fell within the term 'compensation for cost of care incurred during the relevant period', and allowed the defendant to set off the benefits paid against the damages.

16.4.3 Lump sum payments

The Child Maintenance and Other Payments Act 2008 introduced changes to the Social Security (Recovery of Benefits) Act 1997, which provides for the recovery of lump sum payments. The lump sum payments covered include:

(a)   lump sum payments made under the Pneumoconiosis etc (Worker's Compensation) Act 1979; and

(b)   payments under the 2008 Diffuse Mesothelioma Scheme and the Diffuse Mesothelioma Payment Scheme 2014 to people who have contracted diffuse mesothelioma as a result of asbestos exposure in the UK.

In contrast to the system applied to benefits (see **16.4.2** above), under the provisions of the Social Security (Recovery of Benefits) (Lump Sum Payments) Regulations 2008 (SI 2008/1596) the compensator can deduct any amount in respect of a lump sum from any part of the compensation award. However, lump sum payments must be offset against damages for pain and suffering first. Furthermore, if the amount of compensation is less than the lump sum payment, the CRU can only recover an amount up to the equivalent of the gross compensation award. The compensator is liable to repay lump sum payments before repaying recoverable benefits.

EXAMPLE

An award of compensation totalling £60,000 is agreed and broken down as follows: £15,000 for pain, suffering and loss of amenity (PSLA), £25,000 in respect of loss of earnings and £20,000 in respect of loss of mobility.

The CRU certificate lists lump sums totalling £20,000, Income Support totalling £15,000, and Disability Living Allowance (Mobility Component) totalling £10,000.

The compensator must offset the £20,000 lump sum payment from the PSLA first, which would leave an outstanding balance of £5,000. The compensator may then offset from any of the remaining heads of damage, ie the compensator may offset the outstanding balance of £5,000 plus the £15,000 Income Support from the loss of earnings head of damage and the £10,000 DLA (Mobility) from the loss of mobility head of damage.

The claimant has settled their claim for a total of £60,000. Following offsetting, the claimant receives £15,000 from the compensator in addition to the £45,000 the claimant has already received from the state benefits system. Double compensation is thereby avoided.

The compensator pays £15,000 to the claimant and £45,000 to the CRU representing the amount of recoverable benefits and lump sums.

16.5 CONTRIBUTORY NEGLIGENCE

Since 'compensation payment' is defined as the sum falling to be paid to the claimant, it follows that the relevant sum from which benefits can be deducted is that which is paid to the claimant after any deduction for the claimant's contributory negligence. However, the compensator remains liable to pay the full amount of any benefits listed on the certificate regardless of contributory negligence (*Williams v Devon County Council* [2003] EWCA Civ 365). This may have the result after trial that the compensator has to pay a total sum in excess of that which the court has awarded by way of damages.

EXAMPLE

Assume that on a full liability basis the claimant's damages are valued at £10,000 for pain, suffering and loss of amenity (PSLA) and £10,000 for loss of earnings (LE), and that the certificate of recoverable benefit shows that the claimant has received £7,500 in incapacity benefit.

If the claimant is 25% contributorily negligent, the calculation is as follows:

Total damages awarded £15,000 (£7,500 PSLA plus £7,500 LE)

Benefits deducted £7,500 (from LE award)

Defendant pays claimant £7,500

> Defendant repays benefits to CRU £7,500
>
> If the Claimant is 50% contributorily negligent, the calculation is as follows:
>
> Total damages awarded £10,000 (£5,000 PSLA plus £5,000 LE)
>
> Benefits deducted £5,000 (from LE award)
>
> Defendant pays claimant £5,000
>
> Defendant repays benefits to CRU £7,500
>
> In this second calculation, as a result of the finding of 50% contributory negligence, the amount of recoverable benefits now exceeds the sum awarded for the relevant head of damage (LE) against which they can be deducted. However, the defendant must still repay the full amount of benefits to the CRU.

16.6 PROCEDURE

16.6.1 Notifying the CRU

(a)   Section 4 of the 1997 Act requires the compensator to inform the CRU not later than 14 days after receiving the claim.

The notification is made on Form CRU 1 which is sent to the CRU. The information required by the compensator to complete Form CRU 1 includes:

(i)   the full name and address of the claimant;

(ii)   (if known) the date of birth and National Insurance number of that person;

(iii)   the date of the accident or injury (or in the case of disease, the date of diagnosis);

(iv)   the nature of the accident, injury or disease (as alleged by the claimant);

(v)   (if known) the name and address of the claimant's employer and the claimant's payroll number at the relevant time;

(vi)   the name and address of any NHS hospital the claimant has attended as a result of the accident.

(b)   On receipt of Form CRU 1, the CRU will send Form CRU 4 to the defendant. This has a two-fold function:

(i)   it acknowledges receipt of the notification of claim; and

(ii)   the compensator should retain it safely on the file as it will be needed later to obtain the Certificate (ie, the details of the benefit paid or to be paid to the claimant).

(c)   The claim then progresses to the settlement stage.

(d)   When ready to make an offer of compensation, the compensator submits Form CRU 4 to obtain a Certificate.

(e)   The CRU acknowledges receipt of Form CRU 4 (within 14 days).

(f)   The CRU sends the Certificate to the compensator. A copy will also be sent to the claimant's solicitor. The compensator will then settle the compensation claim and pay the relevant amount to the CRU within 14 days of the settlement. The compensator will also complete and send to the CRU Form CRU 102 detailing the outcome of the claim.

Despite the requirement that the CRU be informed of the claim within 14 days of notification of the claim, this is sometimes overlooked by insurance companies. If proceedings are issued and the insurer instructs solicitors, Form CRU 1 should be completed immediately, if this has not already been done. In such circumstances, it may be appropriate for the address of the compensator given on Form CRU 1 to be care of the solicitors, to ensure that the Certificate is forwarded to the solicitors, who are likely to make the compensation payment to the claimant.

When the matter is lodged with the CRU, the claimant's solicitor will be notified and a Form CRU 4R will also be sent to the claimant's representative, which can be used to obtain benefit information (the claimant's solicitor can also obtain benefit details by writing to the DWP). It is important that, prior to negotiating any settlement or accepting any payment into court, the claimant themselves examines the benefit details to ensure that they are correct. It is therefore essential to send a copy of the CRU certificate to the client.

16.6.2 The Certificate

The provision central to the whole system is that no compensation is to be paid until the defendant has obtained a Certificate setting out the recoverable benefits and lump sums. If compensation is paid without obtaining a Certificate, the CRU can still take steps against the defendant to recover the benefits.

The defendant obtains the Certificate by completing and returning Form CRU 4 to the CRU. The defendant must ensure that all the information required by Forms CRU 1 and CRU 4 is given, after which the CRU will acknowledge the form in writing and send the Certificate to the defendant and a copy to the claimant.

The Certificate details:

(a) the amount of relevant benefits paid or likely to be paid by a specified date;

(b) the details of any continuing benefit;

(c) the amount of each recoverable lump sum;

(d) the amount to be repaid in the event of a compensation payment being made;

(e) the date the certificate ceases to be valid.

An example of a Certificate may be found at **Appendix 1(14)**.

16.7 EXEMPT PAYMENTS

Schedule 1, Pt 1 to the 1997 Act and reg 2 of the Social Security (Recovery of Benefits) Regulations 1997, as amended, list the payments which are exempt from offsetting under the Act. These include payments by or under the following:

(a) the FAA 1976;

(b) Criminal Injuries Compensation Authority payments;

(c) vaccine damage payments;

(d) the Macfarlane Trust (established partly under funds from the Secretary of State to the Haemophilia Society) the Eileen Trust and the trust established for persons suffering from variant Creutzfeld-Jakob disease;

(e) British Coal, in accordance with the NCB Pneumoconiosis Compensation Scheme;

(f) cases of hearing loss, where the loss is less than 50db in one or both ears;

(g) the National Health Service (Injury Benefits) Regulations 1974 (SI 1974/1547) and subsequent amendments;

(h) criminal court compensation orders, s 35 of the Powers of Criminal Courts Act 1973;

(i) certain trust funds (in particular 'disaster funds', where more than half of the fund is raised by public subscription);

(j) certain private insurance contracts between the victim and his insurer entered into before the contract;

(k) any redundancy payment already accounted for in the assessment of damages;

(l) any amount which is referable to costs;

(m) any contractual amount paid to an employee by an employer in respect of incapacity for work (eg, occupational sick pay);

(n)   any small payment, as defined in Pt II of Sch 1 to the Social Security (Recovery of Benefits) Act 1997. There are currently no small payment exceptions;

(o)   payment made from the Skipton Fund for the benefit of certain persons suffering from hepatitis C;

(p)   payments made from the London Bombings Relief Charitable Fund established for the benefit of victims, families or dependants of victims of the terrorist attacks carried out in London on 7 July 2005;

(q)   payments made under the Social Security (Infected Blood and Thalidomide) Regulations 2017;

(r)   payments made under the Windrush Compensation Scheme and the Windrush Hardship Fund;

(s)   any payment made for the purpose of providing compensation or support in respect of the fire on 14 June 2017 at Grenfell Tower;

(t)   any payment made by the Post Office or the Secretary of State for the purpose of providing compensation or support in connection with the failings of the Horizon system; or otherwise payable following the judgment in *Bates and Others v Post Office Ltd (No 3)* [2019] EWHC 606 (QB).

16.8   MULTIPLE DEFENDANTS ('COMPENSATORS')

In certain cases, the claimant will sue two or more defendants, and as such, all defendants are jointly and severally liable to reimburse the CRU. However, in practice, it is usual for a sharing agreement to be made as between defendants, whereby the defendants reach an agreement as to how they are to pay the claimant and the CRU.

16.9   CLINICAL NEGLIGENCE

The rules relating to the recovery of benefit apply to clinical negligence claims. Due to their complexity, especially with regard to causation, the CRU has set up a specialist group to deal with the claims, and makes a special request that compensators inform the CRU about clinical negligence claims as soon as the pre-action correspondence is received.

16.10   PART 36 OFFERS

A party who wishes to make a Part 36 offer must first apply for a Certificate of Recoverable Benefit (see **16.6.2**) from the CRU.

Rule 36.22(3) of the CPR 1998 requires a defendant who makes an offer to state whether or not the offer is intended to include any deductible benefits.

Rule 36.22(6) requires the offer to state:

(a)   the amount of the gross compensation;

(b)   the name and amount of any deductible benefit by which that gross amount is reduced; and

(c)   the net amount of compensation after the reduction.

Although Part 36 does not spell it out, guidance from case law suggests that the offer should therefore particularise the various heads of damage and indicate the amount of benefits to be deducted against each head (*Williams v Devon County Council* [2003] EWCA Civ 365).

16.11   INTERIM PAYMENTS

It should be noted that if an interim payment is made, the compensator is liable to repay any relevant recoverable benefits at that stage. Therefore a Certificate of Recoverable Benefit (see **16.6.2**) should be obtained before any voluntary payment or hearing of an application for an interim payment takes place.

16.12 REVIEWS, MANDATORY RECONSIDERATION AND APPEALS

16.12.1 Reviews

Before compensation has been paid the injured person, the compensator or their legal representatives can ask the CRU to review a certificate if there appears to have been a mistake in the recoverable benefits and/or lump sum payments listed, the amounts paid or the period over which they have been paid. A review request should be made in writing and must give the reasons why it is thought the certificate is wrong.

16.12.2 Mandatory reconsideration

If the claim has been settled and the compensator has paid all the monies due as listed on the certificate, it is too late to ask for a review. Instead, a request should be made for a mandatory reconsideration within 1 month of paying the CRU the money due as listed on the certificate. The CRU will then look at all of the evidence and decide if the certificate should be revoked or changed (in which case a full or partial refund will be issued) or confirmed as correct.

16.12.3 Appeals

If you still think the certificate is wrong after receiving a mandatory reconsideration notice (see **16.12.2** above), it is possible to make an appeal. The time limit for the appeal is 1 month from the date on which the mandatory reconsideration notice was sent. The appeal is made in writing and sent directly to Her Majesty's Courts and Tribunal Service (HMCTS).

16.13 RECOVERY OF NHS CHARGES

The CRU operates a similar recovery scheme on behalf of the Government in respect of the cost of NHS treatment given as a result of an accident. Initially the scheme applied only to road traffic accidents, but this was expanded to include all types of accident as from 29 January 2007. The main details of the scheme are as follows.

16.13.1 Key features of the scheme

The relevant legislation is contained in Part 3 of the Health and Social Care (Community Health and Standards) Act 2003 ('the 2003 Act') and associated regulations. The purpose of this legislation is to provide a national administration system, the aim of which is to ensure that the costs of relevant NHS hospital treatment and relevant NHS ambulance costs are recovered in as many cases as possible where compensation has been paid out as a result of a successful personal injury claim. Under s 150 of the 2003 Act, if a compensation payment is made as a result of any physical or psychological injury suffered by a claimant in connection with a personal injury claim against a third party, the third party compensator is liable to pay any relevant NHS treatment charges and any relevant NHS ambulance charges arising out of the claim. The scheme is administered by the CRU.

The NHS charges are calculated according to a tariff. The tariff allows for:

(a) a set fee for patients treated in A&E departments or out-patient clinics (the fee will be the same regardless of the number of out-patient appointments);

(b) a daily rate for patients admitted to hospital.

The precursor to the 2003 Act was the Road Traffic (NHS Charges) Act 1999. This allowed for recovery of NHS treatment charges arising out of road traffic accidents (only) occurring on or after 5 April 1999, including MIB cases, where a successful compensation claim was made. Part 3 of the 2003 Act repealed the 1999 Act, making provision for an expanded scheme to recover the costs of providing treatment to an injured person where that person has made a successful personal injury compensation claim against a third party as set out above. The 2003 Act allows recovery of both NHS hospital treatment costs and NHS ambulance costs in all cases where personal injury compensation is paid, not just following road traffic accidents, but also, for example, following accidents at work. It applies to all accidents which occur on or after 29 January 2007. The 1999 Act continues apply to road traffic accidents that occurred on or after 5 April 1999 but before 29 January 2007.

The scheme applies to injuries only; diseases are excluded from the scheme, unless the disease in question has been contracted as a direct result of an injury that falls within the scope of the scheme. Costs of treatment given by general practitioners in the primary care setting are also not included in the scheme.

There is a limit to the amount of NHS charges that can be recovered, which is known as the 'capped' tariff amount. The tariff for treatment and ambulance costs is reviewed each financial year.

16.13.2 Procedure

In many ways, the NHS costs recovery scheme mirrors the benefit recovery scheme considered above. However, unlike the benefit recovery scheme, NHS charges are not deducted from compensation, so the NHS costs recovery scheme will not affect the amount of damages recovered by the claimant, and if the injury occurs on or after 29 January 2007, the 2003 Act makes provision to take into account contributory negligence, eg a finding of 25% contributory negligence will reduce the NHS charges by 25%.

The procedure is as follows:

(a)   The compensator will apply to the CRU in the usual way by completing Form CRU 1, and must ensure that the form contains the name and address of the hospital where treatment was provided.

(b)   The CRU will send Form CRU 4 to the compensator to acknowledge receipt of Form CRU 1.

(c)   The case progresses to the settlement stage.

(d)   When ready to make an offer to the claimant, the compensator submits Form CRU 4.

(e)   The CRU will provide a Certificate of NHS Charges at the same time as the Certificate of Recoverable Benefit. The Certificate of NHS Charges will specify the name of the NHS Trust or Health Board where the treatment took place, the number of days' admission, the appropriate NHS treatment and ambulance charges.

(f)   The compensator must pay to the CRU the amount shown on the Certificate of NHS Charges within 14 days of making the compensation payment.

The appeal and review procedures for NHS costs recovery are very similar to the appeal and review provisions governing benefit recovery under the Social Security (Recovery of Benefits) Act 1997 (see **16.12** above), although there is no mandatory reconsideration stage and the time limit for making the appeal is 3 months.

16.14 CONCLUSION

Solicitors should exercise care when dealing with this area, to ensure that it is clear whether any offer put forward is net or gross of benefits, and that the benefit figures are correct. In *Hilton International v Martin-Smith* [2001] PIQR P14, it was held that where a party made an error of judgement (in this case, in relation to the amount stated on the Certificate), it did not follow that the court would permit that party to escape its consequences. Similarly, solicitors acting for defendants also need to ensure that benefits listed as recoverable benefits are as a consequence of the accident (see *Eagle Star Insurance v Department of Social Development (Northern Ireland)* (only persuasive) (2001) NICE, 12 February). See also *Williams v Devon County Council* [2003] EWCA Civ 365, [2003] All ER (D) 255 (Mar), concerning details to be included on a Part 36 notice; and *Bruce v Genesis Fast Food Ltd* [2003] EWHC 788 (QB), concerning whether defendants are entitled to take the benefit of any reduction in recoverable benefits when an appeal takes place.

An overview of the recovery of benefits system is set out at **16.16** below.

16.15 FURTHER READING

DWP Guidance Note Z1, *Recovery of benefits and or lump sum payments and NHS charges: technical guidance* (last updated 16 June 2023)

www.gov.uk/government/publications/recovery-of-benefits-and-or-lump-sum-payments-and-nhs-charges-technical-guidance

Kemp and Kemp, *The Quantum of Damages* (Sweet & Maxwell)

16.16 OVERVIEW OF RECOVERY OF BENEFITS

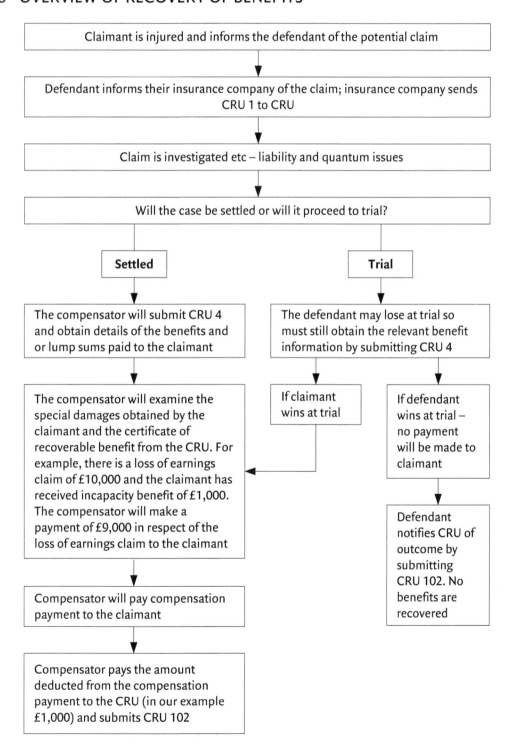

POST-DEATH INVESTIGATIONS

LEARNING OUTCOMES

After reading this chapter you will be able to:

- explain the purpose of an inquest
- take appropriate steps to prepare to represent a client at an inquest
- understand the procedure involved and verdicts that may be given at an inquest
- advise on the possible criminal prosecutions that might follow a fatal accident.

17.1 INTRODUCTION

The personal injury/clinical negligence solicitor must, on occasion, advise either the family of an accident victim who has died, or the person who it is claimed is responsible for the death. There are two main processes in which the solicitor may become involved:

(a) the coroner's inquest; and

(b) a criminal prosecution for:

   (i) manslaughter (corporate or individual);

   (ii) death by dangerous or careless driving; or

   (iii) offences under the HSWA 1974.

Although each process has its own purpose, post-death investigations offer an important opportunity to gain evidence on liability for the civil claim, and both processes are considered below.

17.2 INQUESTS

17.2.1 Background to the Coroners and Justice Act 2009

There was pressure for many years for reform of the coroner system. This was in part due to a series of high-profile disasters, such as Hillsborough in 1989, where the coroner's verdict of 'accidental death' at the first inquests into the deaths of the 96 victims meant that no one was held to account.

In the 1990s, coroners came under further, intense public scrutiny for their actions. For example, there were many concerns raised over the coroner in the *Marchioness* disaster, who ordered the hands of the victims to be cut off for identification purposes. Then there was the Shipman case, where the faking of patients' death certificates highlighted shortcomings in the death certification process.

The Shipman Inquiry (2003) and the Fundamental Review of Death Certification and Investigation (2003) found the level of service provided to bereaved people was inconsistent; family and friends were not always involved in coroners' investigations; there was a lack of leadership and training for coroners; and there was insufficient medical knowledge in the system as a whole.

After many years of consultation, the Coroners and Justice Act 2009 (CJA 2009) came into force on 25 July 2013, together with three new sets of rules which regulate the day-to-day conduct of inquests:

- Coroners (Inquests) Rules 2013 (SI 2013/1616) (the 'Inquests Rules');
- Coroners (Investigations) Regulations 2013 (SI 2013/1629) (the 'Investigations Regulations'); and
- Coroners Allowances, Fees and Expenses Regulations 2013 (SI 2013/1615) and Coroners Allowances, Fees and Expenses (Amendment) Regulations (SI 2018/1127) (the 'Expenses Regulations').

The CJA 2009 introduced a national coroner service for England and Wales, headed by a new Chief Coroner, HHJ Peter Thornton QC. The current Chief Coroner is HHJ Edward Thomas Henry Teague KC. The intention behind the CJA 2009 is to improve the experience of bereaved people coming into contact with the coroner system, giving them rights of appeal against coroners' decisions and setting out the general standards of service they can expect to receive. It is hoped that the new system will be simpler and quicker and will result in a coroner service that meets both the interests of bereaved families and the wider public interest in terms of the quality and effectiveness of investigations. The system also aims to ensure that the knowledge gained from death investigation is applied for the prevention of avoidable death and injury in the future.

After years of campaigning by the Hillsborough families, the original verdicts were quashed by the High Court in December 2012 and new inquests into the Hillsborough deaths have now taken place. After two years of evidence and legal submissions, the jury returned a finding of unlawful killing in respect of all 96 deaths.

17.2.2   What is an inquest?

An inquest is a fact-finding inquiry to establish:

- who has died; and
- how, when and where the death occurred.

It is important to understand that the purpose of an inquest is not to establish any matter of liability or blame. Although it receives evidence from witnesses, an inquest does not have prosecution and defence teams, like a criminal trial; the coroner and all those with 'proper interests' simply seek the answers to the above questions.

An inquest is usually opened soon after a death to record that a death has occurred, to identify the deceased, and to enable the coroner to issue the authority for the burial or cremation to take place without any unnecessary delay. It will then be adjourned until any other investigations and any inquiries instigated by the coroner have been completed. It will usually take an average of 27 weeks to conclude this work, but some cases can take longer than this if the inquiries prove to be complicated. The inquest will then be resumed and concluded. Under the old system, it could sometimes take years before an inquest was held, but r 8 of the Inquests Rules now states that a coroner must complete an inquest within six months of the date on which the coroner is made aware of the death, or as soon as is reasonably practicable after that date.

Sometimes, the coroner may hold one or more hearings before the inquest itself, known as pre-inquest hearings (or pre-inquest reviews), where the scope of the inquest and any matters of concern, including about the arrangements for the hearing, can be considered. The coroner usually invites the properly interested persons and/or their legal representatives to the pre-inquest hearing, where they have the opportunity to make representations to the coroner.

17.2.3 Personnel involved at an inquest

17.2.3.1 The coroner

The coroner is responsible for the inquest procedure, and although appointed by the local government body responsible for the area where the coroner sits (subject to the consent of the Chief Coroner and the Lord Chancellor), the coroner is an independent judicial office holder. To be eligible for appointment as a coroner, a person must now have possessed a relevant legal qualification (barrister/solicitor) for a period of five years. A number of coroners are qualified both as doctors and solicitors/barristers, although this is not a strict requirement of obtaining the post. Those who are legally qualified only normally have significant knowledge of medical matters.

In certain cases, the coroner may sit with an 'assessor', who is a person with specialist knowledge of the matters being considered, for example a consultant anaesthetist in a case where a patient died due to an airway not being maintained. However, the assessor must remain under the control of the coroner and cannot give expert evidence (see R v HM Coroner for Surrey, ex p Wright [1997] 2 WLR 16).

17.2.3.2 The coroner's officer

The coroner is assisted by the coroner's officer, who is usually a serving or ex-police officer and is often the first person with whom the personal injury solicitor will communicate about the case. The coroner's officer will obtain evidence relating to the accident, or liaise with the police if they are carrying out investigations. Their role is important to the solicitor, as they can provide information regarding the investigations which are being carried out and details of the incident, and may provide details of any witnesses the coroner intends to call.

The coroner's officer will notify the relevant parties and/or their solicitors of the inquest date.

17.2.3.3 The assistant coroner

There is one senior coroner for each coroner area, assisted by one or more assistant coroners, who normally stand in when the senior coroner is absent. An assistant coroner will have the same qualifications as a senior coroner but will usually be part time and paid a fee for sitting rather than a salary.

17.2.4 Circumstances which lead to an inquest

The circumstances in which a coroner will become involved in a death are set down in s 1 of the CJA 2009.

If the senior coroner is informed that a dead body is within their jurisdiction (it is the fact that there is a body in their jurisdiction and not where the death occurred that is important), the coroner must as soon as practicable conduct an investigation into the person's death, if the coroner has reason to suspect that a person has died:

(a)   a violent or unnatural death; or

(b)   where the cause of death is unknown; or

(c)   while in custody or otherwise in state detention.

A violent death is normally regarded as one where an injury has occurred, and will normally be apparent, for example when a factory operative falls into machinery and dies.

An unnatural death is not legally defined and it will be a question for the coroner to decide. Certain coroners believe that the phrase should be given its 'ordinary meaning'.

The coroner decides whether the death is natural or unnatural at the coroner's discretion, and this decision may need to be challenged. For example, in R v HM *Coroner for Poplar, ex p Thomas* [1993] 2 WLR 547, a woman died following an asthma attack after there had been a considerable delay in an ambulance reaching her. There was evidence that if she had reached hospital earlier, she might have survived. Was this an unnatural death? The Court of Appeal overturned the decision of the Divisional Court that it was an unnatural death and stated that 'unnatural' was an ordinary word, the meaning of which should be left to the coroner (unless the coroner's decision was unreasonable). If a solicitor believes that the death was unnatural, the coroner's officer must be contacted immediately and informed of the solicitor's interest.

Normally, the police, the GP or the hospital will contact the coroner's officer and inform the coroner of the death. However, on occasion, the relatives of the deceased will contact the coroner's officer, for instance if they believe that there has been an act of clinical negligence. Once the coroner has been informed of the death, the coroner's officer will make preliminary enquiries, and the coroner may then require a post-mortem examination to be made.

Section 6 of the CJA 2009 provides that a senior coroner who conducts an investigation into a person's death must (as part of the investigation) hold an inquest into the death. However, s 4 of the CJA 2009 provides an exception to this rule where a post-mortem examination reveals the cause of death before the inquest begins and the coroner thinks that it is not necessary to continue the investigation. This power to discontinue cannot be used where the deceased died a violent or unnatural death or died in custody or otherwise in state detention. A senior coroner who discontinues an investigation into a death under s 4 must, if requested to do so in writing by an interested person, give to that person as soon as practicable a written explanation as to why the investigation was discontinued.

17.2.5 Post-mortem examinations

Although no absolute obligation is placed upon the coroner, usually the coroner will request that a post-mortem takes place.

Section 14 of the CJA 2009 states that where it is alleged that the death was caused wholly or partly by clinical negligence of a medical practitioner, that practitioner:

(a)   must not make, or assist at, an examination under this section of the body; but

(b)   is entitled to be represented at such an examination.

The coroner must inform the relatives of the deceased, the GP and the hospital (if the deceased died in hospital) of the arrangements for the post-mortem. These are normally referred to as the 'interested parties' and they may be represented at the post-mortem by a doctor.

The post-mortem report is vital evidence, and an immediate request should be made to the coroner for a copy. The report may contain evidence which will assist in establishing civil liability. For example, if the death resulted from a road traffic accident, the pathologist will give a detailed description of the injuries, and photographs will be taken of the body. The pathologist's investigations in respect of this may be vital in indicating the events which occurred prior to the accident, for example whether the deceased was wearing a seat belt. In fatal accident at work cases, the pathologist's report may also be of use in identifying whether the cause of the death resulted from exposure to dangerous materials at work, such as coal dust or asbestos.

If acting for the defendant, the post-mortem may reveal whether there are any intervening illnesses from which the deceased may have died. This may then be used in negotiations, in an attempt to reduce the multiplier in the dependency calculation (see **Chapter 18**). In addition, in a road traffic case, it is important to check the blood alcohol levels to see if the deceased had been drinking at the time of the accident. Such evidence may provide important arguments regarding liability and quantum.

17.2.6 Funding representation at the inquest

The Lord Chancellor has issued guidance on Exceptional Funding for Inquests under s 10 of LASPO 2012. This provides that it may still be possible for a solicitor (with an appropriate contract) to provide legal advice and assistance to a member of the deceased family under what was formerly known as the Legal Help scheme for the initial preparations for an inquest. This can cover all of the preparatory work associated with the inquest, which may include preparing written submissions to the coroner. It can also fund someone to attend the inquest as a 'Mackenzie Friend', to offer informal advice in court, provided that the coroner gives permission.

Funding for representation in the form of advocacy at an inquest is not generally available because an inquest is a relatively informal inquisitorial process, rather than an adversarial one. There are two grounds for granting legal aid exceptionally for representation at an inquest:

(a) it is required by Article 2 of the ECHR; or
(b) where the Director makes a 'wider public interest determination' in relation to the individual and the inquest.

Article 2 inquests are dealt with below at **17.2.17**. A 'wider public interest determination' is a determination that, in the particular circumstances of the case, the provision of advocacy for the individual for the purposes of the inquest is likely to produce significant benefits for a class of person, other than the applicant and members of the applicant's family. In the context of an inquest, the most likely wider public benefits are the identification of dangerous practices, systematic failings or other findings that identify significant risks to the life, health or safety of other persons.

In general, applicants for legal aid must satisfy the eligibility limits as set out in regulations. However, there is a discretion to waive the financial eligibility limits relating to inquests if, in all the circumstances, it would not be reasonable to expect the family to bear the full costs of legal assistance at the inquest. Whether this is reasonable will depend in particular on the history of the case and the nature of the allegations to be raised, for example against agents of the state, the applicant's assessed disposable income and capital, other financial resources of the family, and the estimated costs of providing representation.

As legal aid is only available in exceptional cases, all possible alternative sources of finance should be considered (eg, in a fatal road traffic accident, the deceased's legal expenses insurance may cover the cost of representation for the estate). Immediate enquiries must be made in respect of any claim on any insurance policy and, if appropriate, prior authorisation should be obtained from the insurer. Enquiries should also be made as to whether a trade union will fund representation at the inquest, or whether any *pro bono* service may be able to provide assistance.

Of note, in the case of *King (Administratrix of the Estate of Robert Gadd deceased) v Milton Keynes General NHS Trust* [2004] EWHC 9007 (Costs), it was held that when assessing the costs of civil proceedings, the court did have jurisdiction to award the costs of attending at an inquest if the material purpose was to obtain information or evidence for use in civil proceedings. Similarly, in *Stewart and Howard v Medway NHS Trust* [2004] EWHC 9013 (Costs), the cost of counsel attending an inquest in a clinical negligence case was held to be recoverable. More recently, in *Roach v Home Office* [2009] EWHC 312 (QB), it was held that the costs of attendance at an inquest by both solicitor and counsel were recoverable as costs incidental to subsequent civil proceedings.

If there is a possibility of a clinical negligence claim being brought, any doctor who is required to give evidence will be represented by NHSR solicitors or their defence trade union. Similarly, in a personal injury case, if a civil claim is likely to follow as a result of the death, the employer (eg, in a factory accident) or the driver of the other vehicle (in a road traffic accident) will be represented by solicitors instructed by their respective insurers.

17.2.7   Preparation for the hearing

Rule 13 of the Inquests Rules provides that, where an interested person asks for disclosure of a document, the coroner must provide that document as soon as is reasonably practicable. This includes post-mortem examination reports, any other report provided to the coroner during the course of the investigation and any other document the coroner considers relevant to the investigation.

In some cases, the coroner may hold a 'pre-inquest review' to allow the parties and the coroner to consider matters prior to the actual inquest. The coroner may summarise the evidence that the coroner proposes to call and give the parties the opportunity to suggest any other witnesses that they may wish to call.

Normally, statements will be taken from the proposed witnesses by the coroner's officer or police, and it can be of considerable advantage if these can be obtained beforehand.

It is also important to make enquiries of such bodies as the police, trade union or HSE, which may be able to provide general background information. The more information that is obtained prior to the hearing the better.

When the pathologist gives evidence, they will undoubtedly use medical language, and it is important that the solicitor is able to understand the evidence which is given. Thus, research should be carried out prior to the inquest, so as to become familiar with the potential medical terms that may be used. Consideration should also be given to making a request that blood and tissue samples taken at the post-mortem are preserved, as they may provide important information

In a clinical negligence case, the deceased's medical records should be obtained (see *Stobart v Nottingham Health Authority* [1992] 3 Med LR 284). Once received, they should be placed in an ordered, paginated file, and legible copies made. If the solicitor is instructed by an insurance company on behalf of the deceased's estate, in-depth research should be carried out into the nature of the illness, the usual treatment which is prescribed for the illness, and the usual consequences of and recovery time for the illness. This research will include relevant medical literature, and copies should be taken of any appropriate material. Medical school libraries are generally very helpful with this form of research, and can provide assistance and copying facilities. Research may reveal whether the treatment fell below the level which can reasonably be expected and required of the medical staff.

In addition, a solicitor may seek assistance from an expert who can advise them on how to examine any medical experts giving evidence on behalf of the doctor. Informed examination will test a witness's evidence, and may be useful if civil proceedings are later issued. It is important for the claimant's solicitor to make such detailed preparation, because solicitors acting for a doctor will be experienced in this field and have access to a wide range of sources, including many experts.

17.2.8   Procedure at the inquest

The inquest is formally opened without any significant evidence being given, and the formalities are carried out by the coroner sitting alone (who, for example, will take initial evidence, evidence of identification of the body, issue an order for disposal of the body and adjourn until a more suitable time). Evidence will be called concerning the death at the resumed full hearing, with legal representatives for both sides attending. If appropriate, a jury (see **17.2.9**) will also be in attendance at that time.

Schedule 1 to the CJA 2009 sets out several situations in which a coroner may suspend an investigation and inquest into a death. These relate to when it is likely that certain criminal proceedings will be brought (eg, murder, manslaughter or death by careless or dangerous driving). Rule 25(4) of the Inquests Rules states that a coroner must adjourn an inquest and notify the Director of Public Prosecutions if, during the course of an inquest, it appears to the coroner that the death of the deceased is likely to have been due to a homicide offence and that a person may be charged in relation to that offence.

In such a case, the claimant's solicitor should attend the criminal proceedings and take notes of the trial (see below), as useful evidence may be obtained which can assist in identifying any civil liability for the death.

The majority of evidence at the resumed inquest will usually be given orally by witnesses on oath, but the coroner has power to admit documentary evidence if the coroner believes that the evidence is unlikely to be disputed. However, it is possible to object to such a decision, and a solicitor should do this where they believe that a witness should be called to answer questions (see also R *(Bentley) v HM Coroner for Avon* [2001] EWHC 170 (Admin)). Rules 17 and 18 of the Inquests Rules provide that a coroner may direct that evidence is to be given by video link or from behind a screen when it is in the interests of justice or national security to do so.

The order in which the witnesses are called lies entirely within the discretion of the coroner. However, it is often the pathologist who is the first substantive witness to give evidence. The coroner will normally then examine each witness so that the evidence is heard in the same order as the events leading to the death occurred. The solicitor should make careful notes, as these witnesses may need to be contacted in relation to a potential civil claim. If the witness does not give evidence in accordance with their previous written statement to the coroner, and the interested party is not aware of this, then the coroner must deal with this point (see R *v HM Coroner for Inner London North District, ex p Cohen* (1994) 158 JP 644, DC). Once the coroner has dealt with the witness, each interested party (or the interested party's legal representatives) will be allowed to question the witness. A witness is examined by their own representative last (Inquests Rules, r 21).

An 'interested person' entitled to examine witnesses at an inquest is defined by s 47 of the CJA 2009 and includes:

(a)   a spouse, civil partner, partner, parent, child, brother, sister, grandparent, grandchild, child of a brother or sister, stepfather, stepmother, half-brother or half-sister;

(b)   a personal representative of the deceased;

(c)   a medical examiner exercising functions in relation to the death of the deceased;

(d)   any beneficiary under a policy of insurance issued on the life of the deceased;

(e)   the insurer who issued such a policy of insurance;

(f)   any person whose act or omission, or that of his agent or servant, may, in the opinion of the coroner, have caused, or contributed to, the death of the deceased, or whose employee or agent may have done so;

(g)   any person appointed by a trade union to which the deceased belonged at the time of his death, if the death of the deceased may have been caused by an injury received in the course of his employment or by an industrial disease;

(h)   a person appointed by, or a representative of, an enforcing authority, or any person appointed by a government department to attend the inquest;

(i)   a chief constable;

(j)   the Director General of the Independent Office for Police Conduct in certain circumstances;

(k)   where subsection (5A) applies, the Service Police Complaints Commissioner. Subsection (5A) applies where the death of the deceased is or has been the subject of an investigation directed or carried out by the Service Police Complaints Commissioner under the Armed Forces Act 2006;

(l) a person appointed by a Government department to attend or follow an inquest into the death, or to assist in or provide evidence;

(m) any other person that the senior coroner thinks has a sufficient interest.

The questioning of witnesses at the inquest can be a difficult matter as the strict purpose of the inquest is limited to finding:

(a) who the deceased was;

(b) how, when and where the deceased came by his death;

(c) the particulars required by the Registration Acts to be registered concerning the death.

The Divisional Court has repeatedly reaffirmed that these are the only matters with which the coroner's court is concerned, and the coroner will wish to concentrate on these fundamental points. However, there can be no doubt that many solicitors attend the inquest with a slightly wider agenda, that of trying to identify who was liable for the death and to examine the evidence surrounding the case. Much will depend upon the individual coroner as to the types of questions which are allowed, but the coroner will always limit any questions concerned with civil liability.

To prevent the inquest apportioning blame, r 22 of the Inquests Rules specifically provides that a witness is not obliged to answer any questions tending to incriminate themselves. The witness may be called to the witness box and asked merely to give their name and address. On occasion, no further questions will be put to the witness. However, practice varies widely on this point, and in R v Lincolnshire Coroner, ex p Hay (1999) 163 JP 666, it was held that the privilege against self-incrimination did not give the witness complete immunity against further questioning. The privilege against self-incrimination is against criminal proceedings (and not civil proceedings), and this should be borne in mind when the coroner is deciding if the witness is entitled to claim self-incrimination. The solicitor may have to remind the coroner about this point. If the coroner allows the witness to be questioned, it is for the witness's representative to make the objection if a question is put which might lead to self-incrimination. If the witness answers the question, the witness will waive the privilege.

17.2.9 Juries

The general rule is that an inquest must be held without a jury, but s 7(2) and (3) of the CJA 2009 sets out the exceptions to this rule.

A jury must be summoned where:

(a) the deceased died while in custody or otherwise in state detention, and the death was violent or unnatural, or of unknown cause;

(b) where the death was as a result of an act or omission of a police officer or member of a service police force (defined in s 48) in the purported execution of the officer's duties; or

(c) where the death was caused by an accident, poisoning or disease which must be reported to a government department or inspector. This includes, for example, certain deaths at work.

Although a jury is not required in any other case, the coroner will be able to summon one in any case where the coroner believes there is sufficient reason for doing so.

Section 8 of the CJA 2009 provides that the jury must consist of between seven and 11 people. The senior coroner calls people to attend for jury service by issuing a summons stating the time that they are needed and the place that they must attend. At the outset, the coroner will require jury members to swear they will make a true determination according to the evidence.

A jury will initially be directed by the senior coroner to reach a unanimous determination or finding. If the coroner thinks that the jury have deliberated for a reasonable time without reaching a unanimous verdict, under s 9(2) of the CJA 2009, the coroner may accept a determination or finding on which the minority consists of no more than two persons. The jury spokesperson should announce publicly how many agreed. If there is no agreement by the required number of jurors, the coroner may discharge the jury and summon a completely new jury and the case will be heard again.

17.2.10 Summing up and directions to the jury

If a jury are present, the coroner will sum up the evidence to the jury after the witnesses have given evidence and will direct the jury on points of law. In R v HM *Coroner for Inner London South District, ex p Douglas-Williams* (1998) 162 JP 751, it was held that, in complex cases, it would be good practice for the coroner to prepare a written statement of matters which the law requires in relation to possible verdicts. If such a policy is followed, a solicitor should ask to inspect the statement prior to summing up. If no jury is present, the coroner normally sums up by means of a revision of the evidence and a statement of the conclusions drawn by the coroner.

17.2.11 Reports to prevent future deaths

Sometimes an inquest will show that something could be done to prevent other deaths. If so, at the end of the inquest, the coroner is now under a duty to draw this to the attention of any person or organisation that may have the power to take action under para 7(1) of Sch 5 to the CJA 2009 and r 28 of the Coroners (Investigations) Regulations 2013 (SI 2013/1629) as amended, which states that any report on action to prevent other deaths *must* be sent to the Chief Coroner and to every person whom the coroner believes may have the power to take relevant action. Anyone who receives such a report must send the coroner a written response. These reports (which were previously referred to as rule 43 reports), and the responses to them, are copied to all interested persons and to the Lord Chancellor. A summary of the reports is published twice a year by the Ministry of Justice.

17.2.12 Determinations and findings

Under the CJA 2009, the old terminology of 'inquisition' and 'verdict' has gone. Section 10 of the CJA 2009 requires the coroner – or the jury, where there is one – to make a 'determination' at the end of the inquest as to who the deceased was, and how, when and where the deceased came by their death. This is broadly equivalent to the requirements under the old rules. In an investigation where Article 2 of the ECHR is engaged, the coroner must also include a determination, or direct a jury to include a determination, as to the circumstances of the death.

Section 10(1)(b) also requires the coroner or jury to make a 'finding' at the end of the inquest about the details required for registration of the death. This will normally be, for example, a short finding, such as accident or misadventure, suicide, industrial disease, natural causes, drug related. Where no clear cause of death has been established, the finding will be known as 'open'. Increasingly, coroners make use of 'narrative' findings in which they sum up (usually in a few sentences) how the person came to die.

Section 10(2) makes clear that a determination may not be worded in such a way as to appear to determine any question of criminal liability of any named person or to determine any question of civil liability.

A Record of Inquest (the 'Record') is completed by the coroner at the end of the inquest, which is signed by the coroner and (where there is a jury) jury members who concur with it. The form requires five matters to be dealt with:

(a)   the name of the deceased;

(b)   the medical cause of death;

(c)   how, when and where (and where Article 2 applies, in what circumstances the deceased came by their death);

(d)   the conclusion of the jury/coroner as to the death; and

(e)   the particulars required by the Births and Deaths Registration Act 1953.

The standard Record form gives a list of suggested conclusions, of which the most significant in personal injury/clinical negligence cases are:

(a)   accident or misadventure (the courts have taken the view that any distinction between the two words is undesirable);

(b)   alcohol/drug related;

(c)   industrial disease;

(d)   lawful/unlawful killing;

(e)   natural causes;

(f)   open;

(g)   road traffic collision;

(h)   stillbirth;

(i)   suicide.

The following points should be noted in relation to possible conclusions:

(a)   Accident/accidental death. Even if such a verdict is given, it does not mean that a civil case cannot be brought.

(b)   An open conclusion means simply that there is insufficient evidence to reach a conclusion.

(c)   Suicide or unlawful killing. Until recently, the standard of proof required for a suicide or unlawful killing conclusion to be returned is that of 'beyond reasonable doubt'. However, in R (Maughan) v HM Senior Coroner Oxfordshire and others [2019] EWCA Civ 809, the Court of Appeal determined that the standard of proof to be applied to a suicide verdict should be the civil standard, the balance of probabilities. The Court's view was that, as the purpose of the inquest is merely to find facts, there could be no analogy between coroners' proceedings and criminal proceedings which could justify applying the criminal standard of proof at an inquest. Although not asked to rule on the standard of proof for a verdict of unlawful killing, in obiter statements the Court of Appeal stated that, where unlawful killing arose as an issue, the criminal standard of proof still applied. See also R (on the application of Sharman) v HM Coroner for Inner North London [2005] EWHC 857 (Admin), concerning the returning of a verdict of unlawful killing; and R (on the application of Anderson) v HM Coroner for Inner North Greater London [2004] EWHC 2729 (Admin).

All other conclusions require a burden of proof based on the balance of probabilities.

The Divisional Court has made it clear that the coroner's court does not decide the responsibility for the death. Therefore, conclusions in the coroner's court are framed so as not to identify any individual as being responsible (see also R v HM Coroner for Derby and South Derbyshire, ex p Hart (2000) 164 JP 429 and R v Director of Public Prosecutions, ex p Manning [2000] 3 WLR 463).

17.2.13   Transcripts

At the conclusion of the inquest, the coroner's officer will collect any documents or copy statements which were used during the hearing. A copy of the transcript of the case may be obtained on payment of a fee. (See also R (on the application of the Ministry of Defence) v Wiltshire and Swindon Coroner [2005] EWHC 889 (Admin).)

17.2.14   Representing the family

The inquest can be difficult for lay persons to understand. Lay persons will be unfamiliar with the role of the coroner and may expect that the purpose of the inquest is not to establish how the deceased died but to establish fault.

The procedure that the coroner will follow during the inquest must be explained to the family of the deceased. It will be necessary to discuss the evidence with them and, in particular, to discuss the conclusion. The 'finding' should be explained thoroughly, and the deceased's family should be reminded that the purpose of the inquest and the conclusion is not to apportion blame but to establish by what means the deceased came by their death.

17.2.15 Representing the potential defendant

17.2.15.1 Clinical negligence cases

Requesting records and taking statements

The solicitor for the health authority or NHS Trust should obtain all relevant records, and obtain statements from any medical and nursing staff who have been called by the coroner to give evidence at the inquest.

The solicitor should help the staff by reviewing their statements prior to submission to the coroner. They should ensure that the statements contain only relevant facts and do not offer any opinion which the witness is not competent to give. For example, a house officer should not give an opinion on whether specific parts of the treatment contributed to the death but should restrict their statement to the facts alone.

If it appears from the statements that disciplinary action might be taken against a member of the medical staff (eg, because a mistake in treatment has been made), that person should be advised to seek their own representation from their defence organisation as their interests will conflict with those of the hospital.

The solicitor should advise the medical and nursing staff that the original records will be available at the inquest, and that they are permitted to refer to these.

Purpose, form and limits of inquest

The solicitor should advise the medical and nursing staff about the purpose and form of an inquest, and encourage an attitude of openness and cooperation at the inquest.

Expert evidence

The solicitor may consider obtaining a specialist opinion on the issues arising at the inquest from a hospital consultant (but not from a consultant who is directly involved in the case).

17.2.15.2 Personal injury cases

In a personal injury case, as soon as the solicitor is instructed, they will make contact with the insured and attempt to investigate the matter further. This will normally involve attending at the insured's premises, if the accident was work-based, or at the scene of the accident with the insured, in the case of a road traffic accident. The defendant's solicitor will be under strict instructions from the insurer to formulate a view on liability and attempt to find out as much as possible about the deceased, so that some idea can be obtained about quantum. In a road traffic accident, the inquest will provide early access to the police investigation report (which may have involved a partial accident reconstruction), and useful information, such as whether a seat belt was worn, may become apparent. In the case of an industrial accident, the solicitor investigating the case will normally be concerned with the system of work used or the employment history of the deceased. This may be particularly useful in asbestosis claims, where it may become apparent that the deceased's main exposure to asbestos was during the deceased's employment with another employer.

17.2.16 Publicity at the inquest

There is often publicity attached to inquests. Reporters may request an interview with the key witnesses and, in particular, the family. The appropriate advice to witnesses is at the discretion of the solicitors acting for the parties. Usually, the solicitor representing the hospital or doctors will decline to say anything to the press, to avoid saying anything amounting to an admission in subsequent proceedings, or which may be upsetting to the family. The solicitor should also advise the doctors and nursing staff not to make any comments to the media. In some cases, it may be appropriate, from a public relations point of view, for the hospital to issue a brief statement offering sympathy to the family following the death of the deceased.

If the family wishes to express its anger in a more public forum, the press is usually happy to provide this opportunity. If there are any concerns to which the inquest gave rise, these could be expressed to the press. It is important, however, that the family's solicitor does not get carried away on the tide of emotion and risk slandering any of the individuals concerned.

17.2.17 'Article 2' inquests

Where employees of the state potentially bear responsibility for loss of life (whether by their actions or omissions), the right to life in Article 2 of the ECHR may be engaged. For Article 2 to be engaged, there must be reasonable grounds for thinking that the death may have resulted from a wrongful act on behalf of the state. An example might be a death in custody, either in prison or under police detention, or a death which occurs in an NHS hospital.

In such a case, the state is under an obligation to initiate an effective public investigation by an independent body. The House of Lords (now Supreme Court) ruled that, while a criminal investigation and prosecution may not discharge this obligation, an inquest is likely to do so. The inquest must, however, determine not only the identity of the deceased and when, where and how the death occurred, but also in what circumstances (see *R v HM Coroner for the Western District of Somerset & Another, ex parte Middleton* [2004] UKHL 10). The House of Lords held that, in such circumstances, the inquest 'ought ordinarily to culminate in an expression, however brief, of the jury's conclusion on the disputed factual issues at the heart of the case'.

Whether this more detailed form of inquest will be required will depend on the precise circumstances of the particular case. Only those inquests that are concerned with a possible breach of Article 2 by an agent of the state have this wider scope; other types of inquest may be more limited.

17.3 CRIMINAL PROSECUTIONS

Where an accident results in a fatality, a criminal prosecution of those thought to be responsible will often follow. The procedure adopted in the magistrates' courts and Crown Court for such a prosecution is dealt with in **Criminal Litigation**.

If such a prosecution occurs, the claimant's solicitor should attend at court to obtain details of the circumstances of the accident and take notes of the evidence. If a conviction is obtained, this will be very useful for any civil proceedings that follow, and in these circumstances the relevant insurance company will often settle any claim.

Many insurance policies provide for the cost of defending such criminal charges, and the insurance company will nominate solicitors to act on the insured's behalf. The defendant's insurers will use the proceedings to establish a view on civil, as well as criminal liability.

17.3.1 Criminal prosecution following a fatal road traffic accident

The five offences which may be prosecuted following a fatal road traffic accident are as follows:

(a) *Causing death by dangerous driving* (RTA 1988, s 1). Under s 2 of the RTA 1988, a person is to be regarded as driving dangerously if the standard of driving falls 'far below what would be expected of a competent and careful driver and it would be obvious to a competent and careful driver that driving in that way would be dangerous'. The Sentencing Council has issued a definitive guideline on sentencing in the context of causing death by driving (the 'Guideline') which gives examples of driving behaviour likely to result in this charge. They include aggressive driving, racing or competitive driving, speeding, using a hand-held mobile phone when the driver was avoidably and dangerously distracted by that use, including reading or composing text messages, driving while knowingly deprived of adequate sleep or rest, driving while under the influence of alcohol or drugs, and failing to take prescribed medication or as a result of a known medical condition. Driving above the speed limit, or at a speed inappropriate to the road conditions; knowing that the vehicle has a dangerous defect or is poorly maintained or is dangerously loaded; performing a seriously dangerous manoeuvre; or failing to have proper regard to vulnerable road users are also highlighted in the Guideline. Cyclists, motorcycle riders, horse riders, pedestrians and those working in the road are vulnerable road uses and a driver is expected to take extra care around them.

The maximum penalty in the Crown Court is 14 years' imprisonment with a minimum disqualification of two years with compulsory extended re-test.

(b) *Causing death by careless driving when under the influence of drink or drugs*, or having failed without reasonable excuse either to provide a specimen for analysis or to permit the analysis of a blood sample (RTA 1988, s 3A).

According to s 3ZA of the RTA 1988, careless driving is driving that 'falls below what would be expected of a competent and careful driver'. In comparison with dangerous driving, the level of culpability in the actual manner of driving is lower, but that culpability is increased by the fact that the driver has driven after consuming drugs or alcohol.

The maximum penalty in the Crown Court is 14 years' imprisonment with a minimum disqualification of two years with compulsory extended re-test.

(c) *Causing death by careless or inconsiderate driving* (RTA 1988, s 2B). Careless driving is described in (b) above. Section 3ZA of the RTA 1988 defines careless driving as driving below what would be expected of a competent and careful driver. Inconsiderate driving means driving without reasonable consideration for others/inconveniencing other road users by the driving. Examples of careless driving include overtaking on the inside, emerging from a side road into the path of another vehicle, and tuning a car radio. Examples of inconsiderate driving include flashing of lights to force drivers in front to give way and driving with undipped headlights.

The maximum penalty for this offence is five years' imprisonment with a minimum of 12 months' disqualification.

(d) *Causing death by driving: unlicensed or uninsured drivers* (RTA 1988, s 3ZB). This charge is likely to be prosecuted alongside one of the offences outlined in (a) to (c) above, and is self-explanatory. It carries a maximum penalty of two years' imprisonment with a minimum disqualification of 12 months.

(e) *Causing death by driving: disqualified drivers* (RTA 1988, s 3ZC). As above, this charge is likely to be prosecuted alongside one of the offences outlined in (a) to (c), although this will obviously not always be the case. It carries a maximum penalty of 10 years' imprisonment with a minimum disqualification of 12 months.

Note that s 1A of the RTA 1988 creates the offence of causing serious injury by dangerous driving.

17.3.2 Criminal prosecution following an accident at work

Following a fatal accident at work, the HSE may bring a prosecution under the HSWA 1974 (see **4.9**). It is also possible for an individual (such as a director of a company) to be prosecuted for gross negligence manslaughter.

Where the evidence indicates that a serious criminal offence other than a health and safety offence may have been committed, the HSE is required to liaise with the CPS in deciding whether to prosecute. Health and safety offences are usually prosecuted by the HSE, or by the local authority responsible for enforcement. The CPS may also prosecute health and safety offences, but usually does so only when prosecuting other serious criminal offences, such as manslaughter, arising out of the same circumstances.

There is also the possibility that the CPS could bring a prosecution against an employer for corporate manslaughter under the Corporate Manslaughter and Corporate Homicide Act 2007, which is discussed in more detail below (see **17.3.4**).

17.3.3   Criminal prosecution following clinical negligence

The CPS may bring a prosecution for manslaughter against an individual (such as a doctor or nurse) following a clinical negligence incident which results in the death of a patient. Such a charge will be on the basis that the breach of duty committed was so great as to constitute gross negligence and therefore merits criminal sanctions rather than just a duty to compensate the victim (see R v Adomako [1995] 1 AC 171).

Over the years, a number of doctors have been convicted of manslaughter by gross negligence. In 2003, two senior house officers were so convicted following the death of a man who had been placed in their post-operative care. Following a routine knee operation at Southampton University Hospital, the patient contracted an infection and subsequently died of toxic shock syndrome. The doctors had failed to deal with the clear signs of serious illness, take appropriate blood samples, administer antibiotics or consult senior colleagues. Their appeal against a suspended sentence of 18 months each was dismissed by the Court of Appeal (R v Misra; R v Srivastava [2004] EWCA Crim 2375).

Following their conviction, the CPS also instigated criminal proceedings against the NHS Trust (R v Southampton University Hospital NHS Trust [2006] EWCA Crim 2971) for its failure to discharge its duty under s 3 of the HSWA 1974. This section requires an employer to conduct its undertakings in such a way as to ensure, so far is reasonably practical, that persons not in the employer's employment and who may be affected (in this instance a patient) are not exposed to risks to their health and safety. The Trust had failed to provide enough junior doctors in the Trauma and Orthopaedic Department, and had failed to implement systems for the adequate supervision of staff by consultants. The Trust pleaded guilty, and the initial fine of £100,000 was reduced on appeal to £40,000 on the grounds that the judge had not taken account of the early guilty plea and that the public would suffer as a result of a large fine.

More recently, in R v Mid Staffordshire NHS Foundation Trust (Stafford Crown Court, December 2015), a fine of £500,000 was handed down after the Trust pleaded guilty to charges brought by the HSE following the deaths of four elderly patients between 2005 and 2014.

In August 2016, Honey Rose, a locum optometrist was given a two-year suspended sentence following her conviction for manslaughter at Ipswich Crown Court. She had failed to notice swelling behind the eye of a seven-year-old boy during a routine eye test. The boy died five months later, and the jury found that the failure of the optometrist to spot the problem and refer him for treatment amounted to gross negligence manslaughter. However, the conviction was overturned by the Court of Appeal: although the optometrist had been in breach of duty in failing to examine the internal structure of the child's eye as part of a routine eye examination, this was not enough to establish that she ought reasonably to have foreseen an obvious and serious risk of death at the time the examination was carried out. See R v Rose [2017] EWCA Crim 1168.

See also R v Winter [2018] EWCA Crim 2435; R v Kuddus [2019] EWCA Crim 837; R v Broughton [2020] EWCA Crim 1093; and R (on the application of Canham) v DPP [2021] EWHC 3361 (Admin) on this subject.

It is also now possible that an NHS Trust, Foundation Trust or health authority could be prosecuted for corporate manslaughter (see **17.3.4** below).

17.3.4   Corporate Manslaughter and Corporate Homicide Act 2007

17.3.4.1   The background

The Corporate Manslaughter and Corporate Homicide Act 2007 (CMCHA 2007) came into force on 6 August 2008 in response to problems applying the existing offence of manslaughter by gross negligence to organisations rather than to individuals. The main problem under the then existing criminal law was that, in order for a company or other organisation to be guilty of gross negligence manslaughter, it was necessary for a senior individual (the 'controlling mind'), who might be said to embody the company, to be guilty of the offence. This is sometimes referred to as the 'identification doctrine'.

The matter was examined in *Attorney-General's Reference (No 2 of 1999)* [2000] 2 Cr App R 207, which concerned a train collision at Southall in 1997 in which seven passengers died and 151 were injured. Great Western Trains was prosecuted for manslaughter on the basis that it had allowed the train to be operated with two important safety devices switched off, as a result of which the driver of the train had failed to notice a warning signal. The company was acquitted as there was no human being with whom the company could be identified. On a reference by the Attorney-General, the Court of Appeal stated that the identification doctrine remained the only basis in common law for corporate liability in gross negligence manslaughter.

As a result of the identification doctrine there were very few successful prosecutions for corporate manslaughter. The only successful prosecutions were of small, owner-managed companies, where it was not difficult to pinpoint a senior individual who effectively ran the company, such as in *Kite and Others* (1994) *Independent*, 9 December, where four teenagers drowned while canoeing during an adventure holiday. Also see *R v Kite* [1996] 2 Cr App R (S) 295, where the Court of Appeal upheld the conviction but reduced the sentence.

The perceived insufficiencies in the law led to a sustained campaign for reform, which finally resulted in the offence of corporate manslaughter being introduced by the CMCHA 2007. The offence is intended to work in conjunction with other forms of accountability, such as gross negligence manslaughter for individuals, and other health and safety legislation.

17.3.4.2   The offence

Section 1 of the CMCHA 2007 states:

> (1)   An organisation to which this section applies is guilty of an offence if the way in which its activities are managed or organised—
>
>   (a)   causes a person's death; and
>
>   (b)   amounts to a gross breach of a relevant duty of care owed by the organisation to the deceased.
>
> (2)   An organisation is guilty of an offence ... only if the way in which its activities are managed or organised by its senior management is a substantial element in the breach referred to in subsection (1).

To prove the offence, therefore, the CPS must prove:

(a)   the defendant is a qualifying *organisation*;

(b)   the organisation *causes* a person's death;

(c)   there was a *relevant duty of care* owed by the organisation to the deceased;

(d)   there was a *gross breach* of that duty; and

(e)   a substantial element of that breach was in the way those activities were managed or organised *by senior management*; and

(f)   that the defendant does not fall within one of the *exemptions* for prosecution under the Act.

Therefore the court will have to consider how the fatal activity was managed, or organised, throughout the organisation, including any systems and processes for managing safety and how these were operated in practice. A substantial part of the failure within the organisation must have been at a senior level.

Meaning of 'organisation'

Section 1(2) states the offence applies to the following bodies:

(a)   a corporation;

(b)   a department or other body listed in Sch 1;

(c)   a police force; and

(d)   a partnership, or a trade union or employers' association, that is an employer.

Crown immunity has been a long-established legal doctrine that means that Crown bodies (such as government departments) cannot be prosecuted. Section 11(1) now allows prosecutions under the Act to apply to such bodies. Schedule 1 sets out a list of government departments to which the offence applies.

The Act also applies to a wide range of statutory public bodies which are not part of the Crown, including local authorities and NHS bodies.

Causation

It is not necessary for the management failure to have been the sole cause of death. The prosecution will need to show that 'but for' the management failure (including the substantial element attributable to senior management), the death would not have occurred. The law does not, however, recognise very remote causes, and in some circumstances the existence of an intervening event may mean that the management failure is not considered to have caused the death.

Relevant duty of care

Section 2(1) requires that the relevant duty of care is to be one that is owed under the law of negligence. The Act does not create new duties in addition to those already owed in the civil law of negligence.

The duty must be a relevant one for the offence. Relevant duties are set out in s 2(1) of the Act and include:

(a)   employer and occupier duties;

(b)   duties owed in connection with:

  (i)   supplying goods and services (whether or not for consideration),

  (ii)   construction and maintenance work (note that simply because there is a statutory duty to perform an act, this does not create a relevant duty of care; thus, although a highways authority has a duty to maintain and repair roads (HA 1980, s 41), the failure to do so does not give rise to a duty of care to a motorist in negligence. However, a negligent repair would do so),

  (iii)   other activities on a commercial basis, and

  (iv)   using or keeping plant, vehicles or other things.

Gross breach

Once a relevant duty of care has been established, any breach must fall far below what could reasonably be expected of the organisation in the circumstances (s 1(4)(b)).

This is a matter for the jury to decide, and s 8 sets out factors for the jury to consider. Section 8(2) states that the jury must consider whether health and safety legislation was breached and, if so:

(a)   how serious the breach was (s 8(2)(a)); and

(b)   how much of a risk of death it posed (s 8(2)(b)).

Meaning of 'senior management'

The term 'senior management' is defined in s 1(4) to mean those persons who play a *significant* role in the management of the whole of, or a *substantial* part of, the organisation's activities. This covers both those in the direct chain of management and those in, for example, strategic or regulatory compliance roles.

Neither 'significant' nor 'substantial' is defined, but the former is likely to be limited to those whose involvement is influential, and will not include those who simply carry out the activity.

Whether the activity in question is itself a 'substantial' part of the company's activities will be of great importance in determining if the offence applies, especially where a company has multiple businesses or is a national organisation with regional managers. The test of senior management is wider than the former 'controlling mind', which effectively restricted the offence to actions of directors. A regional manager would probably count, but this may itself depend on the number of regions, the number of higher tiers of management, the diversity of the organisation's activities and the regional manager's own job description.

Exemptions

Corporate manslaughter does not apply to certain public and government functions where there exist wider questions of public policy. So, for example, the Act exempts the military, the police and the emergency services when conducting certain activities, including dealing with emergencies, terrorism and violent disorder.

17.3.4.3 Punishment for corporate manslaughter and health and safety offences causing death

The Sentencing Council issued the Definitive Guideline on Health and Safety Offences, Corporate Manslaughter and Food Safety and Hygiene Offences (the 'Guideline') in February 2016. It sets out the key principles relevant to assessing the seriousness of such offences and the factors that should be taken into account in deciding on an appropriate sentence.

These offences are punishable only on indictment, with a maximum penalty of an unlimited fine. The Guideline states that the fine should meet the objectives of punishment, the reduction of offending through deterrence, and removal of gain through commission of the offence. The fine imposed must be 'sufficiently substantial to have a real economic impact which will bring home to management and shareholders the need to achieve a safer environment for workers and members of the public affected by their actions'. The level of the fine will take into account the turnover of the company in addition to matters of culpability and harm, with the lowest starting point being £300,000 for a business with turnover of up to £2 million.

In addition to a fine, the court can make various ancillary orders:

(a) *Publicity order.* This is available only for offences of corporate manslaughter. A publicity order may require publication of:
   (i) the fact of the conviction;
   (ii) specified particulars of the offence;
   (iii) the amount of any fine; and
   (iv) the terms of any remedial order (see (c) below).
   The Guideline states that a publicity order should ordinarily be imposed in a case of corporate manslaughter. The order should specify the place where the public announcement is to be made (for example, a newspaper or a website) and consideration should also be given to the size of any notice or advertisement required.

(b) *Remedial order.* The Guideline makes clear that a defendant ought, by the time of the sentencing, to have remedied any dangerous practices, and if it has not will be deprived of significant mitigation. Nevertheless, if it still appears to be necessary, a judge may make a remedial order requiring a defendant to address the cause of the accident. The order should be sufficiently specific to make it enforceable.

(c)   *Compensation.* In the majority of cases, the court will conclude that compensation should be dealt with by the civil courts and should make no order for compensation.

17.3.4.4   Corporate manslaughter convictions

According to the Practice Note on LexisNexis 'Corporate Manslaughter – Prosecutions Tracker', there have been 33 successful prosecutions for corporate manslaughter under the CMCHA 2007 since 2010, with additional cases resulting in either an acquittal or acceptance of/being found guilty of charges under the HSWA 1974.

The first company to be convicted under the CMCHA 2007 was Cotswold Geotechnical Holdings Ltd, which was fined £385,000 in February 2011 following the death of an employee who was crushed to death when the sides of an excavated pit collapsed as he was collecting samples. The court took account of the fact that the company was in financial difficulties, and the fine was in fact 116% of the company's turnover.

The second conviction was in May 2012 against JMW Farms, based in Northern Ireland. This was the first corporate manslaughter conviction in Northern Ireland. The company was convicted under the CMCHA 2007 following the death of one of its employees on 15 November 2010. The employee, who was 45 years old, was working at a farm, when he was crushed by a large metal bin, which had fallen from the raised forks of a forklift. The vehicle was being driven by one of the company's directors. The bin had not been properly attached to the forklift. JMW Farms was fined £187,500 plus £13,000 costs.

In July 2012, Lion Steel Equipment Ltd became the third company in the UK to be convicted of corporate manslaughter, and was fined £480,000 and ordered to pay prosecution costs of £84,000. The case followed the death of an employee who suffered fatal injuries when he fell through a fragile roof at the company's site in Hyde, Cheshire in May 2009. The company admitted the offence, part-way through the trial, on the basis that all charges against its directors would be dropped (three men had been charged with gross negligence manslaughter and health and safety charges).

In May 2017, Martinisation (London) Ltd was fined £1.2 million following a conviction for corporate manslaughter. The prosecution arose out of an accident in which two workers died during the refitting of a luxury flat in Knightsbridge. The men were instructed by a director of the company to manually haul a heavy sofa on to a first floor balcony instead of using an elevator which would have cost £848. The railings on the balcony gave way and the men fell to their deaths. The director was also convicted of health and safety offences and sentenced to 14 months in prison and disqualified from being a company director for four years.

On 8 October 2021, Aster Healthcare Ltd, a company which owned and operated a nursing home in Berkshire, was fined £1.04 million following a conviction for corporate manslaughter after Mrs Norris, a vulnerable 93-year-old woman, suffered burns across 12% of her body while being bathed. Mrs Norris had advanced dementia and was losing the ability to communicate. She was bathed by two carers who failed to properly check the water temperature and continued to add hot water. Mrs Norris was taken by ambulance to a specialist burns unit at the Chelsea and Westminster Hospital, where she died three days later. The investigation into her death revealed that the home had longstanding problems in regulating the temperature of the hot water supply. The care home manager and a carer at the home received suspended prison sentences pursuant to charges under the HSWA 1974.

In June 2022 Greenfeeds Ltd (in liquidation) was fined £2 million. One of the directors was sentenced to 13 years' imprisonment, while another was sentenced to 20 months in prison. This followed the deaths of two employees who climbed into a tanker containing pig feed and drowned after being overcome by fumes.

In February 2023, FDA Waste Services Ltd was convicted following a corporate manslaughter trial and fined £640,000 after an employee was fatally injured by a shovel loader when in a recycling yard. A director was convicted of a breach of s 2(1) of the HSWA 1974.

In March 2023, DH Willis & Sons Ltd was convicted following a corporate manslaughter trial and fined £335,000 after an employee fell from a JCB telehandler while undertaking roof repairs and subsequently died. Two directors of this company were acquitted of gross manslaughter but pleaded guilty to offences under s 2 of the HSWA 1974.

Most of the convictions so far have followed guilty pleas by the company, usually in exchange for the dropping of charges against individual directors, and, in several of the more recent convictions, publicity orders were made which required the publication of details of the convictions in trade magazines and local newspapers.

To date, there has been no successful prosecution for corporate manslaughter brought against an NHS Trust. The case against Maidstone and Tunbridge Wells NHS Trust in 2015 arising out of the death of a patient following a caesarean section was dropped due to lack of evidence and a ruling by the judge of no case to answer. In February 2016, Sherwood Rise Ltd became the first care provider in England to be convicted of corporate manslaughter. The conviction related to the death of an 86-year-old woman who died a few days after she was moved out of a residential care home owned by Sherwood. She was found to be dehydrated, malnourished and suffering with untreated bed sores. The company was ordered to pay a fine of £30,000. In addition, the director and acting manager of the company received a prison sentence of three years and two months, after pleading guilty to gross negligence manslaughter. He was also disqualified from being a director for eight years. The individual employed as manager in the care home received a suspended prison sentence and was disqualified from becoming a director for five years.

17.4 CONCLUSION

Inquests and criminal prosecutions are important processes which may be used to gather evidence at an early stage, and the outcome of a criminal prosecution may be extremely influential in establishing liability in a civil claim for compensation. From a personal injury solicitor's point of view, this can be very demanding work, as the client is likely to make considerable demands of the solicitor, both professionally and emotionally. A summary of the main points is set out below at **17.6**.

17.5 FURTHER READING

Matthews, *Jervis on Coroners* (Sweet & Maxwell)

Robottom, Harvey-Sullivan, Weston & Baker, *Coroners Investigations and Inquests* (LexisNexis Butterworths)

LexisNexis Corporate Manslaughter Prosecutions Tracker

17.6 INVESTIGATING FATAL ACCIDENTS

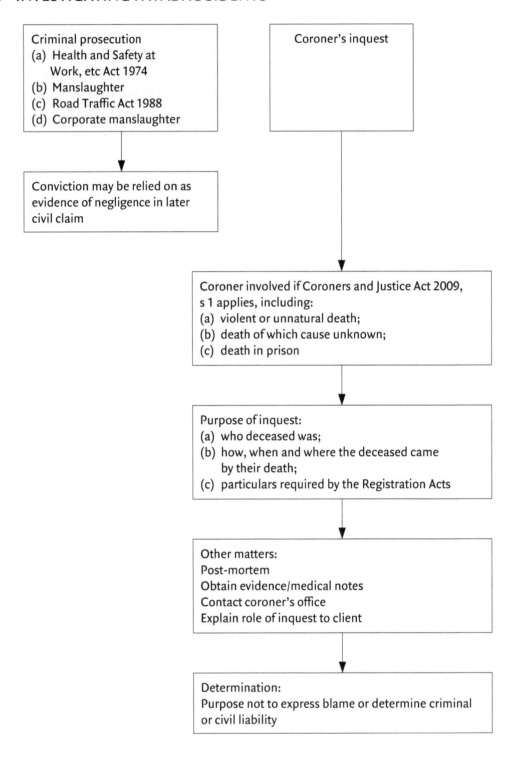

Criminal prosecution
(a) Health and Safety at Work, etc Act 1974
(b) Manslaughter
(c) Road Traffic Act 1988
(d) Corporate manslaughter

Coroner's inquest

Conviction may be relied on as evidence of negligence in later civil claim

Coroner involved if Coroners and Justice Act 2009, s 1 applies, including:
(a) violent or unnatural death;
(b) death of which cause unknown;
(c) death in prison

Purpose of inquest:
(a) who deceased was;
(b) how, when and where the deceased came by their death;
(c) particulars required by the Registration Acts

Other matters:
Post-mortem
Obtain evidence/medical notes
Contact coroner's office
Explain role of inquest to client

Determination:
Purpose not to express blame or determine criminal or civil liability

CHAPTER 18

INTRODUCTION TO FATAL ACCIDENT CLAIMS — PROCEDURE AND QUANTIFICATION

LEARNING OUTCOMES

After reading this chapter you will be able to:

- understand the causes of action available to the estate and dependants of the deceased after a fatal accident
- identify who may claim as a dependant of the deceased
- advise on the heads of damage which may be claimed by the estate of the deceased
- calculate the amount of a dependency claim
- identify who may claim bereavement damages and the amount of those damages.

18.1 INTRODUCTION

This chapter sets out the basic principles involved in assessing damages in personal injury and clinical negligence cases where the victim has died before trial.

There are two elements to a claim in such circumstances:

(a)   the Law Reform (Miscellaneous Provisions) Act 1934 (LR(MP)A 1934), which allows a claim for the benefit of the deceased's estate; and

(b)   the Fatal Accidents Act 1976 (FAA 1976), which allows a claim for the benefit of the dependants and those entitled to an award of bereavement damages.

While the Acts provide two separate causes of action, they are commonly brought together and, to some extent, may overlap. The methods of valuing damages which may be claimed under each Act are considered below.

In certain cases, specific statutes provide for recompense for the deceased's family, such as the Carriage by Air Act 1961 in cases of death arising out of civil aviation accidents. These are not dealt with in this text.

18.2   CAUSE OF ACTION

The LR(MP)A 1934 provides (for the benefit of the deceased's estate) for the continuation of the cause of action to which the deceased was entitled the instant before he died (LR(MP)A 1934, s 1(2)). It does not create a separate cause of action.

The FAA 1976 does create a separate cause of action for the dependants (and those entitled to the award of bereavement damages), but it is based on the pre-condition that the deceased, had he lived, would have been able to sue successfully (FAA 1976, s 1).

Three things follow from this, namely:

(a)   if the deceased had no cause of action then the estate and the dependants have no cause of action;

(b)   any defence that could have been used against the deceased can be used against the estate and the dependants;

(c)   if the deceased was contributorily negligent then the damages of the estate and the dependants are reduced accordingly.

EXAMPLE 1

Tom is driving his car when it collides with a car driven by Sharon. Tom dies as a result of his injuries. He is survived by his widow, Elaine, and his son, Christopher. The accident is entirely the fault of Tom. As a result, neither Tom's estate, nor Elaine or Christopher has any right of action against Sharon.

EXAMPLE 2

Lucy is killed in an accident at work. She is survived by her husband, Tyrone, and daughter, Patricia. Lucy and her employers are equally to blame for the accident. Although Lucy's estate, Tyrone and Patricia may claim against the employers, the damages awarded to each will be reduced by 50%.

In the case of *Jameson and Another v Central Electricity Generating Board and Another* [2000] 1 AC 455, the House of Lords held that in a case where the second co-defendant had paid a compensation payment to the injured person when he was still alive (on a less than full liability basis), this did prevent the dependants bringing a claim under FAA 1976 against the first co-defendant (who was a concurrent tortfeasor) and did amount to a settlement of claim.

Statements of case may be amended to plead a fatal accident claim if the deceased dies during the course of proceedings which were commenced in his name when he was alive. However, once judgment is given or a claim is settled by a living claimant, there can be no subsequent claim by dependants. This is well illustrated by the case of *Thompson v Arnold* [2007] EWHC 1875 (QB). Mrs Thompson commenced proceedings against her GP, Dr Arnold, who had incorrectly diagnosed a lump in her breast as benign. The case was settled for £120,000, in full and final settlement, in January 2000. Mrs Thompson died in April 2002 and, in April 2005, her husband and two daughters as her dependants sought to bring a claim against the defendant under the FAA 1976. Their claim was dismissed on the basis of the previous settlement made by Mrs Thompson during her lifetime. If there is a possibility that a claimant might die of their injuries during the course of proceedings, the best approach (as suggested by Langstaff J in *Thompson v Arnold*) may be to seek an interim payment of equal value to a lifetime award, together with an adjournment of the case. This will preserve the dependant's right to claim under the FAA 1976 in the event of death. Alternatively, a claim for provisional damages could be made (see **15.4**). Section 3 of the Damages Act 1996 makes it clear that a provisional damages award does not bar a claim under the FAA 1976, although the award will be taken into account in assessing damages payable to the dependants under the 1976 Act.

18.3 THE APPOINTMENT OF PERSONAL REPRESENTATIVES

Fatal accident claims are normally representative actions. This means that the personal representative normally brings a claim simultaneously on behalf of the estate under the LR(MP)A 1934 and on behalf of the dependants under the FAA 1976. The grant of probate or letters of administration should therefore be obtained before the claim is commenced.

18.4 DAMAGES UNDER THE LAW REFORM (MISCELLANEOUS PROVISIONS) ACT 1934

Generally, the damages awarded to the estate under the LR(MP)A 1934 are based on the losses for which the deceased could have claimed at the instant before he died. In essence, the estate inherits the deceased's right to sue in respect of the death. Any head of damages that is duplicated between the LR(MP)A 1934 and the FAA 1976 is recoverable only once.

The following heads of damages may be appropriate.

18.4.1 Pain, suffering and loss of amenity (PSLA)

In cases in which a serious injury is followed relatively quickly by death, Chapter 1 of the 16th edition of the *Guidelines for the Assessment of General Damages in Personal Injury Cases* ('the Guidelines') allows for an element of PSLA for the period between injury and death. There are four brackets:

(A) **Full Awareness – £12,540 to £23,810**

Severe burns and lung damage followed by full awareness for a short period and then fluctuating levels of consciousness for between 4 to 5 weeks coupled with intrusive treatment or significant orthopaedic/physical injuries followed by death within a couple of weeks up to 3 months.

(B) **Followed by Unconsciousness – £10,510 to £10,670**

Severe burns and lung damage causing excruciating pain but followed by unconsciousness after 3 hours and death two weeks later.

(C) **Immediate Unconsciousness/Death after Six Weeks – £3,760 to £4,390**

Immediate unconsciousness after injury, and death occurring after six weeks.

(D) **Immediate Unconsciousness/Death within One Week – £1,370 to £2,790**

Immediate unconsciousness, or unconsciousness following very shortly after injury, and death occurring within a week. Where the victim is conscious initially but dies from their injuries the same day, an award towards the bottom of the range will be appropriate, subject to the comments at the start of Chapter 1 of the Guidelines relating to cases of near instant death.

(E) **Mental Anguish – £4,670**

Fear of impending death/reduction in expectation of life.

For the parent of young child suffering such mental anguish for a period of around 3 months.

Until inclusion in the Guidelines in the last few years, there had been no guidance in this area, with parties having to search for authorities in each case, and defendants often argued that there could really be no pain with immediate unconsciousness, so reaching a conclusion that no PSLA award should be made. For example, in *Hicks v Wright* [1992] 2 All ER 65, no damages under this head were awarded by the House of Lords to victims of the Hillsborough disaster for the short period of terror and pain they experienced before death. In *Chouza v Martins and others* [2021] EWHC 1669 (QB) damages of £500 were awarded in a case where the deceased was found to be aware for a maximum of 5 seconds of an impending road traffic collision but died instantaneously on impact. The trial judge decided that pain, suffering and loss of amenity should be taken to include the fear and mental anguish which precedes and is associated with physical injury. The judge found that the £2,500 claimed was too high. The introduction to Chapter 1 of the Guidelines observes that *Hicks* was not cited by the judge in *Chouza*, and therefore that the *Chouza* decision may be per incuriam.

Chapter 1 does not apply to extensive periods of suffering and disability before death, such as in cases relating to asbestos exposure or other cancer claims where reference must be made to the awards for those underlying conditions. For example, Chapter 6 of the Guidelines suggests a bracket of damages for PSLA in a mesothelioma case of £63,650 to £114,460.

Although the above brackets are a useful starting point, every case will be unique and so the amount of the award for pain, suffering and loss of amenity will depend upon the actual level of pain and the length of time over which the pain was experienced. Reference should therefore still be made to case law in order to obtain a more accurate valuation. For example, in *Fallon v Beaumont*, 16 December 1993, CC (Leeds), a 22-year-old man was involved in a high-speed road accident, during which the car in which he was a passenger exploded and burst into flames. He was trapped in the burning car until the emergency services arrived, and was conscious throughout. He died 30 days later. He would have had significant insight into the gravity of his situation and an award of £10,000 (the equivalent of £29,323.61 at September 2023 values) was made for pain and suffering.

The Court of Appeal case of *Kadir v Mistry* [2014] EWCA Civ 1177 concerned a claim for damages for the distress caused by the knowledge of the deceased that she was going to die as a result of the delay by her GP to diagnose that she was suffering from cancer. Section 1(1) of the Administration of Justice Act 1982 provides:

> In an action under the law of England and Wales or the law of Northern Ireland for damages for personal injuries—
>
> (a)   no damages shall be recoverable in respect of any loss of expectation of life caused to the injured person by the injuries; but
>
> (b)   if the injured person's expectation of life has been reduced by the injuries, the court, in assessing damages in respect of pain and suffering caused by the injuries, shall take account of any suffering caused or likely to be caused to him by awareness that his expectation of life has been so reduced.

The appellant/claimant, as personal representative of the deceased's estate, appealed against a decision awarding no damages for pain, suffering and loss of amenity, or for mental anguish, arising from the admitted negligent failure of the respondent/defendant general practitioners to diagnose his late wife with stomach cancer as early as they should have done.

For several months the deceased had been visiting the defendants complaining of various stomach-related symptoms until, in March 2008, she was diagnosed with stomach cancer. She was advised that the cancer was too advanced to treat, and thereafter she received only palliative care until she died in August 2008. She was 32 years old and had four small children. The claimant claimed against the defendant on behalf of himself and the children under the FAA 1976, and on behalf of the deceased's estate under the LR(MP)A 1934.

The defendants admitted liability for the delay in the diagnosis and the consequent delay in treatment.

The claimant gave evidence that in March 2008 the family was told by doctors that the deceased might have survived if she had been diagnosed sooner, and that during a home visit in May 2008 she asked her GP why she was not diagnosed earlier and whether she would have survived if she had been. The trial judge found that if the defendants had not been negligent the deceased would have been diagnosed in June or July 2007, and would probably have lived until July or August 2010. He found that if the deceased had been diagnosed earlier, she would have suffered the same symptoms as she did, albeit later, and would have had to endure intensive and gruelling treatments, so he awarded no damages for pain, suffering and loss of amenity. He also rejected the claim under s 1(1)(b) of the Administration of Justice Act 1982 for damages in respect of mental anguish caused or likely to be caused by the deceased's awareness that her life expectation had been reduced.

Allowing the claimant's appeal, the Court of Appeal held that it was important to bear in mind that there were no special rules for the assessment of damages in cases under the 1934 Act: the court was required to undertake the conventional exercise, namely, decide what pain was occasioned by the negligence. If the court was looking at a living claimant facing an early death, like the deceased, the court inevitably had to compare the facts as they occurred with the likely facts if there had been no negligence. On that basis, the fact that the deceased would have had the same symptoms two years later was relevant, as was the pain of treatment. The judge had been correct on the evidence to refuse the claim for pain, suffering and loss of amenity.

The word 'awareness' in s 1(1)(b) of the 1982 Act did not mean strictly certain knowledge. As a matter of ordinary humanity, if there was good reason for the anguish, it could be inferred that the sufferer would have suffered some. The claimant had given evidence that the deceased had believed that the delay had caused the cancer to spread. The issue of why she was not diagnosed earlier was a live question during her last months. There was plainly material that gave rise to the proper inference that she feared on good objective grounds that her life expectancy had been reduced by the delayed diagnosis. It was necessary to prove that she knew that it was reduced.

No cases had been found that were relevant to the assessment of damages under s 1(1)(b) of the 1982 Act for the deceased's suffering occasioned by her awareness of her reduced life expectancy. On the evidence, her mental anguish was proved for the three-month period from May 2008 until her death. It was important to recognise that there was no psychiatric injury, but there were other important elements: in particular, she was a young woman with four small children; her anguish must have been exacerbated by her knowledge that they would be left without her and that she would not see them grow up. It was proper to take those factors into account. Adopting a broad-brush approach, £3,500 would do justice.

18.4.2 Loss of income

The estate is entitled to claim the lost net earnings of the deceased from the time of the accident until death, calculated in the same way as for a living claimant (see **15.2.1**). No claim can be made for loss of income in respect of any period after that person's death (LR(MP)A 1934, s 1(2)(a)(ii), as amended by the Administration of Justice Act 1982).

18.4.3 Funeral expenses

Funeral expenses are specifically provided for in s 1(2)(c) of the LR(MP)A 1934. The expenses may be claimed provided they are:

(a) reasonable; and

(b) incurred by the estate.

What is 'reasonable' will depend on the individual circumstances of the case, which may include the social standing and ethnicity of the deceased. In *Gammell v Wilson* [1982] AC 27, the court drew a distinction between the cost of the funeral service and a headstone (which was allowed), and the cost of a wake and a memorial to the deceased (which was not allowed).

In *Brown v Hamid* [2013] EWHC 4067 (QB), no award was allowed for funeral expenses on the basis that they would have been incurred shortly in any event. The court found that, even if the defendant had not been negligent, the deceased would have survived for only another 12 months. In *Mosson v Spousal (London) Ltd* [2016] EWHC 53 (QB), it was held to be unreasonable to claim for the cost of a memorial bench or the clothing to be worn at the funeral.

If the expenses are incurred by a dependant of the deceased rather than by the deceased's estate, the dependant may claim the expenses as part of the fatal accidents claim.

On a practical note, it is important to obtain receipts in order to prove all the expenses incurred. Many insurers are amenable to making an immediate interim payment in relation to the funeral expenses, in order to relieve the dependants of some of the immediate expenses and to prevent interest accruing on those expenses.

18.4.4 Value of services rendered by third parties

Services rendered by third parties may include, for example: nursing services rendered by a relative to the deceased up to the time of death; expenses incurred by a third party in assisting in bringing the deceased's body home from abroad; or the costs incurred by relatives in visiting the hospital. The quantum is the proper and reasonable cost of supplying the need. (For the general principles involved, see **Chapter 15**.)

18.4.5 Other losses

Other losses may include, for example, damage to chattels, such as the car the deceased was driving at the time of the incident, or the clothing which he was wearing.

18.4.6 Distribution of damages

Damages under the LR(MP)A 1934 pass to the deceased's estate, and from there to the deceased's beneficiaries according to the deceased's will or the rules of intestacy.

Damages under the LR(MP)A 1934 are, in appropriate cases (eg, where there was a long interval between the accident and the death, and the deceased had been in receipt of recoverable benefits), subject to the Social Security (Recovery of Benefits) Act 1997 (see **Chapter 16**), but are not subject to any other losses or gains to the estate, such as the receipt of insurance money (LR(MP)A 1934, s 1(2)).

18.4.7 Conclusion

In the case of instantaneous death, damages under the LR(MP)A 1934 will normally be limited to damages for funeral expenses, damage to chattels and the relatively modest amounts specified in the Guidelines referred to at **18.4.1**. Where there is a period of survival, the damages may be more extensive but will normally still be severely curtailed by the inability of the estate to claim the lost future income of the deceased.

18.5 DAMAGES UNDER THE FATAL ACCIDENTS ACT 1976

In general terms, there are three possible heads of damages, namely:

(a)   a dependency claim for the financial losses suffered by the dependants of the deceased;

(b)   an award of bereavement damages; and

(c)   a claim for the funeral expenses, if paid by the dependants.

18.5.1 Loss of dependency

To succeed in a dependency claim, the claimant

(a)   must be a dependant as defined by the FAA 1976; and

(b)   must have had a reasonable expectation of financial benefit from the deceased.

18.5.1.1 The statutory meaning of 'dependant'

'Dependant' is defined in s 1(3) of the FAA 1976 as follows:

(a)   the wife or husband or former wife or husband of the deceased;

(aa)   the civil partner or former civil partner of the deceased;

(b)   any person who:

- (i) was living with the deceased in the same household immediately before the date of the death; and
- (ii) had been living with the deceased in the same household for at least two years before that date; and
- (iii) was living during the whole of that period as the husband or wife or civil partner of the deceased;
- (c) any parent or other ascendant of the deceased;
- (d) any person who was treated by the deceased as his parent;
- (e) any child or other descendant of the deceased;
- (f) any person (not being a child of the deceased) who, in the case of any marriage to which the deceased was at any time a party, was treated by the deceased as a child of the family in relation to that marriage;
- (fa) any person (not being a child of the deceased) who, in the case of any civil partnership in which the deceased was at any time a civil partner, was treated by the deceased as a child of the family in relation to that civil partnership;
- (g) any person who is, or is the issue of, a brother, sister, uncle or aunt of the deceased.

The requirement to come within the statutory definition of 'dependant' has resulted in adverse judicial comment (see *Shepherd v Post Office* (1995) *The Times*, 15 June), and the introduction of the cohabitee as a possible claimant ((b) above) by the Administration of Justice Act 1982 was controversial.

In *Fretwell v Willi Betz*, 8 March 2001, CC Sheffield (unreported), the definition of a 'dependant' was challenged, by virtue of the Human Rights Act 1998. The case was settled without any admission as regards the claimant's status as a 'dependant' (the argument concerned a child of the girlfriend who was living with the deceased prior to the accident), but is an illustration of where the Human Rights Act 1998 has been used to challenge what has been argued to be the narrow statutory definition of a 'dependant'.

The requirement under s 1(3)(b) to have been living together for two years prior to the death should be noted, and evidence should be obtained on this point if it is anticipated that the defendant will challenge this (see *Kotke v Saffarini* [2005] EWCA Civ 221). The two year time limit was unsuccessfully challenged in *Swift v Secretary of State for Justice* [2013] EWCA Civ 193, where the appellant relied on the Human Rights Act 1998 (Articles 8 and 14). In terms of the assessment of damages, the FAA 1976 contains a provision that the cohabitee's lack of enforceable right to support is to be taken into account (FAA 1976, s 3(4)). This may mean that a cohabitee will receive less compensation than a lawful spouse or civil partner, as the court may use a lower multiplier in determining the dependency claim. For example, a multiplier of 13 was used for a cohabiting couple, instead of 15 which would have been used if they were married.

18.5.1.2 Further provisions with regard to the meaning of 'dependant'

Section 1(4) of the FAA 1976 (as amended by the Administration of Justice Act 1982) provides:

> ... former wife or husband ... includes a reference to a person whose marriage to the deceased has been annulled or declared void as well as a person whose marriage to the deceased has been dissolved.

In addition:

> ... former civil partner ... includes a reference to a person whose civil partnership with the deceased has been annulled, as well as a person whose civil partnership with the deceased has been dissolved.

Section 1(5) of the FAA 1976 (as amended by the Administration of Justice Act 1982) provides:

- (a) In deducing any relationship for the purposes of subsection [1(3)] any relationship [by marriage or civil partnership] shall be treated as a relationship by consanguinity, any relationship of the half blood as a relationship of the whole blood, and the stepchild of any person as his child;
- (b) an illegitimate person shall be treated as the legitimate child—

(i)   of his mother and reputed father, or

(ii)   in the case of a person who has a female parent by virtue of section 43 of the Human Fertilisation and Embryology Act 2008, the legitimate child of his mother and that female parent.

Thus, for example, in respect of (a) above, the stepbrother of the deceased is treated as his true brother; the uncle of a wife is treated as the husband's uncle.

The Adoption Act 1976 provides that, generally, an adopted child is treated as the natural child of the adopters.

18.5.1.3   Identifying the dependants

It is important to identify all prospective dependants, as s 2(3) of the FAA 1976 provides that 'not more than one action shall lie for and in respect of the same subject matter of complaint' and, as a result, only one claim can be brought. A defendant is entitled to full particulars of all those on whose behalf the claim is being brought. In practice, the particulars of the dependants are set out in the court documentation and generally include details of:

(a)   the age of the dependants;

(b)   their relationship with the deceased;

(c)   the nature of the dependency (eg, the dependant was a minor son wholly supported by the deceased father who was the family breadwinner and who had good promotion prospects).

On occasions, the defendants will argue that a claimant is not a true 'dependant' under the FAA 1976, and this is often resolved by the court ordering a trial of the point as a preliminary issue.

18.5.1.4   The requirement of 'financial loss'

It is not sufficient that the claimant merely satisfies the statutory meaning of 'dependant'. It must be shown in addition that there is a reasonable likelihood that the claimant has or will suffer financial loss as a result of the death of the deceased. In the case of *Thomas v Kwik Save Stores Ltd* (2000) *The Times*, 27 June, the Court of Appeal reaffirmed the principle that, when awarding damages under the FAA 1976, the court was concerned with the financial loss and not the emotional dependency of the claimant on the deceased.

In many cases, the dependants will have a clear and immediate financial loss. For example, where a husband was maintaining his wife and children before his death, the fact that they will suffer financial loss as a result of the husband's death is obvious. In addition to the loss of the deceased's earnings, consideration should be given to whether the dependents have lost any fringe benefits to which he was entitled, such as a company car.

The loss may still be regarded as 'financial' even if there was no expenditure by the deceased, provided the support can be quantified in monetary terms (eg, where the deceased's elderly mother was allowed to live rent-free in the deceased's house before his death, the mother would be able to claim a quantifiable financial loss). If the deceased regularly did DIY, gardening or other jobs around the house, the dependants can claim for the loss of those gratuitous services. In *Crabtree v Wilson* [1993] PIQR Q24 the court valued the deceased's work around the home at £1,500 per annum.

In the case of *Cox v Hockenhull* [1999] 3 All ER 577, the Court of Appeal held that the important point in assessing the dependency was to identify the loss the claimant has suffered as a result of a death. In that case, the deceased's income had been certain State benefits which she and her husband had relied upon. The Court allowed the husband's claim for dependency on the basis that he was dependent on certain benefits that had been received prior to the death and which he no longer obtained after his wife was killed in a road traffic accident.

18.5.1.5   The loss must be as a result of a personal family relationship with the deceased

If the loss to the dependant is, in reality, a loss attributable to a business relationship with the deceased, the claim for loss of dependency will fail (*Burgess v Florence Nightingale Hospital for Gentlewomen* [1955] 1 QB 349).

EXAMPLE

Curtis is killed in a car accident as a result of the negligent driving of Keith. Curtis is survived by his widow, Sofia, and his 6-month-old son, Brodie. Curtis was the sole financial support of Sofia and Brodie. Curtis worked in business with his brother, Jed. As a result of Curtis's death, the business fails and Jed suffers heavy financial losses. Curtis's married sister, Delphine, is very upset at the news of her brother's death.

Sofia and Brodie may claim as defined dependants who suffer financial losses as a result of a family relationship with Curtis.

Jed cannot claim because, although he is a defined dependant, his financial losses are as a result of a business relationship with Curtis.

Delphine cannot claim because, although she is a defined dependant, she has suffered no financial losses (merely grief and sorrow).

18.5.2   Assessing loss of dependency – the traditional method

The award for loss of dependency is ascertained by a multiplicand and multiplier system. The multiplicand is the net annual loss of the dependants; the multiplier is based on the number of years' loss of dependency (ie, the length of time that the claimant would have been dependent on the deceased).

18.5.2.1   The multiplicand – the net annual loss to the dependants

The deceased wage earner

The starting point is to calculate the amount of the deceased's net earnings and deduct the estimated amount representing the sum that would have been spent by the deceased on his own personal and living expenses. The remaining balance will be the dependency multiplicand.

The deceased's net annual earnings must be calculated as at the date of the trial (*Cookson v Knowles* [1979] AC 556). No allowance is made for inflation (*Auty v National Coal Board* [1985] 1 All ER 930), but the deceased's future earning capacity (eg, as result of promotion) must be taken into account. For example, a trainee doctor may have been earning a relatively modest income at the date of death, but their earnings would clearly have increased substantially on qualifying and again on becoming a consultant. Evidence will be needed in support of this, and the best evidence may be from a comparative employee or employees who have gone, or who are going through, the same career structure as the deceased would have done. This evidence could be obtained, for example, from the deceased's trade union or employer.

Conversely, there may be evidence of likely loss of earning capacity, for example because of redundancy.

Calculating the dependency figure

There are two approaches that the courts have considered:

(a)   The 'old' system for calculating the dependency figure is to add up all the financial benefits received by the dependants from the deceased. It is necessary to produce a list of the items which contributed to the annual value of dependency and for the claimant to provide documentary evidence, bills, etc for the year prior to the death. A proportion is then deducted for the deceased's own expenses. For example, the following items have been considered: How much housekeeping money was paid to the wife? How much was spent on the deceased's food? How much was spent on the food for the rest of the family? Who paid how much for the children's shoes, etc? This type of calculation is very difficult and in practice is rarely attempted.

(b)   The customary modern practice, which was established in the case of *Harris v Empress Motors* [1983] 3 All ER 561, is to deduct a percentage from the net income figure to represent what the deceased would have spent exclusively on himself. Conventional percentages are adopted. Where the family unit was husband and wife, the usual figure is one-third. Where the family unit was husband, wife and children, the usual figure is one-quarter. However, it is important to note that each case must be judged on its own facts. The court is willing to depart from the conventional figures where there is evidence that they are inappropriate (*Owen v Martin* [1992] PIQR Q151), for example where the deceased was particularly frugal or a spendthrift. In such circumstances, less or more than the conventional figure should be deducted (see also *Coward v Comex Houlder Diving Ltd*, 18 July 1988, CA and *Dhaliwal v Personal Representatives of Hunt (Deceased)* [1995] PIQR Q56, CA).

Furthermore, it is quite possible that different multiplicands may have to be selected according to different times in the period of dependency. Had he lived, the deceased's financial affairs would not have remained constant throughout his life. Similarly, therefore, the multiplicand will not remain constant either. For example, in the case of a husband with wife and children, 75% of the husband's earnings may be the appropriate initial multiplicand while his children are likely to be dependent. However, from the point where the children can be expected to become independent the multiplicand may be merely two-thirds of the husband's earnings (see also *Coward v Comex Houlder Diving Ltd*, above).

Frequently, both husband and wife would have been earning at the time of death, and in such circumstances the approach adopted is to calculate the dependency as two-thirds or three-quarters (as the case may be) of the total joint net income, less the continuing earnings of the surviving spouse.

EXAMPLE

Mike and Susan both earn £50,000 pa net. They have no children. Mike dies in an accident at work. Two-thirds of their joint income is approximately £66,600 (£100,000 x 66%), but Susan's earnings of £50,000 must be deducted to calculate her dependency claim. Susan's annual loss of dependency is therefore £16,000.

Services rendered by the deceased

The deceased may have been contributing to the support of the family not only in terms of a percentage of his earnings, but also by rendering services to the family free of charge. Examples of such services include:

(a)   DIY jobs (eg, painting the house annually);

(b)   vegetable gardening (therefore saving on grocery bills);

(c)   nursing services to a sick member of the family;

(d)   contributions to childcare.

On the deceased's death, such free services will be lost. The family will have to pay for the services (eg, by employing a decorator) and thus incur a loss. The value of these services can add considerably to the multiplicand. Evidence must be obtained, for example by quotations from the appropriate source.

In *Beesley v New Century Group Ltd* [2008] EWHC 3033 (QB), the claimant's husband had died from malignant mesothelioma as a result of his employment with the defendant company. The court made an award of damages for loss of 'intangible benefits' in respect of the extra value to be attached to help such as domestic services provided by a husband. The court held that there were considerable advantages in having jobs around the house and garden done by a husband in his own time and at his own convenience, rather than having to employ a professional. Accordingly, it awarded the claimant £2,000. See also *Manning v King's College Hospital NHS Trust* [2008] EWHC 3008 (QB), in which similar sums were awarded to the husband and children of the deceased for the loss of personal attention of a wife and mother, 'in recognition that what is lost goes beyond the material'.

The deceased non-wage earner

Where the deceased was a wage earner, the valuation of the multiplicand in the dependency claim is predominantly based on a proportion of the deceased's earnings (see above). This is so whether the deceased was male or female (eg, whether husband, father, wife or mother). It is not uncommon, however, that the deceased was not in paid employment. In this case, the value of the services rendered to the family becomes the vital issue. For example, if the deceased was the wife and mother of the family, and was not a wage earner at the date of her death, the services rendered by her to the family might be quantified in the terms of employing a housekeeper to provide the same services. In *Regan v Williamson* [1976] 1 WLR 305, Watkins J said that in this context 'the word "services" [has] been too narrowly construed. It should at least include an acknowledgement that a wife and mother does not work to set hours, and, still less, to rule'. Accordingly, a value in excess of a housekeeper was awarded in that case. In *Mehmet v Perry* [1977] 2 All ER 529, the claimant widower, on the death of his wife, reasonably gave up his job in order to look after his young children. The starting point for the value of the services of the deceased wife was taken as the husband's loss of earnings.

Claims by parents, if children unmarried

A claim can be made by a parent (who is often unemployed or ill) who was dependent on the support from their unmarried child. When the court considers this type of case, it will have regard to the fact that the child may have married and that the financial assistance provided by the child may have ceased, depending on the facts.

18.5.2.2 The multiplier – the period of loss

Having calculated the multiplicand, the other side of the equation is to calculate the number of years' loss of dependency.

Commencement of period of loss

For nearly 40 years following *Cookson v Knowles* [1979] AC 556, the starting point for calculating the multiplier for future dependency in fatal accident claims was taken to be the date of death, then deducting from it the number of years that had elapsed between death and trial. This approach was at odds with the practice of calculating multipliers in non-fatal cases (see **Chapter 15**) from date of trial and ignored the long-established use of the Ogden tables for calculating future losses, often producing illogical and unjust results.

Cookson was overturned in February 2016 by the landmark case of *Knauer v Ministry of Justice* [2016] UKSC 9, in which the Supreme Court unanimously agreed that the correct approach is to assess the multiplier as at the date of trial (or earlier settlement).

End of the period of loss

In the case of a deceased wage earner, prima facie the number of years' loss will extend to the end of the deceased's working life (ie, usually up to what would have been the deceased's retiring age). Direct evidence should be produced or called on this point. It must be remembered that certain items of loss, such as the claim for the cost of DIY, may extend beyond retirement age, as the deceased would not necessarily have stopped doing DIY when he retired from work.

However, each case will turn upon its own facts, and the period of dependency may end before or after what would have been the normal date of the deceased's retirement. For example, where the deceased was a professional person, he might have been expected to work and support his dependants beyond normal retirement age. Equally, if the deceased would have enjoyed a pension, it may be argued that he would have continued to provide for his dependants beyond normal retirement age (although evidence would be needed to substantiate this: *Auty v National Coal Board* [1985] 1 All ER 930; see **Chapter 15**).

Conversely, the period of dependency may stop before what would have been the normally expected retirement age of the deceased. For example, if the deceased was already in a poor state of health, he may not have been expected to work until normal retirement age, and the financial support for the dependants would therefore have ended earlier. Similarly, if the dependant himself is in a poor state of health and has a short life-expectancy, the period of dependency will be shorter.

What if the dependant's shorter life expectancy has been caused by the negligence of the defendant? This was the case in *Haxton v Philips Electronics UK Ltd* [2014] All ER (D) 138 (Jan). The claimant had developed mesothelioma as a result of handling her husband's work clothes, which had become impregnated with asbestos fibres during his employment with the defendant. After her husband's death from mesothelioma, the claimant issued proceedings against the defendant seeking damages (i) as a dependant, and (ii) in her own right. The defendant admitted liability and damages were agreed, except in respect of her personal claim where she sought a sum to compensate her for the fact that her reduced life expectancy had resulted in a lower dependency claim. Although the claim failed at first instance, the Court of Appeal allowed the claimant's appeal and awarded her an additional £200,000.

Effect of likely divorce or remarriage

Where there is a claim by a widow as dependant, the likelihood that the marriage would have ended in divorce may be taken into account in assessing the period of dependency. In *Owen v Martin* [1992] PIQR Q151, the judge adopted a multiplier of 15, but the Court of Appeal reduced this to 11 on the basis that the widow's attitude towards her marriage vows, as shown by her personal history, led the court to believe that the marriage might not have lasted the whole of the natural life of the deceased. The court should take this approach only provided there is some evidence of likelihood of divorce (*Wheatley v Cunningham* [1992] PIQR Q100). See also *D v Donald* [2001] PIQR Q5, concerning an extra-marital affair. In *O'Loughlin v Cape Distribution Ltd* [2001] EWCA Civ 178, [2001] PIQR Q8, the court confirmed that there was no prescribed method by which damages for loss of dependency had to be identified. The key factor was showing economic loss. However, the widow's prospects of remarriage or actual remarriage are to be ignored (FAA 1976, s 3(3)). Therefore, the period of the widow's dependency on her deceased husband is calculated without regard to the fact that she is or may be financially supported by a new husband.

Conversion of the period of loss to a multiplier

Once the number of years' loss of dependency has been ascertained, this is then converted to a multiplier using the Ogden Tables (see **Chapter 15**) .

18.5.2.3   The multiplication

Having established the appropriate multiplicand and the overall multiplier, one method of calculating the award for loss of dependency is as follows:

(a)   Pre-trial losses – calculate the actual number of years' loss from the date of death until the trial and apply to the multiplicand (or multiplicands).The resulting amount(s) will be treated as special damages and will attract interest.

(b)   Future losses – establish the multiplier using the actuarially recommended method as set out in the Ogden tables and apply to the multiplicand (or multiplicands).

EXAMPLE

Tariq Ahmed is killed in a road traffic accident. At the time of his death, Tariq was 30 years old. Tariq has left a widow, Aneela, aged 29, and twin girls, Fatima and Hanna, aged 9. Tariq was a DIY enthusiast, and performed many decorating and maintenance tasks in the family home. The value of the services to the family was £750 per year. Prior to the accident, Tariq was in good health and was expected to work until he was 65. His net annual earnings at trial have been calculated as £20,000. The case comes to trial three years after the accident when Tariq would have been 33 years old had he lived. Funeral expenses were £1,390.

A simplified schedule of loss for the above example is set out below:

Tariq Ahmed's date of birth	January 1991
Date of accident/death	January 2021
Date of schedule/trial	January 2024
1. BEREAVEMENT DAMAGES	**£15,120**
2. FUNERAL EXPENSES	**£1,390**

3. PAST LOSSES FROM DATE OF DEATH TO DATE OF SCHEDULE/TRIAL

A. Past loss of earnings

Net pre-accident wage £20,000 pa

Reduction for deceased's own needs: 25% so multiplicand = £15,000

1 January 2020 to 1 January 2023 (3 years)   3 x £15,000 = £45,000

B. Other services to family (eg, gardening, housework, DIY)

3 × £750 = £2,250

TOTAL PAST LOSS OF DEPENDENCY	**£47,250**

4. FUTURE LOSSES

A. Future loss of dependency – earnings

Multiplicand = £15,000

Multiplier based on Tariq Ahmed retiring at 65 = 32.33

£15,000 x 32.33 = **£484,950**

B. Future non-financial dependency – gardening, DIY etc

Multiplicand = £750

Multiplier of 56.05

£750 x 56.05 = **£42,037.50**

TOTAL FUTURE LOSS OF DEPENDENCY	**£562,987.50**

SUMMARY

Past (ie pre-trial) losses	£47,250
Future losses	£562,987.50
Bereavement damages	£15,120
Funeral expenses	£1,390
TOTAL	**£626,747.50**

In addition, interest is claimed on the pre-trial loss to the date of trial at half the short-term rate, and on bereavement damages and funeral expenses at the full short-term investment account rate.

The significant factors in the calculation are as follows:

(a)   The length of loss of earnings dependency is likely to be based on the age Tariq would have been at date of trial (33) and his retirement age of 65. This is likely to produce a multiplier of 32.33 using table 9 of the Ogden Tables assuming a rate of return of –0.25% (see **Appendix 6**).

(b)   There is a separate multiplicand based on the value of the services. The length of this dependency would be longer than the earnings dependency, on the assumption that Tariq would have continued to provide these services throughout his lifetime Using table 1 of the Ogden Tables this produces a multiplier of 56.05 assuming a rate of return of –0.25%.

(c)   In practice, the multiplier in respect of the loss of earnings is likely to be further reduced to take account of contingencies other than mortality (see **Chapter 15** and **Appendix 6**).

(d)   Losses in the period between death and trial are treated as special damages and will attract interest. In practice some discount may be made from these past losses to allow for the risk that Tariq may have died anyway in the 3 years between his death and trial.

(e)   The calculation may be split into various sub-calculations to reflect, for example, that for the first nine years after the accident (but for his death) Tariq would have been supporting a wife and children (therefore he might have been expected to spend one-quarter of his net earnings on his own maintenance), but for the remaining 26 years of his working life (after the children became independent) he would have been supporting only a wife (and therefore he might be expected to spend one-third of his net earnings on his own maintenance). Another reason for splitting the calculation may be to reflect any increased earnings because of promotion.

The above example is a simplified calculation to illustrate the general principles of quantifying a claim. In *Knauer*, the method of calculation set out in the explanatory notes to the Ogden tables in respect of fatal claims was endorsed. That method is more complex than the simplified calculation set out above. Such a complex calculation is beyond the scope of this book, and reference should be made to the Ogden tables in practice.

It will be appreciated that, in practice, it will be rare that a person's working and family life can be predicted with such certainty. It should also be remembered that different multipliers must be applied to items that would not have ceased at retirement age. Detailed instructions need to be obtained from the client on this point. In practice, therefore, the facts of a particular case are usually such as to defy precise mathematical calculation. The assessment of dependency damages is a difficult matter, and the court has to anticipate what would have occurred in the future. To assist the court, as much evidence as possible should be obtained. In more complex cases, the use of an actuary to assist in the calculation should also be considered.

18.5.3   Apportionment of the dependency

Whenever there is more than one dependant under the FAA 1976, the court must apportion the damages between them (s 3(1) and (2)). Where a claim is made by a surviving spouse and child, the court's approach is often to assess the claim for dependency of the surviving spouse alone, and then to apportion a small amount ('pocket money') to the child. This approach may be justified on the basis that:

(a)   the surviving spouse will be expected to provide for the child out of their damages;

(b)   compared to the surviving spouse, the period of dependency of the child will often be short (ending probably between the ages of 16 to 21 depending on whether the child is expected to go on to higher education); and

(c)   it avoids repeated applications to the court for the release of invested funds for the benefit of the child.

However, the court is keen to protect the child's interest, and this approach may not be followed in every case. For example, if the surviving spouse is a known spendthrift and cannot be trusted to provide for the child, the court may assess the claims of the surviving spouse and child separately (see *H (A Child) v S (Damages)* [2002] EWCA Civ 792, [2003] QB 965, concerning the protection of any damages for child dependants).

Where the claim involves a minor dependant (or any other protected party), the court's approval of any settlement should be sought, as it will be necessary to satisfy the court that the child's interests are protected.

18.5.4 Bereavement

18.5.4.1 The claimants

The claim for bereavement was until recently open only to the following limited class (not just 'dependants' generally: see **18.5.1.1**). The possible claimants were:

(a)   the spouse or civil partner of the deceased; or

(b)   the parents of a legitimate unmarried deceased minor;

(c)   the mother of an illegitimate unmarried deceased minor.

A cohabitee was excluded from the definition, despite the fact that a cohabitee could pursue a dependency claim, as stated above. However, in *Smith v Lancashire Teaching Hospitals NHS Foundation Trust* [2017] EWCA Civ 1916, the Court of Appeal held that this was incompatible with Article 14 of the European Convention on Human Rights (protection from discrimination) when read with Article 8. It held that what was material was:

> the intimacy of a stable and long term personal relationship, whose fracture due to death caused by another's tortious conduct will give rise to grief which ought to be recognised by an award of bereavement damages, and which is equally and analogously present in relationships involving married couples and civil partners and unmarried and unpartnered cohabitees.

Following the declaration of incompatibility in *Smith*, the Fatal Accidents Act 1976 (Remedial) Order 2020 (SI 2020/1023) amended s 1A of the Fatal Accidents Act 1976 to provide that a cohabiting partner may be eligible for bereavement damages, in addition to the wife, husband or civil partner of the deceased (or, in the case of a minor who has never married or been a civil partner, the parents of the deceased). This came into force on 6 October 2020. Section 1A(4) of the Act provides that, where more than one person is entitled to an award of bereavement damages, the award must be shared equally between them.

A child is not entitled to the award of bereavement on the death of his parent; and in a case where both parents can claim (and no-one else on the facts of the case), the damages are divided equally between them (FAA 1976, s 1A(4)). However, in *Navaei v Navaei*, 6 January 1995, the mother was negligent, and this resulted in the death of her daughter. The father claimed all of the bereavement damages and stated that they should not be shared with the mother. He argued that if he were to be paid only half of the damages, the mother/tortfeasor would be benefiting contrary to public policy. The court held that in bringing a claim under the FAA 1976, a claimant is under a duty to act on behalf of all dependants and the father was allowed only half the damages.

In the case of *Griffiths and Others v British Coal Corporation* (QBD, 23 February 1998), it was held that the FAA 1976 did not require an apportionment of damages for bereavement where there were two causes of death (in this case, smoking and exposure to mine dust), and therefore the claimant recovered the full statutory sum.

The claim for the bereavement award by parents depends on the deceased being a minor at the date of death, not at the date of the accident (*Doleman v Deakin* (1990) *The Times*, 30 January).

18.5.4.2 The amount of the bereavement award

The award is a statutory fixed amount of £15,120. Many people have criticised the level of award. In certain cases, especially those with a media interest, defendants have offered a figure higher than the statutory minimum, so as to avoid allegations by the press that they have undervalued a life. Once entitlement is established, defendants are often amenable to paying this part of the claim early by way of an interim payment.

18.5.5 Funeral expenses

Funeral expenses may be claimed if reasonable and paid by a dependant (FAA 1976, s 3(5)). The question of reasonableness will be a decision on the facts of each case. Reference should be made to previous case law in circumstances where the client puts forward an unusual claim, so as to determine whether the court will regard the claim as reasonable or otherwise.

If the funeral expenses are paid by the estate then they are claimed as part of a LR(MP)A 1934 claim (see **18.4.3**). Clearly, funeral expenses cannot be claimed under both the LR(MP)A 1934 and the FAA 1976.

18.5.6 Disregarding benefits

Section 4 of the FAA 1976 provides:

> In assessing damages in respect of a person's death in an action under this Act, benefits which have accrued or will or may accrue to any person from his estate or otherwise as a result of his death shall be disregarded.

For example, if a dependant receives insurance money as a result of the deceased's death, the dependant does not have to give credit for that money against the FAA 1976 damages. Similarly, if damages awarded to the estate under a LR(MP)A 1934 claim end up in the hands of a dependant by reason of the deceased's will or rules of intestacy, those damages do not necessarily reduce any FAA 1976 damages which may be awarded to that dependant.

See also H (A Child) v S (Damages) [2002] EWCA Civ 792, [2003] QB 965, concerning support now being given by a surviving parent who was unlikely to have supported the children if the death had not occurred.

18.5.7 Recoupment and offsetting of benefits

Any payment made in consequence of a claim under the FAA 1976 is not subject to recoupment under the Social Security (Recovery of Benefits) Act 1997 (see **Chapter 16**).

18.6 INTEREST

Interest on the bereavement damages may be awarded at the full short-term investment rate (*Sharman v Sheppard* [1989] 3 WLUK 121) from the date of death. Interest on funeral expenses is usually awarded at the full rate from the date that they were paid.

The remaining pecuniary losses to the date of the trial are treated as special damages in a fatal injury claim, and therefore are often awarded interest at half the short-term investment rate, although it is arguable that interest can be awarded at the full rate in certain circumstances (see **15.6**). Future pecuniary loss attracts no interest.

18.7 PENSION LOSS

Investigations should be made as to whether there will be a reduced pension fund available to the deceased's dependants due to the early death, and this should be included within the claim if appropriate (see also **15.3.6**). It is likely that an expert accountant will need to be instructed to assist in the calculation of such losses.

18.8 LOSS OF CONSORTIUM

In recent years, there has been a growing trend for separate awards under this head of damages, which is also sometimes referred to as 'loss of intangible benefits'.

It originated in a parent and child context in *Regan v Williamson* [1976] 1 WLR 305, where the sum awarded to the children for loss of services of a mother was increased to reflect the loss of the personal attention and affection which the mother provided and which could not be replaced by a housekeeper or nanny. In *Mehmet v Perry* [1977] 2 All ER 529, separate awards under this head were made to the children and also to the husband.

In *Beesley v New Century Group Ltd* [2008] EWHC 3033 (QB), the principle was extended to loss of a husband, on the basis that Mrs Beesley had lost not only the domestic services that her husband had provided but also the extra value that was derived from having such help provided by a husband and friend rather than an outside contractor.

The sums awarded tend to be fairly modest (between £2,000 and £5,000, depending on the circumstances), on the basis that there is some overlap between this head and bereavement damages (see **18.5.4**), and in the more recent case of *Mosson v Spousal* (see **18.4.3**) the judge refused to make such an award on the basis that it was a claim for 'the sort which bereavement damages were intended to cover'. In *Brown v Hamid* [2013] EWHC 4067 (QB), the judge declined to make a separate award for loss of consortium where the deceased had a limited life expectancy. Nevertheless, the principle of making awards for loss of intangible benefits is now well-established, and consideration should always be given to including such a claim in a fatal case.

18.9 CONDUCT

To avoid conflicts of interest arising, it is good practice to ensure that none of the dependants who could be to blame in whole or part for the accident that resulted in the death are appointed as personal representatives.

The conduct of a fatal accident claim clearly requires sympathy and diplomacy on the part of the solicitor. There are frequently conflicts of personality between the dependants and personal representatives, and this is compounded by the fact that only one claim can be brought in respect of the fatal accident. If, after the fatal accident, it comes to light that the deceased had more than one dependent family, it can be anticipated that any interviews with the deceased's wife may be difficult.

18.10 CONCLUSION

Acting on behalf of the relatives in a fatal accident claim requires the personal injury/clinical negligence solicitor to have tact, sympathy and a detailed understanding of the law involved. It should be appreciated that each case will be dealt with on its own facts, and only broad principles have been established by the case law in this area. In fatal accident cases the court is required to anticipate what would have occurred in the future, which will be different in every case. An overview of damages which may be claimed in fatal cases is set out at **18.12** below.

18.11 FURTHER READING

Kemp and Kemp, *The Quantum of Damages* (Sweet & Maxwell)

18.12 OVERVIEW OF DAMAGES IN FATAL CLAIMS

THE ESTATE
↓
LR(MP)A 1934
↓

If there was a period of survival

Pain, suffering and loss of amenity
- *Was the deceased conscious?*

Loss of income
- *Up to date of death*

Services/care provided
- *Up to date of death*

Damages to personal items
- *Eg car, clothing, jewellery*

Funeral expenses
- *If not claimed under the FAA*

THE DEPENDANTS
↓
FAA 1976
↓

Bereavement
- *£15,120*
- *Spouse/parent/cohabitee?*

Dependency
- *Who are the dependants?*
- *Nature of dependency, eg wages/diy/childcare*

Multiplicand
- *Husband & wife or civil partner $^2/_3$*
- *Husband & wife or civil partner & children $^3/_4$*

Multiplier
- *Assess at date of trial*
- *Split between pre- and post-trial*

Funeral expenses
- *If not claimed under the LR(MP)A*

Loss of consortium/intangible benefits
- *Loss of wife/mother/civil partner/ husband/father*
- *No set figure (£2,000–£5,000 approx)*

CRIMINAL INJURIES COMPENSATION AUTHORITY

LEARNING OUTCOMES

After reading this chapter you will be able to:

- set out the criteria for eligibility to make a claim under the Criminal Injuries Compensation Scheme 2012, and the relevant procedure
- explain how compensation is calculated
- explain when compensation may be withheld or reduced.

19.1 INTRODUCTION

Those who have suffered injury as a result of acts of violence may be unable to take civil proceedings to recover damages, because those responsible are either unknown or have insufficient means to pay compensation. However, blameless victims of crimes of violence in Great Britain who have suffered injuries and associated loss can apply for compensation from a government-funded scheme known as the Criminal Injuries Compensation Scheme 2012, as amended by the Criminal Injuries Compensation Scheme 2012 (Amendment) Instrument 2019 (the 'Scheme'), which is administered by the Criminal Injuries Compensation Authority (CICA). The Scheme is relevant for applications received on or after 27 November 2012.

The Criminal Injuries Compensation Scheme 2012 (Amendment) Instrument 2019 amended the Scheme as from 13 June 2019, by removing the pre-1979 'same roof' rule that could previously be found at para 19 of the Scheme. As a result of this amendment, the Scheme no longer contains a paragraph 19. This change followed the Court of Appeal's ruling in *JT v First-tier Tribunal* [2018] EWCA Civ 1735. The appellant, who was born in 1963, had been sexually assaulted and raped by her step-father in her family home. The abuse started in the 1960s when JT was around five years old, and continued until 1979. She applied for compensation under the Scheme. Her application was refused on the basis of the 'same roof' rule, which existed prior to the Scheme being amended in 2019. This rule stated that an award would not be made in respect of a criminal injury sustained before 1 October 1979 'if, at the time of the incident giving rise to that injury, the applicant and the assailant were living together as members of the same family'. All of the offences committed against JT took place before 1 October 1979. The Court of Appeal found that compensation under the Scheme was a proprietary interest falling within ECHR Article 1 of the First Protocol (and therefore within the ambit of the Human Rights Act 1998) and that the distinction between family and non-family members was discriminatory.

The earlier 2008 scheme was also amended by removing the 'same roof' rule from that earlier statutory scheme.

The types of payment which may be available under the Scheme are:

(a)   injury payments, which are calculated by reference to a tariff (see **19.4.1**);

(b)   loss of earnings payments (see **19.4.2**);

(c)   special expenses payments in respect of injury-related requirements which are not available free of charge from any other source (see **19.4.3**); and

(d)   various payments relating to fatal injuries, which are beyond the scope of this book.

The maximum award payable in relation to one incident, before any reduction (see **19.5**), is £500,000 (para 31), which may fall short of the actual losses suffered by the applicant. However, the Scheme is not designed to provide full financial recompense, but rather to provide some compensation, where there would not otherwise be any, out of the public purse and in recognition of public sympathy for the victim. It is for this reason that the victim must be 'blameless' (see **19.5** below).

The Scheme is both comprehensive and complex and consequently only the basics are dealt with here. For more information, you can find the Scheme, the 2008 Scheme (relevant for applications received prior to 27 November 2012), the application forms and the Guide to the 2012 Compensation Scheme as amended (the 'Guide') at www.gov.uk/government/publications/criminal-injuries-compensation-scheme-2012.

It should be noted that CICA will not cover the costs of making an application under the Scheme and therefore the client will need to fund the matter themselves should the client want a solicitor to deal with the application on their behalf. The client should be advised that free independent advice and help to make the application may be available from Victim Support, Citizens Advice, law centres or welfare rights organisations.

19.2   ELIGIBILITY

In order to be eligible for compensation under the Scheme, an applicant must show that they have sustained a criminal injury which is directly attributable to them being a direct victim of a crime of violence committed in a 'relevant place' (para 4). In the vast majority of cases, and for the purposes of this book, 'relevant place' means Great Britain (para 8), but it also covers, for example, British-controlled aircraft and Her Majesty's ships (see Annex C of the Scheme).

Compensation may also be paid to those who have sustained an injury while taking an exceptional and justified risk in order to remedy or prevent a crime (para 5), to those who have sustained a mental injury as a result of witnessing or being involved in the immediate aftermath of an incident in which a loved one is injured (para 6), or to a qualifying relative of a victim who died as a result of a crime of violence (para 7), but these matters are beyond the scope of this book.

19.2.1   What is a crime of violence?

There is no legal definition of what amounts to a 'crime of violence', but types of crimes of violence which may lead to a payment are set out in Annex B of the Scheme. The following are included, provided the perpetrator acts intentionally or recklessly:

(a)   a physical attack;

(b)   any other act or omission of a violent nature which causes physical injury to a person, eg withholding something that another person needs to stay alive;

(c)   a threat against a person, causing fear of immediate violence in circumstances which would cause a person of reasonable firmness to be put in such fear;

(d)   a sexual assault to which a person did not in fact consent; or

(e)   arson or fire-raising.

However, a crime of violence will not be considered to have been committed for the purposes of the Scheme if an injury:

(a)   resulted from suicide or attempted suicide, unless the suicidal person acted with intent to cause injury to another person;

(b)   resulted from the use of a vehicle, unless the vehicle was used with intent to cause injury to a person (see *Alexander Smith v Criminal Injuries Compensation Authority* (2015), where a man struck by a cyclist on a zebra crossing succeeded in his claim, as the cyclist had ridden his bicycle at him with the intent to injure him);

(c)   resulted from an animal attack, unless the animal was used with intent to cause injury to a person;

(d)   was sustained in the usual course of sporting or other activity to which a person consented by taking part in the activity; or

(e)   was sustained *in utero* as a result of harmful substances willingly ingested by the mother during pregnancy, with intent to cause, or being reckless as to, injury to the foetus.

19.2.2   Residency and nationality

The applicant must meet one of the following residency requirements (paras 10–13):

(a)   ordinarily resident in the UK on the date of the incident;

(b)   a British citizen;

(c)   a close relative of a British citizen;

(d)   a national of a Member State of the European Union (EU) or the European Economic Area (EEA);

(e)   a family member of an EU/EEA national who has the right to be in the UK;

(f)   a national of a State party to the Council of Europe Convention on the Compensation of Victims of Violent Crimes (CETS No 116, 1983);

(g)   a member of Her Majesty's armed forces, or an accompanying close relative of an armed forces member;

(h)   someone identified as a potential victim of human trafficking on or before the date of the application; or

(i)   someone who made an application for asylum to remain in the UK on or before the date of the application for an award.

19.2.3   Matters which may prevent eligibility

It is not necessary for the assailant to have been convicted of an offence in connection with the injury (para 9), and in some cases, the applicant will not know the identity of the offender. However, the following matters will prevent eligibility being established (in relation to incidents happening on or after 1 August 1964 only):

(a)   subject to para 18A (which was inserted as a result of the 2019 amending instrument), an award will not be made to a person who has previously made an application for compensation in respect of the same criminal injury under the Scheme or any other Criminal Injuries Compensation Scheme, irrespective of whether or how that application was finally disposed of (para 18). Following *JT v First-tier Tribunal* (mentioned above), para 18A was inserted into the Scheme to qualify para 18. Paragraph 18A provides that a person who previously made an application under the Scheme or a prior scheme may make a further application in the following circumstances:

(i)   if the injury was sustained on or after 1 August 1964 but before 1 October 1979 ('the relevant period') and an award was withheld in respect of that injury on the basis of the 'same roof' rule;

(ii)   where the injury itself was sustained on or after 1 October 1979 but the incident giving rise to it occurred over a period which began during and ended after the relevant period, and where the award was reduced wholly or partly on the basis of the 'same roof' rule.

(b)   the applicant and the person who caused the injury were adults living together as members of the same family at the time and will continue to do so (para 20); or

(c)   the person who injured the applicant could benefit from the award as a result of a continuing link between that person and the applicant (para 21).

19.2.4   Time limit

Subject to paras 88 and 88A, applications should be made as soon as reasonably practicable and, where the applicant was aged 18 or over at the date of the incident causing the injury, it must be made within two years of the date of the incident (para 87).

Where the applicant was under 18 at the time of the incident, it is advisable that an application is made on their behalf as soon as possible, as it may be more difficult to provide the relevant evidence at a later stage. However, the following time limits apply:

(a)   if the incident was reported to the police before the applicant turned 18, but no application was made on the applicant's behalf, the claim must be made within the period ending on the applicant's 20th birthday; or

(b)   in the case of an incident reported to the police on or after the applicant's 18th birthday, the claim must be made within two years after the date when the incident was first reported to the police.

In both of the above instances, an application will not be accepted unless the claims officer is satisfied that the evidence presented in support of the application means that it can be determined without further extensive enquiries (para 88). The time limits under para 88 do not apply to applicants to whom para 88A applies.

Paragraph 88A of the Scheme makes amendments in respect of time limits to cover applicants either falling within para 18A (amendment following *JT v First-tier Tribunal* to allow those refused or who had their award reduced on the basis of the 'same roof' rule to re-apply to CICA) or who did not make an application before the 2019 amendment date at all because of the 'same roof' rule. The time limit is amended to two years beginning with the day after the 2019 amendment date (13 June 2019) in respect of such applicants; alternatively, two years from the date of the first report to the police if the applicant was a child at the time of the incident and could not have made an application under the Scheme within the time limit (para 88A).

In relation to applicants of any age, in exceptional circumstances, ie where the circumstances of the injury meant that the application could not reasonably have been made within the time limit, CICA may extend the time limit provided it can make a decision without further extensive enquiries (para 89). It does not normally consider the applicant's lack of knowledge of the Scheme to be an 'exceptional reason'.

19.3   PROCEDURE

Applications must be made by filling in CICA's application form and submitting it online or by supplying the relevant details over the telephone. Initially, a regional casework team will handle the application but, once CICA has all the relevant evidence, a claims officer will be assigned to the claim, who will determine the matter on the balance of probabilities.

At all times, the applicant must comply with the obligations set out in paras 91 and 92 of the Scheme. In other words, the applicant must comply with any direction or condition imposed by the claims officer, assist the claims officer as far as reasonably practicable, and provide all information and evidence relevant to the application.

The onus is on the applicant to prove that they are eligible for a payment, and therefore evidence that the applicant meets the residency requirements, and basic medical evidence of the injury suffered, must be provided. The applicant must also provide signed consent for the release of all records relevant to the application to CICA. These might include:

(a) evidence the applicant gave to the police about the incident. The applicant must supply the unique police reference number in the application form. CICA will obtain confirmation from the police that the incident was reported to them and that the applicant's behaviour was not a contributory factor;

(b) criminal records;

(c) medical records; and

(d) where loss of earnings and/or special expenses payments are being claimed, information from the Department for Work and Pensions and/or HM Revenue and Customs.

CICA may require further medical evidence, in which case the applicant will be required to meet the costs of providing initial medical evidence up to maximum of £50. If further medical evidence is required, such as where injuries are complex, the application involves a claim for mental illness, or where there may be pre-existing conditions, the applicant will be required to see their existing doctor or an expert arranged by CICA, and the costs of this will be met by CICA. If the applicant wishes to provide their own medical evidence, CICA will cover the cost only if it relies on the evidence to determine the claim.

19.4 COMPENSATION CALCULATION

Compensation is based on a tariff award for the injuries suffered and, where relevant, compensation for lost earnings and/or special expenses. The minimum award that may be made is £1,000 (para 32) and the maximum award that may be made in respect of one application is £500,000, before any deductions (para 31).

Where injuries are not sufficiently serious to fall under the Scheme, the Hardship Fund introduced by the Government may provide some temporary assistance to very low-paid workers suffering financial hardship as a result of being unable to work due to being a victim of violent crime.

19.4.1 The injury payment (paras 32–41)

In order to determine whether compensation is payable for a certain injury and to calculate the amount due, the claims officer will consult the Tariff of Injuries set out in Annex E of the Scheme. This list sets out descriptions of approximately 400 different types of injuries and, in relation to each one, specifies both the level of seriousness – by means of a figure from 1 (being the least serious) to 20 – and the associated fixed amount of compensation. A Level 1 injury is valued at £1,000 and a Level 20 injury is valued at £250,000. Annex E, Part A of the tariff shows the amount payable in respect of physical and mental injuries. (Part B, which shows the amount payable in respect of fatal injuries, and injuries resulting from sexual and physical abuse, is beyond the scope of this book.)

The following should be noted:

(a) Compensation is not payable under the Scheme unless the injury appears in Annex E, although where an injury does not appear in the list, but is of an equivalent seriousness to an injury which does appear, CICA may refer the matter to the Secretary of State for consideration for inclusion.

(b) Where an applicant is eligible for an injury payment in respect of an injury requiring an operation, no separate payment will be made in respect of scarring arising from that operation (para 35).

(c)   Where an applicant's injury includes the acceleration or exacerbation of an existing condition, the payment will only compensate for the degree of acceleration or exacerbation, will be calculated by reference to such tariff injuries as the claims officer considers appropriate, and will not be paid at all unless the relevant payment is £1,000 or more (para 36).

In order to calculate the total tariff award where there are two or more injuries, the three most serious injuries must be identified and the associated tariffs added together as follows:

(a)   100% of the tariff for the highest rated injury; plus

(b)   30% of the tariff for the second highest injury; plus, where relevant

(c)   15% of the tariff for the third highest injury.

No compensation is payable in respect of any additional injuries (para 37).

19.4.2   Compensation for lost earnings (paras 42–49)

Where an applicant is entitled to a tariff payment and has been unable to work or may be prevented from working in the future as a direct result of the injury, they may also be entitled to be compensated for lost earnings provided they satisfy the following conditions (para 43):

(a)   The applicant must be unable to do any paid work or have a very limited capacity to do such work, ie can work only a few hours of paid work per week. Where the applicant has capacity to do paid work, but the type of work the applicant is able to do is limited as a result of their injuries, a loss of earnings payment will not be made.

(b)   The applicant must be able to demonstrate that they were in work at the time of the incident giving rise to the injury, or show that they had either an established work history, or a good reason for not having such a work history, for the three years immediately prior to the accident. A good reason under the Scheme would be that that applicant was in full-time education, or that the applicant was unable to work due to their age or caring responsibilities.

Payments for loss of earnings are made at a fixed weekly rate, which is the rate of Statutory Sick Pay (SSP) in force at the date when a decision is made regarding the application (£109.40 from 6 April 2023). No such compensation is payable for the first 28 weeks following the date of the accident, and therefore the period to which a loss of earnings payment will relate begins on the first day of the 29th week (para 44).

A loss of earnings payment may relate to earnings lost before an application is determined (past loss of earnings) and any losses which may continue after the determination (future loss of earnings).

A loss of earnings payment in respect of past loss of earnings will be calculated by multiplying the weekly rate of SSP at the date of determination by the number of weeks from the beginning of week 29, treating part weeks as full weeks, and ending on the day the application is determined (para 47).

Payment for future loss of earnings will be calculated by:

(a)   multiplying the weekly rate of SSP at the date of determination by the number of weeks of the period of entitlement. That period begins on the day after the date on which the application is determined and ends when the applicant is no longer incapable of working, or when the applicant reaches retirement age or, where the criminal injury has resulted in a life expectancy below the state pension age, the expected end of the applicant's life (para 48);

(b)   discounting the payment so calculated in accordance with the Tables in Annex F, which set out:

(i)   multipliers to be applied to account for the accelerated receipt of payments, which are found by reference to the number of years of future loss (Table A);

(ii)   discount factors to be applied to a lump sum in respect of loss which starts at a future date, which are also found by reference to the number of years of future loss (Table B); and

(iii)   assumptions in relation to life expectancy, which are calculated by reference to the applicant's age at the date of determination (or death in the case of fatality) (Table C).

19.4.3   Compensation for special expenses (paras 50–56)

Compensation may be paid for special expenses incurred as a result of the injury from the date of the injury, but only where the applicant is eligible for an injury payment and has lost earnings or earnings capacity for longer than 28 weeks.

A special expenses payment will only be made in relation to expenses of the types listed in para 52, such as the applicant's own property or equipment used as a physical aid which was damaged in the incident, NHS prescriptions and dentists or optician's charges, special equipment such as wheelchairs or specially-adapted vehicles, the costs of adaptations to the applicant's home, and costs arising from the administration of the applicant's affairs due to the applicant's lack of mental capacity, provided the following conditions apply (para 51):

(a)   they were/will be necessarily incurred by the applicant on or after the date of the injury as a direct result of the criminal injury giving rise to the injury payment;

(b)   provision, or similar provision, is not available free of charge from another source; and

(c)   the cost is reasonable.

Where the need for special equipment is likely to continue, a claims officer will:

(a)   assess the cost of replacement, taking into account the number of likely replacements;

(b)   deduct the amount for which the applicant's existing equipment could be sold on each occasion; and

(c)   apply an appropriate discount factor in accordance with Table B of Annex F to take account of the fact that a lump sum will be paid in respect of loss which will arise in the future.

Where the need for any other special expenses of a type specified in para 52 is likely to continue, a claims officer will assess the annual cost of the expense and apply the relevant Tables in Annex F (para 53).

A special expenses payment may be withheld or reduced to take account of the receipt of, or entitlement to, social security benefits or insurance payments (paras 54–56), the details of which are beyond the scope of this book.

19.5   WITHHOLDING OR REDUCTION OF AWARD

The Scheme is funded by the Government on the basis that the public are sympathetic to innocent victims of crime and wish to see them supported. Consequently, compensation may be refused or discounted in respect of applications by those who may be seen as morally undeserving of support. In addition, the Scheme must be protected from fraudulent claims and applicants should not be permitted to be over-compensated.

Compensation may be withheld or reduced in the following circumstances:

(a)   where the applicant has failed to report the incident to the police, or has thereafter failed to co-operate with the police or with the CICA (paras 22–24). Generally, the applicant must make a formal report to the police immediately following the incident, and this must be done by the applicant in person, unless the injuries sustained prevent the applicant from doing so. Co-operation with the police includes making a statement, attending identity procedures and giving evidence in court, if required. Co-operation with the CICA includes supplying complete and truthful information, and attending independent medical examinations, if required;

(b)   where the applicant behaved inappropriately either before, or during or after the incident (para 25). This will include where the applicant's consumption of alcohol or illegal drugs caused the applicant to act aggressively or to provoke the attack, where the applicant voluntarily took part in a fight, where the applicant threw the first punch, or where the applicant's use of abusive language or gestures led to the incident. However, this does not include where intoxication through alcohol or drugs made the applicant more vulnerable to becoming a victim of a crime of violence. So, for example, an applicant who was sexually assaulted whilst intoxicated may still be eligible to receive a full award;

(c)   where the applicant has unspent criminal convictions (para 26). Annex D sets out how CICA will determine what effect an unspent criminal conviction will have in respect of the withdrawal or reduction of an award. However, in general terms, an unspent conviction which attracted a custodial or community sentence will result in the withdrawal of the award, whilst a lesser sentence (other than endorsements, penalty points or fines resulting from motoring offences) will result in a reduction in the amount of the award;

(d)   where the applicant's character, other than in relation to an unspent conviction, makes it appropriate to reduce or withhold an award (para 27). CICA will consider evidence relating to involvement with illegal drugs or other crimes, tax evasion or benefit fraud, anti-social behaviour orders and cautions or reprimands;

(e)   where the applicant receives or is awarded criminal injuries compensation or a similar payment, receives an order for damages from a civil court, agrees the settlement of a damages claim, or receives a compensation order or offer made during criminal proceedings (para 85); or

(f)   in relation to payments for special expenses only, where the applicant has received State benefits or insurance payments in respect of the injury (paras 54–56 – see **19.4.3**).

19.6   EXAMPLE

On 10 April 2023, Jacob was attacked in Birmingham city centre as he made his way home from work. He was punched to the ground and kicked repeatedly by assailants who have not been identified. He suffered a depressed fracture of the skull, for which he required surgery, his jaw was dislocated and a front tooth was knocked out. The tooth has been replaced, but his other injuries are continuing to cause him significant difficulties. In addition, he has completely lost his sense of smell. Jacob was unable to work for 40 weeks, but he has now returned to his previous job as a shop assistant. His salary throughout the period when he was unable to work would have been £250 per week, but Jacob received only statutory sick pay of £109.40 per week during this period.

Tariff for injuries: depressed fracture of skull requiring operation = £4,600 (Level A6); dislocated jaw causing continuing significant disability = £3,500 (Level A5); loss of one front tooth = £1,500 (Level A2); total loss of smell = £11,000 (Level A8). Only the three most serious injuries may be considered.

Calculation: 100% of £11,000 (loss of smell) = £11,000; 30% of £4,600 (fractured skull) = £1,380; 15% of £3,500 (dislocated jaw) = £525.

Total for injury = £12,905.

Lost salary: Nothing for first 28 weeks. Thereafter, 12 weeks at the SSP rate of £109.40 per week = £1,312.80. The SSP he has already received is not deductible.

Total payment: £12,905 + £1,312.80 = £14,217.80.

19.7 CONCLUSION

Generally, those who have suffered injury as a result of an act of violence are unable to take civil proceedings against the perpetrator as their attacker is unlikely to have the financial means to pay damages. Where such a situation exists, and it is not possible to hold another individual or body, such as an employer, responsible for the perpetrator's actions, the Criminal Injuries Compensation Scheme may provide compensation to the victim.

As the costs associated with making an application are not recoverable by the applicant, the solicitor should advise the applicant that free assistance may be available elsewhere. However, if the client instructs the solicitor to make the application on the client's behalf, the solicitor should ensure that the client falls within the criteria set out in the Scheme rules and that the procedure for making a claim is followed correctly.

Compensation for injuries suffered is based on a tariff which sets out a comprehensive list of injuries of varying seriousness. Where such an award is made and the victim is unable to work for more than 28 weeks, past and future loss of earnings from the 29th week may also be awarded, as may items of special expense. The total claim cannot exceed £500,000.

Awards may be withheld or reduced as a result of the applicant's conduct before, during or after the incident.

19.8 FURTHER READING AND RELEVANT WEBSITES

Criminal Injuries Compensation Scheme 2012 as amended and A Guide to the Criminal Injuries Compensation Scheme 2012 (Criminal Injuries Compensation Authority)

www.gov.uk/government/publications/criminal-injuries-compensation-scheme-2012

www.gov.uk/guidance/criminal-injuries-compensation-a-guide

CHAPTER 20

CLAIMS ON BEHALF OF CHILDREN AND PROTECTED PARTIES

> **LEARNING OUTCOMES**
>
> After reading this chapter you will be able to:
>
> - identify a child and a protected party
> - understand who might act as a litigation friend, what their duties are, how they are appointed and when their appointment ceases
> - appreciate the court's role in sanctioning settlements involving children and protected parties
> - set out how the money recovered on behalf of a child or protected party will be dealt with.

20.1 INTRODUCTION

The Civil Procedure Rules (CPR), Part 21 and PD 21 set out special provisions relating to proceedings brought or defended by children and protected parties, ie those who lack the mental capacity to conduct proceedings on their own behalf. Many of these provisions apply equally to children and protected parties, for example:

(a) proceedings will usually be conducted on behalf of the child or protected party by a litigation friend (see **20.3**);

(b) the court must approve any settlement of a claim made on behalf of a child or protected party (see **20.4**); and

(c) the court will direct how damages recovered on behalf of a child or protected party will be dealt with (see **20.5**).

20.1.1 Who is a child/protected party?

A child is a person who is not yet 18 years old.

A protected party is a person who lacks capacity, within the meaning of the Mental Capacity Act 2005, to conduct proceedings. In accordance with s 2 of the 2005 Act, a person lacks capacity in relation to a matter if at the material time the person is unable to make a decision for themselves in relation to the matter because of an impairment of, or a disturbance in the functioning of, the mind or brain. It is irrelevant whether the impairment or disturbance is permanent or temporary and a person's age or appearance, or the person's condition or an aspect of their behaviour, which might lead others to make unjustified assumptions about the person's mental capacity, are not of themselves sufficient to establish incapacity.

The principles to be applied when dealing with questions of capacity are set out in s 1 of the 2005 Act as follows:

> (2)   A person must be assumed to have capacity unless it is established that he lacks capacity.
>
> (3)   A person is not to be treated as unable to make a decision unless all practicable steps to help him to do so have been taken without success.
>
> (4)   A person is not to be treated as unable to make a decision merely because he makes an unwise decision.
>
> (5)   An act done, or decision made, under this Act for or on behalf of a person who lacks capacity must be done, or made, in his best interests.
>
> (6)   Before the act is done, or the decision is made, regard must be had to whether the purpose for which it is needed can be as effectively achieved in a way that is less restrictive of the person's rights and freedom of action.

The case of *Dunhill (a protected party by her litigation friend Tasker) v Burgin* [2014] UKSC 18 illustrates how important it is for practitioners to consider whether a party to the proceedings might lack capacity to deal with them. The claimant was an adult woman who had been injured as a result of a road traffic accident, and the modest claim bought on her behalf was settled in the sum of £12,500. Although it was known that she had suffered brain damage, it appears that none of the legal advisers gave any thought as to whether or not she had the capacity to deal with the litigation. Consequently, a litigation friend was not appointed and the court was not asked to approve the settlement. Several years later (when it was realised that a more realistic valuation of the claim might exceed £2,000,000), the Court of Appeal determined that an application made on the claimant's behalf to set aside the settlement, on the grounds of her lack of capacity to manage her affairs at that time and the absence of court approval, should succeed. This decision was subsequently upheld by the Supreme Court.

20.2   LIMITATION

Under s 28(1) and 28(6) of the Limitation Act 1980, where a person under a disability (ie a child or an individual lacking mental capacity) has a cause of action, the three-year limitation period does not start to run until the person ceases to be under a disability.

For a child who is not also a protected party, this is when the person reaches their 18th birthday, which means that they have until their 21st birthday to commence proceedings.

For a protected party, provided the person was incapacitated at the time when the cause of action accrued, disability ceases if and when they regain mental capacity. Where mental incapacity arises after the limitation period has commenced, it will not prevent time from continuing to run. However, an application may be made under s 33 of the LA 1980 to disapply the limitation period (see **7.8**).

20.3   THE LITIGATION FRIEND

A protected party may not conduct proceedings without a litigation friend, and a child must have a litigation friend unless the court orders otherwise (CPR, r 21.2). The court will make an order permitting a child to conduct litigation without a litigation friend only where it is satisfied that the child has sufficient maturity and understanding to deal with the proceedings (*Gillick v West Norfolk & Wisbech Area Health Authority* [1985] UKHL 7).

20.3.1   Who may be the litigation friend?

In accordance with CPR, r 21.4, the following individuals may be a litigation friend:

(a)   in the case of a protected party, a deputy appointed by the Court of Protection under the Mental Capacity Act 2005 with power to conduct proceedings on the protected party's behalf;

(b)   in all other cases, someone who:

(i)   can fairly and competently conduct proceedings on behalf of the child or protected party,

(ii)   has no interests adverse to that of the child or protected party (eg, if a child is injured in a road traffic accident while a passenger in a car being driven by the child's father, the mother should act as litigation friend as the father may become a defendant in the proceedings), and

(iii)   where the child or protected party is a claimant, undertakes to pay any costs which the child or protected party may be ordered to pay in relation to the proceedings, subject to any right they may have to be repaid from the assets of the child or protected party.

This is the case whether the litigation friend is appointed without a court order or with a court order (see CPR, r 21.6(5)).

In the case of a child, the litigation friend will usually be a parent, although another suitable adult may act, for example a grandmother or other person. In the case of a protected party, where the claimant has made a lasting power of attorney, the person named in the power of attorney will usually act. Where there is no suitable person, the Court of Protection will appoint a deputy to act on behalf of the protected party. In circumstances where there is no one suitable and willing to act as the litigation friend, the Official Solicitor will so act subject to their costs being covered.

20.3.2   How is a litigation friend appointed?

Litigation friends are usually appointed without the need for a court order, although such an order will be required where a party to the proceedings other than the child or protected party applies for a litigation friend to be appointed. Consequently, the main reason for a court order is that proceedings have been commenced *against* a child or protected party and the fact that a suitable adult does not step forward to act as litigation friend obliges the claimant to apply for an order. An order will also be required where a litigation friend is to be substituted for an existing one.

In other cases, an order will not be required and a person who wishes to be appointed must follow the procedure set out in CPR, r 21.5 as follows:

(a)   A deputy appointed by the Court of Protection with power to conduct proceedings on a protected party's behalf must file an official copy of the order of the Court of Protection which confers the deputy's power to act.

(b)   Any other person must file a certificate of suitability in Form N235 stating that they satisfy the conditions specified in r 21.4(3). The certificate of suitability must also be served on every person on whom, in accordance with CPR, r 6.13 (service on a parent, guardian, etc), the claim form should be served. See CPR, r 21.5(3)(a) and (b).

This must be done at the time the claim is made if the litigation friend acts for a claimant, and at the time the litigation friend first takes a step in the proceedings if acting for a defendant.

Pursuant to CPR, r 21.5(4), the certificate of suitability must be verified by a statement of truth and must state, in accordance with the prescribed form, that the person:

(a)   agrees to act;

(b)   knows or believes that the claimant/defendant is a child or lacks capacity to conduct the proceedings;

(c)   meets the requirements of CPR, r 21.4(3).

20.3.3 When does the litigation friend's appointment cease?

In accordance with CPR, r 21.9, when a child who is not a protected party reaches the age of 18, the litigation friend's appointment ceases. Where a protected party regains capacity to deal with the proceedings themselves, the litigation friend's appointment continues until it is ended by court order.

Within 28 days after the cessation of the appointment, the child or protected party must serve on other parties and file at court a notice stating that the appointment of the litigation friend has ceased, giving their address for service, and stating whether or not the child or protected party intends to carry on the proceedings. If the child or protected party does not follow these requirements within 28 days after the day on which the appointment of the litigation friend ceases, the court may, on application, strike out the child or protected party's claim or defence.

Where litigation is continuing, the title of the proceedings should be amended in order to reflect the change in the claimant's circumstances, eg 'A B (formerly a child but now of full age)'.

20.4 COURT'S APPROVAL OF SETTLEMENTS

The majority of claims involving children, as with adults, relate to relatively minor injuries where there is a complete recovery after a relatively short period of time and no future losses. Many of these arise as a result of road traffic accidents and therefore fall under the Pre-Action Protocol for Low Value Personal Injury Claims in Road Traffic Accidents, and most of these claims settle without the need for proceedings to be issued.

Whatever the value of the claim, and whether proceedings have been commenced or not, where a claim is made on behalf of a child or a protected party, under CPR, r 21.10 no settlement, compromise or payment (including any voluntary interim payment) and no acceptance of money paid into court shall be valid without the court's approval. The provisions found in both the Pre-Action Protocols for Low Value Claims for payment to be made by the defendant within 10 days of a settlement being reached in Stage 2 (see **21.3.2**) do not apply in relation to children. The RTA Small Claims Protocol also does not apply to children and protected parties – see para 4.3 of that protocol. Approval is always necessary to ensure that the claim is not settled for less than it is worth, that the award is invested appropriately and, where there are future pecuniary losses, periodical payments are considered. Moreover, approval provides the defendant with a valid discharge from the claim. Without this, the child or protected party is not bound by the settlement and is at liberty to bring further proceedings against the defendant at some stage in the future.

20.4.1 Obtaining approval

20.4.1.1 Procedure where settlement is reached prior to issue

In accordance with CPR, r 21.10(2)(b), where an agreement is reached before proceedings have been commenced and the sole purpose is to obtain the court's approval of the settlement, the procedure set out in CPR, Part 8 must be used and the claim must include a request for the court's approval. CPR, r 21.10(3) sets out the supporting information and documentation which must be provided to the court, namely:

(a) a draft consent order setting out the proposed settlement terms. Generally, courts will expect to see the draft consent order in Form N292; although parties may propose their own terms, most judges will reject anything that is not in Form N292;

(b) details of whether and to what extent the defendant admits liability. Where considerations of liability are raised, information relating to any criminal proceedings or an inquest should be provided;

(c) the age and occupation (if any) of the child or protected party. An original birth certificate should be provided. Where funds are to be invested by the Court Funds

Office, the judge must certify on Form CFO 320 (see below) that they have seen the birth certificate;

(d)   the litigation friend's approval of the proposed settlement;

(e)   in larger claims, a copy of any financial advice relating to the proposed settlement;

(f)   a legal opinion on the merits of the settlement. CPR, r 21.10(3)(h) suggests that this can be dispensed with in 'very clear cases', but this does not equate to low value claims. Generally, courts will expect to see an opinion. This will usually be provided by counsel but, in very low value claims, an opinion provided by the claimant's solicitor may be acceptable. The opinion must refer to the appropriate sections of the Judicial College Guidelines for the Assessment of General Damages and relevant case law;

(g)   medical reports and, where appropriate, quantum reports and joint statements material to the opinion mentioned above;

(h)   where appropriate, a schedule of any past and future expenses and losses claimed and any other relevant information relating to the personal injury as set out in PD 16 (statements of case); and

(i)   where the settlement includes periodical payments, the information required by CPR, rr 41.8 and 41.9.

In addition, the claimant's solicitor must provide a Court Funds Office (CFO) Form CFO 320, which is a request for the investment of the damages, completed as far as it can be before the judge has made their decision, and signed by the litigation friend. Where the child or protected party has a building society account, ISA or similar, and the litigation friend proposes that the damages should be invested there rather than in a Court Funds Office account, evidence of the account should be provided. Many judges will allow small amounts to be paid directly to the litigation friend where the judge is satisfied that a suitable savings account exists and that the litigation friend can be trusted to act appropriately in the child's or protected party's best interests. (For further information relating to investment of damages recovered on behalf of children or protected parties, see **20.5**.)

20.4.1.2   Procedure where settlement is reached post-issue

Where settlement is reached after proceedings have been commenced, an application for approval of the settlement should be made in accordance with the procedure set out in CPR, Part 23. Where proceedings had been commenced in the County Court Money Claims Centre, an application to transfer the matter to the preferred County Court hearing centre or a hearing centre convenient for the claimant and litigation friend should be made before an application for approval is submitted.

The only information and documentation which is required to be provided in support of such an application is an opinion on the merits of the settlement plus any documentary evidence material to that opinion, a copy of any financial advice and, where the settlement includes periodical payments, information required by CPR, rr 41.8 and 41.9. Presumably, less information and fewer documents are required than for pre-issue settlements because the court will already have much of the information required, as this will already be on the court file. Nevertheless, the safer approach is to ensure that all the documents and information required by CPR, r 21.10 are made available to the court, as appropriate to the nature and value of the claim, at the approval hearing. Obviously it will not be necessary to issue a Part 8 claim because the proceedings will already have been started on a Part 7 claim form.

20.4.1.3   The approval hearing

The nature of the approval hearing will be the same whether the settlement has been reached before or after issue of proceedings although, of course, larger claims will require more thought and more of the court's time. The primary concern of the court is to ensure that the settlement agreed is a reasonable one in all the circumstances, and that it is in the best interests of the child or protected party. The hearing should not be seen by lawyers as a mere rubber-stamping exercise by the court.

Generally, in lower value claims, defendants will not be present or represented at the hearing. The claimant's representative should attend. Many courts, although not all, will require the litigation friend and a child claimant to attend so that they can be asked about the accident, the injuries, and whether they have fully recovered or not. In circumstances where the child or litigation friend mentions continuing effects which are not dealt with by the medical report, and consequently are not properly compensated for, the court is likely to adjourn the hearing and direct that a further medical report be prepared. If an essential document, such as the birth certificate, is not provided, the matter will be adjourned.

20.5   CONTROL OF MONEY RECOVERED BY OR ON BEHALF OF A CHILD OR PROTECTED PARTY

The court will make directions as to how money recovered by or on behalf of a child or protected party should be dealt with (CPR, r 21.11(1)).

The money must be dealt with in accordance with directions given by the court, and may not be dealt with otherwise.

CPR, r 21.11 provides as follows:

(2)   Directions ... may provide that the money shall be wholly or partly paid into court and invested or otherwise dealt with.

(3)   Where money is recovered by or on behalf of a protected party or money paid into court is accepted by or on behalf of a protected party, before giving directions under this rule, the court will first consider whether the protected party is a protected beneficiary.

(4)   Where a child lacks capacity to manage and control any money recovered by or on behalf of the child, and is likely to remain so on reaching full age, the fund will be administered as a protected beneficiary's fund.

(6)   The representative or litigation friend of the child or protected beneficiary must apply to the court for directions for management of the fund or payment into court (using Form CFO 320 or CFO 320PB to be completed by the judge), stating the nature and terms of any proposed investment vehicle, with appropriate supporting evidence.

(7)   The judge hearing the application may adjourn it and give directions for further information to be provided and, unless the judge directs otherwise, the money recovered will be paid into the court special account pending determination of the application for investment.

20.5.1   Children

CPR, r 21.11(8) provides:

(8)   Where money is recovered for the benefit of a child who is not a protected beneficiary:

(a)   if the court considers it appropriate, it may order that the money be paid directly to the litigation friend to be placed in a bank, building society or similar account for the child's use;

(b)   if the money remains invested in court, it must be paid out to the child when the child reaches the age of 18;

(c)   any investments held in court other than money must either be sold and the proceeds paid to the child, or transferred to the child, when the child reaches the age of 18.

Many cases will involve small amounts of money, usually under £5,000. The general rule of thumb is that the money will be invested in a Court Funds Office account. However, the interest rate is extremely low and, where very small sums are involved, the court may be persuaded to allow the money to be paid to the litigation friend for investment in a building society account, an ISA or some other investment vehicle in the child's name, which may pay a better rate of interest. See the court's power under CPR, r 21.11(8)(a) above. Similarly, the court may also be persuaded to pay all or some of the damages to the litigation friend to be spent for the child's immediate benefit, for example for the purchase of a laptop. However, the court will be slow to do so and will need evidence of the cost of the item or experience to be purchased and of the benefit to the child. Otherwise, the court will order that the money is forwarded to the Court Funds Office for investment.

Where larger sums of money are involved, in making an appropriate order for investment, the court will need to take into account the child's circumstances, including whether the child requires a regular income, capital growth, or both, whether there are any pressing liabilities or requirements, whether the child has other income, and the child's tax position.

The court may appoint the Official Solicitor to be a guardian of the child's estate. Those with parental responsibility must agree, unless the court decides that their agreement can be dispensed with.

When the child reaches 18, any money invested in court must be paid out to the child. See CPR, r 21.11(8)(b) and (c) above.

20.5.2 Protected parties

Before directions are made in a case involving a protected party, the court must determine whether the protected party is a protected beneficiary, ie whether the person lacks the capacity to manage and control the money they have received. Where the person is judged to be a protected beneficiary (CPR, r 21.11(3)), the Court of Protection has jurisdiction to make decisions about how to deal with money recovered in their best interests. The Court of Protection is entitled to make charges for the administration of funds, and provision must be made for such charges in any settlement reached.

Under CPR, r 21.11(9) and (10):

(9)   Where money is recovered for the benefit of a protected beneficiary—

(a)   if the amount is £100,000 or more, subject to (b) below, the court shall direct the litigation friend to apply to the Court of Protection for the appointment of a deputy, after which the fund shall be dealt with as directed by the Court of Protection;

(b)   the procedure in sub-paragraph (a) will not apply where a person with authority to administer the protected beneficiary's financial affairs has been appointed as attorney under a registered enduring power of attorney, or as donee of a registered lasting power of attorney, or as the deputy appointed by the Court of Protection;

(c)   any payment out of money must be in accordance with any decision or order of the Court of Protection;

(d)   if an application to the Court of Protection is required, that application must be made;

(e)   if the Court of Protection so decides, on its own initiative or at the request of the judge hearing the application for investment, an amount exceeding £100,000 may be retained in court and invested in the same way as the fund of a child.

(10)   A request for payment of money from a fund held for the benefit of a child or protected party, or to vary an investment strategy, may be made in writing with appropriate supporting evidence (but without making a formal application) to a Master or District Judge and may be determined without a hearing unless the court directs otherwise.

20.6   CONCLUSION

This chapter merely outlines the most important issues which need to be considered when dealing with a claim involving a child or a protected party. It does not include everything that must be considered, for example the issue of the costs which may be recovered by the claimant's solicitor in these matters. The court always requires solicitors to deal with personal injury and clinical negligence claims competently and professionally, but it will be less tolerant of inadequacies in the services provided when dealing with claims involving children and protected parties. It is therefore incumbent on solicitors to ensure that they are familiar with the relevant issues and the court rules which govern them.

CHAPTER 21

THE PRE-ACTION PROTOCOLS FOR LOW VALUE RTA, EL AND PL CLAIMS

LEARNING OUTCOMES

After reading this chapter you will be able to:

- appreciate when the RTA or EL/PL Protocol for low value claims applies
- understand how to commence a claim through the Claims Portal
- describe the further stages that a claim may go through once commenced
- identify the fixed costs that may be claimed at the end of each stage
- understand how to make an offer to settle under the RTA or EL/PL Protocols
- understand what happens to a case which exits the Portal.

21.1 INTRODUCTION

On 31 July 2013, two new Pre-Action Protocols for Low Value Personal Injury Claims in Road Traffic Accidents (the 'RTA Protocol') and Employers' Liability and Public Liability Claims (the 'EL/PL Protocol') came into force, extending the previous Protocol which had been in force for RTAs from £10,000 to £25,000 and introducing a new procedure for EL or PL claims valued at up to £25,000. Further changes to the RTA Protocol came into force on 6 April 2015, implementing government reforms of low value whiplash claims. Yet further changes have been made following the coming into force on 31 May 2021 of the Whiplash Injury Regulations 2021 (SI 2021/642) and the new Pre-Action Protocol for Personal Injury Claims below the Small Claims Limit in Road Traffic Accidents ('RTA Small Claims Protocol'). See **10.2** for further detail. Solicitors who are instructed to act in RTA, EL or PL cases need to understand how to run these so called 'Portal' claims and so must be familiar with the Low Value Protocols, Practice Direction 8B, and the accompanying regime of fixed costs which are outlined in this chapter. Note that the Low Value RTA Protocol is to be distinguished from the RTA Small Claims Protocol, the latter not being considered in this book other than in passing and in brief. Reference should be made to the RTA Small Claims Protocol in practice as appropriate. The focus in this chapter is on the Low Value Protocols.

21.2 APPLICATION OF THE PROTOCOLS

21.2.1 When will the RTA Protocol apply?

Paragraph 4.1 of the RTA Protocol states that it will apply where:

(a) a claim for damages arises from a road traffic accident which occurs on or after 31 May 2021;

(b) the claim includes damages in respect of personal injury;

(c) the claimant values the claim at no more than the 'Protocol upper limit' (see below); and

(d) if proceedings were started, the small claims track would not be the normal track for that claim. Paragraphs 4.1 and 4.1A set out further detail about this, and see **10.2** for further explanation.

The 'Protocol upper limit' is defined in para 1.2 as:

(a) £25,000 where the accident occurred on or after 31 July 2013; or

(b) £10,000 where the accident occurred on or after 30 April 2010 and before 31 July 2013.

The value is on a full liability basis including pecuniary losses but excluding interest. Paragraph 4.4 states that a claim may include vehicle related damages, but these are excluded for the purposes of valuing the claim under para 4.1.

'Vehicle related damages' are defined as damages for the pre-accident value of the car, vehicle repair, insurance excess and vehicle hire (para 1.1(18)). 'Pecuniary losses' are defined as past and future expenses and losses (para 1.1(14)).

Paragraph 4.5 sets out a number of types of claim to which the RTA Protocol will not apply, including:

(a) claims made to the MIB under the Untraced Drivers Agreement 2017; and

(b) where the claimant or defendant acts as the personal representative of a deceased person or is a protected party.

21.2.2 When will the EL/PL Protocol apply?

Paragraph 4.1 of the EL/PL Protocol states that it applies where:

(a) either:

    (i) the claim arises from an accident occurring on or after 31 July 2013; or

    (ii) in a disease claim, no letter of claim has been sent to the defendant before 31 July 2013;

(b) the claim includes damages in respect of personal injury;

(c) the claimant values the claim at not more than £25,000 on a full liability basis including pecuniary losses but excluding interest ('the upper limit'); and

(d) if proceedings were started, the small claims track would not be the normal track for that claim. Rule 26.6 and para 4.1 of the EL/PL Protocol make clear that the small claims track is not the normal track where the value of any claim for damages for personal injuries (defined as compensation for pain, suffering and loss of amenity), other than a claim arising from a road traffic accident, is more than £1,500.

Paragraph 4.3 sets out claims to which the EL/PL Protocol will not apply, most notably:

(a) claims where the claimant or defendant is the personal representative of a deceased person or a protected party as defined in CPR, r 21.1(2);

(b) claims arising out of the harm, abuse or neglect of a child/protected party;

(c) mesothelioma claims; and

(d) disease claims where there is more than one employer defendant.

21.3 THE THREE STAGES

Both the RTA and the EL/PL Protocols set out a three-stage process. Stages 1 and 2 are pre-litigation. The court becomes involved only at Stage 3, should the claim proceed that far. A summary of each stage is set out below. From 6 April 2015, where a claim is brought under the RTA Protocol for a soft tissue injury, there are additional requirements to follow, primarily in relation to obtaining medical evidence (see **21.4**).

21.3.1 Stage 1

(a) To begin the process, the claimant must complete and send the Claim Notification Form (CNF) to the defendant's insurer. It must be sent electronically via www.claimsportal.org.uk. From 1 June 2015, para 6.3A of the RTA Protocol requires a claimant's legal representative to undertake a search of askCUEPI and to enter the unique reference number generated by that search in the 'additional information' box in the CNF (see **1.4**).

(b) At the same time, the Defendant Only CNF must be sent to the defendant by first class post. This is the only exception to para 5.1 of both Protocols, which provides that all information required by the Protocols must be sent electronically via the claims portal.

There are further detailed provisions to follow in para 6.1 of the EL/PL Protocol where the identity of the insurer is not known or there is no insurance. It is sometimes difficult to establish the identity of insurers in EL/PL claims (due to the passage of time that sometimes elapses before claims are brought), but para 6.1(3) states that the claimant must make a reasonable attempt to identify the insurer and, in an EL claim, must carry out a database search through the Employers' Liability Tracing Office.

(c) The insurer must send to the claimant an electronic acknowledgement the day after receipt of the CNF.

(d) The insurer must complete the 'Insurer Response' section of the CNF and send it to the claimant within:

  (i)   15 days for an RTA claim;

  (ii)   30 days for an EL claim;

  (iii)   40 days for a PL claim.

(e) If the insurer admits liability, the insurer must pay the Stage 1 fixed costs (see below) within 10 days of receiving the Stage 2 settlement pack (see Stage 2 below).

(f) If the insurer does not respond, denies liability, alleges contributory negligence (other than failure to wear a seatbelt in an RTA case), asserts that the information in the CNF is inadequate or, in the case of an RTA claim, notifies the claimant that the defendant considers that the small claims track would be the normal track if proceedings were issued, then the claim exits the Protocol. In an RTA claim, where the date of the accident was on or after 31 May 2021, and where the defendant has notified the claimant that, if proceedings were issued, the small claims track would be the normal track and the parties agree that the RTA Small Claims Protocol applies, then the claimant must start a claim following that protocol, beginning at para 5.3. Otherwise, the claim will proceed under the Pre-Action Protocol for Personal Injury Claims.

(g) Both the RTA and the EL/PL Protocols provide that, before the end of Stage 1, the insurer must apply to the CRU for a certificate of recoverable benefits.

21.3.2 Stage 2

Liability having been admitted, the process now turns to valuation of the claim and settlement.

(a) In an EL claim, the defendant must within 20 days of the admission of liability provide earnings details to verify the claimant's loss of earnings. Under both the RTA and the EL/PL Protocols, the claimant now obtains a medical report. There is no time limit for doing this.

(b)   When ready to value the claim, the claimant sends the Stage 2 settlement pack to the insurer. This includes:

(i)   the medical report(s);

(ii)   any medical records or photographs served with medical reports;

(iii) evidence of all special damages claimed;

(iv)   receipts for disbursements (eg the cost of the medical report);

(v)   any witness statements; and

(vi)   an offer of settlement.

Non-medical reports are not expected to be required as part of the Stage 2 pack, but may be obtained where reasonably required to value the claim. In most cases, witness statements, whether from the claimant or otherwise, will not be required as part of the Stage 2 pack, but they may be provided where reasonably required to value the claim.

(c)   The insurer must respond within 15 days by accepting the offer or making a counter-offer (the 'initial consideration period').

(d)   If the claim is not settled, there follows a 20-day negotiation period (the 'negotiation period').

(e)   Both the initial period and the negotiation period may be extended by agreement.

(f)   An offer to settle by either party will automatically include an agreement to pay Stage 2 fixed costs and disbursements. In some cases, additional advice may be obtained from counsel or a specialist lawyer to assist in valuing any claim over £10,000, recoverable as a disbursement, but this should not be the norm.

(g)   If the insurer does not respond to the Stage 2 settlement pack, the claim exits the RTA or the EL/PL Protocol.

(h)   If the insurer responds but the claim is not settled, the claimant's solicitor prepares a court proceedings pack (CPP) and sends it to the insurer or its nominated solicitor to check for accuracy. The pack includes both parties' comments on disputed heads of damage and both parties' final offers. The insurer has five days to check the pack.

(i)   In addition, except where the claimant is a child, the insurer must pay to the claimant its final offer of damages (net of any CRU benefits and interim payments already made) plus Stage 1 and 2 fixed costs and disbursements within 15 days of receiving the CPP.

21.3.3   Stage 3

(a)   The claimant issues proceedings under CPR, Part 8 in accordance with Practice Direction 8B.

(b)   The defendant must acknowledge service within 14 days.

(c)   It is assumed that the final assessment of damages will be a paper exercise which neither party will attend. However, either party may request an oral hearing.

(d)   The court will notify both parties of the date when a district judge will assess damages.

21.4   SOFT TISSUE INJURY CLAIMS UNDER THE RTA PROTOCOL

21.4.1   Definition of 'soft tissue injury claim'

Paragraph 1.1(16A) of the RTA Protocol defines a soft tissue injury as:

> a claim brought by an occupant of a motor vehicle where the significant physical injury caused is a soft tissue injury and includes claims where there is a minor psychological injury secondary in significance to the physical injury, but excludes any claim which consists of or includes a whiplash injury.

Where such a claim is brought, the RTA Protocol sets out additional requirements, the aim of which (according to para 3.2) is to ensure that:

(a)   the use and cost of medical reports is controlled;

(b)   in most cases only one medical report is obtained;

(c)   the medical expert is normally independent of any medical treatment; and

(d)   offers are made only after a fixed cost medical report has been obtained and disclosed.

21.4.2 Defendant's account of the accident

Although, in most cases where liability is admitted, the defendant's account of an accident will not be relevant, para 6.19A of the RTA Protocol provides that 'In limited cases where it is considered appropriate, the defendant may send their account to the claimant electronically at the same time as the CNF response'.

This will no doubt be of most relevance in so-called 'low velocity' crashes, where the severity of the injuries suffered by the claimant is disputed, and will be used to ask the medical expert to comment on the diagnosis and prognosis based on the defendant's alternative version of events.

21.4.3 Medical reports in soft tissue injury claims

The Protocol provides for fixed cost medical reports, which are defined at para 1.1(10A) as:

> ... a report in a soft tissue injury claim which is from a medical expert who, save in exceptional circumstances –
>
> (a)   has not provided treatment to the claimant;
>
> (b)   is not associated with any person who has provided treatment; and
>
> (c)   does not propose or recommend treatment that they or an associate then provide.

It sets out details of the system for obtaining such reports through an IT Hub known as 'MedCo', which will allocate an independent accredited expert. The relevant provisions in the RTA Protocol are:

> 7.8A   In addition to paragraphs 7.1 to 7.7, and subject to paragraph 7.8B, in a soft tissue injury claim –
>
> (1)   the first report must be a fixed cost medical report from an accredited medical expert selected for the claim via the MedCo Portal (website at: www.medco.org.uk); and
>
> (2)   where the defendant provides a different account under paragraph 6.19A, the claimant must provide this as part of the instructions to the medical expert for the sole purpose of asking the expert to comment on the impact, if any, on diagnosis and prognosis if –
>
> > (a)   the claimant's account is found to be true; or
> >
> > (b)   the defendant's account is found to be true.
>
> 7.8B   In a soft tissue injury claim –
>
> (1)   it is expected that only one medical report will be required;
>
> (2)   a further medical report, whether from the first expert instructed or from an expert in another discipline, will only be justified where –
>
> > (a)   it is recommended in the first expert's report; and
> >
> > (b)   that report has first been disclosed to the defendant; and
>
> (3)   where the claimant obtains more than one medical report, the first report must be a fixed cost medical report from an accredited medical expert selected via the MedCo Portal and any further report from an expert in any of the following disciplines must also be a fixed cost medical report –
>
> > (a)   Consultant Orthopaedic Surgeon;
> >
> > (b)   Consultant in Accident and Emergency Medicine;
> >
> > (c)   General Practitioner registered with the General Medical Council;
> >
> > (d)   Physiotherapist registered with the Health and Care Professions Council.

Additional rules apply in relation to claims which consist of, or include, a claim for whiplash injury or injuries. Paragraph 1.1(20) of the RTA Protocol states that 'whiplash injury' or 'whiplash injuries' means an injury or injuries of soft tissue in the neck, back or shoulder suffered because of driver negligence as defined in s 1 of the Civil Liability Act (CLA) 2018 and as further applied by s 3 of that Act to claims where the duration of the whiplash injury or any of the whiplash injuries: (a) does not exceed, or is not likely to exceed, two years; or (b) would not have exceeded, or would not be likely to exceed, two years but for the claimant's failure to take reasonable steps to mitigate its effect.

Paragraph 7.8C of the RTA Protocol states:

> **7.8C   Claims which consist of, or include, a claim for whiplash injury – Medical Reports**
>
> (1)   The provisions of paragraph 7.8A and 7.8B apply in respect of a medical report obtained under this paragraph, save that—
>
> (a)   any reference to soft tissue injury claim is to be read as referring to a claim which consists of, or includes, a claim for whiplash injury;
>
> (b)   paragraph (2) below applies in place of paragraph 7.8B(2).
>
> (2)   A further report, whether from the first expert instructed or from an expert in another discipline, will only be justified where—
>
> (a)   it is recommended in the first expert's report;
>
> (b)   the first medical report recommends that further time is required before a prognosis of the claimant's injuries can be determined;
>
> (c)   the claimant is receiving continuing treatment; or
>
> (d)   the claimant has not recovered as expected in the original prognosis.

Definition of whiplash injury – Civil Liability Act 2018

Section 1(1) of the Civil Liability Act (CLA) 2018 defines a whiplash injury to mean an injury of soft tissue in the neck, back or shoulder, that is of a description falling within subsection (2), but not including an injury excepted by subsection (3). Section 1(2) states that an injury falls within subsection 2 if it is a sprain, strain, tear, rupture or lesser damage of a muscle, tendon or ligament in the neck, back or shoulder, or an injury of soft tissue associated with a muscle, tendon or ligament in the neck, back or shoulder.

Under s 1(3) of the CLA 2018, an injury is excepted from s 1(2) if:

(a)   it is an injury of soft tissue which is a part of or connected to another injury, and

(b)   the other injury is not an injury of soft tissue in the neck, back or shoulder of a description falling within subsection (2).

21.4.4   Stage 2 settlement pack

In addition to the documents set out at **21.3.2(b)** above, the settlement pack in a soft tissue injury claim must contain the invoice for obtaining the fixed cost medical report and any invoice for the cost of obtaining medical records. Furthermore, para 7.32A provides that:

> … In a soft tissue injury claim, the Stage 2 Settlement Pack is of no effect unless the medical report is a fixed cost medical report. Where the claimant includes more than one medical report, the first report obtained must be a fixed cost medical report from an accredited medical expert selected via the MedCo Portal and any further report from an expert in any of the disciplines listed in paragraph 7.8B(3)(a) to (d) must also be a fixed cost medical report.

A new para 7.A32A has been inserted into the RTA Protocol to reflect the recent changes made by the CLA 2018 and the subsequent Whiplash Injury Regulations 2021 (SI 2021/642), which came into force on 31 May 2021.

Paragraph 7.A32A of the RTA Protocol states:

> Where the claim consists of or includes a whiplash injury—
>
> (1)   the settlement pack must include the fixed cost medical report;
>
> (2)   the claimant's offer in the settlement pack must set out separately—
>
> (a)   the tariff amount; and
>
> (b)   the amount (if any) for damages in respect of any non-whiplash injuries;

(3)   subject to paragraphs (4) and (5) below, the claimant may argue in accordance with the Whiplash Injury Regulations 2021 that there are exceptional circumstances which allow the claimant to seek an uplift on the tariff amount;

(4)   a claimant who makes a request for an uplift under paragraph (3) must state in the settlement pack—

    (a)   the percentage uplift claimed up to a maximum of 20% and the amount claimed; and

    (b)   how the whiplash injury is exceptionally severe; or

    (c)   how the claimant's circumstances increasing the pain, suffering or loss of amenity caused by their whiplash injury are exceptional.

Paragraph 7.32A of the RTA Protocol makes clear:

In a soft tissue injury claim or a claim which consists of, or includes, a claim for whiplash injury, the Stage 2 Settlement Pack is of no effect unless the medical report is a fixed cost medical report. Where the claimant includes more than one medical report, the first report obtained must be a fixed cost medical report from an accredited medical expert selected via the MedCo Portal and any further report from an expert in any of the disciplines listed in paragraph 7.8B(3)(a) to (d) must also be a fixed cost medical report.

The Whiplash Injury Regulations 2021

The Whiplash Injury Regulations 2021 were made by the Lord Chancellor pursuant to powers under the CLA 2018. These Regulations apply to causes of action which accrued on or after 31 May 2021 and they set out a tariff of damages for whiplash injuries. The Regulations refer to 'the Act', which means the CLA 2018.

The tariff of damages payable for whiplash injuries is set out at reg 2 of the Whiplash Injury Regulations 2021:

2   Damages for whiplash injuries

(1)   Subject to regulation 3—

    (a)   the total amount of damages for pain, suffering and loss of amenity payable in relation to one or more whiplash injuries, taken together ('the tariff amount' for the purposes of section 5(7)(a) of the Act), is the figure specified in the second column of the following table; and

    (b)   the total amount of damages for pain, suffering and loss of amenity payable in relation to both one or more whiplash injuries and one or more minor psychological injuries suffered on the same occasion as the whiplash injury or injuries, taken together ('the tariff amount' for the purposes of section 5(7)(b) of the Act), is the figure specified in the third column of the following table—

Duration of injury	Amount – Regulation 2(1)(a)	Amount – Regulation 2(1)(b)
Not more than 3 months	£240	£260
More than 3 months, but not more than 6 months	£495	£520
More than 6 months, but not more than 9 months	£840	£895
More than 9 months, but not more than 12 months	£1,320	£1,390
More than 12 months, but not more than 15 months	£2,040	£2,125
More than 15 months, but not more than 18 months	£3,005	£3,100
More than 18 months, but not more than 24 months	£4,215	£4,345.

(2)   In this regulation, 'duration of injury' means—

    (a)   the duration, or likely duration, of the whiplash injury a person has suffered; or

    (b)   where a person suffers more than one whiplash injury on the same occasion, the whiplash injury of the longest duration, or likely longest duration, suffered on that occasion, if the person were to take, or had taken, reasonable steps to mitigate the effect of that injury or those injuries.

Regulation 3 provides for an uplift on the tariff amounts in exceptional circumstances, but this amount must not exceed the relevant tariff amount by more than 20%. Section 6 of the CLA 2018 and reg 4 of the Whiplash Injury Regulations 2021 make clear that medical evidence from an accredited expert must be obtained and disclosed before an offer or payment to settle a whiplash claim is made or invited.

21.5   INTERIM PAYMENTS

Paragraph 7 of both the RTA Protocol and the EL/PL Protocol set out the procedures for obtaining an interim payment at Stage 2. The claimant must send to the defendant an interim settlement pack (ISP), medical reports and evidence of pecuniary losses and disbursements.

In a claim which consists of or includes a claim for whiplash injury, and to which the RTA Protocol relates, the claimant must specify in the ISP how much of the interim payment relates to the tariff amount set out in the Whiplash Injury Regulations 2021, and the amount (if any) for damages in respect of any non-whiplash injuries. See para 7.14A of the RTA Protocol.

Where the claimant seeks an interim payment of £1,000, the defendant must pay £1,000 within 10 days of receiving the ISP. If the interim payment sought is greater than £1,000, the defendant may offer less than is requested but must pay at least £1,000 to the claimant within 15 days of receiving the ISP.

Where the claim consists of or includes a whiplash injury, the interim payment of £1,000 is to be applied first to the tariff amount. The balance of the £1,000 (if any) is to be applied first to general damages in respect of non-whiplash injuries and any remaining balance to pecuniary losses (RTA Protocol, para 7.17A).

Paragraph 7.44B of the RTA Protocol prohibits the parties from making or accepting any offer or payment in respect of a claim for whiplash injury until after the fixed costs medical report has been disclosed. This is consistent with the requirements of s 6 of the CLA 2018 and reg 4 of the Whiplash Injury Regulations 2021 mentioned above.

21.6   FIXED COSTS

The fixed costs regime in the amended CPR, Part 45 provides for fixed costs to be paid at the end of each stage of the RTA and EL/PL Protocols. The costs are set out in Tables 10 and 11 as follows:

TABLE 10

Fixed costs in relation to the RTA Protocol

Where the value of the claim for damages is not more than £10,000		**Where the value of the claim for damages is more than £10,000**	
Stage 1 fixed costs	£200	Stage 1 fixed costs	£200
Stage 2 fixed costs	£300	Stage 2 fixed costs	£600
Stage 3 Type A fixed costs	£250	Stage 3 Type A fixed costs	£250
Stage 3 Type B fixed costs	£250	Stage 3 Type B fixed costs	£250
Stage 3 Type C fixed costs	£150	Stage 3 Type C fixed costs	£150

TABLE 11

Fixed costs in relation to the EL/PL Protocol

Where the value of the claim for damages is not more than £10,000		**Where the value of the claim for damages is more than £10,000**	
Stage 1 fixed costs	£300	Stage 1 fixed costs	£300
Stage 2 fixed costs	£600	Stage 2 fixed costs	£1300
Stage 3 Type A fixed costs	£250	Stage 3 Type A fixed costs	£250
Stage 3 Type B fixed costs	£250	Stage 3 Type B fixed costs	£250
Stage 3 Type C fixed costs	£150	Stage 3 Type C fixed costs	£150

Type A, B and C fixed costs

Type A fixed costs are the legal representative's Stage 3 costs for a paper hearing, and under both Protocols are £250.00.

Type B costs are additional advocate's costs for conducting an oral Stage 3 hearing and are also £250 for RTA cases and the same for EL/PL Protocol cases, giving a total fee of £500 for an oral Stage 3 hearing in all portals.

Type C fixed costs are the costs for the advice on the amount of damages where the claimant is a child and are £150 in both Protocols.

All fixed costs at all stages are exclusive of VAT, and a further allowance may be made for disbursements such as medical reports and court fees. Where the claim is a soft tissue injury claim, or a claim which consists of, or includes, a claim for a whiplash injury, to which the RTA Protocol applies, limits are placed on the amount that can be claimed for a medical report. CPR, r 45.62 states in this context:

> (2)   Where this rule applies, the only sums (exclusive of VAT) that are recoverable in respect of the cost of obtaining a fixed cost medical report or medical records are as follows –
>
> (a)   obtaining the first report from an accredited medical expert selected via the MedCo Portal: £180;
>
> (b)   obtaining a further report where justified from an expert from one of the following disciplines –
>
> (i)   Consultant Orthopaedic Surgeon (inclusive of a review of medical records where applicable): £420;
>
> (ii)   Consultant in Accident and Emergency Medicine: £360;
>
> (iii)   General Practitioner registered with the General Medical Council: £180; or
>
> (iv)   Physiotherapist registered with the Health and Care Professions Council: £180;
>
> (c)   obtaining medical records: no more than £30 plus the direct cost from the holder of the records, and limited to £80 in total for each set of records required. Where relevant records are required from more than one holder of records, the fixed fee applies to each set of records required;
>
> (d)   addendum report on medical records (except by Consultant Orthopaedic Surgeon): £50; and
>
> (e)   answer to questions under Part 35: £80.
>
> (3)   Save in exceptional circumstances, no fee may be allowed for the cost of obtaining a report to which paragraph (2A) applies where the medical expert –
>
> (a)   has provided treatment to the claimant;
>
> (b)   is associated with any person who has provided treatment; or
>
> (c)   proposes or recommends treatment that they or an associate then provide.
>
> (4)   The cost of obtaining a further report from an expert not listed in paragraph (2A)(b) is not fixed, but the use of that expert and the cost must be justified.

21.7 OFFERS TO SETTLE

If settlement is not reached in a Portal claim, both parties must state their final offer in the Court Proceedings Pack (CPP) prior to the claim being issued. Section II of CPR Part 36 regulates such offers to settle where the parties have followed the RTA or EL/PL Protocols and the claim has proceeded to a hearing at Stage 3.

21.7.1 Form and content of offer

Under CPR, r 36.26, an offer to settle under these provisions is called a 'Protocol offer'. Rule 36.26(2) provides that, to be valid, a Protocol offer must:

(a)   be set out in the CPP; and

(b)   contain the final total amount of the offer from both parties.

Rule 36.27 provides that the offer is deemed to be made on the first business day after the CPP is sent to the defendant. Under CPR, r 36.28, the offer is treated as being exclusive of all interest.

21.7.2 Costs consequences following judgment

As usual, the court will not know the amount of any Protocol offer until the claim has been decided. Rule 36.30 sets out three possible outcomes of the Stage 3 hearing, together with the costs consequences of each outcome:

(a)   *Claimant is awarded damages less than or equal to the defendant's Protocol offer.* The court will order the claimant to pay the defendant's Stage 3 fixed costs and any Stage 3 disbursements under Section IX of Part 45, and interest on those costs from the first business day after the deemed date of the Protocol offer. See CPR, r 45.37.

(b)   *Claimant is awarded more than the defendant's Protocol offer.* The court will order the defendant to pay the claimant's fixed costs under CPR, r 45.30 (including Stage 1 and 2 costs if not already paid), as well as Part 45 Section IX disbursements.

(c)   *Claimant is awarded equal to or more than the claimant's Protocol offer.* The court will order the defendant to pay interest on the whole of the damages at a rate not exceeding 10% above base rate for some or all of the period starting with the date on which the offer was made. In addition, the defendant will be ordered to pay the claimant's fixed costs in r 45.30 and interest on those costs at a rate not exceeding 10% above base rate and an additional amount calculated in accordance with CPR, r 36.17(4)(d).

It should be noted that the amount of judgment is less than the Protocol offer if the judgment is less than the offer once CRU benefits have been deducted (CPR, r 36.31).

21.8 WHAT IF A CLAIM EXITS THE PORTAL?

Claims which are started in the Portal may exit the process, for instance because an allegation of contributory negligence is made, or one party fails to follow the relevant Protocol. Claims which no longer continue under the Protocols cannot subsequently re-enter the process. Where this happens, the Protocols provide that the claims will proceed under the relevant PAP. See also **23.3.1** at (f). Both the Personal Injury PAP and the Disease and Illness Claims PAP provide that in such a case the CNF will serve as the letter of claim.

21.8.1 Fixed costs apply to claims which exit the Portal

CPR, Part 45 contains a fixed costs regime which applies to claims which exit the RTA Protocol or the EL/PL Protocol, the costs of which will be payable on the usual standard basis after they exit the Portal. The detail of this fixed costs regime may be found in Part 45.

CPR, r 45.3 makes provisions for London weighting to apply to fixed costs under some parts of Part 45.

21.8.2　Costs consequences of Part 36 offers after a claim exits the Portal

If a claimant accepts the defendant's Part 36 offer after the date on which the claim left the Portal under either the RTA Protocol or the EL/PL Protocol, then the claimant is entitled to receive Stage 1 and 2 fixed costs in accordance with Table 10 or Table 11 of Practice Direction 45. In addition, the claimant will be liable for the defendant's fixed costs in Tables 12, 14 or 15 of Practice Direction 45 for the stage applicable at the date of acceptance; and any applicable additional fixed costs allowed under Sections I, VI, VII or VIII incurred in any period for which costs are payable to the defendant, less Stage 1 and 2 fixed costs to which the claimant is entitled. See CPR, r 36.23(4) and following.

21.8.3　Claimants who unreasonably fail to follow the Protocols

In order to prevent a claimant from trying to circumvent the rules and deliberately exiting the Portal in order to secure higher costs, CPR, r 45.35 provides as follows:

(1)　This rule applies where the claimant –

    (a)　does not comply with the process set out in the relevant Protocol; or

    (b)　elects not to continue with that process,

    and starts proceedings under Part 7.

(2)　Subject to paragraph (3), where a judgment is given in favour of the claimant but –

    (a)　the court determines that the defendant did not proceed with the process set out in the relevant Protocol because the claimant provided insufficient information on the Claim Notification Form;

    (b)　the court considers that the claimant acted unreasonably –

        (i)　by discontinuing the process set out in the relevant Protocol and starting proceedings under Part 7;

        (ii)　by valuing the claim at more than £25,000, so that the claimant did not need to comply with the relevant Protocol; or

        (iii)　except for paragraph (2)(a), in any other way that caused the process in the relevant Protocol to be discontinued; or

    (c)　the claimant did not comply with the relevant Protocol at all despite the claim falling within the scope of the relevant Protocol,

    the court may order the defendant to pay no more than the fixed costs in rule 45.28 together with the disbursements allowed in accordance with Section IX of this Part.

Paragraph (3) referred to above provides that, where a judgment is given in favour of the claimant but the claimant did not undertake a search of askCUEPI in accordance with para 6.3A(2) of the RTA Protocol, the court may not order the defendant to pay the claimant's costs and disbursements, save in exceptional circumstances. See CPR, r 45.35(3).

21.9　LIMITATION AND PORTAL CLAIMS

Where the limitation period is about to expire and therefore there is insufficient time to comply with the Portal procedure, a Part 8 claim form should be issued using the Stage 3 procedure (see **21.3.3** above) in order to protect the claimant's position. It will then be necessary to apply to the court for a stay of proceedings to enable the parties to comply with the Portal procedure. If the claim is not subsequently settled and exits the Portal, an application may then be made to lift the stay and to request directions for trial.

21.10　CONCLUSION

The extension of Portal claims to all RTA, EL and PL claims up to £25,000, and the reduction in costs that can now be claimed, as well as further recent changes relating to whiplash claims, have been controversial. Many have suggested that whilst the Portal might work for RTAs, which are on the whole relatively straightforward, the complexity in the law relating to EL and PL claims make them unsuitable for such a process. Recent figures suggested that approximately one-third of RTA claims exit the Portal as a result of allegations of contributory negligence. Recent statistics suggest that the drop-out rate at Stage 1 is closer to 50% for EL and EL disease claims and higher still for PL claims.

The amendments to the CPR and Protocols to implement the whiplash reforms are also relatively recent, and it remains to be seen whether they will have the desired effect of decreasing costs and discouraging bogus or exaggerated claims. Amendments made by the Civil Liability Act 2018 and the subsequent Whiplash Injury Regulations 2021, which introduced a tariff for damages in certain whiplash claims, as well as the increase of the small claims limit for RTA claims (subject to exceptions), are likely also to have an impact. See also **1.4.3**, **10.2** and **13.3**.

APPENDICES

Employers' Liability Case Study

INTRODUCTION

The following case study is illustrative of the low-value personal injury cases which form the bulk of the personal injury lawyer's caseload. The documentation charts the basic procedural steps, from instruction, through commencement of proceedings, to settlement. It does not cover all eventualities and not all documents which would be relevant to the case have been provided. As the accident occurred after 30 July 2013, the Pre-action Protocol for Low Value Personal Injury (Employers' Liability and Public Liability) Claims applies.

The claim proceeds as follows:

1   The claimant, Neil Worthing, instructs a firm of solicitors, Goodlaw, in relation to an injury he has suffered whilst in the employment of Guildshire Engineering Limited. A proof of evidence is taken (**Document 1**). The matter is funded by means of a CFA backed up by an AEI policy.

2   Using the Portal, the claimant's solicitors send the Claims Notification Form (CNF) electronically to the Defendant's insurer, Bright Insurance Co Ltd (**Document 2**). At the same time, the Defendant Only Claim Form is sent to the Defendant by first class post.

3   Bright Insurance Co Ltd sends an electronic acknowledgement and instructs Winter Wood & Co, to act on its behalf. A response is sent electronically via the Portal, denying the claim (**Document 3**). The matter therefore exits the Portal and, henceforward, the Pre-action Protocol for Personal Injury Claims applies. The CNF stands as the Letter of Claim.

4   The defendant's solicitors write to the claimant's solicitors setting out their reasons for denying the claim (**Document 4**) and enclosing relevant documents, including the accident report (**Document 5**) and the RIDDOR report (**Document 6**).

5   The claimant's solicitors write to the defendant's solicitors with the aim of appointing a jointly selected medical expert (**Document 7**). They provide three names.

6   The defendant does not raise any objection to those named, one is instructed and a medical report is obtained (**Document 8**).

7   Following receipt of the medical report, the assistant solicitor acting for the claimant conducts research into what the claimant would be entitled to in respect of general damages for pain, suffering and loss of amenity, and he sends an email to his supervising solicitor setting out his findings (**Document 9**).

8   A claim form is issued (**Document 10**) (through the County Court Money Claims Centre), and served with the particulars of claim (**Document 11**), the Schedule of Past and Future Expenses and Losses (**Document 12**) and the medical report.

9   The defendant's solicitors notify the Compensation Recovery Unit (CRU) of the claim by means of Form CRU 1 (**Document 13**). They receive a CRU certificate of repayable benefits (CRU 100) (**Document 14**) which shows that there are no recoverable benefits. A copy is forwarded to the claimant's solicitors.

10   The defence is filed (**Document 15**). The case is provisionally allocated to the fast track and is transferred to the County Court at Christlethorpe.

11   Directions questionnaires are completed by both sides (**Document 16**).

12   Directions are given (**Document 17**).

13   Following disclosure of witness statements, solicitors for the parties discuss a possible settlement, and the claimant subsequently indicates to his solicitors that he wants to

settle. The assistant solicitor acting for the claimant sends an email to his supervising solicitor (**Document 18**).

14 The defendant's solicitors send a Part 36 offer letter to the claimant's solicitors (**Document 19**). The assistant solicitor acting for the claimant consults his client and contacts the defendant's solicitors, asking them for an improved offer. He notes this in an email to his supervising solicitor (**Document 20**).

15 The claimant's solicitors write to the defendant's solicitors accepting the updated offer (**Document 21**) and enclosing a draft consent order (**Document 22**).

DOCUMENT 1 – PROOF OF EVIDENCE

I, Neil Matthew Worthing, of 22 Elstead House, Griffin Road, Christlethorpe, Guildshire GU48 1XX will say:

1.   My date of birth is 14 December 1999 and I am 21 years old. My National Insurance number is WK987999X. I am single and I have lived in rented accommodation at the above address since 4 June 2021.

2.   I am currently a full-time student at Queen Margaret's College, Guildshire, where I am studying law. This is the final year of my degree course. Throughout my years of study, I have taken temporary jobs during the summer breaks in order to help fund my studies.

3.   In June 2021, after the end of term, I was able to get a temporary contract with Guildshire Engineering Limited (GEL) at their factory at 77 Blizzard Lane, Christlethorpe, Guildshire, GU59 2YZ. They manufacture metal tools for industrial use. I was to work on their production line as a process engineer. The contract was to run for 10 weeks from Monday 7 June to Friday 15 August and my take home pay was £296 per week.

4.   When I arrived at the factory on 7 June, I was shown where I was to work by the foreman, Tony Benson. He gave me a short demonstration on how to use the machinery, gave me some written health and safety information, and told me that the Health and Safety Representative would talk to me when he came back from holiday the following Monday. Everything went very well the first week until the last day.

5.   On Friday 11 June 2021, at about 2.30pm, Tony asked me to help Jerry Packman, another process engineer, to move several boxes of widgets from one part of the factory to another. We were to use two metal trolleys, which had handles on each end, to transport the boxes. He told us the boxes were heavy, so we were to move each box between us and keep our backs straight when we were doing it. He said we were to put only four boxes on each trolley. Jerry was mucking about when Tony was talking to us, and Tony told him to listen and behave himself. Jerry is great fun and a bit of a practical joker, but he seems to be in trouble quite a lot.

6.   We stacked the first trolley with four boxes and then I pushed it about three feet further forward. The boxes were heavy so it took considerable effort on my part to move the trolley. Jerry then moved the second trolley to about a foot behind the first one, and we stacked that with four boxes. There was only one box left, so we decided to put this box on the second trolley. Once the fifth box was loaded, Jerry tried to move the trolley, but it wouldn't budge at all. It looked quite funny as Jerry is quite small and skinny. I was standing to the side of the first trolley with my left hand on the handle. I told Jerry to stop being such a weed and to push harder. Suddenly, the trolley he was pushing shot forward and the thumb of my left hand was caught between the handles of the two trolleys. It was excruciatingly painful. The accident happened at around 2.45 pm.

7.   I immediately went to see the first aider, Ayse Caglayan, who examined my thumb and said she thought it might be broken. My hand was already swelling up, and I was in great pain and very distressed. As I am left handed, I was worried about being able to write. Also I was concerned about my ability to play the piano, which is my great passion. I perform as a pianist in the restaurant at the Swan Lake Hotel on Tuesday, Thursday, and Friday evenings from 7pm to 11pm, for which I am paid £80 each Tuesday and Thursday evening and £100 each Friday evening.

8.   As I was unable to drive, Ayse Caglayan drove me to the A&E department at Guildshire Hospital. By the time we arrived, the pain and swelling in my thumb had increased. My left thumb was x-rayed, which confirmed that it had been fractured. A plaster cast was applied to my thumb up to my elbow and I was given a sling. I wore this plaster for two weeks and then a splint for a further two weeks.

9.   Obviously I could not go to work. On Wednesday 16 June, I received a call from Tony Benson. He sounded quite cross. He said that the accident had been due to me mucking about with Jerry and that I hadn't carried out his instructions. He said that he would send me two weeks' wages, which was more than generous and that my services were no longer needed.

10.   A few days later, I received a cheque from GEL in the sum of £592.00 for two weeks' wages – for the week I had worked and for one other week. Because of the injury, I was incapable of working for about four weeks, but when I had recovered enough to work, I was unable to find another job for what remained of the summer break. In addition, I lost money due to being unable to play the piano at the Swan Lake Hotel for a period of 12 weeks. Luckily, they took me back once I was able to play again. I did not claim benefits as I did not think I would be entitled to any.

11.   I was unable to cook or clean, or do anything much after the accident. Consequently, my mother came and stayed with me for two weeks to look after me. She doesn't work, so she didn't lose any money, but it was very inconvenient for her and quite embarrassing for me.

12.   I had a course of five physiotherapy treatments at Guildshire Hospital. I incurred travelling expenses attending these physiotherapy treatments. I travelled in my own car to the hospital, which is a round trip of 10 miles from my flat.

13.   I was then advised to continue with a course of exercises at home. I still do these exercises on a daily basis as I still have restricted movement in my thumb. It continues to give me pain, especially in cold weather, or if I knock or catch it accidentally. Sometimes, it locks when I am trying to grip with my left hand. I can play the piano, but it does hurt towards the end of the four-hour period when I am playing at the hotel. It also hurts when I have been writing for a while, which obviously I have to do at college.

14.   Jerry rang me a few weeks after the accident to apologise and to ask how I was. He told me that he had never received any information or training regarding stacking boxes or moving trolleys, and that GEL had recently had foam placed over the metal handles of all the trolleys in the factory. He asked me not to involve him if I took the matter to court, as he would probably have to give evidence on behalf of his employers.

Signed *Neil Worthing*   15 September 2021

DOCUMENT 2 – CLAIM NOTIFICATION FORM (EL1)

This is a formal claim against you, which must be acknowledged by email immediately and passed to your insurer.

Claim notification form (EL1)
Low value personal injury claims in employers' liability - accident only (£1,000 - £25,000)

Before filling in this form you are encouraged to seek independent legal advice.

Date sent   2 1 / 0 9 / 2 0 2 1

Items marked with (✱) are optional and the claimant must make a reasonable attempt to complete those boxes. All other boxes on the form are mandatory and must be completed before being sent.

What is the value of your claim?   ☐ up to £10,000   ✓ up to £25,000

Please tick here if you are not legally represented?   ☐   *If you are not legally represented please put your details in the claimant's representative section.*

Claimant's representative - contact details	Defendant's details
Name Goodlaw Solicitors	**Defendant's name** Guildshire Engineering Limited
Address 4 College Road Christlethorpe Guildshire Postcode G U 1 4 D Z	**Defendant's address**✱ 77 Blizzard Lane Christlethorpe Guildshire Postcode G U 5 9 2 Y Z
Contact name Mrs Belinda Braithwaite	**Policy number reference (If not known insert not known)** Not known
Telephone number 01483 606099	**Insurer/Compensator name (if known)** Bright Insurance Co. Ltd.
E-mail address bbraithwaite@goodlaw.co.uk	
Reference number BB/WORTH/21/426	

EL1 Claim notification form (04.13)

Section A — Claimant's details

✓ Mr.　　☐ Mrs.　　☐ Ms.
☐ Miss　　☐ Other

Claimant's name

Neil Matthew Worthing

Address

22 Elstead House
Griffin Road,
Christlethorpe
Guildshire

Postcode G U 4 8 1 X X

Date of birth

1 4 / 1 2 / 1 9 9 9

Is this a child claim?　☐ Yes　✓ No

National Insurance number

W K 9 8 7 9 9 9 X

If the claimant does not have a National Insurance
number, please explain why

Occupation

Student

Date of accident

1 1 / 0 6 / 2 0 2 1

If exact accident date is not known please select the
most appropriate date and provide further details in
Section B 1.1

Section B — Injury and medical details

1.1 Please provide a brief description of the injury
sustained as a result of the accident

The claimant's thumb on his left hand was fractured
when it was crushed between the metal handles of
two industrial trolleys. A plaster cast was applied
from the thumb up to the elbow, which remained in
place for two weeks. For a further two weeks, a
splint was in place.

There is some remaining stiffness of the thumb joint,
tenderness, and occasional locking of the joint.

this section continues over the page ▯▷

1.2   Has the claimant had to take any time off work as a result of the accident?   ✓ Yes ☐ No

1.3   Is the claimant still off work?   ☐ Yes ☐ No

If No, how many days in total was the claimant off work?   `45`

1.4   Has the claimant sought any medical attention?   ✓ Yes ☐ No

If Yes, on what date did they first do so?   `1 1 / 0 6 / 2 0 2 1`

1.5   Did the claimant attend hospital as a result of the accident?   ✓ Yes ☐ No

If Yes, please provide details of the hospital(s) attended

> Guildshire Hospital, Grove Road, Guildshire, Christlethorpe, GU34 1HH

1.6   If hospital was attended, was the claimant detained overnight?   ☐ Yes ✓ No

If Yes, how many days were they detained?

Section C — Rehabilitation

2.1   Has a medical professional recommended the claimant should undertake any rehabilitation such as physiotherapy?   ✓ Yes ☐ No ☐ Medical professional not seen

If Yes, please provide brief details of the rehabilitation treatment recommended and any treatment provided including name of provider

> As recommended by the consultant at the Guildshire Hospital, the claimant underwent a course of 5 physiotherapy treatments at Guildshire Hospital. He continues to do a number of exercises at home, as recommended by the physotherapist.

2.2   Are you aware of any rehabilitation needs that the claimant has arising out of the accident?   ✓ Yes ☐ No

If Yes, please provide full details

> The claimant needs to continue to carry out the exercises as mentioned above for the foreseeable future.

Section D — Accident time, location and description

3.1 Estimated time of accident (24 hour clock)

14.45

3.2 Where did the accident happen?

The factory floor at the defendant's factory at Blizzard Lane, Christlethorpe, Guildshire.

3.3 At the time of the accident the claimant was

☑ working at the claimant's own place of work

☐ working in the workplace of another employer

☐ Other (please specify)

3.4 Please explain how the accident happened

The claimant, who is a student, was working at the defendant's factory on a 10 week temporary contract.

At the time of the accident, he and another process engineer, Jerry Packman, were moving boxes of widgets from one part of the factory to another, using two metal trolleys. Once stacked with boxes of widgets, the trolleys were very heavy and difficult to move.

Mr Packman pushed one of the trolleys with some force, causing it to suddenly shoot forward. The claimant had been resting his hand on the handle of the other trolley, and his left thumb was caught in the impact between the handles of two trolleys.

3.5 Was the accident reported?   ☑ Yes   ☐ No   ☐ Not known

If Yes, please confirm the date the accident was
reported and to whom it was reported (if known)

14/06/21 - RIDDOR submitted to the Health & Safety Executive

Section E — Liability

4.1   Why does the claimant believe that the defendant was to blame for the accident?

The accident was caused by the negligence of the defendant, its servants or agents because it:-

1. failed to provide competent fellow workers. Mr Packman was known to the defendant to be a practial joker. He behaved in a reckless manner in pushing the trolley with force, without ascertaining that it was safe to do so. The defendant is vicariously liable for Mr Packman's actions.

2. failed to provide adequate equipment. In view of the likelihood of hands becoming trapped between the handles of trolleys, the handles should have been covered in foam or another suitable material in order to minimise injury. It is understood that the handles were so covered by the defendant following the accident.

3. failed to provide a safe system of work in that insufficient thought had been given to the method by which boxes of widgets should be moved. There were insufficient instructions, safety precautions, warnings and supervision.

In support of the above breaches of duty, the claimant relies on the following breaches of statutory duty.

The Defendant failed:-

(a) to make a proper risk assessment regarding moving the trolleyscontrary to reg 3(1) of the Management of Health and Safety at Work Regulations 1999 (the "Management Regulations") and reg 4(1)(b)(i) of the Manual Handling Operations Regulations 1992 (the "Manual Handling Regulations");

(b) to provide information to its employees on health and safety risks and protective measures contrary to reg 10 of the Management Regulations and reg 8 of the Provision and Use of Work Equipment Regulations 1009 (the "Work Equipment Regulations");

(c) to provide adequate health and safety training to its employess contrary to reg 13 of the Management Regulations and reg 9 of the Work Equipment Regulations;

(d) to ensure the suitability of the trolleys for the purpose for which they were provided contrary to reg 4 of the Work Equipment Regulations.

(e) to ensure that its employees received proper information and training on how to handle loads correctly in the process of moving loaded trolleys contrary to reg 4(1)(b)(ii) of the Manual Handling Regulations;

(f) to take appropriate steps to reduce the risk of injury to employees arising out of the activity mentioned in (e) above to the lowest practicable level contrary to reg 4(1)(b)(ii) of the Manual Handling Regulations.

Section F — Funding

5.1 Has the claimant undertaken a funding
arrangement within the meaning of CPR rule
43.2(1)(k) of which they are required to give
notice to the defendant?

☐ Yes ✓ No

If Yes, please tick the following boxes that apply:

☐ The claimant has entered into a conditional fee agreement in relation to this claim, which provides for a
success fee within the meaning of section 58(2) of the Courts and Legal Services Act 1990

Date conditional fee arrangement was
entered into

☐☐ / ☐☐ / ☐☐☐☐

☐ The claimant has taken out an insurance policy to which section 29 of the Access to Justice Act 1999 applies.

Name of insurance company

Address of insurance company

Policy number

Policy date ☐☐ / ☐☐ / ☐☐☐☐

Level of cover

Are the insurance premiums staged? ☐ Yes ☐ No

If Yes, at which point is an increased
premium payable?

☐ The claimant has an agreement with a membership organisation to meet their legal costs.

Name of organisation

Date of agreement ☐☐ / ☐☐ / ☐☐☐☐

☐ Other, please give details

6

Section G — Other relevant information

Section H — Statement of truth

Your personal information will only be disclosed to third parties, where we are obliged or permitted by law to do so. This includes use for the purpose of claims administration as well as disclosure to third-party managed databases used to help prevent fraud, and to regulatory bodies for the purposes of monitoring and/or enforcing our compliance with any regulatory rules/codes.

Where the claimant is a child the signature below will be by the child's parent or guardian or by the legal representative authorised by them.

☑ I am the claimant's legal representative. The claimant believes that the facts stated in this claim form are true. I am duly authorised by the claimant to sign this statement.

☐ I am the claimant. I believe that the facts stated in this claim form are true.

Signed

Belinda Braithwaite

Date

2 1 / 0 9 / 2 0 2 1

Position or office held
(if signed on behalf of firm or company)

Associate Solicitor

☑ I have retained a signed copy of this form including the statement of truth.

DOCUMENT 3 – RESPONSE TO CNF

Claim notification form (EL1)
Low value personal injury claims in
employers' liability - accident only (£1,000 - £25,000)

Compensator response

Section A — Liability

Please select the relevant statement

Defendant admits: Accident occured

Caused by the defendant's breach of duty

Caused some loss to the claimant, the nature and extent of which is not admitted

The defendant has no accrued defence to the claim under the Limitation Act 1980

☐ The above are admitted

☐ The defendant makes the above admission but the claim will
exit the process due to contributory negligence

If the defendant does not admit liability please provide reasons below

At all material times, the defendant complied with its common law duties to the claimant. It provided competent fellow workers who were adequately trained, instructed and supervised. The trolleys were suitable and safe when used appropriately. Safe systems of work were in place. All statutory obligatons were followed.

The accident was caused by the claimant's own actions in suggesting that one of the trolleys be overloaded with boxes of widgets, in direct contravention of instructions given to him, and in not behaving in a mature and sensible manner.

Section B — Services provided by the compensator - Rehabilitation

Is the compensator prepared to provide
rehabilitation?   ☐ Yes ☐ No

Has the compensator provided rehabilitation?   ☐ Yes ✓ No

If Yes, please provide full details below

Section C — Response information

Date of notification	2 1 / 0 9 / 2 0 2 1
Date of response to notification	0 9 / 1 0 / 2 0 2 1

Defendant's compensator details

Address

Bright Insurance Co. Ltd.
Peacock House
Regents Lane
London WC2 SW4

Contact name

Ralph East

Telephone number

01966 485485

E-mail address

ralpheast@brightinsurance.co.uk

Reference number

GuildshireEL/RE/4321/21

DOCUMENT 4 – LETTER OF DENIAL

Winter Wood & Co Solicitors

Rembrandt House,
Lee Lane, Brampton
Guildshire, GU7 8TU
DX 26438 GUILDSHIRE
Tel: 01483 432143
Fax: 01483 432156

Goodlaw Solicitors
DX 3214 GUILDSHIRE

Our ref: NG/GELTD/21/A48
Your ref: BB/WORTH/21/426
Date: 6/11/2021

Dear Sirs

YOUR CLIENT: Mr Neil Worthing
OUR CLIENT: Guildshire Engineering Limited
ACCIDENT DATE: 11 June 2021

We act for Guildshire Engineering Limited in relation to the above mentioned matter, which has now exited the Portal. As you are aware, our client disputes liability in this matter. Consequently, in furtherance of the Pre-action Protocol for Personal Injury Claims, we write to set out a detailed response to the matters raised in the CNF.

Although it is accepted that Mr Worthing did suffer an injury on 11 June 2021 at our client's premises, the causes of the accident are disputed.

- Our client strongly disputes the allegations that it failed to provide competent fellow workers. Our client provides training to each individual employee in accordance with its legal obligations and insists on the highest levels of behaviour and discipline from its staff. It is our understanding that it was at Mr Worthing's suggestion that an extra box of widgets was placed on one of the trolleys, in direct contravention of the instructions given to him. This made the trolley difficult to manoeuvre, which led directly to the accident. It was your client's inappropriate behaviour which caused his injury.

- The trolleys were, at the time of the alleged accident, suitable in every respect for their intended purpose. Whilst it is true that our client has since placed foam on the handles of the trolleys, this is in no way an acceptance that they were previously unsuitable. These adaptations had been discussed prior to the alleged accident not due to safety issues but because the handles are thin and uncomfortable to push. It is unreasonable to suggest that all hard surfaces in a factory should be covered in foam.

- It is disputed that our client failed to provide a safe system of work. Our client carried out risk assessments as required by Regulation 3 of the Management of Health and Safety at Work Regulations in relation to all activities conducted in their premises. A copy of the pre and post-accident risk assessments are attached. You will note that trolleys are dealt with in paragraph 14.10 of both documents and that no specific risks are identified. There are no risks associated with pushing a trolley provided the person doing the pushing behaves sensibly. It is our client's contention that Mr Worthing was not behaving sensibly at the time of the accident.

- Mr Worthing was provided with appropriate health and safety information and training, both generally and in relation to manual handling. The foreman, Mr Benson, gave him written information on all relevant matters on the first day of Mr Worthing's employment with our client and he also gave specific instructions as to how the boxes of widgets should be moved. In particular he told Mr Worthing that no more than four boxes should be placed on a trolley at one time, which your client chose to ignore. Mr Benson did not give instructions or training on how to push the trolley as this is a matter of common sense.

In addition to the risk assessment mentioned above, we enclose the following documents:

- Copy of your client's contract of employment. Please note the requirement for employees to read the health and safety information and the standards of behaviour required by all employees at all times.
- Copies of all health and safety documents supplied to your client
- Accident book entry
- First aider report
- RIDDOR report to the HSE
- Earnings information

There are no further relevant documents to disclose.

Mr Worthing was dismissed by our client due to his unreasonable behaviour.

This was an unfortunate accident for which we have every sympathy with your client. Nevertheless, we have no offers to make to settle this matter as we do not consider that our client was negligent.

Please note that, should you wish to continue with this matter, we are instructed to accept service of proceedings on our client's behalf.

Yours faithfully,

Winter Wood & Co

DOCUMENT 5 – ACCIDENT REPORT

EMPLOYEE ACCIDENT REPORT

Report number (consecutive)

1. About the person who had the accident

Name	*NEIL MATTHEW WORTHING*
Address	*22 ELSTEAD HOUSE, GRIFFIN ROAD, CHRISTLETHORPE, GUILDSHIRE GU48 1XX*
Position	*PROCESS ENGINEER*

2. About you, the individual filling in this record

If you did not have the accident, write your name and position

Name *AYSE CAGLAYAN*   Position *SECRETARY AND FIRST AIDER*

3. Details of the accident

When it happened.   Date *11/06/21*   Time *2.45pm (approx)*

Where it happened. State location *Factory floor*

How did the accident happen? Give the cause if possible.   *Mr Worthing and another process engineer were using two trolleys to transport components from one part of the factory to another when the thumb of Mr Worthing's left hand became trapped between the handles of the two trolleys.*

If the person who had the accident suffered an injury, give details *Crushed left thumb - fractured*

Signed by *Ayse Caglayan*   Dated *11/06/21*

4. For the employer only

Complete this box if the accident is reportable under the Reporting of Injuries, Diseases and Dangerous Occurrences Regulations 1995 (RIDDOR).

How was it reported? *On-line, electronically*

Signed by *Ayse Caglayan*   Dated *14/06/21*

DOCUMENT 6 – RIDDOR

HSE

Health and Safety
Executive

Report of an injury

Note: this is a preview of your form and does NOT represent the submitted details of your notification, which will include the Notification number for reference

About you and your organisation

Notifier name	Mr Adam Kilbride		
Job title	Works Manager		
Organisation name	Guildshire Engineering Limited		
Address	77 Blizzard Lane Christlethorpe GUILDSHIRE GU59 2YZ		
Phone no	01483 454545	**Fax Number**	01483 454546
Email Address	akilbride@GEL.co.uk		

Where did the incident happen

The incident happened at the above address

About the incident

Incident Date	11/06/2021	Incident Time	14:45
In which local authority did the incident occur (Country, Geographical Area and Local Authority)?			
England, Guildshire, Christlethorpe			
In which department or where on the premises did the incident happen?			
Factory Floor			
What type of work was being carried out (generally the main business activity of the site)?			
All other Manufacturing - Casting of metals - Light metals			

The enforcing authority for the address where the incident happened is HSE

About the kind of accident

Kind of accident	Lifting and handling injuries
Work process involved	Production, manufacturing or processing
Main factor involved	Loss of control of machinery, transport or equipment
What happened	Mr Worthing and a co-worker, Mr Jerry Packman, were transporting boxes of metal parts across the factory floor using two trolleys when his left thumb was caught between the metal handles of the two trolleys.

	It is believed that some horseplay was involved. Mr Packman has been given a written warning regarding his behaviour and Mr Worthing is no longer employed by this company.

About the injured person

Injured persons name	Mr Neil Matthew Worthing		
Injured persons address	22 Elstead House Griffin Road CHRISTLETHORPE Guildshire GU48 1XX		
Phone no	07777 888444	**What was their occupation or job title?**	Process engineer (temporary contract)
Gender	Male	**Age**	21
Work Status	The injured person was one of my employees.		

About the injured person's injuries

Severity of the injury	Injury preventing the injured person from working for more than 7 days		
Injuries	Fracture	**Part of the body affected**	Finger or fingers

DOCUMENT 7 – LETTER PROPOSING MEDICAL EXPERT

Goodlaw Solicitors

4 College Road, Christlethorpe, Guildshire, GU1 4DZ
DX 3214 GUILDSHIRE; Tel: 01483 606060; Fax: 01483 606099

Winter Wood & Co Solicitors
DX 26438 GUILDSHIRE

> Our ref: BB/WORTH/21/426
> bbraithwaite@goodlaw.co.uk
> Your ref: NG/GELTD/20/A48
> Date: 17 November 2021

Dear Sirs,

OUR CLIENT: Mr Neil Worthing
YOUR CLIENT: Guildshire Engineering Limited
ACCIDENT DATE: 11 June 2021

Further to the above matter and in accordance with the pre-action protocol, we write to inform you of our intention to instruct one of the following consultant orthopaedic surgeons to examine our client and prepare a report for these proceedings:

1. Mr G D Cookson, MB ChB, FRCS (Tr & Orth), Crown House, Victoria Drive, Sandford, Storeshire, SS56 6YP.

2. Mr R B Alimi, MB ChB, FRCS (Orth), BSc (Hons), Hampton Hospital, Hampton, Hillshire HS1 89P.

3. Mrs F Field, MB ChB, FRCS (Orth) FRCS (Ed), The Shambles, Greenway, Heston, Scarshire SS35 1QW.

If you have any objections to any of the above, please let us know before 3 December 2021.

Yours faithfully,

Goodlaw Solicitors

DOCUMENT 8 – MEDICAL REPORT

Mr G D Cookson MB ChB, FRCS (Tr & Orth),

Consultant Orthopaedic Surgeon
Crown House, Victoria Drive, Sandford, Storeshire, SS56 6YP
Tel: 01354 787878; Fax: 01358 675675

Our ref: GDC/21/23/WORTHING
Your ref: BB/WORTH/21/426
10 January 2022

This Medical Report is addressed to the Court

1. **Qualifications**

1.1 I am a consultant Orthopaedic and Trauma Surgeon with over 35 years' experience in this field. I became a consultant in 1999. My full CV is attached to this report.

2. **Instructions**

2.1 This medical report was produced on the instructions of Goodlaw Solicitors set out in their letter dated 8 December 2021. I was requested to examine their client, Mr Neil Worthing, who had been injured in an accident at work. The injury was said to be a fracture of the left thumb.

2.2 I interviewed and examined Mr Worthing at Crown House on 10 January 2022. I was also provided with photocopies of his medical records from his GP and from the A&E Department at Guildshire Hospital.

3. **History**

3.1 Mr Worthing is a 22-year-old law student. He is single and lives in rented accommodation with other students. He is left handed.

3.2 Last summer, he was working at a factory owned by Guildshire Engineering Limited on a temporary basis. On 11 June 2021, he was moving boxes of metal components, when his thumb was trapped between the metal handles of two trolleys. He said that the trolleys had been pushed together with some force.

3.3 Immediately after the accident, he was seen by the First Aider at the workplace, who examined his hand and took him to the A&E department at Guildshire Hospital. An examination and x-ray revealed a fracture of the left thumb and, on the advice of the on-call orthopaedic registrar, a POP was applied to the thumb up to the elbow. He was advised to take painkillers and was discharged with a sling. He had difficulty sleeping for the first week and took Nurofen tablets regularly for the first two weeks. He returned to the Fracture Clinic at Guildshire Hospital two weeks after the accident when the plaster was changed to a thumb spika. He was then bandaged for a further two weeks. Mr Worthing subsequently underwent a course of 5 physiotherapy treatments at the hospital.

3.4 Mr Worthing tells me he was unable to work for one month, by which time he had lost his temporary position at the factory. He was unable to find alternative employment for the remainder of the summer vacation. He was unable to play the piano to the standard required by the hotel for a period of 12 weeks.

4. **Previous medical history**

Mr Worthing is a fit and healthy young man. There is nothing in his medical records which could have any bearing at all on the current injury.

5. **Present condition**

Mr Worthing told me that he is still experiencing pain across the back of the metacarpo-phalangeal joint of his left thumb and that the joint often felt stiff. He said that it would sometimes lock, especially if he was holding objects tightly, and on occasions he would drop them. Writing or playing the piano for long periods of time would cause pain and discomfort. Mr Worthing has to do both of these activities on a regular basis as he is a student and plays the piano at a hotel several evenings a week on a commercial basis. He can drive without difficulty. His sleep is not disturbed unless he has been playing the piano at the hotel. On those occasions, he sometimes has to take pain killers in order to get a good night's sleep.

6. **On examination**

The left thumb was not swollen, bruised or discoloured. However, there was light tenderness over the dorsal aspect of the MCP joint. Ligaments and tendons to the thumb appeared to be intact. Resisted movements of the MCP and IP joints of the thumb were possible without pain. He felt, however, that he could not bend the left thumb as well as the right thumb. The grip and pinch grip of the left hand appeared to be normal.

7. **Diagnosis and opinion**

7.1 Undisplaced avulsion fracture base of proximal phalanx radial side left thumb with bruising to IP joint.

7.2 In my opinion, an injury of this nature would have prevented Mr Worthing from working for one month following the accident and from playing the piano competently for a period of three months following the accident.

7.3 Mr Worthing appears to have made a good but not complete recovery from the injury. There appears to be some slight stiffness of the MCP joint of the left thumb with tenderness over the dorsal aspect but resisted movements are pain free. Gripping appears to cause some pain and discomfort, the thumb occasionally 'locks' and he sometimes drops objects.

7.4 On a balance of probabilities, I believe that his symptoms will gradually settle over a period of 18 months from the accident. He will not develop osteoarthritic changes in his left thumb, IP or MCP joints as a result of the injury sustained on 9 June 2020 and his ability to work and pursue leisure activities will not be disadvantaged as a result of these injuries 18 months post-accident.

8. **Declaration**

8.1 I understand that my overriding duty is to the court, both in preparing reports and in giving oral evidence.

8.2 I am aware of and have complied with the requirement of CPR 35, PD35 and the Guidance for the Instruction of Experts in Civil Claims 2015.

8.3 I have set out in my report what I understand from those instructing me to be the questions in respect of which my opinion as an expert is required.

8.4 I have done my best, in preparing this report, to be accurate and complete. I have mentioned all matters which I regard as relevant to the opinions I have expressed. All of the matters on which I have expressed an opinion lie within my field of expertise.

8.5 I have drawn to the attention of the court all matters, of which I am aware, which might adversely affect my opinion.

8.6 Wherever I have no personal knowledge, I have indicated the source of factual information.

8.7 I have not included anything in this report which has been suggested to me by anyone, including the lawyers instructing me, without forming my own independent view of the matter.

8.8 Where, in my view, there is a range of reasonable opinion, I have indicated the extent of that range in the report.

8.9 At the time of signing the report I consider it to be complete and accurate. I will notify those instructing me if, for any reason, I subsequently consider that the report requires any correction or qualification.

8.10 I understand that this report will be the evidence that I will give under oath, subject to any correction or qualification I may make before swearing to its veracity.

8.11 I have attached to this report a summary of my instructions. [not reproduced]

I confirm that I have made clear which facts and matters referred to in this report are within my own knowledge and which are not. Those that are within my own knowledge I confirm to be true and complete professional opinions on the matters to which they refer.

Signed *G D Cookson*   Dated 11/01/22

DOCUMENT 9 – INTERNAL E-MAIL REGARDING DAMAGES

From: Ravinder Omar, Assistant Solicitor, Goodlaw

Sent: 24/01/22

To: Belinda Braithwaite, Associate Solicitor, Goodlaw

Subject: Neil Worthing case – general damages

Hi Belinda,

I have now had the chance to read through the medical report provided by Mr Cookson and, as you have requested, I have researched the general damages position.

With regard to the Guidelines, although we are dealing with a fracture of the thumb on the dominant hand here, I do not believe the injury is serious enough to fall under (u) moderate injury to the thumb, which suggests an award of between £9,670 and £12,590. The Defendant will undoubtedly try to argue that it falls within heading (w) minor injuries to the thumb – a fracture which has recovered in six months – indicating an award of up to £4,750. Mr W's injury is more serious – gripping causes continuing pain and he is still dropping things. The medical expert states this will improve over 18 months from the accident.

Although this injury isn't a dislocation, I suggest that it most logically falls between the two headings I've mentioned, so within heading (v) severe dislocation or soft tissue injury of the thumb, indicating an award of between £6,340 and £7,780. I looked up similar injuries in Kemp on Westlaw Lawtel but there isn't really anything that is completely on a par with the client's injuries. These are the best matches I could find:

- Capon v Rittal CSM Ltd [2009] – 59-year-old male suffered crush injury to both thumbs causing fractures which healed within 2 months. Permanent residual stiffness and sensitivity in both hands in cold weather. PSLA £6,500 (£10,587.63 RPI). Obviously two thumbs involved here, but there would have been some discount applied.

- Pearson v Snax 24 Ltd [2006] – 60-year-old female dislocated middle joint of right thumb, also a laceration. Looks as if right hand is dominant hand (though it doesn't say!). This seems to be a more serious injury as she was left with constant stiffness, a loss of grip and 50% flexion of the interphalangeal joint – injury permanent and she had also suffered from minor arthritis. PSLA £4,500 (£8,021.54 RPI).

- Jones v Manchester City Council [2004] – female – soft tissue strain to dominant right thumb. Satisfactory recovery after 18 months but permanent minor loss of function with intermittent swelling and aching, slight loss of grip strength. Injury less serious than Mr W's but some permanent loss of function. PSLA £3,500 (£6,523.32 RPI).

- Lawrence v Scott Ltd [1998] – older male – crush injury to dominant thumb, fracture of terminal phalanx of thumb – similar sort of injury. No significant pain after 6 months, permanent slight deformity, minor scarring, continuing cold intolerance. Couldn't do DIY for 10 weeks or swimming for 6 mths. PSLA £2,500 (£5,448.28 RPI).

- Moore v Johnston [1987] – older male fractured interphalangeal joint of non-dominant thumb. Left with slight loss of grip in left hand. Small amount of discomfort experienced when practising hobby or archery. Difficulty in picking up small components and operating certain types of lathes. Similar type of injury, but to non-dominant thumb. However, damages also cover concussion to head. PSLA £2,300 (£8,111.06 RPI).

Suggest we aim for an award towards the top end of heading (u) – £7,780. Do you agree?

Ravi

DOCUMENT 10 – CLAIM FORM

Claim Form	**In the** County Court Money Claims Centre

Fee Account no.	G123000
Help with Fees - Ref no. (if applicable)	**H W F** – ☐☐☐ – ☐☐☐

You may be able to issue your claim online which may save time and money. Go to www.moneyclaim.gov.uk to find out more.

	For court use only
Claim no.	N 22 123
Issue date	12 February 2022

SEAL

Claimant(s) name(s) and address(es) including postcode
Mr Neil Matthew Worthing
22 Elstead House
Griffin Road
Christlethorpe
Guildshire GU48 1XX

Defendant(s) name and address(es) including postcode
Guildshire Engineering Limited
77 Blizzard Lane
Christlethorpe
Guildshire
GU59 2YZ

Brief details of claim

The Claimant claims damages for personal injuries suffered and losses and expenses incurred as a result of an accident on 11 June 2021 whilst in the employment of the Defendant, at its factory at 77 Blizzard Lane, Christlethorpe, Guildshire, as a result of the Defendant's negligence.

Value
The Claimant expects to recover more than £10,000 but not more than £25,000. The amount the Claimant expects to recover as general damages for pain, suffering and loss of amenity is more than £1500.

Defendant's name and address for service including postcode	Guildshire Engineering Limited 77 Blizzard Lane Christlethope Guildshire GU59 2YZ		£
		Amount claimed	
		Court fee	£750.00
		Legal representative's costs	
		Total amount	

For further details of the courts www.gov.uk/find-court-tribunal.
When corresponding with the Court, please address forms or letters to the Manager and always quote the claim number.

N1 Claim form (CPR Part 7) (06.22)   © Crown Copyright 2022

Claim no.	N 22 123

You must indicate your preferred County Court Hearing Centre for hearings here
(see notes for guidance)
Christlethorpe, Guildshire

Do you believe you, or a witness who will give evidence on your behalf, are vulnerable in any way which the court needs to consider?

☐ Yes. Please explain in what way you or the witness are vulnerable and what steps, support or adjustments you wish the court and the judge to consider.

☑ No

Does, or will, your claim include any issues under the Human Rights Act 1998?

☐ Yes
☑ No

Claim no.	N 22 123

Particulars of Claim

☐ attached

☑ to follow

Statement of truth

Note: you are reminded that a copy of this claim form must be served on all other parties.

I understand that proceedings for contempt of court may be brought against a person who makes, or causes to be made, a false statement in a document verified by a statement of truth without an honest belief in its truth.

☐ **I believe** that the facts stated in this claim form and any attached sheets are true.

☑ **The claimant** believes that the facts stated in this claim form and any attached sheets are true. **I am authorised** by the claimant to sign this statement.

Signature

R Omar

☐ Claimant

☐ Litigation friend (where claimant is a child or protected party)

☑ Claimant's legal representative (as defined by CPR 2.3(1))

Date

Day	Month	Year
09	02	2022

Full name

Ravinder Omar

Name of claimant's legal representative's firm

Goodlaw Solicitors

If signing on behalf of firm or company give position or office held

Solicitor

Claimant's or claimant's legal representative's address to which documents should be sent.

Building and street

4 College Road

Second line of address

Town or city

Christlethopre

County (optional)

Guildshire

Postcode

G U 1 4 D Z

If applicable

Phone number

01483 606099

DX number

DX 3214 Guildshire

Your Ref.

BB/WORTH/21/426

Email

romar@goodlaw.co.uk

Find out how HM Courts and Tribunals Service uses personal information you give them when you fill in a form:
https://www.gov.uk/government/organisations/hm-courts-and-tribunals-service/about/personal-information-charter

DOCUMENT 11 – PARTICULARS OF CLAIM

Claim No: N 22 123

IN THE COUNTY COURT MONEY CLAIMS CENTRE

BETWEEN

MR NEIL MATTHEW WORTHING   Claimant

and

GUILDSHIRE ENGINEERING LIMITED   Defendant

PARTICULARS OF CLAIM

1.   The Defendant is a manufacturer of industrial tools. At all material times, the Claimant was employed by the Defendant as a process engineer at their factory at 77, Blizzard Lane, Christlethorpe, Guildshire, GU59 2YZ.

2.   At all times, the provisions of the Management of Health and Safety at Work Regulations 1999 ("the Management Regulations"), the Manual Handling Operations Regulations 1992 (the 'Manual Handling Regulations') and the Provision and Use of Work Equipment Regulations 1998 ("the Work Equipment Regulations") applied.

3.   On 11 June 2021, at approximately 2.45pm, whilst acting in the course of his employment, the Claimant and a co-worker Mr Jeremy Packman, were in the process of moving boxes of widgets from one part of the factory to another. They were transporting the boxes on two trolleys both of which had metal handles on each side. The Claimant was standing at the side of the first trolley, with his left hand on the handle, when the second trolley was pushed forward by Mr Packman with force, causing it to slam into the first trolley. The Claimant's left thumb was trapped between the handles of the two trolleys.

4.   The accident was caused or contributed to by the negligence of the Defendant, its servants or agents acting in the course of their employment.

PARTICULARS OF NEGLIGENCE

The Defendant was negligent in that it:

(a)   failed to provide a safe system of work in that the Claimant was not given adequate information, instruction and training in relation to manual handling and health and safety matters;

(b)   failed to provide safe or adequate plant in that the trolleys were not reasonably safe. The handles of the trolleys should have been covered with foam or an alternative appropriate material in order to minimise the risk of injury to employees;

(c)   failed to provide the Claimant with competent fellow workers. The Defendant was aware that Mr Packman was prone to practical jokes and horseplay within the workplace;

(d)   exposed the Claimant to a foreseeable risk of injury;

(e)   breached the following statutory obligations in that the Defendant, its servants or agents:

(i)   failed to make a suitable and sufficient assessment of the risks to health and safety of their employees in relation to the moving of the trolleys contrary to reg 3(1) of the Management Regulations and reg 4(1)(b)(i) of the Manual Handling Regulations;

(ii) failed to provide information to the Claimant and/or Mr Packman on health and safety risks and protective measures that should be adopted, contrary to reg 10 of the Management Regulations and, specifically, failed to provide information and instruction in the use of equipment, namely the trolleys, contrary to reg 8 of the Work Equipment Regulations;

(iii) failed to provide adequate health and safety training to the Claimant and/or Mr Packman contrary to reg 13 of the Management Regulations and, specifically, failed to provide adequate training in the use of equipment contrary to reg 9 of the Work Equipment Regulations;

(iv) failed to ensure the suitability of work equipment, namely trolleys, for the purpose for which they were provided contrary to reg 4 of the Work Equipment Regulations. 4(b) above is repeated;

(v) failed to ensure that the Claimant and/or Mr Packman received proper information and training on how to handle loads correctly in the process of moving loaded trolleys contrary to reg 4(1)(b)(ii) of the Manual Handling Regulations;

(vi) failed to take appropriate steps to reduce the risk of injury to the Claimant arising out of undertaking the operation set out above to the lowest practicable level contrary to reg 4(1)(b)(ii) of the Manual Handling Regulations.

5. By reason of the matters aforesaid the Claimant has suffered pain and injury and sustained loss and damage.

PARTICULARS OF INJURY

The Claimant, who was born on 14 December 1999, suffered a fracture to his left thumb. He has made a good but not complete recovery and continues to suffer from some joint stiffness and tenderness. It is anticipated that he will make a full recovery within 18 months of the accident. Further details of the Claimant's injuries and prognosis are provided in the attached medical report of Mr GD Cookson, Consultant Orthopaedic Surgeon, dated 11 January 2022.

PARTICULARS OF PAST AND FUTURE EXPENSES AND LOSSES
See Schedule attached.

6. The Claimant claims interest on damages pursuant to Section 69 of the County Courts Act 1984 at such rates and for such periods as the Court shall think fit.

AND the Claimant seeks:

(a) Damages; and

(b) Interest pursuant to paragraph 6.

DATED this 9th day of February 2022   SIGNED *Goodlaw Solicitors*

<u>STATEMENT OF TRUTH</u>

I believe that the facts stated in these Particulars of Claim are true. I understand that proceedings for contempt of court may be brought against anyone who makes, or causes to be made, a false statement in a document verified by a statement of truth without an honest belief in its truth.

Signed: *Neil Worthing*

Full name: Neil Matthew Worthing, Claimant

Dated: 9th February 2022

The Claimant's solicitors are Goodlaw Solicitors of 4 College Road, Christlethorpe, Guildshire, GU1 4DZ, where they will accept service of proceedings on behalf of the Claimant.

To: the Defendant
To: the Court Manager

DOCUMENT 12 – SCHEDULE OF PAST AND FUTURE EXPENSES AND LOSSES

IN THE COUNTY COURT MONEY CLAIMS CENTRE   Claim No: N 22 123

BETWEEN

MR NEIL MATTHEW WORTHING   Claimant

and

GUILDSHIRE ENGINEERING LIMITED   Defendant

SCHEDULE OF PAST AND FUTURE EXPENSES AND LOSSES

The Claimant (d.o.b 14 December 1999) was employed by the Defendant and injured at the Defendant's premises on 11 June 2021, when his left thumb was trapped between the metal handles of two trolleys. He suffered a fracture of the left thumb. His hand and arm were placed in a plaster of paris casing for two weeks and his thumb was bandaged for two weeks thereafter. He underwent five physiotherapy treatments, was unable to work for the remaining nine weeks of his contract with the Defendant, or play the piano at the Swan Lake Hotel for twelve weeks.

Loss of earnings

Guildshire Engineering Ltd

Pre-accident weekly net wage = £296

9 weeks @ £296		£2,664	
Less received from employers	£296		
Net loss of earnings		£2,368	

Swan Lake Hotel

Pre-accident weekly net wage = £260

12 weeks @ £260		£3,120	
Total net loss of earnings			£5,488

Travelling expenses

Journeys to and from hospital/outpatients

2 x trips to have PoP/bandages removed		
5 x trips for physiotherapy		
Total 7 x trips		
(10 miles @ 45p per mile £4.50 per trip)	£31.50	
Car parking 7 x £2	£14	
Total		£45.50

Cost of care

4 hours per day for 14 days @ £7 per hour	£392
TOTAL	£5,925.50

INTEREST

Interest will be claimed on the above special damages at half the special account rate from the date of the incident until the date of trial or earlier settlement

STATEMENT OF TRUTH

I believe the facts stated in this schedule are true. I understand that proceedings for contempt of court may be brought against anyone who makes, or causes to be made, a false statement in a document verified by a statement of truth without an honest belief in its truth.

Signed: Neil Worthing

Dated this 9th day of February 2022

DOCUMENT 13 – FORM CRU 1

**Department
for Work &
Pensions**

A claim for compensation
because of an accident or incident

We have many different ways we can communicate with you
If you would like braille, British Sign Language, a hearing loop, translations, large print, audio or something else please tell us.

Mandatory requirements

Please answer all questions. If this form is not completed correctly we may not be able to register the claim.

These are set out in:
- Regulations 3, 6 and 7 of the Social Security (Recovery of Benefits) Regulations 1997, and
- Regulation 7 of the Road Traffic (NHS Charges) Regulations 1999, and
- Regulation 5 of the Personal Injuries (NHS Charges) (General), and Road Traffic (NHS Charges) (Amendment) Regulations 2006.

Please use **BLOCK CAPITALS** if you are filling in this form with a pen.

About the injured person

1. National Insurance (NI) number

W	K	9	8	7	9	9	9	X

2. Surname

WORTHING

3. First forename

NEIL

4. Other forename(s)

MATTHEW

5. Any other known surname(s) for example maiden name

About the injured person continued

6. Title
    For example Mr, Mrs, Miss, Ms.

Mr

7. Gender

    ☐ Female

    ☑ Male

8. Date of birth - DD/MM/YYYY

14/12/1999

9. Date of death (if applicable) - DD/MM/YYYY

10. Address including postcode

22 ELSTEAD HOUSE, GRIFFIN ROAD, CHRISTLETHORPE, GUILDSHIRE, GU48 1XX

Reason for claim

11. Please tell us the date of the accident or alleged clinical negligence.

    DD/MM/YYYY

11/06/2021

About the accident or incident

12. If this compensation claim is because of an accident or condition, please describe the injuries that happened due to that accident. Include the specific body parts involved, for example left arm, left ankle.

We cannot accept 'to be confirmed' or 'not known'.

> FRACTURED LEFT THUMB ARISING FROM AN ACCIDENT AT WORK WHEN THUMB WAS TRAPPED BETWEEN THE HANDLES OF 2 METAL TROLLEYS

Name of disease

13. If compensation is also being claimed for condition(s) before the disease was diagnosed tell us in the box below.

Type of liability

14. Pick **one** option below:

- [✔] employer
- [ ] clinical negligence
- [ ] public
- [ ] motor
- [ ] other - tell us here

About the compensator

15. Name of compensator or compensator's representative

WINTER WOOD & CO. SOLICITORS

16. Full postal address

REMBRANT HOUSE
LEE LANE, BRAMPTON,
GUILDSHIRE, GU7 8TU
DX 26438 GUILDSHIRE

17. On behalf of:
(enter name of compensator if representative's details given above)

BRIGHT INSURANCE CO. LTD

18. Your reference (maximum of 24 characters)

| N | G | / | G | E | L | | T | D | / | 2 | 1 | / | A | 4 | 8 | | | | | | | | |

19. Name of insured or policy holder or car registration

GUILDSHIRE ENGINEERING LIMITED

20. Telephone number

01483 432143

About the injured person's representative

21. Name of representative

GOODLAW SOLICITORS

22. Full postal address

4 COLLEGE ROAD
CHRISTLETHORPE
GUILDSHIRE GU1 4DZ
DX 3214 GUILDSHIRE

23. Your reference (maximum of 24 characters)

| B | B | / | W | O | R | T | H | / | 2 | 1 | / | 4 | 2 | 6 | | | | | | | | | |

About the injured person's representative continued

24. Telephone number

01483 606060

About the hospital(s) attended because of the accident or incident

25. Did the injured person receive NHS treatment because of the incident?

No ☐

Yes ☑

Not yet known ☐

26. Is the compensator the same as the Trust?

No ☑

Yes ☐ If **Yes**, do not complete hospital details.

Please list the hospital(s) in the order the injured person attended.

27. Name of first hospital (if applicable)

GUILDSHIRE HOSPITAL

28. Address including postcode (if applicable)

GROVE ROAD CHRISTLETHORPE GUILDSHIRE GU34 1HH

29. Name of second hospital (if applicable)

30. Address including postcode (if applicable)

If further hospitals attended please provide details on a separate sheet.

What to do now

Send this form to:
Debt Centre Washington
Compensation Recovery Unit
Post Handling Site B
Wolverhampton
WV99 2FR

Or

Email: cru1@dwp.gov.uk

DD/MM/YYYY

Date: 11/02/2022

Why DWP needs personal information and how we treat it

We will treat your personal information carefully. We may use it for any of our purposes.
To learn about your information rights and how we use it, please see our Personal
Information Charter at **www.gov.uk**

DOCUMENT 14 – CRU CERTIFICATE

DWP Department for Work and Pensions	CRU DX68560 Washington 4	Compensation Recovery Unit Post Handling Site B Wolverhampton WV99 2FR

Tel.: 0191-2252377
Fax.: 0191-2252366
Typetalk:-1800101912252377

Our Ref: NLB – 416

Your Ref: BB/WORTH/21/426

Date: 23/02/2022

Below is a copy of the Certificate of Recoverable Benefits sent to Winter Wood & Co.

Please note: This is for information only – no payment is required from you

CRU101

Certificate of Recoverable Benefits

Date of issue: 23/02/2022

Your ref: NG/GELTD/21/A48   Our ref: NBL – 416

Injured person: NEIL M WORTHING

This certificate shows the amount due to the Department for Work and Pensions (DWP), as a result of an accident or injury which occurred on 11/06/2021 to the person named above and is issued in response to your request for a Certificate of Recoverable Benefits which was received on 16/02/2022.

The amount due is NIL. No recoverable benefits have been paid.

This Certificate is valid until 16/08/2022.

Authorized by   S Peters Compensation Recovery Unit
On behalf of the Secretary of State

Issue No. 19988776   **CRU100**

DOCUMENT 15 – DEFENCE

Claim No: N 22 123

IN THE COUNTY COURT MONEY CLAIMS CENTRE

BETWEEN

MR NEIL MATTHEW WORTHING   Claimant

and

GUILDSHIRE ENGINEERING LIMITED   Defendant

———————————

DEFENCE

———————————

1. Paragraphs 1 and 2 of the Particulars of Claim are admitted.

2. As to Paragraph 3, save that it is admitted that the Claimant suffered some accidental injury on 11 June 2021 at the Defendant's premises, the Defendant is unable to admit or deny the remaining allegations and requires the Claimant to prove them.

3. It is denied that the Defendant, its servant or agent, was negligent as alleged in paragraph 4 or at all.

4   As to the Particulars of Negligence in Paragraph 4:

   (i)   4(a) and 4(e)(i)(ii)(iii)(v) and (vi) are denied. In order to ensure a safe system of work was in operation at all times, the Defendant carried out a suitable and sufficient risk assessment on 27 April 2020, a copy of which is attached to this Defence. The Claimant and Mr Packman were provided with appropriate health and safety information and training both generally and in relation to manual handling, orally and in writing. A copy of the written information relevant to this matter is attached to this Defence. The Claimant and Mr Packman received specific instructions not to place more than 4 boxes of widgets on each trolley. In the circumstances, it was not reasonable for the Defendant to provide instructions on how to push a trolley, that being a matter of common sense;

   (ii)   4(b) and 4(e)(iv) are denied. The trolleys were suitable for the purpose for which they were provided;

   (iii) 4(c) is denied. It is admitted that the Defendant was aware of Mr Packman's nature as stated in 4(c), but it is denied that the Defendant failed to provide the Claimant with competent fellow workers. The health and safety information and training mentioned in 4(i) above is provided to all employees, and was provided to Mr Packman. This included clear instructions that practical jokes and horseplay on the Defendant's premises would not be tolerated, and that any such incidents that did arise would lead to investigation and disciplinary action where appropriate. To the Defendant's knowledge, no incidents of horseplay had taken place on the Defendant's premises for at least two years prior to this incident.

   (iv)   4(d) is denied. 4(i) to (iii) are repeated.

5. Further or in the alternative, if, which is not admitted, the Claimant's thumb became trapped between the handles of the trolleys as alleged and this was caused wholly or partly by any inappropriate behaviour on the part of Mr Packman, which is denied, Mr Packman was acting contrary to instructions given to him by the Defendant and was therefore not acting in the course of his employment.

6. Further or in the alternative, if, which is not admitted, the Claimant's thumb became trapped between the handles of the trolleys as alleged, the accident was wholly caused or alternatively materially contributed to by his own negligence.

PARTICULARS OF NEGLIGENCE

The Claimant:

(a)   stacked the second trolley with five boxes instead of four as instructed;

(b)   failed to exercise reasonable care for his own safety by engaging in horseplay with Mr Packman and encouraging him to behave irresponsibly.

7.   The Defendant denies that any pain, injury, loss or damage alleged in Paragraph 5 was caused by any negligence by the Defendant as alleged or at all. The Defendant is not in a position to agree or dispute the contents of the attached medical report of Mr Cookson or the alleged losses and expenses set out in the attached Schedule. Consequently, the Defendant puts the Claimant to strict proof in relation to all damages claimed.

PARTICULARS OF PAST AND FUTURE EXPENSES AND LOSSES

See Counter Schedule attached

DATED this 18th day of February 2022   SIGNED *Winter Wood & Co*

STATEMENT OF TRUTH

The Defendant believes that the facts stated in this Defence are true. I understand that proceedings for contempt of court may be brought against anyone who makes, or causes to be made, a false statement in a document verified by a statement of truth without an honest belief in its truth.

I am duly authorised by the Defendant to sign this statement.

Full name: Jacob Hudson

Signed: *J Hudson*   Position held: Managing Director
18th February 2022

The Defendant's solicitors are Winter Wood & Co, Rembrandt House, Lee Lane, Brampton, Guildshire, GU7 8TU where they will accept service of proceedings on behalf of the Defendant.

To: The Claimant
To: The Court Manager

(Note to readers – the attachments referred to in this Defence are not reproduced)

DOCUMENT 16 – DIRECTIONS QUESTIONNAIRE

Directions questionnaire (Fast track and Multi-track)

In the Christlethorpe County Court	Claim No. N 22 123

To be completed by, or on behalf of,

> Mr Neil Matthew Worthing

who is [1X][2X][3X][∞∞][Claimant][Defendant][Part 20 claimant] in this claim

---

You should note the date by which this questionnaire must be returned and the name of the court it should be returned to since this may be different from the court where the proceedings were issued.

If you have settled this claim (or if you settle it on a future date) and do not need to have it heard or tried, you must let the court know immediately.

If the claim is not settled, a judge will allocate it to an appropriate case management track. To help the judge choose the most just and cost-effective track, you must now complete the directions questionnaire.

You should write the claim number on any other documents you send with your directions questionnaire. Please ensure they are firmly attached to it.

A Settlement

Notes

Under the Civil Procedure Rules parties should make every effort to settle their case before the hearing. This could be by discussion or negotiation (such as a roundtable meeting or settlement conference) or by a more formal process such as mediation. The court will want to know what steps have been taken. Settling the case early can save costs, including court hearing fees.

For legal representatives only

I confirm that I have explained to my client the need to try to settle; the options available; and the possibility of costs sanctions if they refuse to try to settle.

[✓] I confirm

For all

Your answers to these questions may be considered by the court when it deals with the questions of costs: see Civil Procedure Rules Part 44.

The court may order a stay, whether or not all the other parties to the claim agree. Even if you are requesting a stay, you must still complete the rest of the questionnaire.

1. Given that the rules require you to try to settle the claim before the hearing, do you want to attempt to settle at this stage?

[ ] Yes   [✓] No

2. If Yes, do you want a one month stay?

[ ] Yes   [✓] No

3. If you answered 'No' to question 1, please state below the reasons why you consider it inappropriate to try to settle the claim at this stage.

More information about mediation, the fees charged and a directory of mediation providers is available online from www.civilmediation.justice.gov.uk This service provides members of the public and businesses with contact details for national civil and commercial mediation providers, all of whom are accredited by the Civil Mediation Council.

Reasons:

> Attempts to settle were made pre-issue but were unsuccessful. There is no possibility of settlement at this stage, but both parties will reconsider the matter following exchange of documents / witness statements.

B Court

Notes

B1. (High Court only)

The claim has been issued in the High Court. Do you consider it should remain there?   ☐ Yes   ☐ No

If Yes, in which Division/List?

If No, in which County Court hearing centre would you prefer the case to be heard?

High Court cases are usually heard at the Royal Courts of Justice or certain Civil Trial Centres. Fast or multi-track trials may be dealt with at a Civil Trial Centre or at the court where the claim is proceeding.

B2. Trial (all cases)

Is there any reason why your claim needs to be heard at a court or hearing centre?   ☑ Yes   ☐ No

If Yes, say which court and why?

Christlethorpe County Court, as this is local to both parties and their legal representatives.

C Pre-action protocols

You are expected to comply fully with the relevant pre-action protocol.

Have you done so?   ☑ Yes   ☐ No

If you have not complied, or have only partially complied, please explain why.

Before any claim is started, the court expects you to have complied with the relevant pre-action protocol, and to have exchanged information and documents relevant to the claim to assist in settling it. To find out which protocol is relevant to your claim see: www.justice.gov.uk/guidance/courts-and-tribunals/courts/procedure-rules/civil/menus/protocol.htm

D Case management information

D1. Applications

Have you made any application(s) in this claim?   ☐ Yes   ☑ No

If Yes, what for? (e.g. summary judgment, add another party).

For hearing on ☐☐ / ☐☐ / ☐☐☐☐

D1. Applications

It is important for the court to know if you have already made any applications in the claim (or are about to issue one), what they are for and when they will be heard. The outcome of the applications may affect the case management directions the court gives.

D2. Track

If you have indicated in the proposed directions a track attached which would not be the normal track for the claim, please give brief reasons below for your choice.

D2. Track

The basic guide by which claims are normally allocated to a track is the amount in dispute, although other factors such as the complexity of the case will also be considered. Leaflet *EX305 – The Fast Track and the Multi-track*, explains this in greater detail.

2

D Case management information (continued)

D3. Disclosure of electronic documents (multi-track cases only)

If you are proposing that the claim be allocated to the multi-track:

1. Have you reached agreement, either using the Electronic Documents Questionnaire in Practice Direction 31B or otherwise, about the scope and extent of disclosure of electronic documents on each side? ☐ Yes ☐ No

2. If No, is such agreement likely? ☐ Yes ☐ No

3. If there is no agreement and no agreement is likely, what are the issues about disclosure of electronic documents which the court needs to address, and should they be dealt with at the Case Management Conference or at a separate hearing?

```



```

D4. Disclosure of non-electronic documents (all cases)

What directions are proposed for disclosure?

```



```

For all multi-track cases, except personal injury.

Have you filed and served a disclosure report (Form N263) (see Civil Procedure Rules Part 31). ☐ Yes ☐ No

Have you agreed a proposal in relation to disclosure that meets the overriding objective? ☐ Yes ☐ No

If Yes, please ensure this is contained within the proposed directions attached and specify the draft order number.

```

```

E Experts

Do you wish to use expert evidence at the trial or final hearing? ☑ Yes ☐ No

Have you already copied any experts' report(s) to the other party(ies)? ☐ None yet obtained ☑ Yes ☐ No

Do you consider the case suitable for a single joint expert in any field? ☑ Yes ☐ No

There is no presumption that expert evidence is necessary, or that each party will be entitled to their own expert(s). Therefore, the court requires a short explanation of your proposals with regard to expert evidence.

E **Experts** (continued)

Please list any single joint experts you propose to use and any other experts you wish to rely on. Identify single joint experts with the initials 'SJ' after their name(s). Please provide justification of your proposal and an estimate of costs.

Expert's name	Field of expertise (e.g. orthopaedic surgeon, surveyor, engineer)	Justification for expert and estimate of costs
Mr G D Cookson	Consultant orthopaedic surgeon	Evidence as to diagnosis of injury and likely duration of pain / disability £1500 + VAT

F **Witnesses**

Which witnesses of fact do you intend to call at the trial or final hearing including, if appropriate, yourself?

Witness name	Witness to which facts
Mr Neil Worthing - Claimant	The lack of information / traning he received from the Defendant; the accident; the injury and associated losses and expenses.

G **Trial or Final Hearing**

How long do you estimate the trial or final hearing will take?

☑ **less than one day**   ☐ **one day**   ☐ **more than one day**

3 Hrs   State number of days

Give the best estimate you can of the time that the court will need to decide this case. If, later you have any reason to shorten or lengthen this estimate you should let the court know immediately.

Are there any days within the next 12 months when you, an expert or an essential witness will not be able to attend court for trial or final hearing?

You should only enter those dates when you, your expert(s) or essential witnesses will not be available to attend court because of holiday or other commitments.

If Yes, please give details

Name	Dates not available
Mr Worthing Mr Cookson	6-17 June 2022 - exams 15-26 August 2022 - holiday

You should notify the court immediately if any of these dates change.

H   Costs

Do not complete this section if:

    1) you do not have a legal representative acting for you

    2) the case is subject to fixed costs

If your claim is likely to be allocated to the Multi-Track form Precedent H
must be filed at in accordance with CPR 3.13.

I confirm Precedent H is attached. ☐

I   Other information

Do you intend to make any applications in the future?   ☐ Yes   ☑ No

If Yes, what for?

In the space below, set out any other information you consider will help the judge to manage the claim.

Do you believe you, or a witness who will give evidence on your behalf, are vulnerable in any way which the court needs to consider?

☐ Yes. Please explain in what way you or the witness are vulnerable and what steps, support or adjustments you wish the court and the judge to consider.

☑ No

J Directions

You must attempt to agree proposed directions with all other parties. **Whether agreed or not a draft of the order for directions which you seek must accompany this form.**

All proposed directions for multi-track cases must be based on the directions at www.justice.gov.uk/courts/procedure-rules/civil

All proposed directions for fast track cases must be based on CPR Part 28.

Signature

Goodlaw, Solicitors	Date
	0 4 / 0 3 / 2 0 2 2

[Legal Representative for the][~~1st~~][~~2nd~~][~~3rd~~][xxxxxxxx]
[Claimant][~~Defendant~~][~~Part 20 claimant~~]

Please enter your name, reference number and full postal address including details of telephone, DX, fax or e-mail

Goodlaw Solicitors 4 College Road Christlethorpe Guildshire	If applicable	
	Telephone no.	01483 606060
	Fax no.	01483 606099
	DX no.	DX3214 Guild
Postcode G U 1 4 D Z	Your ref.	BB/WorthH1/21/426

E-mail	bbraithwaite@goodlaw.co.uk

DOCUMENT 17 – NOTICE OF ALLOCATION TO FAST TRACK AND DIRECTIONS

To: the Claimant's Solictor

Goodlaw Solicitors
4 College Road
Christlethorpe
Guildshire
GU1 4DZ

In the	COUNTY COURT AT CHRISTLETHORPE
Claim Number	N 22 123
Claimant (including ref)	Mr Neil Matthew Worthing
Defendant (including ref)	Guildshire Engineering Limited
Date	20/04/22

Warning: you must comply with the terms imposed upon you by this order otherwise your case is liable to be struck out or some other sanction imposed. If you cannot comply you are expected to make formal application to the court before any deadline imposed upon you expires.

On 20 April 2022, DISTRICT JUDGE BILLINGHURST, sitting in the County Court at Christlethorpe, considered the papers in the case and **ordered** that:

1. This case is allocated to the fast track

2. (a) Standard disclosure by lists between the parties by 4:00pm on 25 May 2022 and CPR 31.21 shall apply in the event of default.

   (b) Inspection of documents by 4:00pm on 8 June 2022.

3. (a) Statements of witnesses as to fact to be exchanged by 4:00pm on 6 July 2022.

   (b) Witness statements shall stand as evidence in chief.

   (c) Evidence shall not be permitted at trial from a witness whose evidence has not been served in accordance with this order.

4. (a) The Claimant is permitted to rely on the written report of Mr G D Cookson dated 11 July 2022.

   (b) The Defendant shall raise any questions of the said expert in writing by 4:00pm on 20 July 2022 which shall be responded to by 4:00pm on 17 August 2022.

5. (a) The Claimant shall serve an updated schedule of damages by 4:00pm on 24 August 2022 and the Defendant shall serve any counter schedule by 4:00pm on 31 August 2022 both incorporating an estimate of the general range of damages.

   (b) Within 7 days of the exchange of schedules the parties shall communicate and shall agree subject to liability the range of general damages and the extent to which the general damages are agreed and shall agree a case summary setting out the extent of agreement and of disagreement giving reasons for the disagreement.

6. The parties shall file a Listing Questionnaire by 4:00pm on 28 September 2022 together with the case summary directed at 5(b) above.

7. (a) The matter be listed for trial before a District Judge in a 3 week trial window commencing 7 November 2022 with an estimated length of hearing of 3 hours.

   (b) The Claimant shall lodge the trial bundle by no later than 5 days prior to the date of trial.

Dated 20 April 2022

The court office at the County Court at CHRISTLETHORPE is open between 10am and 4pm Monday to Friday. When corresponding with the court, please address forms or letters to the Court Manager and quote the claim number. Tel: 01483 123123 Fax: 01483 123345.

DOCUMENT 18 – INTERNAL E-MAIL RELATING TO OFFER

From: Ravinder Omar, Assistant Solicitor, Goodlaw

Sent: 08/07/22

To: Belinda Braithwaite, Associate Solicitor, Goodlaw

Subject: Neil Worthing case – settlement

Hi Belinda

Just to let you know that we exchanged witness statements with the defendant last week. In his statement Jerry Packman, the guy who was loading the trolleys with Mr W, confirms that it was Mr W who suggested putting the extra box onto the second trolley. He also says that it was Mr W who started messing about with the trolleys, that Mr W pushed his trolley at Mr P's trolley first and then stood about laughing as Mr P tried to push his trolley. That's when the accident happened. In addition, contrary to what he told our client, he is now saying that he did have H&S/manual handling training.

I discussed this with Rosie Smith at Winter Wood on Friday. I said that they couldn't avoid liability. Just handing over H&S info to Mr W isn't sufficient instruction and training, particularly as he has never worked in a factory before. They haven't got any evidence to back up their statement that the foam on the handles was sorted out before the accident and Mr Packman was messing about too. She more or less said she agreed and that she would be talking to her client about making a Part 36 offer on a 25% contrib. basis. The certificate obtained from the CRU shows that there are no repayable benefits. (There are NHS charges which relate to the treatment our client received at hospital, but the defendant has to pay that.)

She was unhappy about our claim for gratuitous care, saying that the number of hours claimed and the amount per hour are unreasonable. She didn't like our mileage rates either but I don't think they'll quibble over a few pounds.

I couldn't get hold of Mr W until this morning. He admitted that Mr P's account was accurate. He is keen to settle and understands that the defendant will want to knock a bit off for contributory negligence. I told him we would wait and see what they offered and then we would talk again.

What do you think?

Ravi

DOCUMENT 19 – PART 36 OFFER LETTER

Winter Wood & Co Solicitors

Rembrandt House,
Lee Lane, Brampton
Guildshire, GU7 8TU
DX 26438 GUILDSHIRE
Tel: 01483 432143
Fax: 01483 432156

Goodlaw Solicitors
DX 3214 GUILDSHIRE

Our ref: NG/GELTD/21/A48
Your ref: BB/WORTH/21/426

Date: 12 July 2022

Dear Sirs

YOUR CLIENT: Mr Neil Worthing
OUR CLIENT: Guildshire Engineering Limited
ACCIDENT DATE: 11 June 2021
PART 36 OFFER – without prejudice save as to costs

We are instructed by our client to put forward the following offer which is made without prejudice save as to costs pursuant to Part 36 of the Civil Procedure Rules 1998:

1. Our client agrees to pay your client the sum of £8,200 inclusive of interest in full and final settlement of all claims your client has or may have against our client in this matter.

2. Our client agrees in addition to pay your client's reasonable costs, including costs that have been incurred up to 21 days after the date you receive this letter, as agreed or, if not agreed within 14 days, to be assessed by detailed assessment.

3. This offer is open for acceptance for 21 days from the date you receive this letter.

We await hearing from you.

Yours faithfully,

Winter Wood & Co

DOCUMENT 20 – INTERNAL E-MAIL RELATING TO PART 36 OFFER

From: Ravinder Omar, Assistant Solicitor Goodlaw

Sent: 15/07/2022

To: Belinda Braithwaite, Principal Solicitor, Goodlaw

Subject: Neil Worthing

Hi Belinda

I telephoned Mr W to inform him of the offer. I talked him through the options and advised him that I thought it was reasonable but perhaps a little on the low side. We agreed that I would speak to the defendant's solicitors to see if I can get them to improve their offer but if not, he wanted to accept their offer.

I then spoke to Rosie Smith at Winter Wood & Co. Their offer is based on generals of £4,800, 25% contributory negligence and some reduction in the claim for gratuitous care. After some negotiation she agreed to increase the total offer to £9,500 which I accepted on Mr W's behalf. I will send a consent order to finalise the matter.

I rang Mr W to tell him the good news – he is delighted!

Ravi

DOCUMENT 21 – ACCEPTANCE LETTER

Goodlaw Solicitors

4 College Road, Christlethorpe, Guildshire, GU1 4DZ
DX 3214 GUILDSHIRE; Tel: 01483 606060; Fax: 01483 606099

Winter Wood & Co Solicitors
DX 26438 GUILDSHIRE

Your ref: NG/GELTD/21/A48
bbraithwaite@goodlaw.co.uk
Our ref : BB/WORTH/21/426
Date: 20 July 2022

Dear Sirs,

OUR CLIENT: Mr Neil Worthing
ADDRESS: 22 Elstead House, Griffin Road, Guildshire, GU48 1XX
ACCIDENT DATE: 11 June 2021

Further to our telephone conversation with Rosie Smith we confirm that our client is prepared to accept your offer of £9,500 in full and final settlement of his claim plus our costs to be assessed if not agreed. Please sign and return the enclosed consent order which we will then file at court.

Yours faithfully

Goodlaw Solicitors

DOCUMENT 22 – DRAFT CONSENT ORDER

Claim No: N 22 123

IN THE COUNTY COURT AT CHRISTLETHORPE

BETWEEN

MR NEIL MATTHEW WORTHING   Claimant

and

GUILDSHIRE ENGINEERING LIMITED   Defendant

<u>CONSENT ORDER</u>

Upon the parties agreeing to settle this matter

AND BY CONSENT

IT IS ORDERED THAT

1. The Defendant pays the Claimant the sum of £9,500.00 in full and final settlement by 4pm on 19 August 2022;
2. The Defendant pays the Claimant's costs of this matter to be assessed on the standard basis if not agreed.

We consent to the terms of this order.	We consent to the terms of this order.
Goodlaw Solicitors	**Winter Wood & Co Solicitors**
Dated 29 July 2022	Dated 28 July 2022

Pre-action Protocol for Personal Injury Claims

1. Introduction

1.1

1.1.1   This Protocol is primarily designed for personal injury claims which are likely to be allocated to the fast track and to the entirety of those claims: not only to the personal injury element of a claim which also includes, for instance, property damage. It is not intended to apply to claims which proceed under—

(a)   the Pre-Action Protocol for Low Value Personal Injury Claims in Road Traffic Accidents from 31 July 2013;

(b)   the Pre-Action Protocol for Low Value Personal Injury (Employers' Liability and Public Liability) Claims;

(c)   the Pre-Action Protocol for the Resolution of Clinical Disputes;

(d)   the Pre-Action Protocol for Disease and Illness Claims; or

(e)   the Pre-Action Protocol for Personal Injury Claims below the small claims limit in road traffic accidents ("the RTA Small Claims Protocol")

1.1.2   If at any stage the claimant values the claim at more than the upper limit of the fast track, the claimant should notify the defendant as soon as possible. However, the "cards on the table" approach advocated by this Protocol is equally appropriate to higher value claims. The spirit, if not the letter of the Protocol, should still be followed for claims which could potentially be allocated multi-track. All parties are expected to consider the Serious Injury Guide in any claim to which that Guide applies (http://www.seriousinjuryguide.co.uk/).

1.2   Claims which exit either of the low value pre-action protocols listed at paragraph 1.1.1(a) and (b) ("the low value protocols") prior to Stage 2, or the RTA Small Claims Protocol, will proceed under this Protocol from the point specified in those protocols, and as set out in paragraph 1.3.

1.3

1.3.1   Where a claim exits a low value protocol because the defendant considers that there is inadequate mandatory information in the Claim Notification Form ("CNF"), the claim will proceed under this Protocol from paragraph 5.1.

1.3.2   Where in a claim under either low value protocol a defendant—

(a)   alleges contributory negligence;

(b)   does not complete and send the CNF Response; or

(c)   does not admit liability,

the claim will proceed under this Protocol from paragraph 5.5.

1.3.3   Where a claim exits the RTA Small Claims Protocol and is directed to this Protocol, the claim will proceed under this Protocol from paragraph 5.5.

1.4

1.4.1   This Protocol sets out conduct that the court would normally expect prospective parties to follow prior to the commencement of proceedings. It establishes a reasonable process and timetable for the exchange of information relevant to a dispute, sets standards for the content and quality of letters of claim, and in particular, the conduct of pre-action negotiations. In particular, the parts of this Protocol that are concerned with rehabilitation are likely to be of application in all claims.

1.4.2   The timetable and the arrangements for disclosing documents and obtaining expert evidence may need to be varied to suit the circumstances of the case. Where one or both parties consider the detail of the Protocol is not appropriate to the case, and proceedings are subsequently issued, the court will expect an explanation as to why the Protocol has not been followed, or has been varied.

1.5   Where either party fails to comply with this Protocol, the court may impose sanctions. When deciding whether to do so, the court will look at whether the parties have complied in substance with the relevant principles and requirements. It will also consider the effect any non-compliance has had on another party. It is not likely to be concerned with minor or technical shortcomings (see paragraphs 13 to 15 of the Practice Direction on Pre-Action Conduct and Protocols).

1.6   The Protocol recommends that a defendant be given three months to investigate and respond to a claim before proceedings are issued. This may not always be possible, particularly where a claimant only consults a legal representative close to the end of any relevant limitation period. In these circumstances, the claimant's solicitor should give as much notice of the intention to issue proceedings as is practicable and the parties should consider whether the court might be invited to extend time for service of the claimant's supporting documents and for service of any defence, or alternatively, to stay the proceedings while the recommended steps in the Protocol are followed.

Litigants in Person

1.7   If a party to the claim does not have a legal representative they should still, in so far as reasonably possible, fully comply with this Protocol. Any reference to a claimant in this Protocol will also mean the claimant's legal representative.

2. Overview of Protocol – General Aim

2.1   The Protocol's objectives are to—

(a)   encourage the exchange of early and full information about the dispute;

(b)   encourage better and earlier pre-action investigation by all parties;

(c)   enable the parties to avoid litigation by agreeing a settlement of the dispute before proceedings are commenced;

(d)   support the just, proportionate and efficient management of proceedings where litigation cannot be avoided; and

(e)   promote the provision of medical or rehabilitation treatment (not just in high value cases) to address the needs of the Claimant at the earliest possible opportunity.

3. The Protocol

An illustrative flow chart is attached at Annexe A which shows each of the steps that the parties are expected to take before the commencement of proceedings.

Letter of Notification

3.1   The claimant or his legal representative may wish to notify a defendant and/or the insurer as soon as they know a claim is likely to be made, but before they are able to send a detailed Letter of Claim, particularly, for instance, when the defendant has no or limited knowledge of the incident giving rise to the claim, or where the claimant is incurring significant expenditure as a result of the accident which he hopes the defendant might pay for, in whole or in part.

3.2   The Letter of Notification should advise the defendant and/or the insurer of any relevant information that is available to assist with determining issues of liability/ suitability of the claim for an interim payment and/or early rehabilitation.

3.3 If the claimant or his legal representative gives notification before sending a Letter of Claim, it will not start the timetable for the Letter of Response. However the Letter of Notification should be acknowledged within 14 days of receipt.

4. Rehabilitation

4.1 The parties should consider as early as possible whether the claimant has reasonable needs that could be met by medical treatment or other rehabilitative measures. They should discuss how these needs might be addressed.

4.2 The Rehabilitation Code (which can be found at: http://www.iua.co.uk/IUA_Member/ Publications) is likely to be helpful in considering how to identify the claimant's needs and how to address the cost of providing for those needs.

4.3 The time limit set out in paragraph 6.3 of this Protocol shall not be shortened, except by consent to allow these issues to be addressed.

4.4 Any immediate needs assessment report or documents associated with it that are obtained for the purposes of rehabilitation shall not be used in the litigation except by consent and shall in any event be exempt from the provisions of paragraphs 7.2 to 7.11 of this Protocol. Similarly, persons conducting the immediate needs assessment shall not be a compellable witness at court.

4.5 Consideration of rehabilitation options, by all parties, should be an on going process throughout the entire Protocol period.

5. Letter of Claim

5.1 Subject to paragraph 5.3 the claimant should send to the proposed defendant two copies of the Letter of Claim. One copy of the letter is for the defendant, the second for passing on to the insurers, as soon as possible, and, in any event, within 7 days of the day upon which the defendant received it.

5.2 The Letter of Claim should include the information described on the template at Annexe B1. The level of detail will need to be varied to suit the particular circumstances. In all cases there should be sufficient information for the defendant to assess liability and to enable the defendant to estimate the likely size and heads of the claim without necessarily addressing quantum in detail.

5.3 The letter should contain a clear summary of the facts on which the claim is based together with an indication of the nature of any injuries suffered, and the way in which these impact on the claimant's day to day functioning and prognosis. Any financial loss incurred by the claimant should be outlined with an indication of the heads of damage to be claimed and the amount of that loss, unless this is impracticable.

5.4 Details of the claimant's National Insurance number and date of birth should be supplied to the defendant's insurer once the defendant has responded to the Letter of Claim and confirmed the identity of the insurer. This information should not be supplied in the Letter of Claim.

5.5

5.5.1 Where a claim no longer continues under either low value protocol, the CNF completed by the claimant under those protocols can be used as the Letter of Claim under this Protocol unless the defendant has notified the claimant that there is inadequate information in the CNF.

5.5.2 Where a claim no longer continues under the RTA Small Claims Protocol, the Small Claim Notification Form or SCNF completed by the claimant can be used as the Letter of Claim under this Protocol.

5.6   Once the claimant has sent the Letter of Claim no further investigation on liability should normally be carried out within the Protocol period until a response is received from the defendant indicating whether liability is disputed.

Status of Letters of Claim and Response

5.7   Letters of Claim and Response are not intended to have the same formal status as a statement of case in proceedings. It would not be consistent with the spirit of the Protocol for a party to 'take a point' on this in the proceedings, provided that there was no obvious intention by the party who changed their position to mislead the other party.

6. The Response

6.1   Attached at Annexe B2 is a template for the suggested contents of the Letter of Response: the level of detail will need to be varied to suit the particular circumstances.

6.2   The defendant must reply within 21 calendar days of the date of posting of the letter identifying the insurer (if any). If the insurer is aware of any significant omissions from the letter of claim they should identify them specifically. Similarly, if they are aware that another defendant has also been identified whom they believe would not be a correct defendant in any proceedings, they should notify the claimant without delay, with reasons, and in any event by the end of the Response period. Where there has been no reply by the defendant or insurer within 21 days, the claimant will be entitled to issue proceedings. Compliance with this paragraph will be taken into account on the question of any assessment of the defendant's costs.

6.3   The defendant (insurer) will have a maximum of three months from the date of acknowledgment of the Letter of Claim (or of the CNF or SCNF where the claim commenced in a portal) to investigate. No later than the end of that period, The defendant (insurer) should reply by no later than the end of that period, stating if liability is admitted by admitting that the accident occurred, that the accident was caused by the defendant's breach of duty, and the claimant suffered loss and there is no defence under the Limitation Act 1980.

6.4   Where the accident occurred outside England and Wales and/or where the defendant is outside the jurisdiction, the time periods of 21 days and three months should normally be extended up to 42 days and six months.

6.5   If a defendant denies liability and/or causation, their version of events should be supplied. The defendant should also enclose with the response, documents in their possession which are material to the issues between the parties, and which would be likely to be ordered to be disclosed by the court, either on an application for pre-action disclosure, or on disclosure during proceedings. No charge will be made for providing copy documents under the Protocol.

6.6   An admission made by any party under this Protocol may well be binding on that party in the litigation. Further information about admissions made under this Protocol is to be found in Civil Procedure Rules ("CPR") rule 14.1A.

6.7   Following receipt of the Letter of Response, if the claimant is aware that there may be a delay of six months or more before the claimant decides if, when and how to proceed, the claimant should keep the defendant generally informed.

7. Disclosure

7.1 Documents

7.1.1   The aim of early disclosure of documents by the defendant is not to encourage 'fishing expeditions' by the claimant, but to promote an early exchange of relevant information to help in clarifying or resolving issues in dispute. The claimant's solicitor can assist by identifying in the Letter of Claim or in a subsequent letter the particular categories of documents which they consider are relevant and why, with a brief explanation of their purported relevance if necessary.

7.1.2   Attached at Annexe C are specimen, but non-exhaustive, lists of documents likely to be material in different types of claim.

7.1.3   Pre-action disclosure will generally be limited to the documents required to be enclosed with the Letter of Claim and the Response. In cases where liability is admitted in full, disclosure will be limited to the documents relevant to quantum, the parties can agree that further disclosure may be given. If either or both of the parties consider that further disclosure should be given but there is disagreement about some aspect of that process, they may be able to make an application to the court for pre-action disclosure under Part 31 of the CPR. Parties should assist each other and avoid the necessity for such an application.

7.1.4   The protocol should also contain a requirement that the defendant is under a duty to preserve the disclosure documents and other evidence (CCTV for example). If the documents are destroyed, this could be an abuse of the court process.

Experts

A.   Claims which do not consist of, or include, a claim for a whiplash injury
(whiplash injury is defined in paragraph 7.12.7)

7.2   Save for cases likely to be allocated to the multi-track, the Protocol encourages joint selection of, and access to, quantum experts, and, on occasion liability experts e.g. engineers. The expert report produced is not a joint report for the purposes of CPR Part 35. The Protocol promotes the practice of the claimant obtaining a medical report, disclosing it to the defendant who then asks questions and/or agrees it and does not obtain their own report. The Protocol provides for nomination of the expert by the claimant in personal injury claims.

7.3   Before any party instructs an expert, they should give the other party a list of the name(s) of one or more experts in the relevant speciality whom they consider are suitable to instruct.

7.4   Some solicitors choose to obtain medical reports through medical agencies, rather than directly from a specific doctor or hospital. The defendant's prior consent to this should be sought and, if the defendant so requests, the agency should be asked to provide in advance the names of the doctor(s) whom they are considering instructing.

7.5   Where a medical expert is to be instructed, the claimant's solicitor will organise access to relevant medical records – see specimen letter of instruction at Annexe D.

7.6   Within 14 days of providing a list of experts the other party may indicate an objection to one or more of the named experts. The first party should then instruct a mutually acceptable expert assuming there is one (this is not the same as a joint expert). It must be emphasised that when the claimant nominates an expert in the original Letter of Claim, the defendant has a further 14 days to object to one or more of the named experts after expiration of the 21 day period within which they have to reply to the Letter of Claim, as set out in paragraph 6.2.

7.7   If the defendant objects to all the listed experts, the parties may then instruct experts of their own choice. It will be for the court to decide, subsequently and if proceedings are issued, whether either party had acted unreasonably.

7.8   If the defendant does not object to an expert nominated by the claimant, they shall not be entitled to rely on their own expert evidence within that expert's area of expertise unless—

(a)   the claimant agrees;

      (b)   the court so directs; or

      (c)   the claimant's expert report has been amended and the claimant is not prepared to disclose the original report.

7.9   Any party may send to an agreed expert written questions on the report, via the first party's solicitors. Such questions must be put within 28 days of service of the expert's report and must only be for the purpose of clarification of the report. The expert should send answers to the questions simultaneously to each party.

7.10   The cost of a report from an agreed expert will usually be paid by the instructing first party: the costs of the expert replying to questions will usually be borne by the party which asks the questions.

7.11   If necessary, after proceedings have commenced and with the permission of the court, the parties may obtain further expert reports. It would be for the court to decide whether the costs of more than one expert's report should be recoverable.

B. Claims for whiplash injury

7.12

7.12.1 The provisions of this paragraph apply to any medical report in support of a claim for whiplash injury, whether or not it is part of a claim for other injuries.

7.12.2 Where there is also a claim for other injuries, the provisions of section A above apply to instructions to and reports from experts in respect of those other injuries. Section A above also applies in respect of the use of any non-medical experts.

7.12.3 In respect of a claim for a whiplash injury, the claimant must follow one of the procedures set out in paragraphs 7.12.4 to 7.12.6.

7.12.4 (a)   The claimant must obtain a fixed cost medical report from an accredited medical expert who is instructed via a search of the online database of medical reporting organisations and medical experts held by MedCo (website at: www.medco.org.uk);

        (b)   in instructing an expert to provide a fixed cost medical report in a claim for whiplash injury, it is expected that in most cases the medical expert will not need to see any medical records;

        (c)   where the claimant lives outside England and Wales, but chooses to be examined for the purposes of a medical report in England and Wales, paragraphs (a) and (b) apply.

7.12.5 Where the claimant obtains a medical report in respect of a more serious injury suffered at the same time as the whiplash injury, the claimant may use that report instead of a report under paragraph 7.12.4 above provided that—

        (a)   the report is from a doctor who is listed on the General Medical Council's Specialist Register; and

        (b)   the report provides evidence of the whiplash injury.

7.12.6 Unless paragraph 7.12.4(c) applies, where the claimant lives outside England and Wales, the medical report in respect of the claim for the whiplash injury (or, if there is more than one report, the first report) must be from a person who is recognised by the country in which they practise as—

        (a)   being a medical expert; and

        (b)   having the required qualifications for the purposes of diagnosis and prognosis of a whiplash injury.

7.12.7 The following definitions apply in paragraph 7.12 and in paragraphs 8.2 and 8.3—

        (a)   'associate' means, in respect of a medical expert, a colleague, partner, director, employer or employee in the same practice and 'associated with' has the equivalent meaning;

    (b)   'accredited medical expert' means a medical expert who is accredited by MedCo to provide medical reports in whiplash injury claims;

    (c)   'fixed cost medical report' means a report in a whiplash injury claim which is from a medical expert who, save in exceptional circumstances—

        (i)   has not provided treatment to the claimant;

        (ii)   is not associated with any person who has provided treatment; and

        (iii)   does not propose or recommend treatment that they or an associate then provide;

    (d)   'MedCo' means MedCo Registration Solutions; and

    (e)   'whiplash injury' means an injury or injuries of soft tissue in the neck, back or shoulder suffered because of driver negligence as defined in section 1 of the Civil Liability Act 2018 and as further applied by section 3 of that Act to claims arising from a road traffic accident on or after 31 May 2021 and where the duration of the whiplash injury or any of the whiplash injuries—

        (i)   does not exceed, or is not likely to exceed, two years; or

        (ii)   would not have exceeded, or would not be likely to exceed, two years but for the claimant's failure to take reasonable steps to mitigate its effect.

8. Negotiations following an admission

8.1

8.1.1   Where a defendant admits liability which has caused some damage, before proceedings are issued, the claimant should send to that defendant—

    (a)   any medical reports obtained under this Protocol on which the claimant relies; and

    (b)   a schedule of any past and future expenses and losses which are claimed, even if the schedule is necessarily provisional. The schedule should contain as much detail as reasonably practicable and should identify those losses that are ongoing. If the schedule is likely to be updated before the case is concluded, it should say so.

8.1.2   The claimant should delay issuing proceedings for 21 days from disclosure of (a) and (b) above (unless such delay would cause his claim to become time-barred), to enable the parties to consider whether the claim is capable of settlement.

8.2   CPR Part 36 permits claimants and defendants to make offers to settle pre-proceedings. Parties should always consider if it is appropriate to make a Part 36 Offer before issuing. If such an offer is made, the party making the offer must always try to supply sufficient evidence and/or information to enable the offer to be properly considered.

    The level of detail will depend on the value of the claim. Medical reports may not Except for any claim for a whiplash injury (for which see paragraphs 7.12 above and 8.3 below), medical reports may not be necessary where there is no significant continuing injury and a detailed schedule may not be necessary in a low value case.

8.3

8.3.1   In a claim that consists of or includes a claim for whiplash injury, the Whiplash Injury Regulations 2021 provide that—

    (a)   no offer may be made, invited or accepted by either party; and

    (b)   no payment may be made by the defendant or accepted by the claimant,

    in respect of the claim for whiplash injury until after the fixed cost medical report has been disclosed.

8.3.2   Any claim for whiplash injury and, if relevant, minor psychological injuries suffered on the same occasion as the whiplash injury, will be valued by reference to the tariffs set out in the Whiplash Injury Regulations 2021.

("Whiplash injury" is defined in paragraph 7.12.7.)

9. Alternative Dispute Resolution

9.1

9.1.1   Litigation should be a last resort. As part of this Protocol, the parties should consider whether negotiation or some other form of Alternative Dispute Resolution ("ADR") might enable them to resolve their dispute without commencing proceedings.

9.1.2   Some of the options for resolving disputes without commencing proceedings are—

(a)   discussions and negotiation (which may or may not include making Part 36 Offers or providing an explanation and/or apology);

(b)   mediation, a third party facilitating a resolution;

(c)   arbitration, a third party deciding the dispute; and

(d)   early neutral evaluation, a third party giving an informed opinion on the dispute.

9.1.3   If proceedings are issued, the parties may be required by the court to provide evidence that ADR has been considered. It is expressly recognised that no party can or should be forced to mediate or enter into any form of ADR but unreasonable refusal to consider ADR will be taken into account by the court when deciding who bears the costs of the proceedings.

9.2   Information on mediation and other forms of ADR is available in the Jackson ADR Handbook (available from Oxford University Press) or at–

https://www.gov.uk/guidance/a-guide-to-civil-mediation

10. Quantification of Loss - Special damages

10.1   In all cases, if the defendant admits liability, the claimant will send to the defendant as soon as reasonably practicable a schedule of any past and future expenses and losses which he claims, even if the schedule is necessarily provisional. The schedule should contain as much detail as reasonably practicable and should identify those losses that are ongoing. If the schedule is likely to be updated before the case is concluded, it should say so. The claimant should keep the defendant informed as to the rate at which his financial loss is progressing throughout the entire Protocol period.

11. Stocktake

11.1   Where the procedure set out in this Protocol has not resolved the dispute between the parties, each party should undertake a review of its own positions and the strengths and weaknesses of its case. The parties should then together consider the evidence and the arguments in order to see whether litigation can be avoided or, if that is not possible, for the issues between the parties to be narrowed before proceedings are issued. Where the defendant is insured and the pre-action steps have been taken by the insurer, the insurer would normally be expected to nominate solicitors to act in the proceedings and to accept service of the claim form and other documents on behalf of the defendant. The claimant or their solicitor is recommended to invite the insurer to nominate the insurer to nominate solicitors to act in the proceedings and do so 7 to 14 days before the intended issue date.

Annex A: Illustrative flow chart

ANNEXE A - ILLUSTRATIVE FLOWCHART OF LIKELY PROGRESSION OF THE CLAIM UNDER THIS PROTOCOL

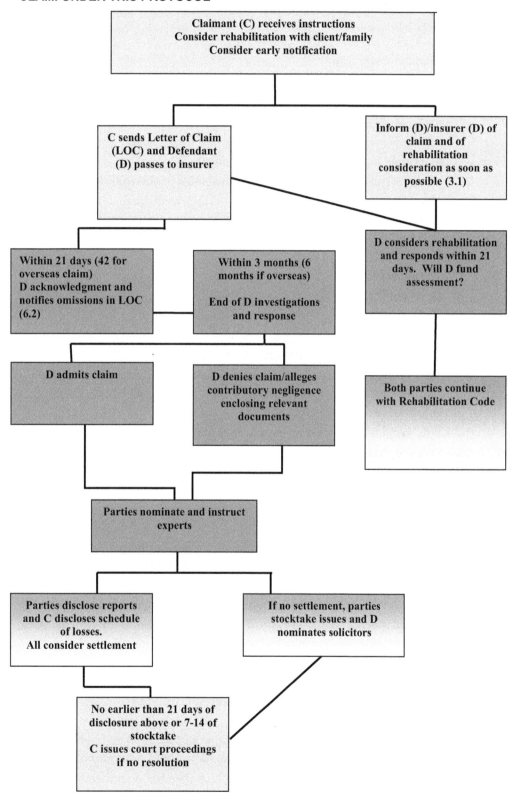

Annex B: Templates for letters of claim and response

B1 Letter of Claim

To

Defendant

Dear Sirs

Re:

Claimant's full name

Claimant's full address

Claimant's Clock or Works Number

Claimant's Employer (name and address)

We are instructed by the above named to claim damages in connection with an **accident at work/road traffic accident/tripping accident**

on day of **(year)** at **(place of accident which must be sufficiently detailed to establish location)**

Please confirm the identity of your insurers. Please note that the insurers will need to see this letter as soon as possible and it may affect your insurance cover and/or the conduct of any subsequent legal proceedings if you do not send this letter to them.

Clear summary of the facts

The circumstances of the accident are:

(brief outline)

Liability

The reason why we are alleging fault is:

(simple explanation e.g. defective machine, broken ground)

We are obtaining a police report and will let you have a copy of the same upon your undertaking to meet half the fee.

Injuries

A description of our clients' injuries is as follows:

(brief outline) The description should include a non-exhaustive list of the main functional effects on daily living, so that the defendant can begin to assess value / rehabilitation needs.

(In cases of road traffic accidents)

Our client (state hospital reference number) received treatment for the injuries at name and address of hospital).

Our client is still suffering from the effects of his/her injury. We invite you to participate with us in addressing his/her immediate needs by use of rehabilitation.

Loss of Earnings

He/She is employed as **(occupation)** and has had the following time off work

(dates of absence). His/Her approximate weekly income is (insert if known).

If you are our client's employers, please provide us with the usual earnings details which will enable us to calculate his financial loss.

Other Financial Losses

We are also aware of the following (likely) financial losses:

Details of the insurer

We have also sent a letter of claim to **(name and address)** and a copy of that letter is attached. We understand their insurers are **(name, address and claims number if known).**

At this stage of our enquiries we would expect the documents contained in parts (insert appropriate parts of standard disclosure list) to be relevant to this action.

A copy of this letter is attached for you to send to your insurers. Finally we expect an acknowledgment of this letter within 21 days by yourselves or your insurers.

Yours faithfully

B2 Letter of response

To Claimant's legal representative

Dear Sirs

Letter of Response

[Claimant's name] v [Defendant's name]

Parties

We have been instructed to act on behalf of [defendant] in relation to your client's accident on [ ]. We note that you have also written to [defendant] in connection with this claim. We [do/do not] believe they are a relevant party because [ ]. [In addition we believe your claim should be directed against [defendant] for the following reasons:

Liability

In respect of our client's liability for this accident we admit the accident occurred and that our client is liable for loss and damage to the claimant the extent of which will require quantification.

Or

admit the accident occurred but deny that our client is responsible for any loss or damage alleged to have been caused for the following reasons:-

Or

do not admit the accident occurred either in the manner described in your letter of claim [or at all] because:

Limitation

[We do not intend to raise any limitation defence]

Documents

We attach copies of the following documents in support of our client's position:

You have requested copies of the following documents which we are not enclosing as we do not believe they are relevant for the following reasons:

[It would assist our investigations if you could supply us with copies of the following documents]

Next Steps

In admitted cases

Please advise us which medical experts you are proposing to instruct.

Please also supply us with your client's schedule of past and future expenses [if any] which are claimed, even if this can only be supplied on a provisional basis at present to assist us with making an appropriate reserve.

If you have identified that the claimant has any immediate need for additional medical treatment or other early rehabilitation intervention so that we can take instructions pursuant to the Rehabilitation Code.

In non-admitted cases

Please confirm we may now close our file. Alternatively, if you intend to proceed please advise which experts you are proposing to instruct.

Alternative Dispute Resolution

Include details of any options that may be considered whether on a without prejudice basis or otherwise.

Yours faithfully

Annex C: Pre-Action Personal Injury Protocol Standard Disclosure Lists

RTA CASES

SECTION A

In all cases where liability is at issue–

(i)   documents identifying nature, extent and location of damage to defendant's vehicle where there is any dispute about point of impact;

(ii)   MOT certificate where relevant;

(iii)   maintenance records where vehicle defect is alleged or it is alleged by defendant that there was an unforeseen defect which caused or contributed to the accident.

SECTION B

Accident involving commercial vehicle as defendant–

(i)   tachograph charts or entry from individual control book;

(ii)   maintenance and repair records required for operators' licence where vehicle

defect is alleged or it is alleged by defendant that there was an unforeseen defect which caused or contributed to the accident.

SECTION C

Cases against local authorities where highway design defect is alleged—

(i)   documents produced to comply with Section 39 of the Road Traffic Act 1988 in respect of the duty designed to promote road safety to include studies into road accidents in the relevant area and documents relating to measures recommended to prevent accidents in the relevant area;

(ii)   any Rule 43 reports produced at the request of a coroner pursuant to Schedule 5 of the Coroners & Justice Act 2009, for accidents occurring in the same locus as one covered by an earlier report.

HIGHWAY TRIPPING CLAIMS

Documents from Highway Authority for a period of 12 months prior to the accident–

(i)   records of inspection for the relevant stretch of highway;

(ii)   maintenance records including records of independent contractors working in relevant area;

(iii)   records of the minutes of Highway Authority meetings where maintenance or repair policy has been discussed or decided;

(iv)   records of complaints about the state of highways;

(v)   records of other accidents which have occurred on the relevant stretch of highway.

WORKPLACE CLAIMS

GENERAL DOCUMENTS

(i)   accident book entry;

(ii)   other entries in the book or other accident books, relating to accidents or injuries similar to those suffered by our client (and if it is contended there are no such entries please confirm we may have facilities to inspect all accident books);

(iii)   first aider report;

(iv)   surgery record;

(v)   foreman/supervisor accident report;

(vi)   safety representative's accident report;

(vii)   RIDDOR (Reporting of Injuries, Diseases and Dangerous Occurrences Regulations) reported to HSE or relevant investigatory agency;

(viii)   back to work interview notes and report;

(ix)   all personnel/occupational health records relating to our client;

(x)   other communications between defendants and HSE or other relevant investigatory agency;

(xi)   minutes of Health and Safety Committee meeting(s) where accident/matter considered;

(xii)   copies of all relevant CCTV footage and any other relevant photographs, videos and/or DVDs;

(xiii)   copies of all electronic communications/documentation relating to the accident;

(xiv)   earnings information where defendant is employer;

(xv)   reports to DWP;

(xvi)   manufacturer's or dealers instructions or recommendations concerning use of the work equipment;

(xvii)   service or maintenance records of the work equipment;

(xviii)   all documents recording arrangements for detecting, removing or cleaning up any articles or substances on the floor of the premises likely to cause a trip or slip;

(xix)   work sheets and all other documents completed by or on behalf of those responsible for implementing the cleaning policy and recording work done;

(xx)   all invoices, receipts and other documents relating to the purchase of relevant safety equipment to prevent a repetition of the accident;

(xxi)   all correspondence, memoranda or other documentation received or brought into being concerning the condition or repair of the work equipment/the premises;

(xxii)   all correspondence, instructions, estimates, invoices and other documentation submitted or received concerning repairs, remedial works or other works to the work equipment/the premises since the date of that accident;

(xxiii)   work sheets and all other documents recording work done completed by those responsible for maintaining the work equipment/premises;

(xxiv)   all relevant risk assessments;

(xxv)   all reports, conclusions or recommendations following any enquiry or investigation into the accident;

(xxvi)   the record kept of complaints made by employees together with all other documents recording in any way such complaints or actions taken thereon;

(xxvii)   all other correspondence sent, or received, relating to our client's injury prior to receipt of this letter of claim;

(xxviii)   documents listed above relating to any previous/similar accident/matter identified by the claimant and relied upon as proof of negligence including accident book entries;

WORKPLACE CLAIMS – DISCLOSURE WHERE SPECIFIC REGULATIONS APPLY

SECTION A - Management of Health and Safety at Work Regulations 1999

Documents including—

(i)   Pre-accident Risk Assessment required by Regulation 3(1);

(ii)   Post-accident Re-Assessment required by Regulation 3(2);

(iii)   Accident Investigation Report prepared in implementing the requirements of Regulations 4, and 5;

(iv)   Health Surveillance Records in appropriate cases required by Regulation 6;

(v)   documents relating to the appointment of competent persons to assist required by Regulation 7;

(vi)   documents relating to the employees health and safety training required by Regulation 8;

(vii)   documents relating to necessary contacts with external services required by Regulation 9;

(viii)   information provided to employees under Regulation 10.

SECTION B– Workplace (Health Safety and Welfare) Regulations 1992

Documents including—

(i)   repair and maintenance records required by Regulation 5;

(ii)   housekeeping records to comply with the requirements of Regulation 9;

(iii)   hazard warning signs or notices to comply with Regulation 17 (Traffic Routes).

SECTION C – Provision and Use of Work Equipment Regulations 1998

Documents including—

(i)   manufacturers' specifications and instructions in respect of relevant work equipment establishing its suitability to comply with Regulation 4;

(ii)   maintenance log/maintenance records required to comply with Regulation 5;

(iii)   documents providing information and instructions to employees to comply with Regulation 8;

(iv)   documents provided to the employee in respect of training for use to comply with Regulation 9;

(v)   risk assessments/documents required to comply with Regulation 12;

(vi)   any notice, sign or document relied upon as a defence to alleged breaches of Regulations 14 to 18 dealing with controls and control systems;

(vii)   instruction/training documents issued to comply with the requirements of Regulation 22 insofar as it deals with maintenance operations where the machinery is not shut down;

(viii)   copies of markings required to comply with Regulation 23;

(ix)   copies of warnings required to comply with Regulation 24.

SECTION D – Personal Protective Equipment at Work Regulations 1992

Documents including—

(i)   documents relating to the assessment of the Personal Protective Equipment to comply with Regulation 6;

(ii)   documents relating to the maintenance and replacement of Personal Protective Equipment to comply with Regulation 7;

(iii)   record of maintenance procedures for Personal Protective Equipment to comply with Regulation 7;

(iv)   records of tests and examinations of Personal Protective Equipment to comply with Regulation 7;

(v)   documents providing information, instruction and training in relation to the Personal Protective Equipment to comply with Regulation 9;

(vi)   instructions for use of Personal Protective Equipment to include the manufacturers' instructions to comply with Regulation 10.

SECTION E – Manual Handling Operations Regulations 1992

Documents including—

(i)   Manual Handling Risk Assessment carried out to comply with the requirements of Regulation 4(1)(b)(i);

(ii)   re-assessment carried out post-accident to comply with requirements of Regulation 4(1)(b)(i);

(iii)   documents showing the information provided to the employee to give general indications related to the load and precise indications on the weight of the load and the heaviest side of the load if the centre of gravity was not positioned centrally to comply with Regulation 4(1)(b)(iii);

(iv)   documents relating to training in respect of manual handling operations and training records.

SECTION F – Health and Safety (Display Screen Equipment) Regulations 1992

Documents including—

(i)   analysis of work stations to assess and reduce risks carried out to comply with the requirements of Regulation 2;

(ii)   re-assessment of analysis of work stations to assess and reduce risks following development of symptoms by the claimant;

(iii)   documents detailing the provision of training including training records to comply with the requirements of Regulation 6;

(iv)   documents providing information to employees to comply with the requirements of Regulation 7.

SECTION G – Control of Substances Hazardous to Health Regulations 2002

Documents including—

(i)   risk assessment carried out to comply with the requirements of Regulation 6;

(ii)   reviewed risk assessment carried out to comply with the requirements of Regulation 6;

(iii)   documents recording any changes to the risk assessment required to comply with Regulation 6 and steps taken to meet the requirements of Regulation 7;

(iv)   copy labels from containers used for storage handling and disposal of carcinogenics to comply with the requirements of Regulation 7(2A)(h);

(v)   warning signs identifying designation of areas and installations which may be contaminated by carcinogenics to comply with the requirements of Regulation 7(2A)(h);

(vi)   documents relating to the assessment of the Personal Protective Equipment to comply with Regulation 7(3A);

(vii)   documents relating to the maintenance and replacement of Personal Protective Equipment to comply with Regulation 7(3A);

(viii)   record of maintenance procedures for Personal Protective Equipment to comply with Regulation 7(3A);

(ix)   records of tests and examinations of Personal Protective Equipment to comply with Regulation 7(3A);

(x)   documents providing information, instruction and training in relation to the Personal Protective Equipment to comply with Regulation 7(3A);

(xi)   instructions for use of Personal Protective Equipment to include the manufacturers' instructions to comply with Regulation 7(3A);

(xii)   air monitoring records for substances assigned a maximum exposure limit or occupational exposure standard to comply with the requirements of Regulation 7;

(xiii)   maintenance examination and test of control measures records to comply with Regulation 9;

(xiv)   monitoring records to comply with the requirements of Regulation 10;

(xv)   health surveillance records to comply with the requirements of Regulation 11;

(xvi)   documents detailing information, instruction and training including training records for employees to comply with the requirements of Regulation 12;

(xvii)   all documents relating to arrangements and procedures to deal with accidents, incidents and emergencies required to comply with Regulation 13;

(xvii)   labels and Health and Safety data sheets supplied to the employers to comply with the CHIP Regulations.

SECTION H – Construction (Design and Management) Regulations 2007

Documents including—

(i)   notification of a project form (HSE F10) to comply with the requirements of Regulation 7;

(ii)   Health and Safety Plan to comply with requirements of Regulation 15;

(iii)   Health and Safety file to comply with the requirements of Regulations 12 and 14;

(iv)   information and training records provided to comply with the requirements of Regulation 17;

(v)   records of advice from and views of persons at work to comply with the requirements of Regulation 18;

(vi)   reports of inspections made in accordance with Regulation 33;

(vii)   records of checks for the purposes of Regulation 34;

(viii) emergency procedures for the purposes of Regulation 39.

SECTION I – Construction (Health, Safety & Welfare) Regulations 1996

Documents including—

(i)   documents produced to comply with requirements of the Regulations.

SECTION J – Work at Height Regulations 2005

Documents including—

(i)   documents relating to planning, supervision and safety carried out for Regulation 4;

(ii)   documents relating to training for the purposes of Regulation 5;

(iii)   documents relating to the risk assessment carried out for Regulation 6;

(iv)   documents relating to the selection of work equipment for the purposes of Regulation 7;

(v)   notices or other means in writing warning of fragile surfaces for the purposes of Regulation 9;

(vi)   documents relating to any inspection carried out for Regulation 12;

(vii)   documents relating to any inspection carried out for Regulation 13;

(viii) reports made for the purposes of Regulation 14;

(ix)   any certificate issued for the purposes of Regulation 15.

SECTION K – Pressure Systems and Transportable Gas Containers Regulations 1989

(i)   information and specimen markings provided to comply with the requirements of Regulation 5;

(ii)   written statements specifying the safe operating limits of a system to comply with the requirements of Regulation 7;

(iii)   copy of the written scheme of examination required to comply with the requirements of Regulation 8;

(iv)   examination records required to comply with the requirements of Regulation 9;

(v)   instructions provided for the use of operator to comply with Regulation 11;

(vi)   records kept to comply with the requirements of Regulation 13;

(vii)   records kept to comply with the requirements of Regulation 22.

SECTION L – Lifting Operations and Lifting Equipment Regulations 1998

Documents including—

(i)   records kept to comply with the requirements of the Regulations including the records kept to comply with Regulation 6.

SECTION M – The Noise at Work Regulations 1989

Documents including—

(i)   any risk assessment records required to comply with the requirements of Regulations 4 and 5;

(ii)   manufacturers' literature in respect of all ear protection made available to claimant to comply with the requirements of Regulation 8;

(iii)   all documents provided to the employee for the provision of information to comply with Regulation 11.

SECTION N – Control of Noise at Work Regulations 1989

Documents including—

(i)   documents relating to the assessment of the level of noise to which employees are exposed to comply with Regulation 5;

(ii)   documents relating to health surveillance of employees to comply with Regulation 9;

(ii)   instruction and training records provided to employees to comply with Regulation 10.

SECTION O – Construction (Head Protection) Regulations 1989

Documents including—

(i)   pre-accident assessment of head protection required to comply with Regulation 3(4);

(ii)   post-accident re-assessment required to comply with Regulation 3(5).

SECTION P – The Construction (General Provisions) Regulations 1961

Documents including—

(i)   report prepared following inspections and examinations of excavations etc. to comply with the requirements of Regulation 9.

SECTION Q – Gas Containers Regulations 1989

Documents including—

(i)   information and specimen markings provided to comply with the requirements of Regulation 5;

(ii)   written statements specifying the safe operating limits of a system to comply with the requirements of Regulation 7;

(iii)   copy of the written scheme of examination required to comply with the requirements of Regulation 8;

(iv)   examination records required to comply with the requirements of Regulation 9;

(v)   instructions provided for the use of operator to comply with Regulation 11.

SECTION R – Control of Noise at Work Regulations 2005

Documents including—

(i)   risk assessment records required to comply with the requirements of Regulations 4 and 5;

(ii)   all documents relating to steps taken to comply with regulation 6;

(iii)   all documents relating to and/or arising out of actions taken to comply including providing consideration of alternative work that the claimant could have engaged to comply with Regulation 7.

SECTION S – Mine and Quarries Act 1954

Documents including—

(i)   documents produced to comply with requirements of the Act.

SECTION T – Control of Vibrations at Work Regulations 2005

Documents including—

(i)   risk assessments and documents produced to comply with requirements of Regulations 6 and 8;

(ii)   occupational health surveillance records produced to comply with Regulation 7.

ANNEX D: Letter of instruction to medical expert

Dear Sir,

Re: (Name and Address)

D.O.B.–

Telephone No.–

Date of Accident –

We are acting for the above named in connection with injuries received in an accident which occurred on the above date. A summary of the main facts of the accident circumstances is provided below. The main injuries appear to have been **(describe main injuries and functional impact on day to day living as in Letter of Claim)**.

In order to assist with the preparation of your report we have enclosed the following documents:

1. Enclosures

2. Hospital Records

3. GP records

Statement of Events

We have not obtained [ ] records yet but will use our best endeavours to obtain these without delay if you request them.

We should be obliged if you would examine our Client and let us have a full and detailed report dealing with any relevant pre-accident medical history, the injuries sustained, treatment received and present condition, dealing in particular with the capacity for work and giving a prognosis.

It is central to our assessment of the extent of our Client's injuries to establish the extent and duration of any continuing disability. Accordingly, in the prognosis section we would ask you to specifically comment on any areas of continuing complaint or disability or impact on daily living. If there is such continuing disability you should comment upon the level of suffering or inconvenience caused and, if you are able, give your view as to when or if the complaint or disability is likely to resolve.

If our client requires further treatment, please can you advise of the cost on a private patient basis.

Please send our Client an appointment direct for this purpose. Should you be able to offer a cancellation appointment please contact our Client direct. We confirm we will be responsible for your reasonable fees.

We are obtaining the notes and records from our Client's GP and Hospitals attended and will forward them to you when they are to hand/or please request the GP and Hospital records direct and advise that any invoice for the provision of these records should be forwarded to us.

In order to comply with Court Rules we would be grateful if you would insert above your signature, the following statement: "I confirm that I have made clear which facts and matters referred to in this report are within my own knowledge and which are not. Those that are within my own knowledge I confirm to be true. The opinions I have expressed represent my true and complete professional opinions on the matters to which they refer".

In order to avoid further correspondence we can confirm that on the evidence we have there is no reason to suspect we may be pursuing a claim against the hospital or its staff.

We look forward to receiving your report within _____ weeks. If you will not be able to prepare your report within this period please telephone us upon receipt of these instructions.

When acknowledging these instructions it would assist if you could give an estimate as to the likely time scale for the provision of your report and also an indication as to your fee.

Yours faithfully,

Updated: Thursday, 19 August 2021   Ministry of Justice

Pre-action Protocol for the Resolution of Clinical Disputes

1 INTRODUCTION

1.1 This Protocol is intended to apply to all claims against hospitals, GPs, dentists and other healthcare providers (both NHS and private) which involve an injury that is alleged to be the result of clinical negligence. It is not intended to apply to claims covered by—

(a) the Pre-Action Protocol for Disease and Illness Claims;

(b) the Pre-Action Protocol for Personal Injury Claims;

(c) the Pre-Action Protocol for Low Value Personal Injury Claims in Road Traffic Accidents;

(d) the Pre-Action Protocol for Low Value Personal Injury (Employers' Liability and Public Liability) Claims; or

(e) Practice Direction 3D – Mesothelioma Claims

1.2 This Protocol is intended to be sufficiently broad-based and flexible to apply to all sectors of healthcare, both public and private. It also recognises that a claimant and a defendant, as patient and healthcare provider, may have an ongoing relationship.

1.3 It is important that each party to a clinical dispute has sufficient information and understanding of the other's perspective and case to be able to investigate a claim efficiently and, where appropriate, to resolve it. This Protocol encourages a cards-on-the-table approach when something has gone wrong with a claimant's treatment or the claimant is dissatisfied with that treatment and/or the outcome.

1.4 This Protocol is now regarded by the courts as setting the standard of normal reasonable pre-action conduct for the resolution of clinical disputes.

1.5

1.5.1 This Protocol sets out the conduct that prospective parties would normally be expected to follow prior to the commencement of any proceedings. It establishes a reasonable process and timetable for the exchange of information relevant to a dispute, sets out the standards for the content and quality of letters of claim and sets standards for the conduct of pre-action negotiations.

1.5.2 The timetable and the arrangements for disclosing documents and obtaining expert evidence may need to be varied to suit the circumstances of the case. Where one or more parties consider the detail of the Protocol is not appropriate to the case, and proceedings are subsequently issued, the court will expect an explanation as to why the Protocol has not been followed, or has been varied.

Early Issue

1.6

1.6.1 The Protocol provides for a defendant to be given four months to investigate and respond to a Letter of Claim before proceedings are served. If this is not possible, the claimant's solicitor should give as much notice of the intention to issue proceedings as is practicable. This Protocol does not alter the statutory time limits for starting court proceedings. If a claim is issued after the relevant statutory limitation period has expired, the defendant will be entitled to use that as a defence to the claim. If proceedings are started to comply with the statutory time limit before the parties have followed the procedures in this Protocol, the parties should apply to the court for a stay of the proceedings while they so comply.

1.6.2 The parties should also consider whether there is likely to be a dispute as to limitation should a claim be pursued.

Enforcement of the Protocol and sanctions

1.7   Where either party fails to comply with this Protocol, the court may impose sanctions. When deciding whether to do so, the court will look at whether the parties have complied in substance with the Protocol's relevant principles and requirements. It will also consider the effect any non-compliance has had on any other party. It is not likely to be concerned with minor or technical shortcomings (see paragraph 4.3 to 4.5 of the Practice Direction on Pre-Action Conduct and Protocols).

Litigants in Person

1.8   If a party to a claim does not seek professional advice from a solicitor they should still, in so far as is reasonably possible, comply with the terms of this Protocol. In this Protocol "solicitor" is intended to encompass reference to any suitably legally qualified person.

    If a party to a claim becomes aware that another party is a litigant in person, they should send a copy of this Protocol to the litigant in person at the earliest opportunity.

2 THE AIMS OF THE PROTOCOL

2.1   The general aims of the Protocol are –

    (a)   to maintain and/or restore the patient/healthcare provider relationship in an open and transparent way;

    (b)   to reduce delay and ensure that costs are proportionate; and

    (c)   to resolve as many disputes as possible without litigation.

2.2   The specific objectives are–

    (a)   to encourage openness, transparency and early communication of the perceived problem between patients and healthcare providers;

    (b)   to provide an opportunity for healthcare providers to identify whether notification of a notifiable safety incident has been, or should be, sent to the claimant in accordance with the duty of candour imposed by section 20 of the Health and Social Care Act 2008 (Regulated Activities) Regulations 2014;

    (c)   to ensure that sufficient medical and other information is disclosed promptly by both parties to enable each to understand the other's perspective and case, and to encourage early resolution or a narrowing of the issues in dispute;

    (d)   to provide an early opportunity for healthcare providers to identify cases where an investigation is required and to carry out that investigation promptly;

    (e)   to encourage healthcare providers to involve the National Health Service Litigation Authority (NHSLA) or their defence organisations or insurers at an early stage;

    (f)   to enable the parties to avoid litigation by agreeing a resolution of the dispute;

    (g)   to enable the parties to explore the use of mediation or to narrow the issues in dispute before proceedings are commenced;

    (h)   to enable parties to identify any issues that may require a separate or preliminary hearing, such as a dispute as to limitation;

    (i)   to support the efficient management of proceedings where litigation cannot be avoided;

    (j)   to discourage the prolonged pursuit of unmeritorious claims and the prolonged defence of meritorious claims;

    (k)   to promote the provision of medical or rehabilitation treatment to address the needs of the claimant at the earliest opportunity; and

    (l)   to encourage the defendant to make an early apology to the claimant if appropriate.

2.3   This Protocol does not—

(a)   provide any detailed guidance to healthcare providers on clinical risk management or the adoption of risk management systems and procedures;

(b)   provide any detailed guidance on which adverse outcomes should trigger an investigation; or

(c)   recommend changes to the codes of conduct of professionals in healthcare.

3 THE PROTOCOL

3.1   An illustrative flowchart is attached at Annex A which shows each of the stages that the parties are expected to take before the commencement of proceedings.

Obtaining health records

3.2   Any request for records by the claimant should–

(a)   provide sufficient information to alert the defendant where an adverse outcome has been serious or has had serious consequences or may constitute a notifiable safety incident;

(b)   be as specific as possible about the records which are required for an initial investigation of the claim (including, for example, a continuous copy of the CTG trace in birth injury cases); and

(c)   include a request for any relevant guidelines, analyses, protocols or policies and any documents created in relation to an adverse incident, notifiable safety incident or complaint.

3.3   Requests for copies of the claimant's clinical records should be made using the Law Society and Department of Health approved standard forms (enclosed at Annex B), adapted as necessary.

3.4

3.4.1   The copy records should be provided within 40 days of the request and for a cost not exceeding the charges permissible under the Access to Health Records Act 1990 and/or the Data Protection Act 1998. Payment may be required in advance by the healthcare provider.

3.4.2   The claimant may also make a request under the Freedom of Information Act 2000.

3.5   At the earliest opportunity, legible copies of the claimant's medical and other records should be placed in an indexed and paginated bundle by the claimant. This bundle should be kept up to date.

3.6   In the rare circumstances that the defendant is in difficulty in complying with the request within 40 days, the problem should be explained quickly and details given of what is being done to resolve it.

3.7   If the defendant fails to provide the health records or an explanation for any delay within 40 days, the claimant or their adviser can then apply to the court under rule 31.16 of the Civil Procedure Rules 1998 ('CPR') for an order for pre-action disclosure. The court has the power to impose costs sanctions for unreasonable delay in providing records.

3.8   If either the claimant or the defendant considers additional health records are required from a third party, in the first instance these should be requested by or through the claimant. Third party healthcare providers are expected to co-operate. Rule 31.17 of the CPR sets out the procedure for applying to the court for pre-action disclosure by third parties.

Rehabilitation

3.9   The claimant and the defendant shall both consider as early as possible whether the claimant has reasonable needs that could be met by rehabilitation treatment or other measures. They should also discuss how these needs might be addressed. An immediate needs assessment report prepared for the purposes of rehabilitation should not be used in the litigation except by consent.

(A copy of the Rehabilitation Code can be found at: http://www.iua.co.uk/IUA_Member/ Publications)

Letter of Notification

3.10 Annex C1 to this Protocol provides a template for the recommended contents of a Letter of Notification; the level of detail will need to be varied to suit the particular circumstances.

3.11

3.11.1 Following receipt and analysis of the records and, if appropriate, receipt of an initial supportive expert opinion, the claimant may wish to send a Letter of Notification to the defendant as soon as practicable.

3.11.2 The Letter of Notification should advise the defendant that this is a claim where a Letter of Claim is likely to be sent because a case as to breach of duty and/or causation has been identified. A copy of the Letter of Notification should also be sent to the NHSLA or, where known, other relevant medical defence organisation or indemnity provider.

3.12

3.12.1 On receipt of a Letter of Notification a defendant should—

(a) acknowledge the letter within 14 days of receipt;

(b) identify who will be dealing with the matter and to whom any Letter of Claim should be sent;#

(c) consider whether to commence investigations and/or to obtain factual and expert evidence;

(d) consider whether any information could be passed to the claimant which might narrow the issues in dispute or lead to an early resolution of the claim; and

(e) forward a copy of the Letter of Notification to the NHSLA or other relevant medical defence organisation/indemnity provider.

3.12.2 The court may question any requests by the defendant for extension of time limits if a Letter of Notification was sent but did not prompt an initial investigation.

Letter of Claim

3.13 Annex C2 to this Protocol provides a template for the recommended contents of a Letter of Claim: the level of detail will need to be varied to suit the particular circumstances.

3.14 If, following the receipt and analysis of the records, and the receipt of any further advice (including from experts if necessary – see Section 4), the claimant decides that there are grounds for a claim, a letter of claim should be sent to the defendant as soon as practicable. Any letter of claim sent to an NHS Trust should be copied to the National Health Service Litigation Authority.

3.16 This letter should contain—

(a) a clear summary of the facts on which the claim is based, including the alleged adverse outcome, and the main allegations of negligence;

(b) a description of the claimant's injuries, and present condition and prognosis;

(c) an outline of the financial loss incurred by the claimant, with an indication of the heads of damage to be claimed and the scale of the loss, unless this is impracticable;

(d) confirmation of the method of funding and whether any funding arrangement was entered into before or after April 2013; and

(e) the discipline of any expert from whom evidence has already been obtained.

3.17 The Letter of Claim should refer to any relevant documents, including health records, and if possible enclose copies of any of those which will not already be in the potential defendant's possession, e.g. any relevant general practitioner records if the claimant's claim is against a hospital.

3.18 Sufficient information must be given to enable the defendant to focus investigations and to put an initial valuation on the claim.

3.19 Letters of Claim are not intended to have the same formal status as Particulars of Claim, nor should any sanctions necessarily apply if the Letter of Claim and any subsequent Particulars of Claim in the proceedings differ.

3.20 Proceedings should not be issued until after four months from the letter of claim. In certain instances it may not be possible for the claimant to serve a Letter of Claim more than four months before the expiry of the limitation period. If, for any reason, proceedings are started before the parties have complied, they should seek to agree to apply to the court for an order to stay the proceedings whilst the parties take steps to comply.

3.21 The claimant may want to make an offer to settle the claim at this early stage by putting forward an offer in respect of liability and/or an amount of compensation in accordance with the legal and procedural requirements of CPR Part 36 (possibly including any costs incurred to date). If an offer to settle is made, generally this should be supported by a medical report which deals with the injuries, condition and prognosis, and by a schedule of loss and supporting documentation. The level of detail necessary will depend on the value of the claim. Medical reports may not be necessary where there is no significant continuing injury and a detailed schedule may not be necessary in a low value case.

Letter of Response

3.22 Attached at Annex C3 is a template for the suggested contents of the Letter of Response: the level of detail will need to be varied to suit the particular circumstances.

3.23 The defendant should acknowledge the Letter of Claim within 14 days of receipt and should identify who will be dealing with the matter.

3.24 The defendant should, within four months of the Letter of Claim, provide a reasoned answer in the form of a Letter of Response in which the defendant should—

    (a)   if the claim is admitted, say so in clear terms;

    (b)   if only part of the claim is admitted, make clear which issues of breach of duty and/or causation are admitted and which are denied and why;

    (c)   state whether it is intended that any admissions will be binding;

    (d)   if the claim is denied, include specific comments on the allegations of negligence and, if a synopsis or chronology of relevant events has been provided and is disputed, the defendant's version of those events;

    (e)   if supportive expert evidence has been obtained, identify which disciplines of expert evidence have been relied upon and whether they relate to breach of duty and/or causation;

    (f)   if known, state whether the defendant requires copies of any relevant medical records obtained by the claimant (to be supplied for a reasonable copying charge);

    (g)   provide copies of any additional documents relied upon, e.g. an internal protocol;

    (h)   if not indemnified by the NHS, supply details of the relevant indemnity insurer; and

    (i)   inform the claimant of any other potential defendants to the claim.

3.25

3.25.1 If the defendant requires an extension of time for service of the Letter of Response, a request should be made as soon as the defendant becomes aware that it will be required and, in any event, within four months of the letter of claim.

3.25.2 The defendant should explain why any extension of time is necessary.

3.25.3 The claimant should adopt a reasonable approach to any request for an extension of time for provision of the reasoned answer.

3.26 If the claimant has made an offer to settle, the defendant should respond to that offer in the Letter of Response, preferably with reasons. The defendant may also make an offer to settle at this stage. Any offer made by the defendant should be made in accordance with the legal and procedural requirements of CPR Part 36 (possibly including any costs incurred to date). If an offer to settle is made, the defendant should provide sufficient medical or other evidence to allow the claimant to properly consider the offer. The level of detail necessary will depend on the value of the claim.

3.27 If the parties reach agreement on liability, or wish to explore the possibility of resolution with no admissions as to liability, but time is needed to resolve the value of the claim, they should aim to agree a reasonable period.

3.28 If the parties do not reach agreement on liability, they should discuss whether the claimant should start proceedings and whether the court might be invited to direct an early trial of a preliminary issue or of breach of duty and/or causation.

3.29 Following receipt of the Letter of Response, if the claimant is aware that there may be a delay of six months or more before the claimant decides if, when and how to proceed, the claimant should keep the defendant generally informed.

4 EXPERTS

4.1 In clinical negligence disputes separate expert opinions may be needed—
- on breach of duty;
- on causation;
- on the patient's condition and prognosis;
- to assist in valuing aspects of the claim.

4.2 It is recognised that in clinical negligence disputes, the parties and their advisers will require flexibility in their approach to expert evidence. The parties should co-operate when making decisions on appropriate medical specialisms, whether experts might be instructed jointly and whether any reports obtained pre-action might be shared.

4.3 Obtaining expert evidence will often be an expensive step and may take time, especially in specialised areas of medicine where there are limited numbers of suitable experts.

4.4 When considering what expert evidence may be required during the Protocol period, parties should be aware that the use of any expert reports obtained pre-action will only be permitted in proceedings with the express permission of the court.

5 ALTERNATIVE DISPUTE RESOLUTION

5.1 Litigation should be a last resort. As part of this Protocol, the parties should consider whether negotiation or some other form of alternative dispute resolution ('ADR') might enable them to resolve their dispute without commencing proceedings.

5.2 Some of the options for resolving disputes without commencing proceedings are—
- (a) discussion and negotiation (which may or may not include making Part 36 Offers or providing an explanation and/or apology)
- (b) mediation, a third party facilitating a resolution ;
- (c) arbitration, a third party deciding the dispute;
- (d) early neutral evaluation, a third party giving an informed opinion on the dispute; and
- (e) Ombudsmen schemes.

5.3 Information on mediation and other forms of ADR is available in the Jackson ADR Handbook (available from Oxford University Press) or at—

https://www.gov.uk/guidance/a-guide-to-civil-mediation

5.4   If proceedings are issued, the parties may be required by the court to provide evidence that ADR has been considered. It is expressly recognised that no party can or should be forced to mediate or enter into any form of ADR, but a party's silence in response to an invitation to participate in ADR might be considered unreasonable by the court and could lead to the court ordering that party to pay additional court costs.

6 STOCKTAKE

6.1

6.1.1 Where a dispute has not been resolved after the parties have followed the procedure set out in this Protocol, the parties should review their positions before the claimant issues court proceedings.

6.1.2 If proceedings cannot be avoided, the parties should continue to co-operate and should seek to prepare a chronology of events which identifies the facts or issues that are agreed and those that remain in dispute. The parties should also seek to agree the necessary procedural directions for efficient case management during the proceedings.

Annex A   ILLUSTRATIVE FLOWCHART

INCIDENT

- Claimant(s) suffers adverse outcome and seeks legal advice.
- C's adviser consider limitation
- C's adviser consider rehabilitation
- C's adviser consider use of complaints process

REQUEST FOR RECORDS

- C requests copies of medical records from D and any relevant third parties
- D provides records - or an explanation as to any delay with 40 days
- If D fails to provide records or explanation C makes pre-action application for disclosure
- C paginates and files any received records

LETTER OF NOTIFICATION

- C sends Letter of Notification (LoN) to D explaining that claim is contemplated
- D acknowledges LoN and confirms where Letter of Claim (LoC) should be sent
- D considers whether to commence investigation and/or obtain expert evidence
- Both parties consider rehabilitation
- Both parties consider limitation

LETTER OF CLAIM

- C sends LoC to D and D's insurer detailing allegations as to breach of duty and causation
- C provides D with copies of relevant records and/or a list of all records obtained
- C sets out chronology of events
- C provides evidence as to condition, prognosis and alleged quantum losses
- Both parties consider rehabilitation

LETTER OF RESPONSE

- D provides C with detailed Letter of Response (LoR) within 4 months
- LoR will set out any admissions or denials as to breach of duty and/or causation
- D identifies relevant medical records not referred to in LoC
- D agree C's chronology or provides alternative chronology
- Both parties consider rehabiliitation

ADR

- Parties consider whether matter can be resolved without further recourse to the court
- Parties consider non-financial resolution (eg. face-to-face explanation, further treatment and/or apology)
- Parties consider financial settlement (without without admission of liability)
- Parties consider rehabilitation

STOCKTAKE

- Parties seektonarrow issues to dispute
- Parties seek to agree chronology and key facts
- Parties seek to identify any matters that could be dealt with as preliminary issues (eg limitation)
- Parties consider rehabilitation
- Parties consider what further expert evidence will be issued
- Parties consider whether Protocol has been complied with

Annex B   FORM FOR REQUESTING MEDICAL RECORDS

Consent form
(Releasing health records under the Data Protection Act 1998)

About this form

In order to proceed with your claim, your solicitor may need to see your health records. Solicitors usually need to see all your records as they need to assess which parts are relevant to your case. (Past medical history is often relevant to a claim for compensation.) Also, if your claim goes ahead, the person you are making the claim against will ask for copies of important documents. Under court rules, they may see all your health records. So your solicitor needs to be familiar with all your records.

Part a – your, the health professionals' and your solicitor's or agent's details

Your full name:	
Your address:	
Date of birth:	
Date of incident:	
Solicitor's or agent's name and address:	
GP's name and address (and phone number if known):	
Name (and address if known) of the hospitals you went to in relation to this incident :	
If you have seen any other person or organisation about your injuries (for example, a physiotherapist) or have had any investigations (for example, x-rays) please provide details.	

Part b – your declaration and signature

Please see the 'Notes for the client' over the page before you sign this form.

To health professionals

I understand that filling in and signing this form gives you permission to give copies of all my GP records, and any hospital records relating to this incident, to my solicitor or agent whose details are given above.

Please give my solicitor or agent copies of my health records, in line with the Data Protection Act 1998, within 40 days.

Your signature: [   ]   Date: [/   /   ]

Part c – your solicitor's or agent's declaration and signature

Please see the 'Notes for the solicitor or agent' over the page before you sign this form.

To health professionals

I have told my client the implications of giving me access to his or her health records. I confirm that I need the full records in this case.   I enclose the authorised fee for getting access to records.

Solicitor's or agent's signature: [   ]   Date: [/   /   ]

Notes for the client

Your health records contain information from almost all consultations you have had with health professionals. The information they contain usually includes:

♦ why you saw a health professional;
♦ details of clinical findings and diagnoses;
♦ any options for care and treatment the health professional discussed with you;
♦ the decisions made about your care and treatment, including evidence that you agreed; and
♦ details of action health professionals have taken and the outcomes.

By signing this form, you are agreeing to the health professional or hospital named on this form releasing copies of your health records to your solicitor or agent. During the process your records may be seen by people who are not health professionals, but they will keep the information confidential.

If you are making, or considering making, a legal claim against someone, your solicitor will need to see copies of all your GP records, and any hospital records made in connection with this incident, so he or she can see if there is anything in your records that may affect your claim. Once you start your claim, the court can order you to give copies of your health records to the solicitor of the person you are making a claim against so he or she can see if any of the information in your records can be used to defend his or her client.

If you decide to go ahead with your claim, your records may be passed to a number of people including:

♦ the expert who your solicitor or agent instructs to produce a medical report as evidence for the case;
♦ the person you are making a claim against and their solicitors;
♦ the insurance company for the person you are making a claim against;
♦ any insurance company or other organisation paying your legal costs; and
♦ any other person or company officially involved with the claim.

You do not have to give permission for your health records to be released but if you don't, the court may not let you go ahead with your claim and, in some circumstances, your solicitor may refuse to represent you.

If there is very sensitive information in the records, that is not connected to the claim, you should tell your solicitor. They will then consider whether this information needs to be revealed.

Notes for the solicitor or agent

Before you ask your client to fill in and sign this form you should explain that this will involve his or her full health records being released and how the information in them may be used. You should also tell your client to read the notes above.

If your client is not capable of giving his or her permission in this form, this form should be signed by:

♦ your client's litigation friend;
♦ someone who has enduring power of attorney to act for your client; or
♦ your client's receiver appointed by the Court of Protection.

When you send this form to the appropriate records controller please also enclose the authorised fees for getting access to records.

If you find out at any stage that the medical records contain information that the client does not know about (for example, being diagnosed with a serious illness), you should discuss this with the health professional who provided the records.

Unless your client agrees otherwise, you must use his or her health records only for the purpose for which the client signed this form (that is, making his or her claim). Under the Data Protection Act you have responsibilities relating to sensitive information. The entire health record should not be automatically revealed without the client's permission and you should not keep health records for any longer than you need them. You should return them to the client at the end of the claim if they want them. Otherwise, you are responsible for destroying them.

Notes for the medical records controller

This form shows your patient's permission for you to give copies of his or her full GP record, and any hospital records relating to this incident, to his or her solicitor or agent. You must give the solicitor or agent copies of these health records unless any of the exemptions set out in The Data Protection (Subject Access Modification) (Health) Order 2000 apply. The main exemptions are that you must not release information that:

♦ is likely to cause serious physical or mental harm to the patient or another person; or
♦ relates to someone who would normally need to give their permission (where that person is not a health professional who has cared for the patient).

Your patient's permission for you to release information is valid only if that patient understands the consequences of his or her records being released, and how the information will be used. The solicitor or agent named on this form must explain these issues to the patient. If you have any doubt about whether this has happened, contact the solicitor or agent, or your patient.

If your patient is not capable of giving his or her permission, this form should be signed by:

♦ a 'litigation friend' acting for your patient;
♦ someone with 'enduring power of attorney' to act for your patient; or
♦ a receiver appointed by the Court of Protection.

You may charge the usual fees authorised under the Data Protection Act for providing the records.

The BMA publishes detailed advice for doctors on giving access to health records, including the fees that you may charge. You can view that advice by visiting www.bma.org.uk/ap.nsf/Content/accesshealthrecords.

This form is published by the Law Society and British Medical Association. (2nd edition, October 2004)

BMA

Crystal
Mark
Clarity
approved by
Plain English Campaign

Annex C   TEMPLATES FOR LETTERS OF NOTIFICATION, CLAIM AND RESPONSE

C1 Letter of Notification

To

Defendant

Dear Sirs

Letter of Notification

Re: [Claimant's Name, Address, DoB and NHS Number]

We have been instructed to act on behalf of [Claimant's name] in relation to treatment carried out/care provided at [name of hospital or treatment centre] by [name of clinician(s) if known] on [insert date(s)].

The purpose of this letter is to notify you that, although we are not yet in a position to serve a formal Letter of Claim, our initial investigations indicate that a case as to breach of duty and/ or causation has been identified. We therefore invite you to commence your own investigation and draw your attention to the fact that failure to do may be taken into account when considering the reasonableness of any subsequent application for an extension of time for the Letter of Response.

Defendant

We understand that you are the correct defendant in respect of treatment provided by [name of clinician] at [hospital/surgery/treatment centre] on [date(s)]. If you do not agree, please provide us with any information you have that may assist us to identify the correct defendant. Failure to do so may result in costs sanctions should proceedings be issued.

Summary of Facts and Alleged Adverse Outcome

[Outline what is alleged to have happened and provide a chronology of events with details of relevant known treatment/care.]

Medical Records 58

[Provide index of records obtained and request for further records/information if required.]

Allegations of Negligence

[Brief outline of any alleged breach of duty and causal link with any damage suffered.]

Expert Evidence

[State whether expert evidence has been obtained or is awaited and, if so, the relevant discipline.]

Damage

[Brief outline of any injuries attributed to the alleged negligence and their functional impact.]

Funding

[If known, state method of funding and whether arrangement was entered into before or after April 2013.]

Rehabilitation

As a result of the allegedly negligent treatment, our client has injuries/needs that could be met by rehabilitation. We invite you to consider how this could be achieved.

Limitation

For the purposes of limitation, we calculate that any proceedings will need to be issued on or before [date].

Please acknowledge this letter by [insert date 14 days after deemed receipt] and confirm to whom any Letter of Claim should be sent. We enclose a duplicate of the letter for your insurer.

Recoverable Benefits

The claimant's National Insurance Number will be sent to you in a separate envelope.

We look forward to hearing from you.

Yours faithfully,

C2 Letter of Claim

To

Defendant

Dear Sirs

Letter of Claim

[Claimant's name] –v- [Defendant's Name]

We have been instructed to act on behalf of [Claimant's name] in relation to treatment carried out/care provided at [name of hospital or treatment centre] by [name of clinician(s) if known] on [insert date(s)]. Please let us know if you do not believe that you are the appropriate defendant or if you are aware of any other potential defendants.

Claimant's details

Full name, DoB, address, NHS Number.

Dates of allegedly negligent treatment

- include chronology based on medical records.

Events giving rise to the claim:

- an outline of what happened, including details of other relevant treatments to the client by other healthcare providers.

Allegation of negligence and causal link with injuries:

- an outline of the allegations or a more detailed list in a complex case;
- an outline of the causal link between allegations and the injuries complained of;
- A copy of any supportive expert evidence (optional).

The Client's injuries, condition and future prognosis

- A copy of any supportive expert report (optional);
- Suggestions for rehabilitation;
- The discipline of any expert evidence obtained or proposed.

Clinical records (if not previously provided)

We enclose an index of all the relevant records that we hold. We shall be happy to provide copies of these on payment of our photocopying charges.

We enclose a request for copies of the following records which we believe that you hold. We confirm that we shall be responsible for your reasonable copying charges. Failure to provide these records may result in costs sanctions if proceedings are issued.

The likely value of the claim

- an outline of the main heads of damage, or, in straightforward cases, the details of loss;

- Part 36 settlement offer (optional);

- suggestions for ADR.

Funding

[State method of funding and whether arrangement was entered into before or after April 2013.]

We enclose a further copy of this letter for you to pass to your insurer. We look forward to receiving an acknowledgment of this letter within 14 days and your Letter of Response within 4 months of the date on which this letter was received. We calculate the date for receipt of your Letter of Response to be [date].

Recoverable Benefits

The claimant's National Insurance Number will be sent to you in a separate envelope.

We look forward to hearing from you.

Yours faithfully

C3 Letter of Response

To

Claimant

Dear Sirs

Letter of Response

[Claimant's name] –v- [Defendant's Name]

We have been instructed to act on behalf of [defendant] in relation to treatment carried out/ care provided to [claimant] at [name of hospital or treatment centre] by [name of clinician(s) if known] on [insert date(s)].

The defendant [conveys sympathy for the adverse outcome/would like to offer an apology/ denies that there was an adverse outcome].

Parties

It is accepted that [defendant] had a duty of care towards [claimant] in respect of [details if required] treatment/care provided to [claimant] at [location] on [date(s)].

However, [defendant] is not responsible for [details] care/treatment provided to [claimant] at [location] on [date(s)] by [name of clinician if known].

Records

We hold the following records...

We require copies of the following records...

Failure to provide these records may result in costs sanctions if proceedings are issued.

Comments on events and/or chronology:

We [agree the chronology enclosed with the Letter of Claim] [enclose a revised chronology of events].

We enclose copies of relevant [records/Protocols/internal investigations] in respect of the treatment/care that [claimant] received.

Liability

In respect of the specific allegations raised by the claimant, the defendant [has obtained an expert opinion and] responds as follows:-

[each allegation should be addressed separately. The defendant should explain which (if any) of the allegations of breach of duty and/or causation are admitted and why. The defendant should also make clear which allegations are denied and why].

Next Steps

The defendant suggests...

[e.g. no prospect of success for the claimant, resolution without admissions of liability, ADR, settlement offer, rehabilitation].

Yours faithfully,"

Pre-action Protocol for Low Value Personal Injury (Employers' Liability and Public Liability) Claims

SECTION I - INTRODUCTION

Definitions

1.1 In this Protocol—

(1) 'admission of liability' means the defendant admits that—

    (a) the breach of duty occurred;

    (b) the defendant thereby caused some loss to the claimant, the nature and extent of which is not admitted; and

    (c) the defendant has no accrued defence to the claim under the Limitation Act 1980;

(2) 'bank holiday' means a bank holiday under the Banking and Financial Dealings Act 1971;

(3) 'business day' means any day except Saturday, Sunday, a bank holiday, Good Friday or Christmas Day;

(4) 'certificate of recoverable benefits' has the same meaning as in rule 36.22(1)(e)(i) of the Civil Procedure Rules 1998.

(5) 'child' means a person under 18;

(6) 'claim' means a claim, prior to the start of proceedings, for payment of damages under the process set out in this Protocol;

(7) 'claimant' means a person starting a claim under this Protocol; unless the context indicated that it means the claimant's legal representative;

(8) 'clinical negligence' has the same meaning as in section 58C of the Courts and Legal Services Act 1990;

(9) 'CNF' means a Claim Notification Form;

(10) 'deductible amount' has the same meaning as in rule 36.22(1)(d) of the Civil Procedure Rules 1998;

(11) 'defendant' includes, where the context indicates, the defendant's insurer or legal representative;

(12) 'disease claim' means a claim within sub-paragraph (14)(b);

(13) 'employee' has the meaning given to it by section 2(1) of the Employers' Liability (Compulsory Insurance) Act 1969;

(14) 'employers' liability claim' means a claim by an employee against their employer for damages arising from—

    (a) a bodily injury sustained by the employee in the course of employment; or

    (b) a disease that the claimant is alleged to have contracted as a consequence of the employer's breach of statutory or common law duties of care in the course of the employee's employment, other than a physical or psychological injury caused by an accident or other single event;

(15) 'legal representative' has the same meaning as in rule 2.3(1) of the Civil Procedure Rules 1998;

(16) 'medical expert' means a person who is—

    (a) registered with the General Medical Council;

    (b) registered with the General Dental Council; or

(c)   a Psychologist or Physiotherapist registered with the Health Professions Council;

(17) 'pecuniary losses' means past and future expenses and losses; and

(18) 'public liability claim'—

(a)   means a claim for damages for personal injuries arising out of a breach of a statutory or common law duty of care made against—

(i)   a person other than the claimant's employer; or

(ii)   the claimant's employer in respect of matters arising other than in the course the claimant's employment; but

(b)   does not include a claim for damages arising from a disease that the claimant is alleged to have contracted as a consequence of breach of statutory or common law duties of care, other than a physical or psychological injury caused by an accident or other single event;

(19) 'Type C fixed costs' has the same meaning as in rule 45.18(2) of the Civil Procedure Rules 1998; and

(20) 'vulnerable adult' has the same meaning as in paragraph 3(5) of Schedule 1 to the Legal Aid, Sentencing and Punishment of Offenders Act 2012

1.2 A reference to a rule or practice direction, unless otherwise defined, is a reference to a rule in the Civil Procedure Rules 1998 ('CPR') or a practice direction supplementing them.

1.3 Subject to paragraph 1.4 the standard forms used in the process set out in this Protocol are available from Her Majesty's Courts and Tribunals Service ('HMCTS') website at www.justice.gov.uk/forms/hmcts—

(1)   Claim Notification Form ('Form EL1', 'Form ELD1' and 'Form PL1'– which are referred to in this Protocol as 'the CNF');

(2)   Defendant Only Claim Notification Form ('Form EL2', 'Form ELD2' and 'Form PL2');

(3)   Medical Report Form ('Form EPL3');

(4)   Interim Settlement Pack Form ('Form EPL4');

(5)   Stage 2 Settlement Pack Form ('Form EPL5');

(6)   Court Proceedings Pack (Part A) Form ('Form EPL6'); and

(7)   Court Proceedings Pack (Part B) Form ('Form EPL7').

1.4 The information required in Form EPL3 may be provided in a different format to that set out in that Form.

Preamble

2.1 This Protocol describes the behaviour the court expects of the parties prior to the start of proceedings where a claimant claims damages valued at no more than £25,000 in an employers' liability claim or in a public liability claim. The Civil Procedure Rules 1998 enable the court to impose costs sanctions where this Protocol is not followed.

Aims

3.1 The aim of this Protocol is to ensure that—

(1)   the defendant pays damages and costs using the process set out in the Protocol without the need for the claimant to start proceedings;

(2)   damages are paid within a reasonable time; and

(3)   the claimant's legal representative receives the fixed costs at each appropriate stage.

Scope

4.1 This Protocol applies where—

(1)   either—

(a)   the claim arises from an accident occurring on or after 31 July 2013; or

(b)   in a disease claim, no letter of claim has been sent to the defendant before 31 July 2013;

(2)   the claim includes damages in respect of personal injury;

(3)   the claimant values the claim at not more than £25,000 on a full liability basis including pecuniary losses but excluding interest ('the upper limit'); and

(4)   if proceedings were started the small claims track would not be the normal track for that claim.

(Rule 26.6 provides that the small claims track is not the normal track where the value of any claim for damages for personal injuries (defined as compensation for pain, suffering and loss of amenity) is more than £1,500.)

4.2   This Protocol ceases to apply to a claim where, at any stage, the claimant notifies the defendant that the claim has now been revalued at more than the upper limit.

4.3   This Protocol does not apply to a claim—

(1)   where the claimant or defendant acts as personal representative of a deceased person;

(2)   where the claimant or defendant is a protected party as defined in rule 21.1(2);

(3)   in the case of a public liability claim, where the defendant is an individual ('individual' does not include a defendant who is sued in their business capacity or in their capacity as an office holder);

(4)   where the claimant is bankrupt;

(5)   where the defendant is insolvent and there is no identifiable insurer;

(6)   in the case of a disease claim, where there is more than one employer defendant;

(7)   for personal injury arising from an accident or alleged breach of duty occurring outside England and Wales;

(8)   for damages in relation to harm, abuse or neglect of or by children or vulnerable adults;

(9)   which includes a claim for clinical negligence;

(10)   for mesothelioma;

(11)   for damages arising out of a road traffic accident (as defined in paragraph 1.1(16) of the Pre-Action Protocol for Low Value Personal Injury Claims in Road Traffic Accidents).

4.4   The fixed costs in rule 45.18 apply in relation to a claimant only where a claimant has a legal representative.

SECTION II – GENERAL PROVISIONS

Communication between the parties

5.1   Subject to paragraphs 6.1 and 6.2, where the Protocol requires information to be sent to a party it must be sent via www.claimsportal.org.uk (or any other Portal address that may be prescribed from time to time). The claimant will give an e-mail address for contact in the Claim Notification Form ("CNF"). All written communications not required by the Protocol must be sent by e-mail.

5.2   Where the claimant has sent the CNF to the wrong defendant, the claimant may, in this circumstance only, resend the relevant form to the correct defendant. The period in paragraph 6.12 starts from the date that the form was sent to the correct defendant.

Time periods

5.3   A reference to a fixed number of days is a reference to business days as defined in paragraph 1.1(3).

5.4   Where a party should respond within a fixed number of days, the period for response starts the first business day after the information was sent to that party.

5.5   All time periods, except those stated in—

(1)   paragraph 6.11 (response);

(2)   paragraph 7.34 (the further consideration period),

may be varied by agreement between the parties.

5.6   Where this Protocol requires the defendant to pay an amount within a fixed number of days the claimant must receive the cheque or the transfer of the amount from the defendant before the end of the period specified in the relevant provision.

Limitation period

5.7   Where compliance with this Protocol is not possible before the expiry of the limitation period the claimant may start proceedings and apply to the court for an order to stay (i.e. suspend) the proceedings while the parties take steps to follow this Protocol. Where proceedings are started in a case to which this paragraph applies the claimant should use the procedure set out under Part 8 in accordance with Practice Direction 8B ("the Stage 3 Procedure").

5.8   Where the parties are then unable to reach a settlement at the end of Stage 2 of this Protocol the claimant must, in order to proceed to Stage 3, apply to lift the stay and request directions in the existing proceedings.

Claimant's reasonable belief of the value of the claim

5.9   Where the claimant reasonably believes that the claim is valued at between £1,500 and £25,000 but it subsequently becomes apparent that the value of the claim is less than £1,500, the claimant is entitled to the Stage 1 and (where relevant) the Stage 2 fixed costs.

Claimants without a legal representative

5.10   Where the claimant does not have a legal representative, on receipt of the CNF the defendant must explain—

(1)   the period within which a response is required; and

(2)   that the claimant may obtain independent legal advice.

Discontinuing the Protocol process

5.11   Claims which no longer continue under this Protocol cannot subsequently re-enter the process.

SECTION III – THE STAGES OF THE PROCESS

Stage 1   Completion of the Claim Notification Form

6.1   (1)   The claimant must complete and send—

(a)   the CNF to the defendant's insurer, if known; and

(b)   the Defendant Only Claim Notification Form ("Defendant Only CNF") to the defendant,

but the requirement to send the form to the defendant may be ignored in a disease claim where the CNF has been sent to the insurer and the defendant has been dissolved, is insolvent or has ceased to trade.

(2)   If—

(a)   the insurer's identity is not known; or

(b)   the defendant is known not to hold insurance cover,

the CNF must be sent to the defendant's registered office or principal place of business and no Defendant Only CNF is required.

(3)   Where the insurer's identity is not known, the claimant must make a reasonable attempt to identify the insurer and, in an employers' liability claim, the claimant must have carried out a database search through the Employers' Liability Tracing Office.

       (4)   In a disease claim, the CNF should be sent to the insurer identified as the insurer last on risk for the employer for the material period of employment.

6.2   If the CNF or Defendant Only CNF cannot be sent to the defendant via the prescribed Portal address, it must be sent via first class post; and this must be done, in a case where the CNF is sent to the insurer, at the same time or as soon as practicable after the CNF is sent.

6.3   All boxes in the CNF that are marked as mandatory must be completed before it is sent. The claimant must make a reasonable attempt to complete those boxes that are not marked as mandatory.

6.4   Where the claimant is a child, this must be noted in the relevant section of the CNF.

6.5   The statement of truth in the CNF must be signed either by the claimant or by the claimant's legal representative where the claimant has authorised the legal representative to do so and the legal representative can produce written evidence of that authorisation. Where the claimant is a child the statement of truth may be signed by the parent or guardian. On the electronically completed CNF the person may enter their name in the signature box to satisfy this requirement.

Rehabilitation

6.6   The claimant must set out details of rehabilitation in the CNF. The parties should at all stages consider the Rehabilitation Code which may be found at: http://www.iua.co.uk/IUA_Member/Publications

Failure to complete the Claim Notification Form

6.7   Where the defendant considers that inadequate mandatory information has been provided in the CNF that shall be a valid reason for the defendant to decide that the claim should no longer continue under this Protocol.

6.8   Rule 45.24(2) sets out the sanctions available to the court where it considers that the claimant provided inadequate information in the CNF.

Response

6.9   The defendant must send to the claimant an electronic acknowledgment the next day after receipt of the CNF.

6.10   If the claimant has sent the CNF to the defendant in accordance with paragraph 6.1(2)—

       (a)   the defendant must send to the claimant an electronic acknowledgment the next day after receipt of the CNF and send the CNF to the insurer at the same time and advise the claimant that they have done so;

       (b)   the insurer must send to the claimant an electronic acknowledgment the next day after its receipt by the insurer;
           and

       (c)   the claimant must then submit the CNF to the insurer via the Portal as soon as possible and, in any event, within 30 days of the day upon which the claimant first sent it to the defendant.

6.11   The defendant must complete the 'Response' section of the CNF ("the CNF response") and send it to the claimant—

       (a)   in the case of an employers' liability claim, within 30 days of the step taken pursuant to paragraph 6.1; and

       (b)   in the case of a public liability claim, within 40 days of the step taken pursuant to paragraph 6.1.

Application for a certificate of recoverable benefits

6.12 The defendant must, before the end of Stage 1, apply to the Compensation Recovery Unit (CRU) for a certificate of recoverable benefits.

Contributory Negligence, liability not admitted or failure to respond

6.13 The claim will no longer continue under this Protocol where the defendant, within the relevant period in paragraph 6.11 —

(1)   makes an admission of liability but alleges contributory negligence;

(2)   does not complete and send the CNF response;

(3)   does not admit liability; or

(4)   notifies the claimant that the defendant considers that—

(a)   there is inadequate mandatory information in the CNF; or

(b)   if proceedings were issued, the small claims track would be the normal track for that claim.

6.14 Where the defendant does not admit liability the defendant must give brief reasons in the CNF response.

6.15 Where paragraph 6.13 applies the claim will proceed under the relevant Pre-Action Protocol and the CNF will serve as the letter of claim (except where the claim no longer continues under this Protocol because the CNF contained inadequate information). Time will be treated as running under the relevant Pre-Action Protocol from the date the form of acknowledgment is served under paragraph 6.9 or 6.10.

(For admissions made in the course of the process under this Protocol, see rule 14.1B.)

(Paragraph 2.10A of the Pre-Action Protocol on Personal Injury and paragraph 6.10A of the Pre-Action Protocol for Disease and Illness Claims provide that the CNF can be used as the letter of claim except where the claim no longer continues under this Protocol because the CNF contained inadequate information.)

Stage 1 fixed costs

6.16 Except where the claimant is a child, where liability is admitted the defendant must pay the Stage 1 fixed costs in rule 45.18 within 10 days after receiving the Stage 2 Settlement Pack.

6.17 Where the defendant fails to pay the Stage 1 fixed costs within the period specified in paragraph 6.16 the claimant may give written notice that the claim will no longer continue under this Protocol. Unless the claimant's notice is sent to the defendant within 10 days after the expiry of the period in paragraph 6.16 the claim will continue under this Protocol.

Stage 2 Medical reports

7.1 The claimant should obtain a medical report, if one has not already been obtained.

7.2 It is expected that most claimants will obtain a medical report from one expert but additional medical reports may be obtained from other experts where the injuries require reports from more than one medical discipline.

7.3 The claimant must check the factual accuracy of any medical report before it is sent to the defendant. There will be no further opportunity for the claimant to challenge the factual accuracy of a medical report after it has been sent to the defendant.

7.4 (1)   The medical expert should identify within the report—

(a)   the medical records that have been reviewed; and

(b)   the medical records considered relevant to the claim.

(2)   The claimant must disclose with any medical report sent to the defendant any medical records which the expert considers relevant.

7.5 Any relevant photograph(s) of the claimant's injuries upon which the claimant intends to rely should also be disclosed with the medical report.

Subsequent medical reports

7.6 A subsequent medical report from an expert who has already reported must be justified. A report may be justified where—

    (1)   the first medical report recommends that further time is required before a prognosis of the claimant's injuries can be determined; or

    (2)   the claimant is receiving continuing treatment; or

    (3)   the claimant has not recovered as expected in the original prognosis.

Non-medical reports

7.7 (1)   In most cases, a report from a non-medical expert will not be required, but a report may be obtained where it is reasonably required to value the claim.

    (2)   Paragraph 7.2 applies to non-medical expert reports as it applies to expert medical reports.

Specialist legal advice

7.8 In most cases under this Protocol, it is expected that the claimant's legal representative will be able to value the claim. In some cases with a value of more than £10,000, an additional advice from a specialist solicitor or from counsel may be justified where it is reasonably required to value the claim.

Details of loss of earnings

7.9 In an employers' liability claim, the defendant must, within 20 days of the date of admission of liability, provide earnings details to verify the claimant's loss of earnings, if any.

Witness Statements

7.10 In most cases, witness statements, whether from the claimant or otherwise, will not be required. One or more statements may, however, be provided where reasonably required to value the claim.

Stay of process

7.11 Where the claimant needs to obtain a subsequent medical report or a report from a non-medical expert the parties should agree to stay the process in this Protocol for a suitable period. The claimant may then request an interim payment in accordance with paragraphs 7.12 to 7.20.

Request for an interim payment

7.12 Where the claimant requests an interim payment of £1,000, the defendant should make an interim payment to the claimant in accordance with paragraph 7.17.

7.13 The claimant must send to the defendant the Interim Settlement Pack and initial medical reports (including any recommendation that a subsequent medical report is justified) in order to request the interim payment.

7.14 The claimant must also send evidence of pecuniary losses and disbursements. This will assist the defendant in considering whether to make an offer to settle the claim.

7.15 Where an interim payment of more than £1,000 is requested the claimant must specify in the Interim Settlement Pack the amount requested, the heads of damage which are the subject of the request and the reasons for the request.

7.16 Unless the parties agree otherwise—

(a)   the interim payment of £1,000 is only in relation to general damages; and

(b)   where more than £1,000 is requested by the claimant, the amount in excess of £1,000 is only in relation to pecuniary losses.

Interim payment of £1,000

7.17   (1)   Where paragraph 7.12 applies the defendant must pay £1,000 within 10 days of receiving the Interim Settlement Pack.

(2)   Sub-paragraph (1) does not apply in a claim in respect of a disease to which the Pneumoconiosis etc. (Workers' Compensation) Act 1979 applies unless there is a valid CRU certificate showing no deduction for recoverable lump sum payments.

Interim payment of more than £1,000

7.18   Subject to paragraphs 7.19 and 7.21, where the claimant has requested an interim payment of more than £1,000 the defendant must pay—

(1)   the full amount requested less any deductible amount which is payable to the CRU;

(2)   the amount of £1,000; or

(3)   some other amount of more than £1,000 but less than the amount requested by the claimant,

within 15 days of receiving the Interim Settlement Pack.

7.19   Where a payment is made under paragraphs 7.18(2) or (3) the defendant must briefly explain in the Interim Settlement Pack why the full amount requested by the claimant is not agreed.

7.20   Where the claim is valued at more than £10,000, the claimant may use the procedure at paragraphs 7.12 to 7.19 to request more than one interim payment.

7.21   Nothing in this Protocol is intended to affect the provisions contained in the Rehabilitation Code.

Application for a certificate of recoverable benefits

7.22   Paragraph 7.23 applies where the defendant agrees to make a payment in accordance with paragraph 7.18(1) or (3) but does not yet have a certificate of recoverable benefits or does not have one that will remain in force for at least 10 days from the date of receiving the Interim Settlement Pack.

7.23   The defendant should apply for a certificate of recoverable benefits as soon as possible, notify the claimant that it has done so and must make the interim payment under paragraph 7.18(1) or (3) no more than 30 days from the date of receiving the Interim Settlement Pack.

Request for an interim payment where the claimant is a child

7.24   The interim payment provisions in this Protocol do not apply where the claimant is a child. Where the claimant is a child and an interim payment is reasonably required proceedings must be started under Part 7 of the CPR and an application for an interim payment can be made within those proceedings.

(Rule 21.10 provides that no payment, which relates to a claim by a child, is valid without the approval of the court.)

7.25   Paragraph 7.24 does not prevent a defendant from making a payment direct to a treatment provider.

Interim payment – supplementary provisions

7.26   Where the defendant does not comply with paragraphs 7.17 or 7.18 the claimant may start proceedings under Part 7 of the CPR and apply to the court for an interim payment in those proceedings.

7.27 Where the defendant does comply with paragraph 7.18(2) or (3) but the claimant is not content with the amount paid, the claimant may still start proceedings. However, the court will order the defendant to pay no more than the Stage 2 fixed costs where the court awards an interim payment of no more than the amount offered by the defendant or the court makes no award.

7.28 Where paragraph 7.26 or 7.27 applies the claimant must give notice to the defendant that the claim will no longer continue under this Protocol. Unless the claimant's notice is sent to the defendant within 10 days after the expiry of the period in paragraphs 7.17, 7.18 or 7.23 as appropriate, the claim will continue under this Protocol.

Costs of expert medical and non-medical reports and specialist legal advice obtained

7.29 (1) Where the claimant obtains more than one expert report or an advice from a specialist solicitor or counsel—
   (a) the defendant at the end of Stage 2 may refuse to pay; or
   (b) the court at Stage 3 may refuse to allow,

   the costs of any report or advice not reasonably required.

   (2) Therefore, where the claimant obtains more than one expert report or obtains an advice from a specialist solicitor or counsel—
   (a) the claimant should explain in the Stage 2 Settlement Pack why they obtained a further report or such advice; and
   (b) if relevant, the defendant should in the Stage 2 Settlement Pack identify the report or reports or advice for which they will not pay and explain why they will not pay for that report or reports or advice.

Submitting the Stage 2 Settlement Pack to the defendant

7.30 The Stage 2 Settlement Pack must comprise—
   (1) the Stage 2 Settlement Pack Form;
   (2) a medical report or reports;
   (3) evidence of pecuniary losses;
   (4) evidence of disbursements (for example the cost of any medical report);
   (5) any non-medical expert report;
   (6) any medical records/photographs served with medical reports; and
   (7) any witness statements.

7.31 The claimant should send the Stage 2 Settlement Pack to the defendant within 15 days of the claimant approving —
   (1) the final medical report and agreeing to rely on the prognosis in that report; or
   (2) any non-medical expert report,
   whichever is later.

Consideration of claim

7.32 There is a 35 day period for consideration of the Stage 2 Settlement Pack by the defendant ("the total consideration period"). This comprises a period of up to 15 days for the defendant to consider the Stage 2 Settlement Pack ("the initial consideration period") and make an offer. The remainder of the total consideration period ("the negotiation period") is for any further negotiation between the parties.

7.33 The total consideration period can be extended by the parties agreeing to extend either the initial consideration period or the negotiation period or both.

7.34 Where a party makes an offer 5 days or less before the end of the total consideration period (including any extension to this period under paragraph 7.32), there will be a further period of

5 days after the end of the total consideration period for the relevant party to consider that offer. During this period ("the further consideration period") no further offers can be made by either party.

Defendant accepts offer or makes counter-offer

7.35   Within the initial consideration period (or any extension agreed under paragraph 7.33) the defendant must either accept the offer made by the claimant on the Stage 2 Settlement Pack Form or make a counter-offer using that form.

7.36   The claim will no longer continue under this Protocol where the defendant gives notice to the claimant within the initial consideration period (or any extension agreed under paragraph 7.33) that the defendant—

(a)   considers that, if proceedings were started, the small claims track would be the normal track for that claim; or

(b)   withdraws the admission of causation as defined in paragraph 1.1(1)(b).

7.37   Where the defendant does not respond within the initial consideration period (or any extension agreed under paragraph 7.33), the claim will no longer continue under this Protocol and the claimant may start proceedings under Part 7 of the CPR.

7.38   When making a counter-offer the defendant must propose an amount for each head of damage and may, in addition, make an offer that is higher than the total of the amounts proposed for all heads of damage. The defendant must also explain in the counter-offer why a particular head of damage has been reduced. The explanation will assist the claimant when negotiating a settlement and will allow both parties to focus on those areas of the claim that remain in dispute.

7.39   Where the defendant has obtained a certificate of recoverable benefits from the CRU the counter offer must state the name and amount of any deductible amount.

7.40   On receipt of a counter-offer from the defendant the claimant has until the end of the total consideration period or the further consideration period to accept or decline the counter offer.

7.41   Any offer to settle made at any stage by either party will automatically include, and cannot exclude—

(1)   the Stage 1 and Stage 2 fixed costs in rule 45.18;

(2)   an agreement in principle to pay a sum equal to the Type C fixed costs of an additional advice on quantum of damages where such advice is justified under paragraph 7.8;

(3)   an agreement in principle to pay relevant disbursements allowed in accordance with rule 45.19; or

(4)   where applicable, any success fee in accordance with rule 45.31(1) (as it was in force immediately before 1 April 2013).

7.42   Where there is a dispute about whether an additional advice on quantum of damages is justified or about the amount or validity of any disbursement, the parties may use the procedure set out in rule 46.14.

(Rule 46.14 provides that where the parties to a dispute have a written agreement on all issues but have failed to agree the amount of the costs, they may start proceedings under that rule so that the court can determine the amount of those costs.)

Withdrawal of offer after the consideration period

7.43   Where a party withdraws an offer made in the Stage 2 Settlement Pack Form after the total consideration period or further consideration period, the claim will no longer continue under this Protocol and the claimant may start proceedings under Part 7 of the CPR.

Settlement

7.44 Except where the claimant is a child or paragraphs 7.46 and 7.47 apply, the defendant must pay—

   (1)   the agreed damages less any—

      (a)   deductible amount which is payable to the CRU; and

      (b)   previous interim payment;

   (2)   any unpaid Stage 1 fixed costs in rule 45.18;

   (3)   the Stage 2 fixed costs in rule 45.18;

   (4)   where an additional advice on quantum of damages is justified under paragraph 7.8, a sum equal to the Type C fixed costs to cover the cost of that advice;

   (5)   the relevant disbursements allowed in accordance with rule 45.19; and

   (6)   where applicable, any success fee in accordance with rule 45.31(1) (as it was in force immediately before 1 April 2013),

   within 10 days of the parties agreeing a settlement.

   (Rule 21.10 provides that the approval of the court is required where, before proceedings are started, a claim is made by a child and a settlement is reached. The provisions in paragraph 6.1 of Practice Direction 8B set out what must be filed with the court when an application is made to approve a settlement.)

7.45 Where the parties agree a settlement for a greater sum than the defendant had offered during the total consideration period or further consideration period and after the Court Proceedings Pack has been sent to the defendant but before proceedings are issued under Stage 3,

   (1)   paragraph 7.44 applies; and

   (2)   the defendant must also pay the fixed late settlement costs in rule 45.23A.

Application for certificate of recoverable benefits

7.46 Paragraph 7.47 applies where, at the date of the acceptance of an offer in the Stage 2 Settlement Pack, the defendant does not have a certificate of recoverable benefits that will remain in force for at least 10 days.

7.47 The defendant should apply for a fresh certificate of recoverable benefits as soon as possible, notify the claimant that it has done so and must pay the amounts set out in paragraph 7.44 within 30 days of the end of the relevant period in paragraphs 7.32 to 7.34.

Failure to reach agreement - general

7.48 Where the parties do not reach an agreement on the damages to be paid within the periods specified in paragraphs 7.32 to 7.34, the claimant must send to the defendant the Court Proceedings Pack (Part A and Part B) Form which must contain—

   (a)   in Part A, the final schedule of the claimant's losses and the defendant's responses comprising only the figures specified during the periods in paragraphs 7.32 to 7.34, together with supporting comments and evidence from both parties on any disputed heads of damage; and

   (b)   in Part B, the final offer and counter offer from the Stage 2 Settlement Pack Form.

7.49 Comments in the Court Proceedings Pack (Part A) Form must not raise anything that has not been raised in the Stage 2 Settlement Pack Form.

7.50 The defendant should then check that the Court Proceedings Pack (Part A and Part B) Form complies with paragraphs 7.48 to 7.49. If the defendant considers that the Court Proceedings Pack (Part A and Part B) Form does not comply it must be returned to the claimant within 5 days with an explanation as to why it does not comply.

7.51 Where the defendant intends to nominate a legal representative to accept service the name and address of the legal representative should be provided in the Court Proceedings Pack (Part A) Form.

7.52 Where the defendant fails to return the Court Proceedings Pack (Part A and Part B) Form within the period in paragraph 7.50, the claimant should assume that the defendant has no further comment to make.

Non-settlement payment by the defendant at the end of Stage 2

7.53 Except where the claimant is a child the defendant must pay to the claimant—

(1) the final offer of damages made by the defendant in the Court Proceedings Pack (Part A and Part B) Form less any—

(a) deductible amount which is payable to the CRU; and

(b) previous interim payment(s);

(2) any unpaid Stage 1 fixed costs in rule 45.18;

(3) the Stage 2 fixed costs in rule 45.18; and

(4) the disbursements in rule 45.19(2) that have been agreed.

7.54 Where the amount of a disbursement is not agreed the defendant must pay such amount for the disbursement as the defendant considers reasonable.

7.55 Subject to paragraphs 7.56 and 7.57 the defendant must pay the amounts in paragraph 7.53 and 7.54 within 15 days of receiving the Court Proceedings Pack (Part A and Part B) Form from the claimant.

7.56 Paragraph 7.57 applies where the defendant is required to make the payments in paragraph 7.53 but does not have a certificate of recoverable benefits that remains in force for at least 10 days.

7.57 The defendant should apply for a fresh certificate of recoverable benefits as soon as possible, notify the claimant that it has done so and must pay the amounts set out in paragraph 7.53 within 30 days of receiving the Court Proceedings Pack (Part A and Part B) Form from the claimant.

7.58 Where the defendant does not comply with paragraphs 7.55 or 7.57 the claimant may give written notice that the claim will no longer continue under this Protocol and start proceedings under Part 7 of the CPR.

General provisions

7.59 Where the claimant gives notice to the defendant that the claim is unsuitable for this Protocol (for example, because there are complex issues of fact or law or where claimants contemplate applying for a Group Litigation Order) then the claim will no longer continue under this Protocol. However, where the court considers that the claimant acted unreasonably in giving such notice it will award no more than the fixed costs in rule 45.18.

Stage 3   Stage 3 Procedure

8.1 The Stage 3 Procedure is set out in Practice Direction 8B.

The 2015 Rehabilitation Code

INTRODUCTION

The Code promotes the collaborative use of rehabilitation and early intervention in the compensation process. It is reviewed from time to time in response to feedback from those who use it, taking into account the changing legal and medical landscape.

The Code's purpose is to help the injured claimant make the best and quickest possible medical, social, vocational and psychological recovery. This means ensuring that his or her need for rehabilitation is assessed and addressed as a priority, and that the process is pursued on a collaborative basis. With this in mind, the claimant solicitor should always ensure that the compensator receives the earliest possible notification of the claim and its circumstances whenever rehabilitation may be beneficial.

Although the objectives of the Code apply whatever the clinical and social needs of the claimant, the best way to achieve them will vary depending on the nature of the injury and the claimant's circumstances. The Code recognises that the dynamics of lesser-injury cases are different to those further up the scale. A separate process is set out for claims below £25,000 (in line with the Civil Procedure Rules definition of low value). Separate provision is also made for soft tissue injury cases as defined in paragraph **1.1(16A)** of the Pre-Action Protocol for Low Value Personal Injury Claims in Road Traffic Accidents.

It is important to stress, however, that even low value injuries can be life-changing for some people. The projected monetary value of a claim is only a guide to the rehabilitation needs of the injured person. Each case should be taken on its individual merits, and the guidelines for higher-value injuries will sometimes be more appropriate for those in the lowest category.

Sections 1 to 3 set out the guiding principles and the obligations of the various parties, and apply to all types of injury. After that, the sections diverge significantly depending on the size of claim.

Although the Code deals mainly with the Immediate Needs Assessment, it encourages all parties to adopt the same principles and collaborative approach right up until the case is concluded. In doing so, it does not stipulate a detailed process. Rather, it assumes that the parties will have established the collaborative working relationships that render a prescriptive document unnecessary.

Ten 'markers' that can affect the rehabilitation assessment, and therefore the treatment, are to be found in the Glossary at the end of the Code. They should be considered in all cases.

With the more serious injuries, it is envisaged that Case Managers will have an essential role to play in assessing the claimant's needs and then overseeing treatment. This Code should be read in conjunction with the Guide for Case Managers and those who Commission them, published separately.

1. **Role of the Code**

   1.1 The purpose of the personal injury claims process is to restore the individual as much as possible to the position they were in before the accident. The Code provides a framework for the claimant solicitor and compensator to work together to ensure that the claimant's health, quality of life, independence and ability to work are restored before, or simultaneously with, the process of assessing compensation.

   1.2 Although the Code is recognised by the relevant CPR Pre-Action Protocols, achieving the aims are more important than strict adherence to its terms. Therefore, it is open to the parties to agree an alternative framework to achieve the early rehabilitation of the claimant.

1.3   Where there is no agreement on liability, the parties may still agree to use the Code. The health and economic benefits of proceeding with rehabilitation at an early stage, regardless of agreement on liability, may be especially strong in catastrophic and other severe cases. Compensators should consider from the outset whether there is a possibility or likelihood of at least partial admission later on in the process so as not to compromise the prospects for rehabilitation.

1.4   In this Code, the expression 'the compensator' includes any person acting on behalf of the compensator. 'Claimant solicitor' includes any legal representative acting on behalf of the claimant. 'Case Manager' means a suitably qualified rehabilitation case manager.

2.   The Claimant Solicitor

2.1   The claimant solicitor's obligation to act in the best interests of their client extends beyond securing reasonable financial compensation, vital as that may be. Their duty also includes considering, as soon as practicable, whether additional medical or rehabilitative intervention would improve the claimant's present and/or longer-term physical and mental well-being. In doing so, there should be full consultation with the claimant and/or their family and any treating practitioner where doing so is proportionate and reasonable. This duty continues throughout the life of the case, but is most important in the early stages.

2.2   It is the duty of a claimant solicitor to have an initial discussion with the claimant and/or their family to identify:

(1)   Whether there is an immediate need for aids, adaptations, adjustments to employment to enable the claimant to perform their existing job, obtain a suitable alternative role with the same employer or retrain for new employment. They should, where practical and proportionate, work with the claimant's employers to ensure that the position is kept open for them as long as possible.

(2)   The need to alleviate any problems related to their injuries.

2.3   The claimant solicitor should then communicate these needs to the compensator by telephone or email, together with all other relevant information, as soon as practicable. It is the intention of this Code that both parties will work to address all rehabilitation needs on a collaborative basis.

2.4   The compensator will need to receive from the claimant solicitor sufficient information to make a well-informed decision about the need for rehabilitation assistance, including detailed and adequate information on the functional impact of the claimant's injuries. There is no requirement for an expert report at this early stage. The information should, however, include the nature and extent of any likely continuing disability and any suggestions that may have already been made concerning rehabilitation and/or early intervention. It should be communicated within 21 days of becoming aware of those injuries or needs once the compensator is known.

2.5   Upon receiving a rehabilitation suggestion from the compensator, the claimant solicitor should discuss it with the claimant and/or their family as soon as practical and reply within 21 days.

2.6   Many cases will be considered under this Code before medical evidence has actually been commissioned or obtained. It is important in these situations that rehabilitation steps are not undertaken that might conflict with the recommendations of treating clinical teams. It is equally important that unnecessary delay is avoided in implementing steps that could make a material difference to the injured person or their family. Early engagement with the compensator is crucial to discuss such issues.

2.7   Whilst generally in catastrophic and other particularly severe cases, it is recommended that an appropriately qualified Case Manager should be appointed before any rehabilitation commences, this may not always be possible even though it should be a priority. Methods of selecting Case Managers are described in paragraphs 7.3 and 7.4. The aim when appointing a Case Manager should be to ensure that any proposed rehabilitation plan they recommend is appropriate and that the goals set are specific and attainable. The Case Manager should, before undertaking an Immediate Needs Assessment (INA) as part of the claims process, make every attempt to liaise with NHS clinicians and others involved in the claimant's treatment, and to work collaboratively with them, provided this does not unduly delay the process. If possible, they should obtain the claimant's rehabilitation prescription, discharge summary or similar, including any A&E records and/or treating consultant's report and medical records.

3. **The Compensator**

3.1 It is the duty of the compensator, from the earliest practicable stage, to consider whether the claimant would benefit from additional medical or rehabilitative treatment. This duty continues throughout the life of the case, but is most important in the early stages.

3.2 If the claimant may have rehabilitation needs, the compensator should contact the claimant solicitor as soon as practicable to seek to work collaboratively on addressing those needs. As set out in paragraph 2.5, the claimant solicitor should respond within 21 days.

3.3 Where a request to consider rehabilitation has been communicated by the claimant solicitor, the compensator should respond within 21 days, or earlier if possible, either confirming their agreement or giving reasons for rejecting the request.

3.4 Nothing in this Code modifies the obligations of the compensator under the Protocols to investigate claims rapidly and, in any event, within the relevant liability response period.

LOWER-VALUE INJURIES

4. **The Assessment Process – lower-value injuries**

4.1 Different considerations apply for soft-tissue injury cases compared to other lower-value cases of £25,000 or below. In all cases, the claimant's solicitor should consider, with the claimant and/or the claimant's family, whether there is a need for early rehabilitation. The results of that discussion should be recorded in section C of the electronic Claims Notification Form, which will be transmitted through the Ministry of Justice Claims Portal to commence the claim. That form requires details of any professional treatment recommendations, treatment already received (including name of provider) and ongoing rehabilitation needs.

4.2 For lower-value injuries generally, this might involve physiotherapy, diagnostics and consultant follow-up, psychological intervention or other services to alleviate problems caused by the injury. In soft-tissue injury cases, in particular, it is understood that there is not always necessarily a requirement for a rehabilitation intervention. It is considered likely that, where there is an initial intervention, it will focus on treating any physical need, for example through physiotherapy.

In all cases, the claimant solicitor should communicate with the compensator as soon as practical about any rehabilitation needs, preferably by electronic means. The mechanism of completion and transmission of the Claims Notification Form should facilitate this process and should take place before any significant treatment has been commenced, subject always to any overriding medical need for urgent treatment.

4.3 Nothing in this Code alters the legal principles that:

1.   Until there has been a liability admission by a compensator (through the Compensator's Response in the Claims Portal), the claimant can have no certainty about the prospect of recovery of any treatment sums incurred.

2.   Until the compensator has accepted a treatment regime in which the number and price of sessions have been agreed, the level of recovery of any such sums will always be a matter for negotiation (most likely through exchange of offers in the portal system), unless the subject of a Court order.

3.   Where a claimant has decided not to take up a form of treatment that is readily available in favour of a more expensive option, the reasonableness of that decision may be a factor that is taken into account on the assessment of damages.

4.4   Unless there is a medico-legal report containing full recommendations for rehabilitation, which both parties are happy to adopt, an initial Triage Report (TR) should be obtained to establish the type of treatment needed. In most cases, the Triage Report will be the only report required. Where both the claimant's solicitor and the compensator agree that further reports are required, the assessment process is likely to have two further stages:

(i)   A subsequent Assessment Report (AR) provided by the healthcare professional who is actually treating the claimant;

(ii)   A Discharge Report (DR) from the treating healthcare professional to summarise the treatment provided.

It is, however, understood within the Code that a treatment discharge summary should routinely be included within the claimant's treatment records.

It is always possible for the Assessment Report (AR) and Discharge Report (DR) to be combined into one document.

4.5   The Triage Report (TR) assessment should be undertaken by an appropriately qualified and experienced person who is subject to appropriate clinical governance structures. Guidance on this may be obtained by reading the British Standards Institute standard PAS 150 or the UKRC Standards. It is permissible under the Code that the assessor providing the Triage Report could also be appointed to implement the recommendations.

4.6   The person or organisation that prepares the Triage and, if appropriate, Assessment and Discharge Reports and/or undertakes treatment should, save in exceptional circumstances, be entirely independent of the person or organisation that provided any medico-legal report to the claimant. In soft-tissue injury cases, the parties are referred to Part 45.29I of the Civil Procedure Rules.

4.7   The Triage and the preparation of any subsequent Assessment and Discharge Report and/or the provision of any treatment may be carried out or provided by a person or organisation having a direct or indirect business connection with the solicitor or compensator only if the other party agrees. The solicitor or compensator will be expected to reveal to the other party the existence and nature of such a business connection before instructing the connected organisation.

4.8   The assessment agency will be asked to carry out the Triage Report in a way that is appropriate to the needs of the case, which will in most cases be a telephone interview within seven days of the referral being received by the agency. It is expected that the TR will be very simple, usually just an email.

4.9   In all cases, the TR should be published simultaneously or made available immediately by the instructing party to the other side. This applies also to treatment reports (AR and DR) where the parties have agreed that they are required. Both parties will have the right to raise questions on the report(s), disclosing such correspondence to the other party.

4.10   It is recognised that, for the Triage Report to be of benefit to the parties, it should be prepared and used wholly outside the litigation process. Neither side can rely on the report in any subsequent litigation unless both parties agree in writing. Likewise, any notes, correspondence or documents created in connection with the triage assessment process will not be disclosed in any litigation. Anyone involved in preparing the Triage Report or in the assessment process shall not be a compellable witness at court. This principle is also set out in the Protocols.

4.11 The compensator will usually only consider rehabilitation that deals with the effects of the injuries that have been caused in the relevant accident. They will not normally fund treatment for other conditions that do not directly relate to the accident unless these conditions have been exacerbated by it or will impede recovery.

5. The Reports – lower-value injuries

5.1 It is expected under the Code that all treatment reporting described in this section will be concise and proportionate to the severity of the injuries and likely value of the claim.

5.2 The Triage Report should consider, where relevant, the ten 'markers' identified at the end of this Code and will normally cover the following headings:

1. The injuries sustained by the claimant;
2. The current impact on their activities of daily living, their domestic circumstances and, where relevant, their employment;
3. Any other relevant medical conditions not arising from the accident;
4. The past provision and current availability of treatment to the claimant via the NHS, their employer or health insurance schemes;
5. The type of intervention or treatment recommended;
6. The likely cost and duration of treatment;
7. The expected outcome of such intervention or treatment.

5.3 The Triage Report will not provide a prognosis or a diagnosis.

5.4 The assessment reports (TR, or any AR or DR) should not deal with issues relating to legal liability and should therefore not contain a detailed account of the accident circumstances, though they should enable the parties to understand the mechanism by which the injury occurred.

5.5 Where agreed as needed, any Assessment Report (AR) will normally have the following minimum headings:

1. Nature, symptoms and severity of injury(ies);
2. Relevance of any pre-existing conditions or injuries;
3. Primary rehabilitation goal and anticipated outcome;
4. Expected duration, number, type and length of treatment sessions;
5. Impact of injuries upon work and or activities of daily living and barriers to recovery and return to work.

5.6 Where agreed as needed, such as where a treatment discharge summary is considered inadequate, any Discharge Report (DR) will normally have the following minimum headings:

1. Current nature, symptoms and severity of injury(ies);
2. Whether the primary rehabilitation goal has been attained;
3. Number, type and length of treatment sessions/appointments attended or missed/ DNAs (Did Not Attend);
4. Current impact of injuries on work or activities of daily living;
5. Whether the claimant has achieved, as far as possible, a full functional recovery;
6. Whether additional treatment is required to address the claimant's symptoms.

In cases where no AR or DR has been agreed, it is expected that the notes and discharge summary of the treatment provider will contain the necessary information.

5.7 The provision as to the report being outside the litigation process is limited to the Triage Report and any notes or correspondence relating to it. Any notes and reports created during the subsequent treatment process will be covered by the usual principle in relation to disclosure of documents and medical records relating to the claimant.

5.8 The compensator will normally pay for the TR within 28 days of receipt. Where the claimant's solicitor and the compensator have agreed that such reports are required, the compensator will also pay for any AR and DR within 28 days of receipt. In either case, the compensator may challenge bills that they believe to be excessive or disproportionate.

5.9 The reporting agency should ensure that all invoices are within reasonable market rates, are clear and provide the following detail:

1. Type of treatment provided, e.g. telephonic CBT, face-to-face physiotherapy;

2. Dates of treatments/sessions attended and DNAs of treatment sessions;

3. Total number of treatments delivered and whether those treatments were provided remotely or in person;

4. Total cost and whether this is for treatment provided or an estimate of future cost.

5.10 Where any treatment has been organised prior to notification to or approval by the compensator, any invoice submitted to the compensator will also need to be accompanied by a discharge summary recording treatment outcome in addition to the information contained in paragraph 5.9 The need for the discharge summary to be included in the treatment records is covered in paragraph 4.4.

5.11 The parties should continue to work together to ensure that the recommended rehabilitation proceeds smoothly and that any further rehabilitation needs continue to be assessed.

6. Recommendations – lower-value injuries

6.1 The compensator will be under a duty to consider the recommendations made and the extent to which funds will be made available to implement the recommendations. The claimant will be under no obligation to undergo intervention, medical or investigation treatment. Where intervention treatment has taken place, the compensator will not be required to pay for treatment that is unreasonable in nature, content or cost.

6.2 The compensator should provide a response to the claimant's solicitor within 15 business days from the date when the TR is disclosed. If the Insurer's Response Form is transmitted via the portal earlier than 15 business days from receipt of the CNF and the TR, the response should be included in the Response Form. The response should include: (i) the extent to which the recommendations have been accepted and rehabilitation treatment will be funded; (ii) justifications for any refusal to meet the cost of recommended rehabilitation and (if appropriate) alternative recommendations. As stated in paragraph 4.3, the claimant may start treatment without waiting for the compensator's response, but at their own risk as to recovering the cost.

6.3 The compensator agrees that, in any legal proceedings connected with the claim, they will not dispute the reasonableness or costs of the treatment they have funded, provided the claimant has undertaken the treatment and it has been expressly agreed and/or the treatment provider has been jointly instructed. If the claim later fails, is discontinued or contributory negligence is an issue, it is not within the Code to seek to recover such funding from the claimant unless it can be proven that there has been fraud/fundamental dishonesty.

6.4 Following on from implementation of the assessment process, the parties should consider and agree at the earliest opportunity a process for ensuring that the ongoing rehabilitation needs of the claimant are met in a collaborative manner.

MEDIUM, SEVERE AND CATASTROPHIC INJURIES

7. **The Assessment Process – medium, severe and catastrophic injuries**

    7.1 The need for and type of rehabilitation assistance will be considered by means of an Immediate Needs Assessment (INA) carried out by a Case Manager or appropriate rehabilitation professional, e.g. an NHS Rehabilitation Consultant. (For further information about Case Managers, refer to the Glossary and The Guide for Case Managers and those who Commission them, published separately.)

    7.2 The Case Manager must be professionally and suitably qualified, experienced and skilled to carry out the task, and they must comply with appropriate clinical governance. With the most severe life-changing injuries, a Case Manager should normally be registered with a professional body appropriate to the severity of the claimant's injuries. The individual or organisation should not, save in exceptional circumstances, have provided a medico-legal report to the claimant nor be associated with any person or organisation that has done so.

    7.3 The claimant solicitor and the compensator should have discussions at the outset to agree the person or organisation to conduct the INA, as well as topics to include in the letter of instruction. The INA should go ahead whether or not the claimant is still being treated by NHS physicians, who should nonetheless be consulted about their recommendations for short-term and longer-term rehabilitation. A fundamental part of the Case Manager's role is to make immediate contact with the treating clinical lead to assess whether any proposed rehabilitation plan is appropriate.

    7.4 The parties are encouraged to try to agree the selection of an appropriately qualified independent Case Manager best suited to the claimant's needs to undertake the INA. The parties should then endeavour to agree the method of instruction and how the referral will be made. When considering options with the claimant, a joint referral to the chosen Case Manager may maximise the benefits of collaborative working. Any option chosen by the parties is subject to the claimant's agreement. In all situations, the parties should seek to agree early implementation of reasonable recommendations and secure funding. In circumstances where trust has been built, it is recommended that the parties agree to retain the Case Manager to co-ordinate the implementation of the agreed rehabilitation plan.

    7.5 With catastrophic injuries, it is especially important to achieve good early communication between the parties and an agreement to share information that could aid recovery. This will normally involve telephone or face-to-face meetings to discuss what is already known, and to plan how to gain further information on the claimant's health, vocational and social requirements. The fact that the claimant may be an NHS in-patient should not be a barrier to carrying out an INA.

    7.6 No solicitor or compensator may insist on the INA being carried out by a particular person or organisation if the other party raises a reasonable objection within 21 days of the nomination. Where alternative providers are offered, the claimant and/or their family should be personally informed of the options and the associated benefits and costs of each option.

    7.7 Objections to a particular person or organisation should include possible remedies such as additional information requirements or alternative solutions. If the discussion is not resolved within 21 days, responsibility for commissioning the provider lies ultimately with the claimant as long as they can demonstrate that full and timely co-operation has been provided.

    7.8 A rehabilitation provider's overriding duty is to the claimant. Their relationship with the claimant is therapeutic, and they should act totally independently of the instructing party.

7.9   The assessment may be carried out by a person or organisation having a direct or indirect business connection with the solicitor or compensator only if the other party agrees. The solicitor and compensator must always reveal any business connection at the earliest opportunity.

7.10   The assessment process should provide information and analysis as to the rehabilitation assistance that would maximise recovery and mitigate the loss. Further assessments of rehabilitation needs may be required as the claimant recovers.

7.11   The compensator will usually only consider rehabilitation that deals with the effects of injuries for which they are liable. Treatment for other conditions will not normally be included unless it is agreed that they have been exacerbated by the accident or are impeding the claimant's recovery.

8.   **The Immediate Needs Assessment (INA) Report – medium, severe and catastrophic injuries**

8.1   The Case Manager will be asked to carry out the INA in a way appropriate to the case, taking into account the importance of acting promptly. This may include, by prior appointment, a telephone interview. In more complex and catastrophic cases, a face-to-face discussion with the claimant is likely.

8.2   As well as the ten 'markers' identified in the Glossary at the end of this Code, the INA should consider the following points, provided doing so does not unduly delay the process:

a.   The physical and psychological injuries sustained by the claimant and the subsequent care received or planned;

b.   The symptoms, disability/incapacity arising from those injuries. Where relevant to the overall picture of the claimant's rehabilitation needs, any other medical conditions not arising from the accident should also be separately noted;

c.   The availability or planned delivery of interventions or treatment via the NHS, their employer or health insurance schemes;

d.   Any impact upon the claimant's domestic and social circumstances, including mobility, accommodation and employment, and whether therapies such as gym training or swimming would be beneficial;

e.   The injuries/disability for which early intervention or early rehabilitation is suggested;

f.   The type of clinical intervention or treatment required in both the short and medium term, and its rationale;

g.   The likely cost and duration of recommended interventions or treatment, their goals and duration, with anticipated outcomes;

h.   The anticipated clinical and return-to-work outcome of such intervention or treatment.

8.3   The INA report will not provide a medical prognosis or diagnosis, but should include any clinically justifiable recommendations for further medical investigation, compliant with NICE guidelines and, where possible, aligned to the NHS Rehabilitation prescription, discharge report or similar. Where recommendations are in addition to or deviate from the NHS recommendations, these should be explained with appropriate justification provided.

8.4   The INA report should not deal with issues relating to legal liability, such as a detailed account of the accident circumstances, though it should enable the parties to understand the mechanism by which the injury occurred.

8.5   The Case Manager will, on completion of the report, send copies to the claimant solicitor and compensator simultaneously. Both parties will have the right to raise questions on the report, disclosing such correspondence to the other party. It is, however, anticipated that the parties will discuss the recommendations and agree the appropriate action to be taken. Subject to the claimant's consent, their GP and/or treating clinical team will also be informed of the INA and its recommendations once funding to proceed has been obtained. In most cases, the INA will be conducted, and the report provided, within 21 days from the date of the letter of referral to the Case Manager.

8.6 For this assessment report to be of benefit to the parties, it should be prepared and used wholly outside the litigation process, unless both parties agree otherwise in writing.

8.7 The report, any correspondence related to it and any notes created by the assessing agency will be deemed to be covered by legal privilege and not disclosed in any proceedings unless the parties agree. The same applies to notes or documents related to the INA, either during or after the report submission. Anyone involved in preparing the report or in the assessment process will not be a compellable witness at court. (This principle is also set out in the Protocols.)

8.8 Any notes and reports created during the subsequent case management process post-INA will be covered by the usual principle in relation to disclosure of documents and medical records relating to the claimant. However, it is open to the parties to agree to extend the provisions of the Code beyond the INA to subsequent reports.

8.9 The compensator will pay for the INA report within 28 days of receipt.

9. Recommendations – medium, severe and catastrophic injuries

9.1 When the Immediate Needs Assessment (INA) report is received, the compensator has a duty to consider the recommendations and the extent to which funds are made available to implement them. The compensator is not required to pay for treatment that is unreasonable in nature, content or cost. The claimant will be under no obligation to undergo treatment.

9.2 The compensator should respond to the claimant solicitor within 21 days of receiving the INA report. The response should include: (i) the extent to which it accepts the recommendations and is willing to fund treatment; and (ii) justifications for any refusal, with alternative recommendations.

9.3 The compensator will not dispute the reasonableness or costs of the treatment, as long as the claimant has undertaken the treatment and it was expressly agreed in advance (or the treatment provider had been jointly instructed). Where there is disagreement, general interim payments are recommended to provide continuity of services with an understanding that recovery of such sums is not guaranteed and will always be a matter for negotiation or determination by a court. Where a claimant has decided not to take up a form of treatment that is readily available in favour of a more expensive option, the reasonableness of that decision may be a factor that is taken into account on the assessment of damages. If the claim later fails or is discontinued or contributory negligence is an issue, the compensator will not seek to recover any agreed rehabilitation funding it has already provided unless it can be proven that there has been fraud/fundamental dishonesty.

9.4 Following implementation of the INA, the parties should consider and attempt to agree, as soon as possible, a collaborative process for meeting the claimant's ongoing rehabilitation needs.

9.5 The overriding purpose of the INA should be to assess the claimant's medical and social needs with a view to recommending treatment rather than to obtain information to settle the claim.

GLOSSARY – THE TEN 'MARKERS'

The ten 'markers' referred to in this Code that should be taken into account when assessing an injured person's rehabilitation needs are summarised below:

1. Age (particularly children/elderly);
2. Pre-existing physical and psycho-social comorbidities;
3. Return-to-work/education issues;
4. Dependants living at home;
5. Geographic location;
6. Mental capacity;
7. Activities of daily living in the short-term and long-term;
8. Realistic goals, aspirations, attainments;
9. Fatalities/those who witness major incidence of trauma within the same accident;
10. Length of time post-accident.

September 2015

The working parties that drew up the 2015 Rehabilitation Code included representatives of ABI, APIL, CMSUK, FOIL, IUA, MASS and PIBA. Although it is for the parties involved in personal injury claims to decide when and how to use the Code, it is envisaged that it should become operational from December 1, 2015.

APPENDIX 6

Actuarial Tables – Extracts

Section B: Contingencies other than Mortality

(a) Introduction

54. As stated in Section A, Tables 3 to 18 of the main Ogden Tables for calculating loss of earnings take no account of risks other than mortality. Likewise, loss of earnings multipliers derived from the Additional Tables make no allowance for risks other than mortality. This section shows how the multipliers in these Tables may be reduced to take account of risks other than mortality by applying reduction factors in Tables A to D.

55. Tables of reduction factors to be applied to the existing multipliers were first introduced in the 2nd edition of the Ogden Tables. These factors were based on work commissioned by the Institute of Actuaries and carried out by Professor S Haberman and Mrs D S F Bloomfield[24]. Although there was some debate within the actuarial profession about the details of the work, and in particular about the scope for developing it further, the findings were broadly accepted and were adopted by the Government Actuary and the other actuaries who were members of the Ogden Working Party when the 2nd edition of the Tables was published and remained unchanged until the 6th edition.

56. Some related work was published in 2002 by Lewis, McNabb and Wass[25]. For the publication of the 6th edition of the Ogden Tables, the Ogden Working Party was involved in further research into the impact of contingencies other than mortality carried out by Professor Richard Verrall, Professor Steven Haberman and Mr Zoltan Butt of City University, London and, in a separate exercise, by Dr Victoria Wass of Cardiff University. Their findings were combined to produce the tables of reduction factors, Tables A to D, given in Section B of the 6th edition.

57. The Haberman and Bloomfield paper relied on data from the Labour Force Surveys for 1973, 1977, 1981 and 1985 and English Life Tables No. 14 (1980-82). The Labour Force Survey (LFS) was originally designed to produce a periodic cross-sectional snapshot of the working age population and collects information on an extensive range of socio-economic and labour force characteristics. Since the winter of 1992/3, the LFS has been carried out on a quarterly basis, with respondents being included in the survey over 5 successive quarters. The research of Professor Verrall *et al* and Dr Wass used panel data from the Labour Force Surveys conducted from 1998 to 2003 to estimate the probabilities of movement of males and females between different employment states, dependent on age, sex, starting employment state and level of disability. These probabilities permit the calculation of the expected periods in employment until retirement age, dependent on the starting employment state, disability status and educational attainment. These working-life expectancies can be compared to the working time to retirement where the person remains in work throughout, to obtain reduction factors which give the expected proportion of time to retirement age which will be spent in employment. The reduction factor is applied to the relevant baseline multiplier from Tables 3 to 18, in order to give a multiplier which takes into account only those periods the claimant would be expected, on average, to be in work. The reduction factors reported in this edition are calculated on the basis of a discount rate of 0%[26] compared to 2.5% in the earlier editions.

---

[24] Work time lost to sickness, unemployment and stoppages: measurement and application (1990), *Journal of the Institute of Actuaries,* 117, 533-595.

[25] Methods of calculating damages for loss of future earnings, *Journal of Personal Injury Law*, 2002 No. 2.

[26] The data is not available to provide reduction factors at -0.25% or -0.75%. However, any difference is thought to be negligible compared to the available reduction factors calculated at 0%.

58.   The factors described in subsequent paragraphs are for use in calculating loss of earnings up to retirement age.   The research did not investigate the impact of contingencies other than mortality on the value of future pension rights. Some reduction to the multiplier for loss of pension would often be appropriate when a reduction is being applied for loss of earnings. This may be a smaller reduction than in the case of loss of earnings because the ill-health contingency (as opposed to the unemployment contingency) may give rise to significant ill-health retirement pension rights. A bigger reduction may be necessary in cases where there is significant doubt whether pension rights would have continued to accrue (to the extent not already allowed for in the post-retirement multiplier) or in cases where there may be doubt over the ability of the pension fund to pay promised benefits. In the case of a defined contribution pension scheme, loss of pension rights may be allowed for simply by increasing the future earnings loss (adjusted for contingencies other than mortality) by the percentage of earnings which the employer contributions to the scheme represent. For further details and an example, see under the subheading "Assessing Pension Losses" in Section C of the explanatory notes.

59.   The methodology of applying the Table A to D reduction factors described below is the suggested method for dealing with contingencies other than mortality and is applicable in most circumstances. The methodology provides for the separate valuation of pre- and post-injury earnings, where the latter accounts for anticipated residual earnings in cases where the claimant is considered capable of working after the injury, whether on an employed or self-employed basis. This will in the majority of cases enable a more accurate assessment to be made of the mitigation of loss. However, there may be some cases when the *Smith v Manchester*[27] or *Blamire*[28] approach remains applicable or otherwise where a precise mathematical approach is inapplicable[29]. For example, there may be no real alternative to a *Smith v Manchester* or *Blamire* award where there is insufficient evidence or too many imponderables for the judge to be able to make the findings necessary to support the conventional multiplicand/multiplier approach[30]. But, merely because there are uncertainties about the future does not of itself justify a departure from the well-established multiplicand/multiplier method and judges should therefore be slow to resort to the broad-brush *Blamire* approach, unless they really have no alternative[31].

60.   The reduction factor approach which follows is for guidance and is not prescriptive. However, the Table A to D reduction factors should generally be used unless there is a good reason to disapply or to adjust them. The suggested reduction factors adjust the baseline multiplier to reflect the average pre- and post-injury contingencies according to the employment risks associated with the age, sex, employment status, disability status and educational attainment of the claimant when calculating awards for loss of earnings and for any mitigation of this loss in respect of potential future post-injury earnings. This method of calculation, based as it is on three broadly defined characteristics, will not capture all the factors which might be expected to affect the claimant's future earnings. Neither is the average for a broad category likely to capture the detail of individual circumstances and characteristics. First, employment history is based on employment status at the time of trial or assessment and does not include details of the claimant's career up to that date. Secondly, educational achievement is measured as three broad groups which are an imperfect proxy for individual human capital and skill level. Thirdly, it can be difficult to place a value on the possible mitigating income when considering

---

27   *Smith v Manchester Corporation* (1974) 17 KIR 1.
28   *Blamire v South Cumbria Health Authority* [1993] PIQR Q1.
29   See *Billett v MOD* [2015] EWCA Civ 773; [2016] PIQR Q1 at para 99; and *Ward v Allies and Morrison Architects* [2012] EWCA Civ 1287; [2013] PIQR Q1 which considered similar wording from the 6th edition of the guidance notes.
30   See *Irani v Duchon* [2019] EWCA Civ 1846, per Hamblen LJ at para 22.
31   See *Bullock v Atlas Ward Structures Ltd* [2008] EWCA Civ 194, per Lord Keene at para 21.

the potential range of impairments and their effect on post-work capability, even within the Ogden definition of disability set out below. For these reasons it may be appropriate in certain circumstances to depart from the published reduction factors in Tables A to D by increasing or reducing the reduction factor to better account for the individual characteristics of the claimant. Some of the circumstances which warrant departure and a methodology to determine the scale of the departure are described below. The examples at the end of this section illustrate the strict application of the reduction factors and also the circumstances and method for making a departure.

61. The reduction factors have not been updated using more recent data from the LFS. They remain based on the data from 1998-2003. Since the introduction of the Equality Act 2010, there have been major changes in the interpretation of disability which has involved a lowering of the threshold of the disability status classification. This is ongoing and is particularly evident in data collected from 2013 onwards. As the definition of disability gets wider and as awareness and acceptance increase, its prevalence rate in the working-age population increases. This is because more people think of themselves as disabled and self-report disability when questioned in surveys. As the prevalence rate increases, the difference in employment risks between disabled and non-disabled people gets narrower. This is not because people with a specific impairment, for example a visual impairment, suffer less employment disadvantage but rather because people with a lower severity of impairment or activity limitation increasingly classify themselves as disabled rather than non-disabled. The employment chances among this bigger group are higher than for those under the narrower definition of disability. While the expanding definition of disability precludes a consistent measure of the disability employment gap, it is advisable to rely upon older data based on a more stable definition of disability and a definition that more closely matches the needs of the Ogden Tables.

62. Whilst the underlying data remain the same, there are three differences to the suggested reduction factors in the 8th edition of the Tables and the way they are calculated. These are as follows:

    (a) Re-calculation of the reduction factors at a discount rate of 0% to reflect the reduction in the personal injury discount rate[32];

    (b) Re-labelling of the education classification to Level 1 (below GCSE level qualification, no qualification or other qualification); Level 2 (A level or equivalent, GCSE or equivalent); Level 3 (higher degree, degree and equivalent, higher education qualification below degree level); and

    (c) Allocation of new qualifications and newly graded qualifications within a re-labelled three-way education classification.

63. Guidance is provided below regarding when it might be appropriate to consider departing from the strict application of the reduction factors and how to estimate the scale of that departure.

(b) The deduction for contingencies other than mortality

64. Under this method, multipliers for loss of earnings obtained from Tables 3 to 18, or, alternatively derived from the Additional Tables, are multiplied by reduction factors to allow for the risk of periods of non-employment.

65. The research by Professor Verrall *et al* and Dr Wass referred to above demonstrated that the key issues affecting a person's future working life are age, sex, employment status, disability status and educational attainment.

66. The definitions of employed/not employed, disabled/not disabled and educational

---

[32]   In England, Wales and Scotland.

attainment used in this analysis and which should be used for determining which reduction factors to apply to the baseline multipliers to allow for contingencies other than mortality are as follows.

(c)   Definition of Employed

67.   *"Employed"*:   In respect of Tables A and C – those who were employed, self-employed or on a government training scheme as at the time of injury.

In respect of Tables B and D – those who are employed, self-employed or on a government training scheme as at the date of assessment / trial.

"Not employed":   All others (including those temporarily out of work, full-time students and unpaid family workers).

(d)   Ogden Definition of Disability

68.   It is important to note that the definition of disability used in the Ogden Tables is not the same as that used in the Equality Act 2010. The Ogden definition of disability is based upon the definition of disability set out in the Disability Discrimination Act (DDA) 1995 (supported by the accompanying guidance notes). This is because this is the definition that applied at the time of the underlying LFS research which underpins the suggested Table A to D reduction factors. In addition to meeting the DDA 1995 definition of disability, the impairment must also be work-affecting by either limiting the kind or amount of work the claimant is able to do. The Ogden definition of disability is defined as follows.

"Disabled person": A person is classified as being disabled if **all three** of the following conditions in relation to ill-health or disability are met:

(i)   The person has an illness or a disability which has or is expected to last for over a year or is a progressive illness; and

(ii)   The DDA1995 definition is satisfied in that the impact of the disability has a substantial[33] adverse effect on the person's ability to carry out normal day-to-day activities[34]; and

(iii)   The effects of impairment limit either the kind **or** the amount of paid work he/she can do.

"Not disabled":   All others

69.   Disability is therefore defined as an impairment that has a substantial adverse effect on a respondent's ability to carry out normal day-to-day activities. Both 'normal' and 'substantial' require interpretation. Normal day-to-day activities are those which are carried out by most people on a daily basis and which include those carried out at work. The meaning of the word 'substantial' has changed over time in both law and common understanding such that the threshold whereby an activity-limitation qualifies as 'substantial' (and therefore amounts to a disability) was lower in 2019 than it was when the data were collected. This is reflected in a higher disability prevalence rate in the working-age population which was around 12% in 1998 and is around 19% in 2019,

---

33   Para 3.2 of the DDA Code of Practice defined substantial as being more than minor or trivial.

34   The reduction factors are based on data from 1998-2003 when disability status was defined by the DDA 1995. Under Schedule 1, para 4 of the DDA, an impairment was taken to affect the ability of the person concerned to carry out normal day-to-day activities only if it affects one of the following: (a) mobility; (b) manual dexterity; (c) physical coordination; (d) continence; (e) ability to lift, carry or otherwise move everyday objects; (f) speech, hearing or eyesight; (g) memory or ability to concentrate, learn or understand; or (h) perception of the risk of physical danger

reflecting an increased reporting of qualifying activity-limiting impairments rather than an increase in the number or severity of such impairments.[35] The issue of severity of disability within the reduction factors underpinned the disagreement in the case of *Billett v MOD*[36] litigated in 2014 and 2015. Mr Billett was disabled under the looser Equality Act 2010 definition but arguably he was not disabled under the tighter Ogden definition of disability because his impairment was not sufficiently limiting relative to the criteria set out below[37].

70.   Criteria (i) to (iii) above, which determine disability status, were self-reported. The guidance notes on the meaning of substantial from the DDA 1995 were available to survey respondents to assist them to self-classify. The guidance notes were not intended to be inclusive or exhaustive and it is not clear to what extent respondents referred to them. The guidance notes were dropped from the Equality Act 2010 and from the LFS survey question in 2013 because they were considered to be overly restrictive in the definition of disability. The guidance notes are reproduced here but should be used with the above caveats in mind.

Mobility - for example, unable to travel short journeys as a passenger in a car, unable to walk other than at a slow pace or with jerky movements, difficulty in negotiating stairs, unable to use one or more forms of public transport, unable to go out of doors unaccompanied.

Manual dexterity - for example, loss of functioning in one or both hands, inability to use a knife and fork at the same time, or difficulty in pressing buttons on a keyboard

Physical co-ordination - for example, the inability to feed or dress oneself; or to pour liquid from one vessel to another except with unusual slowness or concentration.

Problems with bowel/bladder control - for example, frequent or regular loss of control of the bladder or bowel. Occasional bedwetting is not considered a disability.

Ability to lift, carry or otherwise move everyday objects (for example, books, kettles, light furniture) - for example, inability to pick up a weight with one hand but not the other, or to carry a tray steadily.

Speech - for example, unable to communicate (clearly) orally with others, taking significantly longer to say things. A minor stutter, difficulty in speaking in front of an audience, or inability to speak a foreign language would not be considered impairments.

Hearing - for example, not being able to hear without the use of a hearing aid, the inability to understand speech under normal conditions or over the telephone.

Eyesight - for example, while wearing spectacles or contact lenses - being unable to pass the standard driving eyesight test, total inability to distinguish colours (excluding ordinary red/green colour blindness), or inability to read newsprint.

Memory or ability to concentrate, learn or understand - for example, intermittent loss of consciousness or confused behaviour, inability to remember names of family or friends, unable to write a cheque without assistance, or an inability to follow a recipe.

---

[35]   These prevalence rates are DDA and Equality Act 2010 definitions of disability and not the Ogden Tables definition. They are reported by ONS in Table A08: (https://www.ons.gov.uk/employmentandlabourmarket/peopleinwork/employmentandemployeetypes/datasets/labourmarketstatusofdisabledpeoplea08). The prevalence rate on the Ogden tables definition has increased from 11.3% to 13.5% (Jones, M. and Wass, V. J. (2013). "Understanding changing disability-related employment gaps in Britain", 1998-2011. *Work Employment and Society* 27(6), pp. 982-1003 updated to 2019 using LFS April-June 2019).

[36]   *Billett v MOD* [2015] EWCA Civ 773; [2016] PIQR Q1.

[37]   See further Wass V (2015) "Billett v Ministry of Defence: A second bite", Journal of Personal Injury Law, 4 pp. 243-245; and Wass V (2015) "Billett v Ministry of Defence and the meaning of disability in the Ogden Tables", Journal of Personal Injury Law, 1 pp. 37-41.

Perception of risk of physical danger - for example, reckless behaviour putting oneself or others at risk, mobility to cross the road safely. This excludes (significant) fear of heights or underestimating risk of dangerous hobbies.

(e)   Highest educational qualification

71.   Highest educational qualification is used here as a proxy for human capital/skill level, so that those in professional occupations such as law, accountancy, nursing etc who do not have a degree ought to be treated as if they do have one.

72.   Three levels of educational attainment are defined for the purposes of Tables A to D as follows:

Level 3   Higher degree, degree or equivalent, higher education qualification below degree level

Level 2   A level or equivalent (at least one at pass level E), GCSE or equivalent (at least one at pass level A* to C/9 to 4)

Level 1   Low level qualifications below GCSE, no qualifications and other qualifications

73.   The following table gives a more detailed breakdown of the allocation of various types of educational qualification to each of the three categories above and is based on the allocations used in the most recent LFS.

(f)   Categories of highest educational attainment[38]

Level 3 Higher degree, degree or equivalent, higher education qualification below degree level

Higher degree; NVQ level 5; Level 8 Diploma; Level 8 Certificate; Level 7 Diploma; Level 7 Certificate; Level 8 Award; First degree/foundation degree; Other degree; NVQ level 4; Level 6 Diploma; Level 6; Level 7 Award; Diploma in higher education; Level 5 Diploma; Level 5 Certificate; Level 6 Award; HNC/HND/BTEC higher etc; Teaching D further education; Teaching D secondary education; Teaching D primary education; Teaching D foundation stage; Teaching D level not stated; Nursing etc; RSA higher diploma; Other higher education below degree.

Level 2 GCSE A level or equivalent, GCSE grade A* to C, 9 to 4 or equivalent

Level 4 Diploma; Level 4 Certificate; Level 5 Award; NVQ level 3; Advanced/Progression (14-19) Diploma; Level 3 Diploma; Advanced Welsh Baccalaureate; International Baccalaureate; Scottish Baccalaureate; GNVQ/GSVQ advanced; A-level or equivalent; RSA advanced diploma; OND/ONC/BTEC/SCOTVEC National etc; City & Guilds Advanced Craft/Part 1; Scottish 6 year certificate/CSYS; SCE higher or equivalent; Access qualifications; AS-level or equivalent; Trade apprenticeship; Level 3 Certificate; Level 4 Award; NVQ level 2 or equivalent; Intermediate Welsh Baccalaureate; GNVQ/GSVQ intermediate; RSA diploma; City & Guilds Craft/Part 2; BTEC/SCOTVEC First or General diploma etc; Higher (14-19) Diploma; Level 2 Diploma; Level 2 Certificate; Scottish National Level 5; O-level, GCSE grade A*-C, 9-4, or equivalent; Level 3 Award.

---

[38]   Source: Certificate Labour Force Survey User Guide – Volume 3: Details of LFS variables 2019, Highest Qualification, pp 303 -305.
https://www.ons.gov.uk/employmentandlabourmarket/peopleinwork/employmentandemployeetypes/methodologies/labourforcesurveyuserguidance

Level 1 Low level qualifications below GCSE, no or other qualification

NVQ level 1 or equivalent; Foundation Welsh Baccalaureate; GNVQ/GSVQ foundation level; Foundation (14-19) Diploma; Level 1 Diploma; Scottish National Level 4; CSE below grade 1, GCSE below grade C; BTEC/SCOTVEC First or General certificate; SCOTVEC modules; RSA other, Scottish Nationals Level 3; Scottish Nationals below Level 3; City & Guilds foundation/Part 1; Level 1 Certificate; Level 2 Award; YT/YTP certificate; Key skills qualification; Basic skills qualification; Entry level qualification; Entry level Diploma; Entry level Certificate; Level 1 Award; Entry level Award; Other qualification; No qualifications.

74. The research also considered the extent to which a person's future working life expectancy is affected by individual circumstances such as occupation and industrial sector, geographical region and education. The researchers concluded that the most significant consideration was the highest level of education achieved by the claimant and that, if this was allowed for, the effect of the other factors was relatively small. As a result, the Ogden Working Party decided to publish reduction factors which allow for employment status, disability status and educational attainment only. This was a change from the 6th edition of the Ogden Tables compared to previous editions where adjustments were made for types of occupation and for geographical region.

75. A separate assessment is made for (a) the value of earnings the claimant would have received if the injury had not been suffered and (b) the value of the claimant's earnings (if any) taking account of the injuries sustained. The risk of non-employment is significantly higher post-injury where there has been an activity-limiting impairment. The loss is arrived at by deducting (b) from (a).

76. In order to calculate the claimant's loss of earnings had the injury not been suffered, the claimant's employment status and disability status need to be determined as at the date of the injury (or the onset of symptoms resulting in a loss of earnings) giving rise to the claim, so that the correct reduction factor can be selected. For the calculation of future loss of earnings (based on actual pre-injury earnings and also future employment prospects), Tables A and C should be used for claimants who were not disabled at the time of the accident, and Tables B and D should be used for those with a pre-existing disability. In all these tables the three left hand columns are for those who were employed at the time of the accident and the three right hand columns are for those who were not.

77. In order to calculate the value of the actual earnings that a claimant is likely to receive in the future (i.e. after settlement or trial), the employment status and the disability status need to be determined as at the date of settlement or trial. For claimants who meet the Ogden definition of disability defined above at that point in time, Tables B and D should be used. The three left hand columns will apply in respect of claimants actually in employment at the date of settlement or trial and the three right hand columns will apply in respect of those who remain unemployed at that point in time.

78. The factors in Tables A to D allow for the interruption of employment for bringing up children and caring for other dependants.

79. In the case of those who, at the date of the injury, have not yet reached the age at which it is likely they would have started work, the relevant factor will be chosen based on a number of assessments of the claimant's likely employment had the injury not occurred. The relevant reduction factor from the tables needs to be selected on the basis of the level of education the claimant would have been expected to attain, the age at which it is likely the claimant would have started work, together with an assessment as to whether the claimant would have become employed or not. The overall multiplier will also have to be discounted for early receipt by applying the appropriate discount factor

29

from Table 35 to reflect the number of years between the claimant's age at the date of trial and the age at which it is likely that he/she would have started work.

80. In the case of those who at the date of trial have not completed their education/skills acquisition, the relevant education level will be chosen on an assessment of the claimant's likely highest qualification that he/she is likely to have achieved (pre-injury) and is now likely to be achieved (post-injury). It is for this reason that the reduction factors are not available before an individual is old enough to have achieved them, namely aged 16-19 for a degree.

81. In the case of those who, as a result of injury can no longer work in an area which makes use of their qualifications, these qualifications may need to be ignored (see below).

82. Tables A to D include reduction factors up to age 54 only. For older ages the reduction factors tend to increase towards 1 at retirement age for those who are employed and fall towards 0 for those who are not employed. Where the claimant is older than 54, it is anticipated that the likely future course of employment status will be particularly dependent on individual circumstances, so that the use of factors based on averages would not be appropriate. Hence reduction factors are not provided for these older ages.

Table A Loss of earnings to pension age 65: Males – Not disabled

Age at trial	Employed			Non-employed		
	Level 3	Level 2	Level 1	Level 3	Level 2	Level 1
16-19		0.89	0.86		0.87	0.83
20-24	0.91	0.91	0.87	0.88	0.88	0.84
25-29	0.91	0.91	0.88	0.88	0.87	0.83
30-34	0.90	0.90	0.88	0.87	0.86	0.82
35-39	0.88	0.89	0.87	0.85	0.84	0.81
40-44	0.86	0.87	0.86	0.82	0.81	0.79
45-49	0.83	0.85	0.85	0.77	0.77	0.75
50	0.81	0.83	0.84	0.72	0.73	0.71
51	0.80	0.82	0.83	0.69	0.70	0.69
52	0.78	0.81	0.83	0.67	0.67	0.67
53	0.77	0.80	0.82	0.64	0.64	0.64
54	0.76	0.79	0.81	0.60	0.60	0.60

Table B Loss of earnings to pension age 65: Males – Disabled

Age at trial	Employed			Non-employed		
	Level 3	Level 2	Level 1	Level 3	Level 2	Level 1
16-19		0.50	0.29		0.47	0.25
20-24	0.54	0.50	0.34	0.50	0.45	0.24
25-29	0.57	0.50	0.37	0.38	0.40	0.23
30-34	0.57	0.46	0.35	0.39	0.32	0.22
35-39	0.55	0.43	0.35	0.40	0.25	0.19
40-44	0.55	0.43	0.35	0.34	0.21	0.15
45-49	0.53	0.44	0.36	0.27	0.17	0.11
50	0.52	0.46	0.38	0.25	0.16	0.09
51	0.52	0.46	0.38	0.24	0.15	0.09
52	0.52	0.46	0.39	0.23	0.13	0.08
53	0.53	0.46	0.40	0.22	0.13	0.07
54	0.54	0.47	0.41	0.20	0.12	0.06

Table C Loss of earnings to pension age 60: Females – Not disabled

Age at trial	Employed			Non-employed		
	Level 3	Level 2	Level 1	Level 3	Level 2	Level 1
16-19		0.81	0.66		0.78	0.63
20-24	0.88	0.82	0.69	0.86	0.78	0.63
25-29	0.88	0.83	0.72	0.84	0.77	0.64
30-34	0.88	0.84	0.75	0.82	0.77	0.65
35-39	0.88	0.86	0.77	0.81	0.76	0.65
40-44	0.88	0.85	0.79	0.79	0.73	0.62
45-49	0.87	0.84	0.80	0.73	0.65	0.53
50	0.85	0.83	0.80	0.65	0.55	0.44
51	0.84	0.83	0.80	0.62	0.51	0.40
52	0.83	0.83	0.80	0.57	0.46	0.36
53	0.82	0.83	0.81	0.51	0.40	0.32
54	0.82	0.83	0.81	0.45	0.34	0.28

Table D Loss of earnings to pension age 60: Females – Disabled

Age at trial	Employed			Non-employed		
	Level 3	Level 2	Level 1	Level 3	Level 2	Level 1
16-19		0.39	0.22		0.34	0.18
20-24	0.60	0.40	0.22	0.55	0.31	0.16
25-29	0.59	0.42	0.23	0.49	0.31	0.16
30-34	0.59	0.42	0.27	0.44	0.31	0.15
35-39	0.59	0.44	0.31	0.41	0.28	0.14
40-44	0.58	0.48	0.34	0.35	0.24	0.13
45-49	0.58	0.51	0.40	0.26	0.19	0.11
50	0.59	0.54	0.45	0.21	0.15	0.10
51	0.59	0.56	0.47	0.19	0.14	0.09
52	0.60	0.58	0.50	0.18	0.12	0.08
53	0.61	0.61	0.53	0.17	0.11	0.07
54	0.62	0.64	0.57	0.15	0.09	0.06

(g)   Departures from a strict application

83.   Adjustments to the reduction factors since they were introduced in the 6th edition (2007) have proved to be difficult and controversial. It is in the nature of assessing damages that a single estimate based on a group average will be inaccurate for an individual claimant and a certain degree of inaccuracy must be accepted.

84.   There will be many reasons to argue for a departure, but it is important that the departure is made with the following three cautions in mind:

(i)   Reduction factors are based upon group averages which are statistically verifiable;

(ii)   The average is a <u>central</u> estimate and there will be a distribution of observations either side; and

31

(ii)   In the data, most departures will be modest because observations will cluster closely around the central estimate.

85.   The need to depart from a strict application of the reduction factors might arise from characteristics which are relevant to the future loss of earnings but which are not included in the set of characteristics which determine the published estimate, namely age, sex, employment status, highest educational achievement and disability status or because the included characteristics are too broadly defined so that the average does not reasonably represent the claimant.

86.   Characteristics included in the reduction factors are measured at the average, so for example a claimant who dropped out of the education system before reaching their potential highest qualification for positive reasons (such as an offer of employment) might be better represented by a higher educational category. Similarly, claimants whose qualifications are close to the border, for example they may just meet the threshold for a category (for example they are in the GCSE qualification category because they have a single GCSE at the minimum grade for a pass) might be better represented by a lower educational category. However, a full category change may not be required, in which case interpolation between the suggested reduction factors for adjacent categories would facilitate a partial change of category. In such a case the parties may wish to take advice on an adjustment based on outcomes from a more detailed classification.

87.   Employment status is measured at the date of injury and at the date of settlement. A claimant who changed employment status around either of these dates, for example through recruitment to a new position or suffering a job loss from a previous position, perhaps a position of long duration, may require a departure. Claimants who are established in employment in an expanding niche market or in a thriving family firm will face lower than average employment risks for their group. Likewise, claimants who are in temporary work, who have had a chequered employment history or who are restricted by injury to employment in a declining occupation or skill set will face higher than average employment risks for their group.

88.   Where injury precludes use of an educational qualification or skill, a claimant may be better represented by a lower qualification group. For example, a nurse who is now restricted to a basic clerical role would no longer have the employment risks of a graduate. Alternatively, a nurse who was able to transfer to a sedentary role using her nursing skills, for example working as a General Practice nurse or providing telephone or online medical advice, would probably continue to face similar graduate level employment risks.

89.   Disability is perhaps the characteristic where at least one of the parties (sometimes both and in opposite directions) is most likely to seek a departure from a strict application of the reduction factors. Disability is measured as either disabled or not disabled and both categories include different levels of severity of impairment and activity-limitation. The defining characteristics are subjective and context specific. There is often a misconception that impairment and activity-limitation must be severe or at least moderately severe to qualify as a disability. The best available evidence on the severity of impairment which underlies disability in the data used to estimate the reduction factors is reported in Berthoud (2006)[39] and discussed in Wass (2008)[40] and Latimer-Sayer and

---

[39]   Berthoud R (2006) "The employment rates of disabled people", Department for Work and Pensions, Research Paper No 298.

[40]   Wass V (2008) "Discretion in the Application of the New Ogden Six Multipliers: The case of *Connor v Bradman*", *Journal of Personal Injury Law*, 2 pp. 155-164.

Wass (2013)[41]. On a severity scale of 1 to 10 in a sample collected in the Health and Disability Survey 1996-7 and with a disability prevalence rate that matches that found in the data underlying the reduction factors (12%), the median level of severity is 4, 43% lie in the range 1 to 3 (mild), 44% lie in the range 4 to 7 (moderate) and 13% score in the range 7 to 10 (severe). The message here is that the norm for severity is not severe: it is at the mild end of the mild to moderate category. In the circumstances, as long as the claimant meets the above Ogden definition of disability, a departure on the basis of a perceived mild impairment / activity-limitation might not be appropriate (see further under Section B (d) above).

90. When considering whether it is appropriate to depart from the suggested Table A to D reduction factors, it is important to consider how the degree of residual disability may have a different effect on residual earnings depending upon its relevance to the claimant's likely field of work. In this regard there is a distinction between impairment and disability. For example, a lower limb amputation may have less effect on a sedentary worker's earnings than on the earnings of a manual worker. Likewise, cognitive problems may prevent someone from continuing to work in a professional or 'knowledge' capacity where the same problems may not prevent continuing employment in job roles with low cognitive demands. In this context, disability is defined in relation to work and is specific to the skills that are required in a particular job and also to the outstanding effects of the impairment where barriers have not been overcome. Disability is more closely related to employment outcomes than is impairment. So, whilst occupation is irrelevant to impairment (an amputation is the same regardless of the occupation), it is crucial to disability. Disability is the better predictor of employment prospects than the impairment itself and close regard must be given to the effects of the claimant's impairments on his or her future intended occupation.

91. Where a departure is considered to be appropriate, it could be in either direction and it would normally be expected to be modest. Interpolation using a mid-point between the disabled and non-disabled reduction factors is not advised[42]. Disability results in substantial employment disadvantage and therefore applying a mid-point between the pre- and post-injury reduction factors will normally be too great a departure. Professor Victoria Wass, a co-author of the reduction factors, has published advice on when and how to consider an adjustment on the basis of severity of disability[43]. This advice involves using the reduction factors for different employment or educational categories as a guide to the size of the departure rather than the difference between disability categories.

92. All departures will be case-specific. In some cases, it may be difficult to determine the scale of the departure and it may be helpful to consult expert opinion. Expert opinion may also be required to advise upon how the suggested reduction factors should be applied and/or adjusted when the claimant was already disabled at the time of the injury which forms the subject of the claim.

(h) Distinction between Wage Effect and Disability Effect

93. It should be noted that injury causing disability (as defined above) has two separate and distinct effects:

(i)   The first, known as the wage effect, is the reduction in earnings caused by injury, which may result from changing role, working less hours or missing out on

---

41   Latimer-Sayer, W. and Wass, V. (2013) "Ask the Expert: William Latimer-Sayer asks Victoria Wass some questions about the practical application of the Ogden Reduction Factors", Journal of Personal Injury Law, 1, 35-44.

42   See further Wass V (2008) "Discretion in the Application of the New Ogden Six Multipliers: The case of Connor v Bradman", *Journal of Personal Injury Law*, 2 pp. 155-164.

43   See footnotes 40, 41 and 42 above.

promotions. This effect is usually captured by using a different multiplicand for pre- and post-injury net annual earnings, reflecting the change or expected change as a consequence of the injury.

(ii) The second, known as the employment effect, is the impact of the person's disability on their long-term employment prospects. In particular, disability is known to increase job search periods, cause longer periods out of work and is associated with a greater risk of early retirement. Tables A to D seek to capture the disadvantage that the second effect, i.e. a claimant's disability, has on employment prospects.

94. It is a mistake to conflate these two separate and distinct effects[44]. A lower post-injury multiplicand to account for a reduction in earnings following injury does not make any allowance for reduced employment prospects. Assuming that the claimant meets the Ogden definition of disability, then the application of the disability-adjusted reduction factor is also required. There is extensive literature on the impact of both effects of disability, with the employment effect being the most important[45].

(i) Different pension ages

95. The factors in Tables A to D assume retirement at age 65 for males and age 60 for females. It is not possible to calculate expected working lifetimes, assuming alternative retirement ages from the LFS data, since the employment data in the LFS were collected only for the working age population, assumed aged between 16 and 64 for males and between 16 and 59 for females. Where the retirement age is different from age 65 for males or age 60 for females, it is suggested that this should be ignored and the reduction factor and the adjustments thereto be taken from the above tables for the age of the claimant as at the date of trial with no adjustment i.e. assume that the retirement age is age 65 for males and age 60 for females. However, if the retirement age is close to the age at the date of trial, then it may be more appropriate to take into account the circumstances of the individual case.

96. It should be noted that the reduction factors in Tables A to D are based on data for the period 1998 to 2003. Whilst the reduction factors and adjustments allow for the age-specific probabilities of moving into, or out of, employment over a future working lifetime, based on data for the period 1998 to 2003, the methodology assumes that these probabilities remain constant over time; there is no allowance for changes in these age-specific probabilities in future cohorts. Future changes in the probabilities of moving into, and out of, employment are especially difficult to predict. It is also assumed that there will be no change in disability status or educational achievement after the date of the accident.

(j) Early Retirement

97. It should be noted that the lower reduction factors for disabled people in Tables B and D already include an allowance for retiring earlier than the assumed retirements of 65 (for men) and 60 (for women). Sometimes medical evidence will suggest that a claimant who may be able to return to work following injury will now need to retire earlier as a result of the injury than he or she otherwise would have done in the absence of the injury. Since some allowance has already been made in the Table B and D reduction

---

[44] As occurred in the case of *Clarke v Maltby* [2010] EWHC 1201 (QB): see further the commentary in Latimer-Sayer, W. and Wass, V. (2012) Ogden Reduction Factor adjustments since *Conner v Bradman*: Part 1 *Journal of Personal Injury Law*, 2012, No 4, pp 219-230.

[45] The disability employment gap in 2019 was 29 percentage points whereas the disability pay gap is between 10% and 20%. Both are based on the Equality Act 2010 definition of disability: https://www.disabilityatwork.co.uk/

factors to reflect the average increased risk of early retirement post-injury, adopting a base multiplier to calculate residual earnings with an earlier retirement age than the base multiplier used to calculate but for the injury earnings may amount to a double discount.

(k) Summary

98. In summary to perform a loss of earnings calculation applying the methodology set out in this section, the process is as follows:

(1) Choose the table relating to the appropriate sex of the claimant and retirement age. Where the claimant's retirement age differs from that assumed in Tables 1 to 34, the Additional Tables can be used to calculate the appropriate multiplier or the procedure set out under the "interpolation" and "Different retirement ages" subheadings of Section A of the explanatory notes should be followed.

(2) Choose the appropriate discount rate column (currently -0.25% in England and Wales; -0.75% in Scotland; and, pending further legislation, by default still 2.5% in Northern Ireland).

(3) In that column find the appropriate figure for the claimant's age at trial ("the basic multiplier").

(4) When calculating loss of earnings, Tables 3 to 18 or the Additional Tables should be used when a multiplier/multiplicand approach is appropriate. If it is, the basic multiplier should be adjusted to take account of contingencies other than mortality. These contingencies include the claimant's employment and disability status and educational qualifications. The basic multiplier should be multiplied by the appropriate figure taken from Tables A to D to give the employment risks adjusted multiplier. If there is a good reason to depart from the suggested reduction factor, it may be necessary at this stage to modify the resulting figure further to allow for circumstances specific to the claimant.

(5) Multiply the net annual loss (the multiplicand) by the employment risks adjusted multiplier to arrive at a figure which represents the capitalised value of the future loss of earnings.

(6) If the claimant has a residual earning capacity, allowance should be made for any post-accident vulnerability on the labour market: the following paragraphs show the suggested way of doing this, although there may still be cases where a *Smith v Manchester* award is appropriate.

Where it is appropriate to do so, repeat steps 1 to 5 above, replacing the pre-injury employment and disability status with the post-injury employment and disability status in step 4 and replacing the net annual loss by the assumed new level of net earnings at step 5. It will only be necessary to reconsider the claimant's educational attainments if these have changed between the accident and the date of trial or settlement.

The result will represent the capitalised value of the claimant's likely post-accident earnings

(7) Deduct the sum yielded by step 6 from that yielded by step 5 to obtain the net amount of loss of earnings allowing for residual earning capacity. Where the above methodology is used there will usually be no need for a separate *Smith v Manchester* award.

Appendix A – Technical Note

1. The purposes of the tables and the application of the multipliers are set out in Section A of the explanatory notes. The main set of tables provide multipliers at rates of return ranging from -2.0% to +3.0%, in steps of 0.5%, along with inclusion of multipliers at the prescribed rates of discount at the date of publication of -0.25% for England and Wales and -0.75% for Scotland.

2. The assumptions underlying the calculation of the multipliers have been set by the Ogden Working Party following detailed consideration of the relevant issues and the latest available data.

3. The multipliers have been calculated assuming the average date of trial, or settlement, is 2022. This date has been chosen as providing multipliers which will be appropriate for award settlements occurring over the next four or five years, after which it is anticipated a new edition of the Ogden Tables will be produced. Further information on the construction of the multipliers are available on request from GAD using enquiries@gad.gov.uk.

4. The multipliers are assumed to be applicable to the average member of the United Kingdom population and allow for future projected changes in mortality based on the projected mortality rates underlying the 2018-based principal population projections for the United Kingdom, published by the Office for National Statistics (ONS) in October 2019[81].

5. The multipliers in the 8th edition are generally lower than those in the 7th edition, especially in respect of losses after retirement age. This is because over the last decade there has been a stalling of mortality improvements at most ages with little increase in projected life expectancies. As a result, the 2008-based population projections (which were used in the 7th edition of the tables) have proved more optimistic over the short term than the actual outturn, and the 2018-based projections assume lower life expectancies for a given age in 2022 than the 2008-based projections had done. Section A of the explanatory notes provides further details on the mortality assumptions and discusses how the multipliers may be amended if the claimant is deemed to have atypical life expectancy.

6. In addition to the main set of tables, Additional Tables have been produced using the same assumptions which can be used to derive multipliers for loss of pension or to split multipliers into shorter periods, for example where variable levels of earnings or care costs are assumed payable over different age periods. These Additional Tables are provided at rates of discount of -0.25%, -0.75% and 0%. These include the rates of discount prescribed for use in England & Wales and in Scotland at the date of publication. If the prescribed rates in any of the jurisdictions are changed in future, further supplementary tables will be provided.

7. In addition to the tables of multipliers we have also derived the factors for Table E (which provides factors for discounting pre-trial damages to allow for the risk the deceased would not have survived to provide a dependency for the full period to the date of trial or cessation of dependency) and Table F (which provides factors to apply to post-trial damages to allow for the risk that the deceased would not have survived to the date of trial). The factors in both of these tables were calculated using the same mortality rates used for calculating the multipliers but assuming the date of death was in 2020, which

---

[81] The mortality rates used for the calculations are not published directly by ONS but have been derived from data provided by ONS giving the projected death rates assumed for the United Kingdom as a whole at the start of the projections process. These were converted into the format and age definition required for calculating the multipliers. There are a variety of other data sets published by ONS from which the mortality rates required could be derived. These can give slightly different results in some cases to the multipliers calculated for Ogden 8. The mortality rates used for the calculations are available from GAD on request at enquiries@gad.gov.uk.

is believed a reasonable assumption for most fatal accident cases reaching trial between 2020 and 2025.

8. The mortality projections do not include any allowance for the possible effects of the COVID-19 pandemic on future mortality, as the projections used were published before the outbreak of the pandemic. At this stage, the full impact of the COVID-19 pandemic is not known and will remain uncertain until further evidence has been established. In general, whilst pandemics may affect mortality rates in the short term, the effects on longer term rates may be relatively slight. For example, the main result may be the bringing forward of deaths that would have occurred anyway in the next few years so that longer-term mortality rates would be expected to remain relatively unaffected. The position may need to be reviewed in due course once the implications of the COVID-19 pandemic become more apparent to ensure that the mortality rates used in these projections remain fit for purpose.

Limitations and professional compliance

9. The multipliers and other actuarial analysis outlined in this publication have been calculated and carried out in accordance with the applicable Technical Actuarial Standard: TAS 100 issued by the Financial Reporting Council (FRC). The FRC sets technical standards for actuarial work in the UK.

July 2020 Government Actuary's Department

Table 1 Multipliers for pecuniary loss of life (males)

Age at date of trial	Multiplier calculated with allowance for projected mortality from the 2018-based population projections and rate of return of:													Age at date of trial
	-2.00%	-1.50%	-1.00%	-0.75%	-0.50%	-0.25%	0.00%	0.50%	1.00%	1.50%	2.00%	2.50%	3.00%	
0	254.93	189.83	144.12	126.51	111.60	98.93	88.13	70.95	58.19	48.57	41.20	35.48	30.97	0
1	249.12	186.26	141.94	124.81	110.27	97.90	87.34	70.49	57.93	48.43	41.14	35.47	30.98	1
2	242.63	182.15	139.32	122.71	108.60	96.56	86.26	69.79	57.47	48.14	40.95	35.34	30.90	2
3	236.22	178.06	136.70	120.61	106.90	95.19	85.16	69.07	57.00	47.82	40.74	35.20	30.80	3
4	229.95	174.03	134.10	118.51	105.21	93.83	84.05	68.34	56.52	47.50	40.52	35.05	30.70	4
5	223.80	170.07	131.52	116.43	103.53	92.47	82.95	67.61	56.04	47.18	40.30	34.90	30.60	5
6	217.79	166.17	128.98	114.37	101.86	91.11	81.84	66.88	55.54	46.84	40.08	34.75	30.49	6
7	211.91	162.33	126.46	112.33	100.20	89.76	80.74	66.14	55.05	46.51	39.85	34.59	30.38	7
8	206.16	158.55	123.96	110.30	98.54	88.40	79.63	65.40	54.54	46.16	39.61	34.42	30.27	8
9	200.53	154.83	121.50	108.28	96.89	87.05	78.53	64.65	54.03	45.81	39.37	34.26	30.15	9
10	195.02	151.17	119.05	106.28	95.25	85.71	77.42	63.89	53.51	45.46	39.12	34.08	30.03	10
11	189.62	147.57	116.63	104.29	93.62	84.36	76.31	63.13	52.99	45.09	38.87	33.90	29.90	11
12	184.35	144.03	114.24	102.32	92.00	83.02	75.20	62.37	52.46	44.72	38.61	33.72	29.77	12
13	179.19	140.55	111.88	100.37	90.38	81.68	74.09	61.60	51.93	44.35	38.34	33.53	29.63	13
14	174.14	137.12	109.54	98.44	88.78	80.35	72.98	60.83	51.39	43.97	38.07	33.34	29.49	14
15	169.20	133.75	107.23	96.52	87.18	79.02	71.87	60.06	50.84	43.58	37.80	33.14	29.35	15
16	164.38	130.44	104.94	94.61	85.59	77.70	70.76	59.28	50.29	43.19	37.51	32.93	29.20	16
17	159.67	127.19	102.69	92.73	84.02	76.38	69.66	58.50	49.74	42.79	37.23	32.72	29.04	17
18	155.06	124.00	100.46	90.87	82.46	75.07	68.56	57.72	49.18	42.39	36.94	32.51	28.89	18
19	150.57	120.86	98.26	89.02	80.91	73.76	67.46	56.93	48.62	41.98	36.64	32.29	28.73	19
20	146.18	117.78	96.09	87.19	79.37	72.46	66.36	56.15	48.05	41.57	36.34	32.07	28.56	20
21	141.89	114.76	93.95	85.39	77.84	71.17	65.27	55.36	47.48	41.15	36.03	31.85	28.39	21
22	137.69	111.78	91.83	83.60	76.32	69.89	64.17	54.57	46.90	40.73	35.72	31.61	28.22	22
23	133.59	108.86	89.73	81.82	74.82	68.60	63.08	53.77	46.32	40.30	35.40	31.38	28.04	23
24	129.58	105.99	87.66	80.06	73.32	67.33	61.99	52.97	45.73	39.87	35.08	31.13	27.86	24
25	125.66	103.16	85.62	78.31	71.83	66.05	60.90	52.17	45.14	39.42	34.74	30.88	27.67	25
26	121.83	100.38	83.59	76.58	70.34	64.78	59.81	51.36	44.54	38.97	34.41	30.62	27.47	26
27	118.08	97.65	81.59	74.87	68.87	63.52	58.72	50.55	43.93	38.52	34.06	30.36	27.27	27
28	114.42	94.97	79.62	73.17	67.41	62.26	57.63	49.74	43.32	38.05	33.71	30.09	27.06	28
29	110.84	92.33	77.67	71.49	65.96	61.00	56.55	48.92	42.70	37.59	33.35	29.81	26.84	29
30	107.35	89.74	75.74	69.82	64.52	59.75	55.46	48.10	42.08	37.11	32.98	29.53	26.62	30
31	103.93	87.20	73.84	68.18	63.09	58.51	54.38	47.28	41.45	36.63	32.61	29.24	26.40	31
32	100.60	84.71	71.96	66.54	61.67	57.28	53.31	46.46	40.82	36.14	32.23	28.95	26.17	32
33	97.34	82.25	70.11	64.93	60.26	56.05	52.23	45.64	40.19	35.65	31.85	28.65	25.93	33
34	94.16	79.85	68.28	63.33	58.86	54.82	51.16	44.81	39.54	35.15	31.46	28.34	25.69	34
35	91.06	77.48	66.47	61.75	57.48	53.61	50.09	43.98	38.90	34.64	31.06	28.02	25.43	35
36	88.02	75.16	64.69	60.19	56.10	52.40	49.02	43.15	38.25	34.13	30.66	27.70	25.18	36
37	85.06	72.89	62.93	58.64	54.74	51.19	47.96	42.32	37.59	33.62	30.25	27.37	24.91	37
38	82.17	70.66	61.20	57.11	53.39	50.00	46.90	41.49	36.94	33.09	29.83	27.04	24.64	38
39	79.36	68.47	59.49	55.60	52.05	48.81	45.85	40.65	36.28	32.57	29.40	26.70	24.37	39
40	76.61	66.32	57.80	54.10	50.72	47.63	44.80	39.82	35.61	32.03	28.98	26.35	24.08	40
41	73.92	64.21	56.14	52.63	49.41	46.46	43.75	38.99	34.94	31.49	28.54	26.00	23.80	41
42	71.30	62.14	54.51	51.17	48.11	45.30	42.71	38.15	34.27	30.95	28.10	25.64	23.50	42
43	68.75	60.12	52.89	49.72	46.81	44.14	41.68	37.32	33.59	30.40	27.65	25.27	23.20	43
44	66.26	58.13	51.30	48.30	45.53	42.99	40.65	36.48	32.91	29.84	27.19	24.89	22.89	44
45	63.82	56.18	49.73	46.89	44.27	41.85	39.62	35.64	32.23	29.28	26.73	24.51	22.57	45
46	61.45	54.26	48.18	45.49	43.01	40.71	38.59	34.80	31.54	28.71	26.26	24.12	22.24	46
47	59.13	52.38	46.65	44.11	41.76	39.59	37.57	33.96	30.85	28.14	25.78	23.72	21.91	47
48	56.86	50.54	45.14	42.75	40.52	38.46	36.55	33.12	30.15	27.56	25.30	23.31	21.56	48
49	54.65	48.73	43.66	41.40	39.30	37.35	35.54	32.28	29.45	26.97	24.80	22.90	21.21	49
50	52.50	46.95	42.19	40.06	38.08	36.24	34.53	31.44	28.74	26.38	24.30	22.47	20.85	50
51	50.39	45.21	40.75	38.74	36.88	35.14	33.52	30.59	28.03	25.78	23.80	22.04	20.48	51
52	48.34	43.50	39.32	37.44	35.69	34.05	32.52	29.75	27.32	25.17	23.28	21.60	20.11	52
53	46.34	41.83	37.92	36.15	34.51	32.96	31.52	28.90	26.60	24.56	22.76	21.15	19.72	53
54	44.38	40.19	36.53	34.88	33.34	31.89	30.53	28.06	25.88	23.95	22.23	20.70	19.33	54
55	42.48	38.58	35.17	33.63	32.18	30.82	29.55	27.22	25.16	23.33	21.69	20.23	18.92	55
56	40.63	37.01	33.84	32.40	31.04	29.77	28.57	26.38	24.43	22.70	21.15	19.76	18.51	56
57	38.83	35.48	32.53	31.18	29.92	28.72	27.60	25.55	23.71	22.07	20.61	19.29	18.10	57
58	37.09	33.98	31.24	29.99	28.81	27.69	26.64	24.72	22.99	21.45	20.06	18.81	17.67	58
59	35.39	32.52	29.98	28.82	27.72	26.68	25.70	23.89	22.27	20.82	19.51	18.32	17.25	59
60	33.75	31.10	28.75	27.67	26.64	25.68	24.76	23.07	21.56	20.19	18.95	17.83	16.81	60
61	32.15	29.71	27.54	26.54	25.59	24.69	23.84	22.26	20.84	19.56	18.39	17.34	16.37	61
62	30.60	28.36	26.36	25.43	24.55	23.72	22.93	21.46	20.13	18.93	17.83	16.84	15.93	62
63	29.10	27.05	25.20	24.34	23.53	22.76	22.02	20.66	19.42	18.30	17.27	16.34	15.48	63
64	27.65	25.76	24.06	23.28	22.53	21.81	21.13	19.87	18.72	17.67	16.71	15.83	15.03	64
65	26.23	24.51	22.95	22.23	21.54	20.88	20.25	19.08	18.02	17.04	16.14	15.32	14.57	65
66	24.87	23.30	21.87	21.21	20.57	19.97	19.39	18.31	17.32	16.41	15.58	14.81	14.10	66
67	23.55	22.12	20.82	20.21	19.63	19.07	18.54	17.54	16.63	15.79	15.01	14.30	13.64	67
68	22.27	20.97	19.79	19.23	18.70	18.19	17.70	16.79	15.94	15.17	14.45	13.78	13.17	68
69	21.04	19.86	18.78	18.28	17.79	17.33	16.88	16.04	15.26	14.55	13.88	13.27	12.70	69

continued

64

Table 1 Multipliers for pecuniary loss of life (males) *continued*

Age at date of trial	Multiplier calculated with allowance for projected mortality from the 2018-based population projections and rate of return of:													Age at date of trial
	-2.00%	-1.50%	-1.00%	-0.75%	-0.50%	-0.25%	0.00%	0.50%	1.00%	1.50%	2.00%	2.50%	3.00%	
70	19.84	18.78	17.80	17.34	16.90	16.48	16.07	15.30	14.59	13.93	13.32	12.75	12.22	70
71	18.69	17.73	16.85	16.43	16.03	15.64	15.27	14.57	13.92	13.32	12.76	12.23	11.74	71
72	17.58	16.72	15.92	15.54	15.18	14.83	14.49	13.86	13.26	12.71	12.20	11.71	11.26	72
73	16.51	15.73	15.02	14.68	14.35	14.03	13.73	13.15	12.61	12.11	11.64	11.20	10.79	73
74	15.47	14.78	14.14	13.84	13.54	13.26	12.98	12.46	11.97	11.52	11.09	10.68	10.31	74
75	14.48	13.87	13.29	13.02	12.76	12.50	12.25	11.78	11.34	10.93	10.54	10.17	9.83	75
76	13.53	12.98	12.47	12.23	11.99	11.77	11.54	11.12	10.73	10.35	10.00	9.67	9.35	76
77	12.62	12.14	11.68	11.47	11.26	11.05	10.85	10.48	10.12	9.79	9.47	9.17	8.88	77
78	11.75	11.32	10.92	10.73	10.54	10.36	10.19	9.85	9.53	9.23	8.95	8.68	8.42	78
79	10.92	10.55	10.19	10.02	9.86	9.70	9.54	9.24	8.96	8.69	8.44	8.19	7.96	79
80	10.14	9.81	9.50	9.35	9.20	9.06	8.92	8.66	8.40	8.16	7.94	7.72	7.52	80
81	9.39	9.10	8.83	8.70	8.57	8.45	8.33	8.09	7.87	7.66	7.45	7.26	7.08	81
82	8.69	8.44	8.20	8.09	7.97	7.86	7.76	7.55	7.35	7.17	6.99	6.82	6.65	82
83	8.03	7.81	7.60	7.50	7.40	7.31	7.22	7.03	6.86	6.70	6.54	6.39	6.24	83
84	7.41	7.22	7.04	6.95	6.87	6.78	6.70	6.54	6.39	6.25	6.11	5.97	5.84	84
85	6.83	6.67	6.51	6.43	6.36	6.28	6.21	6.08	5.94	5.82	5.69	5.58	5.46	85
86	6.29	6.14	6.01	5.94	5.88	5.82	5.75	5.63	5.52	5.41	5.30	5.20	5.10	86
87	5.78	5.66	5.54	5.48	5.43	5.37	5.32	5.22	5.12	5.02	4.93	4.84	4.75	87
88	5.31	5.20	5.10	5.05	5.01	4.96	4.91	4.82	4.74	4.65	4.57	4.49	4.42	88
89	4.87	4.78	4.70	4.65	4.61	4.57	4.53	4.45	4.38	4.31	4.24	4.17	4.10	89
90	4.47	4.39	4.32	4.28	4.25	4.21	4.18	4.11	4.05	3.98	3.92	3.86	3.81	90
91	4.10	4.03	3.97	3.94	3.91	3.88	3.85	3.79	3.74	3.68	3.63	3.58	3.53	91
92	3.76	3.70	3.65	3.62	3.60	3.57	3.55	3.50	3.45	3.40	3.36	3.31	3.27	92
93	3.45	3.40	3.36	3.33	3.31	3.29	3.27	3.23	3.18	3.14	3.11	3.07	3.03	93
94	3.17	3.13	3.09	3.07	3.05	3.03	3.01	2.98	2.94	2.91	2.87	2.84	2.81	94
95	2.92	2.88	2.85	2.83	2.82	2.80	2.78	2.75	2.72	2.69	2.66	2.63	2.61	95
96	2.69	2.66	2.63	2.61	2.60	2.58	2.57	2.54	2.52	2.49	2.47	2.44	2.42	96
97	2.47	2.45	2.42	2.41	2.40	2.38	2.37	2.35	2.33	2.31	2.28	2.26	2.24	97
98	2.28	2.25	2.23	2.22	2.21	2.20	2.19	2.17	2.15	2.13	2.12	2.10	2.08	98
99	2.10	2.08	2.06	2.05	2.05	2.04	2.03	2.01	2.00	1.98	1.96	1.95	1.93	99
100	1.94	1.93	1.91	1.90	1.90	1.89	1.88	1.87	1.85	1.84	1.82	1.81	1.80	100

65

Table 2   Multipliers for pecuniary loss of life (females)

Age at date of trial	Multiplier calculated with allowance for projected mortality from the 2018-based population projections and rate of return of:													Age at date of trial
	-2.00%	-1.50%	-1.00%	-0.75%	-0.50%	-0.25%	0.00%	0.50%	1.00%	1.50%	2.00%	2.50%	3.00%	
0	268.92	198.89	150.02	131.29	115.47	102.08	90.69	72.66	59.34	49.35	41.74	35.86	31.23	0
1	262.78	195.13	147.74	129.51	114.09	101.01	89.87	72.18	59.07	49.21	41.67	35.83	31.24	1
2	256.07	190.92	145.09	127.40	112.41	99.67	88.80	71.49	58.63	48.92	41.49	35.72	31.16	2
3	249.45	186.75	142.43	125.28	110.72	98.31	87.71	70.79	58.18	48.63	41.30	35.59	31.08	3
4	242.97	182.63	139.81	123.18	109.03	96.96	86.62	70.09	57.71	48.32	41.10	35.45	30.99	4
5	236.62	178.58	137.20	121.09	107.35	95.61	85.54	69.38	57.25	48.02	40.89	35.32	30.89	5
6	230.41	174.59	134.63	119.02	105.68	94.26	84.45	68.66	56.78	47.70	40.68	35.18	30.80	6
7	224.34	170.66	132.08	116.96	104.02	92.92	83.36	67.94	56.30	47.38	40.47	35.03	30.70	7
8	218.39	166.80	129.56	114.92	102.37	91.57	82.27	67.22	55.82	47.06	40.25	34.88	30.60	8
9	212.56	163.00	127.07	112.89	100.72	90.23	81.17	66.49	55.33	46.73	40.02	34.73	30.49	9
10	206.86	159.25	124.60	110.88	99.08	88.90	80.08	65.76	54.83	46.39	39.79	34.57	30.38	10
11	201.29	155.57	122.15	108.89	97.45	87.56	78.99	65.02	54.33	46.05	39.56	34.41	30.27	11
12	195.83	151.95	119.74	106.91	95.83	86.23	77.90	64.28	53.83	45.70	39.32	34.24	30.15	12
13	190.49	148.38	117.35	104.95	94.22	84.91	76.80	63.54	53.32	45.35	39.07	34.07	30.03	13
14	185.27	144.88	114.98	103.00	92.62	83.59	75.71	62.79	52.80	44.99	38.82	33.89	29.90	14
15	180.16	141.43	112.64	101.08	91.02	82.27	74.62	62.04	52.28	44.63	38.57	33.71	29.78	15
16	175.17	138.04	110.33	99.16	89.44	80.95	73.53	61.28	51.75	44.26	38.31	33.53	29.64	16
17	170.28	134.71	108.05	97.27	87.87	79.65	72.44	60.52	51.22	43.89	38.04	33.34	29.51	17
18	165.50	131.43	105.79	95.39	86.30	78.34	71.35	59.76	50.69	43.51	37.77	33.14	29.37	18
19	160.83	128.21	103.56	93.53	84.75	77.04	70.26	58.99	50.14	43.12	37.50	32.94	29.22	19
20	156.26	125.04	101.35	91.68	83.20	75.75	69.17	58.22	49.60	42.73	37.22	32.74	29.08	20
21	151.79	121.92	99.16	89.85	81.67	74.45	68.09	57.45	49.04	42.33	36.93	32.53	28.92	21
22	147.42	118.86	97.01	88.04	80.14	73.17	67.00	56.67	48.49	41.93	36.63	32.32	28.76	22
23	143.14	115.84	94.87	86.23	78.62	71.88	65.91	55.89	47.92	41.52	36.33	32.10	28.60	23
24	138.95	112.87	92.76	84.45	77.10	70.60	64.83	55.11	47.35	41.10	36.03	31.87	28.43	24
25	134.86	109.96	90.67	82.68	75.60	69.32	63.74	54.32	46.77	40.68	35.72	31.64	28.26	25
26	130.85	107.09	88.60	80.92	74.11	68.05	62.65	53.52	46.19	40.25	35.40	31.40	28.08	26
27	126.94	104.26	86.56	79.18	72.62	66.78	61.57	52.73	45.60	39.81	35.07	31.15	27.89	27
28	123.11	101.49	84.54	77.45	71.15	65.52	60.48	51.93	45.01	39.37	34.74	30.90	27.70	28
29	119.36	98.76	82.54	75.74	69.68	64.26	59.40	51.12	44.41	38.92	34.40	30.65	27.51	29
30	115.70	96.08	80.57	74.05	68.22	63.00	58.32	50.32	43.81	38.47	34.05	30.38	27.31	30
31	112.13	93.45	78.62	72.37	66.78	61.75	57.24	49.51	43.20	38.00	33.70	30.11	27.10	31
32	108.63	90.86	76.70	70.71	65.34	60.51	56.16	48.70	42.58	37.54	33.35	29.84	26.89	32
33	105.21	88.32	74.80	69.07	63.91	59.27	55.09	47.88	41.96	37.06	32.98	29.56	26.67	33
34	101.87	85.82	72.92	67.43	62.49	58.04	54.01	47.06	41.34	36.58	32.61	29.27	26.44	34
35	98.61	83.36	71.06	65.82	61.09	56.81	52.94	46.24	40.71	36.09	32.23	28.97	26.21	35
36	95.42	80.95	69.23	64.22	59.69	55.59	51.87	45.42	40.07	35.60	31.85	28.67	25.97	36
37	92.30	78.57	67.42	62.63	58.30	54.37	50.80	44.59	39.43	35.10	31.45	28.36	25.73	37
38	89.25	76.24	65.63	61.07	56.92	53.16	49.73	43.77	38.78	34.59	31.05	28.05	25.48	38
39	86.27	73.96	63.87	59.51	55.55	51.95	48.67	42.93	38.13	34.08	30.65	27.72	25.22	39
40	83.37	71.71	62.12	57.97	54.20	50.75	47.61	42.10	37.47	33.56	30.23	27.39	24.95	40
41	80.52	69.50	60.40	56.45	52.85	49.56	46.55	41.27	36.81	33.03	29.81	27.06	24.68	41
42	77.75	67.33	58.70	54.94	51.51	48.37	45.49	40.43	36.14	32.50	29.38	26.71	24.40	42
43	75.03	65.20	57.02	53.45	50.18	47.19	44.44	39.59	35.47	31.96	28.95	26.36	24.11	43
44	72.38	63.11	55.36	51.97	48.87	46.01	43.39	38.74	34.79	31.41	28.51	26.00	23.82	44
45	69.79	61.05	53.73	50.51	47.56	44.84	42.34	37.90	34.11	30.86	28.05	25.63	23.51	45
46	67.27	59.04	52.11	49.07	46.26	43.68	41.29	37.05	33.42	30.30	27.59	25.25	23.20	46
47	64.80	57.06	50.52	47.63	44.97	42.52	40.25	36.20	32.73	29.73	27.13	24.86	22.88	47
48	62.39	55.11	48.95	46.22	43.70	41.37	39.21	35.36	32.03	29.16	26.65	24.47	22.56	48
49	60.03	53.21	47.40	44.82	42.43	40.22	38.17	34.50	31.33	28.58	26.17	24.07	22.22	49
50	57.74	51.33	45.87	43.43	41.18	39.09	37.14	33.65	30.63	27.99	25.68	23.66	21.88	50
51	55.50	49.50	44.36	42.07	39.94	37.96	36.12	32.80	29.92	27.40	25.19	23.24	21.53	51
52	53.31	47.70	42.88	40.72	38.71	36.84	35.09	31.95	29.21	26.80	24.69	22.82	21.17	52
53	51.18	45.94	41.41	39.38	37.49	35.72	34.08	31.10	28.49	26.20	24.18	22.39	20.80	53
54	49.10	44.21	39.97	38.06	36.28	34.62	33.07	30.25	27.77	25.59	23.66	21.95	20.42	54
55	47.08	42.52	38.55	36.76	35.09	33.53	32.06	29.40	27.05	24.98	23.14	21.50	20.04	55
56	45.10	40.86	37.16	35.48	33.91	32.44	31.06	28.55	26.33	24.36	22.61	21.04	19.64	56
57	43.18	39.24	35.78	34.22	32.75	31.37	30.07	27.70	25.60	23.74	22.07	20.58	19.24	57
58	41.31	37.65	34.43	32.97	31.59	30.30	29.08	26.86	24.88	23.11	21.53	20.11	18.84	58
59	39.49	36.10	33.11	31.74	30.46	29.25	28.11	26.02	24.15	22.48	20.98	19.64	18.42	59
60	37.72	34.58	31.80	30.53	29.33	28.20	27.14	25.18	23.42	21.85	20.43	19.15	18.00	60
61	35.99	33.09	30.52	29.34	28.22	27.17	26.18	24.34	22.69	21.21	19.87	18.66	17.57	61
62	34.31	31.64	29.26	28.16	27.13	26.15	25.22	23.51	21.96	20.57	19.31	18.17	17.13	62
63	32.68	30.22	28.02	27.01	26.05	25.14	24.27	22.68	21.23	19.93	18.74	17.66	16.68	63
64	31.09	28.83	26.81	25.87	24.98	24.14	23.34	21.85	20.50	19.28	18.17	17.15	16.23	64
65	29.55	27.48	25.61	24.75	23.93	23.15	22.41	21.03	19.77	18.63	17.59	16.64	15.77	65
66	28.05	26.15	24.44	23.65	22.89	22.17	21.49	20.21	19.05	17.98	17.01	16.12	15.30	66
67	26.59	24.86	23.30	22.57	21.88	21.21	20.58	19.40	18.32	17.33	16.42	15.59	14.82	67
68	25.18	23.61	22.18	21.51	20.87	20.26	19.68	18.59	17.59	16.68	15.84	15.06	14.34	68
69	23.81	22.38	21.08	20.47	19.89	19.33	18.80	17.79	16.87	16.03	15.25	14.52	13.86	69

continued

66

Table 2 Multipliers for pecuniary loss of life (females) *continued*

Age at date of trial	Multiplier calculated with allowance for projected mortality from the 2018-based population projections and rate of return of:													Age at date of trial
	-2.00%	-1.50%	-1.00%	-0.75%	-0.50%	-0.25%	0.00%	0.50%	1.00%	1.50%	2.00%	2.50%	3.00%	
70	22.48	21.19	20.00	19.45	18.92	18.41	17.92	17.00	16.16	15.38	14.65	13.98	13.36	70
71	21.19	20.03	18.96	18.45	17.97	17.50	17.06	16.22	15.44	14.73	14.06	13.44	12.87	71
72	19.95	18.90	17.93	17.48	17.04	16.62	16.21	15.45	14.74	14.08	13.47	12.90	12.37	72
73	18.76	17.81	16.94	16.53	16.13	15.75	15.38	14.69	14.04	13.44	12.88	12.36	11.87	73
74	17.60	16.76	15.97	15.60	15.25	14.90	14.57	13.94	13.35	12.80	12.29	11.81	11.36	74
75	16.49	15.74	15.04	14.70	14.38	14.07	13.77	13.20	12.67	12.17	11.71	11.27	10.86	75
76	15.43	14.76	14.13	13.83	13.54	13.27	13.00	12.48	12.00	11.55	11.13	10.73	10.36	76
77	14.41	13.81	13.25	12.99	12.73	12.48	12.24	11.78	11.35	10.94	10.56	10.20	9.86	77
78	13.43	12.90	12.40	12.17	11.94	11.72	11.50	11.09	10.70	10.34	10.00	9.67	9.36	78
79	12.49	12.03	11.59	11.38	11.18	10.98	10.79	10.42	10.08	9.75	9.44	9.15	8.87	79
80	11.60	11.19	10.80	10.62	10.44	10.27	10.10	9.77	9.46	9.17	8.90	8.63	8.39	80
81	10.75	10.39	10.05	9.89	9.73	9.58	9.43	9.14	8.87	8.61	8.36	8.13	7.91	81
82	9.94	9.63	9.33	9.19	9.05	8.92	8.79	8.53	8.29	8.06	7.85	7.64	7.44	82
83	9.18	8.90	8.65	8.52	8.40	8.28	8.17	7.95	7.73	7.53	7.34	7.16	6.98	83
84	8.45	8.22	7.99	7.89	7.78	7.68	7.58	7.38	7.20	7.02	6.85	6.69	6.53	84
85	7.77	7.57	7.37	7.28	7.19	7.10	7.01	6.84	6.68	6.53	6.38	6.24	6.10	85
86	7.13	6.95	6.79	6.71	6.63	6.55	6.48	6.33	6.19	6.05	5.92	5.80	5.68	86
87	6.53	6.38	6.24	6.17	6.10	6.03	5.97	5.84	5.72	5.60	5.49	5.38	5.28	87
88	5.97	5.85	5.72	5.66	5.61	5.55	5.49	5.38	5.28	5.18	5.08	4.99	4.90	88
89	5.46	5.35	5.25	5.20	5.15	5.10	5.05	4.96	4.87	4.78	4.69	4.61	4.53	89
90	4.99	4.90	4.81	4.77	4.72	4.68	4.64	4.56	4.48	4.41	4.33	4.26	4.20	90
91	4.56	4.48	4.41	4.37	4.34	4.30	4.26	4.20	4.13	4.06	4.00	3.94	3.88	91
92	4.18	4.11	4.04	4.01	3.98	3.95	3.92	3.86	3.80	3.75	3.70	3.64	3.59	92
93	3.83	3.77	3.71	3.69	3.66	3.63	3.61	3.56	3.51	3.46	3.41	3.37	3.33	93
94	3.51	3.46	3.41	3.39	3.37	3.34	3.32	3.28	3.24	3.20	3.16	3.12	3.08	94
95	3.22	3.18	3.14	3.12	3.10	3.08	3.06	3.03	2.99	2.95	2.92	2.89	2.85	95
96	2.96	2.92	2.89	2.87	2.85	2.84	2.82	2.79	2.76	2.73	2.70	2.67	2.64	96
97	2.71	2.68	2.65	2.64	2.62	2.61	2.60	2.57	2.54	2.52	2.49	2.47	2.44	97
98	2.49	2.46	2.44	2.43	2.41	2.40	2.39	2.37	2.34	2.32	2.30	2.28	2.26	98
99	2.29	2.26	2.24	2.23	2.22	2.21	2.20	2.18	2.16	2.14	2.13	2.11	2.09	99
100	2.10	2.08	2.07	2.06	2.05	2.04	2.03	2.02	2.00	1.98	1.97	1.95	1.94	100

Table 7   Multipliers for loss of earnings to pension age 60 (males)

Age at date of trial	Multiplier calculated with allowance for projected mortality from the 2018-based population projections and rate of return of:													Age at date of trial
	-2.00%	-1.50%	-1.00%	-0.75%	-0.50%	-0.25%	0.00%	0.50%	1.00%	1.50%	2.00%	2.50%	3.00%	
16	69.56	61.36	54.38	51.29	48.43	45.78	43.32	38.93	35.14	31.86	29.01	26.53	24.36	16
17	67.17	59.44	52.84	49.90	47.18	44.66	42.32	38.12	34.49	31.33	28.58	26.18	24.07	17
18	64.83	57.55	51.31	48.53	45.95	43.55	41.32	37.31	33.83	30.80	28.15	25.82	23.78	18
19	62.54	55.70	49.81	47.17	44.72	42.44	40.32	36.49	33.16	30.25	27.70	25.46	23.48	19
20	60.30	53.87	48.32	45.82	43.50	41.34	39.32	35.68	32.49	29.70	27.25	25.09	23.17	20
21	58.11	52.07	46.84	44.49	42.29	40.24	38.33	34.86	31.82	29.14	26.79	24.70	22.86	21
22	55.96	50.31	45.38	43.16	41.09	39.15	37.33	34.03	31.14	28.58	26.32	24.31	22.53	22
23	53.86	48.56	43.94	41.85	39.89	38.06	36.34	33.21	30.45	28.00	25.84	23.91	22.20	23
24	51.80	46.85	42.51	40.54	38.70	36.97	35.34	32.38	29.75	27.42	25.35	23.50	21.85	24
25	49.78	45.16	41.10	39.25	37.51	35.88	34.35	31.54	29.05	26.83	24.85	23.08	21.50	25
26	47.80	43.50	39.70	37.97	36.34	34.80	33.35	30.70	28.34	26.23	24.35	22.65	21.13	26
27	45.86	41.86	38.31	36.69	35.16	33.72	32.36	29.86	27.63	25.62	23.83	22.21	20.76	27
28	43.96	40.25	36.94	35.43	34.00	32.65	31.37	29.01	26.90	25.01	23.30	21.76	20.37	28
29	42.10	38.66	35.59	34.18	32.84	31.57	30.38	28.17	26.18	24.38	22.77	21.30	19.97	29
30	40.28	37.10	34.25	32.93	31.69	30.51	29.39	27.31	25.44	23.75	22.22	20.83	19.57	30
31	38.50	35.57	32.92	31.70	30.54	29.44	28.40	26.46	24.70	23.11	21.66	20.35	19.15	31
32	36.76	34.05	31.61	30.48	29.41	28.38	27.41	25.60	23.95	22.46	21.10	19.85	18.72	32
33	35.05	32.57	30.32	29.27	28.28	27.33	26.42	24.74	23.20	21.80	20.52	19.35	18.27	33
34	33.38	31.10	29.03	28.07	27.15	26.28	25.44	23.87	22.44	21.13	19.93	18.83	17.82	34
35	31.74	29.66	27.77	26.88	26.04	25.23	24.45	23.00	21.67	20.45	19.33	18.30	17.35	35
36	30.13	28.24	26.51	25.70	24.93	24.18	23.47	22.13	20.90	19.77	18.72	17.76	16.87	36
37	28.56	26.85	25.27	24.53	23.82	23.14	22.49	21.26	20.12	19.07	18.10	17.20	16.37	37
38	27.03	25.48	24.05	23.37	22.73	22.11	21.51	20.38	19.34	18.37	17.47	16.64	15.86	38
39	25.52	24.13	22.83	22.23	21.64	21.07	20.53	19.50	18.54	17.66	16.83	16.06	15.34	39
40	24.05	22.80	21.64	21.09	20.56	20.05	19.55	18.62	17.75	16.93	16.17	15.47	14.80	40
41	22.61	21.49	20.45	19.96	19.48	19.02	18.58	17.73	16.94	16.20	15.51	14.86	14.25	41
42	21.19	20.20	19.28	18.84	18.41	18.00	17.60	16.84	16.13	15.46	14.83	14.24	13.68	42
43	19.81	18.94	18.12	17.73	17.35	16.98	16.63	15.95	15.31	14.71	14.14	13.60	13.10	43
44	18.46	17.69	16.97	16.63	16.29	15.97	15.66	15.05	14.48	13.94	13.44	12.96	12.50	44
45	17.13	16.46	15.84	15.54	15.24	14.96	14.68	14.15	13.65	13.17	12.72	12.29	11.88	45
46	15.83	15.26	14.71	14.45	14.20	13.95	13.71	13.25	12.81	12.39	11.99	11.61	11.25	46
47	14.55	14.07	13.60	13.38	13.16	12.95	12.74	12.34	11.95	11.59	11.24	10.91	10.59	47
48	13.30	12.89	12.50	12.31	12.12	11.94	11.77	11.42	11.10	10.78	10.48	10.19	9.92	48
49	12.08	11.74	11.41	11.25	11.09	10.94	10.79	10.50	10.23	9.96	9.71	9.46	9.23	49
50	10.88	10.60	10.33	10.20	10.07	9.94	9.82	9.58	9.35	9.13	8.92	8.71	8.51	50
51	9.70	9.47	9.26	9.15	9.05	8.95	8.85	8.65	8.46	8.28	8.11	7.94	7.77	51
52	8.54	8.36	8.19	8.11	8.03	7.95	7.87	7.72	7.57	7.42	7.28	7.15	7.02	52
53	7.40	7.27	7.14	7.08	7.02	6.96	6.90	6.78	6.66	6.55	6.44	6.34	6.23	53
54	6.29	6.19	6.10	6.05	6.01	5.96	5.92	5.83	5.75	5.66	5.58	5.50	5.43	54
55	5.20	5.13	5.06	5.03	5.00	4.97	4.94	4.88	4.82	4.76	4.70	4.65	4.59	55
56	4.12	4.08	4.04	4.02	4.00	3.98	3.96	3.92	3.88	3.84	3.81	3.77	3.73	56
57	3.07	3.04	3.02	3.01	3.00	2.99	2.97	2.95	2.93	2.91	2.89	2.87	2.85	57
58	2.03	2.02	2.01	2.00	2.00	1.99	1.99	1.98	1.97	1.96	1.95	1.94	1.93	58
59	1.01	1.00	1.00	1.00	1.00	1.00	1.00	0.99	0.99	0.99	0.99	0.98	0.98	59

Table 8   Multipliers for loss of earnings to pension age 60 (females)

Age at date of trial	Multiplier calculated with allowance for projected mortality from the 2018-based population projections and rate of return of:													Age at date of trial
	-2.00%	-1.50%	-1.00%	-0.75%	-0.50%	-0.25%	0.00%	0.50%	1.00%	1.50%	2.00%	2.50%	3.00%	
16	70.09	61.81	54.76	51.63	48.74	46.07	43.59	39.16	35.34	32.03	29.16	26.65	24.46	16
17	67.69	59.89	53.22	50.25	47.50	44.95	42.59	38.35	34.69	31.50	28.73	26.31	24.18	17
18	65.35	57.99	51.69	48.88	46.27	43.84	41.59	37.54	34.03	30.97	28.30	25.95	23.89	18
19	63.05	56.13	50.18	47.52	45.04	42.74	40.59	36.73	33.37	30.43	27.85	25.59	23.60	19
20	60.80	54.30	48.68	46.16	43.82	41.63	39.59	35.91	32.70	29.88	27.40	25.22	23.29	20
21	58.60	52.49	47.20	44.82	42.60	40.53	38.60	35.09	32.02	29.32	26.94	24.84	22.98	21
22	56.44	50.72	45.74	43.49	41.40	39.43	37.60	34.27	31.34	28.76	26.47	24.45	22.65	22
23	54.32	48.96	44.29	42.17	40.19	38.34	36.60	33.44	30.65	28.18	26.00	24.05	22.32	23
24	52.25	47.24	42.85	40.86	39.00	37.25	35.60	32.60	29.95	27.60	25.51	23.64	21.98	24
25	50.21	45.54	41.43	39.56	37.81	36.16	34.60	31.77	29.25	27.01	25.01	23.22	21.62	25
26	48.22	43.87	40.02	38.27	36.62	35.07	33.61	30.93	28.54	26.41	24.50	22.79	21.26	26
27	46.27	42.22	38.63	36.99	35.45	33.99	32.61	30.08	27.82	25.80	23.99	22.35	20.88	27
28	44.36	40.60	37.25	35.72	34.27	32.91	31.61	29.23	27.10	25.18	23.46	21.90	20.50	28
29	42.49	39.00	35.89	34.46	33.11	31.83	30.62	28.38	26.37	24.56	22.92	21.44	20.10	29
30	40.65	37.43	34.54	33.21	31.95	30.76	29.62	27.53	25.63	23.92	22.38	20.97	19.69	30
31	38.86	35.89	33.21	31.98	30.80	29.69	28.63	26.67	24.89	23.28	21.82	20.49	19.28	31
32	37.10	34.36	31.89	30.75	29.66	28.62	27.64	25.81	24.14	22.63	21.25	19.99	18.84	32
33	35.38	32.86	30.59	29.53	28.52	27.56	26.65	24.94	23.39	21.97	20.67	19.49	18.40	33
34	33.69	31.39	29.30	28.32	27.39	26.50	25.65	24.07	22.62	21.30	20.08	18.97	17.94	34
35	32.04	29.94	28.02	27.12	26.27	25.45	24.66	23.20	21.85	20.62	19.48	18.44	17.47	35
36	30.42	28.51	26.75	25.93	25.15	24.39	23.67	22.32	21.07	19.93	18.87	17.89	16.99	36
37	28.84	27.10	25.50	24.75	24.04	23.35	22.68	21.44	20.29	19.23	18.25	17.34	16.49	37
38	27.28	25.71	24.27	23.58	22.93	22.30	21.70	20.55	19.50	18.52	17.61	16.77	15.98	38
39	25.76	24.35	23.04	22.42	21.83	21.26	20.71	19.67	18.70	17.80	16.96	16.18	15.46	39
40	24.27	23.01	21.83	21.27	20.74	20.22	19.72	18.78	17.89	17.07	16.30	15.59	14.92	40
41	22.81	21.68	20.63	20.13	19.65	19.19	18.74	17.88	17.08	16.33	15.63	14.97	14.36	41
42	21.38	20.38	19.45	19.00	18.57	18.15	17.75	16.98	16.26	15.58	14.95	14.35	13.79	42
43	19.98	19.10	18.27	17.88	17.50	17.12	16.76	16.08	15.43	14.82	14.25	13.71	13.20	43
44	18.61	17.84	17.11	16.76	16.43	16.10	15.78	15.17	14.59	14.05	13.54	13.05	12.59	44
45	17.27	16.60	15.96	15.66	15.36	15.08	14.80	14.26	13.75	13.27	12.81	12.38	11.97	45
46	15.95	15.37	14.82	14.56	14.30	14.05	13.81	13.34	12.90	12.47	12.07	11.69	11.32	46
47	14.66	14.17	13.70	13.47	13.25	13.04	12.83	12.42	12.04	11.67	11.32	10.98	10.66	47
48	13.40	12.98	12.58	12.39	12.21	12.02	11.84	11.50	11.17	10.85	10.55	10.26	9.98	48
49	12.16	11.81	11.48	11.32	11.16	11.01	10.86	10.57	10.29	10.02	9.77	9.52	9.28	49
50	10.94	10.66	10.39	10.26	10.13	10.00	9.88	9.64	9.41	9.18	8.97	8.76	8.56	50
51	9.75	9.53	9.31	9.20	9.10	9.00	8.90	8.70	8.51	8.33	8.15	7.98	7.82	51
52	8.58	8.41	8.24	8.15	8.07	7.99	7.91	7.76	7.61	7.46	7.32	7.18	7.05	52
53	7.44	7.31	7.18	7.11	7.05	6.99	6.93	6.81	6.69	6.58	6.47	6.37	6.26	53
54	6.32	6.22	6.13	6.08	6.03	5.99	5.94	5.86	5.77	5.69	5.61	5.53	5.45	54
55	5.22	5.15	5.08	5.05	5.02	4.99	4.96	4.90	4.84	4.78	4.72	4.67	4.61	55
56	4.14	4.09	4.05	4.03	4.01	3.99	3.97	3.93	3.89	3.86	3.82	3.78	3.75	56
57	3.08	3.05	3.03	3.02	3.01	2.99	2.98	2.96	2.94	2.92	2.90	2.88	2.85	57
58	2.03	2.02	2.01	2.01	2.00	2.00	1.99	1.98	1.97	1.96	1.95	1.94	1.93	58
59	1.01	1.01	1.00	1.00	1.00	1.00	1.00	1.00	0.99	0.99	0.99	0.99	0.98	59

Table 9   Multipliers for loss of earnings to pension age 65 (males)

Age at date of trial	Multiplier calculated with allowance for projected mortality from the 2018-based population projections and rate of return of:													Age at date of trial
	-2.00%	-1.50%	-1.00%	-0.75%	-0.50%	-0.25%	0.00%	0.50%	1.00%	1.50%	2.00%	2.50%	3.00%	
16	81.53	70.81	61.85	57.93	54.33	51.03	48.00	42.64	38.09	34.21	30.88	28.02	25.54	16
17	78.89	68.74	60.23	56.49	53.06	49.90	46.99	41.85	37.46	33.71	30.48	27.70	25.29	17
18	76.31	66.71	58.62	55.06	51.79	48.77	45.99	41.05	36.83	33.21	30.08	27.38	25.03	18
19	73.79	64.71	57.04	53.65	50.53	47.65	44.99	40.25	36.19	32.70	29.68	27.05	24.77	19
20	71.32	62.74	55.47	52.25	49.28	46.53	43.99	39.45	35.55	32.18	29.26	26.72	24.50	20
21	68.90	60.81	53.92	50.86	48.03	45.42	42.99	38.65	34.90	31.66	28.84	26.38	24.23	21
22	66.53	58.91	52.39	49.49	46.80	44.31	41.99	37.84	34.25	31.13	28.41	26.03	23.94	22
23	64.21	57.03	50.87	48.12	45.57	43.20	41.00	37.03	33.59	30.59	27.97	25.67	23.65	23
24	61.94	55.18	49.37	46.77	44.35	42.10	40.00	36.22	32.93	30.05	27.53	25.31	23.35	24
25	59.71	53.37	47.88	45.42	43.13	41.00	39.00	35.40	32.26	29.50	27.07	24.93	23.04	25
26	57.53	51.58	46.41	44.09	41.92	39.90	38.01	34.58	31.58	28.94	26.61	24.55	22.72	26
27	55.39	49.81	44.96	42.77	40.72	38.80	37.01	33.76	30.89	28.37	26.13	24.15	22.39	27
28	53.30	48.08	43.52	41.46	39.53	37.71	36.02	32.93	30.20	27.79	25.65	23.75	22.05	28
29	51.25	46.37	42.10	40.16	38.34	36.63	35.02	32.10	29.51	27.21	25.16	23.34	21.70	29
30	49.25	44.70	40.69	38.87	37.16	35.55	34.03	31.26	28.81	26.62	24.66	22.91	21.35	30
31	47.28	43.04	39.30	37.59	35.98	34.47	33.04	30.43	28.10	26.02	24.15	22.48	20.98	31
32	45.36	41.42	37.92	36.33	34.82	33.40	32.05	29.59	27.38	25.41	23.64	22.04	20.60	32
33	43.48	39.82	36.56	35.07	33.66	32.33	31.07	28.75	26.66	24.79	23.11	21.59	20.22	33
34	41.64	38.25	35.22	33.83	32.51	31.26	30.08	27.90	25.94	24.17	22.57	21.13	19.82	34
35	39.83	36.70	33.89	32.59	31.37	30.20	29.10	27.05	25.21	23.54	22.03	20.66	19.41	35
36	38.07	35.18	32.57	31.37	30.23	29.15	28.11	26.20	24.47	22.90	21.47	20.17	18.99	36
37	36.34	33.68	31.27	30.16	29.10	28.09	27.13	25.35	23.73	22.25	20.91	19.68	18.56	37
38	34.65	32.21	29.99	28.96	27.98	27.05	26.16	24.49	22.98	21.60	20.33	19.18	18.12	38
39	33.00	30.76	28.72	27.77	26.87	26.00	25.18	23.64	22.23	20.93	19.75	18.66	17.66	39
40	31.38	29.33	27.47	26.60	25.76	24.97	24.20	22.78	21.47	20.26	19.16	18.14	17.20	40
41	29.79	27.93	26.23	25.43	24.67	23.93	23.23	21.91	20.70	19.58	18.55	17.60	16.72	41
42	28.24	26.55	25.00	24.27	23.58	22.90	22.26	21.05	19.93	18.89	17.94	17.05	16.23	42
43	26.73	25.20	23.79	23.13	22.49	21.88	21.29	20.18	19.15	18.20	17.31	16.49	15.72	43
44	25.24	23.87	22.59	21.99	21.42	20.86	20.32	19.31	18.37	17.49	16.67	15.91	15.21	44
45	23.79	22.55	21.41	20.87	20.35	19.84	19.36	18.43	17.58	16.77	16.03	15.33	14.67	45
46	22.36	21.26	20.24	19.75	19.28	18.83	18.39	17.56	16.78	16.05	15.37	14.73	14.12	46
47	20.96	19.99	19.08	18.64	18.22	17.82	17.43	16.68	15.97	15.31	14.69	14.11	13.56	47
48	19.60	18.74	17.93	17.55	17.17	16.81	16.46	15.79	15.16	14.57	14.01	13.48	12.98	48
49	18.26	17.50	16.80	16.46	16.13	15.81	15.50	14.90	14.34	13.81	13.31	12.84	12.39	49
50	16.94	16.29	15.67	15.37	15.09	14.81	14.53	14.01	13.51	13.04	12.60	12.18	11.77	50
51	15.66	15.09	14.56	14.30	14.05	13.81	13.57	13.11	12.68	12.27	11.87	11.50	11.14	51
52	14.40	13.91	13.46	13.24	13.02	12.81	12.61	12.21	11.84	11.48	11.13	10.81	10.49	52
53	13.16	12.75	12.37	12.18	12.00	11.82	11.64	11.31	10.98	10.68	10.38	10.10	9.82	53
54	11.95	11.61	11.29	11.13	10.98	10.83	10.68	10.40	10.12	9.86	9.61	9.37	9.14	54
55	10.76	10.48	10.22	10.09	9.96	9.84	9.72	9.48	9.26	9.04	8.83	8.62	8.43	55
56	9.60	9.37	9.16	9.06	8.96	8.86	8.76	8.57	8.38	8.20	8.03	7.86	7.70	56
57	8.45	8.28	8.11	8.03	7.95	7.87	7.79	7.64	7.50	7.35	7.21	7.08	6.95	57
58	7.33	7.20	7.08	7.01	6.95	6.89	6.83	6.72	6.60	6.49	6.38	6.28	6.18	58
59	6.24	6.14	6.05	6.00	5.96	5.91	5.87	5.78	5.70	5.62	5.54	5.46	5.38	59
60	5.16	5.09	5.03	4.99	4.96	4.93	4.90	4.84	4.78	4.73	4.67	4.61	4.56	60
61	4.10	4.05	4.01	3.99	3.97	3.95	3.93	3.89	3.86	3.82	3.78	3.75	3.71	61
62	3.05	3.03	3.00	2.99	2.98	2.97	2.96	2.94	2.92	2.89	2.87	2.85	2.83	62
63	2.02	2.01	2.00	2.00	1.99	1.99	1.98	1.97	1.96	1.95	1.94	1.93	1.92	63
64	1.00	1.00	1.00	1.00	1.00	1.00	0.99	0.99	0.99	0.99	0.99	0.98	0.98	64

Table 10   Multipliers for loss of earnings to pension age 65 (females)

Age at date of trial	Multiplier calculated with allowance for projected mortality from the 2018-based population projections and rate of return of:													Age at date of trial
	-2.00%	-1.50%	-1.00%	-0.75%	-0.50%	-0.25%	0.00%	0.50%	1.00%	1.50%	2.00%	2.50%	3.00%	
16	82.35	71.48	62.41	58.43	54.79	51.45	48.38	42.96	38.36	34.43	31.07	28.17	25.67	16
17	79.71	69.41	60.78	57.00	53.52	50.32	47.38	42.17	37.73	33.94	30.68	27.87	25.43	17
18	77.12	67.38	59.18	55.57	52.25	49.20	46.38	41.38	37.11	33.44	30.28	27.55	25.18	18
19	74.58	65.37	57.59	54.16	50.99	48.07	45.38	40.58	36.47	32.93	29.88	27.23	24.92	19
20	72.10	63.39	56.02	52.75	49.74	46.95	44.38	39.78	35.83	32.42	29.47	26.90	24.65	20
21	69.66	61.45	54.46	51.36	48.49	45.84	43.38	38.98	35.19	31.90	29.05	26.56	24.38	21
22	67.28	59.53	52.92	49.98	47.25	44.72	42.38	38.17	34.53	31.37	28.62	26.21	24.10	22
23	64.94	57.65	51.40	48.61	46.02	43.61	41.38	37.36	33.88	30.84	28.18	25.86	23.81	23
24	62.65	55.79	49.89	47.25	44.79	42.51	40.38	36.55	33.21	30.29	27.74	25.49	23.51	24
25	60.40	53.96	48.39	45.90	43.57	41.40	39.38	35.73	32.54	29.74	27.28	25.12	23.20	25
26	58.20	52.16	46.91	44.56	42.36	40.30	38.38	34.91	31.86	29.18	26.82	24.73	22.88	26
27	56.05	50.38	45.45	43.23	41.15	39.20	37.38	34.08	31.18	28.62	26.35	24.34	22.56	27
28	53.94	48.64	44.00	41.91	39.95	38.11	36.39	33.25	30.49	28.04	25.87	23.94	22.22	28
29	51.88	46.92	42.57	40.60	38.75	37.02	35.39	32.42	29.79	27.46	25.38	23.53	21.88	29
30	49.85	45.23	41.16	39.31	37.57	35.93	34.39	31.58	29.09	26.86	24.88	23.11	21.52	30
31	47.87	43.56	39.76	38.02	36.39	34.85	33.40	30.74	28.38	26.26	24.37	22.68	21.16	31
32	45.93	41.92	38.37	36.75	35.21	33.77	32.41	29.90	27.66	25.66	23.86	22.24	20.78	32
33	44.03	40.31	37.00	35.48	34.05	32.69	31.41	29.05	26.94	25.04	23.33	21.79	20.40	33
34	42.17	38.72	35.64	34.23	32.89	31.62	30.42	28.21	26.21	24.42	22.79	21.33	20.00	34
35	40.35	37.16	34.30	32.98	31.74	30.55	29.43	27.35	25.48	23.78	22.25	20.86	19.59	35
36	38.56	35.62	32.97	31.75	30.59	29.49	28.44	26.50	24.74	23.14	21.69	20.37	19.17	36
37	36.82	34.11	31.66	30.53	29.45	28.43	27.45	25.64	23.99	22.49	21.12	19.88	18.74	37
38	35.11	32.62	30.36	29.32	28.32	27.37	26.46	24.77	23.23	21.83	20.55	19.37	18.30	38
39	33.43	31.15	29.08	28.12	27.19	26.32	25.48	23.91	22.47	21.16	19.96	18.86	17.84	39
40	31.79	29.71	27.81	26.92	26.08	25.27	24.49	23.04	21.71	20.48	19.36	18.33	17.37	40
41	30.18	28.29	26.55	25.74	24.96	24.22	23.51	22.17	20.93	19.80	18.75	17.78	16.89	41
42	28.61	26.89	25.31	24.57	23.86	23.18	22.52	21.29	20.15	19.10	18.13	17.23	16.39	42
43	27.07	25.51	24.08	23.41	22.76	22.14	21.54	20.41	19.36	18.40	17.50	16.66	15.88	43
44	25.56	24.16	22.87	22.26	21.67	21.10	20.56	19.53	18.57	17.68	16.85	16.08	15.36	44
45	24.08	22.83	21.66	21.11	20.58	20.07	19.58	18.64	17.77	16.95	16.19	15.48	14.82	45
46	22.63	21.51	20.47	19.98	19.50	19.04	18.60	17.75	16.96	16.22	15.52	14.87	14.27	46
47	21.21	20.22	19.29	18.85	18.43	18.02	17.62	16.86	16.14	15.47	14.84	14.25	13.69	47
48	19.82	18.95	18.13	17.74	17.36	16.99	16.64	15.96	15.32	14.72	14.15	13.61	13.11	48
49	18.46	17.70	16.98	16.63	16.30	15.97	15.66	15.06	14.49	13.95	13.44	12.96	12.50	49
50	17.13	16.46	15.84	15.54	15.24	14.96	14.68	14.15	13.65	13.17	12.72	12.29	11.88	50
51	15.82	15.25	14.71	14.45	14.20	13.95	13.71	13.24	12.80	12.38	11.99	11.61	11.25	51
52	14.54	14.06	13.59	13.37	13.15	12.94	12.73	12.33	11.95	11.59	11.24	10.91	10.59	52
53	13.29	12.88	12.49	12.30	12.12	11.93	11.76	11.42	11.09	10.77	10.48	10.19	9.91	53
54	12.07	11.72	11.40	11.24	11.08	10.93	10.78	10.49	10.22	9.95	9.70	9.45	9.22	54
55	10.86	10.58	10.32	10.19	10.06	9.93	9.81	9.57	9.34	9.12	8.91	8.70	8.50	55
56	9.68	9.46	9.24	9.14	9.04	8.94	8.84	8.64	8.45	8.27	8.10	7.93	7.77	56
57	8.53	8.35	8.18	8.10	8.02	7.94	7.86	7.71	7.56	7.41	7.27	7.14	7.01	57
58	7.39	7.26	7.13	7.07	7.01	6.95	6.89	6.77	6.65	6.54	6.43	6.33	6.23	58
59	6.28	6.19	6.09	6.05	6.00	5.96	5.91	5.82	5.74	5.66	5.58	5.50	5.42	59
60	5.19	5.13	5.06	5.03	5.00	4.97	4.93	4.87	4.81	4.76	4.70	4.64	4.59	60
61	4.12	4.08	4.04	4.02	4.00	3.98	3.96	3.92	3.88	3.84	3.80	3.77	3.73	61
62	3.07	3.04	3.02	3.01	3.00	2.98	2.97	2.95	2.93	2.91	2.89	2.87	2.85	62
63	2.03	2.02	2.01	2.00	2.00	1.99	1.99	1.98	1.97	1.96	1.95	1.94	1.93	63
64	1.01	1.00	1.00	1.00	1.00	1.00	1.00	0.99	0.99	0.99	0.99	0.98	0.98	64

Index